Perspectives on the Formation of the Book of the Twelve

Beihefte zur Zeitschrift für die alttestamentliche Wissenschaft

Herausgegeben von
John Barton · F. W. Dobbs-Allsopp
Reinhard G. Kratz · Markus Witte

Band 433

De Gruyter

Perspectives on the Formation
of the Book of the Twelve

Methodological Foundations – Redactional Processes – Historical Insights

Edited by
Rainer Albertz, James D. Nogalski
and Jakob Wöhrle

De Gruyter

MIX
Papier aus verantwor-
tungsvollen Quellen
FSC
www.fsc.org   FSC® C016439

ISBN 978-3-11-028334-1
e-ISBN 978-3-11-028376-1
ISSN 0934-2575

Library of Congress Cataloging-in-Publication Data

A CIP catalog record for this book has been applied for at the Library of Congress.

Bibliographic information published by the Deutsche Nationalbibliothek

The Deutsche Nationalbibliothek lists this publication in the Deutsche
Nationalbibliografie; detailed bibliographic data are available in the Internet
at http://dnb.dnb.de.

© 2012 Walter de Gruyter GmbH & Co. KG, Berlin/Boston

Printing: Hubert & Co. GmbH & Co. KG, Göttingen
∞ Printed on acid-free paper

Printed in Germany

www.degruyter.com

Preface

The current volume contains essays from the international conference "Perspectives on the Formation of the Book of the Twelve" that took place January 14–16, 2011 at the Westfälische Wilhelms-Universität Münster. The question of the development of the Book of the Twelve has been explored intensively over the last twenty years. Comprehensive models have been put forward and numerous individual studies have been treated. The goal of the conference was to bring together the primary protagonists of this field of inquiry. Scholars from both sides of the Atlantic came together to investigate points of scholarly consensus, to lay out problems that have not yet been solved satisfactorily, and to develop perspectives for further research. These scholars included the pioneers who put forward the initial proposals as well as scholars of the second generation who have just recently developed their own theses about the development of the Twelve.

We want to thank all those who enabled the conference to take place and the current volume to appear. The Deutsche Forschungsgemeinschaft and the University of Münster's International Office and Cluster of Excellence "Religion and Politics" generously financed the meeting. Students and doctoral candidates at the University provided invaluable help, especially Ruth Ebach, Dagrun Pflüger and Svenja von Rönn.

We also sincerely thank the editors of BZAW – Prof. Dr. John Barton, Prof. Dr. F.W. Dobbs-Allsopp, Prof. Dr. Reinhard G. Kratz and Prof. Dr. Markus Witte – for accepting this volume into their series, as well as Sabina Dabrowski, Dr. Albrecht Döhnert and Dr. Sabine Krämer at Walter de Gruyter for the engaging editorial care they provided.

Our gratitude goes to Dr. Paul L. Redditt for his extensive help in polishing the English for those essays composed by non-native speakers. We also thank those same authors for presenting their essays in English to provide the volume a wider audience. Finally, we want to thank Vera Bongert und Corinna Pfannkuche for compiling the index.

Münster / Waco, April 2012

Rainer Albertz
James D. Nogalski
Jakob Wöhrle

Contents

Methodological Issues

Editorial Issues

Historical Issues

Issues Concerning the Canon

Appendix

Methodological Issues

So Many Cross-References!
Methodological Reflections on the Problem of Intertextual Relationships and their Significance for Redaction Critical Analysis

JAKOB WÖHRLE

Westfälische Wilhelms-Universität Münster

Introduction

20 years ago, Old Testament scholarship found a new object: The Book of the Twelve.[1] Previously, scholars primarily focused on the individual books of this corpus. They asked about the formation, the structure, the intention or the historical backgrounds of the books of Hosea, Joel, Amos, and the other prophetical books in this collection. But they did not ask about the formation or the intention of the Book of the Twelve as a whole.

This changed in the 1990s. Scholars like James Nogalski, Erich Bosshard-Nepustil, and Aaron Schart elaborated for the first time comprehensively the thesis that the Book of the Twelve is not a mere collection of twelve individual books, but the product of a long-term redactional process.[2] According to their view the individual books were collected in several stages and on each redactional level these books underwent general redactions unifying the content of the individual books to an overall message.

The basis for this new approach is the identification of numerous intertextual relationships between the individual books in the Book of the Twelve.[3] These books are connected by literal cross-references, by similar headings, and by other common features with regards to form and content. To give just a few examples: Hos 4:1 and Mic 6:2 summon

---

1   For the following remarks cf. the research reviews Schart, *Entstehung*, 6–21; idem, "Redaktionsgeschichte," 13–33; Redditt, "Formation," 1–26; Wöhrle, *Sammlungen*, 3–24.

2   Nogalski, *Precursors*; idem, *Processes*; Bosshard-Nepustil, *Rezeptionen*; Schart, *Entstehung*.

3   Cf. for example Nogalski, *Precursors*, 20–57, who speaks of the "catchword phenomenon." Cf. idem, "Intertextuality."

the people to hear "because Yhwh has a legal dispute against the inhabitants of the land/his people" (כי ריב ליהוה עם־יושבי הארץ/עמו); Joel
2:13 and Jonah 4:2 characterize Yhwh as "gracious and merciful, slow
to anger and of great kindness, one who relents from doing evil"
(חנון ורחום ... ארך אפים ורב־חסד ונחם על־הרעה); Joel 3:5 and Obad
17 promise that "on mount Zion will be deliverance" (בהר ציון ... תהיה
פליטה); Joel 4:18 and Amos 9:13 predict that "the mountains will drip
sweet wine" (נטף ההרים עסיס); Zech 1:3 and Mal 3:7 call to repent with
the words "Return to me and I will return to you" (שובו אלי ... ואשוב[ה]
אליכם). Additionally, several passages in the Book of the Twelve deal
with similar topics like the day of Yhwh (Joel 1–4; Amos 5:18–20; Obad
15; Zeph 1:7–18; Mal 3:23–24), the nations' pilgrimage to mount Zion
(Mic 4:1–4; Zeph 3:10; Zech 8:20–23; 14:16–19) or the coming of a new
king (Amos 9:11; Mic 5:1–4; Zech 9:9–10).

Redaction critical approaches take note of these intertextual relationships and explain them as the product of deliberate redactional
processes. On this basis, at least a small consensus has been achieved
regarding the earliest collections of the Book of the Twelve: the exilic
Book of the Four comprising the books of Hosea, Amos, Micah, and
Zephaniah, and the Haggai-Zechariah-Corpus.[4] But it has to be admit-
ted that no consensus about the further development of this corpus has
been reached.[5]

The reasons for the diverging results of current research may be
manifold. But one of the reasons has to do with the aforementioned
intertextual relationships. It is far from clear how to integrate the many
intertextual relationships detected within the Book of the Twelve into a
solid redaction critical model. To state this more concretely: it remains
unclear how to prove whether and which intertextual relationships are
indeed the product of one and the same redaction with some degree of
certainty.[6]

Thus, the following considerations will treat the problem of intertextual relationships and their significance for redaction critical analy-

---

4   The existence of an exilic Book of the Four was proposed, for example, by Nogalski,
     Precursors, 176–178; Schart, *Entstehung*, 156–233; Albertz, *Exilszeit*, 164–185; idem,
     "Exile," 232–251; Zenger, *Einleitung*, 520; Wöhrle, *Sammlungen*, 51–284; idem, "Fu-
     ture," 608–627. That the books of Haggai and Zechariah once formed a common col-
     lection was already assumed in the year of 1896 by Klostermann, *Geschichte*, 213; cf.
     Beuken, *Haggai-Sacharja 1–8*, 331–336; Nogalski, *Precursors*, 256; Redditt, *Haggai*, 12.
     42–43; Wöhrle, *Sammlungen*, 285–385; idem, "Formation."
5   Cf. Wöhrle, *Abschluss*, 2–14.
6   This is one of the most important reasons for the critique against current research on
     the formation of the Book of the Twelve; cf. Ben Zvi, "Books," esp. 135–137; idem,
     "Twelve Hypothesis," 85–96; Rudnig-Zelt, "Genese," 359 note 25.

sis. The article will, first, deal with the phenomenon of intertextuality and draw some methodological consequences for reconstructing the formation of the Book of the Twelve. In a second step, as an illustration of the methodological considerations and as a test case, the article will present the results for one redactional level.

1. Intertextuality and the Formation of the Book of the Twelve

1.1 The Phenomenon of Intertextuality

It was Julia Kristeva, a French-Bulgarian literary theorist, who brought the term "intertextuality" into use. In her article "Le mot, le dialogue et le roman" from 1966 Kristeva defines "intertextuality" not as a specific characteristic of an individual text, but as a general characteristic of any given text.[7] According to Kristeva, any text exists in relationship to other texts. Even more, any text is in relationship with the whole anterior literary corpus. Thus, Kristeva says:[8]

> "... tout texte se construit comme mosaïque de citations, tout texte est absorption et transformation d'un autre texte."

Notably enough, Kristeva in her definition of intertextuality does not refer to texts as concrete individual texts.[9] For Kristeva, text is rather a general term encompassing culture, history, or society. Kristeva acts on the assumption of a universal, infinite space of texts, out of which concrete texts arise and with which they are in relationship. Thus, Kristeva uses the term "intertextuality" in a broad, general sense.

Different from her definition, in the subsequent debate – in literary as well as in biblical studies – this term came to be used in a narrower sense.[10] With the term "intertextuality" scholars now mostly describe the phenomenon of concrete interrelationships between concrete individual texts and based upon this understanding they ask for the intention of literary cross-references.

Such a restricted application of the term "intertextuality" was anathema to Kristeva. For her, the term was misused "dans le sens ba-

---

7   Kristeva, "Mot;" (ET: "Word"). For Kristeva's approach see, for example, Pfister, "Konzepte," 1–11; van Wolde, "Texts," 1–4; Steins, *Bindung*, 48–56; Schmitz, *Literaturtheorie*, 91–92.

8   Kristeva, "Mot," 146 (ET: "... any text is constructed as a mosaic of quotations; any text is the absorption and transformation of another." [Kristeva, "Word," 66]).

9   Kristeva, "Mot," 145–146 (ET: "Word," 65–66); cf. Pfister, "Konzepte," 6–7.

10   Cf. Pfister, "Konzepte," 11–30; van Wolde, "Texts," 4–7; Schmitz, *Literaturtheorie*, 92–97.

nal de 'critique des sources'."[11] She gave up this term and henceforth she spoke about "transposition." However, the question of how to explain intertextual relationships – be it banal or not – remained.

This question raises serious methodological problems. The main problem is evident, but important to note. Intertextual relationships can be explained in several ways. First, one can distinguish between intentional and unintentional relationships.[12] Since texts, as Kristeva correctly pointed out, do not arise out of an empty space, but out of a space of given texts, of given culture, history, and society, not every intertextual relationship between two texts has to be explained as an intentional relationship. It could also be that two texts react to the same cultural, historical, or social circumstances or that they simply use the same common formulations or common motifs. Additionally, it could be that two texts independently cite the same source text.

Second, when dealing with an intentional intertextual relationship between two texts, several kinds of literary dependency can be distinguished.[13] In a simplified model, three cases are possible:

- text A is dependent upon text B
- text B is dependent upon text A
- text A and text B trace back to the same author

Intertextuality is thus a phenomenon to be handled with care. On its own, intertextuality is just a descriptive term pointing to the interrelatedness of any given literature. But explaining this interrelatedness in more detail requires more sophisticated differentiation. One has to distinguish between intentional and unintentional intertextual relationships, and one has to distinguish between different kinds of literary dependency. Working on a model for the formation of a literary corpus like the Book of the Twelve, these claims have to be considered.

1.2 Methodological Consequences for Reconstructing the Formation of the Book of the Twelve

In previous research biblical scholars often based their work on the formation of the Book of the Twelve by examining a certain part of the Book of the Twelve, and out of the insights gained from these parts they drew consequences for the whole corpus. For example, James No-

---

11 Kristeva, *Révolution*, 60 (ET: "in the banal sense of 'study of sources'" [*Revolution*, 60]).
12 Cf. for example Helbig, *Intertextualität*, 45.
13 For the problem of determining the direction of literary dependencies, cf. for example Carr, "Method."

galski, at first, focused upon the opening and the concluding chapters of the individual books.[14] Other scholars started by examining an individual book or an individual tradition mentioned in several books. Aaron Schart worked on the book of Amos,[15] Burkard Zapff analyzed the book of Micah,[16] Martin Beck focused upon those passages mentioning the day of Yhwh.[17] In a second step, they looked for comparable features within the rest of the Book of the Twelve and on this basis they developed a model for the formation of the whole corpus.

Without a doubt, all of these scholars have done a lot of work to reach plausible results for the formation of the Book of the Twelve. Many of their hypotheses, especially for the earlier layers, are still valid, and they paved the way for further research on the Book of the Twelve.

The approach chosen by these scholars bears, however, one important risk. The insights gained from one specific part of the Book of the Twelve are transferred to the other parts of this corpus without sufficient control. But as the previously noted considerations of the phenomenon of intertextuality showed, common features between two different texts can be explained in many different ways. Intertextual relationships can be unintentional. They can be caused by similar cultural, historical, and social circumstances. They can be traced back to common formulations, common motifs, or to quotations of a common source text. And as mentioned above, even in the case of intentional intertextual relationships three different kinds of literary dependency are possible.

Against this background, the following methodological demands are appropriate.[18] First, any model for the reconstruction of the Book of the Twelve has to be based on a redaction critical analysis of all the individual books. Only in a second step can it then be asked whether the redactional layers detected within the individual books are connected by common features and thus trace back to the same hand. Ideally, this procedure makes it possible to show that the individual books, from a certain time forward, show comparable redactional processes.[19]

---

14 Nogalski, *Precursors*; idem, *Processes*.
15 Schart, *Entstehung*.
16 Zapff, *Studien*.
17 Beck, *Tag YHWHs*.
18 Cf. Wöhrle, *Sammlungen*, 24–27.
19 This does not mean that every redactional layer has to be detected in every book. It is important, however, that from a certain time forward the redactional development of an individual book shows correspondences to the redactional development of the other books.

Such an approach has considerable advantages. It helps to avoid transferring insights gained from one part of the Book of the Twelve to other parts without some further control. Additionally, based on a redaction critical analysis of each book it is possible to demonstrate whether literary cross-references were brought into the individual books on the same redactional level or whether one passage was brought into the corpus after the other.

However, this approach still poses an important problem. Even if the individual books show comparable redactional processes, this discovery need not lead to the assumption that a redactional layer detected in one book and a redactional layer in another book, which were brought in at the same time and which show common features, trace back to the same hand. Based on the aforementioned considerations on intertextual relationships, it could also be that these common features are unintentional. They could, for example, be caused by the fact that both texts react to the same cultural, historical, or social circumstances.

This problem can be solved, however, by a second methodological demand. The redaction critical approach has to be combined with a composition critical approach.[20] It has to be shown that the individual additions of a certain redactional layer detected in several books form an overall structure. Only in this case, is it possible to say with sufficient certainty that the common features of secondary passages found in different books lead one to the conclusion that these passages were added by one and the same hand.

The fact that intertextual relationships can be explained in different ways thus leads to the methodological demands that the reconstruction of the formation of the Book of the Twelve has to be based on a redaction critical analysis of each book and that the redaction critical findings have to be combined with composition critical considerations. By so doing, composition critical observations function as a cross-check for redaction critical assumptions. Additionally, by following this process, diachronic and synchronic approaches – often seen as alternatives in biblical studies – can be combined since both the formation and the structure of each redactional layer up to the canonical form of the Book of the Twelve are taken into account. Finally, the composition critical observations can help to explain the intention of the individual redactional layers in more detail.

---

20 Already Albertz, "Exile," 235–236, put in this methodological claim for reconstructing the formation of the Book of the Twelve; cf. Werlitz, *Redaktion*, 1–14.

In what follows, this methodological approach will be illustrated by casting a quick glance at the results for one redactional level of the Book of the Twelve, the Grace-Corpus.[21]

2. A Test Case:
The Grace Formula in the Book of the Twelve

One of the most obvious intertextual relationships within the Book of the Twelve is the quotation of the so called grace formula known from Exod 34:6 that appears in Joel 2:13 and in Jonah 4:2.[22] Both passages describe God's character with the same words as being "gracious and merciful, slow to anger and of great kindness, one who relents from doing evil" (חנון ורחום ... ארך אפים ורב־חסד ונחם על־הרעה).

Scholars debate how to define the direction of the literary dependency between these two passages. The most common view is held by scholars like Erich Bosshard-Nepustil, Aaron Schart, or Jörg Jeremias who argue that Joel 2:13 represents the earliest instance of the Exodus passage within the Book of the Twelve and that Jonah 4:2 depends upon Joel.[23] Other scholars like Siegfried Bergler or Hermann Spieckermann articulate the dependency from the opposite direction and claim that Joel 2:13 depends upon Jonah 4:2.[24] Additionally, Ernst Sellin and Hans Walter Wolff proposed that both passages independently took up a common source text.[25] And Raymond C. van Leeuwen supposed that Joel 2:13 and Jonah 4:2 trace back to the same hands.[26] Thus, nearly every possible hypothesis is on the table.

However, the evidence becomes even more complicated when one takes into account that in addition to Joel 2:13 and Jonah 4:2, several other passages within the Book of the Twelve cite parts of the grace formula. Jonah 3:10, Mic 7:18–20, Nah 1:2b, 3a, and Mal 1:9a show striking terminological correspondences to the grace formula mentioned in Joel 2:13 and Jonah 4:2. This phenomenon raises the question of how to explain the literary relationship of all of these passages.

---

21 Cf. Wöhrle, *Abschluss*, 363–419; idem, "Reflection."
22 The term "grace formula" (Gnadenformel) was established by Spieckermann, "Barmherzig," 3. Concerning Exod 34:6 and the parallels to this formula cf., for example, Scharbert, "Formgeschichte," 130–150; Dentan, "Affinities," 34–51; Scoralick, *Güte*, 10–203; Franz, *Gott*, 111–153.
23 Nogalski, *Processes*, 273 note 79; Bosshard-Nepustil, *Rezeptionen*, 424; Schart, *Entstehung*, 288; Jeremias, *Joel*, 107.
24 Bergler, *Joel*, 230–233; Spieckermann, "Barmherzig," 15–16 with note 41.
25 Sellin, *Zwölfprophetenbuch*, 126; Wolff, *Dodekapropheton 2*, 58.
26 Van Leeuwen, "Wisdom," 31–49.

Beginning with the previously mentioned methodological considerations, this question will be answered, first, by treating the formation
of these passages, second, by asking about their compositional relationship, and third, by outlining the intention of these passages.

2.1 The Redactional Character of the Individual Passages

The first passage to cite the grace formula within the Book of the
Twelve is Joel 2:12–14:

> 2:12 But now, oracle of Yhwh, turn to me with all your heart,
>   with fasting, with weeping, and with mourning.
>   13 And rend your heart, and not your garments,
>   and turn to Yhwh your God,
>   for he is gracious (חַנּוּן) and merciful (רַחוּם),
>   slow to anger (אֶרֶךְ אַפַּיִם), and of great kindness (חֶסֶד),
>   and he relents from doing evil (נִחָם עַל־הָרָעָה).
>   14 Who knows if he will turn and relent and leave a blessing
>   behind him,
>   grain offering and drink offering for Yhwh, your God?

In Joel 2:12–14 the people of Yhwh are summoned to repent, and this
summons is motivated in Joel 2:13 by a quotation of the grace formula.
Yhwh's gracious and merciful character, described in this formula,
offers the reason to hope that Yhwh will react to the repentance of the
people and turn to them again.

Interestingly enough, the subsequent passage in Joel (2:15–17) cites
another call for repentance. According to Joel 2:15–17 the people will be
gathered from the oldest to the youngest, and the priests will pray to
Yhwh and ask him to spare his people.

Thus, Joel 2:12–14 and Joel 2:15–17 are doublets. Both passages put
forward a call to repent, and they explain the concrete behavior re-
quested from the people. Additionally, the first passage in Joel 2:12–14
is directed to the people as a whole, but the second passage Joel 2:15–17
begins with a summons to gather the people.[27] These observations
strongly speak for the assumption that Joel 2:12–14 is a secondary addition to the growing book of Joel.[28]

The next quotations of the grace formula can be found in the book
of Jonah. Here, verses Jonah 3:6–4:2 are noteworthy:

---

27 Not without reason Sellin, *Zwölfprophetenbuch*, 126; Loretz, *Regenritual*, 51, thought
     that Joel 2:12–14 had its original place after Joel 2:15–17. However, they could not re-
     ally explain why this passage should have been transposed to its current position.
28 Thus already Duhm, "Anmerkungen," 186; Hölscher, *Profeten*, 432.

3:6 Then the word came to the king of Nineveh; he arose from his throne, took of his robe, put on sackcloth and sat in ashes.

7 He issued a proclamation and it said: In Nineveh by the decree of the king and his nobles: No person or animal, no herd or flock, may eat anything; they shall not feed, nor shall they drink water.

8 Men and beast must put on sackcloth and cry mightily to God. Every one shall turn from their evil ways and from the violence that is in their hands.

9 Who knows if God will turn and relent, and turn away from his burning wrath, so that we may not perish?

10 God saw their works, that they turned from their evil way, and God relented from doing the evil (נחם על־הרעה) that he had said he would bring upon them, and he did not do it.

4:1 This made Jonah very indignant, and he became angry.

2 He prayed to Yhwh and said: O Yhwh, isn't this what I said would happen when I was still in my own country? That was why I tried to flee to Tarshish, for I knew that you are a gracious (חנון) and merciful (רחום) God, slow to anger (ארך אפים) and of great kindness (חסד), one who relents from doing the evil (נחם על־הרעה).

Jonah 3:6–4:2 narrates a sequence of actions: the king of Nineveh calls his people to repent; God forgives the people of Nineveh; and the prophet Jonah gets angry about that forgiveness. This passage quotes the grace formula twice. Jonah 3:10 cites the phrase "God relented from doing the evil ..." (נחם על־הרעה), and Jonah 4:2 cites the whole formula using exactly the same phraseology as Joel 2:13.

Concerning the formation of this passage, it is interesting to note that the previous verse (3:5) already mentions that the people of Nineveh believed in God, and that they fasted and put on sackcloth. Thus, the king's call to repent in Joel 3:6–9 lags behind this description.[29] Additionally, Jonah 3:5 and 3:6–9 show interesting terminological differences. For example, in 3:5 the term גודל characterizes the older people, but in 3:7, it refers to the officials of the king. Jonah 3:5 uses the verb לבש to describe the dressing of the people with sackcloth, while 3:6, 8 use the verb כסה. Finally, Jonah 3:5 describes the fasting of the people with the term צום, while 3:7 uses the formulation טעם מאומה.

---

29 Many scholars have recognized that the king's call to return in Jonah 3:6–9 lags behind the description of the people's repentance in 3:5; cf. Marti, *Dodekapropheton*, 255; Wolff, *Dodekapropheton 3*, 120; Lux, *Jona*, 134 with note 176; Krüger, "Wachstum," 48; Jeremias, *Joel*, 100. Most of these scholars assume, however, that Jonah 3:6–9 explains the background for the previously mentioned events. However, Jonah 3:6–9 does not give any clear hint that the speech of the king took place at an earlier point in time and caused the people's repentance mentioned in 3:5.

These observations suggest that Jonah 3:6–4:2 is a secondary addition.[30] What should be stated, but cannot be shown in detail here is that these verses are part of a broader redactional reworking of Jonah focusing upon the conditions and the theological background of divine forgiveness.[31]

Further allusions to the grace formula can be found in the concluding verses of the book of Micah in Mic 7:18–20:

> 7:18 Who is a God like you pardoning iniquity
>   and passing over the transgression of the remnant
>   of his heritage?
>   He does not retain his anger forever,
>   because he delights in kindness (חסד).
>   19 He will again show mercy against us (ירחמנו),
>   he will subdue our iniquities,
>   and 'he will' throw all 'our sins'[32] into the depths of the sea.
>   20 You will give truth to Jacob,
>   kindness (חסד) to Abraham,
>   as you have sworn to our fathers from the days of old.

Mic 7:18–20 reflects upon the gracious character of Yhwh. In so doing, it takes up the terms kindness (חסד) and mercy (רחם) known from the grace formula.

While the preceding passage Mic 7:8–17 predicts judgment against foreign nations, this perspective is absent in Mic 7:18–20. These verses are formulated as a prayer to God and they deal with the iniquities of the people and God's willingness to show mercy against them. Thus, Mic 7:18–20 is a secondary addition to this book.[33]

Comparable observations can be made in Nah 1:2b, 3a:

> 1:2b Yhwh takes vengeance on his adversaries
>   and he rages against his enemies.
>   3a Yhwh is slow to anger (ארך אפים), and great in power,
>   and he never lets go unpunished.

---

30 Cf., with differences regarding the details, Weimar, "Jon 4,5," 107–108; Krüger, "Wachstum," 48.

31 Based on a redaction critical analysis of the whole book of Jonah, the primary layer of this book comprises Jonah 1:1–5a, 7, 8aαb, 9, 11–13, 15; 2:1, 11; 3:1–5; 4:5, 6*(without יהוה and without להציל to גדולה), 7–9, while the secondary layer presenting a theological reflection on divine forgiveness consists of Jonah 1:5b, 6, 8aβ, 10abα, 14, 16; 2:2–10; 3:6–10; 4:1–4, 6*(יהוה) and להציל to גדולה), 10–11; cf. Wöhrle, *Abschluss*, 365–399; idem, "Reflection," 3–5.

32 Read with LXX (ἀπορριφήσονται … τὰς ἁμαρτίας ἡμῶν) והשליך and חטאותנו; cf. Jeremias, *Joel*, 220.

33 Cf. Wolff, *Dodekapropheton 4*, 189–192, who argued that Mic 7:18–20 is an originally indepent unit secondarily added to the book of Micah.

Nah 1:2b, 3a presents Yhwh as a vengeful God who punishes his adversaries. With the characteristic phrase "slow to anger" (אֶרֶךְ אַפַּיִם) this passage again refers to the grace formula.

In the present form of the book Nah 1:2b, 3a is part of the theophanic psalm (1:2–8). This psalm is shaped as an acrostic.[34] Nah 1:2b, 3a, however, does not fit into the acrostic. It stands in between the א-line in Nah 1:2a and the ב-line in Nah 1:3b. This interruption suggests that Nah 1:2b, 3a is also a later addition.[35]

The same holds true for Mal 1:9a:

> 1:9a But now, entreat the face of God,
> and he will be gracious to us (חנן).

Mal 1:9a calls a group to repent to Yhwh and motivates this call with the promise that Yhwh will be gracious. Thus, Mal 1:9a refers to Yhwh's gracious character using the term חנן known from the grace formula.[36]

Remarkably enough, Mal 1:9a is formulated in the 1st person plural, while its direct context in Mal 1:8, 9b–14 is written as divine speech. Additionally, according to Mal 1:9a, the invocation of God is the condition for his forgiveness, while the rest of Mal 1:6–14 is concerned with accurate offerings. This change of perspective suggests that Mal 1:9a is also a secondary addition.[37]

The redaction critical considerations show that all the passages within the Book of the Twelve citing the grace formula (Joel 2:12–14; Jonah 3:6–4:2; Mic 7:18–20; Nah 1:2b, 3a; Mal 1:9a) are later additions. This secondary character could suggest that these passages trace back to one and the same hand working on the whole Book of the Twelve. However, the methodological reflections presented previously caution us that the intertextual relationships between these passages could also be unintentional. For example, it is possible that different redactors working independently of one another, referred to the same source text. Important to this discussion, several other passages outside the Book of the Twelve also cite the grace formula (Num 14:18; Ps 86:15; 103:8; 145:8; Neh 9:17). Thus, the redaction critical results have to be connected with composition critical observations.

---

34 Cf. for example Seybold, *Nahum*, 19; Perlitt, *Nahum*, 8; Roth, *Israel*, 238–241.
35 Elliger, *Propheten*, 3–4; Nogalski, *Processes*, 105–107; Schart, *Entstehung*, 243; Perlitt, *Nahum*, 8; Roth, *Israel*, 241, et al.
36 Cf. Meinhold, *Maleachi*, 120.
37 Thus already Lescow, "Strukturen," 207, for Mal 1:9 as a whole.

2.2 The Composition of the Grace-Corpus

Regarding the compositional relationship of the passages citing the grace formula, at first on a general level, the distribution of these passages over the Book of the Twelve is remarkable:[38]

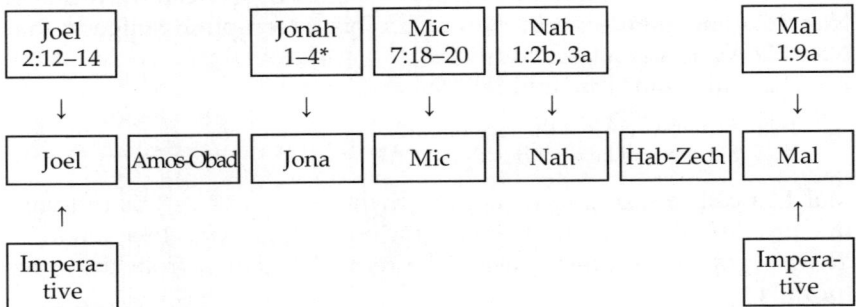

Joel 2:12–14		Jonah 1–4*	Mic 7:18–20	Nah 1:2b, 3a		Mal 1:9a
↓		↓	↓	↓		↓
Joel	Amos-Obad	Jona	Mic	Nah	Hab-Zech	Mal
↑						↑
Imperative						Imperative

These passages were incorporated into the books of Joel, Jonah, Micah, Nahum, and Malachi at the beginning, in the middle, and at the end of the corpus. Additionally, it is remarkable that only the additions in Joel 2:12–14 and Mal 1:9a, and thus only the first and the last addition, include an imperative directed to the addressees of the book (Joel 2:13; Mal 1:9a). With Joel 2:12–14 and Mal 1:9a the appeal to turn to Yhwh, decisive in these two passages, now frames the whole corpus.

Finally, and most important, the distribution of the individual elements of the grace formula is notable:

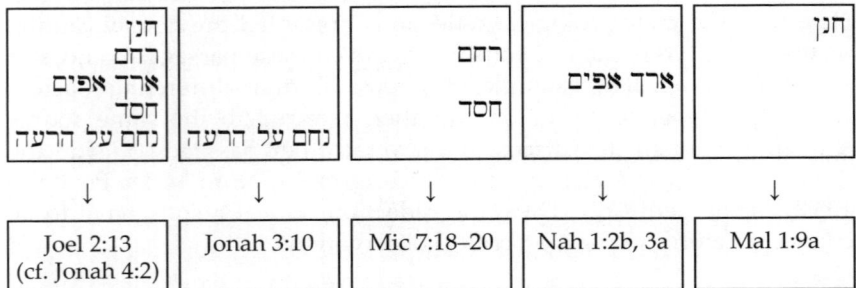

חנן רחם ארך אפים חסד נחם על הרעה	נחם על הרעה	רחם חסד	ארך אפים	חנן
↓	↓	↓	↓	↓
Joel 2:13 (cf. Jonah 4:2)	Jonah 3:10	Mic 7:18–20	Nah 1:2b, 3a	Mal 1:9a

---

38 The following considerations presuppose that the book of Hosea has not been part of the Grace-Corpus. For the assumption that the book of Hosea was part of the exilic Book of the Four, but was taken out of this collection and was not re-integrated into the Book of the Twelve until a very late stage, see the detail in Wöhrle, *Sammlungen*, 450–453; idem, *Abschluss*, 429–437.

The whole formula is cited in Joel 2:13 and Jonah 4:2. Within the other additions just one or two individual terms of the grace formula are mentioned. Interestingly enough, within these passages every individual element of the grace formula of Joel 2:13 // Jonah 4:2 is taken up exactly once more. The phrase נחם על־הרעה is mentioned in Jonah 3:10, the terms חסד and רחם in Mic 7:18–20, ארך אפים in Nah 1:3a, and חנן in Mal 1:9a. That means, the grace formula, completely cited in Joel 2:13 // Jonah 4:2, is taken up step by step fragmented in its elements in Jonah 3:10; Mic 7:18–20; Nah 1:2b, 3a; Mal 1:9a.

Thus, the secondary additions to the books of Joel, Jonah, Micah, Nahum, and Malachi influenced by the grace formula indeed constitute an all-encompassing composition. This linking can be taken as distinct evidence that these passages trace back to one and the same redaction. The result of this redactional reworking of the Book of the Twelve is a new corpus of prophetical books with a new aggregate intention: the Grace-Corpus.

2.3 The Intention of the Grace-Corpus

The Grace-Corpus concerns itself with the question of Yhwh's willingness to forgive. Based upon older prophetic writings, taken up by the redactors of this corpus, it specifies the conditions, the theological background, and the limits of divine forgiveness.

For this purpose, at first, the additions in Joel 2:12–14 and Mal 1:9a frame the entire corpus and call the people to repent. Thus, from its edges, the Grace-Corpus can be understood as a broad appeal to turn to Yhwh.

However, the Grace-Corpus is not only determined by this call to repent. It also explains why Yhwh is willing to react to the repentance of the people. For this reason the additions made by the redactors of this corpus continuously refer to the grace formula. For them the description of God's character presented in this formula is the theological key for understanding God's willingness to forgive.

Thus, at the beginning of the corpus, in Joel 2:12–14, the call to repent in Joel 2:12, 13a is motivated by a quotation of the grace formula. Because of God's gracious and merciful character it is possible that he will save his people from the agricultural distress mentioned in Joel 1:1–2:11. The subsequent promise in Joel 2:18–27, according to which Yhwh will end the distress, can now be understood as the initial evidence that he indeed reacts to the repentance of the people and turns to them with grace.[39]

In the middle of the grace-corpus, the book of Jonah gives another broad portrayal of Yhwh's willingness to forgive. Jonah 1–3 presents a threefold description of how Yhwh reacts to the repentance of a certain group of people, and the final chapter citing the grace formula in Jonah 4:2 gives the theological reason for divine forgiveness. Additionally, Jonah 3:10 emphasizes one specific element of the grace formula: Yhwh relents from doing evil (נחם על־הרעה).[40] Exemplified by the fate of Nineveh, the book of Jonah points out that Yhwh is willing to cancel the judgment he had planned to do.

At the end of the book of Micah, 7:18–20 mentions two further elements of the grace formula: Yhwh's mercy (רחם) and his kindness (חסד). This last word of the book of Micah thus gives a theological explanation of the twofold way from judgment to salvation in the preceding book (Mic 1–3 / 4–5 and Mic 6:1–7:7 / 7:8–17). According to Mic 7:18–20 the mercy and kindness of Yhwh is the reason that the judgment oracles given in Mic 1–3; 6:1–7:7 do not represent the final word from Yhwh because he, as documented in Mic 4–5; 7:8–17, is willing to forgive.

At the beginning of the book of Nahum, a book with harsh words of judgment against the city of Nineveh, Nah 1:2b, 3a takes up the phrase "slow to anger" (ארך אפים) from the grace formula. This passage points out that Yhwh's willingness to forgive has its limits. Yhwh, though slow to anger, is ultimately able and willing to act in anger and to punish his adversaries.[41]

Thus, in the middle of the grace corpus, the books of Jonah, Micah, and Nahum develop Yhwh's willingness to forgive in two directions. The book of Jonah describes how Yhwh again and again relents from the evil he had planned to do. The book of Micah presents a twofold way from judgment to salvation and the end of the book (7:18–20) emphasizes Yhwh's mercy and kindness as the reason for this change. However, the book of Nahum states that Yhwh's willingness to forgive has its limits. Although Yhwh is slow to anger, he is able and willing to act in anger.

At the end of the Grace-Corpus, Mal 1:9a presents another call to repent. Additionally, this small passage takes up the last missing element of the grace formula, חנן, emphasizing Yhwh's gracious behavior. Thus, Mal 1:9a, as a concluding remark, states again that repentance is

---

39 For this interpretation of Joel 2 cf. Jeremias, *Joel*, 6.
40 For the term רחם cf. Jeremias, *Reue*, and the new monograph Döhling, *Gott*.
41 Cf. for example Scoralick, *Güte*, 195–196; Franz, *Gott*, 261–262; Roth, *Israel*, 247–248.

the condition of Yhwh's willingness to forgive and that Yhwh will react to this repentance.

On the redactional level of the Grace-Corpus the growing Book of the Twelve thus gets a theological superstructure. The Book of the Twelve now gives a theological explanation for the manifold ways from judgment to salvation presented within the prophetical writings collected in this corpus. Based on the grace formula, this corpus mentions Yhwh's gracious and merciful character as the reason for his willingness to forgive and it specifies the conditions and the limits of divine forgiveness.

Conclusion

The phenomenon of intertextuality raises serious methodological problems. These problems are caused by the fact that intertextual relationships can be explained in many different ways. Literary connections can be intentional or unintentional, and even in case of an intentional interrelationship several kinds of literary dependency are possible.

Any model for the formation of the Book of the Twelve has to consider these problems and must be built upon a solid methodological foundation. At least two methodological claims seem appropriate. First, the starting point for reconstructing the formation of the Book of the Twelve should be a complete redaction critical analysis of every individual book. Second, redaction critical observations have to be combined with composition critical considerations. In this way it is possible to prove whether two interrelated passages from two different books trace back to the same hand and are thus the product of redactional work on the growing Book of the Twelve as a whole. Additionally, the intention of such redactional work can be described in more detail.

Thus, the explanation of intertextual relationships is by no means banal, but an important and illuminating task that provides insights both on a historical and on a theological level.

References

Albertz, R. *Die Exilszeit: 6. Jahrhundert v. Chr.* Biblische Enzyklopädie 7. Stuttgart: Kohlhammer, 2001.
– "Exile as Purification: Reconstructing the 'Book of the Four.'" Pp. 232–251 in *Thematic Threads in the Book of the Twelve*. Edited by P.L. Redditt and A. Schart. BZAW 325. Berlin: de Gruyter, 2003.

Beck, M. *Der "Tag YHWHs" im Dodekapropheton: Studien im Spannungsfeld von Traditions- und Redaktionsgeschichte*. BZAW 356. Berlin: de Gruyter, 2005.

Ben Zvi, E. "Twelve Prophetic Books or 'The Twelve': A Few Preliminary Considerations." Pp. 125–156 in *Forming Prophetic Literature: Essays on Isaiah and the Twelve*. Edited by J.W. Watts and P.R. House. FS J.D.W. Watts. JSOTSup 235. Sheffield: Sheffield Academic Press, 1996.

– Is the Twelve Hypothesis Likely from an Ancient Readers' Perspective. Pp. 47–96 in *Two Sides of a Coin: Juxtaposing Views on Interpreting the Book of the Twelve / the Twelve Prophetic Books*. Edited by idem and J.D. Nogalski. Analecta Gorgianna 201. Piscataway: Gorgias Press, 2009.

Bergler, S. *Joel als Schriftinterpret*. BEATAJ 16. Frankfurt: Lang, 1988.

Beuken, W.A.M. *Haggai–Sacharja 1–8: Studien zur Überlieferungsgeschichte der frühnachexilischen Prophetie*. SSN 10. Assen: Van Gorcum, 1967.

Bosshard-Nepustil, E. *Rezeptionen von Jesaia 1–39 im Zwölfprophetenbuch: Untersuchungen zur literarischen Verbindung von Prophetenbüchern in babylonischer und persischer Zeit*. OBO 154. Fribourg: Universitätsverlag and Göttingen: Vandenhoeck & Ruprecht, 1997.

Carr, D. "Method in Determination of Direction of Dependence: An Empirical Test of Criteria Applied to Exodus 34,11–26 and its Parallels." Pp. 107–140 in *Gottes Volk am Sinai: Untersuchungen zu Ex 32–34 und Dtn 9–10*. Edited by M. Köckert and E. Blum. Veröffentlichungen der Wissenschaftlichen Gesellschaft für Theologie 18. Gütersloh: Gütersloher, 2001.

Dentan, R.C. "The Literary Affinities of Exodus xxxiv 6f." *VT* 13 (1963) 34–51.

Döhling, J.-D. *Der bewegliche Gott: Eine Untersuchung des Motivs der Reue Gottes in der Hebräischen Bibel*. Herders biblische Studien 61. Freiburg: Herder, 2009.

Duhm, B. "Anmerkungen zu den Zwölf Propheten." *ZAW* 31 (1911) 1–43.81–110.161–204.

Elliger, K. *Die Propheten Nahum, Habakuk, Zephanja, Haggai, Sacharja, Maleachi*. Vol. 2 of *Das Buch der zwölf kleinen Propheten*. ATD 25. 3rd ed. Göttingen: Vandenhoeck & Ruprecht, 1956.

Franz, M. *Der barmherzige und gnädige Gott: Die Gnadenrede vom Sinai (Exodus 34, 6–7) und ihre Parallelen im Alten Testament und seiner Umwelt*. BWANT 160. Stuttgart: Kohlhammer, 2003.

Helbig, J. *Intertextualität und Markierung: Untersuchungen zur Systematik und Funktion der Signalisierung von Intertextualität*. Heidelberg: Winter, 1996.

Hölscher, G. *Die Profeten: Untersuchungen zur Religionsgeschichte Israels*. Leipzig: Hinrichs, 1914.

Jeremias, J. *Die Reue Gottes: Aspekte alttestamentlicher Gottesvorstellung*. Biblisch-theologische Studien 31. 2nd ed. Neukirchen-Vluyn: Neukirchener, 1997.

– *Die Propheten Joel, Obadja, Jona, Micha*. ATD 24,3. Göttingen: Vandenhoeck & Ruprecht, 2007.

Klostermann, A. *Geschichte des Volkes Israel: Bis zur Restauration unter Esra und Nehemia*. München: Beck, 1896.

Kristeva, J. "Le mot, le dialogue et le roman." Pp. 143–173 in *Σημειωτική: Recherches pour une sémanalyse*. Edited by eadem. Paris: Éditions du Seuil, 1969.

– *La révolution du langage poetique: L'avat-garde a la fin du XIXᵉ siècle: Lautréamont et Mallarmé.* Paris: Éditions du Seuil, 1974.
– "Word, Dialogue, and Novel." Pp. 64–91 in *Desire in Language: A Semiotic Approach to Literature and Art.* Edited by eadem. Oxford: Blackwell, 1980.
– *Revolution in Poetic Language.* New York: Columbia University Press, 1984.
Krüger, T. "Literarisches Wachstum und theologische Diskussion im Jona-Buch." Pp. 41–65 in *Kritische Weisheit: Studien zur weisheitlichen Traditionskritik im Alten Testament.* Edited by idem. Zürich: Pano, 1997.
Lescow, T. "Dialogische Strukturen in den Streitreden des Buches Maleachi." *ZAW* 102 (1990) 194–212.
Loretz, O. *Regenritual und Jahwetag im Joelbuch: Kanaanäischer Hintergrund, Kolometrie, Aufbau und Symbolik eines Prophetenbuches.* UBL 4. Altenberge: CIS, 1986.
Lux, R. *Jona: Prophet zwischen 'Verweigerung' und 'Gehorsam': Eine erzählanalytische Studie.* FRLANT 162. Göttingen: Vandenhoeck & Ruprecht, 1992.
Marti, K. *Das Dodekapropheton.* KHC 13. Tübingen: Mohr, 1904.
Meinhold, A. *Maleachi.* BKAT 14,8. Neukirchen-Vluyn: Neukirchener, 2006.
Nogalski, J. *Literary Precursors to the Book of the Twelve.* BZAW 217. Berlin: de Gruyter, 1993.
– *Redactional Processes in the Book of the Twelve.* BZAW 218. Berlin: de Gruyter, 1993.
– "Intertextuality and the Twelve." Pp. 102–124 in *Forming Prophetic Literature: Essays on Isaiah and the Twelve.* Edited by J.W. Watts and P.R. House. FS J.D.W. Watts. JSOTSup 235. Sheffield: Sheffield Academic Press, 1996.
Perlitt, L. *Die Propheten Nahum, Habakuk, Zephanja.* ATD 25,1. Göttingen: Vandenhoeck & Ruprecht, 2004.
Pfister, M. "Konzepte der Intertextualität." Pp. 1–30 in *Intertextualität: Formen, Funktionen, anglistische Fallstudien.* Edited by U. Broich and idem. Tübingen: Max Niemeyer, 1985.
Redditt, P.L. *Haggai, Zechariah and Malachi.* New Century Bible Commentary. Grand Rapids: Eerdmans, 1995.
– "The Formation of the Book of the Twelve: A Review of Research." Pp. 1–26 in *Thematic Threads in the Book of the Twelve.* Edited by idem and A. Schart. BZAW 325. Berlin: de Gruyter, 2003.
Roth, M. *Israel und die Völker im Zwölfprophetenbuch: Eine Untersuchung zu den Büchern Joel, Jona, Micha und Nahum.* FRLANT 210. Göttingen: Vandenhoeck & Ruprecht, 2005.
Rudnig-Zelt, S. "Die Genese des Hoseabuches: Ein Forschungsbericht." Pp. 351–386 in *Textarbeit: Studien zu Texten und ihrer Rezeption aus dem Alten Testament und der Umwelt Israels.* Edited by K. Kiesow and T. Meurer. FS P. Weimar. AOAT 294. Münster: Ugarit-Verlag, 2003.
Scharbert, J. "Formgeschichte und Exegese von Ex 34,6f und seiner Parallelen." *Bib* 38 (1957) 130–150.
Schart, A. *Die Entstehung des Zwölfprophetenbuchs: Neubearbeitungen von Amos im Rahmen schriftenübergreifender Redaktionsprozesse.* BZAW 260. Berlin: de Gruyter, 1998.
– "Zur Redaktionsgeschichte des Zwölfprophetenbuchs." *VF* 43 (1998) 13–33.

Schmitz, T.A. *Moderne Literaturtheorie und antike Texte: Eine Einführung.* Darmstadt: Wissenschaftliche Buchgesellschaft, 2002.

Scoralick, R. *Gottes Güte und Gottes Zorn: Die Gottesprädikationen in Exodus 34,6f und ihre intertextuellen Beziehungen zum Zwölfprophetenbuch.* Herders biblische Studien 33. Freiburg: Herder, 2002.

Sellin, E. *Das Zwölfprophetenbuch.* KAT 12. Leipzig: Deichert, 1922.

Seybold, K. *Nahum, Habakuk, Zephanja.* ZBK 24,2. Zürich: Theologischer Verlag, 1991.

Spieckermann, H. "Barmherzig und gnädig ist der Herr ..." *ZAW* 102 (1990) 1–18.

Steins, G. *Die "Bindung Isaaks" im Kanon (Gen 22): Grundlagen und Programm einer kanonisch-intertextuellen Lektüre.* Herders biblische Studien 20. Freiburg: Herder, 1999.

van Leeuwen, R.C. "Scribal Wisdom and Theodicy in the Book of the Twelve." Pp. 31–49 in *In Search of Wisdom.* Edited by L.G. Perdue. FS J.G. Gammie. Louisville: Westminster, 1993.

van Wolde, E. "Texts in Dialogue with Texts: Intertextuality in the Ruth and Tamar Narratives." *BibInt* 5 (1997) 1–28.

Weimar, P. "Jon 4,5: Beobachtungen zur Entstehung der Jonaerzählung." *BN* 18 (1982) 86–109.

Werlitz, J. *Redaktion und Komposition: Zur Rückfrage hinter die Endgestalt von Jesaja 40–55.* BBB 122. Berlin: Philo, 1999.

Wöhrle, J. *Die frühen Sammlungen des Zwölfprophetenbuches: Entstehung und Komposition.* BZAW 360. Berlin: de Gruyter, 2006.

– "The Formation and Intention of the Haggai–Zechariah Corpus." *Journal of Hebrew Scriptures* 6.10 (2006) 1–14.

– *Der Abschluss des Zwölfprophetenbuches: Buchübergreifende Redaktionsprozesse in den späten Sammlungen.* BZAW 389. Berlin: de Gruyter, 2008.

– "'No Future for the Proud Exultant Ones': The Exilic Book of the Four Prophets (Hos., Am., Mic., Zeph.) as a Concept Opposed to the Deuteronomistic History." *VT* 58 (2008) 608–627.

– "A Prophetic Reflection on Divine Forgiveness: The Integration of the Book of Jonah into the Book of the Twelve." *Journal of Hebrew Scriptures* 9.7 (2009) 1–17.

Wolff, H.W. *Dodekapropheton 2: Joel und Amos.* BKAT 14,2. 2nd ed. Neukirchen-Vluyn: Neukirchener, 1975.

– *Dodekapropheton 3: Obadja und Jona.* BKAT 14,3. Neukirchen-Vluyn: Neukirchener, 1977.

– *Dodekapropheton 4: Micha.* BKAT 14,4. Neukirchen-Vluyn: Neukirchener, 1982.

Zapff, B.M. *Redaktionsgeschichtliche Studien zum Michabuch im Kontext des Dodekapropheton.* BZAW 256. Berlin: de Gruyter, 1997.

Zenger, E. *Einleitung in das Alte Testament.* 7th ed. Stuttgart: Kohlhammer, 2008.

Synchronic and Diachronic Concerns in Reading the Book of the Twelve Prophets

MARVIN A. SWEENEY
Claremont School of Theology
Claremont Graduate University

I

The questions of the literary form and compositional history of the Book of the Twelve Prophets has emerged as a major concern in recent scholarship. Interpreters have increasingly recognized that Book of the Twelve Prophets as a whole stands as a literary work in its own right as well as a presentation of its twelve constitutive prophetic books.[1] Although a number of models have been put forward, the redaction-critical readings of Nogalski, Schart, Wöhrle, and others have emerged as an important force in contemporary critical scholarship.[2] In general, these scholars have developed a model that traces the compositional history from an initial late-monarchic or exilic book of four prophets that grew through a series of stages into the full form of the Twelve Prophets that emerged in the Hellenistic period. The model has been quite influential in central European scholarship, in large measure due to the appeal of diachronically-oriented redaction-critical models among German-speaking scholars, but it has less of a following in North American and English-speaking circles where more synchronically-oriented canonical and literary models are becoming increasingly influential.[3]

The division between these two approaches is both unnecessary and counterproductive to the larger interests of modern, critical scholarship. Indeed, developments in redaction-critical methodology call explicitly for a combination of synchronic and diachronic strategies in reading biblical texts. Several methodological issues must be considered.

---

1   For discussion of the Book of the Twelve, see esp. Sweeney, *Twelve Prophets*, 1:xv-xlii; Redditt, "Formation," 1–26; Wöhrle, *Sammlungen*, 1–27.
2   Nogalski, *Precursors*; idem, *Processes*; Schart, *Entstehung*; Wöhrle, *Sammlungen*; idem, *Abschluss*; see also Zapff, *Studien*.
3   See, e.g., Conrad, *Zechariah*; Ben Zvi, *Micah*; idem, *Hosea*.

First is the synchronic question of the final form of the text at hand
and its role in setting the agenda for diachronic study of the text.[4] Classical redaction-critical method frequently presupposes that redaction-
criticism appears near the end of the sequence of methodological steps
because of the secondary nature of redactional additions to the text.[5]
But Rolf Knierim argues that biblical exegesis must grapple with redaction-critical concerns at the outset, beginning with consideration of the
final form of the text, insofar as biblical texts come to us from the hands
of their presumed final redactors who would have expanded and
shaped the text according to their own concerns and understanding of
the text at hand.[6] Interpreters cannot assume at the outset that a text is
the product of redaction or that the interpretation of the final form of
the text is self-evident. Rather, the final form of the text must be critically analyzed first to understand fully the organization, conceptualization, and concerns of the text as a whole. Only then may the text be
probed for evidence of earlier levels of composition that must be reconstructed as well as the settings from which those levels of composition
would have derived. Indeed, explicit reference to later settings within
the literature in question is crucial, such as the references to Cyrus in
Isa 44:28 and 45:1 that provide a key argument to demonstrating the
exilic setting of Second Isaiah. This issue is of particular importance to
current research on the Book of the Twelve insofar as contemporary
scholars often presume textual discontinuity without first understanding the organizational patterns and underlying conceptualization of the
final form of the text. This problem is particularly acute when one considers the thin formal and linguistic bases, such as alleged Deuteronomistic language, as well as the influence of later theological categories,
such as eschatology and the Day of YHWH, on which much of contemporary redaction-critical work proceeds in reading the Book of the
Twelve.

Second is the synchronic and diachronic problem of textual criticism. For the most part, biblical scholars are trained to view textual
versions, such as the Septuagint, Dead Sea Scrolls, Targums, Peshitta,
Vulgate, etc., as treasure troves for improving the reading of the Masoretic text. But as text critical research has developed during the twentieth century and beyond, scholars have learned to recognize that the
versions have their own distinctive literary characters and theological
or hermeneutical outlooks that mark them as literary-theological works

4   See Sweeney, "Formation," 113–126; idem, "Form Criticism," 58–89.
5   Richter, *Exegese,* 165–173; Hayes and Holladay, *Biblical Exegesis,* 127–138; cf. Steck,
     Exegesis, 75–93.
6   Knierim, "Criticism," 123–165; cf. idem, "Form Criticism," 435–468.

in their right.[7] Although versions such as the LXX may be translated from an underlying Hebrew text, the interpretation of a version such as the LXX is not necessarily dependent upon an understanding of the proto-Masoretic text or other Hebrew versions from which it might be derived. Such an observation has tremendous ramifications for reading the Book of the Twelve and reconstructing its compositional history, especially when we consider that the Septuagint forms of the book – with their variety of sequences in the orders of the twelve constituent books – differ markedly from the Masoretic form and its well-known order of books. Given this consideration, it is not entirely clear that the MT represents the earliest form of the Book of the Twelve that would then stand as the foundation for redaction-critical work. Analysis of the Book of the Twelve must begin with the synchronic task of assessing the final forms of the versional texts in question, e.g., the Septuagint, Masoretic, and other relevant forms, to address the diachronic question of their respective socio-religious, socio-political, and historical settings. Only then may work turn to the diachronic process of reconstructing the literary growth that led to those textual forms.

Third is the problem of evaluating textual coherence or more properly the lack thereof, which has been the primary basis for identifying the literary seams that point to redactional layers in a biblical text for well over a century. John Barton calls this methodological procedure into question by raising the issue of the so-called disappearing redactor.[8] The disappearing redactor refers to a redactor who has done the work of redaction so well that the literary seams are no longer evident, thereby depriving critics of one of the primary criteria employed in redaction-critical research. The issue is further complicated by advances in literary criticism, insofar as literary scholars such as Meir Sternberg have demonstrated the importance of the role of textual gapping, in which textual discontinuity so often functions as a deliberate means employed to signal elements of plot and characterization within a single text.[9] Scholars must now reckon with the possibility that a coherent text in fact is a redactional text and a discontinuous or gapped text may well be the work of an original author. Again, this issue is of particular importance to study of the Book of the Twelve, which comprises twelve relatively coherent and discrete prophetic books in an order that is inherently unstable. Given the differences in the sequence of the constituent books, we cannot presume a specific sequence among

---

7   See e.g., van der Kooij, *Textzeugen;* idem, *Oracle.*
8   Barton, *Reading,* 45–60.
9   Sternberg, *Poetics.*

the books or even that there was a collection of books prior to the present forms of the Twelve.

Fourth is the question of how biblical books are received and read. Modern literary criticism has correctly challenged the traditional diachronic notion of the author as the governing factor in the interpretation of literature. For most of the twentieth century, modern scholarship has proceeded on the basis of the view that the reconstruction of the earliest levels of texts in relation to their earliest settings gives us access both to the original text forms and to the setting and intentions of its original authors. But modern reader response criticism raised the question of the role of the reader in the construction of literature, i.e., to what extent do the reader's concerns govern the interpretation of literature and indeed construct the text insofar as those concerns then set the agenda for interpretation?[10] Indeed, modern scholarship is replete with examples in which New Testament concerns are read back into the text of the Hebrew Bible. The interpretation of the phrase, והיה באחרית הימים, "and it shall come to pass in later days," in Mic 4:1 and Isa 2:2 has so frequently been interpreted as a signal of the text's eschatological concerns. But such an interpretation is based on the LXX rendition of the phrase, καὶ ἔσται ἐπ᾽ ἐσχάτων, "and it will come to pass upon the end of days," and later Second Temple period and NT concerns with eschatology. Comparison with the usage of the Akkadian cognate of the phrase, *ana aḥrat ūmī*, literally, "in the back of days," and examination of והיה באחרית הימים in context demonstrates that it simply refers to the future, not to an eschatological scenario as has been presumed by so many interpreters working under the influence of the LXX rendition of the phrase and its understanding in relation to NT concerns.[11] Concern with the text's reception does not negate concern with the text's author as some modern literary critics contend. Rather, reader response and reception criticism open a discussion as to how texts are interpreted in later times and contexts as a complement to attempts to reconstruct the intentions of the author. Such concerns have important implications for reading the Book of the Twelve, especially when we consider that visions of restoration in the monarchic period might have a very different construction when they are read in the Persian, Hellenistic, or Greco-Roman periods and beyond.

With these considerations in mind, this paper assesses the final forms of the Septuagint and Masoretic versions of the Book of the Twelve Prophets in an effort to understand their distinctive orders of presentation and to reconstruct socio-political, socio-religious, and his-

---

10   See McKnight, "Reader," 230–252; cf. Conrad, *Isaiah*; idem, *Prophets*.
11   Seebass, "*'aḥărît*," 210–212; cf. De Vries, *Revelation*, 89–95.

torical settings in which each form would have been produced. The paper presupposes my earlier redaction-critical analyses of the books of Hosea, Amos, Micah, Zephaniah, Nahum, and Habakkuk within the Book of the Twelve presented in my study of the role played by King Josiah's program of religious reform and national restoration in the composition of biblical literature.[12] My earlier analyses of these books argued that Hosea, Amos, Zephaniah, Nahum, and Habakkuk are discrete compositional wholes that were composed in relation to specific concerns and settings in the late-monarchic period. Micah, however, shows evidence of having been redacted to address concerns with the Babylonian exile.

Analysis of both the final forms of the Book of the Twelve and its constituent prophetic books points to a very different model for reading the Book of the Twelve as a whole and for reconstructing its compositional history. This paper argues that the LXX order of the book represents the original sequence of the Book of the Twelve that dates to the early Persian period whereas the MT represents a later order of books that may be placed in relation to the efforts of Ezra and Nehemiah later in the Persian period to restore Jerusalem as the holy center of post-exilic Judah.

II

The Book of the Twelve Prophets appears in a variety of forms, including the Masoretic text, a variety of Septuagint forms, several forms known from the manuscripts of the Judean wilderness, and others. An assessment of these forms is necessary in order to determine the basis on which analysis of the Book of the Twelve as a whole can proceed.[13]

The Masoretic Hebrew text of the Twelve Prophets constitutes a long recognized standard form of the text, including a standard order of its constituent prophetic books. The MT order includes Hosea, Joel, Amos, Obadiah, Jonah, Micah, Nahum, Habakkuk, Zephaniah, Haggai, Zechariah, and Malachi. This order is not mentioned in the Talmudic discussion of the order of the biblical books (b Baba Batra 14b). It does appear in Masoretic Hebrew manuscripts beginning with the Cairo Codex of the Prophets, which dates to 896 C.E., and it is generally recognized as the oldest manuscript of the Masoretic version of the Prophets. The MT order also appears in two manuscripts of the Book of the

---

12 Sweeney, *Twelve Prophets*; cf. idem, *King*, ad loc.
13 Sweeney, *Twelve Prophets*, 1:xxvii–xxxix; idem, "Sequence," 175–188.

Twelve from the Judean wilderness, including the Wadi Murabba`at Twelve Prophets scroll (Mur 88), which dates to the second century C.E., and the Naḥal Ḥever Greek Twelve Prophets Scroll (8ḤevXIIgr), which dates to the late first century B.C.E.[14] Although Barthélemy views the Naḥal Ḥever Greek XII Prophets scroll as an early example of the so-called *kaige* recension of the Septuagint, its very wooden translation style – including instances when it simply transliterates a Hebrew term whose meaning is not clear – its close adherence to the proto-Masoretic text, and its adoption of the proto-Masoretic order of the Twelve Prophets indicates that it is not a recensional text at all. Instead, the Naḥal Ḥever Greek Twelve Prophets scroll must be considered as a somewhat crude local translation of the proto-Masoretic text not unlike that witnessed in the Wadi Murabba`at Twelve Prophets scroll.[15] The proto-MT order of the Twelve Prophets was also employed in the Vulgate, which was produced by Jerome in the fourth century B.C.E. on the basis of Jewish sources available at the time.

The Greek manuscript tradition witnesses a wide variety of orders in the presentation of the Book of the Twelve Prophets, but a number of the earliest uncial manuscripts present the order Hosea, Amos, Micah, Joel, Obadiah, Jonah, Nahum, Habakkuk, Zephaniah, Haggai, Zechariah, and Malachi.[16] These manuscripts include Codex Vaticanus, which dates to the fourth century C.E.; Codex Sinaiticus, which also dates to the fourth century C.E.; Codex Alexandrinus, which dates to the fifth century C.E.; Codex Marchalianus, which dates to the sixth century C.E.; and Codex Basiliano-Venetus, which dates to the eighth–ninth century C.E. This order also appears in the canon lists of Pseudo-Gelasius (decret. De libr.), falsely attributed to the late-fifth century Pope Gelasius, and Codex Claromontanus, which dates to the fifth or sixth century C.E. The relatively early dates of these manuscript witnesses indicate an early LXX order which continues to appear in critical editions of the LXX. Although this order is not explicitly cited in the Babylonian Talmud, the Talmud's discussion of the order of books raises the possibility of a historical sequence, including Hosea, Isaiah, Amos, and Micah, which may presuppose the order now found in the early LXX uncials.

Other orders are also known, but none appears as consistently as those of the (proto-)MT and early-LXX traditions, and so they need not be considered.[17] Altogether, these orders demonstrate great fluidity in

---

14   See Milik, "Rouleau," 181–205; Tov, *Prophets*.
15   Barthélemy, *Devanciers*; cf. my discussion in *Zephaniah*, 26–28.
16   See Swete, *Introduction*, 125–128.129–132.197–230.
17   For discussion, see Jones, *Formation*; Ben Zvi, "Twelve Prophetic Books," 125–156.

the reading of the sequence of the Book of the Twelve so that we must establish which order of the book likely represents the earliest form of the Book of the Twelve Prophets.

In my earlier work on sequence of the Book of the Twelve, I have identified distinctive conceptualizations underlying our two primary text forms.[18] The LXX sequence begins with Hosea, Amos, and Micah, which has generally been understood to represent an interest in grouping the books historically in the LXX, but close attention to the order of these three books indicates that this is not the case at all. Amos cites events associated with the Israelite-Aramaean wars of the late-ninth and early-eighth century B.C.E., and makes no overt references to the Assyrian empire. Hosea is very much concerned with Israel's alliance with Assyria, initiated under King Jehu (r. 842–815 B.C.E.) and continued by his descendants through the reigns of King Jeroboam ben Joash (786–746 B.C.E.) and King Zechariah ben Jeroboam (746 B.C.E.). Micah presupposes the Assyrian invasion of Judah by Sennacherib in 701 B.C.E. and even describes his own experience in fleeing from his hometown of Moresheth-Gath on the border between Judah and Philistia, which is precisely where Sennacherib struck. The chronology of these three prophets must be Amos, Hosea, and Micah rather than Hosea, Amos, and Micah. Chronology therefore does not satisfactorily explain the sequence.

Although chronology may be influential, insofar as Hosea, Amos, and Micah are all eighth century prophets, another principle must explain their order. Concern with the anticipated judgment against the northern kingdom of Israel emerges as the principle that motivates the sequence of these books. Hosea is explicit in condemning the northern kingdom – and to a lesser extent, Judah – insofar as he employs the metaphor of his own failed marriage with Gomer to explain YHWH's plans for judgment against the purportedly faithless bride Israel (Hos 1–2). But Hosea also envisions the reunification of Israel and Judah under a Davidic king as part of the process of restoration (Hos 3:1–5). Amos clearly condemns northern Israel, particularly for its alleged crimes of social justice against his native Judah (Amos 2:6–16). He, too, calls for the restoration of Davidic rule over Israel and Judah (Amos 9:11–15). Micah has much criticism for the kings of northern Israel, whose decisions led to the invasion of his homeland, but he has plenty of critique for the Davidic kings who followed in their northern counterparts' footsteps, ultimately costing Micah his home (Micah 1–3). For all of Micah's dissatisfaction with the kings, the book envisions a Da-

---

18   Sweeney, *Twelve Prophets*, 1:xxvii–xxxix; idem, "Sequence," 175–188.

vidic king who will overthrow the nations that threaten Israel – but it
does so in relation to the aftermath of Babylonian exile (Micah 4–5).

Micah's critique of the northern and southern kings then leads us to
Joel, which portrays YHWH's defeat of the threats posed by the nations
to Jerusalem. Indeed, Joel's frequent intertextual citations frequently
take up Obadiah, which follows in the LXX sequence.[19] Obadiah focuses on judgment against Edom, one of the nations that threatened Jerusalem in Judean history. Jonah takes up the question of YHWH's mercy
to Nineveh, thereby preserving the very city that would one day destroy northern Israel and subjugate Judah. Jonah's position prior to Nahum is auspicious in the LXX form of the Book of the Twelve. Nahum celebrates the downfall of Nineveh, the Assyrian oppressor
spared in Jonah that went on to destroy Israel and subjugate Judah.
Habakkuk establishes that YHWH has brought the Chaldeans, i.e., neo-
Babylonians, to threaten Jerusalem but will ultimately defeat them for
their alleged arrogance and crimes (Hab 1–2). Zephaniah warns Jerusalem to adhere to YHWH or suffer the consequences. Haggai calls upon
the people of Persian-period Jerusalem to rebuild the Temple. Zechariah portrays the significance of rebuilding the Temple, anticipating
YHWH's defeat of the oppressor nations who have subjugated the city.
Finally, Malachi calls for adherence to YHWH's Torah and Temple as
the bases for restoring the ruptured covenant.

Altogether, the LXX sequence of the Book of the Twelve points to
an interest in the fate of the northern kingdom of Israel and its implications for Jerusalem and Judah. Just as northern Israel would suffer punishment for its failure to adhere to YHWH's will, so Jerusalem and Judah would suffer the same fate if they did not learn the lesson. But once
the punishment was over, YHWH would act to restore Jerusalem and
the people at large, who would then be expected to adhere to YHWH's
expectations. Indeed, Micah correlates the concern with northern Israel's punishment with the question of restoration following the Babylonian exile. But the Babylonian exile does not otherwise become an explicit concern until much later in the sequence of the Twelve when
Habakkuk questions YHWH concerning the presence of the Babylonians in Judah and Haggai, Zechariah, and Malachi presuppose settings
in the aftermath of the Babylonian exile.

When we turn to the MT sequence of the Book of the Twelve, we
see a different set of concerns in which the fate of Jerusalem appears to
be highlighted throughout. The MT begins with Hosea's portrayal of
the disruption of the covenant and its implications for northern Israel,

---

19   For discussion of Joel's intertextual citations of Obadiah and other biblical works, see
      esp. Bergler, *Joel*.

but it immediate turns to Joel with its interest in the threat posed to Jerusalem by the nations. It then returns to Amos's indictment of northern Israel, but then it turns in Obadiah to an indictment of Edom, which is well-known for its role in the Babylonian destruction of Jerusalem and the Temple. Micah's diatribes against the northern and then the southern kings precedes YHWH's efforts to save Nineveh from judgment once the people of the city repented. With Nahum's celebration of the downfall of Nineveh, Jerusalem's deliverance from oppression once again comes to the forefront. Habakkuk focuses on Judah – with obvious implications for Jerusalem – in his dialog with YHWH concerning the presence of the Chaldeans, and his anticipation of YHWH's deliverance once the punishment of the land is complete. Haggai, Zechariah, and Malachi are all expressly concerned with Jerusalem and the Temple.

The differing sequences of books and the underlying concerns that come to expression in these sequences demand consideration of the socio-religious, historical, and political settings that would have produced each. When we see the concern with the northern kingdom of Israel in the LXX sequence, with its focus on judgment against Israel, its anticipation of reunification under a Davidic king, its focus on judgment against Jerusalem, and finally its interest in the restoration of Jerusalem, we see a concern that is initially rooted in the reigns of Hezekiah and Josiah. Both monarchs are portrayed as engaging in Temple reform and revolt against their Assyrian overlords with an eye to reasserting Davidic rule over the territory and people of the former northern kingdom of Israel. Of course, with the inclusion of clearly post-exilic books, such as Haggai, Zechariah, and Malachi, the monarchic period cannot serve as the setting for the full form of the LXX version of the book. But the concern with northern Israel's experience as a model for that of Jerusalem and the anticipation of full restoration points most decidedly to the early Persian period, when the restoration of the Temple pointed to the possibility of the nations' recognition of YHWH's worldwide sovereignty by the nations and the potential for the restoration of Davidic rule over all Israel once again. Later periods, such as the later-Persian, Hellenistic, or Hasmonean periods, do not qualify. The later-Persian period sees no overt interest in the restoration of Israel and Judah or even of Davidic kingship. The Hellenistic period likewise sees no interest in the reunification of Israel and Judah or the restoration of Davidic kingship, particularly after Alexander the Great brutally suppressed Samaria but established an alliance with Jerusalem. The Hasmonean period sees no restoration of Davidic kingship as the Hasmoneans, who actually restored Jerusalem's rule over northern Israel,

were not Davidic. But interest in the restoration of the Davidic monarchy emerges during the period of Hasmonean rule as the Judean population becomes increasingly dissatisfied with their Hasmoneans rulers.

When we turn to the concern with Jerusalem throughout the Masoretic sequence of the Twelve, we see that it is concerned with the potential threats to Jerusalem and YHWH's plans to restore the city and
Temple once the threats have passed. Such concerns might well find
their impetus in the post-Josian monarchic period, but the inclusion of
clearly post-exilic books, such as Haggai, Zechariah, and Malachi, point
to later periods. Although concern with northern Israel still appears, its
focus has been diluted by the deliberate highlighting of Jerusalem's
fate, both in terms of judgment and restoration, throughout. Although
the building of the Temple and Zerubbabel's return to Jerusalem might
have ignited hopes for the reunification of Israel and Judah in the early
Persian period, no such reunification appears to be contemplated in
later periods. The portrayal of the administrations of Nehemiah and
Ezra focus on the restoration of Jerusalem throughout, but the relationship with Samaria is invariably portrayed as one of conflict and threat
against Jerusalem. Likewise, the concluding emphasis on adherence to
YHWH's Torah and Temple fits well with the Ezra-Nehemian setting.
Although concerns with the restoration of Davidic kingship also appear
throughout the sequence, they are a distant vision to be realized once
the full period of punishment is over. Later periods again do not qualify. Jerusalem is not threatened during the Hellenistic period as indicated by Alexander's alliance with the city and the subsequent period of
Ptolemaic rule. Although the Seleucid dynasty clearly threatens Jerusalem, the rise of the Hasmonean dynasty precludes the restoration of
Davidic rule.

Although both forms of the Book of the Twelve are extant for centuries to come, it appears that the LXX sequence, with its interest in the
fate of northern Israel as a model for Jerusalem's and Judah's future, is
the earlier form of the book. Indeed, the close intertextual relationships
between Joel and Obadiah, on the one hand, and Jonah and Nahum, on
the other hand, appear to support such a contention. Consequently, any
theory of the redactional formation of the Book of the Twelve Prophets
must account for the LXX sequence of books.

III

Two major conclusions may be drawn from this discussion. First, we cannot assume that the Masoretic text provides us with a full basis for engaging in redaction-critical work on the Book of the Twelve. The variety of text forms of the Book of the Twelve indicates a fluid order in their presentation that must be assessed in order to determine which sequence constitutes the earliest form of the book. Although the proto-Masoretic form of the book is known from the Judean Desert, the LXX order of the books appears to be the earliest insofar it presents a concern with judgment against the northern kingdom of Israel that serves as a paradigm for understanding judgment against Jerusalem and Judah prior to restoration of the whole. Such concerns would have originated in the reigns of Kings Hezekiah and Josiah of Judah who sought to bring the territory and population of the northern kingdom of Israel back under Davidic rule, but of course such an ambition was never realized during the reign of either king. Such concerns persisted through the early Persian period, however, when the rebuilding of the Jerusalem Temple was believed to portend the restoration of the house of David and the recognition of YHWH's sovereignty in Jerusalem throughout the entire world. The MT sequence indicates an interest in the fate of Jerusalem, including its punishment and its restoration, which is best set in the period of Ezra and Nehemiah and continued through the Second Temple period.

Second, the differing orders of the constituent books of the Book of the Twelve indicate that these books must be viewed as discrete compositions within the whole that can be shifted in sequence according to an overarching view of their respective significance within the larger form of the Book of the Twelve. Such an observation undermines views that each book is the product of gradual growth that was at least in part designed to shape them for their specific places within the Book of the Twelve. Indeed, my earlier individual analyses of Hosea, Amos, Micah, Zephaniah, Nahum, and Habakkuk demonstrate that, with the exception of Micah, each is preoccupied with a set of concerns relevant to the historical settings identified within the book for each. Only Micah shows an interest in the Babylonian exile which would point to a potential interest in the overarching viewpoints of the book as a whole. There is little effort to correlate the books as a whole through their superscriptions, although Nogalski, Schart, Wöhrle, and others are likely correct in noting sub-collections within the whole, such as Hosea, Amos, Micah, and Zephaniah, or Haggai, Zechariah, and Malachi. Nevertheless, it is unlikely that overarching concerns with an eschatological day of

YHWH or the like has played a role in the redactional-correlation of these books. Such an agenda is not consistently applied throughout the books of the Twelve nor are the Day of YHWH and other passages pertaining to the future markedly eschatological in relation to the concerns of their compositional settings. Rather, such concerns are read into the text by later readers. Instead, Micah appears to have been redacted with an eye to addressing the concerns of the Babylonian exile, but it is not clear that this redaction took place with an eye to shaping the Book of the Twelve.

In sum, the Book of the Twelve must be viewed as both a literary work in and of itself, albeit in each of its extant forms witnessed by the MT, LXX, and other versions, as well as a collection of twelve independently composed prophetic books that have been brought together to form the whole.

References

Barthélemy, D. *Les devanciers d'Aquila*. VTSup 10. Leiden: Brill, 1963.

Barton, J. *Reading the Old Testament: Method in Biblical Study*. Louisville: Westminster John Knox, 1996.

Ben Zvi, E. "Twelve Prophetic Books or the Twelve? A Few Preliminary Considerations." Pp. 125–156 in *Forming Prophetic Literature: Essays on Isaiah and the Twelve in Honor of John D.W. Watts*. Edited by J.W. Watts and P.R. House. JSOTSup 235. Sheffield: Sheffield Academic Press, 1996.

−   *Micah*. FOTL 21B. Grand Rapids: Eerdmans, 2001.

−   *Hosea*. FOTL 21A part 1. Grand Rapids: Eerdmans, 2005.

Bergler, S. *Joel als Schriftinterpret*. BEATAJ 16. Frankfurt: Lang, 1988.

Conrad, E.W. *Reading Isaiah*. OBT. Minneapolis: Fortress, 1991.

−   *Zechariah*. Readings. Sheffield: Sheffield Academic Press, 1999.

−   *Reading the Latter Prophets: Towards a New Canonical Criticism*. JSOTSup 376. London: T&T Clark, 2003.

De Vries, S.J. *From Old Revelation to New: A Tradition-Historical and Redaction-Critical Study of the Temporal Transitions in Prophetic Prediction*. Grand Rapids: Eerdmans, 1995.

Hayes, J.H. and Holladay, C.R. *Biblical Exegesis: A Beginner's Handbook*. Louisville: Westminster John Knox, 2007.

Jones, B.A. *The Formation of the Book of the Twelve: A Study in Text and Canon*. SBLDS 149. Atlanta: Scholars Press, 1995.

Knierim, R. "Form Criticism Reconsidered." *Int* 27 (1973) 435–468.

−   "Criticism of Literary Features, Form, Tradition, and Redaction." Pp. 123–165 in *The Hebrew Bible and its Modern Interpreters*. Edited by D.A. Knight and G.M. Tucker. Chico: Scholars Press, 1985.

McKnight, E.V. "Reader Response Criticism." Pp. 230–252 in *To Each its Own Meaning: An Introduction to Biblical Criticisms and their Application*. Edited by S.L. McKenzie and S.R. Haynes. Louisville: Westminster John Knox, 1999.

Milik, J.T. "Rouleau des Douze Prophètes." Pp. 181–205 in *Les grottes de Murab-ba`at*. Edited by P. Benoit et al. DJD 2. Oxford: Clarendon, 1961.

Nogalski, J.D. *Literary Precursors to the Book of the Twelve*. BZAW 217. Berlin: de Gruyter, 1993.

– *Redactional Processes in the Book of the Twelve*. BZAW 218. Berlin: de Gruyter, 1993.

Redditt, P.L. "The Formation of the Book of the Twelve: A Review of Research," Pp. 1–26 in *Thematic Threads in the Book of the Twelve*. Edited by idem and A. Schart. BZAW 325. Berlin: de Gruyter, 2003.

Richter, W. *Exegese als Literaturwissenschaft: Entwurf einer alttestamentlichen Literaturtheorie und Methodologie*. Göttingen: Vandenhoeck & Ruprecht, 1971.

Schart, A. *Die Entstehung des Zwölfprophetenbuchs. Neubearbeitungen von Amos im Rahmen schriftenübergreifender Redaktionsprozesse*. BZAW 260. Berlin: de Gruyter, 1998.

Seebass, H. "*'aḥărît.*" *TDOT* 1 (1977) 210–212.

Steck, O.H. *Old Testament Exegesis: A Guide to the Methodology*. SBLRBS 39. Atlanta: Scholars Press, 1998.

Sternberg, M. *The Poetics of Biblical Narrative: Ideological Literature and the Drama of Reading*. Bloomington: Indiana University Press, 1985.

Sweeney, M.A. "Formation and Form in Prophetic Literature." Pp. 113–126 in *Old Testament Interpretation: Past, Present, and Future*. Edited by J.L. Mays et al. FS G.M. Tucker. Nashville: Abingdon, 1995.

– "Form Criticism." Pp. 58–89 in *To Each its Own Meaning: An Introduction to Biblical Criticisms and their Application*. Edited by S.L. McKenzie and S.R. Haynes. Louisville: Westminster John Knox, 1999.

– *The Twelve Prophets*. 2 vols. Berit Olam. Collegeville: Liturgical, 2000.

– *King Josiah of Judah: The Lost Messiah of Israel*. Oxford: Oxford University Press, 2001.

– *Zephaniah*. Hermeneia. Minneapolis: Fortress, 2003.

– "Sequence and Interpretation in the Book of the Twelve." Pp. 175–188 in *Form and Intertextuality in Prophetic and Apocalyptic Literature*. Edited by idem. FAT 45. Tübingen: Mohr, 2005.

Swete, H.B. *An Introduction to the Old Testament in Greek*. New York: KTAV, 1968.

Tov, E. *The Greek Minor Prophets Scroll from Naḥal Ḥever (8ḤevXIIgr)*. DJD 8. Oxford: Clarendon, 1990.

van der Kooij, A. *Die alten Textzeugen des Jesajabuches: Ein Beitrag zur Textgeschichte des Alten Testaments*. OBO 35. Fribourg: Universitätsverlag and Göttingen: Vandenhoeck & Ruprecht, 1981.

– *The Oracle of Tyre: The Septuagint of Isaiah XXIII as Version and Vision*. VTSup 71. Leiden: Brill, 1998.

Wöhrle, J. *Die frühen Sammlungen des Zwölfprophetenbuches: Entstehung und Komposition*. BZAW 360. Berlin: de Gruyter, 2006.

– *Der Abschluss des Zwölfprophetenbuches. Buchübergreifende Redaktionsprozesse in den späten Sammlungen*. BZAW 389. Berlin: de Gruyter, 2008.

Zapff, B.M. *Redaktiongeschichtliche Studien zum Michabuch im Kontext dem Dodekapropheton*. BZAW 256. Berlin: de Gruyter, 1997.

The Case of Edom in the Book of the Twelve: Methodological Reflections on Synchronic and Diachronic Analysis

RUTH SCORALICK

Eberhard Karls Universität Tübingen

1. Introduction

Mal 1:1   A pronouncement.
The word of YHWH to Israel through Malachi.

2 I love you, says YHWH.
But you say, "How do you love us?"
Is not Esau Jacob's brother? saying of YHWH.
Yet Jacob I have loved,

3 but Esau I have hated.
I have made his hill country a desolation
and his heritage a desert for jackals.

4 If Edom says,
"We are shattered but we will rebuild the ruins,"
thus says YHWH of hosts:
They may build, but I will tear down.
They will be called "region of wickedness,"
and "the people with whom YHWH is angry forever."

5 Your own eyes shall see this,
and you, you shall say:
"Great is YHWH over the region of Israel."[1]

The last time that Edom is mentioned in the Book of the Twelve is in this disturbing passage. It is the beginning of the book of Malachi.[2] God declares his love for Israel – and it seems that when asked to prove it, to demonstrate it, he points to his hatred of Esau. This hatred shows in the fate of the land of Edom in past and present, and even into an unlimited future: a land and people under the wrath of God – forever.

---

1   The translation of this last sentence is debated, some understand "great ... beyond the borders of Israel" (e.g. NRSV). I follow the plausible arguments listed by Meinhold, *Maleachi*, 23–24.55.

2   Whenever I speak of "Hosea" or "Malachi" etc. in the following pages, this refers to the books, not to any person.

I find the reasoning in the text hard to follow: How does hatred of someone demonstrate love for someone else? In what way does the devastation of Edom show YHWH's greatness in Israel? If election by God is at play, as many think, how are we to understand what is said of the non-elect in this passage? Is "not being elected" and being hated and actively rejected by God the same thing? If not, what was Esau/Edom's fault? What kind of knowledge does the text presuppose to be understood in a coherent way?

My aim in the following pages is twofold: I want to gain insights concerning the problems connected to Mal 1:2–5, and I want to present elements of a synchronic study of Edom in the Twelve that will help to reflect on fundamental hermeneutical and methodological issues in recent research. It is not my intention to discuss hermeneutics and methodology in the abstract. Rather, Edom in the Twelve and a synchronic, canonical approach will serve as a case study.

Finding elements of unity and coherence in the Book of the Twelve has been among the most exciting discoveries in research over the last fifteen years. There is no need to repeat the history of research at this point. A lot of work has been done on motifs, threads, patterns and shared vocabulary in the Twelve.

Redaction critical studies with an eye to larger units than the individual books of the Twelve have flourished, and work in that perspective is still in progress – as this volume shows. These studies with their methodological premises have been questioned and challenged by works from a tradition-critical perspective.[3] The floor is open for discussion.

Studies written from a different hermeneutical and methodological angle altogether do not seem to be quite as numerous, at least not in the German language. I especially refer to approaches that may be called canonical, relating the textual data not to the intentions of authors/redactors but analyzing them with respect to the reading process and interpreting this in the horizon of a community's canon of scripture. The point of interest is not the production of the text and its circumstances, but the literary context in a biblical canon and the way the text guides the reading processes. It is along these lines that the following reflections will proceed.

---

3   Cf. especially the studies of Beck, *Tag*, and Gärtner, *Summe*.

2. Recent Observations on Mal 1:2–5

Recently Rainer Kessler has put forward a short but profound study of Mal 1:2–5 that can be read as a canonical approach, even though Kessler did not intend it as such.[4] For Kessler, Mal 1:2–5 is not only organized according to the pattern of a disputation, it also shows a break between Mal 1:2–3 and v. 4–5. The text moves from Jacob and Esau in v. 2–3 to Edom and Israel in v. 4–5. At the same time, the verbal system shows a change from looking to the past to speaking about the future.[5] And there is the semantic move from preference and rejection in the family context, which can be expressed with the term "hatred" in Hebrew, to the total condemnation of Edom in v. 4–5. This movement and this condemnation, for Kessler, can only be understood by considering the intertextuality with Torah and Prophets and realizing that the latter texts are combined.[6]

> It is interesting to see that there is another voice in recent research that does not share the traditional view of Mal 1:2–5 as perfectly coherent. Jakob Wöhrle also underlines the break between v. 2–3 and 4–5.[7] For him it indicates a change of theme too: the future of Edom and the future insight of Israel (v. 5) are not answers to the present question of how God's love can be seen. At the same time these verses do not seem to fit into the context of Malachi. They represent the only mention of a foreign people in the book. While Mal 1:2–3 consider the question of God's love of his people, Mal 1:4–5, for Wöhrle, constitute a word of judgment against Edom. This is a later addition occasioned by Mal 1:2–3 mentioning Esau. The addition, Mal 1:4–5, according to Wöhrle belongs to a late redaction ("Fremdvölkerschicht II") that covers almost all sections concerning Edom in the Twelve.[8]

---

4 Kessler, "Jakob;" cf. his article, p. 223–236, in this volume. Kessler emphasizes Malachi's significant position in a TaNaK-structured canon: Malachi closes the Book of the Twelve and is the last book of the (Former and Latter) Prophets (Jos–Mal). Its last verses signal a closing function for Torah and Prophets together ("Jakob," 209). For a canonical reading, other structures of canon could and should be considered as well, and there are varieties of order in the Book of the Twelve. In several places (e.g. "Jakob," 219) Kessler mentions an author of Malachi and reflects on his possible knowledge of texts, which proves that his approach is not canonical.
5 Kessler, "Jakob," 214–215.
6 Cf. Kessler, "Jakob," 220: "Im Folgenden will ich zeigen, dass ... vor allem der Übergang von der grundlosen Zurücksetzung des Bruders Esau zur bedingungslosen Verurteilung Edoms, nicht verstanden werden kann, wenn man die zahlreichen intertextuellen Bezüge auf Tora und Prophetie nicht erkennt. Meine These ist, dass es sich dabei nicht um die punktuelle Aufnahme einzelner Motive oder Stichworte, sondern um ein bewusstes Zusammenlesen der Bezugstexte handelt."
7 Cf. Wöhrle, *Abschluss*, 219–222.
8 Wöhrle, *Abschluss*, 222. Wöhrle, ibid., 264–287, fits Mal 1,4–5 into his "Fremdvölkerschicht II" (Joel 4:4–8, 18–21; Amos 1:9–12; 9:12a, 13aβb; Obad 1–16, 17b, 18–21; Zech

Most scholars agree, that love and hate in Mal 1:2–5 are rhetorically not
on the same level. The point that is made in the passage concerns God's
love of Israel; mentioning his hatred is subordinate to that purpose. In
line with that notion, Kessler emphasizes that only God and Israel
speak to each other, Esau/Edom is left out of the communication, even
though it is cited in a soliloquy (Mal 1:4).

Love and hate, or election and rejection rest in God's free choice.
Once the text moves out of the familial context of the brothers Jacob
and Esau onto the plane of the people Israel and Edom, this raises the
question whether national interests are projected into God's will. Some
scholars think so.[9] Kessler tries to show that this is not necessarily, or at
least not exclusively, the case.

3. Rainer Kessler's proposal regarding Mal 1:2–5

Kessler sketches the way that readers will understand the textual move
in Malachi. They will fill in the gap by knowledge from the Torah and
Prophets. There is a pattern in the Torah's presentation of pairs of
brothers in the book of Genesis (cf. Cain and Abel, Ishmael and Isaac,
Jacob and Esau). Not being preferred is a status that can be accepted –
then all is well – or it can lead to unjust actions. The textual move in
Mal 1:2–5 lets readers suppose that things went badly with Esau/Edom.
The Torah supplies the necessary information for that. In the book of
Genesis the brothers Jacob and Esau themselves end up peacefully, yet
the story of their descendants in Num 20:14–21, Edom's denial to let
Israel pass through its land, explains how Edom becomes a "wicked
land" in the perspective of Mal 1:4–5. The word גבול (Num 20:16–17,
21), that occurs in both texts, is an important link.

Kessler, together with Arndt Meinhold and others, sees a justifica-
tion of God's primary choice in this outcome. "Die zunächst nicht be-
gründete Zurücksetzung des einen Bruders findet durch das Verhalten
seiner Nachfahren ihre nachträgliche Rechtfertigung."[10]

At the same time, Mal 1:3b, 4–5 refers to prophetic announcements
of doom about Edom. This can be seen on the level of shared vocabu-

---

9:2–6, 8, 11–13; 10:6–10, 12; 14:4, 6–10, 11*; Mal 1:1, 4–5) from Hellenistic times (mid
4th to mid 3rd century), that formed most of the book of Obadiah and integrated an
already existing form of the book of Malachi, exactly because Mal 1:2–3 concerned
Edom. The aim of this redaction is to apply the already existent hope on YHWH's
action against foreign peoples to a new situation. The historical background is the
capture of Jerusalem by Ptolemaios I ca. 302 B.C.E. (cf. ibid., 216–217).

9   E.g. Rudolph and Mason; cf. Kessler, "Jakob," 212–213.
10   Kessler, "Jakob," 222, the whole quotation is set in italics in the article.

lary (e.g. the root שׁמם).[11] The prophetic texts accuse Edom for diverse reasons. Kessler sees various historical experiences in their background that all together have led to an almost unsurpassable hatred of Edom. The announcements are seen as fulfilled in Malachi. The land of Edom is devastated and will stay that way into an unlimited future. The reasoning against Edom in prophetic texts, together with Num 20, justifies the judgment on Edom in Mal 1:2–5. Readers will supply the information from Torah and Prophets to understand the development of Esau/Edom in Mal 1:2–5 from being rejected or not preferred to being judged for unethical behavior.

Then how did the loved and elected Jacob/Israel develop, what does its present look like? Kessler emphasizes that Mal 1:2–5 is the opening of the book of Malachi and cannot be understood fully without considering the text that follows. Only Mal 1:2–5 concerns a foreign people, the rest of the book discusses inner-Israelite problems and conditions. The fourth and especially the sixth and last section (Mal 2:17–3:5 and 3:13–21) discuss the separation of the righteous and wicked on the coming day of YHWH. There are significant connections to the opening of the book. The structure of communication once again excludes one group, this time the wicked (3:1, 18, 19, 21, cf. רשׁעה in 1:4). The root בנה occurs in both passages (3:15; 1:4 twice). This way, the contrast of Edom and Israel of Mal 1 is set side by side with the contrast of righteous and wicked in Israel. For Kessler, this signifies that Mal 1:2–5 in the first place does not treat a contrast of nations but the contrast between righteous and violent behavior. This contrast is specified on the one hand by looking at Israel and Edom, and on the other hand by looking at conditions inside Israel.[12] To become like Edom is a possibility for parts of Israel, or, as Kessler puts it: Edom becomes a mirror for Israel.

In other words Kessler tries to demonstrate that there is a case to be made concerning Edom, that its present and – according to Mal 1:4–5 – lasting devastation is a consequence of justice being done. This could happen to Israel or parts of Israel too.

---

11   Kessler points to Jer 49:13; Ezek 25:13; Ezek 35; Joel 4:19; Obad 7. Mal 1:2–5 presents the fulfillment of these announcements (Kessler, "Jakob," 223). The vocabulary in v. 3b is rather important for the argumentation, while at the same time this is text from before the break in Mal 1:2–5.

12   "Es geht also, so lässt sich vom Schluss der Maleachi-Schrift rückblickend sagen, im ersten Wort nicht um einen nationalen Gegensatz, sondern um den Gegensatz von Gerechtigkeit und Gewalttätigkeit. Er findet auf das Verhältnis Israels zu Edom, aber auch auf die Verhältnisse innerhalb Israels Anwendung." (Kessler, "Jakob," 226, set in italics).

4. Considering the Context in the Book of the Twelve

I want to re-read Kessler's interpretation of Mal 1:2–5 from a decidedly
canonical position, following the MT-order of the text. The most important modification will be the emphasis on the nearest literary context,
the Book of the Twelve. Kessler refers to such elements on the same
level with reference to other prophetic books, but in a canonical reading
they gain a privileged position. Readers of the Twelve arrive at the
beginning of Malachi with knowledge and expectations that have been
formed to a large part by reading the book. Certain words and concepts
may have gained a characteristic profile related to the context of the
Twelve. Certain expectations arise that may be called up or fulfilled by
a very short reference. Such references may remain cryptic, when not
seen in the larger horizon. The Book of the Twelve in its first three
parts, Hosea, Joel and Amos, to my mind, confronts readers with two
decisive aspects. On the one hand, there are two cases where the text
engages its readers immediately, reaching out to them across the times,
only presupposing that they identify themselves with "Israel."[13] One is
Hos 11, especially Hos 11:8–9, and the other is the call to return to
YHWH in Joel 2:12–13. Hos 11 presents theology in a very literal sense:
at its core God is speaking about himself to Israel. Joel 2:12–13 is God's
call to Israel, transmitted by a prophet, to return and repent. Both texts
are quintessential to the Book of the Twelve concerning its theological
outlook and intended impact. Both can be read as elements that re-call
and re-enact foundational texts from the Pentateuch: the disclosure of
the name of God with its dramatic exegesis in Exod 32–34.[14] On the
other hand, right from the start, beginning with the placement of Joel
after Hosea, and continuing with the ties that can be seen between the
books, readers are taught the strategy to connect books and supply data
lacking in one from another. That way, readers of the Twelve will not
be clueless when they reach the book of Amos and arrive at the turning
point from wrath to mercy (Amos 9:7–8).[15] Similarly, they may learn
how the devastation of Edom shows God's love of Israel.

Observations from the context of the Twelve can strengthen some
of Kessler's arguments. The "wicked" in Mal 3:19–21 read in this context will remind readers of Edom, but not just from the characteristics listed by Kessler. The reference to them as זֵדִים (parallel to כָּל־עֹשֵׂה רִשְׁעָה)
in Mal 3:19 has its only lexical equivalent in the Twelve in Edom's זָדוֹן

---

13   On the hermeneutical questions of Christian readings of these texts see Dohmen and
     Stemberger, *Hermeneutik*.
14   Cf. Scoralick, *Güte*.
15   Cf. Steins, *Gericht*.

(Obad 3). The picture of both groups becoming stubble (קַשׁ) to be burned by the coming day of YHWH reminds one of Joel 2:5 (the day of YHWH) and Obad 18 (Edom).[16] These points, if elaborated, could strengthen Kessler's interpretation. At the same time, the book of the Twelve in two prominent places accuses Edom of violence (חָמָס against Judah in Joel 4:19; in Obad 10 against "your brother Jacob"). This will have to be taken seriously for the interpretation of Mal 1:2–5.

In other words the motif of the brotherhood of Jacob and Esau and the mention of the fate of Edom (the land as well as the people) gain specific connotations in Malachi when this book is read as the last book of the Twelve.

4.1 God's Love for Jacob/Israel

For a long time now scholars have recognized that Malachi contains echoes of images, themes and verbal formulations from the book of Hosea. There seems to be a characteristic correspondence between the opening and closing of the Book of the Twelve. Erich Zenger summarizes it:

> "Die Bücher Hosea und Maleachi haben durch ihre Anfangs- bzw. Schlussposition eine herausgehobene strukturelle und hermeneutische Funktion. Hos ist das am stärksten geschichtstheologisch imprägnierte Prophetenbuch; mit seinem intensiven Rückgriff auf die Anfänge Israels (Jakob; Exodus, Wüstenwanderung und Landnahme) entwirft es den theologischen Horizont für die im Zwölfprophetenbuch folgende Unheils- und Heilsankündigung. Vor allem stellt es die unendliche Liebe JHWHs zu seinem Volk Israel als das Fundament seines Zorns und seiner letztendlich rettenden Zuwendung heraus ... Der letzte Vers des Buchs (14,10) fasst schließlich die ganze Geschichte JHWHs mit seinem Volk und der Völkerwelt als ein Scheidungsgericht zwischen Gerechten und Treulosen zusammen. Genau diese beiden Perspektiven (JHWHs Liebe zu Israel sowie die Geschichte als Trennung der Gerechten und der Gottlosen) werden im Buch Maleachi aufgegriffen."[17]

One may add that the topic of God's special relationship to the land (of Israel) that is addressed almost at the beginning of Hosea (cf. Hos 1:2), and which recurs at a crucial point in the book of Joel (2:18), reaches its conclusion in Malachi in the dichotomy between Edom and Jacob. Edom is the "country of wickedness" (Mal 1:4) in contrast to the expec-

---

16 Mal 3:19 can serve as a reinterpretation of Obad 18. The third mention of קַשׁ, Nah 1:10, remains enigmatic, but fits into a scenario of judgment too.

17 Zenger, *Einleitung*, 519.

tation that the addressed people, the בני יעקב, will be the "land of delight" (ארץ חפץ, Mal 3:12).[18]

Concerning Mal 1:2–5, it is the motif of God's love that is of special interest now. Hosea speaks characteristically of God's love for Israel that is threatened to the point of being overcome by his (just) anger. Two of the three parts of Hosea (Hos 1–3; 4–11; 12–14) literally speak of the "case," the ריב of God against Israel/Juda (Hos 4:1; 12:3, cf. 2:4). God has every reason to show himself no longer merciful (cf. Hos 1:6–7) and to end the relationship with Israel, even taking back his name (cf. the implications in Hos 1:9). Thus, the beginning of the book announces the "case" and the following texts argue it. Using a memorable image, the pattern of the three parts of the book, read synchronically, has been compared by Norbert Lohfink to waves of God's mounting wrath that break at their highest point and turn to love.[19] Hosea 11 is the central theological text that speaks of the breaking of the wave, the "Herzensumsturz," as Jörg Jeremias has called it, the turning of God's heart within him.[20] Remarkably, this text is presented as spoken by God herself. At its most dramatic moment, when the final breaking of the relationship is at hand, God addresses Ephraim/Israel and lets it (and the readers) participate in an inner experience ("How can I give you up, Ephraim? ..."; Hos 11:8–9). Jan-Dirk Döhling has recently analyzed this text judiciously.[21] He points out that Hos 11 does not present readers with an insight into God's ever-loving nature, as is often thought. The text rather draws readers into God's own inner struggle, one that is not merely a struggle of the past but of the present. This struggle can relate in various ways to readers' experiences of their own situation and its theological interpretation. Döhling writes:

> "Inhaltlich spannt sich der Bogen in 11,1–11 vom Rückblick auf den Beginn des Gott-Israel-Verhältnisses, Gottes stetiger Fürsorge und Israels stetigen Übertretungen (1–4), über die Beschreibung des gegenwärtigen Zustandes (5–7) bis in die (ferne) Zukunft einer erneuerten Beziehung. Die V. 8f. entziehen sich dabei durch ihre kompositorische Geschlossenheit, die Partikel איך, die direkte Anrede und durch die Verschiebung des Fokus von Israels

---

18 The word about Edom being "called the wicked country" in Mal 1:4, even if the word "country" (גבול) is used, fits into this line of thought and presents a negative counterpart. These remarks do not contradict Kessler's observations about Mal 1:4 and Num 20, but rather add a further dimension. See also Morgan, "Land", and Scoralick, "Quelle."

19 Lohfink, "Zornesglut," 188: "Jede dieser Wellen wird vom Sturmwind des Zorns vorangetrieben, jede bricht sich und wird zur Liebe. Dreimal wird das Problem aufgeworfen, dreimal erfährt es die Antwort."

20 Cf. Scoralick, Güte, 145–160.

21 Döhling, Gott, 304–364. His focus is on Hos 11:8–9, but is not restricted to these verses.

Verhalten und Ergehen auf das Ergehen und Verhalten Gottes zwar einerseits der exakten Einfügung in dieses temporale Gefüge. Durch ihre Stellung zwischen dem unmittelbar drohenden Unheil (V.5–7) und dem künftigen Heil (10f.) behaupten sie aber andererseits in diesem Gefüge die Möglichkeit je neuer Gegenwart dieses Wandels und beteiligen den Leser gleichsam in Echtzeit an Gottes Wandel."[22]

Read in this way, Hos 11:8–9 is reminiscent of the disclosure and the interpretations of God's name in Exodus (3:14; 33:19; and 34:6–7). The name of God is one of the key motifs of the Book of the Twelve from beginning (cf. Hos 1:9) to end (cf. Zech 14:9; Mal 1:11).[23] It is bound up with the central narrative in the Torah (Exod 32–34) that interprets God's name and his way. This text is recalled in several passages, Hos 11 being one of them.[24]

Hos 11, with the quality of the ever new presence of its core verses, is the theological basis for the book of the Twelve read as a whole. This concept of God's love does not exclude the possibility and reality of catastrophic historical events, as Döhling has convincingly argued and Hos 11:1–7 show. But it is the basis for the calls to Israel to return "even now" that echo throughout the book and reach out to the actual readers, beginning with the book of Joel (Joel 2:12–13). This concept is the basis of hope for the future of Israel. It is not conceived as a certainty resulting from God's eternally unchanging nature, but from his name as revealed in the Torah, a name that that is ever new and ever the same in its presence.

From the beginning, Hosea speaks of Israel as undeserving, as misunderstanding and rejecting God's love. This attitude reaches far back into history, as the book demonstrates (cf. Hos 11:1 "... out of Egypt I called my son"). Its last part, Hos 12–14 reaches furthest back to the ancestor Jacob himself. Jacob's twin brother Esau is also mentioned, even if not by name. Hos 12:4 reads בבטן עקב את־אחיו. Esau is present as Jacob's brother, together with him in the womb.[25] Obviously the verb of the sentence is conceived as a play on the name of Jacob. The meaning is controversial. Does the verb have an openly negative meaning (e.g. "he cheated") or is a rather neutral understanding possible (e.g.

---

22 Döhling, Gott, 307.
23 Cf. also Mic 4:5 ("we will walk in the name of YHWH, our God, forever and ever") in between.
24 For Exod 32–34 being a subtext from the Torah that is being re-called and re-enacted cf. (for Hosea, Joel and Amos) Döhling, Gott; with regard to Amos alone cf. Steins, Gericht.
25 If Hos 12:5b (also) alludes to the meeting of Jacob and Esau, it shows a positive perception of Esau.

"he grabbed the heel")?[26] The presentation of Jacob in Hos 12 remains partially enigmatic. Jacob is certainly not, however, portrayed as part of a glorious past.[27] Jacob is not painted in colors that explain God's love for him.

The book of Malachi refers to Jacob in a similar way. Mal 3:8–9 employs a paronomastic wordplay on Jacob's name (like Hos 12:4). This time the root קבע qal ("to rob") is used, and the text addresses the descendants of Jacob (בני יעקב),[28] a group that includes the implicit readers. If the Book of the Twelve presents one of the twin brothers Jacob and Esau with a tendency to evil that is already linked to his name, a tendency that can be verified in the behavior of the descendants, this person does not seem to be Esau/Edom but Jacob.

Read in the context of the Twelve, the opening of the book of Malachi does not recall the reader's knowledge about Esau and Jacob directly from the book of Genesis, but rather the interpretation that this constellation has been given in the book of the Twelve, starting with Hos 12. Concerning the concept of election, as treated in Malachi's counterpart Hosea, this knowledge implies that the Book of the Twelve underlines the freedom of God's choice more than anything else. Hosea's God is not rationally in love with Israel, he is desperately in love. The book makes that very clear. Supposing that Hosea sets the tone for the Twelve in that matter – as there is good reason to believe – and that this theme is taken up at the beginning of Malachi (אהב), Kessler's reflections on how Edom/Esau's (im)moral behavior justifies his not being elected in the first place lose much of their plausibility. The *ratio* of God's choice may be presented differently in other biblical texts, but in the Book of the Twelve, Jacob/Israel's 'good behavior' of in the past is definitely not the issue.

Read in the context of the Twelve, the point of the opening of Malachi does not seem to lie in Edom being judged and laid waste – that has happened to Israel too, as the book admits. Rather, the point lies in this judgment being pronounced "forever" (Mal 1:4).

The difference can be illustrated with a text from the first chapter of Zechariah. There, the same verb as in Mal 1:4b, זעם, is used of YHWH's attitude towards the cities of Juda in Zech 1:12. Yet it is not the final

---

26   In other words, is it a reference to Gen 25:26 or rather to 27:36? Cf. the translation by Wolff, *Dodekapropheton 1*, 266: "im Mutterleib hinterging er seinen Bruder." Andersen and Freedman, *Hosea*, 593 opt for "he grabbed his ... heel."

27   Cf. Jeremias, *Hosea*, 153, who speaks of "Bruderbetrug" and writes: "Für Hosea sind alle positiven Züge der alten Erzählungen über die zwielichtige Jakobsgestalt verbannt." (see also 158). Recently cf. Irsigler, "Streit."

28   Cf. Meinhold, *Maleachi*, 310–311, who remarks on the connection with Hos 12:4 and with the Jacob tradition in Genesis.

word. YHWH's זעם in Zech 1 is limited to seventy years. Then the forces expressed by the roots רחם, נחם and קנא change the situation again (cf. Hos 2:3 רחם; Hos 11 נחם and Joel 2:18 קנא). As Hos 11 shows at the beginning of the Twelve, there is hope that God cannot let go of his love. Yet this is God's love of Israel. For Edom, things might be different. There might be a real end.[29]

4.2 Edom in the Book of the Twelve

The Book of the Twelve is the prophetic book that stresses the brotherhood of Edom and Israel most. Among the prophetic books, only the Book of the Twelve presents Edom explicitly as Israel's brother. "It is striking and undoubtedly not accidental, that in three books of the Twelve Edom is called Israel's brother (Amos 1:11; Obad 10; Mal 1:2–5), whereas the Major Prophets *do not* mention Edom's brotherhood."[30] Reading canonically, the brotherhood of Edom to Israel refers back to the book of Genesis, where Jacob's twin brother Esau is variously identified as Edom or called the father of Edom (Gen 25:30; 36:1, 8–9, 43). This reference to the Torah is underscored further by a second characteristic. Esau's name occurs nine times in the Twelve: seven times Esau is mentioned in Obadiah, the book about Edom, and twice at the beginning of Malachi, also in close connection to Edom.[31] The only other prophetic book that mentions Esau in connection with Edom (or at all) is Jeremiah (49:8, 10), where it appears as part of a passage with close parallels to Obadiah.[32]

This characteristic element of the Twelve recalls Kessler's remark that the fault of Edom is defined for readers by reaching back to the Torah. In the story in Num 20, when Edom does not let Israel pass

---

29   Yet the "forever" is not directly part of a quotation of God's words, but a citation of what will be said about them, presumably by the nations of the world. The difference to the related section Mal 3:6–12 is interesting: When Israel's positive future is envisioned it is the voice of the nations that will pronounce them happy (Mal 3:12), but the cause for that is given as spoken by God "because you, you will be a land of delight, says the Lord of hosts." There is an interesting parallel in the book of Joel. When the land is desolate, all Israel shall assemble and the priests shall pray to YHWH and ask him to have pity and not to let the people and nations of the world defy Israel and its God (Joel 2:17; cf. Exod 32:12; Deut 9:26–28). "And YHWH became jealous for his land and had pity on his people" (Joel 2:18). Priests and prophet that intercede with God for Israel are missing for Edom (but cf. "5. Conclusion" of this article).

30   Dicou, *Edom*, 113–114.

31   The name Esau occurs in Obad 6, 8, 9, 18 (twice), 19, 21; Mal 1:2, 3.

32   Cf. the article of Nogalski, p. 89–107, in this volume.

through its land, one finds explicit mention of the brotherhood of the
two people. Moses sends messengers to the king of Edom and has them
say, "Thus says your brother Israel" (Num 20:14). At the same time the
message to the king of Edom also contains an account of the events
surrounding the Exodus. In remarkable contrast to the reaction of
Jethro (Exod 18:1, 8–12), who acclaims the greatness of Israel's God
(Exod 18:11), "Edom"'s only reaction is to deny Israel passage through
its land, first threatening Israel with the sword and then, after a second
plea, reacting with military force and בְּיָד חֲזָקָה. This last phrase is used
in the Torah in the context of the "competition" between Pharaoh and
God and afterwards in praise and in confessional statements of God's
strength as shown in the Exodus (cf. Exod 3:19; 6:1; 13:9 etc. as well as
e.g. Deut 26:8). Edom, Israel's brother, reacting against Israel בְּיָד חֲזָקָה,
implicitly aligns itself with Egypt.[33]

In a way, that reaction makes it more plausible that Num 20 could
be a background text for Mal 1:2–5, as Kessler suggests. Not letting
another people pass through one's territory does not, however, seem to
constitute an act of injustice that obviously deserves (everlasting?) destruction. The narrative in Num 20 itself seems to downplay the significance of the offense when v. 21 dryly refers to Israel's reaction: "... so
Israel turned away from them (וַיֵּט יִשְׂרָאֵל מֵעָלָיו)" (Num 20:21).

Rather, the outrage occurs on different levels. On the one hand, it is
behavior towards a brother, as the text emphasizes. On the other hand,
it is behavior that implies no reaction, or rather, a negative reaction to
the saving acts of God in the Exodus as recounted by Moses. The example of Jethro in Exod 18 shows that a different response is possible.
Edom seems to be a nation that does not hear. Thirdly, the militant
animosity mirrors the behavior of Egypt in its competition with God,
but on an advanced level, because the events of the Exodus from Egypt
are already known.

When Israel simply chooses another route, it might seem as if there
was an unsettled score with Edom. When Edom is mentioned for the
first time in the Twelve, in Joel 4:19, it is in parallelism to Egypt as a
country that will be devastated for former misdeeds. Of the nine explicit references to Edom in the Book of the Twelve,[34] this seems to be one
of the most debated and enigmatic ones. As has been seen and dis-

---

33 Similarities with the painting of Egypt and the Pharao in Exod 1 are even more
    striking in Num 22:2–7.
34 "Edom" is explicitly mentioned in Joel 4:19; Amos 1:6, 9, 11; 2:1; 9:12; Obad 8 and
    Mal 1:4. Reading "Edom" against the MT in Mic 2:12 does not seem probable to An-
    dersen and Freedman, *Micah*, 331.340.

cussed now for a long time, Joel 4:19 is the first of the verses referring to Edom that connects the books of Joel, Amos, and Obadiah, which is also taken up at the beginning of Malachi.

4.3 Egypt and Edom in Joel 4:19

A brief look at the book of Joel and its function in the reading process of the Book of the Twelve is necessary at this point. The book of Joel is of special relevance for the Twelve. It is centered on the theme of the day of YHWH for Zion and the world. The day of YHWH is presented as a day of catastrophe from different angles and with a complex literary technique of overlapping metaphorical worlds. At the core of the presentation is an urgent call to return to YHWH that aims at becoming immediate to readers of all times ("Even now: return to me").[35] While Joel 1–2 concentrate on Zion/Jerusalem and Israel, even if the scenario is cosmic, the following sections in Joel 3–4 seem to present a kaleidoscope of pictures concerning God's judgment against all people and their relationship to Zion/Jerusalem (Israel). Joel 3 is of central relevance in these pictures. It speaks of the outpouring of YHWH's spirit on all flesh that will turn everybody in Israel to prophets.[36] God will give signs (מוֹפְתִים) that announce the coming of his day. Read in the context of the book of Joel with its references to the plague (or sign) narratives of the book of Exodus, these signs recall this connection too, though this is not elaborated. For Irmtraud Fischer, the description of the signs points back to the theophany in the context of Exodus and Sinai.[37] The text according to Fischer relates an epiphany of God to all mankind. All Israel will take over the function of Moses, the prophet. In Joel 3 it is Zion that is painted in colors of Sinai for all people.[38] Fascinating as this interpretation is, it still needs some elaboration. The text itself is very terse.

In any case, with Joel 3:5 the scenario remarkably turns to individuals regardless of ethnic categories. Everyone who calls on the name of YHWH will be saved.[39] This hope can be read as the horizon for the following chapter Joel 4, that speaks of the day of YHWH as the judg-

---

35 Cf. Scoralick, "Auch jetzt noch."
36 This is an important instance of the thematic thread in the Twelve that reflects on prophets in Israel and on Israel itself acting as prophet to the nations.
37 Fischer, *Gotteskünderinnen*, 245.
38 "Joel 3,3–5 beschreibt damit ein Theophaniegeschehen, wie es vom Sinai her bekannt ist, und versetzt es an den Zion." (Fischer, *Gotteskünderinnen*, 246).
39 Cf. Jeremias, *Joel*, 43–44.

ment day for the nations (Joel 4:2, 12). Joel 4:17 signals the end of this passage.

The next verse, Joel 4:18, adds a new aspect to the picture. Judah's paradisaic future is portrayed as a well-watered land with a spring emanating from the house of YHWH and is contrasted with two desolate countries. Joel 4:19 states: "Egypt shall become a desolation and Edom a desolate wilderness, because of the violence done to the people of Judah, in whose land they have shed innocent blood." The "desolate wilderness" (מדבר שממה) that is announced for Edom seems to have come true in Mal 1:3b, where the two nouns are split up in a parallelism referring to Edom. Yet the terms are not very specific (cf. Joel 2:3). Scholars have wondered why Egypt and Edom are singled out in this way at the end of Joel.[40] The combination is singular and has provoked several explanations and evoked rather far reaching theories.

Following Hans Walter Wolff, the combination of Egypt and Edom in Joel 4:19 is sometimes explained in relation to prophetic tradition. Egypt and Edom are mentioned (separately) in prophetical texts connected with the day of YHWH (cf. Ezek 30; Jer 46; Isa 34), sometimes together with the word שממה.[41]

At the same time, Wolff also considers Egypt and Edom as archetypal enemies ("Erbfeinde").[42] Enmity towards Edom is connected with the fall of Jerusalem (cf. Obad 10–16; Lam 4:21; Ps 137:7). Concerning Egypt, Wolff refers to Exod 1:15–22 and 1 Kgs 14:25–26; 2 Kgs 23:29. The combination of the two remains singular.

A different approach understands the naming of Egypt and Edom together as pointing back to historical events. Those events have been variously identified, e.g. as connected with Nebuchadnezzar's actions (cf. Jer 27; Ezek 29). Recently Jakob Wöhrle has connected the verse with a redactional layer ("Fremdvölkerschicht II") from Hellenistic times. For him, the combination of Egypt and Edom in Joel 4:19 can serve as a basis for historical hypotheses.[43]

---

40   E.g. Dicou, *Edom*, 35.80–81.
41   Wolff, *Dodekapropheton 2*, 101.
42   Wolff, *Dodekapropheton 2*, 110. Barton, *Joel*, 110, considers the possibility too, but thinks that instead of Edom probably Assyria or Babylon would have been named as 'traditional' enemies. Therefore he rather reckons with a reference to contemporary events involving Edom.
43   See Wöhrle, *Abschluss*, 216–217: "Angesichts der Tatsache, dass Joel 4,19 frühestens ins fortgeschrittene 4. Jh. datiert werden kann, ist dieser Vers somit ein Beleg dafür, dass zu dieser Zeit von Ägypten wie von Edom her Übergriffe auf judäisches Gebiet stattgefunden haben. Und dies könnte, auch wenn die genaueren Umstände zugegebenermaßen im Dunkeln liegen, darauf hindeuten, dass die Edomiter im Zusammenhang der Eroberung Jerusalems durch die Ptolemäer auch selbst gegen Jerusalem vorgegangen sind."

Joel 4:19, 21 speak of the Judeans, not of the Israelites, and that to some extent obscures the reference to the Torah. Also, as has often been pointed out, the syntactical reference of the suffixes of "in their land" to the Judeans might seem obvious. That would not support the reference back to Egypt and Edom in the Pentateuchal narratives. Yet this is not the only possible construal, and the text may have several facets.[44]

The literary context indicates a connection of Joel 4:19 with Joel 4:1–17. There the judgment of the nations has already been described as well as its outcome (Joel 4:17). Joel 4:18–21 adds a look at the results. Why then does Judah's paradisial future have to be contrasted with the bad fate of the land of Edom and Egypt? Joel 4:19b, 21a implies that the cause is past misdeeds against Judah that will be dealt with by God. Joel 4:21 is notoriously difficult but probably speaks of not leaving bloodshed against Judah unpunished ("And I should leave their blood unpunished? I will not leave [it] unpunished.").[45] The phrase remotely recalls Jer 49:12, which refers to Edom and is part of the text that is closely related to Obadiah. But at the same time it recalls Exod 34:7 (ונקה לא ינקה), which is part of the interpretation of God's name: he does not leave unpunished.

The acts that will be punished are characterized as חמס, violence, and שפך דם נקי, shedding of innocent blood. These are rather general phrases.[46] The paradisial overtones of the description of the land of Judah may refer readers back to the primeval history. Then the two misdeeds remind of the story of the flood and its ending. חמס, violence, corrupted the earth in the eyes of God (Gen 6:11). Gen 9:6 concerns the shedding of human blood. Egypt and Edom, read against that background, appear in the guise of forces of chaos.

At the same time Judah is also painted with colors of the Promised Land. Compared with the parallel line in Amos (Amos 9:13b), Joel 4:18 differs by mentioning flowing milk. Scholars sometimes take this as a reference (even if an obscure one) to the description of the promised land (cf. Exod 3:8, 17; 13:5 etc.). In that context, Egypt and Edom might be named as two enemy countries in the two decisive phases of the Pentateuch account of God's history with his people: the Exodus from Egypt on one side and the difficulties caused by people who hinder the entrance into the land on the other side. Edom would stand for the second category because of Num 20 and perhaps also because of the motif of brotherhood, that makes its case special. Other texts single out

44　Rudolph, *Joel*, 87–88; Crenshaw, *Joel*, 201.
45　Cf. Scoralick, *Güte*, 174–175.
46　Cf. Isa 59:6–7 and its correspondence with Prov 1:16. Jeremias, *Joel*, 54, calls the deeds "nur generell charakterisiert."

these two phases, even if they do not concentrate on Edom, e.g. Ps 136 (Egypt in v. 10–13; Sichon and Og in v. 14–22) and Mic 6:3–5.

It may be noted that the devastation of Egypt and Edom is mentioned once more in the Twelve – at the end of Zechariah and the beginning of Malachi, if the two texts are read in sequence. Zech 14, the last chapter of the book of Zechariah, has been called a summation of prophecy. It contains references to most of the texts that treat the day of YHWH in the Book of the Twelve, and there are significant references to the Torah (cf. Zech 14:9 and Deut 6:4–5). Egypt is mentioned in a very prominent place that (like in Joel 4) concerns events after the day of YHWH is over. Zech 14:15 speaks of the remnant of all the people coming to Jerusalem to worship the king YHWH and to celebrate Sukkot. The following verses in Zech 14:17–19 concern the case of משפחות הארץ that will not worship. There will be no rain for these "families of the earth."

The following verse, 14:18, specifically mentions Egypt, but it is not at all clear what is being said.[47] Some scholars wonder whether this reference is merely an addition because Egypt does not depend on rain but rather on the water of the Nile.[48] Others ask whether actual historical events occasioned the addition.[49] In any case, Egypt is treated as an example among the nations of the future (Zech 14:19). Continuing to read with Mal 1, Edom is joined to this picture, either in the same vein, but with a much harsher verdict, or as a contrast.[50]

5. Conclusion

Reading Mal 1:2–5 in the context of the Book of the Twelve will let readers arrive at the beginning of the last book with certain expectations and certain concepts in mind. My observations and remarks concern only a small portion of those ideas. To present the overall picture would mean to follow the threads and patterns that are woven into Mal 1:2–5 as they reach back into the whole Book of the Twelve.

---

47 Cf. the discussion in Gärtner, Summe, 69 with note 231: "Das Verständnis dieses Teilsatzes ist bisher ungeklärt." She translates "Und wenn die Sippe Ägyptens nicht hinaufzieht und nicht kommt, dann wird über sie nicht sein" following the Targum in relating this to the Nile not rising.
48 Beck, Tag, 223: "V. 18f. ist ... als Glosse zu begreifen: da Ägypten durch die Überflutungen des Nils bewässert wird, muss der Interpolator klarstellen, dass auch Ägypten der gleiche Schlag – nun weit zu denken als Trockenheit – treffen wird."
49 Cf. Beck, Tag, 226, for references.
50 Beck, Tag, 226 note 102, rejects the idea of a reminiscence to Joel 4:19 in Zech 14:18 because Edom is not mentioned too. Mal 1:2–5 might supply that.

This article has focused on one of those threads. The theme of Israel's election – or of God's special love for Jacob/Israel – is prominent right at the beginning of the Twelve in Hosea and runs through the whole book. It is coupled with the motif of Israel's turning away from God, with Hos 11 providing the basic pattern. For Israel, hope exists that there will always be the possibility to return (cf. Hos 11:8–9; Joel 2:12–14). This return is not necessarily possible for other nations. Yet one might ask whether a text like the ending of the book of Micah, with its hymnal praise of God's forgiveness (Mic 7:18–20), does not also contain hope for the people of the world, perhaps even coupled with the idea of Israel interceding like a prophet with God on their behalf.[51] Then Mal 1:2–5 might not necessarily be conceived as the last word about Edom, even if the book of Malachi does not develop this thought further. In that way, the disturbing contrast of Israel and Edom at the beginning of the book of Malachi may not only have to be read in light of the issue of (individual?) justice but also in the context of the drama of Israel and the nations with regard to Israel's function of intermediary of God's name and word to the world.

References

Andersen, F.I. and Freedman, D.N. *Hosea: A New Translation with Introduction and Commentary*. AB 24. New York: Doubleday, 1980.
Barton, J. *Joel and Obadiah: A Commentary*. OTL. London: Westminster, 2001.
Beck, M. *Der "Tag YHWHs" im Dodekapropheton: Studien im Spannungsfeld von Traditions- und Redaktionsgeschichte*. BZAW 356. Berlin: de Gruyter, 2005.
Crenshaw, J.L. *Joel: A New Translation with Introduction and Commentary*. AB 24C. New York: Doubleday, 1995
Dicou, B. *Edom, Israel's Brother and Antagonis: The Role of Edom in Biblical Prophecy and Story*. JSOTSup 169. Sheffield: JSOT Press, 1994.
Döhling, J.-D. *Der bewegliche Gott. Eine Untersuchung des Motivs der Reue Gottes in der Hebräischen Bibel*. Herders biblische Studien 61. Freiburg: Herder, 2009.
Dohmen, C. and Stemberger, G. *Hermeneutik der Jüdischen Bibel und des Alten Testaments*. Stuttgart: Kohlhammer, 1996.
Fischer, I. *Gotteskünderinnen: Zu einer geschlechterfairen Deutung des Phänomens der Prophetie und der Prophetinnen in der Hebräischen Bibel*. Stuttgart: Kohlhammer, 2002.
Gärtner, J. *Jesaja 66 und Sacharja 14 als Summe der Prophetie: Eine traditions- und redaktionsgeschichtliche Untersuchung zum Abschluss des Jesaja- und des Zwölfprophetenbuches*. WMANT 114. Neukirchen-Vluyn: Neukirchener, 2006.
Irsigler, H. "Der Streit um die Identität Israels in der vorexilischen Prophetie. Besonders am Beispiel von Hosea 12." Pp. 59–86 in *Die Identität Israels*.

---

51   The MT of Mic 7:19b can suggest that (see Scoralick, *Güte*, 191–192).

Entwicklungen und Kontroversen in alttestamentlicher Zeit. Edited by idem. Herders biblische Studien 56. Freiburg: Herder, 2009.

Jeremias, J. *Der Prophet Hosea.* ATD 24,1. Göttingen: Vandenhoeck & Ruprecht, 1983.

– *Die Propheten Joel, Obadja, Jona, Micha.* ATD 24,3. Göttingen: Vandenhoeck & Ruprecht, 2007.

Kaminsky, J.S. *Yet I loved Jacob: Reclaiming the Biblical Concept of Election.* Nashville: Abingdon Press, 2007.

Kessler, R. "Jakob und Esau als Brüderpaar in Mal 1,2–5." Pp. 209–229 in *Diasynchron: Beiträge zur Exegese, Theologie und Rezeption der Hebräischen Bibel.* Edited by T. Naumann and R. Hunziker-Rodewald. FS W. Dietrich. Stuttgart: Kohlhammer, 2009.

Krause, J.J. "Tradition, History, and Our Story: Some Observations on Jacob and Esau in the Books of Obadiah and Malachi." *JSOT* 32 (2008) 475–486.

Langer, G. (ed.) *Esau: Bruder und Feind.* Göttingen: Vandenhoeck & Ruprecht, 2009.

Lohfink, N. "'Ich komme nicht in Zornesglut' (Hos 11,9): Skizze einer synchronen Leseanweisung für das Hoseabuch." Pp. 163–190 in *Le Dieu qui vient.* Edited by R. Kuntzmann. FS B. Renaud. Paris: Cerf, 1995.

Meinhold, A. *Maleachi.* BKAT 14,8. Neukirchen-Vluyn: Neukirchener, 2006.

Morgan, D.M. "Land and Temple as Structural and Thematic Marks of Coherence for the Hebrew Edition of the Book of the Twelve." *BN* 145 (2010) 37–55.

Rudolph, W. *Joel – Amos – Obadja – Jona.* KAT 13,2. Gütersloh: Gütersloher, 1971.

Scoralick, R. "'Auch jetzt noch' (Joel 2,12a). Zur Eigenart der Joelschrift und ihrer Funktion im Kontext des Zwölfprophetenbuches." Pp. 47–70 in *"Wort JHWHs, das geschah ..." (Hos 1,1): Studien zum Zwölfprophetenbuch.* Edited by E. Zenger. Herders biblische Studien 35. Freiburg: Herder, 2002.

– *Gottes Güte und Gottes Zorn: Die Gottesprädikationen in Ex 34,6f und ihre intertextuellen Beziehungen zum Zwölfprophetenbuch.* Herders biblische Studien 33. Freiburg: Herder, 2002.

– "JHWH als Quelle der Fruchtbarkeit und das Motiv vom Gottesgarten in der Prophetie: Beobachtungen anhand des Zwölfprophetenbuches." Pp. 318–342 in *Mythisches in biblischer Bildsprache: Gestalt und Verwandlung in Prophetie und Psalmen.* Edited by H. Irsigler. QD 209. Freiburg: Herder, 2004.

Steins, G. *Gericht und Vergebung. Re-Visionen zum Amosbuch.* SBS 221. Stuttgart: Katholisches Bibelwerk, 2010.

Wöhrle, J. *Der Abschluss des Zwölfprophetenbuches: Buchübergreifende Redaktionsprozesse in den späten Sammlungen.* BZAW 389. Berlin: de Gruyter, 2008.

Wolff, H.W. *Dodekapropheton 1: Hosea.* BKAT 14,1. Neukirchen-Vluyn: Neukirchener, 1961.

– *Dodekapropheton 2: Joel und Amos.* BKAT 14,2. Neukirchen-Vluyn: Neukirchener, 1969.

Zenger, E. (ed.) *Einleitung in das Alte Testament.* 7th ed. Stuttgart: Kohlhammer, 2008.

Editorial Issues

Hosea in the Book of the Twelve

ROMAN VIELHAUER

Georg-August-Universität Göttingen

Many recent studies on the books of the prophets have concluded that the Twelve Minor Prophets may be construed as a unit.[1] This assumption is based first, but not solely on the observation that in all extant textual traditions the Twelve Prophets are delivered to us as an entity.[2] In addition, features within the text also serve to corroborate the idea of a well-conceived composition comprising the books from Hosea to Malachi. On the one hand, the collocation of the twelve books shows a certain chronological order, i.e. from the Assyrian (Hosea to Nahum) via the Babylonian (Habakkuk to Zephaniah) to the Persian (Haggai to Malachi) period. On the other hand, one can detect various thematic and terminological cross references, which interrelate the Twelve Prophets and serve to unify the collection of scriptures.[3] Hence, it does not come as a surprise that even in antiquity authors could refer to "the Twelve" as a coherent entity, which Jerome even described as *one* book.[4]

Still, the Book of the Twelve can only to a limited extent be compared to other prophetic books. For, unlike the books of Isaiah, Jeremiah, and Ezekiel, and according to its self-conception, the Book of the Twelve does not represent a coherent entity, but a collection of twelve well-defined, discrete books. Their collocation may simply be owing to

---

1 Cf. Schart, *Entstehung*, 6–21; idem, "Redaktionsgeschichte;" idem, "Zwölfprophetenbuch;" Redditt, "Research;" idem, "Formation;" Beck, *Tag*, 1–23; Wöhrle, *Sammlungen*, 3–24; idem, *Abschluss*, 2–14; Nogalski, "Book," 12–30; Kratz, "Hosea und Amos im Zwölfprophetenbuch."
2 This assessment applies to the Masoretic Text as well as the Septuagint and the Vulgate. It most likely also applies to the manuscripts of the Twelve Prophets found at Murabba'at und Naḥal Ḥever. The Qumran attestations, however, are not as unambiguous as they are often made out to be; cf. Tov, "Texts," 132; Brooke, "Prophets;" Guillaume, "Reconsideration;" Kratz, "Hosea und Amos in den Schriften vom Toten Meer," 359–362.
3 Cf. Nogalski, "Intertextuality;" idem, "Themes;" Redditt and Schart, *Threads*.
4 Jerome prefaced the Book of the Twelve in the Vulgate by noting: "unum librum esse duodecim prophetarum." The oldest attestation is assumed to be found in Sir 49:10. For further references to the Book of the Twelve in antiquity, cf. e.g. Nogalski, *Precursors*, 2–3; Redditt, "Production," 26–30.

their brevity,[5] and their thematic and terminological similarity "can be easily explained in terms of the general discourse of the period," as has been argued e.g. by Ehud Ben Zvi.[6] Thus, unlike the books of Isaiah, Jeremiah, and Ezekiel, one cannot simply presuppose that the Book of the Twelve was subject to an intentional literary redaction. Rather, an alleged unity of the Book of the Twelve needs first to be demonstrated.

Within the context of the Book of the Twelve, the book of Hosea proves to be especially challenging. Given its position at the beginning of the composition, a particularly vivid redactional activity might be expected. Yet, the opposite is true. Cross references to the other Minor Prophets constitute an exception in the book of Hosea! Thematically speaking, for instance, the "Day of Yhwh," which is of great importance in the subsequent books, remains unmentioned in the book of Hosea.[7] Even the destiny of the foreign nations seems irrelevant to Hosea.[8] Jakob Wöhrle attempts to explain this observation by assuming a temporal detachment of the book of Hosea from the Book of the Twelve,[9] while Susanne Rudnig-Zelt bids farewell to the hypothesis of a Book of the Twelve altogether.[10]

However, there is no denying that the book of Hosea is to some extent cross-referenced with the other books of the Twelve.[11] Among them, references can be detected that, by and large, suggest comprehensive redactional activity. In my view, four texts in particular could be considered redactional compositions serving to incorporate the book of Hosea into the evolving Book of the Twelve: 1) the superscription in Hos 1:1; 2) the symbolic action performed by Hosea in Hos 3; 3) the call to penitence in Hos 14:2–4; and 4) the cessation of divine patience in Hos 1. These passages will be considered in what follows.

---

5   Cf. already *b. B. Bat.* 14b.

6   Ben Zvi, "Hypothesis," 95; cf. idem, "Books," 136–137.

7   Cf. Rudnig-Zelt, "Genese," 359; Barton, "Day," 76; Beck, *Tag*, 64–66; Schwesig, "Stimmen," 238; Wöhrle, *Sammlungen*, 57.451. Ever since Rendtorff, "Book;" idem, "Day," recognized the Day of Yhwh to be a unifying theme within the Book of the Twelve, some have attempted to prove that this theme also existed within the book of Hosea; cf. e.g. Scoralick, *Güte*, 150; Nogalski, "Day(s);" Schwesig, *Rolle*, 74–77.287. Tellingly, Rendtorff, "Book," 85; idem, "Day," 263, identifies an inclusion of "Day of Yhwh" statements within the Book of the Twelve, only within Joel to Malachi.

8   Cf. Wöhrle, *Abschluss*, 431–432; regarding the view on foreign peoples cf. also Roth, *Israel*.

9   Wöhrle, *Sammlungen*, 450–453; idem, *Abschluss*, 429–437.

10   Rudnig-Zelt, "Genese," 358–359. Doubts regarding the hypothesis of the Book of the Twelve are further entertained by Ben Zvi, "Books;" idem, "Hypothesis;" Spronk, "Hosea;" Perlitt, *Propheten*, XIV-XVI.

11   Cf. e.g. Watts, "Frame;" Braaten, "God;" Nogalski, "Themes."

1. The Superscription in Hos 1:1

Undoubtedly, the superscription in Hos 1:1 represents the most explicit indication of a deliberate incorporation of the book of Hosea into the Book of the Twelve. This is corroborated, on the one hand, by the dating, which presents itself in line with the rough chronological order of the Book of the Twelve. On the other hand, it agrees significantly with other superscriptions found within the composition. Let us thus take a closer look.

As with the superscriptions of the books of Joel, Amos, Micah, and Zephaniah, Hos 1:1 follows the so-called "dabar" pattern.[12] The generic classification is succeeded by the name of the prophet, which, in this instance, is further identified through the name of the father.

The dating mentions the kings ruling over both the northern and southern kingdom during Hosea's prophetic period. Mentioned are Uzziah, Jotham, Ahaz, and Hezekiah as sovereigns of Judah, and Jeroboam II as sovereign of Israel. None of these kings plays an important role in the book of Hosea itself. Yet, they are encountered again in the superscription of the books of Amos and Micah: Jeroboam II and Uzziah in Amos, the Judean kings Jotham, Ahaz, and Hezekiah in Micah. Hence, the names of the kings chosen for the superscription of the book of Hosea seem to be synchronized with the books of Amos and Micah.[13]

A further superscription following the "dabar" pattern is the one found in the book of Zephaniah, which expands the time frame to the reign of Josiah. The book of Joel, on the other hand, remains undated. For a number of scholars, the similarities of these superscriptions in the books of Hosea, Amos, Micah, and Zephaniah represent perhaps the most crucial observation in favor of a Book of the Four, which is considered a predecessor of the Book of the Twelve.[14] Yet, the conformity of the superscriptions alone does not suffice to corroborate that hy-

---

12   For a classification cf. Koch, "Profetenbuchüberschriften," 166–170; Wöhrle, *Samm-
     lungen*, 32–44.
13   Further noteworthy, is the synchronism with the book of Isaiah – the superscription
     in Isa 1:1 mentions the exact same order of Judean kings as does Hos 1:1 (or Amos
     1:1 and Mic 1:1 combined) – which makes Hosea (just as Amos and Micah) appear a
     coeval with Isaiah. The names of the kings, again, might be considered original in
     the book of Isaiah, where they are encountered in the further context of the prophet-
     ic book (for Uzziah see Isa 6:1; 7:1; for Jotham see Isa 7:1; for Ahaz see Isa 7:1, 3, 10,
     12; 14:28; 38:8; for Hezekiah see Isa 36–39), and a secondary addition in the Book of
     the Twelve inspired by their mentioning in the book of Isaiah; cf. Hitzig, *Propheten*, 6;
     Bosshard-Nepustil, *Rezeptionen*, 349; Rudnig-Zelt, *Hoseastudien*, 106; more cautiously:
     Wöhrle, *Sammlungen*, 47–48.
14   Cf. Nogalski, *Precursors*, 84–89; Schart, *Entstehung*, 39–49; Albertz, *Exilszeit*, 166–167;
     idem, "Exile," 237; Wöhrle, *Sammlungen*, 29–50.

pothesis.[15] Another look at the kings mentioned in the superscription of Hos 1:1 helps to clarify that the staggered resumption of those kings in the superscriptions of the books of Amos and Micah appears to connect the book of Hosea with a larger interscriptural context. Whether this cross reference is, however, original or whether it represents a link created only secondarily, cannot be deduced without consulting further significant linkages that connect the book of Hosea with other books of the Minor Prophets. Hence, we will now continue with an analysis of the symbolic action performed by Hosea in Hos 3.

2. The Symbolic Action Performed by Hosea in Hos 3

Hos 3 is part of the composition Hos 1–3, which thematically addresses the marriage of the prophet as a metaphor for Israel's relation toward her God. According to the texts' surface, the events mentioned in the chapters are to be considered sequential: Hos 1 narrates Hosea's marriage as well as the birth of three children; Hos 2 describes the separation from the wife (v. 4–15) and the prospect of her re-acceptance (v. 16–25); while Hos 3 continues with the reunion of husband and wife.

Yet, this connection seems to be secondary in nature. Said chapters already differ substantially regarding their form: Hos 1 is designed as a third-person-narrative, while Hos 2 represents a divine speech, and Hos 3 has the prophet speak for himself. Such formal discrepancies are accompanied by incongruencies as regards content. While the narrative accounts in chapters 1 and 3 deal with Hosea's marriage to Gomer,[16]

---

15   The fact that the superscription of the book of Amos differs from those of the book of Hosea, Micah, and Zephaniah (דברי עמוס instead of דבר־יהוה), however, does not necessarily rule out the hypothesis of a "Book of the Four" (critically: Koch, "Profetenbuchüberschriften," 168; Rudnig-Zelt, "Genese," 359). Rather, it could be a sign of an older superscription being incorporated (cf. Schart, *Entstehung*, 40.50; Albertz, *Exilszeit*, 167; idem, "Exile," 237; Wöhrle, *Sammlungen*, 37–38).

16   It is widely disputed whether Hos 1 and Hos 3 refer to one and the same woman or two distinct women. Already Wellhausen, *Propheten*, 104, noted in this regard: "Natürlich ist es die Gomer bat Diblaim, die Hosea noch einmal lieben soll. Denn die Bedeutung geht verloren, wenn die hier erwähnte Person nicht die selbe ist wie in Kap. 1. Wenn Hosea ein neues Weib nehmen soll, das zu ihm bis dahin in keiner Beziehung gestanden hat, das also auch, wenn es אהבת רע ומנאפת heisst, nicht ihm, sondern einem Dritten die Ehe gebrochen hat, was soll das für das Verhältnis Jahves zu Israel besagen? will er das treulose Israel, das Weib seiner Jugend verstossen und dafür ein neues Volk, ein anderes Weib nehmen – aber nicht etwa ein reines und treues, sondern eins, das auch schon die Ehe gebrochen hat, nur nicht ihm? Das wäre Aberwitz. Es widerspricht zudem völlig der folgenden Deutung: sowie Jahve die Kinder Israel lieb hat, trotzdem sie sich fremden Göttern zuwenden. Vielmehr, nur

the divine speech in Hos 2 directly addresses God's marital relationship with Israel. Hos 1, on the other hand, only treats the issue of marriage marginally, being primarily concerned with the children conceived in it and the symbolic names given to them. The children are not mentioned again in Hos 3. Rather, the characteristic distinction between wife and children is annihilated in this chapter. The wife has here become a symbol representing the sons of Israel.

As I have attempted to show elsewhere, the above incongruencies are best explained by assuming a gradual growth of the three chapters at hand.[17] In this regard, Hos 3 seems to represent the latest addition,[18] since a certain lack of independence cannot be denied. For, apart from the fact that the protagonist would remain unidentified without the preceding context, Hos 3 presupposes Hosea's marriage with Gomer and God's marriage with Israel, as described in chapter 1 and 2, as well as the separation of the spouses described in chapter 2. Chapters 1 and 2, on the other hand, do not require further continuation. Both wife and children of the unhappy marriage have fallen from grace (1:2–2:15). For both, however, one finds the prospect of a return (2:16–25). In this context, Hos 2:25 refers to the children begotten in Hos 1, thus creating a link between the two chapters.

In the course of the reunion with the once scorned wife, Hos 3 reports, on a metaphoric level, the withdrawal of king, prince, sacrifice, massebah, ephod, and teraphim, i.e. of all things, which according to the text separate Israel from her God. This conception has led Rainer Albertz and Jakob Wöhrle[19] to suggest an interrelationship between this passage and those texts within the Book of the Four that also announce a purifying judgment.[20] In combination with other texts,[21] these texts

---

in Bezug auf Hosea kann אהבת רע ומנאפת gesagt sein; das Weib hat ihm die Ehe gebrochen."

17   Cf. Vielhauer, *Werden*, 127–158.

18   Cf. e.g. Marti, *Dodekapropheton*, 33–34; Levin, *Verheißung*, 239–240; Yee, *Composition*, 57–64; Wacker, *Figurationen*, 217–220; Rudnig-Zelt, *Hoseastudien*, 75–77; Wöhrle, *Sammlungen*, 230–233; Vielhauer, *Werden*, 133–137; Kessler, "Hosea 3," 576.

19   Albertz, *Exilszeit*, 164–185; idem, "Exile;" Wöhrle, *Sammlungen*, 51–284; idem, "Future."

20   In addition to Hos 3:1–5, Albertz and Wöhrle include Amos 9:7–10; Mic 5:9–13; Zeph 1:4–6 and Zeph 3:11–13.

21   According to Albertz, "Exile," 251, the redaction is palpable in the following passages: Hos 1:5, 7; 3:1bβ; 4:1*, 15; 8:1b, 6a, 14; 11:5b; Amos 1:1b, 9–10, 11–12; 2:4–5, 10–12; 3:1b*, 7; 5:25(?); 8:11–12; 9:7–10; Mic 1:1, 5b–7, 13bβ; 5:8(?), 9–13; Zeph 1:1, 3–6, 13b, 17aβ; 2:3a; 2:5–3:8bα*, 11–13 (without 2:7, 9, 10–11; 3:8bβ–10). Wöhrle, *Sammlungen*, 245; idem, "Future," 610, refers to the following texts: Hos 1:1; 3:1–4, 5*; 4:1abα, 10, 15; 8:1b, 4b–6, 14; 13:2–3; 14:1; Amos 1:1*; 2:4–5, 9–12; 3:1b, 7; 4:13*; 5:11, 25–26; 7:10–17; 8:5, 6b, 11–12; 9:7–10; Mic 1:1, 5b–7, 9, 12b; 5:9–13; 6:2–4a, 9aα, 10–15; Zeph 1:1, 4–6, 13b; 2:1–2, 3*, 4–6, 8–9a; 3:1–4, 6–8a, 11–13.

form a redactional layer within the Book of the Four "which in a broader sense can be called Deuteronomistic."[22] Alongside the above mentioned superscriptions, this material creates the Book of the Four in the
first place. However, these two scholars disagree on whether the redactor of the Book of the Four was already familiar with Hos 3 as a part of
the once independent pre-Deuteronomistic book of Hosea and used it
as a source of inspiration (Albertz) or whether Hos 3 represents a Deuteronomistic addition to the book of Hosea composed specifically for
the interscriptural context of the Book of the Four (Wöhrle).

First, let us discuss the Deuteronomistic character of Hos 3. In my
opinion it is evident that this chapter presupposes Deuteronomistic
theology and terminology.[23] This assumption is not only corroborated
by the distinctive phrase פנה אל אלהים אחרים in v. 1, which one encounters elsewhere in the OT only in Deut 31:18, 20 (cf. Deut 29:17;
30:17). Furthermore, the critique of offerings, massebahs, ephod, and
teraphim, as well as the reciprocal character of love between God and
Israel have several parallels in Deuteronomistic literature.[24] Yet, the
figure of thought represented in Hos 3 extends beyond the conception
described above. To be sure, Israel's transgression – in line with Deuteronomistic literature – simultaneously consists of a lack of reverence for
the deity and the worship of foreign gods (violation of the first commandment). However, it never suggests avoiding the foreign deities
and returning to God. Instead, Hos 3:1 speaks of God's love *in spite of*
Israel's lack of requited love.[25] It is only when God withdraws all the
factors separating Israel from her deity that she can return to him – an
endeavor, which she could never have accomplished on her own. Thus,
Hos 3 introduces an alternative to the Deuteronomistic conception,
while presupposing both its terms and its content.[26] Both the awareness
of Israel's need for God's forgiveness and the certainty of his grace
form a constitutive element of this specific Deuteronomistic interpreta-

22 Wöhrle, "Future," 610.
23 Cf. Vielhauer, *Werden*, 135, and Yee, *Composition*, 57–64; Wöhrle, *Sammlungen*, 232–
    233; Rudnig-Zelt, "Propheten."
24 The similarities with the Deuteronomic-Deuteronomistic conception of "love" have
    long been recognized; cf. e.g. von Rad, "Gottesvolk," 89; Wolff, *Hosea*, 76; Yee, *Com-
    position*, 58.60; Vielhauer, *Werden*, 135. Wöhrle, *Sammlungen*, 232, mentions parallels
    to the cultic accusations of DtrH.
25 Hence, all attempts to reconstruct a calamitous original layer for Hos 3 – e.g. by
    considering v. 5 a later addition – fail; cf. the discussion in Wacker, *Figurationen*, 214–
    220, and more recently Kessler, "Hosea 3."
26 With regard to the intention of the "Exilic Book of the Four," Wöhrle, "Future,"
    likewise subtitles his article "a Concept Opposed to the Deuteronomistic History;"
    cf. already idem, *Sammlungen*, 275–282. To what extent it might be reasonable to
    speak of a *deuteronomistic* concept, however, remains disputable.

tion. In historical-theological terms texts such as Exod 34:6–7; Num 14:18–19 or Jer 31:31–34 represent the closest parallels to Hos 3.[27]

Even if Jakob Wöhrle is correct in arguing that Hos 3 represents an addition within the Book of Hosea that presupposes Deuteronomistic theology and terminology, the question remains whether the chapter needs to be considered a constituent text of the "Book of the Four" redaction – a fact, which had already been contested by Rainer Albertz: "Da Hos 3,5 noch nicht die Restvorstellung von Zeph 3,13 kennt, geht diese Erwartung einer zukünftigen Umkehr nicht auf den VPR (i.e., the Four-Prophets-Redactor) zurück."[28] This statement is supported by the following observation: The anticipated return of the Israelites is described by בקש את יהוה in Hos 3:5. Within the Deuteronomistic redaction of the Book of the Four identified by Albertz and Wöhrle, the only other two attestations of the phrase are found in Zeph 1:6 and 2:3,[29] i.e. toward the end of the alleged Book of the Four. Wöhrle takes this as a sign for a deliberate framing of the Book of the Four through the motif of a search of God: "So steht von den äußeren Rändern her also die gesamte Zusammenstellung der vier Prophetenbücher unter der Hoffnung, daß das Volk durch das Gericht hindurch wieder zu Jhwh umkehren wird."[30] Yet, is it really possible to combine the ideas of Hos 3 and Zeph 1:6; 2:3 so readily? Zeph 1:4–6, which displays a purifying judgment, announces the annihilation of those who do not seek Yhwh ("I will cut off from this place ... those ... who do not seek Yhwh");[31] while Zeph 2:3, which is part of the call to penitence in Zeph 2:1–3, describes the search for Yhwh as a possible way to salvation from doom ("Seek Yhwh, ... perhaps you may be hidden on the day of

---

27 With regard to this particular interpretation of Deuteronomism cf. especially Schmid, *Buchgestalten*, 302–304; Spieckermann, "Herr;" idem, "Love." There is, hence, no need to attribute Hos 3:1b or parts thereof to a Deuteronomistic redaction (as it is done by e.g. Jeremias, *Hosea*, 55; Seifert, *Reden*, 131; Schart, *Entstehung*, 170; Albertz, *Exilszeit*, 181; idem, "Exile," 246).

28 Albertz, *Exilszeit*, 181–182; cf. his assumption in idem, "Exile," 240: "Both passages [sc. Hos 3:1–5 and 14:2–4] ... do not fit the redactional concept totally."

29 Further attestations within the Book of the Twelve: Hos 5:6 and Zech 8:21, 22.

30 Wöhrle, *Sammlungen*, 251.

31 Zephaniah 1:4 initially mentions the annihilation of a group referred to as שאר הבעל. The understanding of that term has always posed problems, cf. already the ancient versions. The parallel encountered in Isa 14:22 (כרת Hiphil + שם // שאר) might indicate that the term refers to the totality of the destruction rather than implying that only a remnant of Baal was still left for destruction; with regard to this discussion cf. e.g. Spieckermann, *Juda*, 204; Ben Zvi, *Study*, 64–67. Albertz's view in "Exile," 241, "that the strange expression ... can only be understood in the wider horizon of the Book of the Four. It includes all that remained after Hosea's damnation of Baalism" (cf. idem, *Exilszeit*, 172; Wöhrle, *Sammlungen*, 248; cf. already Schart, *Entstehung*, 209), is, in any case, far-reaching.

Yhwh's wrath!"). Neither statement, however, represents a perspective consistent with the one introduced in Hos 3. There, a search for Yhwh is not even expected from Israel. Rather, the search results from a divine intervention.[32] Thus, I think it more reasonable to refrain from including Hos 3 into an alleged Book of the Four redaction.[33] Let us instead take a closer look at another Hosean text, which may once have served to integrate Hosea into the Book of the Twelve: the call to penitence in Hos 14:2–4.

3. The Call to Penitence in Hos 14:2–4

One encounters Hos 14:2–4 within the concluding salvation prophecy of Hos 14:2–9, which can be divided into two parts: the prophetic plea for repentance in Hos 14:2–4 and the divine assurance of forgiveness in Hos 14:5–9. Hos 14:2–9 constitutes a redactional text that draws deliberately on essential statements provided by the preceding context while simultaneously combining those statements and directing them toward a goal. This understanding derives from a detailed analysis of Jörg Jeremias.[34] The logic of the composition has likewise been described aptly by Jeremias. Certainly, the assurance of forgiveness is given only *after* the plea for repentance. Yet, the loving devotion and the healing of Israel's inability to repent, which is implied in this assurance, actually *precede* the plea for repentance.[35]

---

32 Hos 3 shares this realistic view of humankind with other texts in the book of Hosea, such as Hos 11 or 14, which likewise refer to Israel's inability to return, which is only overcome through the initiative of the deity. Regarding Hos 11 and 14, cf. Vielhauer, *Werden*, 13–42.181–205. Among the texts announcing a purifying judgment, and which according to Albertz and Wöhrle form the backbone of the Book of the Four, Hos 3 finds its closest content parallel in Mic 5:9–13. The latter, however, has recently been identified by Jeremias, *Propheten*, 194, as an Early Hellenistic addition – at the earliest – to the book of Micah, which even presupposes Zech 9:9–10.

33 With regard to Wöhrle, *Sammlungen*, 229–240, the loss of Hos 3 would constitute the loss of his most crucial reference text for identifying the "Book of the Four" redaction within the book of Hosea, since the interrelation of that passage with texts such as Hos 8:4b–6 or 13:2–3 seems to be one, if not the most important, such criterion. It is true that Wöhrle verifies both the secondary nature and the "Deuteronomistic" provenance of such texts, which he ascribes to his "Book of the Four" redaction. Yet, those criteria are hardly conclusive, especially when one considers that ever since Gale Yee's analysis, an increasing number of texts within the book of Hosea have been discovered that meet such presuppositions without fitting in with any specific redactional layer (cf. Yee, *Composition*; Nissinen, *Prophetie*; Wacker, *Figurationen*; Pfeiffer, *Heiligtum*; Rudnig-Zelt, *Hoseastudien*; Vielhauer, *Werden*).

34 Jeremias, "Eschatologie," 231–233; idem, *Hosea*, 169–174.

35 Jeremias, "Eschatologie," 232; idem, *Hosea*, 169; cf. already Wolff, *Hosea*, 302.

As Aaron Schart has demonstrated, however, plea and assurance may not constitute a coherent, original composition.[36] For, unlike v. 5–9, the plea for repentance in v. 2–4 is not explained by the promised healing of Israel's transgression (v. 5), but by the observation that Israel has stumbled (v. 2b: כי כשלת בעונך), i.e. by the notion of enforced judgment. When combined with formal observations, a literary separation may be suggested since v. 2–4 speak to Israel in the second person while v. 5–9 speak about Israel in the third person. Since the suffixes in v. 5 would remain unidentified without consulting the preceding (v. 2–4), one may further assume that v. 5–9 were added at a later time. Consequently, the literary core of Hos 14:2–9 may be considered the plea for repentance in v. 2–4, which would once have concluded the book of Hosea.

Hos 14:2–4 consists of a plea for repentance phrased in the singular (v. 2), while its elaboration as a penitential prayer (v. 3–4) shows plural forms. It is interrelated with the preceding context of the book in several ways. The issue of "repentance" (שוב) is encountered throughout the book of Hosea. While previously, however, Israel's deficiency (2:9–10; 5:15–6:6; 12:7–10) and even unwillingness (7:10; 11:5) to return was depicted in several ways, 14:2–4 demands Israel to return to "Yhwh, your God." The phrase יהוה אלהיך is mentioned twice within chapters 12–13 (12:10; 13:4) and refers to the deity who brought Israel up from Egypt and thus proved to be her sole savior. Now that Israel has stumbled because of her transgression – cf. the identical description (כשל בעון) in 5:5 – and the catastrophe has occurred, she will turn to her God. But how is this return to be understood? According to the book's tendency toward a critique of offerings (cf. 5:6; 6:6), 14:3 suggests offering "our lips as bulls." Material offerings are replaced by personal confession that includes the renunciation of all powers on whom Israel had pinned its hopes for deliverance (cf. 1:7; 13:4, 10 ישע) instead of trusting its God, whether those powers be "Assyria" (cf. 5:13; 7:11; 8:9; 12:2), the "charger" (סוס, cf. 1:7), or the "work of our hands" (מעשה, cf. 8:4–6; 13:2).

It is solely owing to God's mercy, according to v. 4b, that Israel is once again granted the opportunity to repent and return.[37] With the

---

36 Schart, *Entstehung*, 174; cf. Pfeiffer, *Heiligtum*, 161–162.

37 Cf. already Keil, *Commentar*, 117; Schart, *Entstehung*, 174. Thus, it is not advisable to eliminate v. 4b on literary-critical grounds (as do e.g. Marti, *Dodekapropheton*, 106; Wolff, *Hosea*, 301; Jeremias, *Hosea*, 172). The arguments brought forth in this regard – the uncommon grammatical construction with אשר (cf. however GKC §158b) and the lack of terminological interrelations with v. 2–4a – are not sufficient, especially since the commitment to Yhwh who has mercy on the orphans fits in with the preceding rejection of any delusive human help. This image is also encountered in some

term רחם this final verse draws upon Hosea's second child Lo-Ruchama, mentioned at the beginning of the book (1:6; cf. 2:6). This allusion neutralizes the name's calamitous implication (cf. 2:25). At the same time the image evokes the portrayal of Israel as an orphan in Hos 11. As God had then accepted the orphan in place of a son (11:1), 14:4b now inspires the well-founded confidence that Israel, orphaned anew due to her refusal to repent (11:5), will again find mercy before her deity, will be restored as God's child, and will be granted the opportunity to repent.

With regard to a theological-historical classification of Hos 14:2–4, the following issues are important. As already implied, the passage at hand looks back on the downfall of the northern kingdom. Moreover, as Jörg Jeremias demonstrated, both the language and the subject matter suggest a Judean influence, especially with regard to the statement found in v. 4:[38] The motif of confidence in military power, an issue of only marginal importance in the book of Hosea (cf. 10:13), draws on typical Isaian terminology, especially using the term סוס (cf. Isa 2:7; 30:16; 31:1–3).[39] The reproach of worshipping "the work of our hands" (מעשה ידינו) may likewise point to a Judean provenance, since one primarily encounters the phrase in the context of Deuteronomic-Deuteronomistic literature and literature dependent thereon (Deut 4:28; 27:15; 2 Kgs 19:18; 22:17; 2 Chr 32:19; 34:25; Ps 115:4; 135:15; Isa 2:8; 17:8; 37:19; Jer 1:16; 10:3; 25:6–7; 32:30; 44:8; Mic 5:12).[40] One may thus conclude that Hos 14:2–4 aims at Judean readers.[41] A more exact classification of the theological provenance of this passage is, however, disputed among scholars. Some scholars, following Jeremias, assume Hos 14:2–4 to be the work of Hosean disciples who followed the prophet closely in time and content and seem responsible for the composition of the book of Hosea.[42] Others, like Gale Yee and Aaron Schart, plead for a considerably later dating of this passage and relate it to Deuteronomistic theology and terminology.[43]

---

psalms (Ps 10:14, 18; 68:6; 146:9) where it portrays an Israel entirely dependent upon the deity.

38   Jeremias, "Eschatologie," 231–232; idem, *Hosea*, 169–172.
39   Cf. already Wellhausen, *Propheten*, 133: "Verstehn kann das nur, wer Isa. 30 kennt."
40   This is also true for Hos 8:4–6 and 13:2; cf. e.g. Yee, *Composition*, 189–193.248–251; Wacker, *Figurationen*, 233–235; Pfeiffer, *Heiligtum*, 129–171; Wöhrle, *Sammlungen*, 233–236; Vielhauer, *Werden*, 174–175.180. These are the reproaches within the book of Hosea which might be considered the closest parallel to 14:4.
41   Cf. Jeremias, "Eschatologie," 232.
42   Cf. e.g. Naumann, *Erben*, 139–140.144.170–172; Seifert, *Reden*, 234; Albertz, *Exilszeit*, 182; idem, "Exile," 246, following Jeremias, "Eschatologie," 231–233; idem, *Hosea*, 169–172.
43   Yee, *Composition*, 132–135; Schart, *Entstehung*, 173–176.

Indeed, the plea for repentance in Hos 14:2–4 shows many similarities with the late Deuteronomistic penitential theology, the basic texts of which might be considered Deut 4:29–31 and 30:1–10.[44] All of the above texts portray an Israel who suffered divine judgment. Against this background, Israel is offered new prospect for the future through penitence (Deut 4:30; 30:1–3; Hos 14:2). In all these texts, Israel's return is rooted in God's mercy (Deut 4:31; Hos 14:4b: רחם) and consists primarily in the observance of his commandments (Deut 30:2, 8, 10; cf. 4:30; in Hos 14:4 in keeping the first two commandments by dissociating from Assyria, charger, and idols as saviors alongside Yhwh, cf. 13:4, 10 ישׁע). Thus, it might not be coincidental that Israel's repentance in Deut 4:30; 30:2 and Hos 14:2 is expressed through the rare phrase שׁוב עד, further attestations of which with Israel as the subject are only found in Isa 9:12; Lam 3:40; Joel 2:12; and Amos 4:6, 8, 9, 10, 11.[45] Considering the preceding observations we may conclude that the author of Hos 14:2–4 was closely familiar with this late form of Deuteronomism.

Apart from the late verse Joel 2:12, the rare phrase שׁוב עד, is only encountered within the Book of the Twelve in the plea for repentance in Hos 14:2–4 and the review of Israel's refusal to return in Amos 4. This observation has led Aaron Schart[46] to suggest an interrelationship between the latter two texts, a relationship which he attributes to a comprehensive Deuteronomic-Deuteronomistic inspired redaction that established the Book of the Four.[47] In this regard, Hos 14:2–4 calls Israel to penitence because of its stumbling. Only when Israel refused to do penance on multiple occasions – as stated in Amos 4 – does Amos 5:2 acknowledge that "the virgin of Israel has fallen; she will rise no more!"

---

44 With this regard cf. Knapp, *Deuteronomium 4*, 91–106.154–157; Graupner and Fabry, "שׁוב," 1155–1156. An interrelation of Hos 14:2–4 and Deut 4:29–31; 30:1–10 are further assumed by Keil, *Commentar*, 117; Kaiser, *Gott*, 2:58–59.

45 Further attestations are encountered in Job 22:23 with Job as a subject and Isa 19:22 with Egypt as the subject.

46 Schart, *Entstehung*, 160–162.175–176.

47 Schart, *Entstehung*, 156, designates the Book of the Four as the "D-Korpus" (abbreviated: "DK"), to point out "daß zwar eine auffallende Nähe zu Konzeption und Sprache deuteronomistischer Texte festzustellen ist, daß aber andererseits Unterschiede zu notieren sind, die eine einfache Gleichsetzung mit diesen aus Gründen der Klarheit der Nomenklatur nicht geraten erscheinen lassen." According to Schart the following passages can be considered compositions by the DK redaction (*Entstehung*, 317): Hos 1:1, 2b*; 2:6; 3:1*; 4:1a*; 5:1–2*; 8:1b; 14:2–4; Amos 1:1, 2, 9–12; 2:4–5, 10–12; 3:1b, 7; 4:6–11*; 5:11, 25–26*; 8:4–7, 11–12; 9:7–10; Mic 1:1, 2, 5a, 6–7, 13b; 2:3*; 6:2–16*; Zeph 1:1, 6, 13b, 17aβ. Within the book of Hosea itself, the contribution of DK solely consists of Hos 14:2–4 and some few discrete additions.

This could, indeed, constitute an excellent nexus. But was it intended as such? Considering the perspective of the book of Amos, we need to admit that it may make more sense to introduce the refusal to repent in Amos 4, if preceded by a corresponding statement.[48] With regard to Hosea, no such reference can be verified. The plea for repentance represents a satisfactory conclusion of the book. There is no hint that Hos 14:2–4 requires further elaboration or explanation. On the contrary, as I have attempted to show, the references in Hos 14:2–4 draw on earlier Hosean passages. The final reference of God's mercy (רחם) may be considered an inclusion-like allusion to the beginning of the book (1:6; cf. 2:6). Hence, it seems reasonable to assume that the literary horizon of Hos 14:2–4 might not extend beyond the book of Hosea itself. Let us take one final look at the announcement of a cessation of divine patience in Hos 1.

4. The Cessation of Divine Patience in Hos 1

In Hos 1 three children are born to the prophet, whose symbolic names herald the downfall of the northern kingdom: the downfall of kingship (v. 4), the downfall of statehood (v. 6), and the destruction of the elect (v. 9). As Christoph Levin has convincingly shown, the basic narrative of the birth account presupposes the Isaian report on Maher-shalal-hash-baz in Isa 8:1–4.[49] Thus, one may assume Hos 1 to have been composed in Judah. It is, however, unlikely that Hos 1 attempts to issue a warning against the northern kingdom on the occasion of the Syro-Ephraimite War, as does its reference text in Isa 8:1–4.[50] In this case, the author of Hos 1 would most likely have refrained from calling the enemy in the north "my people" (v. 9).[51] Rather, Hos 1 seems to reflect retrospectively on the downfall of the northern kingdom.[52] This demise is explained by Israel's "harlotry, forsaking Yhwh" (Hos 1:2b), i.e. by apostatizing from Yhwh and worshipping foreign deities (violation of the first commandment). Hos 1 shares this view with texts of Deutero-nomistic tradition (cf. e.g. 1 Kgs 12–14; 2 Kgs 17). This joint perspective is corroborated by the fact that Hos 1 includes terminology primarily

48 Cf. Schart, *Entstehung*, 162. However, it might be considered that the author of Amos 4:6–11 encountered the plea for repentance in the context of an admonition, which did not speak explicitly of שׁוב, such as Am 3:13–14.
49 Levin, *Verheißung*, 236–237; cf. also Vermeylen, "Osée 1," 200–202; Rudnig-Zelt, *Hoseastudien*, 90.
50 Thus Levin, *Verheißung*, 238–239.
51 Cf. Kratz, "Israel," 16–17.
52 Cf. e.g. Jeremias, *Hosea*, 29–30; Vermeylen, "Osée 1," 203.

encountered in Deuteronomistic literature: the phrase מאחרי יהוה (v.
2bγ; cf. Num 14:43; Josh 22:16, 18, 23, 29; 1 Sam 12:20; 2 Kgs 17:21; 2 Chr
25:27; 34:33; Zeph 1:6), the phrase זנה אחרי (v. 2bβ; cf. Exod 34:15, 16;
Lev 17:7; 20:5, 6; Num 15:39; Deut 31:16; Judg 2:17; 8:27, 33; 1 Chr 5:25;
Ezek 6:9; 16:34; 20:30; 23:30), the designation of kingship as ממלכות (v.
4bβ; cf. Josh 13:12, 21, 27, 30, 31; 1 Sam 15:28; 16:3; Jer 26:1), and the
covenant formula, which, apart from Hos 1:9[53] and the dependent formulation in Hos 2:25, is first encountered in Deuteronomic-Deuteronomistic literature. Thus, these observations suggest that Hos 1 presupposes both Deuteronomistic theology and terminology.[54]

The name of the first child refers to kingship. Unlike the following
two names the interpretation of the first name addresses an individual
case entailing an individual guilt. The name alludes to the annihilation
of the house of Ahab during the revolt of Jehu, described in 2 Kgs 9–10.
With regard to both Hos 1 and 2 Kgs 9–10 the reproach to worship foreign gods is of crucial importance.[55] The evaluation of Jehu's action,
however, could not be more different. 2 Kgs 9–10 is in favor of him
because he abolished the house of Ahab and with it the cult of Baal. For
this reason, he receives a promise that his dynasty would last to the
fourth generation (2 Kgs 10:30). Indeed, Jehu is the only northern king,
of whom it is said that he has "done well in executing what is right in"
Yhwh's eyes (2 Kgs 10:30). Hos 1, on the other hand, considers Jehu's
action to be a punishable blood debt.[56] The divergent judgment may
best be explained by assuming that Hos 1 was already cognizant of the
interpretation offered in 2 Kgs 9–10 and mentions Jehu precisely because of his positive depiction in the Book of Kings. Hos 1:4 equals
Jehu's action against the house of Ahab with Ahab's behavior toward
Naboth (1 Kgs 21), thus creating a succession of bloodshed (cf. Hos 1:4
with 2 Kgs 9:26) that seals the fate of the northern kingdom. By drawing on Jehu, the author of Hos 1 even condemns the sole king of the
northern kingdom who, according to the Book of Kings, was granted a
positive evaluation.

The name of the second child renounces Yhwh's mercy shown to
the house of Israel. As Aaron Schart has pointed out, the divine word "I

53 Probably אלהיכם with regard to Hos 2:25; cf. already Wellhausen, *Propheten*, 99.
54 Cf. also Rudnig-Zelt, *Hoseastudien*, 88–94. It is true that the provenance of the cove-
    nant formula is highly uncertain and that v. 2bβγ.4bβ pose some literary difficulties.
    Yet, even if the latter were considered later additions (cf. e.g. Vermeylen, "Osée 1,"
    194–195), the seemingly Deuteronomistic reproach of harlotry in the sense of wor-
    shipping foreign gods would remain a constituent of v. 2 and could not be excluded
    from its immediate context without alterations of the extant text.
55 2 Kgs 9:22 even uses the same terminology as Hos 1: זנונים.
56 This contrast has long been recognized; cf. already the paraphrase in the Targum.

will no longer have mercy on the house of Israel!" in Hos 1:6 presupposes the end of divine patience described in the cycle of Amos' visions (Amos 7:1–3, 4–6, 7–8; 8:1–2), where the deity, after two successful intercessions by the prophet, concludes "I will spare them no longer" (Amos 7:8; 8:2) using the analogous terminology לוֹא אוֹסִיף עוֹד.[57] The change of emphasis over against Amos' visions is represented by the change of terminology regarding "the people." While the initial two visions speak of "Jacob" (Amos 7:2, 5), the final two address "my people Israel" (Amos 7:8; 8:2). It seems fair to assume that both terms refer to Israel as the elect.[58] Hos 1:6, on the other hand, speaks of "the house of Israel." And within the book of Hosea (1:4, 6; 5:1; 6:10; 12:1) this expression exclusively refers to the statehood of the northern kingdom.[59] Thus, Hos 1 restricts the withdrawal of divine mercy to the northern kingdom.

By negating the covenant formula,[60] the name of the third child, eventually renounces Israel's relationship with her God: "You are not my people and I am not your God!"[61] (Hos 1:9).

Looking at the observations above, several texts may be seen as the decisive force behind the composition of Hos 1 – among them a text from the Book of the Twelve, namely the visions of Amos. It was this explicit reference that – in combination with other observations – caused Aaron Schart to suggest a Two-Prophets-Scroll, consisting of Hosea and Amos and representing a pre-stage of the reconstructed, Deuteronomic-Deuteronomistic inspired Book of the Four.[62] If, as I assume, Deuteronomistic theology already forms the background of Hos 1, a pre-Deuteronomistic dating of said chapter seems, however, rather unlikely. The explicit reference in Hos 1 to the visions of Amos might undoubtedly suggest that both books were transmitted in one scroll. Yet, it does not necessarily imply that both books were consid-

---

57   Schart, *Entstehung*, 116–120; cf. Jeremias, "Rezeptionsprozesse," 38–39; Vermeylen, "Osée 1," 197–200; Rudnig-Zelt, *Hoseastudien*, 93.

58   Cf. the line of arguments by Jeremias, "Jakob;" idem, *Amos*, 98–105.

59   Wolff, *Amos*, 199–200, also rendered this idea plausible for the book of Amos.

60   The recourse to the covenant formula might be inspired by Amos' "The end has come upon my people (עמי) Israel!" (Amos 8:2); cf. Schart, *Entstehung*, 119; Vermeylen, "Osée 1," 198.200.

61   Textus emendatus following Hos 2:25 אל היכם; cf. already Wellhausen, *Propheten*, 99.

62   Schart, *Entstehung*, 101–155, following contemplations made by Jeremias, "Anfänge." Schart, ibid., 316, considers the following passages genuine contributions of the redaction: Hos 1:2*, 3–4, 5(?), 6, 8–9; 4:1abβ; 5:1*; 11:11 (only נאם יהוה); 13:14bβ; Amos 2:8aβbβ, 9(?); 3:1a, 2, 13–14; 5:12a; 6:8; 7:9, 11b(?), 17bβ; 8:3, 14; 9:3 (only מנגד עיני), 4b. Again, the scope of genuine contributions made by this redaction within the book of Hosea is relatively small: apart from Hos 1*, it merely includes a few discrete additions.

ered a unity.[63] It remains uncertain how to read the text as one entity. Specifically, one may ask, to what extent does comprehension of the book of Hosea benefit from being read as constituting a union with the book of Amos.[64] In my view the book of Hosea does not require a continuation, not even Hos 1. It is true that the naming of the children and the threat their names bear, is introduced abruptly into the context of the book of Hosea. Why God's mercy ceases remains unexplained. Yet, it is implied in the course of the next chapters, which successively offer explanations, until Hos 13:14, near the end of the book, mentions that "Compassion is hidden from my sight!"[65] Thus, I would be cautious about attributing more importance to the reference pointing toward the visions of Amos than to the allusions hinting at the Book of Kings or Isaiah. The observation only shows that the visions of Amos form a literary background for Hos 1.[66] It does not allow for the conclusion, though, that Hos 1 was deliberately composed to integrate the book of Hosea into an evolving Book of the Twelve.

Conclusion

A review of selected passages from the book of Hosea that seem, on the one hand, particularly apt for verifying the integration of the book of Hosea into an evolving Book of the Twelve and have, on the other hand, often been considered programmatic texts of an assumed pre-redaction of the Book of the Twelve, has led to the following results: Apart from the superscription in Hos 1:1 no text has proven to be composed explicitly for the book's incorporation into the Book of the Twelve or one of its pre-stages, respectively. The superscription merely suggests a loose connection to the Book of the Twelve. It interrelates the

---

63   Wöhrle, *Sammlungen*, 241–244, is likewise sceptical.
64   Schart, *Entstehung*, 153, is also somewhat sceptical: "Die Erstposition von Hos bringt wohl auch zum Ausdruck, daß die Tradenten Trad-Am im Licht von Hos gelesen haben, und nicht umgekehrt."
65   Cf. Schart, *Entstehung*, 119–120: "Im weiteren Verlauf der Hoseaschrift wird ohne Zweifel eben dies geleistet. Begründungen werden nachgetragen, warum das Königtum Israels, ja ganz Israel zum Untergang verurteilt ist. ... In Hos 13,14 wird ausdrücklich die Zurücknahme der Reue Jahwes festgestellt. ... Damit erst ist eingetreten, was bereits in Hos 1 festgestellt war: kein Erbarmen mehr. Der Rahmen von Hos hat sich geschlossen."
66   Cf. Schart, *Entstehung*, 137: "Man muß also ... annehmen, daß die Amos-Tradenten und die Hosea-Tradenten miteinander im Austausch standen. ... Ein 'Austausch' zwischen beiden Tradentenkreisen muß ... am ehesten so vorgestellt werden, daß dem einen die Schrift des anderen vorgelegen hat. ... Dieses Modell ist schon sehr erklärungskräftig, vielleicht reicht es sogar aus, um alle Phänomene zu erklären."

book of Hosea with the chronological frame of the Book of the Twelve and aims to portray Hosea as a coeval of Amos and Micah.[67] Whether the superscription was composed in conjunction with the superscriptions of Amos and Micah or whether the synchronism represents a later harmonization cannot be deduced with certainty by considering the superscription alone. The fact that the book of Hosea does not include additional, identifiable traces of a comprehensive redactional activity relating the book to the other Minor Prophets, rather suggests that we here have to deal with a late interlinkage.[68]

At first glance, this might be an unsatisfying result. Yet, it might also suggest that the Minor Prophets, and especially the book of Hosea, were thought of as discrete books more vigorously than assumed and than their textual tradition would imply.[69] At least the early reception of the books in Qumran, suggests that the Minor Prophets were understood as discrete books as well. Among the pesharim discovered at Qumran, no single pesher on the Book of the Twelve as a coherent unit was found, while several pesharim relating to discrete Minor Prophets are attested.[70] Moreover, a textual signal within the book of Hosea itself

---

67   As with Isaiah.
68   Hos 4:15 and 8:14 might be considered discrete additions referring to the book of Amos (in the case of Hos 8:14 possibly even a reference to Mic 5:10), cf. Jeremias, "Anfänge," 38–41; idem, *Hosea*, 71.112; Schart, *Entstehung*, 154–155; Albertz, *Exilszeit*, 181; idem, "Exile," 246–247; Wöhrle, *Sammlungen*, 238–239; Pfeiffer, *Heiligtum*, 65–68.138. However, compositionally, those verses that might not be attributed to the same literary layer are merely loosely connected to their respective context so that a relative or absolute chronological classification can hardly be achieved. Suggestions range from the 7th century B.C.E. (Jeremias) to the exilic (Albertz, Wöhrle) or (late) post-exilic period (Schart, Pfeiffer). The fact that the verses in question presuppose "die schon abgeschlossene Komposition der Hoseakapitel, ... also das schriftliche Hoseabuch oder zumindest Teile davon" (Jeremias, "Anfänge," 40), favors a late composition.
69   Jeremias, *Propheten*, 121, has recently reached a similar conclusion with regard to the book of Micah: "In der umstrittenen Frage, ob das Buch Micha als Einzelbuch oder (und gegebenenfalls: ab wann) im Kontext des Zwölfprophetenbuches gedeutet werden will, ist angesichts der Fülle an gegenwärtigen Ansichten und Thesen Behutsamkeit geboten. Ich selber würde meinen, dass die entscheidenden Stadien des Wachstums des Buches sich im Kontext des Michabuches als Einzelbuch vollzogen haben."
70   As to the pesharim cf. the (yet not replaced) edition by Horgan, *Pesharim*; idem, "Pesharim." Whether the attestation of combined citations, especially with regard to the Damascus Document, might be considered an indication that the Book of the Twelve was construed as a unity, as Brooke, "Prophets," 37–39, suggests, is highly uncertain, since such combined quotations also involve biblical books other than the Book of the Twelve (cf. Kratz, "Hosea und Amos in den Schriften vom Toten Meer," 363). Considering the interpretation of the book of Hosea within the Dead Sea Scrolls, it might be deduced that at least the book of Hosea was construed as a discrete book; cf. Vielhauer, *Werden*, 207–223; idem, "Hosea."

has the reader concentrate on the individual book rather than on the Book of the Twelve, when the final sapiential verse (Hos 14:10) summarizes the book as follows:[71] "Whoever is wise, let him understand these things; whoever is discerning, let him know them. For the ways of the Lord are straight, and the righteous walk in them, but the sinners stumble in them."

References

Albertz, R. *Die Exilszeit: 6. Jahrhundert v. Chr.* Biblische Enzyklopädie 7. Stuttgart: Kohlhammer, 2001.
- "Exile as Purification: Reconstructing the 'Book of the Four'." Pp. 232–251 in *Thematic Threads in the Book of the Twelve*. Edited by P.L. Redditt and A. Schart. BZAW 325. Berlin: de Gruyter, 2003.
Barton, J. "The Day of Yahweh in the Minor Prophets." Pp. 68–79 in *Biblical and Near Eastern Essays*. Edited by C. McCarthy and J.F. Healey. FS K.J. Cathcart. JSOTSup 375. London: T&T Clark, 2004.
Beck, M. *Der "Tag YHWHs" im Dodekapropheton: Studien im Spannungsfeld von Traditions- und Redaktionsgeschichte*. BZAW 356. Berlin: de Gruyter, 2005.
Ben Zvi, E. *A Historical-Critical Study of the Book of Zephaniah*. BZAW 198. Berlin: de Gruyter, 1991.
- "Twelve Prophetic Books or 'The Twelve': A Few Preliminary Considerations." Pp. 125–156 in *Forming Prophetic Literature*. Edited by J.W. Watts and P.R. House. FS J.D.W. Watts. JSOTSup 235. Sheffield: Sheffield Academic Press, 1996.
- *Hosea*. FOTL. Grand Rapids: Eerdmans, 2005.
- "Is the Twelve Hypothesis Likely from an Ancient Readers' Perspective?" Pp. 47–96 in *Two Sides of a Coin: Juxtaposing Views on Interpreting the Book of the Twelve / the Twelve Prophetic Books*. Edited by idem and J.D. Nogalski. Analecta Gorgiana 201. Piscataway: Gorgias Press, 2009.
Bosshard-Nepustil, E. *Rezeptionen von Jesaia 1–39 im Zwölfprophetenbuch: Untersuchungen zur literarischen Verbindung von Prophetenbüchern in babylonischer und persischer Zeit*. OBO 154. Freiburg: Universitätsverlag and Göttingen: Vandenhoeck & Ruprecht, 1997.
Braaten, L.J. "God Sows: Hosea's Land Theme in the Book of the Twelve." Pp. 104–132 in *Thematic Threads in the Book of the Twelve*. Edited by P.L. Redditt and A. Schart. BZAW 325. Berlin: de Gruyter, 2003.
Brooke, G.J. "The Twelve Minor Prophets and the Dead Sea Scrolls." Pp. 19–43 in *Congress Volume Leiden 2004*. Edited by A. Lemaire. VTSup 109. Leiden: Brill, 2006.
Graupner, A. and Fabry, H.-J. "שוב." *ThWAT* 7 (1993) 1118–1176.

---

71 For Hos 14:10 as the hermeneutic key for the book of Hosea as a whole cf. e.g. Sheppard, *Wisdom*, 129–136; Jeremias, *Hosea*, 174; Kratz, "Erkenntnis," 302–303; Ben Zvi, *Hosea*, 313–317; Vielhauer, *Werden*, 201–203.

Guillaume, P. "A Reconsideration of Manuscripts Classified as Scrolls of the Twelve Prophets (XII)." *Journal of Hebrew Scriptures* 7.16 (2007).

Hitzig, F. *Die zwölf kleinen Propheten.* 2nd ed. Kurzgefasstes exegetisches Handbuch zum Alten Testament 1. Leipzig: Weidmannsche Buchhandlung, 1852.

Horgan, M.P. *Pesharim: Qumran Interpretations of Biblical Books.* CBQMS 8. Washington: Catholic Biblical Association of America, 1979.

–   "Pesharim." Pp. 1–193 in *Hebrew, Aramaic, and Greek Texts with English Translations.* Vol. 6B of *Pesharim, Other Commentaries, and Related Documents.* Edited by J.H. Charlesworth et al. The Princeton Theological Seminary Dead Sea Scrolls Project 6B. Tübingen: Mohr and Louisville: Westminster John Knox, 2002.

Jeremias, J. "Zur Eschatologie des Hoseabuches." Pp. 217–234 in *Die Botschaft und die Boten.* Edited by J. Jeremias and L. Perlitt. FS H.W. Wolff. Neukirchen-Vluyn: Neukirchener, 1981.

–   *Der Prophet Hosea.* ATD 24,1. Göttingen: Vandenhoeck & Ruprecht, 1983.

–   *Der Prophet Amos.* ATD 24,2. Göttingen: Vandenhoeck & Ruprecht, 1995.

–   "Die Anfänge des Dodekapropheton: Hosea und Amos." Pp. 34–54 in *Hosea und Amos: Studien zu den Anfängen des Dodekapropheton.* Edited by idem. FAT 13. Tübingen: Mohr, 1996.

–   "Jakob im Amosbuch." Pp. 257–271 in *Hosea und Amos: Studien zu den Anfängen des Dodekapropheton.* Edited by idem. FAT 13. Tübingen: Mohr, 1996.

–   "Rezeptionsprozesse in der prophetischen Überlieferung – am Beispiel der Visionsberichte des Amos." Pp. 29–44 in *Rezeption und Auslegung im Alten Testament und in seinem Umfeld.* Edited by R.G. Kratz and T. Krüger. OBO 153. Freiburg: Universitätsverlag and Göttingen: Vandenhoeck & Ruprecht, 1997.

–   *Die Propheten Joel, Obadja, Jona, Micha.* ATD 24,3. Göttingen: Vandenhoeck & Ruprecht, 2007.

Kaiser, O. *Der Gott des Alten Testaments: Theologie des Alten Testaments.* 3 vols. Göttingen: Vandenhoeck & Ruprecht, 1993–2003.

Keil, C.F. *Biblischer Commentar über die Zwölf Kleinen Propheten.* 3rd ed. Biblischer Commentar über das Alte Testament III,4. Leipzig: Dörffling und Franke, 1888.

Kessler, R. "Hosea 3 – Entzug oder Hinwendung Gottes?" *ZAW* 120 (2008) 563–581.

Knapp, D. *Deuteronomium 4: Literarische Analyse und theologische Interpretation.* GTA 35. Göttingen: Vandenhoeck & Ruprecht, 1987.

Koch, K. "Prophetenbuchüberschriften: Ihre Bedeutung für das hebräische Verständnis von Profetie." Pp. 165–186 in *Verbindungslinien.* Edited by A. Graupner et al. FS W.H. Schmidt. Neukirchen-Vluyn: Neukirchener, 2000.

Kratz, R.G. "Israel als Staat und als Volk." *ZTK* 97 (2000) 1–17.

–   "Erkenntnis Gottes im Hoseabuch." Pp. 287–309 in *Prophetenstudien: Kleine Schriften II.* Edited by idem. FAT 74. Tübingen: Mohr, 2011.

–   "Hosea und Amos im Zwölfprophetenbuch." Pp. 275–286 in *Prophetenstudien: Kleine Schriften II.* Edited by idem. FAT 74. Tübingen: Mohr, 2011.

- "Hosea und Amos in den Schriften vom Toten Meer." Pp. 359–379 in *Prophetenstudien: Kleine Schriften II*. Edited by idem. FAT 74. Tübingen: Mohr, 2011.

Levin, C. *Die Verheißung des neuen Bundes in ihrem theologiegeschichtlichen Zusammenhang ausgelegt*. FRLANT 137. Göttingen: Vandenhoeck & Ruprecht, 1985.

Marti, K. *Das Dodekapropheton*. KHC 13. Tübingen: Mohr, 1904.

Naumann, T. *Hoseas Erben: Strukturen der Nachinterpretation im Buch Hosea*. BWANT 131. Stuttgart: Kohlhammer, 1991.

Nissinen, M. *Prophetie, Redaktion und Fortschreibung im Hoseabuch: Studien zum Werdegang eines Prophetenbuches im Lichte von Hos 4 und 11*. AOAT 231. Kevelaer: Butzon & Bercker and Neukirchen-Vluyn: Neukirchener, 1991.

Nogalski, J.D. *Literary Precursors to the Book of the Twelve*. BZAW 217. Berlin: de Gruyter, 1993.

- "Intertextuality and the Twelve." Pp. 102–124 in *Forming Prophetic Literature*. Edited by J.W. Watts and P.R. House. FS J.D.W. Watts. JSOTSup 235. Sheffield: Sheffield Academic Press, 1996.

- "The Day(s) of YHWH in the Book of the Twelve." Pp. 192–213 in *Thematic Threads in the Book of the Twelve*. Edited by P.L. Redditt and A. Schart. BZAW 325. Berlin: de Gruyter, 2003.

- "Recurring Themes in the Book of the Twelve: Creating Points of Contact for a Theological Reading." *Int* 61 (2007) 125–136.

- "One Book and Twelve Books: The Nature of the Redactional Work and the Implications of Cultic Source Material in the Book of the Twelve." Pp. 11–46 in *Two Sides of a Coin: Juxtaposing Views on Interpreting the Book of the Twelve / the Twelve Prophetic Books*. Edited by E. Ben Zvi and idem. Analecta Gorgiana 201. Piscataway: Gorgias Press, 2009.

Perlitt, L. *Die Propheten Nahum, Habakuk, Zephanja*. ATD 25,1. Göttingen: Vandenhoeck & Ruprecht, 2004.

Pfeiffer, H. *Das Heiligtum von Bethel im Spiegel des Hoseabuches*. FRLANT 183. Göttingen: Vandenhoeck & Ruprecht, 1999.

Redditt, P.L. "The Production and Reading of the Book of the Twelve." Pp. 11–33 in *Reading and Hearing the Book of the Twelve*. Edited by J.D. Nogalski and M.A. Sweeney. SBLSymS 15. Atlanta: Society of Biblical Literature, 2000.

- "Recent Research on the Book of the Twelve As One Book." *CurBS* 9 (2001) 47–80.

- "The Formation of the Book of the Twelve: A Review of Research." Pp. 1–26 in *Thematic Threads in the Book of the Twelve*. Edited by idem and A. Schart. BZAW 325. Berlin: de Gruyter, 2003.

- and Schart, A. (ed.) *Thematic Threads in the Book of the Twelve*. BZAW 325. Berlin: de Gruyter, 2003.

Rendtorff, R. "How to Read the Book of the Twelve as a Theological Unity." Pp. 75–87 in *Reading and Hearing the Book of the Twelve*. Edited by J.D. Nogalski and M.A. Sweeney. SBLSymS 15. Atlanta: Society of Biblical Literature, 2000.

- "Alas for the Day! The 'Day of the LORD' in the Book of the Twelve." Pp. 253–264 in *Der Text in seiner Endgestalt: Schritte auf dem Weg zu einer Theolo-*

gie des Alten Testaments. Edited by idem. Neukirchen-Vluyn: Neukirchener, 2001.

Roth, M. *Israel und die Völker im Zwölfprophetenbuch: Eine Untersuchung zu den Büchern Joel, Jona, Micha und Nahum*. FRLANT 210. Göttingen: Vandenhoeck & Ruprecht, 2005.

Rudnig-Zelt, S. "Die Genese des Hoseabuches: Ein Forschungsbericht." Pp. 351–383 in *Textarbeit: Studien zu Texten und ihrer Rezeption aus dem Alten Testament und der Umwelt Israels*. Edited by K. Kiesow and T. Meurer. FS P. Weimar. AOAT 294. Münster: Ugarit-Verlag, 2003.

– *Hoseastudien: Redaktionskritische Untersuchungen zur Genese des Hoseabuches*. FRLANT 213. Göttingen: Vandenhoeck & Ruprecht, 2006.

– "Vom Propheten und seiner Frau, einem Ephod und einem Teraphim – Anmerkungen zu Hos 3:1–4, 5." *VT* 60 (2010) 373–399.

Schart, A. *Die Entstehung des Zwölfprophetenbuchs: Neubearbeitungen von Amos im Rahmen schriftenübergreifender Redaktionsprozesse*. BZAW 260. Berlin: de Gruyter, 1998.

– "Zur Redaktionsgeschichte des Zwölfprophetenbuchs." *VF* 43 (1998) 13–33.

– "Das Zwölfprophetenbuch als redaktionelle Großeinheit." *TLZ* 133 (2008) 227–246.

Schmid, K. *Buchgestalten des Jeremiabuches: Untersuchungen zur Redaktions- und Rezeptionsgeschichte von Jer 30–33 im Kontext des Buches*. WMANT 72. Neukirchen-Vluyn: Neukirchener, 1996.

Schwesig, P.-G. *Die Rolle der Tag-JHWHs-Dichtungen im Dodekapropheton*. BZAW 366. Berlin: de Gruyter, 2006.

– "Sieben Stimmen und ein Chor: Die Tag-*Jhwhs*-Dichtungen im Zwölfprophetenbuch." Pp. 229–240 in *Die unwiderstehliche Wahrheit: Studien zur alttestamentlichen Prophetie*. Edited by R. Lux and E.-J. Waschke. FS A. Meinhold. Arbeiten zur Bibel und ihrer Geschichte 23. Leipzig: Evangelische Verlagsanstalt, 2006.

Scoralick, R. *Gottes Güte und Gottes Zorn: Die Gottesprädikationen in Exodus 34,6f und ihre intertextuellen Beziehungen zum Zwölfprophetenbuch*. Herders biblische Studien 33. Freiburg: Herder, 2002.

Seifert, B. *Metaphorisches Reden von Gott im Hoseabuch*. FRLANT 166. Göttingen: Vandenhoeck & Ruprecht, 1996.

Sheppard, G.T. *Wisdom as a Hermeneutical Construct: A Study in the Sapientializing of the Old Testament*. BZAW 151. Berlin: de Gruyter, 1980.

Spieckermann, H. *Juda unter Assur in der Sargonidenzeit*. FRLANT 129. Göttingen: Vandenhoeck & Ruprecht, 1982.

– "Barmherzig und gnädig ist der Herr ..." *ZAW* 102 (1990) 1–18.

– "God's Steadfast Love: Towards a New Conception of Old Testament Theology." *Bib* 81 (2000) 305–327.

Spronk, K. "Hosea als Onderdeel van het Boek van de Twaalf Profeten." *ACEBT* 17 (1999) 23–35.

Tov, E. "The Biblical Texts from the Judean Desert – An Overview and Analysis." Pp. 128–154 in *Hebrew Bible, Greek Bible and Qumran: Collected Essays*. Edited by idem. TSAJ 121. Tübingen: Mohr, 2008.

Vermeylen, J. "Osée 1 et les prophètes du VIIIᵉ siècle." Pp. 193–206 in *Schriftaus-legung in der Schrift.* Edited by R.G. Kratz et al. FS O.H. Steck. BZAW 300. Berlin: de Gruyter, 2000.

Vielhauer, R. *Das Werden des Buches Hosea: Eine redaktionsgeschichtliche Untersu-chung.* BZAW 349. Berlin: de Gruyter, 2007.

– "Reading Hosea at Qumran." Pp. 91–108 in *The Mermaid and the Partridge: Essays from the Copenhagen Conference on Revising Texts from Cave Four.* Edit-ed by G.J. Brooke and J. Høgenhaven. STDJ 96. Leiden: Brill, 2011.

von Rad, G. "Das Gottesvolk im Deuteronomium." Pp. 9–108 in *Gesammelte Studien zum Alten Testament II.* Edited by R. Smend. TB 48. München: Kai-ser, 1973.

Wacker, M.-T. *Figurationen des Weiblichen im Hosea-Buch.* Herders biblische Studien 8. Freiburg: Herder, 1996.

Watts, J.D.W. "A Frame for the Book of the Twelve: Hos 1–3 and Malachi." Pp. 209–217 in *Reading and Hearing the Book of the Twelve.* Edited by J.D. Nogals-ki and M.A. Sweeney. SBLSymS 15. Atlanta: Society of Biblical Literature, 2000.

Wellhausen, J. *Die kleinen Propheten: Übersetzt und erklärt.* 4ᵗʰ ed. Berlin: de Gruy-ter, 1963.

Wöhrle, J. *Die frühen Sammlungen des Zwölfprophetenbuches: Entstehung und Kom-position.* BZAW 360. Berlin: de Gruyter, 2006.

– *Der Abschluss des Zwölfprophetenbuches: Buchübergreifende Redaktionsprozesse in den späten Sammlungen.* BZAW 389. Berlin: de Gruyter, 2008.

– "'No Future for the Proud Exultant Ones': The Exilic Book of the Four Prophets (Hos., Am., Mic., Zeph.) as a Concept Opposed to the Deutero-nomistic History." *VT* 58 (2008) 608–627.

Wolff, H.W. *Dodekapropheton 1: Hosea.* BKAT 14,1. Neukirchen-Vluyn: Neukir-chener, 1961.

– *Dodekapropheton 2: Joel und Amos.* BKAT 14,2. Neukirchen-Vluyn: Neukir-chener, 1969.

Yee, G.A. *Composition and Tradition in the Book of Hosea: A Redaction Critical In-vestigation.* SBLDS 102. Atlanta: Scholars Press, 1987.

The Function of the Book of Joel for Reading the Twelve

JÖRG JEREMIAS

Philipps-Universität Marburg

More than any other single book except Zech 9–14 among the Twelve Prophets, the book of Joel is full of cross references to other parts of the Twelve. This is true especially for chapters 1–2, on which the present paper will concentrate. Yet this observation is not too surprising, since Joel is a very late prophet according to the majority of scholars who have dealt with his book.[1] Nearly all the cross references in the book of Joel can be explained by the assumption that Joel learned from older prophets, taking up their ideas, expanding and modifying them. Only once does Joel legitimate himself by referring to an immediate word of God (2:19). Usually he and his traditionists refer to former prophetic utterances, which they may even cite literally (2:12; 3:5). There are good reasons to call Joel's prophecy "learned prophecy."[2]

Still, in its present position the book of Joel precedes the other books of the Twelve with the exception of Hosea, at least in the order of MT. Therefore, it serves a kind of hermeneutical key to the Twelve. A reader of, say, Amos and Zephaniah will have read Joel before coming to them in his or her scroll and will understand Amos and Zephaniah in line with Joel's message, though the historical Joel learned from Amos and Zephaniah and modified them both. Consequently, we have to distinguish between two different trends of interpretation. While Amos and Zephaniah strongly influenced Joel, the book of Joel by its position among the Twelve influences the meaning of the books of Amos (Obadiah, Jonah) and Zephaniah. This process of double influence will be the subject of the following pages.

---

1   For the most important reasons to date the book cf. Wolff, *Joel*, 2–4.8–12; Jeremias, *Propheten*, 2–5.
2   Wolff, *Joel*, 12; Jeremias, "Prophetie," 97–111.

I

The one and only subject of the book of Joel is the "Day of the Lord." The term יוֹם יְהוָה appears in each of the four chapters of the book. There is no other context in the Old Testament, where it is used more often. Yet, as James Nogalski has noticed many years ago, none of these instances sounds very original:

> "When one isolates the Day-of-YHWH references in Joel, virtually every one has a close (if not verbatim) parallel in the Book of the Twelve."[3]

Joel has learned from his predecessors, especially from Amos and Zephaniah, and Jakob Wöhrle is correct in claiming that Zeph 1 is the most important source for the description of the Day of the Lord in Joel.[4] Thus, the ideal reader should come to know the books of Amos and Zephaniah first in order to understand the entire message of Joel.

Still, the concept of the Day of the Lord in Joel is very different from that in Amos and Zephaniah, as will be shown, and Joel determines the understanding of the concept of Amos, Obadiah, and Zephaniah by the very fact that the book of Joel (in the Hebrew transmission of the text) is positioned in front of those books. Joel thus serves a hermeneutical function. If Joel deliberately is taking up the main characteristics of the Day of the Lord described in the books of his predecessors Amos and Zephaniah, and if he apparently is interested in the continuity of this concept, the decisive question then is this: why did his traditionists position his book in front of these earlier books? What is new in Joel's dealing with the Day of the Lord?

Answering these questions sounds like a simple task, but its weight and importance can hardly be overestimated. The book of Joel is the only book in the Old Testament that points to the possibility of salvation when the coming of the Day of the Lord is announced. To be more precise: the book of Joel (ch. 1–2) is *the only book in the Old Testament daring to speak of the survival of a whole generation in Israel in the context of the Day of the Lord.*[5] The position of the book of Joel in front of the first mention of the Day of the Lord in Amos thus changes the character of the Day of the Lord completely; moreover, it changes the essence of Old Testament eschatology. For Amos and Zephaniah nobody can escape the threatening coming of the Day of the Lord. Amos 5:18–19 reads:

---

3   Nogalski, "Joel," 104–105.
4   Wöhrle, *Sammlungen,* 437–438.444–445.457.
5   Zeph 2:3 reckons on the salvation of very few single persons, but with the reservation of the famous prophetic "perhaps," to which we shall return when dealing with Joel 2:14.

5:18 The Day of YHWH is darkness and not light.
19 As when a man flees from a lion – and a bear will meet him; or when he reaches home and leans his hand to the wall – and a snake bites him.

For Amos on the issue of the Day of the Lord there is only one single certainty: everyone dies, no matter how the day is realized. As God's creation of the world started with the creation of light, thus darkness ("without a gleam," v. 20) symbolizes the revocation of creation.

Zephaniah even increases this picture of death without any hope. I cite Zeph 1:14–16:

1:14 Near is the great day of the Lord, nearing very swiftly.
The sound of the day of the Lord: bitterly shrieks then a warrior.
15 A day of wrath is that day:
a day of distraint and distress,
a day of devastation and desolation,
a day of darkness and gloom,
a day of clouds and dense fog,
16 a day of trumpet blast and siren,
against the fortified cities and against the lofty corner towers.[6]

In this highly poetic text with no finite verb, very different traditional motifs are mixed in order to describe the terrifying horror of the Day of the Lord as comprehensively as possible. "Clouds and dense fog" remind one of the mighty appearances of YHWH against his enemies in descriptions of theophany; "darkness and gloom" take up the subject of Amos to depict the loss of divine shelter and of life. "Trumpet blast and fortified cities" remind one of wars with heavy losses, and in the center שאה and משאה describe destruction and devastation of all life and of all fertile land. But the decisive theme of this all embracing terror stands in front of all five word-pairs just mentioned; it stands alone with its full weight: "A day of wrath is that day." The wrath of God appears in the Old Testament where punishment is no longer possible that is appropriate for a single, specific guilty act. The wrath of God is without measure and without limit. Nobody can survive it. The five word-pairs of tradition and of new formation (the word-pair in the center) explain the work of the wrath of YHWH. This wrath leads to death and to devastation everywhere.

In Joel the terrifying character of the Day of the Lord is by no means weakened. Quite the contrary, it is intensified to a level where further intensification is hardly possible. In Joel 2:1–11, one of the most sophisticated texts in the whole Old Testament, an even greater mix-

---

6   Translation by Berlin, *Zephaniah*, 85.

ture of traditions is found than in Zeph 1,[7] and this mixture appears in combination with pictures and parables changing so quickly that readers are confused about whether a terrifying human army or a hungry multitude of locusts is described.[8] Apparently, the author of the text aims at this "confusion," because he wants to describe a phenomenon that transcends typical understandings of either possibility. His description of an undefeatable, hostile army is full of references to former prophetic texts surpassing all of them by their combination. It ends in a vision of cosmic destruction and in the horrifying statement that nobody but YHWH is the leader of the superhuman destructive army.

But – having Isa 13 and Zeph 1 in mind, the main texts which Joel 2:1–11 is referring to – the reader should notice that *one of the most important ideas of Isa 13 and Zeph 1 is missing: the wrath of YHWH.*[9] Both Isa 13 and Zeph 1 intend to describe the effect of YHWH's wrath on his "day," which for them is by definition a day of wrath. This is by no means true for Joel. *Instead* of the devastating, all-devouring wrath of YHWH which is without measure and without limit, there suddenly and unexpectedly *follows an invitation to return to YHWH* introduced by: "Yet even now." In other words, one finds this invitation even in the face of God's destructive army, even at the beginning of the Day of the Lord.

The vocabulary used is worth investigating. For many years it has been observed that Joel does not choose the most common phrase for "return." He does not speak of the return of Israel *from* guilty ways (שוב מן). He does not stress or even hint at the sins of the people – quite the contrary. Instead, Joel speaks of his hope for the return of his generation *to* YHWH (שוב עד). Schart and especially Nogalski have shown convincingly that Joel here is learning from Hosea, i.e. the last chapter of the book of Hosea, where the שוב עד is the central idea (Hos 14:2).[10] But, as I demonstrated thirty years ago in my commentary to Hosea, the reason given in Hos 14 for the possibility of Israel returning to YHWH is that YHWH promises "to heal Israel's apostasy," because his wrath already "*has* turned away from him" (v. 5).[11] If the wrath of YHWH were still threatening Israel, no healing of Israel's apostasy and no return to God would be possible, even though Israel might be willing to move.

---

7   Cf. among others Meinhold, "Rolle," 206–223; Scoralick, "Jetzt," 48–59.
8   For the first interpretation cf. Wolff, *Joel*, 43–57; for the second Rudolph, *Joel*, 49–58.
9   Cf. Jeremias, *Zorn*, 180–184.
10   Schart, *Entstehung*, 176.266; Nogalski, "Joel," 94–99.
11   Jeremias, *Hosea*, 170–171.

II

What then is *the reason that Joel dares to show a way of salvation* even at the imminent experience of the Day of the Lord, which in tradition is a day of devastation without any hope? There are numerous reasons; I mention only the two most important ones.

1. Joel opens the eyes of his contemporaries to the possibility that *the Day of the Lord is embedded already in any extreme distress* like in the drought and in the locusts of his own time. He is the first and only prophet that not only warns his own generation of the coming of the Day of the Lord, but claims that they are already experiencing the dreaded effects of this day, though the day is only beginning and has not yet reached its full power. For Joel, with the utter lack of food removing the possibility of celebrating the typical service for God, the drought functions transparently for any other distress like a locust plague and a military invasion. Only cumulatively do all these different kinds of suffering serve as appropriate descriptions of the frightening Day of the Lord. Humans can only respond adequately to any of these experiences when they take into account its potential development into more extreme distress that ultimately leads to the Day of the Lord. Thus, present experience and eschatological threat for Joel are not two different subjects, but are different aspects of one single subject. One can be influenced by human conduct; the other can't. Therefore, Joel is the first prophet who not only expects the Day of the Lord for the future, but who already detects its roots in the present.

2. *Joel relies upon the famous description of God's characteristics in Exod 34:6–7.* These verses are often cited in postexilic texts of the Old Testament: "YHWH, YHWH: a God compassionate and gracious, slow to anger but abounding in steadfast love and faithfulness." *But Joel comments upon and qualifies this confession* from two directions.

a. The confession stresses the incomparability of God's grace and his anger ("slow to anger but abounding in steadfast love"); but for Joel this use of the comparative is not enough, since the Day of the Lord *is* a day of anger and wrath in tradition. Therefore, Joel skips the following passage in Exod 34:7 ("yet he does not leave the guilty unpunished") and instead reads: *"ready to relent over calamity"* (וְנִחָם עַל־הָרָעָה). "To relent over calamity" – related to the Day of the Lord! – means no less than to spare Israel from the final judgment, or more precisely to spare the present generation from the final judgment. For Joel, too, the Day of the Lord in its full power *has* to come, because so many prophets have predicted it.

We cannot tell for sure whether this keen addition to the traditional confession of God's mercy was influenced by the visions of Amos (Amos 7:3, 6) or by Hosea (Hos 11:9), who first used the idea of the repentance of God. The phrase of Joel 2:14 is closer to, nearly identical with, the result of Moses' famous intercession on Mt. Sinai/Horeb in Exod 32:14. There Moses' petition was able to spare his people from God's destructive wrath, which would have led to Israel's end. As well in Joel 2 as in Exod 32 the continued existence of Israel is at stake, depending upon God's willingness to repent from his destructive plans. Will he repent?

b. There is a second addition to the traditional confession of Exod 34:6–7 in Joel 2. It is the weighty *prophetic "perhaps"* used by Amos and Zephaniah when speaking of their hope for the salvation of a few righteous men from divine judgment. They say "perhaps," because they have not received a special word of God for their hope (Amos 5:15; Zeph 2:3). Joel takes up this way of speaking in a more modern term ("who knows"): "Who knows? He may turn and relent and leave a blessing behind him ..." This prophetic "perhaps" has often been misinterpreted, as if its meaning was: nobody knows for sure. Joel's intention is quite different: His "perhaps" is *a sign of firm personal conviction* intentionally leaving room for God's freedom in view of the knowledge of the coming of the terrible character of the Day of the Lord.

In his days Joel's hope did not fail. At the end of chapter 2 the reader is informed: "Then YHWH became jealous for his land and he had pity on his people and YHWH answered and said to his people ..." (Joel 2:18–19). A whole series of promises follows: partly already experienced in the time of the book of Joel (the end of the drought), mostly transcending everyday experience and expected for the future.

III

What was *the intention of the book of Joel* after all? A group of modern exegetes favors the idea that the book of Joel was written for its present context within the Book of the Twelve.[12] For me personally this theory seems very unlikely. Joel is the only prophetic book in the Old Testament presenting its intention at the very outset by using a kind of prologue. *This prologue states the intention of the book quite clearly*, as I tried to demonstrate extensively a year ago.[13] It stresses mainly two points:

---

12   Among them are Nogalski, *Processes*, 276, and especially idem, "Joel," 105–109; Schneider, *Unity*, 84; Wöhrle, *Sammlungen*, 445–447.
13   Jeremias, "Weinstock," 355–358.

1. The book starts with a call to the elders and to the inhabitants of the land to tell its story to their sons in order that their sons tell their sons about it and they tell a future generation. Why is the call to deliver Joel's message given this urgently? A first hint is given by the observance that the addressees of the call (elders and inhabitants of the land) are the same as those being called in 1:14 to an official fast which according to 2:15–17 leads to the end of the drought. Apparently, not only a hint at the unusual need of the drought and locusts is the focus of the urgent call, but the whole horizon of the imminent threat of the Day of the Lord and its final avoidance. This broad horizon is confirmed by the verb used. "To tell" (ספר pi.) the sons means much more than mere oral transmission. At other places telling future generations is the subject either of hymns or of psalms of thanksgiving. In the hymns the "miracles" of God are the subject of such a "telling" (Ps 9:2; 26:7; 40:6 etc.) or else his "glorious deeds" (Ps 9:15; 78:4; 79:13 etc.) or his "honor" verified in his deeds (Ps 19:2; 96:3) or his mighty deeds of the past in favor of his people (Ps 44:2; 48:14). Otherwise "telling" is a central term of the psalms of thanksgiving. These psalms have a double function: to praise the Lord for his action of healing or saving etc. which is done in direct address, and "to tell" the congregation, how God changed the need of the person who has called the congregation for worship. The aim of this "telling" is to strengthen the trust of the congregation in God in case of their own distress.[14] Thus, by the use of "telling" the future generations, any reader of the book of Joel knows in advance that she or he is informed of an unexpected act of divine salvation in order to learn for her or his own generation, how to be saved when a similar need like the drought in the days of Joel is experienced.

2. Yet, the aim of the call to tell is not to turn away the drought. Joel 1:2 takes care to deny that anything comparable to the story told in the book has ever happened in history before (Joel 1:2). In fact, this statement is by no means interested in history. Its essence is explicitly taken up in Joel 2:2, which describes the terrible army of YHWH on YHWH's frightening day. But when YHWH's superhuman army is described, Joel 2:2 deliberately intensifies the incomparability of Joel 1:2 by stating not only that nothing comparable *has* ever happened, but also that nothing comparable *will* ever appear.[15] By this intensification it becomes evident that the Day of the Lord is the focus of the book of Joel from its very beginning. "Telling" future generations is not necessary to prepare them for dealing with severe needs like Joel's drought, but it is

---

14   For the details cf. Crüsemann, *Studien*, 210–284.
15   This intensification first was used by Exod 10 which is hinted at in Joel 1–2; cf. Müller, *Zukunft*, 41–57; Jeremias, "Weinstock," 358–360.

required if they are to know how to survive the deadly, imminent Day
of the Lord. Judging by its prologue, the book of Joel has an evident,
though implicit, didactic function.

IV

What, then, is *the effect* of reading the Twelve with this concept of the
book of Joel in mind?[16] Because of space limitations I shall show this
effect only for the book of Amos, the book that immediately follows
Joel in the Hebrew order of the prophetic books. In the case of Amos,
we stand on firm ground when relating the message of Joel to Amos,
because both books in their final form are tied together by two nearly
identical "bridging" verses. In the case of Joel 4:16a it is evident that it
cites the "motto" of the book of Amos, Amos 1:2,[17] while in the case of
Joel 4:18 parallel to Amos 9:13b the priority is not so certain.[18]

Without attempting a complete analysis, I choose three instances
for my demonstration of Joel's influence of reading the book of Amos:
Amos 4, Amos 5, and the visions.

1. In *Amos 4:6–13*, probably added to 4:4–5 in exilic times, a whole
chain of missed opportunities to return to YHWH (שוב עד as in Joel
2:12 and Hos 14:2) is enumerated, always ending in the refrain: "but
you did not return to me, says YHWH." Having read the book of Joel
before turning to Amos, the reader is forced to listen carefully, especially to v. 9, where it says: "Locusts were eating your fig trees and olive
trees, but you did not return to me, says YHWH." This statement
sounds nearly like a citation of Joel, but this time with a negative result:
the distress of the locusts did not lead to Israel's repentance. The whole
passage read in its context in the book of Amos already sounds very
urgent; it seems to speak of a last chance for Israel to turn to God. Having Joel in mind this urgency is even intensified: Has Israel already
missed her last chance?

The poem in Amos 4:6–13 reaches its climax in v. 12: "Therefore,
thus I will do to you, Israel! Because I will do thus to you, prepare to
meet your God, Israel!" Perhaps the indefinite "thus" in "thus I will do
to you" is already leading the reader to relate Amos 4:12 to the book of

---

16 Joel 3 and Joel 4 were probably added rather soon (cf. among others Jeremias,
    Propheten, 3–5) and did not change the intention of the older book of Joel decisively.
17 Cf. the arguments of Nogalski, "Intertextuality," 105–108.
18 Wöhrle, *Sammlungen,* 437.449, has concluded that the book of Joel was added to the
    exilic Book of the Four (Hosea, Amos, Micah, and Zephaniah) prior to other books of
    the Twelve. This theory would correspond to many of my own observations.

Joel and to keep the horror of the Day of the Lord in mind. Certainly, the final imperative does so: "Prepare to meet your God, Israel!" In a book of Amos read separately, this readiness to meet God would probably hint at Moses' (Exod 34:2) and Israel's (Exod 19:11, 15) readiness to meet God (cf. Exod 19:17) on the peak or at the base of Mt. Sinai, stressing that in the coming confrontation with God the continued existence of God's relation to Israel will be at stake. Read with Joel in mind, the meeting with God takes on the characteristics of the Day of the Lord. While Joel's generation understood that the drought and the locusts which threatened their daily life actually transcend everyday experience to serve as signs of the imminence of the Day of the Lord, the congregation of Amos 4:6–12 did not return to YHWH when the locusts came. Can the meeting with God in its character of a final event mean anything but death for them? Yet, Amos 4 leads to Amos 5.

2. Amos 5, indeed, opens up with the famous dirge on the virgin Israel having died much too early (Amos 5:2). Death remains the dominant subject of the whole chapter, before the Day of the Lord finally becomes the explicit subject (Amos 5:18–20). Yet, in between, there is a sudden glimpse of life. God says: "Seek me and you shall live!" (Amos 5:4). What precisely does this call to seek God have in mind? Immediately after 5:4, the reader is informed about false ways of seeking God ("Don't seek Bethel ...!"). How then does this "seeking God" lead to life realized in a context of extensive death? The reader concentrating on the book of Amos has to wait until v. 14–15 inform him that seeking God begins with seeking good ("Seek good and not evil, that you may live!"). The reader, having understood the book of Joel before, will know in advance: only worship in which hearts and not (only) garments are torn, will lead to God and to his repentance from bringing death (Joel 2:12–14).

3. My last example is taken from the four visions of Amos in Amos 7–8. These four visions are arranged in pairs running parallel: In the first pair Amos' intercession with God reaches its goal; in the second pair there is no further room for any prophetic intercession because Amos has to learn that God's patience has reached a limit. The first pair of visions shows Amos a huge multitude of locusts and a terrible drought in cosmic dimensions. Together with Schart[19] I am convinced that Joel, by describing the distress of his time using pictures of both a locust plague and a drought, hints at the first two visions of Amos.[20] In any case, a reader with the book of Joel in mind is urged to notice the parallel. In Joel the locusts and the drought developed into the deadly

---

19   Schart, *Entstehung*, 262.
20   Jeremias, *Propheten*, 19–20.

Day of the Lord, but the Day of the Lord had been avoided by the worship of the congregation, by the honest return to God. By analogy, the visions of Amos will be understood in a similar way. The second pair of visions in Amos seems to lead to an "end of my people Israel" (Amos 8:2), but for a reader coming from the book of Joel this "end" is not inevitable. YHWH stays the "one ready to relent over/to repent from calamity" (Joel 2:13) as he has already shown both in the time of Joel and in the first two visions of Amos (Amos 7:3, 6).

Reading Amos separately, the visions show that God's patience with his guilty people has reached a definite limit. Reading Amos after Joel, the visions show that locusts and drought which may lead to the end of Israel manifest an even greater distress. Yet, this distress, though unsurpassable in the light of God's final judgment at his terrible "Day," in the end is designed to lead Israel back to God. Once the dimension of the Day of the Lord has reached this goal Israel will receive all the aspects of final salvation described in Joel 2, as well as Joel 4 and Amos 9.

Looking back from this final objective of God's actions, the Day of the Lord, as terrible as that day appears, in the end represents an extreme means for God to lead Israel to the salvation he has prepared for her. True, for Joel God is judge and savior at the same time; but by no means is God judge and savior to the same degree. Already when he plans to bring the terrible Day of the Lord to his people – as he is forced to do – God hopes he will not have to implement it. Rather, God hopes to spare his people and to bring salvation to them. This is his true intention and by it he stays the "one who relents over/ who repents from calamity" (Joel 2:13).

References

Barton, J. *Joel and Obadiah*. OTL. Louisville: Westminster John Knox, 2001.
Bergler, S. *Joel als Schriftinterpret*. BEATAJ 16. Frankfurt: Lang, 1988.
Berlin, A. *Zephaniah*. AB 25A. New York: Doubleday, 1994.
Crüsemann, F. *Studien zur Formgeschichte von Hymnus und Danklied in Israel*. WMANT 32. Neukirchen-Vluyn: Neukirchener, 1969.
Jeremias, J. *Der Prophet Hosea*. ATD 24,1. Göttingen: Vandenhoeck & Ruprecht, 1983.
– "Gelehrte Prophetie: Beobachtungen zu Joel und Deuterosacharja." Pp. 97–111 in *Vergegenwärtigung des Alten Testaments: Beiträge zur biblischen Hermeneutik*. Edited by C. Bultmann et al. FS R. Smend. Göttingen: Vandenhoeck & Ruprecht, 2002.
– *Die Propheten Joel, Obadja, Jona, Micha*. ATD 24,3. Göttingen: Vandenhoeck & Ruprecht, 2007.

– "'Der Weinstock verdorrt, der Feigenbaum verwelkt' (Joel 1,12): Bedrohte Existenz in Joel 1." Pp. 346–361 in *Essen und Trinken in der Bibel*. Edited by M. Geiger et al. FS R. Kessler. Gütersloh: Gütersloher, 2009.

– *Der Zorn Gottes im Alten Testament: Das biblische Israel zwischen Verwerfung und Erwählung*. Biblisch-Theologische Studien 104. 2nd ed. Neukirchen-Vluyn: Neukirchener, 2011.

Meinhold, A. "Zur Rolle des Tag-JHWHs-Gedichts Joel 2,1–11 im XII-Propheten-Buch." Pp. 206–223 in *Verbindungslinien*. Edited by A. Graupner et al. FS W.H. Schmidt. Neukirchen-Vluyn: Neukirchener, 2000.

Müller, A.K. *Gottes Zukunft: Die Möglichkeit der Rettung am Tag JHWHs nach dem Joelbuch*. WMANT 119. Neukirchen-Vluyn: Neukirchener, 2008.

Nogalski, J.D., *Redactional Processes in the Book of the Twelve*. BZAW 218. Berlin: de Gruyter, 1993.

– "Intertextuality in the Twelve." Pp. 102–124 in *Forming Prophetic Literature*. Edited by J.W. Watts and P.R. House. FS J.D.W. Watts. JSOTSup 235. Sheffield: Sheffield Academic Press, 1996.

– "Joel as 'Literary Anchor' for the Book of the Twelve." Pp. 91–109 in *Reading and Hearing the Book of the Twelve*. Edited by idem and M.A. Sweeney. SBLSymS 15. Atlanta: Society of Biblical Literature, 2000.

Rudolph, W. *Joel – Amos – Obadja – Jona*. KAT 13,2. Gütersloh: Gütersloher, 1971.

Schart, A. *Die Entstehung des Zwölfprophetenbuchs: Neubearbeitungen von Amos im Rahmen schriftenübergreifender Redaktionsprozesse*. BZAW 260. Berlin: de Gruyter, 1998.

Schneider, D.A. *The Unity of the Book of the Twelve*. Diss. Yale, 1979.

Scoralick, R. "'Auch jetzt noch' (Joel 2,12a): Zur Eigenart der Joelschrift und ihrer Funktion im Kontext des Zwölfprophetenbuches." Pp. 47–69 in *"Wort JHWHs, das geschah ..." (Hos 1,1): Studien zum Zwölfprophetenbuch*. Edited by E. Zenger. Herders biblische Studien 35. Freiburg: Herder, 2002.

Wöhrle, J. *Die frühen Sammlungen des Zwölfprophetenbuches: Entstehung und Komposition*. BZAW 360. Berlin: de Gruyter, 2006.

Wolff, H.W. *Dodekapropheton 2: Joel und Amos*. BK 14,2. 3rd ed. Neukirchen-Vluyn: Neukirchener, 1985.

Not Just another Nation:
Obadiah's Placement in the Book of the Twelve

JAMES D. NOGALSKI

Baylor University

Introduction

I recently suggested that finding agreement (or at least narrowing the disagreements) for dating the editorial work of the six writings in the Book of the Twelve whose superscriptions do not contain dates needed to explore more fully the use of "cultic source blocks" to accomplish editorial agendas.[1] That essay explored how the editorial adaptation and the placement of pre-existing theophanic hymns at the beginning of Nahum and the end of Habakkuk served the redactor's literary and theological agenda. Recognizing the editorial elements produces a coherent rhetorical function in reading Micah, Nahum, and Habakkuk sequentially.

The current essay continues this line of investigation by considering the composition of Obadiah in light of its location in the Book of the Twelve. Doing so raises a methodological question: Have models of the redactional growth of the corpus that comes to be known as the Twelve moved too quickly to explain literary and theological tensions within the writings by postulating "redactional layers" without fully considering whether these tensions may be explained by the adaptation of source material for a writing's *Sitz im Buch*?

Unlike Nahum and Habakkuk, the editorial work in Obadiah does not involve the attachment of a cultic hymn to a pre-existing corpus. Nevertheless, the book of Obadiah almost certainly represents an adaptation of source material that was initially composed for another purpose. The reason, however, for the selection and arrangement of this material has not been given the attention it deserves. This essay shall explore this question from two directions. First, it will delineate evidence for understanding Obadiah as a composite piece of literature that combines (through ordering, editing, and composition) at least three brief units, at least two of which originated in another context. Second,

---

1 See Nogalski, "One Book," 30–39.

the essay will argue that the motivation for arranging these units derives not from a desire to record the sayings of an anonymous prophet,
but that this arrangement instead owes its shape to its literary location,
its *Sitz im Buch*. Further, by taking seriously the idea that the Book of
the Twelve represents the literary context for understanding Obadiah,
one can plausibly explain many of the book's literary abnormalities, its
macrostructural flow, and its role in the broader corpus. Fundamentally, these assertions recognize the role of Edom in Obadiah does not
merely, or even primarily, serve as a cipher for any nation. Rather, in
Obadiah Edom means Edom.[2]

1. Structural and Thematic Parallels
between Obadiah and Amos 9

1.1 The Placement of Obadiah

In the history of scholarship, a few scholars have noted that the placement of Obadiah in the Book of the Twelve resulted from a *compiler's*
decision to place it beside Amos because of the fortuitous reference to
the "possession" of "Edom" in Amos 9:12, two keywords which also
appear in Obad 17–18. In many respects, this combination, they argue,
could represent a thematic summary of Obadiah as a whole.[3] Consequently, these scholars assume correctly that the context in the Book of
the Twelve influenced the location of Obadiah.

   However, assuming an editor merely copied a completed collection
of anti-Edom sayings onto a scroll at the end of Amos because one
verse contained two key concepts in Obadiah does not provide an adequate explanation for Obadiah's placement for two reasons: 1) the parallels between Amos 9:12 and Obad 17–18 only begin to scratch the
surface of the common motifs, wording, and structural components of
Amos 9 and Obadiah; and 2) the idea that a completed Obadiah was
placed beside a completed Amos based upon the presence of two
common words begs a larger question: namely, why these two words?
More should be said about both of these reasons: documenting parallel
vocabulary, structural components, and themes between Amos 9 and

---

2   Contra those who see Edom primarily as a type for all nations, such as Jenson, *Oba-
     diah*, 7; House, *Unity*, 82; Stuart, *Hosea*, 421–422. One should take full account of the
     references to Edom when interpreting Obadiah. For a comparative example, see
     Struppe, *Obadja*, 52–53.
3   E.g., Cassuto, "Sequence," 5–6.

Obadiah on the one hand, and considering the possession of Edom in the postexilic context on the other.

Given the difference in genres between Amos 9 and Obadiah, as well as the history of interpretation that has largely treated the individual writings in the Book of the Twelve as entirely independent of one another, one can hardly be surprised that these two passages are rarely treated together. However, the sheer volume of lexical and thematic parallels, combined with observations regarding the transitional markers of Obadiah that match those of Amos 9, requires an explanation that goes beyond coincidence.

1.2 Amos 9

One first needs to consider Amos 9 as a composite literary entity in its own right. Amos 9 begins the fifth and final "vision" of Amos (9:1–4) in which the prophetic spectator envisions the destruction of Israel. While scholars have often noted the uniqueness of this vision compared to the first four visions, no one doubts that 9:1–4 plays a key role in the book by demonstrating with finality god's judgment upon the northern kingdom. Together with the concluding doxology (9:5–6), these verses once likely concluded Amos prior to the addition of 9:7–15*, verses whose promissory nature stands in stark contrast to anything that has preceded in Amos.[4] This promissory material, in its current form, reflects two units: the first (9:7–10) reflects a debate about the nature of election and a remnant in which two sides of the debate are presented; the second unit (9:11–15) represents a composite eschatological promise that God will restore the Davidic kingdom and provide for the land's fertility. In short Amos 9 begins with destruction and ends with promise: the destruction of Israel and the promise of a restored Davidic kingdom.

While Amos 9 almost certainly reflects more than one hand in shaping its final form as the conclusion to Amos, two verses stand out for their thematic connections forward to Obadiah (Amos 9:12) and backward to Joel (Amos 9:13b, which cites Joel 4:18a). The promise to restore the Davidic kingdom by rebuilding it reads more smoothly if these short comments were not present, so one can easily imagine these two verses as an editor's parenthetical foreshadowing (9:12) and rehearsal (9:13) of Obadiah and Joel respectively.

---

4   Amos 9:7–10 and 9:11–15 represent additions to the chapter. See the more detailed explanation of the complex unity of these verses in Wolff, *Joel*, 345–346.351–352; Nogalski, *Precursors*, 104–121.

1.3 Amos 9 and Obadiah: Structural and Thematic Parallels

Thus, Amos 9 has its own literary integrity, composite though it may be, which generally makes sense within the developmental history of Amos. Nevertheless, a comparison of Amos 9:1–15 with Obadiah reveals a number of significant parallels that go well beyond the thematic foreshadowing of Amos 9:12, as can be seen in the following chart.

Structural and Thematic Elements		Amos	Obadiah
Vision		9:1	1
Five אם ("if/though") clauses		9:2–4	4–5
No escape from YHWH: "From there I will bring them/you down"		9:2	4
Destruction & remnant motifs (using agricultural imagery)		9:7–10	5
Thematic shifts/ text markers:	הלוא "is it not"	9:7 (twice)	5 (twice) 8 (1st word)
	ביום ההוא "on that day"	9:11	8 (2nd word)
	נאם יהוה "utterance of YHWH"	9:7, 8, 13	8 (3rd word)
Day(s) of *Judah's* restoration/ destruction		9:11(ביום ההוא) 9:13 (ימים באים)	11–14 (ביום 10xs)
Introduction with eschatological "day" of punishment on nations and restoration of Judah		9:11	15
Allusion to destruction of Jerusalem		9:11	16
Restoration of Davidic kingdom		9:11–12	19–20
"Possession" of Edom and other nations		9:12	17–18, 19–20
Restoration of captivity/exiles		9:14	19–20
Concluding promise for restoring the kingdom		9:15	21

To understand these parallels, one should see them in light of their rhetorical function in Obad 1–5, 8–9, 10–14+15b, and 15a, 16–21.

Obadiah 1–5. Comparing the differences between Obad 1–5 and its parallel in Jer 49:14–16, 9, one can plausibly explain most of the variations between the Jeremiah and the Obadiah parallel as changes in

Obadiah's sources that reflect elements from Amos 9:1–4. First, Amos
9:1–4 contains five concessive clauses constructed with מִשָּׁם ... אִם
("though ... from there"). While Obad 1–5 contains only one clause with
this construction, it does contain five clauses that begin with אִם. The
parallel text and Jer 49 contains only two such clauses. The phrase
"from there I will bring them down" in Amos 9:2 parallels the same
phrase in Obad 4, except the latter has a second masculine singular
pronoun ("from there I will pull you down). This phrase, "from there I
will pull them/you down" appears in only one other text, namely Jer
49:16, the very passage (Jer 49:14–16) that parallels Obad 1–4.

Second, the superscription in Obad 1 labels Obadiah as a "vision,"
even though the subsequent verses do not conform to what one would
traditionally expect as a vision. By contrast, no one doubts that Amos
9:1–4 should be interpreted as a vision.

Third, after Obad 1–4 closely parallels Jer 49:14–16, Obad 5 reaches
backward and picks up Jer 49:9 but inverts the order of the two halves
of the verse by placing 49:9b prior to 49:9a.[5]

Jer 49:9b	... or (אִם) thieves at night, would they destroy (שָׁחַת) their sufficiency?
Obad 5a	If (אִם) thieves come to you – or (אִם) destroyers (שֹׁדֵד) at night – how (אֵיךְ) you would be ruined (דָּמָה) – would they not (הֲלוֹא) steal their sufficiency?
Obad 5b	or (אִם) grape harvesters come to you, would they not (הֲלוֹא) leave gleanings?
Jer 49:9a	If (אִם) grape harvesters came to you, (would they) not (לֹא) leave gleanings?

Obad 5 (= Jer 49:9b, a) uses agricultural metaphors to depict the thematic content of the destruction and (the lack of) a remnant for Edom.
Amos 9:7, 8–10 also uses agricultural metaphors to explain Israel's destruction (Amos 9:7//Obad 5a) and the existence of a remnant (Amos
9:8–10//Obad 5b). In essence, the compiler of Obadiah draws upon and
yet inverts Jer 49:9b, a to create a thematic parallel to Amos 9:7–10, although the application of these thematic elements to Edom, as opposed
to Israel, means that the parallel also displays a hermeneutic of ironic
reversal. Whereas Israel will be destroyed (Amos 9:7), a remnant will
remain (Amos 9:8–10). By contrast, the agricultural metaphors of Obad
5 articulate a situation in which Edom will be destroyed (Obad 5a) but

---

5   See Nogalski, *Processes*, 66.

no remnant will remain (Obad 5b). This hermeneutical perspective will reappear in several places in Obadiah.

Thus, these five verses in Obadiah draw upon a parallel text (Jer 49:14–16, 9), but they do so in a way that suggests a deliberate, intentional mirroring of the vocabulary, structure, and thematic development of Amos 9:1–10. Nevertheless, these similarities should not hide differences in the rhetorical aims of Obad 1–5 and Amos 9:1–10: whereas both Israel and Edom will be destroyed, a remnant will remain for Israel (Amos 9:7–10, 11–15), but not for Edom.

These thematic and structural parallels between Amos 9 and Obadiah do not stop with the parallels of Obad 1–5. Much of the remaining material in Obadiah also exhibits structural or thematic parallels with Amos 9.

Obad 8–9. The syntactical and transitional markers in Obadiah represent essentially the same markers, and in roughly the same order, as those in Amos 9. As already noted, the term "vision" in the superscription of Obad 1 essentially evokes and summarizes the final vision of Amos (9:1–4). Relatedly, the presence of םשׁמ ... םא along with a fivefold use of םא in Obad 1–5 corresponds to the five םשׁמ ... םא clauses in Amos 9:1–4.

Beyond Obad 1–5, the syntactically cumbersome triple formula beginning the transitional verse in Obad 8 ("Surely, on that day, utterance of YHWH") mirrors the same transitional markers in Amos 9, where "surely" (אולה) appears twice in Amos 9:7; "on that day" appears in Amos 9:11; and "utterance of YHWH" appears in 9:7, 8, 13.

This transitional trio marks the beginning of a saying (Obad 8–9) that essentially functions as an inclusio to the entire, composite anti-Edom collection of Jeremiah 49:7–22.[6]

Obad 8	Jer 49:7
On that day, says the LORD, I will destroy *the wise out of Edom*, and understanding out of Mount Esau.	Concerning Edom. Thus says the LORD of hosts: Is there no longer *wisdom in Teman*? Has counsel perished from the prudent? Has their *wisdom* vanished?
Obad 9	Jer 49:22
Your *warriors* shall be shattered, O *Teman*, so that everyone from Mount Esau will be cut off.	Look, he shall mount up and swoop down like an eagle, and spread his wings against Bozrah, and the heart of the *warriors of Edom* in that day shall be like the heart of a woman in labor.

---

6 Nogalski, *Processes*, 67; Raabe, *Obadiah*, 197.

Hence, not only does Obad 8–9 contain the same structural elements as Amos 9:7–15, the content of these two verses also alludes to the first and last Edom oracle in the Jeremiah collection of 49:7–22: the destruction of the wise (Jer 49:7) and the warriors (Jer 49:22) of Teman/Edom. This is the same collection, needless to say, where the parallels to Jer 49:14–16, 9 appear.

Obad 10–14. A subtle thematic and phonetic phenomenon appears with Amos 9:13 and Obad 10–14. Amos 9:11 combines the sound of ב with the word יום in the word ביום that begins the verse (on that day; ביום ההוא). Amos 9:13 transitions to a new promise with the phrase "behold the days are coming ..." The days to which Amos 9:13 alludes refers to a time of promise for Israel as the coming days, ימים באים, a phrase that also combines the sound of ב with the word יום – albeit in reverse order.

Interestingly, ten times Obad 10–14 uses the singular form of "day" preceded by the preposition ב, which means that in Amos 9:11, 13 the coming days (ימים באים; ביום ההוא) of promise for God's people are contrasted in Obadiah with ten references to something happening "on a day" (ביום) of judgment.[7] Thus, even the eschatological day phrases in Amos 9:11 and the plural ימים באים of Amos have a parallel in Obadiah, except that the "day" of judgment in Obad 10–14 refers to Judah's punishment (as opposed to Judah's restoration in Amos 9:13), while condemning Edom's behavior. Rhetorically, these verses serve as (implicit) accusations against Edom – as will be discussed below.

Obad 15a, 16–21. The thematic parallels continue in Obad 15a, 16–21, where the "day" of Judah's judgment in Obad 10–14 gives way to a promise concerning the day of YHWH as punishment on the nations and restoration of Judah. Nevertheless, restoration presumes destruction, further underscoring the need for Obad 10–14: to explain the reason for Edom's judgment *and* to convey the relationship of Edom's judgment to the judgment on Judah.

These verses have long been recognized in many circles as an independent unit artfully attached to Obad 10–14, 15b. Not only does 15a, 16–21 change subject, it changes the dominant style of address. The preceding verses consistently refer to Edom in the second person singular, whereas Obad 15a, 16–21 address Judah using second masculine plural forms. This block of verses also coalesces thematically with Amos 9:11–15.

Amos 9:11 introduces the final promissory unit of Amos with the editorial transition ("on that day" of restoration) while Obad 15a begins

---

7   The forms include: עמד + ביום, שבות, אח, נכר, אבד, צרה (twice), and איד (three times).

with a reference to the "day of YHWH" against "all the nations." Amos 9:12 further explicates "that day" as a time when the fallen booth of David will possess Edom and "all the nations" called by YHWH's name.

Amos 9:11 alludes obliquely to the destruction of Jerusalem in terms of the fallen booth of David that will be restored and rebuilt, while Obad 16 refers to Jerusalem's destruction using the "cup of wrath tradition" that plays a prominent role in Jeremiah's oracles against the nations (OAN). Amos 9:11–12 articulates its promise as restoration of the Davidic kingdom (fallen booth of David, rebuilt as in the days of old, all the nations over whom my name is called). Restoration of the Davidic kingdom, using different terminology and specifying surrounding regions, also underlies the articulation of the promise of Obad 19–20 (possession of Esau's mountain, Philistine territory, Samarian territory, Gilead, etc.).

Amos 9:12 calls for the "possession" of Edom and other nations, while Obad 17 refers to Jerusalem's "possession" of those who dispossessed them. Obad 18 goes on to identify these enemies as the "house of Esau." The possession of Edom by Israel leads directly to possession of other nations and territories in Obad 19–20, so that the exiles who are reclaiming territory essentially reconstitute the idealized borders of David's kingdom with Jerusalem at the center. The repossession of these territories essentially surrounds Jerusalem in Obad 19–20:

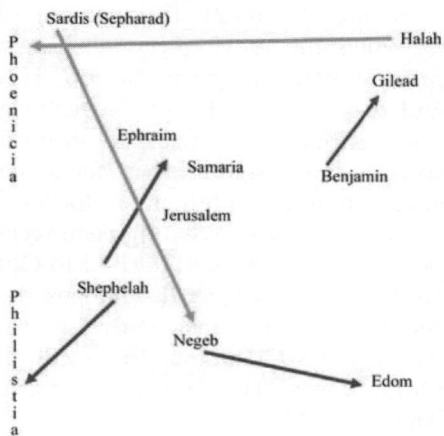

And the Negeb will possess the Mountain of Esau,
And the Shephelah (will possess) the Philistines.
And they will possess the field of Samaria,
And Benjamain (will possess) Gilead.
And the exiles of this force belonging to the sons of Israel who are among the Canaanites as far as Zarephath.[8]
And the exiles of Jerusalem who are in Sepharad (Sardis), they will possess the cities of the Negeb.

---

8   Alternatively: The exiles of the Israelites who are in Halah [will possess] the Canaanites [Phoenicia] as far as Zarephath.

The first wave (v. 19) describes the retaking of territory that had been lost, with Jerusalem essentially in the center. The second wave describes reinforcement of territory that was vacated during the first wave (Negeb) or the second wave (Phoenicia).

Amos 9:14 promises to "restore the fortunes" and rebuild the cities while Obad 19–20 promises the retaking of the territory in the return of the exiles to Judah. Amos 9:15 offers a concluding promise of enduring restoration of the people to the land while Obad 21 offers its concluding promise of the restoration on Mount Zion and rule over Esau as signs of YHWH's enduring kingship.

The parallels between these two texts are clear, but admittedly of a different character than those between Obad 1–5, 8–9 and Jer 49:7–22. How does one account for these similarities between Amos 9 and Obad 1–21?

2. Source Material, Adaptation, and Composition

Obadiah reflects at least three sources blocks (1–9; 10–14+15b; and 15a+16–21), adapted or composed by the compiler to fit the literary context and to serve a rhetorical purpose.[9] Several observations about the adaptation of the source material and the function of these sources to the rhetorical aims of Obadiah in general are now in order.

2.1 Obad 1–5, 6–9

As noted, Obad 1–5 draws from Jer 49:14–16, 9, but the verses have been adapted, when compared to that text. The direction of borrowing derives from the compiler of Obadiah borrowing and adapting Jeremiah's Edom oracle (49:7–22). While some suggest we cannot determine the direction of borrowing, recent redactional studies are largely united in suggesting that Obadiah borrows from Jeremiah.[10] The evidence for

---

9   The extent of the parallels between Obadiah and Amos make it highly unlikely that the similarities can be explained merely by the placement of one completed text next to another, contra Barton, *Joel*, 116–117, who relies on Ben Zvi, "Twelve Prophetic Books," 130–138, to ascribe similarities to unintentional verbal echoes of other prophetic texts.

10 Barton, *Joel*, 125–126, doubts the dependence can be determined, despite the work of Raabe, *Obadiah*, 22–31, who evaluates numerous allusions to Jeremiah and concludes: "The hypothesis that Obadiah reused and adapted material from Jeremiah best accounts for the evidence" (31). Ben Zvi, *Obadiah*, 53, also remains skeptical. For those who conclude Obadiah is dependent upon Jeremiah, see Nogalski, *Processes*,

this assertion does not rely exclusively upon the parallels to Amos 9 created by the compiler.

The strongest single piece of evidence derives from the 3fs pronominal suffix in Obad 1 whose antecedent must be Edom: "Rise up! Let us rise against it (3fs) for battle." The command, "rise up," contains a masculine plural imperative, followed by a first-person cohortative ("let us rise") in which the speaker identifies himself as part of the group who is called to attack "it." The word "it" represents the feminine singular pronominal suffix as the object of the preposition. The antecedent in Obad 1 can only refer to Edom, but countries normally take a masculine singular gender, and nowhere else does Obadiah refer to Edom with a feminine pronoun. By contrast, the parallel text (Jer 49:14) also has a feminine singular pronominal suffix, but this suffix has as its antecedent the city Bozrah in 49:13. Cities, in contrast to countries, do normally take feminine singular antecedents. As such, the pronoun in Jeremiah makes perfect sense, whereas its presence in Obadiah is syntactically unique.

A second line of evidence for Obadiah's use of Jeremiah appears in the expansionary elements in Obad 4 (compared to Jer 49:16) and in the expanded sentence in Obad 5a (compared to Jer 49:9b). Obad 4 inserts a poetic line that complicates the syntax while presuming the subject, verb, and direct object of the simpler line. It also changes the introductory particle from כִּי to אִם. The result of this insertion is twofold: it adds two אִם particles in comparison to the Jeremiah source text, and the inserted line elevates the parallelism to the stars rather than merely assuming a high nest (as in Jer 49:16). This parallel comes closer to the comparative heights of Amos 9 (especially the mention of "heaven" in 9:2; and in the doxology of 9:6). This heightened contrast into the stars introduces the verbal parallel with Amos: "from there I will bring you down." This phrase appears five times in Amos, but elsewhere only in Jer 49:16 and Obad 4. It likely sparked the compiler's interest in the Edom oracles of Jeremiah in the first place.

The compiler of Obadiah inverts the parallel between Obad 5a, b and Jer 49:9b, a. In so doing, the Obadiah compiler borrows the verb from Jer 49:9a to introduce 49:9b (whereas that verb is assumed by Jer 49:9b in the Jeremiah context). The use of Jer 49:9 also adds the final three אִם particles, including two in the source text and one in the in-

61–74; Schart, *Entstehung*, 270–271; Jeremias, *Joel*, 63–65; Sweeney, *Twelve Prophets*, 1:282, and Wöhrle, *Abschluss*, 195–201. Weiser, *Propheten*, 207, gives little attention to the issue, but simply seems to presume Obadiah borrows from Jeremiah. Jeremiah scholarship also generally concurs on this point. See especially, Lundbom, *Jeremiah 37–52*, 325.

serted material of Obad 5. This additional אם particle brings to five the number of אם particles in Obad 14–16, the same number as in Amos 9:2–4, while the Jeremiah parallels have only two such particles.

These observations account for many of the differences between Obadiah and its Jeremiah 49 parallels. The compiler chose a compatible text as a starting point, but made minor adjustments to the text to strengthen parallels with Amos 9.

2.2 Obadiah 15a, 16–21

Obadiah 15a, 16–21 also appears to be an originally independent oracle that has been attached to Obad 1–14, 15b. The reasons why it represents a new unit are widely recognized.[11] First, the forms of address change from the singular direct address of Edom that dominates 1–14 to masculine plural forms that address the people of Judah.

Second, the theme of the day of YHWH introduced by Obad 15a differs from 1–14, where the reference to the day of YHWH alludes to Jerusalem's day of reckoning (10–14), although it is not incompatible with the reference in Obad 8 to "on that day" when the wise and discerning of Edom will be destroyed. Obad 8, it was already suggested, comes from the hand of the compiler.

Third, the target of the oracle is not merely Edom, unlike the focus on Edom in Obad 1–14. The target of the day of YHWH, according to Obad 15a, is "all the nations."

Fourth, Obad 16–21 presumes Israel will attack Edom. By contrast, Obad 1 introduces the first unit in a way that announces that the nations will punish Edom.

Despite wide acceptance that 15a, 16–21 represents a preexisting unit, several commentators dispute the cohesion of the verses, mostly with respect to the second wave of attacks in Obad 19–20. For example, Wolff describes 15a, 16–21 oddly. On the one hand, in his commentary he refers to 1–14, 15b as "a single unit, in spite of a number of difficulties," and he separates 15a, 16–21 as a "passage."[12] On the other hand, he does not mean an author's singular composition by these designations. He seems to assume a model whereby individual sayings were compiled in written form after becoming fixed in oral transmission. When describing the "form" of Obad 15a, 16–21, Wolff refers to the "rhetorical unit" as being comprised of *two* sayings (15a, 16–17 and 18),

---

11   See Rudolph, *Joel*, 296; Wolff, *Obadiah*, 37–38, 62; Barton, *Joel*, 118–119.
12   Wolff, *Obadiah*, 37.

100   James D. Nogalski

a "two-stage addition" (19–20), and a conclusion to the book (21).[13] Rudolph sees 15a, 16–18 as a unit from Obadiah, while he labels 19–21 as *Anhänge* (additions), but he also describes Obad 21 as consistent with genuine Obadiah speech material.[14] Barton divides 15a, 16–21 into two parts (15a+16–18 and 19–21).[15] Raabe extensively details the wide variety of divisions of units in Obadiah, delineating three models of composition that result in at least nine different explanations of the various units.[16] Consequently, Raabe opts to treat the entirety as a single composition, preferring to consider the endeavor of determining its sources as too speculative to be reliable or to produce a coherent reading.[17]

Barton, who otherwise is not particularly receptive to the idea of the Book of the Twelve affecting the shape of individual writings, offers a very interesting take upon Obad 19–20:

> "The oracle thus spells out in detail the hopes probably implied in Isa 55:4–5 and Amos 9:11–12. One could see Obad 19–20 as a kind of commentary on or detailed working out of the underlying oracle that appears toward the end of the book of Amos (itself regarded by most commentators as a postexilic addition to the words of Amos)."[18]

In fact, Barton is more correct than he realizes in that the entire act of compiling Obadiah owes its shape to Amos 9. The structural, lexical, and thematic parallels between Amos 9 and Obadiah, once observed, require more explanation than typically provided. Obad 19–20 does not merely serve as a commentary to portions of Amos 9. Rather, the entire book adapts pre-existing anti-Edom sayings to draw a parallel between

---

13   Wolff, *Obadiah*, 62.
14   Rudolph, *Joel*, 311–318.
15   Barton, *Joel*, 150–158 respectively, for the two units, and he also dates 15a, 16–21 to the late Persian or early Hellenistic period (123) even as he dates 1–14, 15b near to the time of Jerusalem's destruction. In other words, he dates the passages approximately 250 years apart from one another. He offers no real motivation for what caused this addition other than a general propensity to add eschatological material to the end of prophetic collections. Schniedewind, *Bible*, makes a compelling case that support for the collection of literature changes from royal patronage to cultic centers in the Persian period. However, when he argues (139–164) that only a small amount of material was produced in the Persian period, he overstates the case since he does not adequately deal with the possibility of Mizpah as a place where religious scribes relocated following the loss of the temple. See Albertz, *Exilszeit*, 65–68; idem, *History*, 241–242.370–373.
16   Raabe, *Obadiah*, 14–18.
17   Raabe, *Obadiah*, 18, states: "Despite the amount of diversity displayed in it (Obadiah), the book does present itself as a literary and structural unit, a unity that invites the reader to make coherent sense of the book's contents by interpreting the parts as integrally related to each other rather than as self-contained and self-defining units."
18   Barton, *Joel*, 157. Compare his skepticism elsewhere about the Twelve's editing affecting the shape of the writings: ibid., 116–117.

the destruction of the northern kingdom and the anticipated destruction of Edom.

In addition to these critical assessments, one should also note the curious reference to the day of wrath tradition, which connects Obad 15–17 conceptually to the OAN of Jeremiah (especially in the LXX version). Obadiah 15a announces the nearness of the day of YHWH on all the nations. The reason for the pronouncement is given in Obad 16: "because you (2mp) have drunk upon my holy mountain, all the nations will drink (3mp) continually." The plural "you" must be interpreted as an address to Judah in this verse. Consequently, Obad 16 presumes a situation in which prior judgment against Judah inaugurates judgment on the nations.

The "drinking" in Obad 16 draws upon the "cup of wrath tradition" which assumes judgment will come upon Jerusalem, but that judgment will not stop when Jerusalem's punishment is complete. Rather, Jerusalem's judgment will inaugurate a series of judgments as the day of YHWH begins to unfold. This cup of wrath imagery plays a prominent role in Jeremiah's oracles against the nations. This tradition finds its fullest expression in Jer 25:15–29 (the original conclusion to Jeremiah's OAN that appears in the MT at the end of the corpus), but it also appears in Isa 51:17–23 (where the cup's effects are first described and then removed by passing to unnamed tormenters). It also appears in Ezek 23:31–32 (where personified Lady Jerusalem receives the cup from her sister Samaria); Lam 4:21 (against Edom); Hab 2:12 (against Babylon); and within Jeremiah in the oracles against Edom (49:12) and Babylon (51:7).

Thus, in both Jeremiah and the Twelve, the cup of wrath to be drunk by the nations is applied both to Edom and Babylon. This connection between the refrains of Jeremiah's Edom and Babylon oracles increases the likelihood that the dependence upon Jeremiah by the Obadiah compiler had access to a version of Jeremiah in which the OAN were still in the middle of the book. One cannot, of course, prove this case absolutely, but this cup of wrath imagery is certainly suggestive.[19]

---

19 The case is complicated, of course, and requires further exploration. See, for example, the discussion of the uncharacteristic extra wording in the LXX version of Jer 49:16 and Obad 4 in Ben Zvi, *Obadiah*, 67–68.

2.3 Obad 10–14

Obadiah 10–14 may constitute a third preexisting source, but it more likely represents the longest compositional element from the compiler of Obadiah.[20] However, no one disputes its function in Obadiah. It provides the reason why Edom will be punished, but the formulation of these accusations is expressed as a future event to be avoided: "You shall not gloat, rejoice," etc. (Obad 12–14). These vetitive forms represent a classic *"vaticinium ex eventu"* (prophecy after the fact).

Literarily Obadiah *anticipates* Edom's destruction on the day of YHWH at a point in the Book of the Twelve where Israel's destruction has just been documented (Amos 9:1–4). At the end of the Twelve, Mal 1:2–5 presumes that Edom's punishment is under way,[21] while Obadiah largely presumes the punishment has not yet happened – even though the reason for Edom's punishment has occurred.

This dichotomy is quite similar to the dichotomy of Jerusalem's destruction in the Book of the Twelve and in Isaiah.[22] These prophetic scrolls either "anticipate" Jerusalem's destruction in Hosea–Zephaniah, or its aftermath is presumed in Haggai–Malachi. In the same way, Obadiah "anticipates" Edom's destruction while Mal 1:2–5 presumes its judgment has begun.

The same dynamic happens in Isaiah with the destruction of Edom and Jerusalem. Isaiah 34–35 anticipate Jerusalem and Edom's destruction, where Isaiah 40-55 presumes Judah's punishment as a past event (replaced by restoration) while Isa 63:1–6 narrates Edom's destruction by YHWH as a past event.

3. Why Edom and When Was Obadiah Compiled?

Positive and negative traditions regarding Edom can be found in biblical traditions. Positive traditions include 1) theophanies related to YHWH's appearance in Edom, 2) Edom as a home for wisdom, and 3) traditions about Edom's "brotherhood" with Israel through their respective progenitors Esau and Jacob.

---

20   It has a thematic parallel to Amos 9, though the parallel comes via the relentless combination of ב and יום. Caution is warranted at this point, however, because the dovetailing of 15b and 15a suggests two preexisting units were "woven" together. If so, then 10–14 could be the continuation of 1–9, as a kind of midrash on Jer 49:7–22, combined with images from Ezekiel.

21   Cf. the article of Scoralick, p. 35–52, in this volume.

22   See Nogalski, "Teaching," 252–253.

1) Texts depicting Edom as the home of YHWH include Deut 33:2; Judg 5:4; and Hab 3:3. All three present a theophany that associates YHWH with Edom, the first two even using Seir and Sinai in parallel. This theophanic connection attests to an ancient association of the worship of YHWH in Edom. Hab 3:3 is often cited as ancient poetry.[23] The other two passages existed by the end of the seventh century. External evidence for the ancient association of YHWH with Edom also appears in two inscriptions from Kuntillit Ajrud (late 9th century or early 8th century). Together these inscriptions show an intriguing connection between the worship of YHWH in Samaria and in Edom:[24]

The inscription on Pithos A testifies:

"Say to Yehal[lel'el] and to Yo'asah and [to Z]: I bless you by *Yahweh of Samaria* and by his asherah."

Inscription 2 on Pithos B from the same site reads:

"Amaryau says: say to my lord: Is it well with you? I bless you by *Yahweh of Teman* and by his asherah. May he bless you and keep you and be with my lord."

This evidence has no direct connection to Obadiah, but it demonstrates that traditions rooted in the worship of YHWH have a long history, one that precedes the textual traditions of biblical texts. The fact that Obadiah inverts this theophanic tradition after 587 shows how long these common traditions lingered, even if the details are too obscure to postulate the exact circumstances. These traditions also suggest that ancient associations between Edom, Israel, and Judah help explain the location of Obadiah in the Book of the Twelve, and why it may have been important to insert a literary work that drew attention to the parallel fates of Israel and Edom.[25]

2) Edom also connotes wisdom. Job 1:1–3 claims that Job comes from Uz (associated with Edom in Lam 4:21). In Job, Eliphaz comes from Teman, located in Edom.

3) Brother traditions include the Jacob cycle and Deut 2:4. The Jacob cycle relates the story of Esau and Jacob as the twin sons of Isaac and Rebekah (though the story resolves through an uneasy truce). Compared to the stories of the Ammonites and Moabites (Gen 19:30–38), these stories operate with a different set of assumptions. Deut 2:4–5

23 Anderson, "Prayer," 58–59.
24 Hadley, *Cult*, 121–129 (translations on 121 and 125); see also Dever, "Asherah," 32–34 (notes 5.27.45).
25 In most assessments of the order in which the writings were incorporated into the Twelve, Jonah represents a late arrival to the corpus. See Nogalski, *Processes*, 270–273; Schart, *Entstehung*, 289–291; Wöhrle, *Abschluss*, 396.

alludes to Esau's descendants as Jacob's brothers, implicitly explaining why Israel does not take Edomite territory when it conquers the promised land.

Negative traditions reverse these same motifs in prophetic literature as a whole, with Obadiah transposing more of these positive characteristics than any other writing. Isa 63:1–6 inverts the Edomite theophany tradition. This late text depicts YHWH coming from Edom (63:1) with blood on his garments after destroying Edom and "the peoples" (63:3, 6) on the "day of vengeance" (63:4). This text almost certainly alludes to Isaiah 34, which anticipates "the day of vengeance" (34:8) directed against Edom (34:5) and the peoples (34:1).[26]

Several prophetic judgment oracles reject the wisdom of Edom tradition. Significantly, both Jer 49 and Obadiah do so, though the material is not a direct citation (Jer 49:7–8; Obad 7, 8–9). In both prophetic texts, the wisdom of Edom evaporates as the wise will be destroyed.

Edom and brotherhood serve as the backdrop for two denunciations of Edom's betrayal. Amos 1:11–12, often considered an exilic addition to the OAN of Amos, condemns Edom for "pursuing his brother with the sword." Obad 10–14 expresses similar ideas by condemning Edom's behavior toward its brother on the day of Jacob's (= Judah's) calamity. Mal 1:2–5 describes Esau's (= Edom) misfortune as punishment from YHWH to affirm YHWH's preference for Jacob (= Judah).

Within prophetic writings, the combination of Edom's wisdom and brotherhood appears only in the Book of the Twelve. Jeremiah (49:7) refers to Edom's wisdom, but does not refer to Edom as a brother. Isaiah and Ezekiel do neither. Obadiah combines a wide range of punishments against Edom. It reverses the positive traditions of Edom as brother and as the home of wisdom. Ezekiel's anti-Edom statements accuse Edom of participation in Jerusalem's overthrow, like Obadiah.

When was Obadiah compiled? In Ezek 25:12–14, the text anticipates Israel taking vengeance for YHWH against Edom (Obad 18) because they grievously injured the "house of Judah" and "my people Israel." Ezekiel 35:5 accuses Edom of retaliation because they "gave over the people of Israel to the power of the sword at the time of their calamity" (איד; see Obad 13), and according to 35:10, Edom also tried to "possess" Israel, making Israel and Edom one nation, but under Edomite rule.[27]

---

26 Steck, "Untersuchungen," 209–211.
27 Dating Ezekiel 35 can be done only in general terms. The situation described in Ezek 35:10 assumes Edomite incursion. According to Pohlmann, *Prophet*, 1:34, the bulk of Ezekiel 35 entered the corpus with the *gola*-oriented redaction responsible for most of the book, though the date of the source material in Ezek 35:5, 10–11 is earlier.

The adaptation of Jeremiah's OAN by Obadiah, probably occurred at a time before the expanded MT version moved those OAN out of their original location following Jer 25:13. Dating the oracles in Jer 49:7–22 depends upon several factors.[28] Nevertheless, most commentators do not date these materials too far into the sixth century.[29] The Obadiah adaptations were made in light of Amos 9 at a point after the expansions of 9:7–10 and 9:11–15*, which suggests the early Persian period as the *terminus ante quem*, but before the proto-MT of Jeremiah relocated the OAN to the end of that corpus. Mal 1:2–5 presumes Edom's punishment is underway, and alludes to Obadiah, marking the *terminus ad quem*. The collection of OAN for prophetic texts could perhaps stem from a point after Ezra/Nehemiah reforms which emphasized the need for separatism from other nations. Edom plays no role, however, in Ezra–Nehemiah, suggesting Edom could have already been in decline during the time of Ezra–Nehemiah. Of course, even this relative chronology only limits the dates somewhat for Obadiah because the dates of Malachi and Ezra–Nehemiah are very much in dispute.

Pohlmann dates this redaction to some point near the end of the fifth century. By contrast, Zimmerli, *Ezekiel*, 1:9–11, gives more credence to the date formulae in 14 superscriptions, that date oracles between 593–571 B.C.E., and he thus dates the book around that time. More specifically, Zimmerli, *Ezekiel*, 2:234, argues that Ezekiel 35–36 was collected prior to the return of exiles with Zerubbabel. By contrast, Tuell, *Ezekiel*, 241–242, emphasizes the allusions to the ancestor stories, but ibid., 2–3, he considers the final editing of the book to have taken place in the fifth century, during the latter half of the reign of Darius II (522–485). Hence, the date of Ezekiel 35 can be confidently fixed between 571 and 400, though Tuell's position of the early fifth century probably reflects more of a consensus at this point.

28 Lundbom, *Jeremiah 37–52*, 325, argues that scholars typically date Jer 49:7–22 too late because they read these verses "through the refracted lens of Obadiah and other OT passage of late date." He avers that nothing in these Edomite oracles requires that one assumes the oracles postdate Jerusalem's destruction. His observations should raise caution. Nevertheless, he overstates the case since it is hard to imagine that 49:12 does not already presume Jerusalem's destruction. Edom did not experience Babylonian devastation at the same time as Jerusalem, but evidence suggests they did experience Babylonian attacks during the reign of Nabonidus (556–539). See Lundbom, *Jeremiah 37–52*, 331. It is difficult to say with certainty at what date the proto-MT and the LXX source material were separated from one another. Some see this division as quite early; so Lundbom, *Jeremiah 1–20*, 57–62, who thinks one copy of the Jeremiah corpus was taken to Egypt (by Baruch) and another was taken to Babylon, with the Babylonian version undergoing more editorial activity thereafter. By contrast, most others see the division coming in the late Persian period; so Stulman, "Jeremiah," 222–224. In either case, an early sixth century date for the oracles themselves means they would have been available, though it makes more sense that these oracles were preserved in Judah than in Babylon or Egypt.

29 Jones, *Jeremiah*, 512–513.

Summary

Thematic and structural parallels exist between Obadiah and Amos 9, and these parallels display an intricate awareness of and interplay with the Edom collection (Jer 49) and with the cup of wrath tradition (Jer 25). Most likely, a compiler adapted existing source material in Obad 1–5 and 16–21 with the compiler's own compositional material in 8–9 and 10–14.

References

Albertz, R. *A History of Israelite Religion in the Old Testament Period*. 2 vols. Translated by J. Bowden. OTL. Louisville: Westminster John Knox, 1994.
– *Die Exilszeit. 6. Jahrhundert v. Chr*. Biblische Enzyklopädie 7. Stuttgart: Kohlhammer, 2001.
Anderson, J. "Awaiting an Answered Prayer: The Development and Reinterpretation of Habakkuk 3 in its Contexts." *ZAW* 123 (2011) 57–71.
Barton, J. *Joel and Obadiah*. OTL. Louisville: Westminster John Knox, 2001.
Ben Zvi, E. *Obadiah: A Historical-Critical Study of the Book of Obadiah*. BZAW 242. Berlin: de Gruyter, 1996.
– "Twelve Prophetic Books or 'the Twelve': A Few Preliminary Considerations." Pp. 125–156 in *Forming Prophetic Literature: Essays on Isaiah and the Twelve in Honor of John D. W Watts*. Edited by J.W. Watts and P.R. House. JSOTSup 235. Sheffield: Sheffield Academic Press, 1996.
Cassuto, U. "The Sequence and Arrangement of the Biblical Sections." Pp. 1–6 in vol. 1 of *Biblical and Oriental Studies*. Translated by I. Abrams. Jerusalem: Magnes Press, 1973.
Dever, W.G. "Asherah, Consort of Yahweh? New Evidence from Kuntillet Ajrûd." *BASOR* 255 (1984) 21–37.
Hadley, J.M. *The Cult of Asherah in Ancient Israel and Judah*. New York: Cambridge University Press, 2000.
House, P.R. *The Unity of the Twelve*. JSOTSup 97. Sheffield: Sheffield Academic Press, 1990.
Jenson, P.P. *Obadiah, Jonah, Micah: A Theological Commentary*. Library of Hebrew Bible / Old Testament Studies 496. New York: T&T Clark, 2008.
Jeremias, J. *Joel, Obadja, Jona, Micha*. ATD 24,3. Göttingen: Vandehoeck & Ruprecht, 2007.
Jones, D.R. *Jeremiah*. New Century Bible. Grand Rapids: Eerdmans, 1992.
Lundbom, J.R. *Jeremiah 1–20*. AB 21A. New York: Doubleday, 2004.
– *Jeremiah 21–36*. AB 21B. New York: Doubleday, 2004.
– *Jeremiah 37–52*. AB 21C. New York: Doubleday, 2004.
Nogalski, J.D. *Literary Precursors to the Book of the Twelve*. BZAW 217. Berlin: de Gruyter, 1993.
– *Redactional Processes in the Book of the Twelve*. BZAW 218. Berlin: de Gruyter, 1993.

- "One Book and Twelve Books: The Nature of the Redactional Work and the Implications of Cultic Source Material." Pp. 1–46 in *Two Sides of a Coin: Juxtaposing Views on Interpreting the Book of the Twelve / the Twelve Prophetic Books.* Edited by Ehud Ben Zvi and idem. Analecta Gorgianna 201. Piscataway: Gorgias Press, 2009.
- "Teaching Prophetic Books." *PRSt* 36 (2009) 251–256.

Pohlmann, K.-F. *Der Prophet Hesekiel/Ezechiel.* 2 vols. ATD 22,1–2. Göttingen: Vandenhoeck & Ruprecht, 1996.

Raabe, P.R. *Obadiah.* AB 24D. New York: Doubleday, 1996.

Rudolph, W. *Joel – Amos – Obadja – Jona.* KAT 13,2. Gütersloh: Gütersloher, 1971.

Schart, A. *Die Entstehung des Zwölfprophetenbuchs: Neubearbeitungen von Amos im Rahmen schriftenübergreifender Redaktionsprozesse.* BZAW 260. Berlin: de Gruyter, 1998.

Schniedewind, W.M. *How the Bible Became a Book: The Textualization of Ancient Israel.* Cambridge: Cambridge University Press, 2004.

Steck, O.H. "Zu jüngsten Untersuchungen von Jes 56,9–59,21; 64,1–6." Pp. 192–213 in *Studien zu Tritojesaja.* BZAW 203. Berlin: de Gruyter, 1991.

Struppe, U. *Die Bücher Obadja, Jona.* Neuer Stuttgarter Kommentar. Altes Testament 24,1. Stuttgart: Katholisches Bibelwerk, 1996.

Stuart, D. *Hosea – Jonah.* WBC 31. Waco: Word, 1987.

Stulman, L. "Jeremiah, Book of." *New Interpreter's Dictionary of the Bible* 3 (2008) 220–235.

Sweeney, M.A. *The Twelve Prophets.* Berit Olam. 2 vols. Collegeville: Liturgical, 2000.

Tuell, S. *Ezekiel.* NIBCOT 15. Peabody: Hendrickson, 2009.

Weiser, A. *Die Propheten Hosea, Joel, Amos, Obadja, Jona, Micha.* ATD 24,1. Göttingen: Vandenhoeck & Ruprecht, 1985.

Wöhrle, J. *Der Abschluss des Zwölfprophetenbuches: Buchübergreifende Redaktionsprozesse in den späten Sammlungen.* BZAW 389. Berlin: de Gruyter, 2008.

Wolff, H.W. *Joel and Amos: A Commentary on the Books of the Prophets Joel and Amos.* Translated by W. Janzen et al. Hermeneia. Philadelphia: Fortress, 1977.

- *Obadiah and Jonah.* Translated by M. Kohl. Minneapolis: Augsburg, 1986.

Zimmerli, W. *Ezekiel.* 2 vols. Translated by R.E. Clements. Hermeneia. Philadelphia: Fortress, 1979.

The Jonah-Narrative within the Book of the Twelve[*]

AARON SCHART

Universität Duisburg-Essen

The book of Jonah is certainly strange within its context in several respects. It is obvious that the author of the narrative and the redactor who placed Jonah into the Book of the Twelve must be different persons. In this paper I would like to ask in what way Jonah is tied into the Twelve. Answering this question will also help discover why it was included at all. The interest is not so much in the surface of the final text but in the redactional activity that led to this text. Therefore it is of primary importance to detect the traces that the redactor left when Jonah was incorporated into the Twelve. This will help to understand more fully at what stage of the development of the Twelve the narrative of Jonah was added into the collection. As a prerequisite to this question it is imperative to undertake a source-critical analysis, i.e., to investigate whether the text of Jonah is a unified literary work by one author or whether later additions to the text can be detected.

1. Global Narrative Structure

The book of Jonah is a unique and special book within the Twelve Prophets in many respects. Most obviously it contains neither a collection of prophetic sayings nor poetically crafted lyrics; rather it represents a narrative, a tale about a prophet. At first glance, the story has a straightforward plot and a simple style marked by a penchant for lexical repetition, as if the author was quite restricted in his or her vocabulary. Such "Leitwörter," as Buber has called them, are used with great frequency and give the text great cohesion. By implication, the reader has easily detectable signals available regarding how to conceptualize the progression of the narrative.[1]

---

[*]   I would like to thank Jonathan Robker for improving the English of this article.
[1]   This stylistic device has been worked out quite impressively by several scholars, see Wolff, *Studien*, 29–58; for an overview over the research history see Jeremias, "Jonabuch," 96–104.

The global structure of the narrative is likewise structured in a simple, straightforward way; the division into two parts of nearly equal length is basic: chs. 1–2 and 3–4. Both parts have a similar structure.[2] Let me recall the most obvious indicators. God's command to Jonah to go to Nineveh is first refused (1:1–3), whereas in the second part it is obeyed (3:1–3a). In each part Jonah delivers a message to strangers who are threatened by perishing (n.b. אבד in 1:6, 14; 3:9): the sailors in 1:4–16 and the people of Nineveh in 3:3b–10. These strangers act first as a collective (1:5; 3:5), but then a nameless representative comes in: the captain (1:6) and the king (3:6). In both cases the strangers hope to be saved by Jonah's God, but at the same time state that God's act of salvation is not assured (1:6, 3:9). In sharp contrast to this attitude, it is emphasized that Jonah would rather die than allow God to act differently than Jonah himself expects (1:12; 4:3–8). At the end of each part is a scene involving only God and Jonah situated in a miraculous natural environment. Within the miraculous fish Jonah cries to God (ch. 2), whereas under the wondrous plant outside of the city God tries to convince Jonah that God's grace does indeed extend to Nineveh. Whether God succeeds is left open. The text ends with a question, but one has to notice that the story includes a further element: Jonah's reaction to this question, namely his stubborn silence. The rhetorical effect of this element is that it is ultimately up to the reader to answer in Jonah's stead.

In sum, the Jonah narrative is a neatly structured story in child-like language. As a result, it is difficult to discover breaks in the narrative coherence that could imply different literary layers. But before I come to source-criticism, it is imperative to determine the genre of the narrative.

2. Genre

As is universally acknowledged, the narrative is fictitious throughout. The world of the text is in many respects incompatible with our normal world experience. Most famously, the episode with the fish remains simply absurd. And it does not help if one transforms the fish into a whale. This problem already bothered the scholars of the Enlightenment. Heinrich Adolph Grimm, for example, who lived from 1747–1813 and was the last professor of the old University of Duisburg, proposed the thesis that the Jonah narrative recounts Jonah's dream from the point in the narrative where Jonah falls asleep within the hull of the

---

2   See Wolff, *Studien*, 76.

ship (1:5) until he was spit out on the land again (2:11).[3] However, massive breaks with normal reality occur throughout the whole of the book. The repentance of an evil city like Nineveh is equally as improbable as a trip within the belly of a fish. So, what we have here is a thought-experiment, a totally unrealistic narrative that only serves didactic purposes.

However, the mood in which the didactic goal is brought home is humorous and comical. There are so many details in the story where even the modern reader, who consumes the most drastic forms of humor every evening on television and is therefore oversaturated with comedy, must at least smile. I do not doubt that the ancient hearers laughed wholeheartedly, when they heard the story.

In many cases the humor takes on the shape of irony, and even parody. There are many self-contradictions in the behavior of Jonah that ironically let him appear as a fool: he flees before God's order, even though he knows that God "had made the sea and the dry land" (1:9); and he wants to die because he and his message – as opposed to Elijah in 1 Kings 19:4 – had not failed, but had been too successful!

From my perspective this humorous understanding of the novella is the most plausible explanation for the many ridiculous features. Jonah is a satire: In the form of the character Jonah a specific position is caricatured and ridiculed.[4]

Let me hasten to add that the notion of "satire" does not imply that the narrative excludes reliable and serious insights. Quite the contrary: a satire seeks to reveal the absurdity of the opponent's position with a serious didactic intention. Millar Burrows described the striving for truth correctly:

> "The truth which the story brings home to the reader is thus twofold: Compassion is supreme in God's way with his creatures; and it is a universal compassion, extending to all of them equally. What is satirized in the behavior of Jonah is a self-centered, arrogant attitude which denies or ignores these two basic truths."[5]

---

3   Grimm, *Prophet Jonas*.
4   I follow here the position of Good, "Jonah," and others; see Jeremias, "Jonabuch," 107–109; Schart, *Entstehung*, 283–287.
5   Burrows, "Literary Category," 102.

3. Jonah Ridicules Joel

After having established that Jonah is a satire, the next step is to identify the position that it seeks to satirize. Here, I am convinced that we
find ourselves in the lucky position that the foil against which Jonah is
directed is preserved in the writing of Joel. There are some very clear
verbal connections that demonstrate that Jonah must be read with Joel
in mind. Joel is cited verbatim, but the contexts in which the citations
are set show that Jonah does the opposite of what he confesses. Jonah
presupposes Joel and needs a reader who is familiar with this writing;
otherwise one would miss a good deal of the ironic potential of the
narrative. This is important already for the reader of the independent
book of Jonah, but even more so for the reader of the final Book of the
Twelve, who will discover more intertextual relations, for example to
Hosea.[6]

4. Source Criticism

After the form-critical analysis has been achieved the source-critical
task can be undertaken. Most interpreters of Jonah perceive this book
as a literary unity written by a single author in one situation. However,
some source critics have tried to find literary breaks within even this
smooth narrative. The most recent attempt comes from Jakob Wöhrle.[7]
Wöhrle has assembled an extensive sampling of source-critical arguments. However, the basic problem is that Wöhrle and others do not
give full credence to the humorous and satirical character of the narrative. I do not want to evaluate all of the arguments here, but only those
where I think that the understanding of Jonah as a satire solves the
problems of the alleged breaks in narrative coherence.[8]

---

6   Scoralick, *Güte*, 182–184, demonstrates what a reading looks like that uses Joel as
    hermeneutical frame for Jonah. In addition, she notices connections to Hosea: e.g.,
    the name of the prophet "Jonah," which means "dove," reminds the reader of Hos
    7:11 and 11:11, where Israel is identified as a dove. In turn, the prophet Jonah must
    be understood as representing Israel. "Die Jonaschrift wird so zum Midrasch über
    das von Joel her gelesene Kapitel Hos 11. Dabei ist die 'zitternde Umkehr' des Pro-
    pheten Jona/Israel in der Schrift nicht erzählt, sie muß vom Leser angenommen oder
    erhofft werden." (ibid., 183).
7   Wöhrle, *Abschluss*, 365–399.
8   For a refutation of the common source-critical arguments on the basis of a non-
    satirical understanding see Gerhards, *Studien*, 14–55. As rightly noted by Wöhrle,
    however, some of his arguments are not convincing.

Let me start with Jonah 1:5b–6. According to Wöhrle this short passage, in which the captain of the ship approaches the sleeping Jonah and asks him to contribute his share to rescue the boat, is not well integrated into the narrative flow. One of his arguments is that it remains unclear whether Jonah followed the captain's imperative.[9] However, I see no unclear situation here: Since no reaction of Jonah is recorded, it is clear that he did not obey but remained silent. It is only in the fish that he turns to his God, thus doing as the captain demanded of him. Those scholars who claim that Jonah joined the sailors and prayed to YHWH do so without any hint in the text. They infer this simply because they assume that Jonah, being a pious man, would not resist adhering to such an urgent wish of a desperate or dying man.[10] But if the satirical attitude is accepted, it is completely in line with the characterization of Jonah that he refuses to pray to God in this moment. The narrator's presupposition that Jonah did pray to God is precluded, as it would imply that he gave up his resistance to YHWH's command to go to Nineveh, just as Jeremias accurately noted.[11] There is no break in coherence once one realizes that the narrator is ridiculing the narrative figure of Jonah.

A second tension within the flow of the narrative is found in 1:11. Wöhrle stresses the fact that the sailors twice question Jonah in a similar way. And, although it would not have been necessary, the narrator introduces the speech of the sailors with a narrative introduction in the second case, too.[12] However, this phenomenon should not be perceived as a tension, but as an artistic narrative technique: the reader has to imagine a lasting phase of silence between the sailors' first and second question. Within this phase the sailors begin to grasp that Jonah has run away from his God, whereas, at the same time, Jonah gains no further insight, but becomes even more stubborn.

> 1:10 Then the men were even more afraid, and said to him, "What is this that you have done!" For the men knew that he was fleeing from the presence of the Lord (because he had told them so).[13]

---

9   Wöhrle, *Abschluss*, 366.
10   Marti, *Dodekapropheton*, 250; Rudolph, *Joel*, 342.
11   Jeremias, *Joel*, 87: "Es würde implizieren, dass Jona schon jetzt zum Gang nach Ninive bereit wäre. Er ist aber noch im Schlusskapitel lieber zum Tod bereit, als dass er Gottes Verhalten gegenüber Ninive zustimmen würde (4,3.8f)."
12   Wöhrle, *Abschluss*, 369–370.
13   The short sentence in parentheses is in my opinion the only secondary insertion into the text of Jonah. It is an isolated gloss by a reader who did not understand, how the sailors could have recognized from the short confession in 1:9 that Jonah was *fleeing* from YHWH, unless Jonah had told them so (Wöhrle, *Abschluss*, 369 with note 14). However, this reader did not understand that the word "fleeing" stems from the narrator and not from the sailors. The narrator wanted to characterize the sailors *to*

11 Then they said to him, "What shall we do to you, that the sea may
quiet down for us?" For the sea was growing more and more tem-
pestuous. (NRSV)

Even in this situation, in which Jonah can see the astonishing religious
sensibility of the sailors, he remains quiescent; it is only after they ask
him a second time that Jonah offers his advice as to what should be
done. Stubborn as he is, he chooses rather to die instead of obeying
God's will to preach to Nineveh.

All in all, the sailors and their captain serve as foils against which
Jonah is ridiculed. Their piety cannot be attributed to a later layer but
provides a fitting contrast to the characterization of the stubborn Jonah,
who must be urged to break his silence and only thereafter utters some
words. It is completely unnecessary to assume an earlier layer that was
secondarily expounded.

A third place where a source-critical break is often assumed is the
psalm in Jonah 2:3–10. However, the psalm is totally in place and does
not stand in tension to its context once one is inclined to perceive the
psalm as a satirical presentation of a hypercritic. It is totally in line with
chapter 1 that Jonah chooses the genre of a prayer of thanksgiving, as
he thinks that he has escaped a mission that he cannot accept.

In addition to the well-known arguments that he cites approvingly,
Wöhrle emphasizes that it is not a good narrative style to disclose the
end of the period within the belly of the fish to the reader in advance:
"Hier ist schon auffällig, dass der Prophet nach Jona 2,1 drei Tage und
drei Nächte im Bauch des Fisches war. Es wird also von vornherein ein
festes Ende der Zeit im Fisch angegeben."[14]

However, the point of the narrative is not to provide the end date of
the sojourn within the fish in advance. The three days and the three
nights is the time span that Jonah waits before he begins to pray and
finally concedes to the captain's wish (1:6). Again Jonah is portrayed as
remaining in silence for three days, presumably until he can take it for
granted that he has escaped successfully.

Fourthly, many interpreters identify Jonah 4:5 as an addition because Jonah's trip out of the city is a strange reaction to God's question
and it comes too late. It would be much more fitting immediately after
Jonah has delivered his message (Jonah 3:4). Following Lohfink, it is
sometimes assumed that the *wayyiqtol*-Forms in Jonah 4:5 are used in
the sense of a pluperfect and refer back to the time described in Jonah

---

the reader as extraordinary sensible and sharp-minded: they understood intuitively
without words and explanation what really was going on.
14 Wöhrle, *Abschluss*, 374.

3:4.[15] But, as Wöhrle rightly states, this is impossible on grammatical grounds: there is no case, where a *wayyiqtol* can be used in this sense.[16] But Wöhrle uses the old argument that Jonah 4:5 perfectly follows 3:4, insofar as he thinks that the text between 3:5 (!) and 4:5 must be secondarily inserted. Again, the supposed tension disappears as soon as one is willing to see the humor and the exaggeration. The narrator presupposes that God does not wait 40 days but recants immediately after God has seen the exceptional way in which the king of Nineveh reacted to Jonah's short message.[17] It does not matter whether all of the citizens will follow the king's command. In sharp contrast to God, Jonah is not impressed by the reaction to his message; at least it does not change his attitude towards Nineveh. Before the 40 days that Jonah has pronounced as the period before the city's overthrow, he leaves the wicked city because he does not want to be eliminated with it. Outside of the city he undertakes something like a sit-in (*Sitzstreik*). Wöhrle interprets this as if Jonah wants to see what the city's inhabitants will do, whether they all will obey the king's command.[18] However, in my view Jonah wants to see what *God* will do. He wants to urge God to return from God's repentance and destroy the city, so that his announcement of the 40 days will finally come true. He cannot and does not want to believe that YHWH indeed spares the city for a lengthy period of time.

In sum, as soon as one recognizes the satirical mood of the book of Jonah, no convincing arguments that would justify the hypothesis of two distinct literary layers remain. Even the psalm is an original part of the book. The narrative once existed independently outside the Book of the Twelve. Since the entire story in the book is located outside of the geographical boundaries of Israel, it may be the creation of a diaspora-community that criticizes hardliners in their homeland and makes fun of their fear that the capital of the foreign nation is a big evil city. Quite to the contrary, the notion of the wicked foreign city, as is maintained, is an unjustified projection of hypocrites. It is a mystery but at the same time a gift that this polemical work was inserted into the Book of the Twelve, where the foil against which Jonah was written in the first place, namely Joel, already had its place. I suppose that it was the result of a compromise between the diaspora and Jerusalem. Jonah was integrated on the one hand and Malachi on the other.

---

15 Lohfink, "Jona," esp. 190–193.
16 Wöhrle, *Abschluss*, 374.383 with notes 61–62.
17 This is a striking contrast to King Jehoiakim in Jer 36:1.
18 Wöhrle, *Abschluss*, 384.

5. Reading Jonah within the Framework of the Twelve:
The Position of Jonah before Nahum

Turning now to the question how Jonah was integrated into the Twelve, one first has to deal with the different places of Jonah within the sequence of the Twelve in the different manuscript traditions. The main point of difference between the MT and the mainstream of the Greek tradition is that Jonah precedes Micah in MT but Nahum in LXX. The best explanation for this difference is that the Book of the Twelve was reordered when it was translated into Greek. The writings Hosea, Amos and Micah were transposed to the front, whereas the sequence of the rest of the writings was left untouched.[19] Especially noteworthy is the fact that already in the Hebrew tradition there is one manuscript, 4QXII[a], that contains Jonah after Malachi.[20] This sequence difference may be due to the fact that Jonah came into the Book of the Twelve very late and its place was initially disputed.

The second point to make is that the satirical character of the story was in some way lost because the fictitious world of the Jonah narrative was integrated into the real historical world, with which the other eleven prophets were dealing. The symbolic name "Jonah" (= "dove") now designated a real person, namely "Jonah ben Amittai," the prophet mentioned in 2 Kings 14:25.[21] At least that is most likely the reason why Jonah was inserted into the chain of the prophets after Amos and Obadiah. The narrative was read as a historical report of something that really happened, not as a fictive scenario.

After these preliminary remarks we can now turn to the thematic coherence between the message of the narrative about the stubborn prophet Jonah and the rest of the Book of the Twelve.[22] In this respect it is obvious that the attitude towards the nations is the biggest problem regarding conceptual coherence. There is some variation between the other prophets when they denounce the final fate of the nations. Joel seems to imply that the nations will be eliminated by YHWH at the end of days (Joel 4). Others imagine that the nations will be included in some way into the salvation of Israel. The narrative of Jonah, however, goes far beyond that. Its main message is that even a big evil city like

---

19   See Schart, "Zwölfprophetenbuch (2008)," 229–230.
20   That Jonah followed Mal is the opinion of the editio princeps: Ulrich et al., *Qumran*. This thesis is challenged by Guillaume, "Malachi-Jonah."
21   It is possible that the patronym "Ben Amittai" was added only at this stage.
22   I now follow the Masoretic text. For an intriguing reflection on how the different sequences affect the reading of the Book of the Twelve see Gerhards, "Jona/Jonabuch."

Nineveh that deserves nothing more than complete destruction – at least from the point of view of the oppressed little towns – is not as bad as one might expect. If you make your way to its middle and deliver a godly message, then you'll find the people alert, sensitive, god-fearing and willing to repent. And this is true to such an extent that even God is impressed and renounces his plan to punish the city. God's mercy extends even to a city that has never heard of YHWH.

The contrast between negative and positive views is most clearly stated in the case of Jonah and Nahum. Nahum differs sharply from Jonah concerning the possibility of Nineveh's repentance. Nahum's prophecy leaves no room for repentance whatsoever. Nahum is convinced that God will totally destroy this center of oppression, exploitation, and violence. And the prophet seems to take delight in envisioning how the wrath of God will deal with this foreign superpower. That Nineveh will and can turn away from its behavior is totally unimaginable to the author. The only solution is that YHWH executes his punishment. In this point, Nahum is completely in line with the narrative figure Jonah, who also wanted to see Nineveh destroyed, but Nahum disagrees with the narrative of Jonah, which shows that God's essence leads God to spare even Nineveh.

The sharp contrast between God's behavior in the narrative about Jonah and God's behavior in Nahum has long puzzled the readers of the Book of the Twelve. As far as I can see, there are three solutions to the problem. The first is that the repentance of Nineveh did not last for long. After a couple of years they not only returned to their evil conduct but did worse, in that they attacked Israel, Judah and Jerusalem. This behavior can be inferred from the report in 2 Kgs 18:13ff and within the Book of the Twelve from Mic 5:4, where Assyria seems to represent a massive threat to Judah. Most of all, the writing of Nahum is the proof that Nineveh must have returned to its bad behavior. Otherwise Nahum's fierce accusations and predictions of doom would be unjustified. That a nation can return to bad conduct after it has experienced God's mercy and repentance is well attested in the case of Israel itself. This reading strategy can be found already in Pirke de Rabbi Eliezer.[23]

A second option has been proposed by Jeremias, who thinks that the narrative of Jonah illustrates God's innermost and final will, namely that God's mercy even extends to the most guilty people, if they are capable of radical repentance (Jonah) and passionately ask for his will (Mic 4:1ff), whereas the severe punishment that Nahum envisions only represents God's temporary will.[24] Viewed in this way the reader of the

---

23   See Schart, *Entstehung*, 27–28; Ego, "Repentance;" Scoralick, *Güte*, 185.
24   Jeremias, *Joel*, 81.

Twelve has to learn that God's will to show mercy even to Nineveh
was missed by two prophets immediately following each other: first the
prophet Jonah, second Nahum.

The third option would be to see an implied criticism of the character Jonah. Jonah's fault was not to mistrust the repentance of Nineveh,
but to announce a very short time span before the end of Nineveh
would come about. The period of 40 days, after which the city will be
overthrown, was not part of God's command, but the prophet's own
invention, presumably placed into his message out of wishful thinking,
because he wanted this event so desperately. In the end God fulfilled
what the prophet had anticipated, but more than 100 years later.[25] The
prophet Jonah should not have excluded the possibility of repentance
on the side of Nineveh and the side of God. Although he was ultimately right with his assessment that Nineveh was bad and that it would
never really change its essence and therefore would be punished some-
day, Jonah's judgment came too early because God gives even the
worst nations the chance to repent and wants God's prophets to take
this task seriously. It is totally unacceptable that a prophet wants God
to obey to his own will and does not serve God's will.

6. Traces of Redactional Activities Related to the Inclusion of Jonah within the Twelve

Let us now consider at what stage of the development of the Twelve
the narrative of Jonah was included and whether traces of redactional
activities can be detected that are placed outside of the narrative of
Jonah, but nevertheless stem from the same redactor who included
Jonah. As several studies have shown, it is very probable that the Book
of the Twelve grew in such a way that writings were included into
different multi-volume precursors to the Twelve and at the same time
some passages were inserted in order to balance out the tensions that
the inclusion brought into the conceptual coherence of the Twelve.
Different authors have identified such passages that look as though
they are connected to the Jonah-redaction. Most impressive is Wöhrle's
thesis of a *Gnadenkorpus*.

Wöhrle proposes the thesis that a redactor inserted the book of Jonah in order to establish a corpus comprising twelve writings: Joel,
Amos, Obad, Jonah, Mic, Nah, Hab, Zeph, Hag, Zech, Deutero-Zech

---

25   At least this is the case, if one identifies the narrative character within Jonah with the
     figure mentioned in 2 Kings 14:25.

(counted as an independent writing) and Mal. This redactor at the same time thoroughly reworked the narrative of Jonah and inserted some passages in four other books: Joel 2:12–14; Mic 7:18–20; Nah 1:2b, 3a; Mal 1:9a.[26] All these passages demonstrate a similar interest in the compassionate essence of YHWH. Besides this global thematic coherence some passages deliberately cite or allude to the famous definition of YHWH's character in the context of the Sinai-theophany in Exod 34:6, designated as *Gnadenformel*:[27]

> 34:6 The LORD, the LORD, a God merciful and gracious, slow to anger, and abounding in steadfast love and faithfulness. (NRSV)

In addition, some passages share words and concepts. In some cases the lexical overlap is significant, in others not so much. All in all, as Wöhrle himself admits, these observations can equally be explained by other theories and models.[28] What gives Wöhrle's hypothesis of a *Gnadenkorpus* special strength is his argument that the redactional passages within the *Gnadenkorpus* show a clear intention to provide the corpus with a unifying structure. Wöhrle visualizes this structure with the following table:[29]

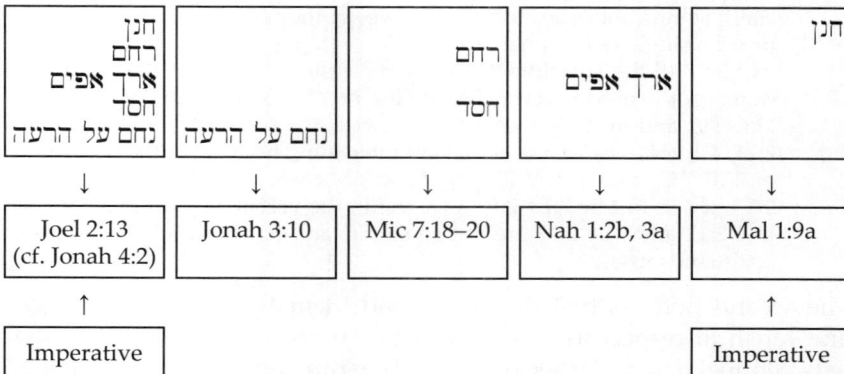

חנן רחם ארך אפים חסד נחם על הרעה	נחם על הרעה	רחם חסד	ארך אפים	חנן
↓	↓	↓	↓	↓
Joel 2:13 (cf. Jonah 4:2)	Jonah 3:10	Mic 7:18–20	Nah 1:2b, 3a	Mal 1:9a
↑				↑
Imperative				Imperative

Table 1: The *Gnadenkorpus* according to Jakob Wöhrle

---

26 Vgl. Wöhrle, *Abschluss*, 400. The redactional layer in Jonah comprises: Jonah 1:5b, 6, 8aβ, 10abα, 14, 16; 2:2–10; 3:6–10; 4:1–4, 6*(יהוה) and להציל to הגדולה), 10–11.
27 Wöhrle, *Abschluss*, 401.
28 Wöhrle, *Abschluss*, 406–407.
29 Wöhrle, *Abschluss*, 408.

The table shows that the redactional passages in the first and the last writing begin with an imperative and in this way build a kind of frame around the corpus. The first appearance of the *Gnadenformel* in Joel 2:13 gives a complete version of the concepts mentioned in Exod 34:6, whereas in the subsequent writings, that is those except Joel and Jonah, every word is repeated exactly one time. If these were all of the allusions to Exod 34:6 in the Book of the Twelve, this neat structure would be quite impressive and a good argument to think of the *Gnadenkorpus* as a unified and self-contained redactional unit. However, if you look at it more closely, it becomes obvious that Wöhrle does not provide the whole picture.

The first point to make is that the degree of grammatical agreement between the various phrases differs from how Wöhrle actually presents it:

- The adjective חַנּוּן does not show up in Mal 1:9a. Only the Verb חָנַן appears. The root חנן, however, is also attested in Hos 12:5 and Amos 5:15. It is right that in Mal we do have a וְעַתָּה, which is similarly found in Joel 2:12, but in Joel 2:12 the exact wording is וְגַם־עַתָּה, which is certainly different. On the other hand, there is a striking and famous affinity to Amos 5:15, insofar as אוּלַי is attested in both places and in a comparable context. As a result, the reference from Mal 1:9 to Joel 2:12 is not especially significant or exclusive. The words they have in common cannot prove a single redactional layer.
- In Mic 7:19 the adjective רַחוּם is not attested, but the verb רחם is. The same root is used seven times in Hos 1:6, 7; 2:3, 6, 25 (2x); 9:14; 14:4, in Hab 3:2, and in Zech 1:12; 10:6. Likewise, the noun חֶסֶד is used in Hos 2:21; 4:1; 6:4, 6 (which is especially interesting because of the occurrence of חֶסֶד חָפֵץ as in Mic 7:18); 10:12; 12:7; Mic 6:8; Zech 7:9 (roots חֶסֶד and רחם just as in Mic 7:18–20). As a result, the verbal connections between Joel 2:12 and Mic 7:19 are not so significant that Wöhrle's thesis really commends itself.

The second point is that the verbal and thematic relationship of Joel and Jonah in respect to Exod 34:6 is by far more significant than that between Joel and the other writings. This can sufficiently be explained with the thesis that Jonah cited Joel because the author of the narrative of Jonah wanted to ridicule the writing of Joel, but that the redactor who alluded to Exod 34:6 in the other writings was a different person. In contrast, it is unlikely that the same redactor worked in such a markedly distinct manner within the different writings.

The third point is that Wöhrle rightly points to the fact that Joel 2:13 contains an imperative, but he does not mention that the specific form, the imperative שׁוּבוּ "return!" picks up the same imperative of Hos 14:3. It is especially noteworthy that the command to return is doubled in Hos 14:2–3 and Joel 2:12–13 as well: Hos 14:2 and Joel 2:12 construe the

imperative with the preposition עַד and are followed immediately by a
second imperative of שׁוּב, this time construed with the preposition אֶל
(Hos 14:3; Joel 2:13). In addition, the topic of repentance using שׁוּב is
very strong in Zech 1:2–6 and shows up ultimately in Mal 3:7. The topic
of repentance and the *Gnadenformel* are heavily intertwined in Joel 2:12–
14 and in Jonah 3. Therefore it is unwise to construe a literary layer by
concentrating solely on the *Gnadenformel*.

The fourth point is that one has to consider the wider context of the
Gnadenformel in Exod 34, since there are some more significant verbal
agreements. In Exod 32:14 it is stated: "And the LORD changed his mind
about the disaster that he planned to bring on his people" (NRSV). This
is exactly the sentiment expressed in Jonah 3:10! Nineveh experiences
the same mercy of God that allowed Israel to survive after the incident
with the golden calf at Mount Sinai. Israel nevertheless had to suffer
severe punishment after God repented, whereas Nineveh's punishment
seems to be nullified altogether.

The fifth point concerns Mal 1:9a. The opening imperative "Now,
entreat God's face!" is reminiscent of Exod 32:11 where it is stated with
the same verb "But Moses entreated YHWH."

All of the citations are shown in table 2.

In summary, Wöhrle is right that there is a chain of passages that
cite or allude to the *Gnadenformel* as attested in Exod 34:6. As in the case
of Exod 34 (and Num 14:18) it is important to note that God does not
need any prerequisites from the people in order to forgive. But this
analysis gives only part of the picture.

First, it is obvious that the verbal agreements that Wöhrle has observed are only significant in the case of Joel and Jonah. However, the
connection between these two can better be explained by the thesis that
the author of the narrative of Jonah deliberately cited and alluded to
Joel, whereby a good reason for that would be the satirical character of
Jonah. Apart from Joel and Jonah, the lexical overlap with the other
writings does not justify the hypothesis of a *Gnadenkorpus*. In turn, the
redactional passages that Wöhrle has isolated share some vocabulary of
greater significance with passages and writings that do not belong to
Wöhrle's *Gnadenkorpus*. Especially noteworthy is the allusion of Mic
7:18 to Hos.

Second, within the Book of the Twelve it is especially noteworthy
that the most important passage, which Wöhrle considers to be of basic
importance because it contains a complete set of the concepts of the
Gnadenformel, namely Joel 2:12–13, includes a call to repentance. This
call definitely picks up Hos 14:2–3 in many respects. In addition, the
concept and some of the words are also used in Zech 1:2–3 and Mal 3:7.

	Exod 32–34	Hos 14:2–3	Joel 2:12–13	Jonah 3–4	Mic 7:18–20	Nah 1:3	Mal 3:7
Imperative: Return to me!		שׁובה ישׂראל עד יהוה אלהיך / שׁובו אל יהוה	שׁבו עד־יהוה אלהיכם / שׁבו אלי				שׁובו אלי ואשׁובה אליכם
	Exod 32:11						Mal 1:9b
God entreated	ויחל משׁה את פני יהוה אלהיו						ועתה חלו־נא פני־אל
	Exod 34:6–7			Jonah 4:2			
YHWH	יהוה יהוה			כי־אל	כי־אל כמוך	יהוה	
compassionate	אל רחום		יהוה	וחנון			
gracious	וחנון		חנון	חנון			
slow to anger	ארך אפים		ארך אפים	ארך אפים		אפים	
lovingkindness and truth	ורב־חסד ואמת		ורב־חסד	חסד רב	וחסד נשׂא עון ועבר על־פשׁע		
keeping mercy	נצר חסד לאלפים				לא־החזיק לעד אפו		
forgiving	נשׂא עון ופשׁע וחטאה				מי־אל כמוך נשׂא עון ועבר על־פשׁע		
relenting			ונחם על־הרעה	ונחם על־הרעה			
			Joel 4:18				
not clearing the guilty	ונקה לא ינקה					ונקה לא ינקה	
	Exod 32:14			Jonah 3:10			
God relents	וינחם יהוה על־הרעה			וינחם האלהים על־הרעה			
	אשׁר דבר לעשׂות לעמו			אשׁר־דבר לעשׂות להם			

Table 2: Intertextual Relations between Exod 32–34 and Texts in the Twelve

The theme of repentance definitely is an important thematic thread within the Twelve.

Third, citations of passages within the vicinity of Exod 32–34 demonstrate that the redactor was aware of the wider context of the *Gnadenformel*.

In sum, the hypothesis that there was a *Gnadenkorpus* is unlikely as Wöhrle has reconstructed it. The thesis of a redactional layer across several writings of the *Gnadenkorpus* is, at least in the case of the book of Jonah, not convincing because the claims that there are massive thematic tensions within the narrative do no justice to the satirical character of the narrative. In addition, the passages that Wöhrle has identified as belonging to the redaction do not form a significant self-contained structure. The verbal agreements between the passages do not stem from the work of a single redactor, but from different authors instead. There are several highly significant allusions to Exod 34:6 within Wöhrle's redactional passages, but they are not limited to these passages. Highly significant allusions to the *Gnadenformel* and other phrases from the Sinai episode can be found elsewhere, too. The alleged central passage of the redaction in Joel 2:12–13 contains an important element that Wöhrle ignores, namely an urgent call to repentance with a double occurrence of the imperative שׁובו. This alludes clearly to Hos 14:2–3, a passage that, according to Wöhrle, is not part of the *Gnadenkorpus*. The topic of return to YHWH is taken up prominently in Zech 1, where it is stated that the people finally followed this command. And it occurs in the final chapter of the Twelve, in Mal 3:7. Wöhrle should have considered these passages also to be part of the redaction that inserted Jonah into the Book of the Twelve. Wöhrle proposes that Hos was not part of the *Gnadenkorpus* because he cannot detect clear verbal connections between Hos and the rest of the corpus. However, there is no reason to speculate in this direction, because the verbal and conceptual agreement between Joel 2:12–13 and Hos 14:2–3 is very significant.[30]

7. Other Editorial Passages Related to the Inclusion of Jonah

The book of Jonah brought an important idea into the Book of the Twelve, namely that the nations, even those with the worst behavior, can experience the very same merciful imminence and essence of

---

30   Scoralick, *Güte*, has dealt extensively with the question how Exod 34:6–7 is interwoven in the Book of the Twelve. She has noted many intertextual relations with Hos.

YHWH as Israel. The mercy of God does not extend exclusively to Israel.[31] Even more so, the ethnically mixed group of sailors and the Ninevites can serve as an impressive example for Israel showing how a perfect return to God can be achieved. This measure of positive attitude concerning the nations is unparalleled in the rest of the Twelve and counterbalances the many negative passages about the nations. Several authors have proposed the hypothesis that some passages that display a positive attitude towards the nations are connected to the redaction that inserted Jonah into the Twelve.

7.1 Possible Connections to Jonah in Mic 7

In Mic 7:19a the suffix in the 1st person plural is unclear. Within the context it is plausible that the suffix refers to the nations rather than to Israel. If this were so, the verse would imply that YHWH will forgive the nations their sins in a similar way to Israel, although this meaning of the text is neither straight-forward nor easily understandable within its context.[32]

Metzner has proposed that the last additions to Mic, which can be found in Mic 7:11b, 12b, and 19b, contain a positive attitude towards the nations that can be paralleled to that of the book of Jonah.[33] In Mic 7:11b she translates "jener Tag, die Schranke entfernt sich."[34] This somewhat cryptic statement is taken as having a metaphorical sense: "Im Zusammenhang mit V.12 ist an das Fallen der nationalen Schranken zu denken: die Frommen der ganzen Erde, voran die Diaspora aus Ägypten und Assyrien, werden zum geschützten Ort kommen."[35] Although this understanding of the somehow cryptic passage seems a bit far-fetched, it is certainly worth thinking about, because it is completely imaginable that a reader of the Book of the Twelve or its precursors sought guidance for how to understand the shift concerning the nations from Jonah to Micah.

---

31 Wöhrle, *Abschluss*, 396.
32 Nogalski, *Precursors*, 153, puts it this way: "This allusion seeks to draw a parallel between the 'salvation' of Jonah and the 'salvation' of the congregation in 7:19b." There is also a verbal connection to Jonah 2:4: The combination of the substantive מצלה together with the verb שלך in the hiphil is attested in both cases (Nogalski, ibid., 153; Metzner, *Kompositionsgeschichte*, 166–167); however, the word מצלה probably has been inserted secondarily; see Jeremias, *Joel*, 89.
33 Metzner, *Kompositionsgeschichte*, 183.
34 Metzner, *Kompositionsgeschichte*, 195.
35 Metzner, *Kompositionsgeschichte*, 165.

7.2 Connections to Jonah in Malachi

Within Malachi there is one short statement concerning the nations that has always puzzled the readers of this book.[36] Mal 1:11 (cf. 14b) states:

> 1:11 For from the rising of the sun to its setting,
> my name is great among the nations,
> and in every place incense is offered to my name,
> and a pure gift.
> Yes, my name is great among the nations,
> says YHWH Zebaoth.

It is indeed astonishing how the author states as a fact that people who do not belong to Israel and may not have even heard the name YHWH bring a pure offering to YHWH. As a consequence, many scholars perceive this statement as directed towards the distant future.[37] However the grammatical construction of a sentence with a participle and a second nominal phrase does not refer to a future event but expresses the notion that an action is durative, i.e., that it continues through time at the time of the speaker. The second proposal is that the author is not thinking of non-Israelites, but of members of the diaspora that live all over the world distancing themselves from the cults of other gods and bringing offerings to YHWH where they are. However, this meaning is speculative.

If one assumes the straight-forward sense, that non-Israelites worship YHWH outside of the land of Israel, Jonah provides two good examples of how this could be imagined in its narrative!

In Jonah 1:16 the sailors very probably should be imagined as a heterogeneous and religiously diverse group of non-Israelites in that each person prays to his own god. After the sea has calmed down – even while still on the ship! – they offered a sacrifice to YHWH and took a vow (Jonah 1:16). This matches the idea of Mal 1:11 exactly: Non-Israelites offer their gifts to YHWH, the god of Israel, who they know and address by name, but they do not need to go to Jerusalem or to another temple.[38] Every place qualifies as a satisfactory location for sacrifice to YHWH. And they serve as a positive example for Jonah, the Hebrew (Jonah 1:9), who knows YHWH's essence so well (Jonah 4:2),

---

36 See for example Weyde, *Prophecy*, 146–149.
37 Already the King James Version did so.
38 This is noted for example by Roth, *Israel*, 153–155; he is right that Zeph 2:11 likewise envisions a worship of YHWH by the nations, but for the distant future.

but refuses to obey or to pray to his god, even should the consequence be his own death.[39]

In addition, Jonah 3 envisions the people of Nineveh as positively outstanding. They are depicted as serving only one God, who is identified with YHWH by the narrator, although they themselves do not know the real name of this God. As a consequence, the Ninevites turn with their repentance to the God they know. They cannot address YHWH by name because Jonah has not given them the chance to do so. Nevertheless, YHWH is impressed so much by this conduct that he recants immediately. Again, one can infer that the narrative demonstrates how foreigners who do not even know the name of YHWH can serve him in a much better way than the prophet Jonah.[40]

This picture stands in sharp contrast to the prayer of Jonah, who is portrayed as a hardline nationalist and who does not give up the idea that YHWH is bound to the temple in Jerusalem. In Jonah 2:5 and 2:8 his desire for the temple is expressed vividly with the same phrase. In Jonah 2:8b it even has an ironic twist to it:

> 2:8 "And my prayer came to you, into your holy temple." (NRSV)

The phrase אֶל־הֵיכַל קָדְשֶׁךָ cites Pss 5:8 and 138:2. There the person who prays is located physically at the temple in front of the temple building (הֵיכָל). In the case of Jonah, however, his longing for the temple is so intense that he even wants his prayer to stop by Mount Zion before it reaches God.

In sum, the conduct of the sailors is the only example within the Twelve that positively proves that Mal 1:11, 14 is not an eschatological hope but an option that can be realized within history. Jonah illustrates what Mal 1:11, 14 states: that the nations can be a positive foil for venerating YHWH in Israel! This conceptual coherence between Jonah and the redactor who inserted Mal 1:11, 14b into Mal make it a probable assumption that the redactor who inserted Jonah into the Twelve also inserted Mal 1:11, 14b.[41]

---

39 This concept parallels the self-understanding of Cyrus as expressed in his edict transmitted in Ezra 1:2–4; (6:3–5, 9; 7:12). He addresses YHWH and acts truly on his behalf, although he never visited the land of Israel.

40 Wöhrle, *Abschluss*, 395.

41 Bosshard-Nepustil, *Rezeptionen*, 421–428, postulates a layer that comprises the first literary layer in the Book of Jonah, Zeph 2:11, 3:1–7, and the first layer in Malachi and dates it into the period of Artaxerxes III Ochus. However, many source-critical reconstructions of his thesis are unwarranted. Wöhrle, *Abschluss*, 358–360, perceives Zeph 2:11 as isolated gloss that is not part of a layer, and also Mal 1:11a is seen as an isolated gloss "ohne größere Bedeutung für die Entstehung des Maleachibuches oder gar des Zwölfprophetenbuches" (ibid., 263).

8. Conclusion

The source-critical hypothesis of a *Gnadenkorpus* proposed by Wöhrle undoubtedly has its merits, insofar as he has put the focus on important aspects that the inclusion of the Book of Jonah brought into the Book of the Twelve. However, the hypothesis has its limits. The source-critical analysis of the narrative of Jonah has overlooked its satirical character and therefore misunderstood some humorous and ironic elements as unmotivated tensions that justify the assumption of different layers. In other cases the borders of the *Gnadenkorpus* have not been convincingly demonstrated. It is especially unfortunate to exclude Hos from the *Gnadenkorpus*, as Wöhrle has ignored significant citations and allusions that suggest the contrary. Wherever one detects redactional traces that are connected to Jonah they belong to the latest layers in that writing, as is probable in the case of Mic and Mal. As a consequence, it is safe to assume that Jonah belonged to the final redaction of the Book of the Twelve.

The narrative of Jonah changed the message of the Twelve as a whole significantly in several respects. First, as Wöhrle has rightly noticed, YHWH's mercy is underscored, whereas his anger is downplayed. The author of Jonah alludes to the events at Mount Sinai as a kind of proof-text, presumably because he wanted to show that his understanding of God's mercy is drawn from YHWH's own self-disclosure. In contrast to the situation at Mount Sinai, YHWH's mercy is extended to the nations within Jonah. Jonah also stresses the necessity for people to repent and to return to YHWH. This topic was already important at many stages of the development of the Twelve, but with the inclusion of Jonah it was given a new twist. Some representatives of the nations serve as positive examples for Israel.

References

Bosshard-Nepustil, E. *Rezeptionen von Jesaia 1–39 im Zwölfprophetenbuch: Untersuchungen zur literarischen Verbindung von Prophetenbüchern in babylonischer und persischer Zeit.* OBO 154. Fribourg: Universitätsverlag and Göttingen: Vandenhoeck & Ruprecht, 1997.

Burrows, M. "The Literary Category of the Book of Jonah." Pp. 80–107 in *Translating and Understanding the Old Testament.* Edited by H.T. Frank and W.L. Reed. Nashville: Abingdon, 1970.

Ego, B. "The Repentance of Nineveh in the Story of Jonah and Nahum's Prophecy of the City's Destruction – A Coherent Reading of the Book of the Twelve as Reflected in the Aggada." Pp. 155–164 in *Thematic Threads in the*

Book of the Twelve. Edited by P.L. Redditt and A. Schart. BZAW 325. Berlin: de Gruyter, 2003.

Gerhards, M. *Studien zum Jonabuch*. Biblisch-theologische Studien 78. Neukirchen-Vluyn: Neukirchener, 2006.

–   "Jona/Jonabuch." wibilex (2008).

Good, E.M. "Jonah: The Absurdity of God." Pp. 39–55 in *Irony in the Old Testament*. Edited by idem. London: S.P.C.K., 1965.

Grimm, H.A. *Der Prophet Jonas, aufs neue übersetzt und mit erklärenden Anmerkungen herausgegeben von Heinrich Adolph Grimm, Doct. u. Professor der Theologie auf der königlich. Preussischen Universität zu Duisburg*. Düsseldorf: Dänzer, 1789.

Guillaume, P. "The unlikely Malachi-Jonah Sequence (4QXIIa)." *Journal of Hebrew Scriptures* 7 (2007).

Jeremias, J. "Das Jonabuch in der Forschung seit Hans Walter Wolff." Pp. 93–140 in Wolff, H.W. *Studien zum Jonabuch*. Edited by idem. Neukirchen-Vluyn: Neukirchener, 2003.

–   *Die Propheten Joel, Obadja, Jona, Micha*. ATD 24,3. Göttingen: Vandenhoeck & Ruprecht, 2007.

Lohfink, N. "Und Jona ging zur Stadt hinaus (Jona 4,5)." *BZ* 5 (1961) 185–203.

Marti, K. *Das Dodekapropheton*. KHC 13. Tübingen: Mohr, 1904.

Metzner, G. *Kompositionsgeschichte des Michabuches*. Europäische Hochschulschriften XXIII,635. Frankfurt: Lang, 1998.

Nogalski, J. *Literary Precursors to the Book of the Twelve*. BZAW 217. Berlin: de Gruyter, 1993.

Roth, M. *Israel und die Völker im Zwölfprophetenbuch: Eine Untersuchung zu den Büchern Joel, Jona, Micha und Nahum*. FRLANT 210. Göttingen: Vandenhoeck & Ruprecht, 2005.

Rudolph, W. *Joel, Amos, Obadja, Jona*. Mit einer Zeittafel von Alfred Jepsen. KAT 13,2. Gütersloh: Gütersloher Verlagshaus, 1971.

Schart, A. *Die Entstehung des Zwölfprophetenbuchs: Neubearbeitungen von Amos im Rahmen schriftenübergreifender Redaktionsprozesse*. BZAW 260. Berlin: de Gruyter, 1998.

–   "Das Zwölfprophetenbuch als redaktionelle Großeinheit." *TLZ* 133 (2008) 227–246.

–   "Das Zwölfprophetenbuch." *wibilex* (2007).

Scoralick, R. *Gottes Güte und Gottes Zorn: Die Gottesprädikationen in Exodus 34,6f und ihre intertextuellen Beziehungen zum Zwölfprophetenbuch*. Herders biblische Studien 33. Freiburg: Herder, 2002.

Ulrich, E. et al. *Qumran cave 4: X: The Prophets*. DJD 15. Oxford: Clarendon, 1997.

Weyde, K.W. *Prophecy and Teaching: Prophetic Authority, Form Problems, and the Use of Traditions in the Book of Malachi*. BZAW 288. Berlin: de Gruyter, 2000.

Wöhrle, J. *Der Abschluss des Zwölfprophetenbuches: Buchübergreifende Redaktionsprozesse in den späten Sammlungen*. BZAW 389. Berlin: de Gruyter, 2008.

Wolff, H.W. *Studien zum Jonabuch*. Mit einem Anhang von J. Jeremias. 3rd ed. Neukirchen-Vluyn: Neukirchener, 2003.

The Book of Micah –
the Theological Center of the Book of the Twelve?[1]

BURKARD M. ZAPFF

Katholische Universität Eichstätt-Ingolstadt

In the context of the past twenty years' research concerning the composition and growth of the Book of the Twelve, the Book of Micah is one of the books attracting particular attention for various reasons.[2] First, due to its heading, which refers to various kings of the southern kingdom of Judah and thus establishes a chronological setting for the prophetic message received by Micah, the Book of Micah seems to make particular reference to the prophetic writings of Hosea, Amos and Zephaniah.[3] Indeed, the heading of Hosea parallels that of Micah in presenting "Jotham, Ahaz and Hezekiah" as the ruling kings of Judah so that Micah is characterized as a contemporary of Hosea. Second, the judgment against the northern kingdom proclaimed by Amos and Hosea undergoes an expansion within Micah.[4] In Micah, judgment is first directed against Samaria, the capital of the northern kingdom, as described in Mic 1:5, but judgment also reaches the capital of the southern kingdom, Jerusalem, including its Temple Mount. Mic 3:12 announces destruction to the latter. Thus, the correspondence between Hosea and Micah, which the heading of Micah establishes through its chronological reference to the heading of the Book of Hosea, attempts to provide a provisional conclusion to a sequence of YHWH's acting in judgment which extends across several writings in the Book of the Twelve.

A third striking characteristic of Micah is its intertextual relationship with Isaiah, intertextuality of a kind only paralleled by Joel. It is manifest in Mic 1:1, which not only presents Micah as a younger contemporary to Isaiah by means of its chronology of kings (1:1a) but also contains (in 1:1b) clear allusions to Isa 1:1 and 2:1. Concerning the contents, I would just mention the pilgrimage of the nations in Mic 4:1–3,

---

1   Regarding the title cf. Scoralick, *Güte*, 186; Kessler, "Buch," 139.
2   Cf. Nogalski, *Precursors*, 123–170; Zapff, *Studien*; idem, "Völkerperspektive;" Schart, *Entstehung*, 177–201.257.258; Metzner, *Kompositionsgeschichte*; Kessler, *Micha*; Roth, *Völker*; Wöhrle, *Sammlungen*, 138–189; idem, *Abschluss*; Jeremias, *Propheten*, 113–232.
3   Schart, *Entstehung*, 39.
4   Schart, *Entstehung*, 221.

which parallels Isa 2:2–4, and the so-called motif of the nations' attack in Mic 4:11–13, which is to be compared with Isa 17:12–14, and to the announcement of Israel's purification in Mic 5:9–13, which is to be compared with Isa 2:6–21.[5]

Fourth and finally, one should note the position of Micah within the Masoretic order of the writings comprising the Book of the Twelve. Being the sixth book, not only is its position precisely in the middle but the Masoretes themselves define Mic 3:12 as the center of the Book of the Twelve, too.[6]

These few but quite striking observations suffice to raise a question of the compositional and theological function that could be attributed to the Book of Micah within the thematic flow of the Book of the Twelve, assuming of course that the Book of the Twelve really intends to be read as a whole. In my view, this last-mentioned assumption is supported by quite a number of indications that I will discuss in detail at a later point.

The aim of my statement is first to document the most important results of the past few years' research on the Book of Micah, and while doing so I will refer to the question of whether Micah may be an integral part of a theological conception of the Book of the Twelve. In a second section I will put forward a number of observations supporting the conclusion that the Book of Micah in its current form represents something like a theological core of the Book of the Twelve, where important themes are concentrated and mark a kind of dividing line within the Book of the Twelve. Subsequently, I will articulate a few desiderata which in my view have consequences for further research work on Micah within the context of the Book of the Twelve.

1. Recent Research on Micah in the Context of Research on the Book of the Twelve

I would first like to distinguish between an approach exclusively referring to Micah as a corpus and another type of research which heuristically takes into consideration a possible integration of the Book of Micah into the context of either a book comprising several of the Prophets or the contemporary Book of the Twelve.

a) The point of departure of modern research on Micah is a thesis already put forward by Stade which says that if any textual material at

---

5   Cf. Renaud, *Formation*, 265.
6   Scoralick, *Güte*, 186.

all that would allow us to hear the very voice of the historical prophet called Micah, it could only be found in Mic 1–3.[7] The argument is simple but still convincing. It refers to Jer 26:18, which quotes Mic 3:12 and thus characterizes Micah exclusively as a prophet of doom. Consequently, this characterization means that chapters 4–7, which in essential parts consist of prophecies of salvation, are likely later supplements added to an original version of Micah. As we will see, however, the literary character of these additions and the internal relationships between each of the sections are being discussed quite controversially. In the context of these supplements, consisting mainly of prophecies of salvation, Mic 1–3 also seem to have been modified by various redactional expansions. Among these expansions, for example, most scholars include Mic 2:12–13, although its meaning and its assignment to a corresponding stage in redactional history are fiercely disputed due to the extremely difficult text-critical findings. Estimations vary from those proposing a prophecy of salvation for Israel,[8] which some interpreters would even like to attribute to Micah's opponents,[9] to others suggesting an additional prophecy of doom, one that was subsequently supplemented by a prophecy of salvation in v. 13b – as has recently been held by Wöhrle.[10] All the arguments have been exchanged on this case, I think, and no further certainty can be achieved.

As to the genesis of the *earliest form* of the Book of Micah, there are two opposing positions within recent scholarship, namely those of Schart and Jeremias. Whereas Schart wants to understand the Book of Micah as a deliberate supplement to an already existing corpus of two prophets comprising Amos and Hosea,[11] Jeremias holds that the book was first composed independently as a "summary report" (*Rechenschaftsbericht*) of the prophet's work.[12] On this level, too, I consider it quite difficult to obtain sufficient clarity, but I would rather opt for Jeremias' position. In fact, it is striking that the earliest parts of the Book of Micah, which are most likely to be found in the area of Mic 1:3–3:12, make the prophet quite similar to Isaiah. To illustrate, one may compare the motif of the prophet's nakedness in Mic 1:8 and Isa 20, or the critique against the upper class's attempts to increase their property

---

7   Stade, "Bemerkungen," 164–165.
8   Cf. Zapff, *Studien*, 15–40.
9   Cf. van der Woude, "Micah," 256–257.
10   Wöhrle, *Sammlungen*, 148–153, following a thesis of Mays, "Purpose," 279; idem, *Micah*, 76.
11   Schart, *Entstehung*, 201: "Eine völlig selbständige Michaschrift hat es vermutlich nie gegeben."
12   Jeremias, *Propheten*, 116: "Wahrscheinlich lag den Kernkapiteln 1–3 des Michabuches ein *Rechenschaftsbericht des Propheten* zugrunde."

holdings at the expense of the ordinary family farm in Mic 2:2 and Isa 5:8. Conversely, a connection with Amos and Hosea is established through Mic 1:5–7, where the doom coming upon Samaria is made the subject matter. This passage, however, is probably a later supplement.[13] As a result, Micah appears in the earliest form of the book rather as a "little" Isaiah and is only related to Hosea and Amos by means of a *later* redactional adaptation.

Although there is, as already mentioned, a broad consensus about Mic 4–5 being later supplements, the literary critical delimitations as well as the assignment of the individual parts to redaction-historical stages are disputed.[14] Nonetheless I hold that the following sufficiently reliable assignments can be made.

1. A number of texts in Mic 4–5 imply that Israel faces a serious emergency, and these texts should be situated in the context of the Exile. Among them is, for example, Mic 4:9–10+14.[15]

2. Moreover, Mic 4:11–13 contains the motif of an as yet unsuccessful attack against Zion by the nations. In contrast to the use of this motif in the Book of Isaiah and in Psalms 46 and 48, it is interesting that here it is not YHWH himself who brings release, but Zion that is characterized by means of the image of a bull and is equipped by YHWH with appropriate weapons – mentioned are horns of iron and hooves of bronze. Similarly Zion also proves to be superior to her enemies in Mic 5:7b+8. Interestingly, she is also described in the form of an animal metaphor in v. 7b.

3. By contrast, Mic 5:14 tells of a direct intervention by YHWH against a number of nations that are referred to as "disobedient." As has been noted repeatedly in the more recent publications, this verse relates to Mic 1:2, where "all nations" have been required to listen.[16]

4. Apart from these three groups of texts which above all see the nations under the aspect of hostility, annihilation and doom, other texts can be found which open the prospect of salvation to the nations. One of them is the previously mentioned pilgrimage of the nations in Mic 4:1–3, where salvation is imparted to the nations because of their orientation towards YHWH's law, a text which is known to have a parallel in Isa 2:2–4. Another of these texts is Mic 5:6, where salvation is granted

---

13 Jeremias, *Propheten*, 116, considers Mic 1:3–7 as an exilic text: "Es geht den Versen um den Aufweis analoger Schuld beider Städte [scil. Samaria and Jerusalem], die zu ihrem analogen Geschick geführt hat."
14 Cf. Zapff, *Studien*, 41–49; Wöhrle, *Sammlungen*, 197.
15 Zapff, *Studien*, 82: "spätvorexilisch;" Jeremias, *Propheten*, 179: "Rückblick (auf) die Not der letzten Wochen Jerusalems vor seiner Zerstörung;" Wöhrle, *Sammlungen*, 192: "frühe Exilszeit."
16 Cf. Lescow, "Analyse," 80; Cuffey, *Coherence*, 197.

to the nations through Israel insofar as it works among the nations like beneficent dew and rain.

5. Besides these groups of texts to be described as "hostile" or "friendly" towards the nations, we find texts containing the subject of Israel's restoration and the reestablishment of its kingdom. They either announce YHWH himself as king as in Mic 4:7, or they expect an earthly king as in Mic 5:1–5. In the latter text this king's character oscillates between singular and plural.

6. Finally, Mic 5:9–13 recounts judgment executed by YHWH which is obviously directed against Israel, or to be more precise against certain entities in Israel who are obstructing the true worship of YHWH. A striking characteristic of this text is the fact that it is related to Isa 2:6–22 by means of various catchwords. Among these are, for example, the "soothsayers" (עננים[מ]) in Isa 2:6b and Mic 5:11b, or the "horses" (סוסים) and "chariots" (מרכבות) in Isa 2:7 and Mic 5:9b.

The dual references to the Book of Isaiah in Mic 4–5, plus the motif of the nations' unsuccessful attack against Zion, create a framework around the two chapters, as Renaud has pointed out.[17] Similarly to Isa 2:2–4 and 2:6ff, this frame links the pilgrimage of the nations at the end of the days with a purification of Israel.

At first sight, the diversity of themes in Mic 4–5 seems to be confusing. Thus Schart, for instance, holds that the passage results from the discourse between various theological circles in postexilic Israel.[18] This may indeed be true for the various differing positions represented here, but on the level of the present *canonical text* there are various signals in the textual flow of Mic 4–5 which show that at least one of the various redactional adaptations made an effort to reshape this diversity into a tense unity. This assumption seems to be confirmed by the references to

17 Renaud, *Formation*, 120; cf. Vermeylen, *Prophète*, 2:594.
18 Schart, *Entstehung*, 257: "Die Art und Weise, wie man in diesen Kapiteln konträre Ansichten unverbunden aneinander gereiht hat, läßt m.E. die These zu, hier habe ganz bewußt eine Diskussion als solche dokumentiert werden sollen. Sich gegenseitig widersprechende theologische Positionen wurden miteinander konfrontiert, ohne dass ein Kompromiß beide Positionen abschließt. Da beide Positionen als vertretbar erschienen, sollte sich wohl die Leserschaft im Verlauf des Abschreitens der Argumente beider Seiten ihr eigenes Urteil bilden."
   In my opinion a deficiency of Wöhrle's redaction-critical Analysis of Mic 4–5 lies in the fact that it more or less lacks an explanation of what the statement of Mic 4–5 as a whole may either mean on the canonical level of the text or at least on the level of one of the preceding redactional revisions coming close to the canonical text. It is true that the different layers of the text have to be distinguished from each other, but Wöhrle does not sufficiently take into consideration the manner in which the later redactional expansions include the earlier texts into their theological concepts. A diachronic analysis should always be completed by a synchronic one!

the Book of Isaiah found in both framework texts of Mic 4 and 5. These references continue the tendency of adapting the Book of Micah to the model of Isaiah. This tendency, already documented in the earliest parts of the book, could be called an "Isaianization" of Micah.

Another important observation for understanding the two chapters as one composition is the *chronological structure* created by means of the obviously deliberate use of the chronological indicators "now" (עתה) and "but now" (ועתה), which refer to the present. Clearly set off from these markers, the texts introduced by "and in the last days it shall come to pass" (והיה באחרית הימים) in Mic 4:1 and "in that day" (ביום ההוא) in Mic 4:6 and 5:9 unambiguously refer to a later period of time. It appears questionable to me whether a further distinction has to be made here as Wöhrle requires[19] because the formulaic expression "in that day" in Mic 4:6 seems to refer to a day mentioned before. The antecedent can only be the preceding indication of time in Mic 4:1. So two texts are confronted with each other here which describe a present and a future time. Regarding content, it is notable that the texts pointing to the future first announce the salvation of the nations going on pilgrimage to Jerusalem, thus for example Mic 4:1–3, then the salvation of Israel, as does Mic 4:6–7, whereas Mic 5:9–14 predicts 1) a purifying judgment against those subjects in Israel which obstruct the worship of YHWH, and 2) a judgment against the nations which do not obey. Thus a concentrically formed framework is arranged around Mic 4–5 which in its center primarily describes the distress of the present era, but which already anticipates judgment against the nations in the near future. A problem of this view remains the identification of the time in Mic 5:4 and 5:6. In fact, both are introduced by "and it will be" (והיה), which could indicate a future perspective but is not directly connected with "in that day" (ביום ההוא). Therefore Gärtner wants to assume a *third level of time* here which is situated between the present time described and that future time.[20] To me, this suggestion appears to be the most adequate view as will be confirmed by a contextual reading of Micah within the setting provided by the books of Jonah and Nahum.

In summary, we can say that the diversity of themes in Mic 4–5 is explained on the level of the canonical text by situating the action in two different chronological levels: the present distress combined with Israel's triumph over its enemies, and a future pilgrimage of the nations, alongside a restitution of Israel that includes both the simultaneous return of the Diaspora under YHWH's kingship and a final purifi-

19　Wöhrle, *Sammlungen*, 159.
20　Gärtner, *Jesaja*, 169: "Mi 5,6f. zielt auf die Zeit zwischen Jetzt-Zeit und End-Zeit, wie es durch den Anschluss mit והיה an die Jetzt-Texte unterstrichen wird."

cation of Israel combined with a final judgment against those nations which are disobedient. In this context it is interesting that the pilgrimage of the nations and the judgment against the nations are obviously regarded as two eschatological alternatives. This is a view that seems to be derived from the Book of Isaiah, too, when comparing, for example, the close relations between Isa 2:1–4, which is the nations' pilgrimage to Zion, and Isa 13, where a judgment against Babylon widens to a universal judgment.[21]

We now turn to Mic 7 skipping Mic 6 due to limited space. Mic 6:1–8 may have been the conclusion of an earlier version of the Book of Micah,[22] and in the present textual flow of Micah, it can be read as a more detailed description of YHWH's final purifying judgment on his people.

During the past years Micah 7, the concluding chapter of Micah, has attracted increased interest among scholars too. To a certain degree, agreement has been reached in so far as a redaction-critical distinction has to be made between Mic 7:1–7 and Mic 7:8–20.[23] As noted by Jeremias, Mic 7:1–7 is a text composed in view of and as an updating of Mic 3.[24] Continuing, Mic 7:4 is likely to be a later supplement providing a link with the future days mentioned in Mic 7:11–12.[25]

Another point of wide agreement is that Mic 7:8–20 is not, as was formerly assumed, a liturgical piece of text which once had been handed down independently[26] but a concluding text composed for Micah referring in various ways to the present text of Micah and intended to be read – at least at its end – as a kind of liturgical response of Israel responding to the text of Micah.[27] Various authors of more recent studies understand Mic 7:8–20 theologically as an overarching tie providing the material unity of Micah.[28] Thus numerous catchword and thematic

21 Cf. Zapff, *Prophetie*, 27.32.314.
22 The exegetical judgments of the literary character of this text are quite differing: Schart, *Entstehung*, 204, counts Mic 6:2–16* to the "D-Redaktion," whereas Jeremias, *Propheten*, 120, thinks that Mic 6:1–8 is a postexilic redactional expansion of the book of Micah independent of Mic 4–5. Further expansions were added to it in Mic 6:9–16 and 7:1–7. According to Kessler, *Micha*, 47, Mic 6:1–7:7 is an expansion originating from a former edition of the book of Micah (Mic 1–5) in the Persian period; Wöhrle, *Sammlungen*, takes a differing view and counts Mic 7:1–7 already to the first layer of the Book of Micah, whereas some parts of Mic 6 (6:2–4a, 9aαb, 10–15) belong to a later so-called "dtr. redactional expansion."
23 Cf. Zapff, *Studien*, 128ff.
24 Jeremias, *Propheten*, 213: "Deutlicher noch als 6,1–8 will 7,1–7 aktualisierende Auslegung von Mi 3 bieten."
25 Zapff, *Studien*, 215.
26 Stade, "Streiflichter," 164–171; Gunkel, "Michaschluß," 16.
27 Zapff, *Studien*, 213–236.
28 Jeremias, *Propheten*, 219.

links can be found between Micah 7 and the core of Micah.[29] The
redactional history of Mic 7:8–20 now as before remains a matter of
dispute.[30] More recent studies here tend to assume a stage-by-stage
process of text growth in which later supplements of the type of
redactional expansions directly refer to already existing texts. Such
relations can especially be observed between Mic 7:8–10 and 7:14–17, a
fact already noted by Renaud.[31] Thus the gloomy description of Zion's
situation in v. 8 "when I sit in darkness" (כי אשב בחשך) corresponds to
v. 14b, which tells about those who "solitarily dwell in the forest" (שכני
לבדד יער). Equally in v. 9c Zion's confidence that YHWH will lead her
to the light (יוציאני לאור), fits the commemoration of the days of the
Exodus from Egypt expressed in v. 15a: כימי צאתך מארץ מצרים. Finally the humiliation of the female enemy in v. 10a, too, has an equivalent
in the humiliation of the nations, which according to v. 17a shall "lick
the dust like a serpent" (ילחכו עפר כנחש). The series of equivalents
could be continued.[32] Nonetheless Jeremias is right to note a number of
differences, too, such as the fact that only Zion's female enemy is quoted as giving a lampooning speech about Zion's fall but not the nations,
as well as the fact that the fate of the nations is evaluated in a much
more lenient manner than that of the hostile woman.[33] From this perspective Jeremias draws the conclusion that Mic 7:14–17 is a later
redactional expansion of Mic 7:8–10 that seeks to include the nations,
whereas I have considered the two texts as a literary unity. In my opinion, this question cannot be answered by a view of the text which is
limited to the Book of Micah. Rather, the relations between the acrostic
in Nah 1:2–8 and Mic 7 are to be taken into consideration. From this
vantage point, one may propose, on the one hand, that Micah 7 was
written with regard to this semi-acrostic, but also the other way round
that the semi-acrostic was adapted in some instances in context with
the insertion of Mic 7:8–20.[34] An interesting question is that of the relationship between the female enemy's lampooning speech as cited in
Mic 7:10b and Joel 2:17d. As was seen by Wöhrle,[35] the latter passage
puts that lampoon "Where is their God?" into the mouth of the nations.
By contrast, Mic 7:10b limits the speech to Zion's female enemy, which
results in a more positive view of the nations and leads to their conversion to YHWH in v. 17.

---

29   Cf. Zapff, *Studien*, 232–236.
30   Cf. Wöhrle, *Abschluss*, 140.400.
31   Renaud, *Formation*, 370.
32   Cf. Zapff, *Studien*, 208–209.
33   Jeremias, *Propheten*, 223.
34   Cf. Zapff, *Studien*, 268–273.
35   Wöhrle, *Sammlungen*, 388.

More problematic, however, is the understanding of Mic 7:11–13. The conclusion that Micah 7:11 is intended to be read in the context of the previous verse becomes clear from two essential observations. First, the emphatically positioned expression "now" (עתה) in v. 10d is important here. This expression is separated from "day" (יום) in v. 11a and from "that day" (יום הוא) in v. 12a. By this means two levels of time are again introduced. Being connected by catchword, "the day" here obviously relates to the "day of your watchmen" mentioned in Mic 7:4b. Second, we have to note the scribal reference from v. 10 and 11 to Isa 5:5 using the catchwords "now" (עתה); "into what has been trampled underfoot" (למרמס), and "your wall/his wall" (גדריך/ו). The two catchwords "into what has been trampled underfoot" and "wall" are resumed in reverse order here, and the rebuilding of Zion's wall is contrasted with the breaking down of the vine's wall in Isa 5:5. In Micah, by contrast, it is Zion's enemy who turns "into what has been trampled underfoot" as had happened to Zion previously. In contrast to Jeremias[36] I consider it quite improbable in this context that the scribal reference to Isa 5:5 should only have been created by means of v. 11 and its contrast between Zion's fate and that of her enemy. In fact, already on the level of v. 10a–c, the fate of Zion's enemy is similarly contrasted with that of Zion. This is last but not least indicated by the catchword connection established between v. 10a and 10c through ראה, which sets Zion's triumphant seeing against the enemy's seeing.

The distinction of time introduced through Mic 7:10d and v. 11a clearly reminds one of what we have already encountered in Mic 4–5. With respect to their contents, Mic 7:11–12 are considered among the most difficult verses of Micah and have been subject to differing interpretations due to grave text-critical problems.[37] But, in fact, their subject seems to be a restoration of Zion and a return of the Diaspora communities. The latter assumption particularly suggests itself because of the similarity with Isa 27:13.[38]

Another big problem is v. 13. The verse announces a judgment that will leave the earth as a desert. Even if one qualifies this verse, as does Jeremias, by means of literary critical arguments as a later supplement critical of the nations, one cannot avoid asking what the supplementing author may have had in mind regarding its relationship to the subsequent text which not only speaks about humiliation but also about a conversion of the nations. We may here have a modified version of the concept of a distinction between nations subject to judgment and saved

36 Jeremias, *Propheten*, 226.
37 Cf. Nogalski, *Precursors*, 167; Wöhrle, *Sammlungen*, 181–185.
38 Cf. Zapff, *Studien*, 186.

nations. That distinction is known from Mic 4–5, although its sense would now be that the nations saved are those which have escaped the judgment and converted to YHWH. Its background could be a corresponding concept which is found in tritoisaianic redactional expansions.[39]

Finally, the fourth section Mic 7:18–20 is seen by many of the recent studies as a further supplement in the sense of a redactional expansion dating from the Hellenistic era. Both Jeremias and Wöhrle count this text as one of the latest adaptations of Micah.[40] Within the book, Mic 7:18–20 refers to the opening passage (Mic 1:2–7) by treating the subject matter of Israel's sin and by appealing to YHWH's forgiveness in view of his judgment announced there because of Israel's sin.[41] Moreover, reference is made to the guilt which has been the subject matter of Mic 7:9. In this context, Jeremias discerns a clear theological discrepancy within Mic 7:8–20. In v. 9, Israel's guilt is considered to have been paid for by the experience of the exile, whereas v. 18–20 state that YHWH's unmerited willingness to forgive sins is the reason Israel is still alive.[42] But such a discrepancy cannot be established based upon v. 9. This verse only deals with Zion "bearing YHWH's wrath." This fact, however, causes a further action of YHWH that leads Israel to the light. No mention is made here of Israel having paid for its guilt. This situation corresponds exactly with the idea found in v. 18, which states that YHWH does not retain his anger but will now carry the burden of guilt.

The conclusion to be drawn regarding the possible redaction history of Mic 7 is that, because of the relevant texts being tightly interwoven with each other, the usual instruments of literary and redaction criticism do not allow one to identify Mic 7:8–20 beyond doubt either as a text forming a literary unit or as a product of various redactional expansions. A synchronic reading of the text reveals the following structure. First, we obviously have a distinction here between various levels of time. Thus the "day of your watchmen" mentioned in Mic 7:4b refers to a day of judgment whose consequences are depicted in Mic 7:8–10. The humiliation of Zion's enemy in v. 10, by contrast, seems to relate to the present whereas in v. 11–12 the day of Zion's restoration and the return of the Diaspora describes a moment in the future. Also situated in future are obviously the humiliation of the nations and their conversion to YHWH in v. 14–17.

---

39   Cf. Isa 66:19–20.
40   Jeremias, *Propheten*, 121; Wöhrle, *Abschluss*, 403–404: "zweite Hälfte des 3.Jh."
41   Jeremias, *Propheten*, 230; Kessler, *Micha*, 309–310.
42   Jeremias, *Propheten*, 223–224.

A comparison of this statement with Micah 4–5 reveals both common features and significant differences. Corresponding elements are found in Mic 4:11bβ and Mic 7:10d. Thus, in the first passage the nations want to feast their eyes on Zion (ותחז בציון עינינו) whereas in 7:10d Zion expects exactly the same for herself: "My eyes shall feast on her" (עיני תראינה בה). The fact that the root חזה is here replaced by ראה results from the catchword connection within the verse, where, as already explained, the enemy's "seeing" corresponds with Zion's "seeing." A notable difference is that Mic 4 and 5 do not mention a past day of judgment but only the consequences of the judgment from which Zion is suffering. In Micah 7 a distinction is made, but this time not between the nations who are disobedient and those who are obviously obedient, but between a female enemy who at first remains anonymous and the nations which, after a universal judgment and their own humiliation, *altogether* convert to YHWH. Yet, a characteristic common to both passages is the fact that the events described take place on two different levels of time.

When we try to read Micah 4–5 and 7 in their full context, then the nations' behavior and their respective fates, which are originally meant to be an alternative, develop to the effect that in the end it is only Zion's "enemy" who perishes. By contrast, Mic 5:14 and 7:13 together with Mic 7:17b state that each of the nations convert to YHWH after a final judgment. This conception will be reaffirmed by a contextual reading of the Book of Micah, as I would like to show in my next point.

In a second step I will turn to the question of possible relationship between the book of Micah and its current context in the Book of the Twelve according to the Masoretic order.

b) The question of the relationship between a book of Micah and a book of several or twelve prophets is answered by scholars in quite different ways. This is not least due to the problem that it is not certain whether the sequence of the scriptures in the Hebrew Bible is original, and whether the sequence had quasi canonical authority and thus intentionally provided a certain direction of reading. This uncertainty also explains the caution exercised in a number of more recent publications when it comes to reading and understanding Micah in an overarching context. This finds expression in two recent German commentaries on Micah. Kessler, for example, treats this problem in a three-page chapter of his commentary, where he very briefly gives a subtly differentiated sketch of the problem and lists a number of possible points of reference between the scripture of Micah and scriptures of the later Book of the Twelve.[43] One of these is, for example, the above-mentioned description of the judgment against Samaria in the opening chapter of Micah, which according to Kessler is not comprehensible without previously reading Hosea and Amos.[44] Further, he notes an interesting characteristic of the use of the Grace Formula in Mic 7:18–19, which according to him is likely to have been written with knowledge of Amos 7:8.[45] Even more cautious on this point than Kessler is Jeremias, who touches this question in only few passages and argues in his introduction that the final redactor's negative statements about the nations – which according to him include Mic 1:2; 5:8, 14; 6:1 and 7:13 – have to be read from the perspective of the entire Book of the Twelve.[46]

A different point of view has been advanced by authors such as Nogalski, Schart, and most recently Wöhrle. They have in common that they want to understand redaction-historical processes within the Book of Micah against the background of the growth of a book comprising several of the Prophets or, respectively, of the Book of the Twelve. A still different approach to the point has been chosen by Scoralick, who reads the Scripture of Micah in the current context of the Book of the Twelve and largely dispenses with the application of diachronic questions, yet without denying their possibility.[47]

With reference to these works and to the results of the studies about the scripture of Micah concisely described in the preceding point, the following statements can be made. There is no doubt that the scripture of Micah in its present form displays a clear ambivalence in respect of the nations' behavior and future fate. This is underlined by the above-mentioned framework of the book as found in Mic 1:2 and Mic 5:14, where the subject matter concerns nations called to listen or, respectively, nations refusing to follow this call and therefore subjugated to YHWH's judgment. If, as is now mostly accepted, Mic 1:2 is really among the latest texts in Micah, then the question arises what the contents of the message to be "listened to" might be? When the analysis remains limited to the Book of Micah, then the answer follows to a certain degree from Mic 4–5, where indeed a universal perspective is opened relating to the nations' salvation and doom (compare especially the pilgrimage of the nations). The fact that the nations expect "torah" from YHWH suggests a concept of listening which generally corre-

---

43   Kessler, *Micha*, 51–53.
44   Kessler, *Micha*, 52.
45   Kessler, *Micha*, 52.
46   Jeremias, *Propheten*, 121.
47   Scoralick, *Güte*, 207.

sponds to Deuteronomistic usage of the word. Although this may not
be the equivalent of the original use of "torah" in Mic 4:2, it may well
be a later comprehension of this text by the redactor responsible.

Strikingly, Micah is surrounded by two writings (Jonah and Nahum) which reflect precisely this same ambivalence about the nations'
fate. Due to their present canonical positions they may be called something like paradigms for possible future fates of the nations: either salvation or doom. In this context, however, Mic 7:8–20 unfolds a scene in
which after a judgment *all* the remaining nations convert to YHWH
whereas, according to Nahum, Nineveh will perish. Against this background Jonah's position before Nahum implies that this sequence not
only proposes alternatives that the nations are facing but also the *difference* between Nineveh's behavior and that of the nations. These nations
convert to YHWH according to Mic 7:17, whereas Nineveh's conversion is only of a limited duration so that the city falls into definite destruction. Yet, this distinction is also expressed in Mic 7:8–20, where the
fate of Zion's enemy is contrasted with that of the rest of the nations. In
my opinion the resulting conclusion is that Zion's anonymous enemy
in Mic 7:8–10 should indeed be identified with Nineveh.[48]

Next I would like to show that this interpretation, which is founded
on the current sequence of the writings, can also be confirmed by observations relating to details, namely that there are noticeable relationships between Jonah and Micah. For example: Zion is characterized in
Mic 7:8–20 in a similar way as in Jonah.[49] The relationships primarily
concern the characterization of Jonah in the psalm of Jonah (2:3–10).
Thus, for example, Zion's confidence that YHWH will lead her to the
light has an analogy in the psalm of Jonah when Jonah confesses that
YHWH will bring him up from the grave. Jonah's turning to YHWH, as
depicted in Jonah 2:3–10, is the precondition for Nineveh's conversion
and salvation to be initiated by the prophetic message of doom. Similar
considerations analogously apply to Zion's confession of confidence in
Mic 7:8–9, which through Zion's salvation becomes a precondition of
the nations' conversion to YHWH. Scholarly studies have repeatedly
noted the two catchword connections between Mic 7:19b and Jonah
2:4a:[50] "you have cast all our sins into the depths of the sea" (ותשליך
במצלות ים כל חטאותם) and "you cast me into the deep, into the heart
of the seas" (ותשליכני מצולה בלבב ימים), as well as the fact that both
Jonah and Micah contain references to the grace formula in Exod 34:6–7
(compare Jonah 4:2 and Mic 7:18). Concerning the redactional history, it

48 Against Jeremias, *Propheten*, 224, who thinks of Edom for tradition-historical reasons.
49 Cf. Zapff, *Studien*, 259–261.
50 Nogalski, *Precursors*, 153; Scoralick, *Güte*, 184.

can be inferred from this relationship that both Jonah and Micah have been subject to redactional adaptations made in relation to each other.

Similar observations can be made in the semi-acrostic poem of Nahum, which, according to the evidence given by Nogalski, has catchword connections with Micah 7.[51] There are two connections to be mentioned which are particularly prominent. The first one is the reference of Nah 1:2+3a to the formula of grace in Ex 34:6–7, which includes some characteristic modifications,[52] and the second one is the use of the catchword "enemy" אֹיֵב in Nah 1:2b, which is also found in Mic 7:8 and 10. A striking feature of the latter is that "enemies" now occur in the plural and have a personal suffix. Obviously, Nah 1:2b adds the enemy of Zion to the number of YHWH's enemies. The one who is Zion's enemy is equally YHWH's enemy. By referring to the grace formula both an intense link with the final passage of Micah and a connection with Jonah are established so that this threefold use of the grace formula, which simultaneously modifies the formula, results in one integral message: YHWH grants his grace for an honest conversion, even to Nineveh, YHWH grants his grace to his people by virtue of his oath to the fathers, but YHWH refuses to grant his grace to his enemies including the enemies of Zion.[53]

From this point new light may be shed upon Mic 5:6–7. If Israel were to be understood as a collective Jonah and, conversely, if Jonah in the Psalm of Jonah as a collective character representing Israel, then the attitude towards him would be decisive for a future salvation.

2. The Book of Micah as the Theological Center of the Book of the Twelve?

On the basis of these observations I will conclude with a number of statements concerning the question which is the title of this contribution: Is the Book of Micah a kind of theological *center* of the Book of the Twelve? Indeed it is striking that references to the so-called grace formula in Exod 34:6–7 manifest themselves in various writings within the Book of the Twelve. In this context, Wöhrle maintains that references to the grace formula can be observed not only in Joel, Jonah, Micah and

---

51 Cf. Nogalski, *Processes*, 107–111.115–117; Zapff, *Studien*, 268–273.
52 Scoralick, *Güte*, 194, is right to stress the contrast between the wording of Nah 1:2 and that of Mic 7:18. Thus YHWH's intervention in favor his people and against its enemy is accentuated in so far as the enemy of his people becomes the enemy of YHWH himself.
53 Cf. Zapff, *Studien*, 273–276.

Nahum but also in Malachi 1:9a,[54] where it says: "And now, I pray you, entreat the face of God, *that he may be gracious to us*" (וְעַתָּה חַלּוּ־נָא פְנֵי־אֵל וִיחָנֵנוּ). Additionally, Scoralick considers that a thematic reference to the divine predicates of Exod 34:6–7, which is intensified by linguistic affinities, can also be noted in the Book of Hosea.[55] Accordingly the Book of the Twelve would be marked by references to the grace formula in its opening, middle and concluding parts, with a conspicuous accumulation in the areas of Jonah, Micah and Nahum. The center of the Book of the Twelve would thus, through the example of Nineveh, clarify the question of a correct understanding of the grace formula with respect to Israel and the nations. Since Israel, which has been humiliated by the events of the exile, recognizes its guilt and is able to refer to the promises given to the fathers, it will enhance its future prospects as well as find forgiveness thanks to the grace formula. Similar gifts may even be obtained by Nineveh, which embodies all that is opposed to YHWH and Israel, if Nineveh's conversion is honest and lasting. In the opposite case, Nineveh will be subject to doom.

Besides this question, which is answered in a central passage of the Book of the Twelve, one should note that Micah treats other core themes of the Book of the Twelve, too. One of these concerns the future prospects of Israel and Zion. In Micah the doom descending upon Samaria and Jerusalem comes to a provisional end (see Mic 3:12). With the pilgrimage of the nations to Mount Zion, which is placed in a position marking a turning point, a radical change takes place beginning in Mic 4. This change continues with the restoration of Zion expected in Mic 7. In fact, from the book of Micah onward the thematic focus is generally, although not exclusively, on the restoration of Zion/Israel and the return of the Diaspora. Indeed, it appears repeatedly and with increasing intensity. Here I would only point to Nah 2:1–2, the final passage of Zephaniah (3:14–20), and, of course, Haggai and the final passage of Zechariah. Thus, also in this respect, Micah seems to be a kind of *dividing line* in the Book of the Twelve.

Finally, only in Micah are the relationship and the future prospects between the nations and Israel so carefully taken into consideration. It is notable that, beyond the expectation of an imminent judgment against the nations, the future prospects of salvation are also developed in favor of some portion of the nations. Interestingly, this subject matter

---

54 Wöhrle, *Abschluss*, 404.
55 Scoralick, *Güte*, 160: "Der Bezug auf die Gottesprädikationen aus Ex 34,6f. ist auf inhaltlicher Ebene deutlich und wird durch sprachliche Berührungspunkte verstärkt. Es bleibt jedoch bei Andeutungen."

is once more set out in the final passages of Zephaniah and Zechariah.[56] In both instances, a prospect of salvation is held out after a message of doom against the nations. Eventually, the end of Micah (combined with Nahum) continues and resolves the issue concerning a nation whose bitter hostility against Zion causes it to perish.

Last but not least, within Micah, the nations' prospect of salvation is accompanied by a final purification of Israel. This concept is also echoed at the end of the Book of the Twelve in Mal 3.

So Micah may indeed be characterized as a kind of *center* of the Book of the Twelve due to both its subject matter and its position, which is marked by the grace formula. A striking feature is the fact that, in various ways, Micah is marked by the influence of the Book of Isaiah, as has been illustrated. Even if the question of the original location of the text about the pilgrimage of the nations is left open,[57] at least the sequence of judgment against Israel, exile, and judgment against the nations combined with the distinction between the nations regarding their judgment or salvation reminds one of theological lines which are also found in prominent locations within Isaiah, namely in the redactional expansions of Trito-Isaiah. If the Book of Isaiah is considered as a kind of compendium of Israel's prophecy, then this also applies to a certain degree to its smaller and younger brother, the book of Micah. From this point of view, I would only like to emphasize a desideratum concerning the further research on Micah which Kessler has already formulated in his commentary.[58] When concentrating on the relations between Micah and the Book of the Twelve, interpreters should not neglect its relationship to the tradition of Isaiah. As the studies of Steck,[59] Bosshard-Nepustil,[60] and Gärtner[61] have shown, the Book of the Twelve seems to have been adapted to its final form within similar theological circles as the Book of Isaiah. Obviously Isaiah was seen as something like the perfect example of prophecy. Therefore it is not surprising that such a composition inspired by Isaiah is also found in the center of the Book of the Twelve. Thus, Micah represents something like a reminder of important statements of the Book of Isaiah within the Book of the Twelve.

---

56   Cf. Gärtner, *Jesaja*, 324.326, who speaks of a thematic distinction between the nations' assault and the nations' pilgrimage to Mount Zion in Zech 14.
57   For the discussion cf. Zapff, *Studien*, 64–74; Wöhrle, *Abschluss*, 346–351.
58   Kessler, *Micha*, 51.
59   Steck, *Abschluß*.
60   Bosshard, "Beobachtungen;" idem, *Rezeptionen*.
61   Gärtner, *Jesaja*.

References

Bosshard, E. "Beobachtungen zum Zwölfprophetenbuch." *BN* 40 (1987) 30–62.

Bosshard-Nepustil, E. *Rezeptionen von Jesaia 1–39 im Zwölfprophetenbuch: Untersuchungen zur literarischen Verbindung von Prophetenbüchern in babylonischer und persischer Zeit.* OBO 154. Fribourg: Universitätsverlag and Göttingen: Vandenhoeck & Ruprecht, 1997.

Cuffey, K.H. *The Coherence of Micah: A Review of the Proposal and a New Interpretation.* Diss. Drew University, 1987.

Gärtner, J. *Jesaja 66 und Sacharja 14 als Summe der Prophetie: Eine traditions- und redaktionsgeschichtliche Untersuchung zum Abschluss des Jesaja- und des Zwölfprophetenbuches.* WMANT 114. Neukirchen-Vluyn: Neukirchener, 2006.

Gunkel, H. "Der Micha-Schluß: Zur Einführung in die literaturgeschichtliche Arbeit am AT" *ZS* (1924) 145–178.

Jeremias, J. *Die Propheten Joel, Obadja, Jona, Micha.* ATD 24,3. Göttingen: Vandenhoeck & Ruprecht, 2007.

Kessler, R. *Micha,* Herders theologischer Kommentar zum Alten Testament, Freiburg: Herder, 1999.

– "Das Buch Micha als Mitte des Zwölfprophetenbuchs: Einzeltext, redaktionelle Intention und kontextuelle Lektüre." Pp. 139–148 in *"Wort JHWHs, das geschah…" (Hos 1,1).* Edited by E. Zenger. Herders biblische Studien 35. Freiburg: Herder, 2002.

Lescow, T. "Redaktionsgeschichtliche Analyse von Micha 1–5." *ZAW* 84 (1972) 46–85.

Mays, J.L. *Micah. A Commentary.* OTL. Philadelphia: Westminster John Knox, 1976.

– "The Theological Purpose of the Book of Micah." Pp. 276–288 in *Beiträge zur alttestamentlichen Theologie.* Edited by H. Donner et. al. FS W. Zimmerli. Göttingen: Vandenhoeck & Ruprecht, 1977.

Metzner, G. *Kompositionsgeschichte des Michabuches.* Europäische Hochschulschriften 635. Frankfurt: Lang, 1998.

Nogalski, J.D. *Literary Precursors to the Book of the Twelve.* BZAW 217. Berlin: de Gruyter, 1993.

– *Redactional Processes in the Book of the Twelve.* BZAW 218. Berlin: de Gruyter, 1993.

Renaud, B. *La formation du livre de Michée: Tradition et Actualisation.* EtB. Paris: Librairie Lecoffre, 1977.

Roth, M. *Israel und die Völker im Zwölfprophetenbuch: Eine Untersuchung zu den Büchern Joel, Jona, Micha und Nahum.* FRLANT 210. Göttingen: Vandenhoeck & Ruprecht, 2005.

Schart, A. *Die Entstehung des Zwölfprophetenbuchs: Neubearbeitungen von Amos im Rahmen schriftenübergreifender Redaktionsprozesse.* BZAW 260. Berlin: de Gruyter, 1998.

Scoralick, R. *Gottes Güte und Gottes Zorn: Die Gottesprädikationen in Ex 34,6f. und ihre intertextuellen Beziehungen zum Zwölfprophetenbuch.* Herders biblische Studien 33. Freiburg: Herder, 2002.

Stade, B. "Bemerkungen über das Buch Micha." *ZAW* 1 (1881) 161–172.

–   "Streiflichter auf die Entstehung der jetzigen Gestalt der alttestamentlichen Prophetenschriften." *ZAW* 93 (1903) 153–171.

Steck, O.H. *Der Abschluß der Prophetie im Alten Testament: Ein Versuch zur Frage der Vorgeschichte des Kanons.* Biblisch-Theologische Studien 17. Neukirchen-Vluyn: Neukirchener, 1991.

van der Woude, A.S. "Micah in Dispute with the Pseudoprophets." *VT* 19 (1969) 244–260.

Vermeylen, J. *Du Prophète Isaïe à l`Apocalyptique: Isaïe, I-XXXV, miroir d' un demimillénaire d'expérience religieuse en Israël.* 2 vols. EBib. Paris: Librairie Lecoffre, 1978.

Wöhrle, J. *Die frühen Sammlungen des Zwölfprophetenbuches: Entstehung und Komposition.* BZAW 360. Berlin: de Gruyter, 2006.

–   *Der Abschluss des Zwölfprophetenbuches: Buchübergreifende Redaktionsprozesse in den späten Sammlungen.* BZAW 389. Berlin: de Gruyter, 2008.

Zapff, B.M. *Schriftgelehrte Prophetie – Jes 13 und die Komposition des Jesajabuches: Ein Beitrag zur Erforschung der Redaktionsgeschichte des Jesajabuches.* FB 74. Würzburg: Echter, 1995.

–   *Redaktionsgeschichtliche Studien zum Michabuch im Kontext des Dodekapropheton.* BZAW 256. Berlin: de Gruyter, 1997.

–   "Die Völkerperspektive des Michabuches als 'Systematisierung' der divergierdenden Sicht der Völker in den Büchern Joel, Jona und Nahum? Überlegungen zu einer buchübergreifenden Exegese im Dodekapropheton." *BN* 98 (1999) 86–99.

Three Minor Prophets and the Major Empires: Synchronic and Diachronic Perspectives on Nahum, Habakkuk, and Zephaniah

Universität Bern

The twelve books of the Dodekapropheton are basically chronologically arranged. Even though there are differences between the Hebrew and the Greek Bible in the first half of the book, namely in the positioning of Joel and Micah, in both the MT and LXX each of the six prophets was understood to be acting in the period of time when both Israel and Judah existed. In the second half of the book, where the orders of both canonical versions correspond with one another, there was apparently no doubt concerning the chronologic attribution. The last three books (Hag–Zech–Mal) represent the Persian times, while the three books in front of them (Nah–Hab–Zeph) represent the time of Assyrian and Babylonian sovereignty over Judah, after Israel no longer existed.

This assignment is understandable. In Nah–Hab–Zeph the kingdom of Israel no longer plays a role. Judah stands alone while the Neo-Assyrian and Neo-Babylonian empires oppose it. The opponent is present in Nah and Zeph under the name "Assyria" (Nah 3:18; Zeph 2:13), but mainly in the guise of its capital Nineveh (Nah 2–3; Zeph 2:13–15).[1] In comparison, the "Chaldeans" appear on the scene in Hab (1:6), a term used for the Neo-Babylonian empire in Jer as well.

Though the classification of Nah–Hab–Zeph into the Assyrian-Babylonian era makes complete sense, the order of the books startles: Why is Hab, where Babylon is the opponent, placed *between* Nah and Zeph, which are about Assyria, and not placed *after* them? We can try to obtain answers by first conducting a synchronic analysis and afterwards a diachronic analysis.

---

1   Nineveh was the Assyrian capital since King Sennacherib (705–681).

1. Synchronic Reading –
or: The Northern Great Empire in Nah–Hab–Zeph

There is no doubt among scholars that a book of *twelve* prophets didn't exist before the late-Persian, possibly the Hellenistic times. From the Assyrian and Babylonian era in the history of Judah, which is treated in Nah–Hab–Zeph, this means a chronological span of up to half a millennium! It is quite conceivable that the contours of both Mesopotamian empires (Assyria and Babylon) had merged by that time. The endpoint of this development can be seen in the book of Daniel, originating in the second century. In both visions of Dan 2 and Dan 7, the seer envisions four empires. The first one (the most precious by comparison) is identified explicitly with Nebuchadnezzar's Babylon (Dan 2:38). The following kingdoms are then associated with Media, Persia, and Hellas. Assyria has vanished from sight, or disappeared from memory, even though the first animal in the second vision is a winged lion (Dan 7:4), a symbol well known from Assyrian (as well as Babylonian) iconography. It was different for Herodotus (around 470 B.C.E.), with whom the world empire visions in Dan share extensive material. For him, the first of the world empire is the (Neo-)Assyrian, the second the Median (not the Babylonian!), and the third the Persian.[2]

One explanation for the conspicuous sequence of Nah–Hab–Zeph could be that the historical sequence Assyria–Babylonia(–Persia) faded from the collective Jewish memory as time passed. "Nineveh" and "the Chaldeans" would then stand equally for a previous great Mesopotamian empire that cast its shadow over the history of Judah. Thus considered, the order Nah/Assyria – Hab/Babylon – Zeph/Assyria could be held as almost artificial, because they would form some kind of an *inclusio*: a popular device for the composition of exactly the prophetic traditional material as well.[3]

Of course the great northern empire doesn't always play the same role in Nah, Hab and Zeph. Moreover, a chiasmus appears. In Nah 2–3 the prophet, quite angry, attacks the Assyrian metropolis as immoderately greedy and unscrupulously immoral and imagines how the unprincipled, proud city will soon be humiliated and plundered. In Hab

---

2   Herodotus I 95.130; cf. Koch, *Daniel 1–4*, 203, with the presumption that the Greek Historian drew this out of Persian sources (and, if so, above all the year dates: 520 years for the Assyrians, 128 for the Medes, then the Persians).

3   Cf. only Hos 1 / 2 / 3; Amos 1–2 / 3–6 / 7–9. For Micah cf. Otto, "Techniken," 119–150. Chiastic or concentric compositions can as well be observed in the redaction of legal literature (e.g. the Covenant Code Exod 21–23) or in narrative literature (e.g. the stories of Jacob Gen 27–33 or the narration of Absalom's riot 2 Sam 16–19).

1:5–10 the prophet learns in an auditory experience that the Chaldeans would move forward with irresistible military power, with God's consent. In Zeph 2:13–15 again, the prophet threatens Assyria and its capital, which says in a boastful way about itself: "Me and none else!" Viewing this sequence synchronically and with the assumption that the redactors remembered only *one* Mesopotamian major power, then they draw here a subtle historical picture. To become fully aware of this, Jonah, the preceding book (in both canonical versions) has to be included. Already in this book, which is set fictively in the time of Jeroboam II, i.e., before the encroachment of Assyria into the southern Levant,[4] the metropolis Nineveh appears full of "spite" (Jonah 1:2). Admittedly God succeeds, with the reluctant help of Jonah, in causing the Ninevites to turn around, whereupon God can spare them. However, the conversion did not last. Why else would Assyria have attacked Israel and Judah and provoked Nahum's rage against the "whore" Nineveh?

Sure enough, the Anti-Nineveh-Texts in Nah 2–3 are not declared to be God's word; instead the prophet speaks in understandable outrage. But then, in Hab 1, God himself speaks – and he doesn't hold out the prospect of the complete and immediate destruction of the horrible enemy, but its irresistible intrusion! In the end of his auditory experience, the prophet learns that the arrival of the superpower would be of a passing nature; it would be wrecked by its own self-apotheosis (... "his God is his own power," 1:11). Zeph 2 builds on this understanding. Assyria and Nineveh effectively form the target and the end point in a series of words of God, which are directed against the enemies in the west, east, south, and north. This goal means God even puts a stop to this greatest and most dangerous hostile power of all.

Consecutively and synchronically read, the statements about the great northern empire in Nah–Hab–Zeph lead to the following proposition: Judah had every reason to be very much afraid of the empire and hoped, understandably, that God would disable this major power in time (Nah). But God decided to give it a free hand (Hab). In the end, however, divine judgment had to strike it (Zeph). This is an unveiled theodicy regarding God's seeming inaction facing the decay of the states of Israel. The Hab judgment happened not because the major power was insurmountable or because Yahweh was powerless. Instead it was part of the plan of history to let the horrible enemy do as he liked for some time. God's own people should first be chastised, but then their tormentor should be wiped out.

---

4   Cf. 2 Kgs 14:24 and Dietrich, "Ninive," 239–254.

The creators of the Book of the Twelve probably thought this course of action eye-opening, not only regarding the past, meaning the Assyro-Babylonian era, but also subsequently. In the same way as the Mesopotamian major power had to carry out harmful, but time-limited action against Israel, after which God withdrew the power from them, Israel could count on the final end of every further foreign rule, whether it be the Persians or the Greeks. The visions in Dan 2 and 7 get to the heart of this insight: no global empire is eternal; moreover, the time of this world will end.

The sequence of Nah–Hab–Zeph might be interpreted this way while reading synchronically. But of course, there are also reasons for the assuming that those composing the Book of the Twelve weren't completely free to choose the order of the books and that the proffered reflections weren't *causal* for the sequence Nah–Hab–Zeph. Rather, the sequence just appears afterwards as meaningful.

2. Diachronic Analysis –
or: The Great Empires Assur and Babylon
in Nahum, Habakkuk and Zephaniah

There exists large consensus among scholars that the redactional processes which led in the end to the Dodekapropheton began well before the Persian or the Hellenistic era. Theses about a Two-prophets-book (Hos–Am) in the 7th century, which was enlarged to a Four-prophets-book (Hos–Am–Mi–Zeph) in the 6th century,[5] and was completed with a Two-prophets-book Hag–PrSach in the 5th century have found a wide agreement.

If this consensus is accurate, Zeph would have been involved at a quite early stage in the emerging prophetic anthology.[6] But it remains open when Nah and Hab were added and why they were placed *before* Zeph. To answer this question, the history of origins of Nah and Hab has to be considered.

In my opinion,[7] the prophet *Nahum* acted around mid-7th-century, when the Assyrian empire was still fully intact, but was already being shaken by the murderous civil war between the Assyrian king Ashur-

---

5   In favour of this hypothesis argue many authors, from Wolfe, "Editing," 90–130, to Wöhrle, "Future," 608–627. But see the recent objections of Levin, "Vierprophetenbuch."

6   This conclusion does not prevent a later extension of the booklet, of course; but we can leave it at that here. Cf. to it Kessler, "Hinkende," 93–101. Cf. also Gerstenberger, "Hymnus," 102–112.

7   Cf. Dietrich, "Nahum / Nahumbuch," 737–742.

banipal and his brother Shamash-shum-ukin who resided in Babylon. Contrary to Nahum's hopes, Nineveh was not destroyed at that time. Judah was, and remained, firmly in the hand of the Assyrian footman Manasseh (696–641). Nahum's attacks turned against both: against the metropolis of the great empire (Nah 2:4–3:19) and against the ruling class in Judah, who borrowed its power from Assyria's might (which is still discernible in the current text of Nah 1:9–2:3). It need not be decided here whether Nahum originally recited his messages orally or whether he wrote them down literarily. Nevertheless, the poetically artificial Nineveh-poems let one think the latter.

The political situation in Judah changed quite soon after Manasseh's (late) death. His son and successor Amon became the victim of a palace coup after governing only one year, whereupon the Am-ha-aretz killed the king's murderer and placed the eight years old Josiah on the throne (2 Kgs 21:23–24). This group had existed at least since the removal of queen Athalia, i.e. since the mid-9th-century, as an active political group. The downfall of Assyrian power came about during Josiah's regnal period (639–609), and Judah disentangled itself from Assyria's shadow. A foreshadowing sign of this decline might have been Babylon's liberation from Assyrian rule under Nabopolassar in the year 625. Only three years later Josiah carried out his reform (was it a coincidence?). The reform acted on Deuteronomic maxims and seems to have led to the abolition of the Assyrian celestial cults.[8] In 612, Nineveh was destroyed and Nahum's expectation came true in a triumphal, but ghastly way.

Habakkuk, too, might have appeared and acted during the Assyrian era, probably a little bit later than Nahum. Habakkuk's attention wasn't directed toward the major power at first, but toward the ruling class in Judah. He stated, that it was committing "oppression and violence;" "torah" and "justice" had become powerless, and the "righteous one" was at the mercy of the "wrongdoer" (Hab 1:2–4). Unlike the prophets of the eighth century, Habakkuk does not speak directly to the men responsible (maybe this would have been far too dangerous under the regime of Manasseh), but he does lament before God. And God answers: The Chaldeans will rise and will overrun the land (1:5–8) – which probably means: within a short time the regime in Jerusalem along with the major power that supports it will be swept away.

Apparently, this announcement wasn't fulfilled as soon as the prophet had hoped.[9] So, again, he turns to God and asks in a reproach-

---

8   Cf. 2 Kgs 23 and the groundbreaking monograph of Spieckermann, *Juda*, esp. 71–138.
9   I.e., we are indeed still situated in the Assyrian era, which, for some in Judah, was going on way too long.

ful tone (Hab 1:12): "Haven't you been YHWH, my holy God, at all times?" The prophet continues: "You have appointed him to judge." To whom does the pronoun "him" refer? In my opinion it can only be Assyria. Assyria is mentioned also in Isa 10:5 as God's "rod of fury" and "stick of wrath," but there Assyria is also immediately accused of arbitrary acts and haughtiness and threatened with condemnation (Isa 10:5–15). In this sense, Habakkuk calls upon God, though he doesn't seem to have the major power in mind as much as its henchmen in Judah: "Your eyes are too pure to behold bad things and you are not able to watch hardship. Why do you watch the unfaithful and delay when the wrongdoer devours the righteous?" (Hab 1:12–13) Again, the prophet receives an answer: He should write down the "vision" – which means probably the announcement of the approaching of the Babylonians (1:5–8) –, because it will stay valid "until the determined time" (2:2–3). Thus YHWH undertakes the task of making sure that the Chaldeans will really come.

And how they came! In an unimaginably quick way, they took the Assyrian empire off its hinges. In Judah, the hope of better days arose. Deuteronomy, if it has been the guideline of Josiah's reform, contains not only cultic, but also social legislation, which largely accounts for the prophetic critique. But before this reform legislation could actually become effective, the Assyrian giant, which was itself falling, drew Judah into a political abyss. When, at Megiddo, Josiah faced Pharaoh Necho, who came to Assyria's aid, Necho "killed him, when he saw him" (2 Kgs 23:29). This sounds oddly casual, as if Josiah didn't have troops with him – or as if they would not have fought for him. Nonetheless, Necho couldn't save Assyria, just as he could not hinder Babylon from succeeding Assyria. Thus, Judah, after a short Egyptian interlude, came under Babylonian sovereignty with the well-known catastrophic ending.

What happened during the time of the Babylonian Exile to the heritage of Nahum and Habakkuk? With *Nah* it is obvious that wherever "Nineveh" is mentioned, "Babylon" was heard. But after they had been severely punished, the attacks on the Judean ruling classes were changed into a comforting message reminding one of Deutero-Isaiah's message of the liberation of Judah (from the Babylonian yoke): "Behold the feet of a messenger on the mountains, who announces peace. Celebrate, Judah, and fulfill your vows ... YHWH establishes again the sovereignty of Jacob" (Nah 2:1a, 3a; cf. Isa 52:7).

The *Hab*-tradition was submitted to a similar change during the exilic period. Its pro-Babylonian tone was turned into an anti-Babylonian one. The Chaldeans would no longer advance to put a stop to the exploiters within Judah, but "he" – probably the king of Babylon – now becomes an exploiter himself: "He comes for an act of violence;" "he gathers prisoners of war like sand;" "he laughs about every fortress;" "his power is his God" (Hab 1:9–11). Habakkuk's social critique was changed so that it did not target the local holders of power, but instead targeted the occupying power. For instance, whereas Habakkuk had threatened a ruthless (and certainly a Judean) collector of taxes (2:6–7), this exploiter becomes now one, who "has plundered many nations" and who will therefore soon be "plundered by the rest of the nations" (2:8). Of course, this refers to Babylon. Habakkuk had flung a "Woe!" against one who "builds a city on blood" (2:12) – an accusation that is raised in a different place against Manasseh.[10] But this woe now becomes a lament that someone lets "the nations labor for nothing" (2:13). Of course, this text again refers to Babylon. The series of woes in 2:6–17 was originally intended socio-critically, but it concludes with a polemic against idols that reminds one of Deutero-Isaiah. It is probably also directed against Babylon's pantheon (2:18–19).

With this polemic against idols, the exilic book of Hab ended. It would be more correct to say, the exilic book of Nah and Hab ended. Rainer Kessler[11] developed the thesis, and supported it with good arguments, that Nah and Hab – like Hos and Amos or Hag and PrZech – were combined together into a Two-prophets-book, before they were later included in the Book of the Twelve. In my opinion, this incorporation took place in the course of the described exilic reworking of both books. Thus, on the one hand, they also received the very similar, but elsewhere within the Dodekapropheton unique headings: "The burden over Nineveh, book of the vision of Nahum, the Elkoshite" (Nah 1:1) and: "The burden which Habakkuk the prophet saw" (Hab 1:1). The noun מַשָּׂא and the root חזה are linked in this way only here.[12] On the other hand, the names of the two speakers including the designation of origin of one of them ("from Elkosh") and the title of the other ("the prophet") might belong to the older traditional material.

The order of sequence of the two books is only logical: Nah had the Assyrians in mind as an opponent, while Hab had the Babylonians. In their present linkage, they tell approximately the following: In the same way that Nahum predicted the end of Nineveh and this end actually came, so the end of Babylon, predicted by Habakkuk, will come as well.

---

10   Cf. 2 Kgs 21:16; Jer 22:13–15.
11   Kessler, "Nahum–Habakuk," 137–145.
12   Solitary they can also be found elsewhere: מַשָּׂא in Mal 1:1, חזה in Amos 1:1; Obad 1;
      Mic 1:1.

The double book Nah–Hab is therefore meant as a book of comfort to Judah moaning under the yoke of the Babylonians.

When the book of Nah–Hab was later inserted into the emerging larger anthology of prophets, probably in the middle to late Persian period, it was enlarged at the beginning and at the end and thus made compatible with its new context. The two psalms Nah 1:2–8 and Hab 3 were added then.[13] Presumably, the psalms should be seen in connection with a similarly late text in Jonah: the song of the prophet in the fish's stomach.[14] If this thesis is accurate, the Four-prophets-book (Hos–Am–Mi–Zeph) was at that time not only enlarged by Nah–Hab, but also by Jonah – and probably also by the second Two-prophets-book Hag–PrZech, and perhaps Obad and Joel.

This assumption is also compatible with existing hypotheses about the emergence of the Book of the Twelve. For instance, after a Four-prophets-book (Hos, Am, Mi, Zeph), Aaron Schart[15] reckons with three continually growing collections: a "Nahum-Habakuk-Komposition" (including Nah and Hab), a "Haggai-Sacharja-Korpus" (containing Hag and Zech 1–8), and a "Joel-Obadja-Korpus" (adding Joel and Obad), before in the end the whole corpus is complete. In my opinion, the separation of these three intermediate levels is hard to prove. They should be combined into one level that also includes Jonah. Jakob Wöhrle discerns for the (late) 5th and the 4th century two levels, the first of which – the replacing of Hos by Joel within the Four-prophets-book – seems unconvincing to me. The second step is quite near to my own proposal: Wöhrle's "Fremdvölker-Korpus I" includes Hag, Zech 1–8 and Nah (unfortunately not Hab and Jonah).

Why Zeph (the last part of the Four-prophets-book) was placed behind Nah–Hab in the big arrangement supposed here is easily comprehensible: Each of the three books speaks about the Assyro-Babylonian era. It didn't seem possible to separate the double book Nah–Hab. It wasn't even necessary, because the order of sequence, as it now stands, makes perfect sense, as shown in the beginning of this paper.

The several interspersed texts of psalms that were now in the anthology of the prophets in the Persian period suggest a liturgical use for the corpus. Linked to that cultic use one should note an unremarkable,

---

13 The double amplification also met the aesthetic standards, because it extended a chiasmus, which already characterized the exilic double book Nah–Hab A) *Psalm* (Nah 1:2–8); B) accusation of inner social wrongs (Nah 1:9–2:3); C) accusation of the foreign power (Nah 2:4–3:19); C') announcement/accusation of the foreign power (Hab 1:1–2:5); B') accusation of inner social wrongdoers (Hab 2:4–19); A') *Psalm* (Hab 3:1–19).

14 Cf. Mathys, *Dichter*, 218–227. See recently Jeremias, "Psalm," 203–214.

15 Schart, *Entstehung*.

yet important issue. The Psalm of Habakkuk (Hab 3:1–19) was not attached directly to the exilic polemic against idols in Hab 2:18–19, but
was attached by means of a connecting link, one that puts the virulence
of YHWH in opposition to the lack of power of the idols: "YHWH is in
his holy temple.[16] The whole earth – quiet before him!" (2:19). The cultic
call in 2:20 ("quiet before him!"; הס מפניו) resounds quite similarly
three other times in the Book of the Twelve: in Amos 6:10, Zeph 1:7,
and Zech 2:17. The earliest reference might be the one in Zeph 1:7; the
other three were inserted redactionally during the Persian period: at
the end of Nah–Hab (Hab 2:19), the book preceding Zeph; at the beginning of Hag–PrZech (Zech 2:17), the book succeeding Zeph; and close
to the beginning of the entire corpus, in the book of Amos (6:10). In this
way a subtle arc emerged, standing on four columns and stretching
nearly over the entire Dodekapropheton.

References

Dietrich, W. "Nahum / Nahumbuch." *TRE* 23 (1994) 737–742.
–   "Ninive in der Bibel." Pp. 239–254 in *Theopolitik: Studien zur Theologie und
      Ethik des Alten Testaments*. Edited by idem. Neukirchen-Vluyn: Neukir-
      chener, 2002.
Gerstenberger, E.S. "Der Hymnus der Befreiung im Zefanjabuch." Pp. 102–112
      in *Der Tag wird kommen: Ein interkontextuelles Gespräch über das Buch des Pro-
      pheten Zefanja*. Edited by W. Dietrich and M. Schwantes. SBS 170. Stuttgart:
      Katholisches Bibelwerk, 1996.
Jeremias, J. "Der Psalm des Jona (Jona 2,3–10)." Pp. 203–214 in *Was ist der
      Mensch, dass du seiner gedenkst? (Psalm 8,5): Aspekte einer theologischen An-
      thropologie*. Edited by M. Bauks et al. FS Bernd Janowski. Neukirchen-
      Vluyn: Neukirchener, 2008.
Kessler, R. "'Ich rette das Hinkende, und das Versprengte sammle ich': Zur
      Hirtenmetaphorik in Zef 3." Pp. 93–101 in *Der Tag wird kommen: Ein inter-
      kontextuelles Gespräch über das Buch des Propheten Zefanja*. Edited by W. Diet-
      rich and M. Schwantes. SBS 170. Stuttgart: Katholisches Bibelwerk, 1996.
–   "Nahum-Habakuk als Zweiprophetenschrift: Eine Skizze." Pp. 137–145 in
      Gotteserdung: Beiträge zur Hermeneutik und Exegese der Hebräischen Bibel.
      Edited by idem. BWANT 170. Stuttgart: Kohlhammer, 2006.
Koch, K. *Daniel 1–4*. BKAT 22,1. Neukirchen-Vluyn: Neukirchener Verlag, 2005.
Levin, C. "Das 'Vierprophetenbuch': Ein exegetischer Nachruf." *ZAW* 123
      (2011) 221–235.
Mathys, H.-P. *Dichter und Beter: Theologen aus spätalttestamentlicher Zeit*. OBO
      132. Fribourg: Universitätsverlag and Göttingen: Vandenhoeck &
      Ruprecht, 1994.

---

16   The "temple" of course is the second one, built from 520–515 B.C.E.

Otto, E. "Techniken der Rechtssatzredaktion israelitischer Rechtsbücher in der Redaktion des Prophetenbuches Micha." *SJOT* 5 (1991) 119–150.

Schart, A. *Die Entstehung des Zwölfprophetenbuchs: Neubearbeitungen von Amos im Rahmen schriftenübergreifender Redaktionsprozesse.* BZAW 260. Berlin: de Gruyter, 1998.

Spieckermann, H. *Juda unter Assur in der Sargonidenzeit.* FRLANT 129. Göttingen: Vandenhoeck & Ruprecht, 1982.

Wöhrle, J. *Die frühen Sammlungen des Zwölfprophetenbuches: Entstehung und Komposition.* BZAW 360. Berlin: de Gruyter, 2006.

– *Der Abschluss des Zwölfprophetenbuches: Buchübergreifende Redaktionsprozesse in den späten Sammlungen.* BZAW 389. Berlin: de Gruyter, 2008.

– "'No Future for the Proud Exultant Ones': The Exilic Book of the Four Prophets (Hos., Am., Mic., Zeph.) as a Concept Opposed to the Deuteronomistic History." *VT* 58 (2008) 608–627.

Wolfe, R.E. "The Editing of the Book of the Twelve." *ZAW* 53 (1935) 90–130.

Time and Situational Reference in the Book of Haggai: On Religious- and Theological-Historical Contextualizations of Redactional Processes

MARTIN LEUENBERGER

Westfälische Wilhelms-Universität Münster

1. Introduction

1.1 Hag–IZech in the Book of the Twelve

The argument which will be presented here begins with the well-founded thesis *that Hag–IZech* (or Hag–Zech–Mal*)[1] follow after a deep – probably even the deepest – break in the Book of the Twelve and thus *represent a – or even the – fundamental redeployment in the thematic sequence of the Twelve* as a composition. This broad consensus is based upon synchronic as well as diachronic observations and evaluations:

(1) *Synchronically*, it is an elementary, widely accepted observation that the transition from Zeph to Hag represents the most striking change within the sequence of the Book of the Twelve: (a) The Biblical narrative of history leaps over the exilic period by attaching the Neo-Babylonian constellation in the Book of Zephaniah (after Obad; Hab–Nah) directly to reports of the building of the new temple in the Persian era promoted by Haggai (and further pursued in the books of Zechariah and Malachi). Hag–IZech moreover presents a distinctive theology of history. (b) In both books, the high priest Joshua and the governor or special emissary Zerubbabel perform a central leadership function. (c) Thematically, the historical-theological perspective is manifested by the progression from judgment against Israel-Judah and the nations (in Nah–Zeph)[2] to the temple-centered restitution of Israel in the midst of the nations (in Hag–Zech).[3] (d) In addition, Hag–Zech differs from the

---

1   Unless otherwise indicated, in this article Zech/IZech designates more precisely Zech 1–8.
2   See already Kaiser, *Grundriß*, 2:106, and others.
3   Cf. Bosshard and Kratz, "Maleachi;" Steck, *Abschluß*, 33–55.

rest of the Book of the Twelve also with respect to the chronological system of headings and subheadings,[4] which date the events described in the books exactly to the day in the first years of Darius I.

In sum, one can state with Aaron Schart: "Der tiefste Einschnitt liegt zwischen Zeph und Hag: An dieser Stelle wird das babylonische Exil mit einer Schweigepause übergangen."[5]

(2) *Diachronically*, these findings led the newer redaction-critical research with good reason to surmise that the Haggai-Zechariah-corpus forms the concluding pivot point of the redaction history of the Twelve – in contrast to the Two-Prophets-Book (Hos–Am respectively) to the Four-Prophet-Book Hos–Am–Mi–Zeph[6] as the (older) nucleus in the front section of the Book of the Twelve.

1.2 A Two-Prophets-Book: Hag–IZech

In this context, several scholars have argued for the redaction-historical hypothesis of a Two-Prophets-Book Hag–IZech*.[7] If one leaves open the controversy concerning the affiliation of the Malachi core,[8] then the question arises whether a connection between Hag and IZech – which is indicated by the strong compositional arguments mentioned – marks the literary beginning of the books or whether it represents only a later editorial combination.

The following points speak in favor of the second option and is presently favored by a large majority: (a) Haggai and Zechariah are preserved as two separate prophetic books, although they represent virtually "twin prophets"[9] regarding their general time and thematic frame. (b) However, a more precise examination reveals differences in the chronological system as well as in the thematic range. (c) More precisely, there are close cross references of the book of Haggai to specific areas within the book of Zechariah, in particular to Zech 1:1–7 and to ch. 7–8,[10] suggesting a corresponding redaction-historical connection.

---

4   Cf. hereto Wöhrle, *Sammlungen*, 29–50.367–385.
5   Schart, "Redaktionsgeschichte," 20.
6   For Hos–Am* see esp. Jeremias, "Dodekapropheton;" Schart, *Entstehung*, 101–155; Schmid, "Nebiim," 374; for Hos–Am–Mic–Zeph see Nogalski, *Processes*, 274–275; Schart, *Entstehung*, 156–233; Wöhrle, *Sammlungen*, 51–284; idem, "Future;" Schmid, "Nebiim," 375.
7   Cf. esp. Lux, "Zweiprophetenbuch;" Wöhrle, *Sammlungen*, 285–385 (Lit.); Hallaschka, *Haggai*, 314–320 (summary).
8   See hereto e.g. Nogalski, *Processes*, 201–202, and recently Wöhrle, *Abschluss*, 219–263.
9   Lux, *Prophetie*, VI.
10   See for an overview Meyers and Meyers, *Haggai*, XLIX.LIV.

1.3 State of research

I will now outline the current state of research. The redaction-historical approach, for good reasons, presently constitutes a prominent branch of exegesis of the prophets. One can safely begin with the basic consensus that in Hag (and IZech) a process of successive editorial/redactional formations took place.[11] This process reckons, more precisely, "mit einer nicht allzu komplexen Entstehungsgeschichte beider Bücher."[12]

Following the initial fundamental observations on and evaluations of the catchword-phenomenon, namely at the seams of the books, by *James Nogalski*[13] in the early 1990s, *Jakob Wöhrle* has recently reexamined the entire Book of the Twelve. Integrating broad areas of research, he has submitted a relatively careful, manageable model, which he justifies solidly.[14] For Haggai, Wöhrle plausibly differentiates between a core (*Grundschrift*[15]), two formative redactions (*Haggaichronik*;[16] *Fremdvölker-Korpus I*[17]), and isolated additions (*Einzelzusätze*[18]). In the present context it is worth mentioning that Hag and Zech were connected for the first time in the first half of the 5th century B.C.E.[19] The redactors only add productively to Zech (1:1–7, 14aβ–17aα; 2:10–14; 4:9b; 6:15; 7:1, 7, 9–14; 8:1–5, 7–8, 14–17, 19b), while Hag is taken over unchanged, with the exception of being (deuteronomistically) conditioned by inserting the conversion of the people (Zech 1:1–7) which precedes the divine care (*göttliche Zuwendung*) in Zech 1–8. Later (approx. 400 B.C.E.), the nations-corpus I (*Fremdvölker-Korpus I*) combines Hag–IZech with Joel–Amos–Mic–Zeph and adds Nah and IIZech.

> The model's outline is rather convincing. Less compulsory seems to me excluding Hag 2:11–14 from the basic layer, especially if one assumes a historic prophet who then is expected to be heavily shaped by priestly categories on the one hand. On the other hand one may dispute the allocation of 2:23 to the core.

In contrast, the hypothesis presented by *Martin Hallaschka* proceeds in a considerably more radical and differentiated manner, starting with a

---

11 Cf. hereto my short summary: Leuenberger, "Herrschaftsverheißungen," 105–108 (Lit.), and recently Wöhrle, *Sammlungen*, 285–287; Hallaschka, *Haggai*, 2–14.
12 Hallaschka, *Haggai*, 4, following Boda (see however 7–14 for "komplexere Entstehungsmodelle").
13 Nogalski, *Precursors*; idem, *Processes*.
14 Cf. Wöhrle, *Sammlungen*, 285–385; idem, *Abschluss*, 14–18 and passim.
15 Hag 1:2, 4–11, 12b, 13; 2:3, 4*, 5aβ, b, 9, 15–16, 18abβ, 19, 23.
16 Hag 1:1, 3, 12a, 14–15; 2:1–2, 4*, 10, 20, 21a.
17 Hag 2:6–8, 21b, 22.
18 Hag 2:5aα, 11–14, 17, 18bα.
19 The so-called word-redaction (see Wöhrle, *Sammlungen*, 367–385).

core of 6 verses from Haggai and 5 verses from Zechariah: "Der Grundbestand des Haggai-Buchs besteht aus zwei Worten (1,4.8; 2,3.9a), die den Tempel zum Thema haben."[20] After independent expansions, according to him, the connection of both books takes place for the first time by the dating in Zech 1:7 and related texts concerning on the one hand the renewed dwelling of Yhwh in the temple (1:16–17; 2:10–14*) and on the other hand Zerubbabel (4:6–10*). As with Wöhrle, Hallasch-ka argues this combination of books leaves no direct traces in the book of Haggai. Only later do various overarching redactions take place in Hag–Zech*.[21] The limited range of his analysis, however, yields no comprehensive perspective on the formation of the Book of the Twelve.

> This conclusion results more or less stringently from a consistently used subtraction method, which Hallaschka, however, neither justifies nor reflects upon methodically. Therefore, it, remains unclear, how he estimates the efficiency and function of his model (for instance with regard to the literary-historical cogency).

Surveying these examples focused on recent German-speaking studies, it is obvious that the present redaction-historical research remains within a relatively restricted range of hypotheses. At the origin of all these models and of the redaction-historical approach in general stands the basic assumption that prophecy functions to interpret history in terms of the author's actual present. This observation implies the possibility of reconstructing developments within prophetic texts in correspondence to historical processes.[22]

1.4 Research Perspectives

From this current standpoint, we can formulate four perspectives for further research:

(1) Essential is, as Jakob Wöhrle has emphasized,[23] a *methodical reflection* of developing redaction-historical hypotheses (including the relevant criteria such as catchwords and conceptual levels): Exegesis needs constant accompanying hermeneutics.

---

20   Hallaschka *Haggai*, 315; see 316 similar for Zech: "Am Beginn des Sacharja-Buchs stehen zwei kurze Visionen (Sach 1,8.9a.10.11b; 2,5–6)" (see similar for Hag and Zech Kratz, "Hosea," 281).

21   In Hag, diverse additions are to be found in 2:6–7, then 2:8 (after 450 B.C.E., possibly already Hellenistic), finally 2:20–23 was added (see Hallaschka, *Haggai*, 66–70.103–120; cf. his article, p. 171–189, in this volume).

22   Cf. e.g. Steck and Schmid, "Heilserwartungen," 9.

23   See his article, p. 3–20, in this volume.

(2) Equally important, it seems to me, would be substantive *concrete examples of* individual *cases*, since the constant movement between exegetical theory and practice has to be proven.

(3) On the *literary level*, the modeling can no longer take place within the range of single books, but must always keep in view the horizon of the Book of the Twelve, since overarching aspects usually begin to take effect during relatively early phases of book developments. In my view, this change constitutes an inevitable insight of the newer research, affecting the book of Haggai on several layers.

(4) Finally, an urgent desideratum consists in the effort to embody redaction-historical models more firmly by correlating them with *religious- and theological-historical constellations*. Thus it is possible, on the one hand, at least at salient points, to corroborate the redaction history of the Book of the Twelve historically, thereby securing the additional internal stratifications.[24] On the other hand, the religious- and theological-historical contextualizations provide sharper profiles for the corresponding redactional layers and allow one to determine their historical purposes.

In the second part of this paper, I will now try to implement these suggestions by means of a concrete example: the nationwide restitution of Israel in Hag 2:6–9 and 2:20–23.

2. The Nationwide Restitution of Israel (Hag 2:6–9, 20–23)

2.1 The Setting of Haggai

The book of Haggai 'happens' directly on the horizon of the temple's re-establishment. This theological-historical *time of change* marks the birth of postexilic prophecy, and it has gained more intensive scholarly attention over the last two decades.[25] This change concerns not only the literary presentation of what happened, but also proves (despite the criticism esp. of Diana Edelman) to be reliable historically.[26]

---

24 Cf. esp. the article of Albertz, p. 303–318, in this volume.
25 Responsible for this trend are mainly the redaction-historical quest for the formation and composition of the Book of the Twelve as a unity on the one hand, and the fundamentally changed understanding of prophecy on the other hand, for which the learned and scripture-based "prophetische Prophetenauslegung" (Steck) until the 2nd century B.C.E. is of central relevance.
26 Cf. Edelman, *Origins*; Dequeker, "Darius;" but see the refutation of Klein, "Contemporaries;" see also esp. Uehlinger, "Policy," 336–337; Willi-Plein, *Haggai*, 11–16, and most recently Hallaschka, *Haggai*.

With regard to the literary and redaction history, this reliability applies to the origins of Hag and Zech, and possibly to the hypothesis of a Two-Prophets-Book reported above (1.2). If so, this Two-Prophets-Book would then synthesize the preceding materials at a time that was still quite close to the events. In effect, this synthesis amounts to locating the core tradition of Hag and Zech – and possibly also the Two-Prophets-Book – in the religious- and theological-historical horizon of the second temple's founding. This contextualization is at present widely acknowledged, allowing us to move a step further.

2.2 Hag 2:6–9, 20–23

It is rather interesting to see that the general constellation of the book of Haggai – centering around overcoming the agrarian-economic distress in Jerusalem at the end of the exile by building the new temple – is very clearly transcended in the two sections of *Hag 2:6–9, 20–23*: They take into account a universal cosmos and national horizon, and they also vary with respect to formal and literary-critical aspects.[27]

כי כה אמר יהוה צבאות	6	For thus says Yhwh Zebaot:
עוד אחת מעט היא		Once again, in a little while,
ואני מרעיש את־השמים		I will shake the heavens
ואת־הארץ		and the earth
ואת־הים ואת־החרבה	7	and the sea and the dry land!
והרעשתי את־כל־הגוים		And I will shake all the nations,
ובאו חמדת כל־הגוים		and the treasure of all nations shall come,
ומלאתי את־הבית הזה		and I will fill this house with
כבוד אמר יהוה צבאות		splendor, says Yhwh Zebaot.
לי הכסף	8	The silver is mine,
ולי הזהב		and the gold is mine –
נאם יהוה צבאות		says Yhwh Zebaot.
גדול יהיה כבוד הבית הזה	9	The latter splendor of this house
האחרון מן־הראשון		will be greater than the former,[28]
אמר יהוה צבאות		says Yhwh Zebaot.
ובמקום הזה אתן		And in this place I will give
שלום נאם יהוה צבאות		prosperity – says Yhwh Zebaot.

---

27   See below the reference in note 30.
28   Due to the Hebrew Syntax (see Joüon and Muraoka, *Grammar*, §§139a.143h, but see Rudolph, *Haggai*, 41) this understanding is more probable than the alternative: "Greater will be the splendor of this latter house than the one of the former."

Schematically this order of events can be represented as depicted in the following graphic:

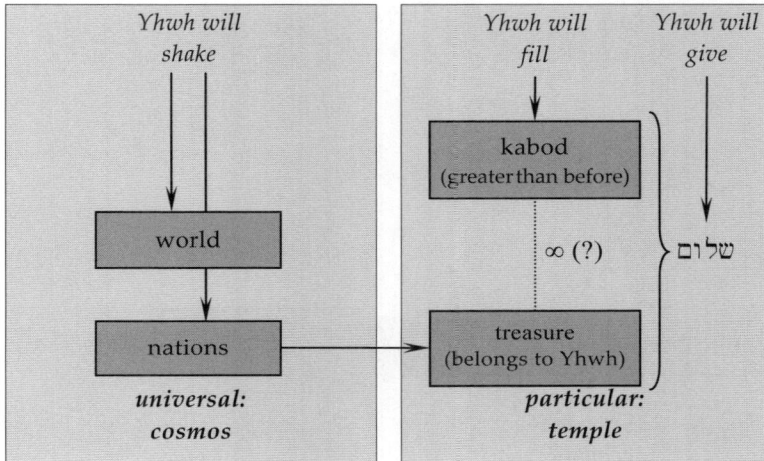

Yhwh will shake		Yhwh will fill	Yhwh will give
		kabod (greater than before)	
world		∞ (?)	שלום
nations	→	treasure (belongs to Yhwh)	
universal: cosmos		**particular: temple**	

The second passage runs as follows:

ויהי דבר־יהוה שנית אל־חגי	20	And the word of Yhwh came a second time to Haggai
בעשרים וארבעה לחדש לאמר		on the 24th day of the month:
אמר אל־זרבבל	21	Speak to Zerubbabel,
פחת־יהודה לאמר		governor of Judah:
אני מרעיש את־השמים		I am about to shake the heavens
ואת־הארץ		and the earth,
והפכתי כסא ממלכות	22	and I will overthrow the throne of kingdoms;
והשמדתי חזק ממלכות הגוים		and I will destroy the strength of the kingdoms of the nations,
והפכתי מרכבה ורכביה		and I will overthrow the chariots and their riders;
וירדו סוסים ורכביהם		and the horses and their riders will fall,
איש בחרב אחיו		each one by the sword of his brother.
ביום ההוא נאם־יהוה צבאות	23	On that day – says Yhwh Zebaot –,
אקחך זרבבל בן־שאלתיאל עבדי		I will take you, o Zerubbabel, son of Shealtiel, my servant –
נאם־יהוה		says Yhwh –,
ושמתיך כחותם		and will make you like a signet ring,
כי־בך בחרתי		for I have chosen you –
נאם יהוה צבאות		says Yhwh Zebaot.

Again, the sequence of action gives a rather similar impression to the one in 2:6–9:

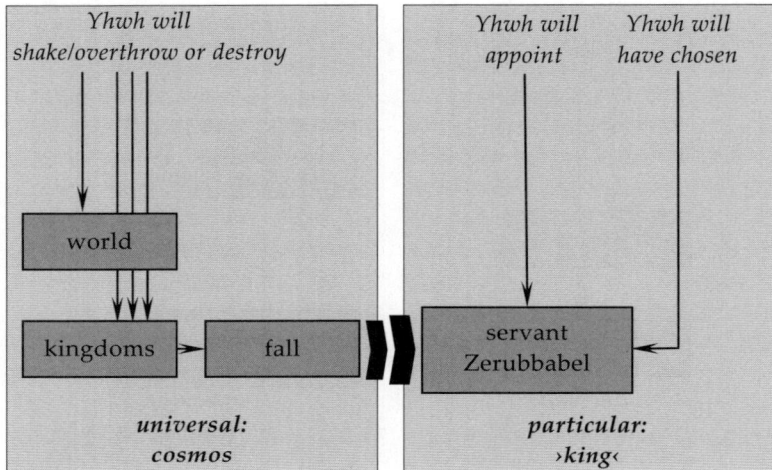

Yhwh will shake/overthrow or destroy	Yhwh will appoint	Yhwh will have chosen
world		
kingdoms → fall	servant Zerubbabel	
universal: cosmos	particular: ›king‹	

In both cases a change to restitution takes place and is depicted as a concentrated movement from a universal start to a particular end. The movement anticipates events in the very near future that move from a universal shaking of sky, earth and nations (judgment on the nations by YHWH) to the particular salvation centered around the temple (2:6–9) and the chosen ›king‹ (2:20–23) in the midst of a well-ordered cosmos.

> Naturally, differences exist in the details, differences which transcend categories that refer to the temple, the king, and their constituent parts. Hag 2:6–9 is part of the argument in the word of God encompassing 2:1–9, while 2:20–23 constitutes the fourth word of God in its entirety. Taken together with the emphasis on the book's conclusion (Achtergewicht), it seems probable that we have here a final, compositional (and probably also a redaction-historical) accent. Also of interest is the aforementioned perspective on the nations which appears only in 2:22 where it accentuates total judgment against the nations, while 2:7–8 only describes the effect of the nations' shaking – the treasures come to Jerusalem (how this transfer happens is not stated). The fate of the nations is left open in 2:7–8.
>
> This development can be understood within the book's dynamic.[29] At the same time, however, it shows clearly that the theme of the nations plays a (contextually differing) auxiliary function with regard to the restitution of Israel – no matter how one evaluates this development redaction-

---

29 The nations first bring treasures into Jerusalem, where the nations nevertheless will be destroyed (cf. Joel 4:12–17). This by no means unambiguous reading is further complicated by the time frame of 2:6–9, 20–23.

historically. Finally, it is worth noting that in 2:20–23 an objective corresponding to the שלום-state (2:9) is missing, possibly indicating that 2:6–9
and 2:20–23 involve different phases of formation.

2.3 Hag 2:6–9, 20–23 as Updates (*Fortschreibungen*)

Current redaction-historical models agree to some extent, and in my
view justifiably so, in considering both sections to be later updates
(*Fortschreibungen*), although the judgments for that conclusion diverge
in detail.[30] On the whole one can state that literary-critical observations,
combined with conceptual features, establish one of the most probable
redactional layers in the book of Haggai,[31] which possibly complements
other additions, even though such a differentiated rolling corpus as
Hallaschka, for example, proposes remains unverifiable.

2.4 Religious- and Theological-Historical
Contextualization of Hag 2:6–9, 20–23

Now, is it possible to make plausible this conceptually distinct, redactional layer more precisely with regard to the postexilic history of religion and theology? It is noteworthy that recent research has proposed a
Hellenistic dating of texts dealing with a judgment over the nations and
the cosmos. This placement, however, should be reexamined and, in
my view, modified in favor of a *late Persian origin*.

(1) In particular, according to Steck, the prophetic announcements
of a general judgment against the nations and the world reflect the
collapse of the Persian ecumenism. This ecumenism was understood as
worldwide pacification[32] and as "weltweite *Ordo*-Erfahrung sonderglei-
chen" (unprecedented universal experience of order).[33] A similar assessment is quite common and is advocated for instance also by Konrad
Schmid.[34]

---

30 See my overview: Leuenberger, *Gott*, 242–245 (Lit.).
31 With regard to content and redaction-historical arguments, it is very unlikely that
    2:6–9, 21b–22 can be linked with the early Persian revolts during the first years of
    Darius I. (against Meyers and Meyers, *Haggai*, 53; Albertz, "Restoration," 7; Lux,
    "Völkertheologie," 111).
32 See esp. Steck, *Abschluß*, 25–60.73–111; idem, *Studien*, 163–164; Steck and Schmid,
    "Heilserwartungen," 9–10.33–34.
33 Steck and Schmid, "Heilserwartungen," 33; more cautious Steck, *Prophetenbücher*,
    119.
34 Cf. Schmid, *Literaturgeschichte*, 192–194; idem, *Buchgestalten*, 181–185.305–309.

166   Martin Leuenberger

Concretely, Hallaschka also interprets Hag 2:20–23 in this sense. According to him, the section dates from Hellenistic time, because "seit dem Alexanderzug nun tatsächlich nach der 200jährigen *pax persica* die Throne der Königreiche umstürzen."[35]

(2) Nevertheless, one must ask whether this argumentation is really conclusive. Already a quick historical glance shows that the events and conditions in the western part of the Persian Empire were extremely and continually chaotic, at least during its last century. Namely, during the reign of Darius II (424–404 B.C.E.), Artaxerxes II (404–359/8 B.C.E.) and (soon also under) Artaxerxes III (359/8–338 B.C.E.), numerous rebellions, revolts and changes of power dominate the picture.[36]

(3) Against this background, a late Persian emergence of texts emphasizing universal judgment against the nations appears much more plausible in term of the history of religion and theology, possibly dating sometime between the late fifth century (beginning with Darius II in 424 B.C.E.) and the middle of the fourth century.

Of course, this briefly proposed thesis requires more detailed exploration than is possible here. But if this suggestion withstands critical scrutiny, the redaction-historical dating of the relevant texts by Jakob Wöhrle (for his *Fremdvölker-Korpus I*)[37] and others[38] would gain valuable religious- and theological-historical support.

> Of course, the text corpora would have to be discussed and differentiated more extensively. First of all, there seem to be theological-historical differences portraying a general judgment against the nations (with different nuances),[39] a cosmic world-judgment, and so-called apocalyptic conceptions of judgment. Secondly, consistant themes (esp. the issue of the nations) also show different profiles in an intertemporal perspective.

---

35 Hallaschka, *Haggai*, 138 cf. 69–70.117; Steck and Schmid, "Heilserwartungen," 33. The controversial expression כסא ממלכות "throne(s) of the kingdoms" (v. 22) cannot exclusively be connected with either the Persian or the Hellenistic Period (see besides the commentaries esp. Lux, "Völkertheologie," 115–118).
36 Cf. Briant, *History*, 588–690; Miller and Hayes, *History*, 524–527; Donner, *Geschichte*, 431–437; cf. specifically for Hag Wöhrle, *Abschluss*, 161–164.
37 Hag 2:6, 20 possesses strong cross-references to Joel: Only in Hag 2:6, 20 and Joel 4:16 the shaking (רעש) refers to heaven and earth (see further for heaven Joel 2:10); this indicates probably a significant redaction-historical link (cf. in more detail Wöhrle, *Abschluss*, 139–171 [Lit.]).
38 See for Hag 2:6–7 e.g. Gärtner, *Summe*, 328.
39 Cf. hereto the *Fremdvölker-Korpus I* and *II* of Wöhrle (*Abschluss*, 23–171.191–287).

3. Conclusion

After a short review of current redaction-historical research on Hag and IZech, notably on the hypothesis of a Two-Prophets-Book Hag–IZech*, a few perspectives for further research were noted, particularly focusing on the need for correlating redaction-historical models with religious- and theological-historical constellations.

Next, an attempt was made to concretize this correlative task for Hag 2:6–9, 20–23 with respect to the expectation of a restitution for Israel by judgment against the nations and a universal judgment. Contrary to the frequent dating in the early Hellenistic era, this constellation fits much better in the late Persian period when, notably, the western part of the empire was in more or less constant uproar. If this placement is correct, then quite a distinctive redactional stage of the formation of the Book of the Twelve can be embedded in the religious- and theological-historical context of the late Persian period and it can be understood more precisely against this background.

References

Albertz, R. "The Thwarted Restoration." Pp. 1–17 in *Yahwism after the Exile: Perspectives on Israelite Religion in the Persian Era*. Edited by idem and B. Becking. Studies in Theology and Religion 5. Assen: Van Gorcum, 2003.

Bosshard, E. and Kratz, R.G. "Maleachi im Zwölfprophetenbuch." *BN* 52 (1990) 27–46.

Briant, P. *From Cyrus to Alexander: A History of the Persian Empire*, Winona Lake: Eisenbrauns, 2002.

Dequeker, L. "Darius the Persian and the Reconstruction of the Jewish Temple in Jerusalem (Ezra 4:24)." Pp. 67–92 in *Ritual and Sacrifice in the Ancient Near East*. Edited by J. Quaegebeur. OLA 55. Leuven: Peeters, 1993.

Donner, H. *Geschichte des Volkes Israel und seiner Nachbarn in Grundzügen*. 2 vols. GAT 4,1–2. 3rd ed. Göttingen: Vandenhoeck & Ruprecht, 2001.

Edelman, D.V. *The Origins of the 'Second' Temple: Persian Imperial Policy and the Rebuilding of Jerusalem*. London: Equinox, 2005.

Gärtner, J. *Jesaja 66 und Sacharja 14 als Summe der Prophetie: Eine traditions- und redaktionsgeschichtliche Untersuchung zum Abschluss des Jesaja- und des Zwölfprophetenbuches*. WMANT 114. Neukirchen-Vluyn: Neukirchener, 2006.

Hallaschka, M. *Haggai und Sacharja 1–8: Eine redaktionsgeschichtliche Untersuchung*. BZAW 411. Berlin: de Gruyter, 2010.

Jeremias, J. "Die Anfänge des Dodekapropheton: Hosea und Amos." Pp. 34–54 in *Hosea und Amos: Studien zu den Anfängen des Dodekapropheton*. Edited by idem. FAT 13. Tübingen: Mohr, 1996.

Joüon, P. and Muraoka, T. *A Grammar of Biblical Hebrew*. 2 vols. SubBi 14,1–2. Rome: Pontificio Istituto Biblico, 1991.

Kaiser, O. *Grundriß der Einleitung in die kanonischen und deuterokanonischen Schriften des Alten Testaments*. 3 vols. Gütersloh: Gütersloher, 1992–1994.

Klein, R.W. "Were Joshua, Zerubbabel, and Nehemiah Contemporaries? A Response to Diana Edelman's Proposed Late Date for the Second Temple." *JBL* 127 (2008) 697–701.

Kratz, R.G. "Hosea und Amos im Zwölfprophetenbuch." Pp. 275–286 in *Prophetenstudien: Kleine Schriften II*. Edited by idem. FAT 74. Tübingen: Mohr, 2011.

Leuenberger, M. "Herrschaftsverheißungen im Zwölfprophetenbuch: Ein Beitrag zu seiner thematischen Kohärenz und Anlage." Pp. 75–111 in *Prophetische Heils- und Herrschererwartungen*. Edited by K. Schmid. SBS 194. Stuttgart: Katholisches Bibelwerk, 2005.

– *Gott in Bewegung: Religions- und theologiegeschichtliche Beiträge zu Gottesvorstellungen im alten Israel*. FAT 76. Tübingen: Mohr, 2011.

Lux, R. "'Wir wollen mit euch gehen …' Überlegungen zur Völkertheologie Haggais und Sacharjas." Pp. 107–133 in *Gedenkt an das Wort*. Edited by C. Kähler et al. FS W. Vogler. Leipzig: Evangelische Verlagsanstalt, 1999.

– "Das Zweiprophetenbuch: Beobachtungen zu Aufbau und Struktur von Haggai und Sacharja 1–8." Pp. 191–217 in *"Wort Jhwhs, das geschah …" (Hos 1,1): Studien zum Zwölfprophetenbuch*. Edited by E. Zenger. Herders biblische Studien 35. Freiburg: Herder, 2002.

– *Prophetie und Zweiter Tempel: Studien zu Haggai und Sacharja*. FAT 65. Tübingen: Mohr, 2009.

Meyers, C.L. and Meyers, E.M. *Haggai, Zechariah 1–8: A New Translation with Introduction and Commentary*. AB 25B. New York: Doubleday, 1987.

Miller, J.M. and Hayes, J.H. *A History of Ancient Israel and Judah*. 2nd ed. London: SCM, 2006.

Nogalski, J.D. *Literary Precursors to the Book of the Twelve*. BZAW 217. Berlin: de Gruyter, 1993.

– *Redactional Processes in the Book of the Twelve*. BZAW 218. Berlin: de Gruyter, 1993.

Rudolph, W. *Haggai – Sacharja 1–8 – Sacharja 9–14 – Maleachi: Mit einer Zeittafel von A. Jepsen*. KAT 13,4. Gütersloh: Gütersloher, 1976.

Schart, A. *Die Entstehung des Zwölfprophetenbuchs: Neubearbeitungen von Amos im Rahmen schriftenübergreifender Redaktionsprozesse*. BZAW 260. Berlin: de Gruyter, 1998.

– "Zur Redaktionsgeschichte des Zwölfprophetenbuchs." *VF* 43 (1998) 13–33.

Schmid, K. *Buchgestalten des Jeremiabuches: Untersuchungen zur Redaktions- und Rezeptionsgeschichte von Jer 30–33 im Kontext des Buches*. WMANT 72. Neukirchen-Vluyn: Neukirchener, 1996.

– "Hintere Propheten (Nebiim)." Pp. 313–412 in *Grundinformation Altes Testament: Eine Einführung in Literatur, Religion und Geschichte des Alten Testaments*. Edited by J.C. Gertz. 3rd ed. Uni-Taschenbücher 2745. Göttingen: Vandenhoeck & Ruprecht, 2008.

– *Literaturgeschichte des Alten Testaments: Eine Einführung*. Darmstadt: WBG, 2008.

Steck, O.H. *Der Abschluß der Prophetie im Alten Testament: Ein Versuch zur Frage der Vorgeschichte des Kanons*. Biblisch-theologische Studien 17. Neukirchen-Vluyn: Neukirchener, 1991.

– *Studien zu Tritojesaja*. BZAW 203. Berlin: de Gruyter, 1991.

– *Die Prophetenbücher und ihr theologisches Zeugnis: Wege der Nachfrage und Fährten zur Antwort*. Tübingen: Mohr, 1996.

Steck, O.H. and Schmid, K. "Heilserwartungen in den Prophetenbüchern des Alten Testaments." Pp. 1–36 in *Prophetische Heils- und Herrschererwartungen*. Edited by K. Schmid. SBS 194. Stuttgart: Katholisches Bibelwerk, 2005.

Uehlinger, C. "Figurative Policy, Propaganda und Prophetie." Pp. 297–349 in *Congress Volume Cambridge 1995*. Edited by J.A. Emerton. VTSup 66. Leiden: Brill, 1995.

Willi-Plein, I. *Haggai, Sacharja, Maleachi*. ZBK 24,4. Zürich: Theologischer Verlag, 2007.

Wöhrle, J. *Die frühen Sammlungen des Zwölfprophetenbuches: Entstehung und Komposition*. BZAW 360. Berlin: de Gruyter, 2006.

– *Der Abschluss des Zwölfprophetenbuches: Buchübergreifende Redaktionsprozesse in den späten Sammlungen*. BZAW 389. Berlin: de Gruyter, 2008.

– "'No Future for the Proud Exultant Ones': The Exilic Book of the Four Prophets (Hos.; Am.; Mic.; Zeph.) as a Concept Opposed to the Deuteronomistic History." *VT* 58 (2008) 608–627.

From Cores to Corpus:
Considering the Formation of
Haggai and Zechariah 1–8

MARTIN HALLASCHKA

Georg-August-Universität Göttingen

1. Brief Review of Recent Research

The books of Haggai and First Zechariah show certain similarities. Both books deal with the construction of the second temple. Both books emphasize the role of Zerubbabel, the governor, and Joshua, the High Priest, as leaders of the Judean community. Each book contains a system of chronological data which refers to the reign of Darius I (cf. Hag 1:1, 15a; 1:15b–2:1,[1] 10, 18, 20; Zech 1:1, 7; 7:1). And in both cases the dates are combined with the word event formula (*Wortereignisformel*) to introduce the oracles, thus providing a framework for Haggai's and Zechariah's prophecies. Moreover, the chronological data of Haggai and Zechariah 1–8 can be combined so that the two books present a chronological sequence ranging from the second to the fourth year of king Darius.

Because of these similarities and connections Klostermann in the late 19th century assumed that Haggai and Zechariah 1–8 originally had been part of one single temple building account edited by Zechariah himself before the oracles of the two prophets were separated and rearranged in the shape of the books we know today.[2]

In the second half of the 20th century the purpose and theological milieu of the editorial framework of Haggai and Zechariah was discussed. Beuken's seminal work on Haggai and Zechariah 1–8 needs to be mentioned specifically.[3] Beuken held that Haggai and Zechariah 1–8

---

1   The regnal year notice of Hag 1:15b most likely belongs to the date given in 2:1. Otherwise the regnal year would not be mentioned in the introduction to the second oracle, cf., e.g., Wolff, *Dodekapropheton*, 40–41; Rudolph, *Haggai*, 30 note 15a; Beuken, *Haggai*, 48–49; Willi-Plein, *Haggai*, 29; Floyd, *Prophets*, 255; Sweeney, *Micah*, 529.533. Pace, e.g., Assis, "To Build," 519–522; Wöhrle, *Sammlungen*, 292–294.

2   Cf. Klostermann, *Geschichte*, 213.

3   Cf. Beuken, *Haggai*.

were edited by one rather late redaction that he assigned to a chronistic milieu.[4]

Beuken's hypothesis subsequently met with critique from various scholars who proposed that neither themes nor terminology of the editorial framework were exclusively chronistic but rather showed similarities with deuteronomistic or priestly writings and might be assigned to an early Persian period-redaction which could more generally be located in a temple milieu.[5]

In his survey of recent research on Haggai and Zechariah Boda noted two trends:

> "First of all, there has been a general trend among recent scholars to move the date of the composition of Haggai and Zechariah 1–8 closer to the dates offered in the superscriptions ... Secondly, recent work on the redaction of Haggai and Zechariah reveals a trend toward simplicity."[6]

One example of this trend is the commentary by Meyers and Meyers.[7] According to Meyers and Meyers, Haggai and First Zechariah form a "composite work"[8] or a "single compendious work"[9] which was edited after the last date given in Zech 7:1, i.e. December 518 B.C.E., and before the rededication of the temple in 515 B.C.E. which is not reported in Haggai and Zechariah. Meyers and Meyers substantiate their hypothesis with the thematic, structural, and terminological similarities in Haggai and Zechariah that I have mentioned previously.[10]

While those who propose the theory of a single redaction comprising both prophetic writings stress the similarities some scholars have recently pointed at the differences between the two books. Differences can be found in the framework, not only between the books but also within each of them:

---

4   Cf. Beuken, *Haggai*, 27–183.331–336. Beuken distinguishes between the chronistic circle responsible for the final edition of Haggai–Zechariah and the Chronicler's school of 1–2 Chronicles and Ezra–Nehemiah. Some of the formulations and theological concepts that, according to Beuken, suggest the chronistic background of the redaction of Haggai and Zechariah 1–8 include the following: The use of the word event formula with בְּיַד, the formulation רוּחַ + עוּר, the concern for the prophets' role and success, the characterization of the rebuilding of the temple as covenantal duty, the hope of the continuation of the Davidic dynasty, the interest in the history of Israel, and the rejection of the Samaritan cult. Before Beuken, Bloomhardt, "Poems," 156, and Ackroyd, "Studies (Part 1)," 173; idem, "Studies (Part 2)," 1; idem, "Book," 152.155–156, had already suggested that Haggai and Zechariah underwent a chronistic redaction.

5   Cf. esp. Mason, "Purpose," 413–421.

6   Boda, *Research*, 4.

7   Cf. Meyers and Meyers, *Haggai*.

8   Meyers and Meyers, *Haggai*, xliv.

9   Meyers and Meyers, *Haggai*, xlvii.

10 Cf. Meyers and Meyers, *Haggai*, esp. xliv–xlviii.

	Date		Sequence	ביד	אל	המלך	Patronymic
Hag 1:1	01.06.02	29.08.520	Y/M/D	x		x	
Hag 1:15b–2:1	21.07.02	17.10.520	Y/M/D	x		x	
Hag 2:10	24.09.02	18.12.520	D/M/Y		x		
Hag 2:20	24.09.02	18.12.520	D/(M)		x		
Zech 1:1	–.08.02	–.10./11.520	M/Y		x		x
Zech 1:7	24.11.02	15.02.519	D/M/Y		x		x
Zech 7:1	04.09.04	07.12.518	Y/D/M		x	x	

The word event formula is used with ביד in Hag 1:1; 2:1[11] and with אל in Hag 2:10, 20; Zech 1:1, 7; and 7:1.[12] Only the date formulae in Zech 1:7; 7:1 contain the name of the month while the others just give the number. In Zech 7:1 Zechariah's patronymic is missing but it is mentioned in Zech 1:1, 7. In Hag 1:1; 1:15b–2:1; and Zech 7:1 Darius is called המלך but not in Hag 2:10; Zech 1:1, 7.[13] Only in Zech 1:1 is the precise day not given with the date formula. Also the order of day, month and year is inconsistent within the chronological system of Haggai and Zechariah. And the chronological sequence of the dating system is interrupted by Zech 1:1, for this first date in the book of Zechariah predates the last date in the book of Haggai (cf. Hag 2:10, 18, 20).

Thematic differences can be added. While the book of Haggai concentrates on issues concerning the reconstruction of the temple, the book of First Zechariah, especially the night vision cycle (Zech 1:7–6:8), offers a broader concept of reorganizing Jerusalem and Judah, and the prologue and epilogue of Zechariah (Zech 1:1–6; 7:1–8:23) have a strong ethical impetus that is based on penitential prayer tradition.[14] Visions and their angelic interpretation cannot be found in Haggai.

According to Kessler and Boda for example, because of formal and thematic differences Haggai and Zechariah should not be seen as a unified piece of literature.[15] Kessler explains the similarities in the date formulae as scribal conventions and comes to the conclusion that Haggai and Zechariah should be treated as two separate books.[16] Boda states: "The content of Zech 1–8 cannot be explained solely by reference

---

11   Cf. Hag 1:3 (without date).
12   Cf. Zech 4:8; 6:9; 7:4, 8; 8:18 (without date).
13   Hag 2:20 repeats the date of 2:10 without the year.
14   On the impact of penitential prayer tradition on the prologue and epilogue of Zechariah see Boda, "Zechariah," 61–67.
15   Cf. Kessler, *Book*, 56–57; Boda, "Zechariah," 51–54.
16   Cf. Kessler, *Book*, 56–57. Kessler reckons with the possibility "that Zechariah 1–8 was written to complement the text of Haggai which was *already in existence*" (Kessler, *Book*, 57, original emphasis). On this possibility cf. already Mason, "Purpose," 421.

to the rebuilding of the Second Temple and thus should not be fused together with Hag 1–2 to form a unified collection."[17]

Despite the differences between Haggai and Zechariah, however, the similarities mentioned above cannot be ignored. Wöhrle points out that the incipits of Haggai and Zechariah are exceptional within the *corpus propheticum*. Even if Hag 1:1 uses בְּיַד and Zech 1:1 uses אֶל, according to Wöhrle both verses are similar since they are the only superscriptions in the *corpus propheticum* that begin with a date formula followed by a word event formula.[18]

Though Zechariah transcends the theme of rebuilding the temple, it is mentioned explicitly (cf. Zech 1:16; 3:7; 4:6–10; 6:12–15; 8:9). As with Haggai, Zech 4:6–10 and 8:9 mention the laying of the temple's foundations and like the book of Haggai, Zech 8:9–13 regards this as the turning point from the time of curse to the time of blessing.

Since neither the hypothesis that Haggai and Zechariah were edited solely as a single volume that created a unified work nor the assumption that Haggai and Zechariah had never been combined seem sufficient to account for the current form of the text, more complex models of their redaction history have been presented in recent years.

Albertz and Lux each identify two different redactional processes that formed a Haggai-Zechariah-Corpus. Albertz assigns the introductory formulae in Haggai (Hag 1:1–3*, 13–15; 2:1–2, 4*, 10, 20) and Zech 8:9–13 to a first redactional layer and the prologue (Zech 1:1–6) and the composition of the epilogue of Zechariah (Zech 7:1–8:19), together with Hag 2:5a and Zech 6:15b, to a second redactional layer.[19]

According to Lux, Haggai's oracles are linked with Zechariah's night visions by a redaction creating the date formulae not only in Haggai but also in Zech 1:7; 7:1 and incorporating the oracles Zech 8:9–13. A later redaction added Zech 1:1–6 and Zech 7:7–14 so that Zechariah's call for repentance predates the laying of the foundations reported in Hag 2:10, 18, 20.[20]

Kratz assumes various redactional levels and literary expansions (*Fortschreibungen*) within Haggai and Zechariah.[21] Thus the literary growth of the editorial framework is linked to the additions to the

---

17 Boda, "Zechariah," 54.
18 "Doch auch hier ist und bleibt die prinzipielle Übereinstimmung der beiden Einleitungen auffällig, die eben darin besteht, daß beide Male überhaupt zunächst eine Datierung gefolgt von einer Wortereignisformel angegeben wird, was sich so bei keinem anderen Prophetenbuch des Alten Testaments findet." (Wöhrle, *Sammlungen*, 369).
19 Cf. Albertz, *Religionsgeschichte*, 484.
20 Cf. Lux, "Zweiprophetenbuch," 4–26; idem, "Konditionierung," 227–240.
21 Cf. Kratz, "Tempel," 67–69; idem, "Serubbabel," 79–92.

oracular material of both prophetic books. Since the date in Zech 1:1 predates Hag 2:10, 18, 20, Kratz presupposes that Zech 1:1 was originally added to Hag 1:1–2:9.[22]

Last but not least, Wöhrle's hypothesis has to be mentioned.[23] Regarding methodology, his approach is founded on an important and necessary proposition: Wöhrle insists on analyzing the redaction history of the discrete books of Haggai and Zechariah first before turning to the question whether a connection between the two existed.[24]

The different formulations of the dates in Haggai and Zechariah respectively lead Wöhrle to the conclusion that the dating system in Haggai and Zechariah is no original unit. Wöhrle assigns the editorial framework of Hag (1:1, 3, 12a, 14–15; 2:1–2, 4*, 10, 20, 21a) to a redaction labeled "Haggai-Chronicle" that was implemented in the primary layer which had arranged Haggai's oracles to show that the people's obedience to Haggai's call to rebuild the temple is the precondition for Yahweh's blessing.[25] According to Wöhrle the "Haggai-Chronicle rearranges the words of the primary layer ... to a narrative report, which describes how the people ... obeyed the prophet and built the temple."[26] Only a few pieces of text were later inserted into the Haggai-Chronicle, mainly the question of impurity of the people (Hag 2:11–14) and oracles against the nations (Hag 2:6–8, 21b, 22) which Wöhrle assigns to a redactional reworking of the Book of the Twelve (*Fremdvölkerschicht I*).[27]

In Zechariah Wöhrle identifies a rather extensive "word-redaction" that adds the date formulae in Zech 1:1, 7; 7:1 and oracular material (1:2–6, 14aβ–17aα; 2:10–14; 4:9b; 6:15; 7:1, 7, 9–14; 8:1–5, 7–8, 14–17, 19b) to the night visions and the question about fasting in Zech 7–8. The intention of the "word-redaction" is to call for repentance (cf. esp. the prologue of Zech 1:1–6), and repentance is linked to doing social justice (cf. the expansions in Zech 7–8).[28]

Because of the different formulations of the dates and because of the different intentions of the Haggai-Chronicle and the word-redaction Wöhrle concludes that both cannot belong to the same layer. Since the date formulae are still very similar and since Zech 1:1 predates the last date in Haggai to interrelate Zechariah's prophetic minis-

---

22 Cf. Kratz, "Tempel," 68.
23 Cf. Wöhrle, *Sammlungen*, 288–385; idem, "Formation," 2–14.
24 Cf. Wöhrle, *Sammlungen*, 287; idem, "Formation," 4. Cf. idem, *Sammlungen*, 24–27, for Wöhrle's general methodological considerations to analyzing the Book of the Twelve.
25 Cf. Wöhrle, *Sammlungen*, 317–320.
26 Wöhrle, "Formation," 5.
27 Cf. Wöhrle, *Sammlungen*, 320–321; idem, *Abschluss*, 23–171.
28 Cf. Wöhrle, *Sammlungen*, 362–380.

try to that of Haggai, Wöhrle infers that the word-redaction is dependent on the Haggai-Chronicle whose date formulae served as a model
for Zechariah. Thus the books of Haggai and Zechariah were connected
by a redaction that can only be found in Zech 1–8.[29]

In the models of Lux, Kratz and Wöhrle the overlap of the last date
in Haggai and the first in Zechariah plays an important role for the
question how and when the two writings were connected. For Wöhrle
the different introductory formulae are one indicator that the dates in
Haggai and Zechariah were implemented by two distinct hands.

Moving beyond Wöhrle, however, the diversity of the formulae
within the discrete books should be taken into account as well.[30] In
Haggai it is noteworthy that only in the first and second date formula is
the word event formula used with בְּיַד (Hag 1:1; 1:15b–2:1, cf. 1:3),
whereas in the third and fourth case אֶל is used (Hag 2:10, 20) thus corresponding with the book of Zechariah (Zech 1:1, 7; 7:1, cf. 4:8; 6:9; 7:4,
8; 8:18). Hag 1:1 and 1:15b–2:1 have the same sequence year/month/day,
while Hag 2:10 and Zech 1:7 have the sequence day/month/year. In
contrast to Hag 1:1 and 1:15b–2:1 but in accordance with Zech 1:1, 7,
Hag 2:10 omits the title הַמֶּלֶךְ for Darius. The oracular introduction of
Hag 2:20 is unique in mentioning that the word of Yahweh came a second time to Haggai on the same day.

In the book of Zechariah all date formulae are different from each
other. Zech 1:1 omits the precise day and the name of the month, and
the order of day, month and year in Zech 1:7; 7:1 is dissimilar. Zech 7:1
does not give Zechariah's patronymic but Darius bears the title הַמֶּלֶךְ.
Both features are singular in Zechariah but correspond with the book of
Haggai which does not give a patronymic of the prophet and names
Darius הַמֶּלֶךְ in the first and second date formula. However, the sequence year/day/month and the position of the word event formula in
Zech 7:1 is unique.

If any of these observations hint at literary growth of the editorial
framework it needs to be cross-checked by the analysis of the formation
of each individual book.

---

29 Cf. Wöhrle, "Formation," 9–12; idem, *Sammlungen*, 367–374.
30 See the chart above page 173.

2. The Formation of the Books of Haggai and Zechariah 1–8

In this paper I can outline the formation of Haggai and Zechariah only very briefly and only refer to the main stages of redaction.[31]

2.1 The Formation of the Book of Haggai

Concerning the redaction history of the book of Haggai, most scholars agree that an editorial framework was secondarily added to the actual oracles.[32] Yet, the redaction historical analysis of the literary growth of both the oracular material (cf. Hag 1:4–11; 2:3–9, 11–19, 21–23) and the framework (cf. Hag 1:1–3, 12–15; 2:1–2, 10, 20) needs further differentiation.

The core material of Haggai can be found in two short oracles concerning the building of the temple and its glory (Hag 1:4, 8 and 2:3, 9a):[33] In the present text of Hag 1 the question (v. 4) and the command (v. 8) pertaining to the rebuilding of the temple are interrupted by the description of the poor conditions the people are facing,[34] which therefore is a later insertion. While Hag 1:8 is the climax of the first oracular unit[35] and focuses on the future,[36] the next verses (v. 9–11) resume and vary the theme of the futility curses in v. 6 and look once more back to the past.[37] Thus Hag 1:9–11 can be identified as secondary addition(s) to chap. 1 after the insertion of v. 5–7.[38]

In the final form of Hag 2 a question about the glory of the temple (2:3) and its response (2:6–9) that the future glory will be greater than the former glory are interrupted by the address and encouragement in

---

31 For a more detailed analysis cf. Hallaschka, *Haggai*.
32 Cf., e.g., Ackroyd, "Studies (Part 1)," 166–173; Beuken, *Haggai*, esp. 331–336; Mason, "Purpose," 413–421; Wolff, *Dodekapropheton*, 3–6; Reventlow, *Propheten*, 5–6; Tollington, *Tradition*, 19–23; idem, "Readings," 196–200; Kratz, "Tempel," 69; Wöhrle, *Sammlungen*, 288–294; Lux, "Zweiprophetenbuch," 4–8. Pace, e.g., Floyd, "Nature," esp. 473; Kessler, *Book*, 53–56.
33 Cf. Kratz, "Serubbabel," 88–91.
34 See below.
35 Cf., e.g., Steck, "Haggai," 357.366; Beuken, *Haggai*, 185–186; Verhoef, *Books*, 21.64; Assis, "Composition," 6.
36 Cf. Wolff, *Dodekapropheton*, 32.
37 Cf. Steck, "Haggai," 357; Wöhrle, *Sammlungen*, 295.
38 Cf. Ackroyd, "Studies (Part 1)," 167–168; Horst, *Propheten*, 205; Steck, "Haggai," 364–372; Rudolph, *Haggai*, 35; Koch, "Volk," 212; Nogalski, *Precursors*, 219; Wöhrle, *Sammlungen*, 297, who separate Hag 1:9–11 from v. 4–8 but regard it as a parallel oracle of v. 4–8.

v. 4–5.[39] Moreover, v. 6–8 which introduce the theme of the shaking of the nations and are not very closely connected to the context, can be delineated as an expansion of the original answer.[40] Also v. 9b, which promises peace using typically Deuteronomistic formulations, is a secondary addition.[41] Thus, only v. 9a is the original answer to v. 3,[42] taking up the catchwords ‏ראשון‎, ‏הבית הזה‎, ‏כבוד‎ from v. 3.[43]

The earliest oracles in the book of Haggai (Hag 1:4, 8 and 2:3, 9a) most probably had a short introduction that could have consisted of a date formula, a word event formula and the reference to the prophet Haggai (cf. 1:1*[44] and 1:15b–2:1). Both sayings have a similar structure using the same pattern of rhetorical question and reply. Both oracles use the stylistic device of antithesis. The two oracles are interconnected by several catchwords: ‏הבית הזה‎ (1:4; 2:3, 9a), ‏כבוד/כבד‎ (1:8; 2:3, 9a), emphatic ‏אתם‎ (1:4; 2:3), ‏עתה/עת‎ (1:4; 2:3). The compilation and combination of the two oracles 1:4, 8 and 2:3, 9a reveal the intention to create a small collection of prophetic sayings pertaining to the temple rebuilding. Most probably, these oracles can be dated to the time before or during the temple restoration.

At a next stage the theme of blessing and curse was added to the core material ("Fluch-und-Segen-Bearbeitung"). As has been noted by other scholars before, the exhortations ‏שימו לבבכם על דרכיכם‎ and futility curses in Hag 1:5–7 interrupt the question about the present state of the temple (1:4) and the command to build the temple in Hag 1:8 which is the actual answer to the question posed in 1:4. The exhortations in Hag 1:5–7 that reflect upon the past are complemented by the call to reflect upon the future in 2:15–19*. The latter is also introduced by the formula ‏ועתה שימו נא לבבכם‎ and promises Yahweh's future blessings from the day when the foundations of the temple will be laid.[45] Unlike the oldest oracles in 1:4, 8; 2:3, 9a, Hag 2:15, 18 uses ‏היכל‎ instead of ‏בית‎. Both units of this expansion use and vary the model of

---

39 Cf. Ackroyd, "Studies (Part 1)," 168; Beuken, *Haggai*, 51–52; Mason, *Tradition*, 193; Kratz, "Serubbabel," 88.

40 Cf. Kratz, "Serubbabel," 88; Wöhrle, *Sammlungen*, 300–302. On Hag 2:6–8 and its parallel in 2:21 see also below.

41 Cf. Beuken, *Haggai*, 60–64; Kratz, "Serubbabel," 88. Hag 2:9b cites Jer 14:13b: In contrast to the false prophets in Jer 14, Haggai legitimately prophesies peace to the people.

42 Cf. Kratz, "Serubbabel," 88–89.

43 Also the orcales in 2:10–14, 15–19, 20–23 are secondary additions to 2:3, 9a, see below.

44 Only: ‏בשנת שתים לדריוש המלך בחדש הששי ביום אחד לחדש היה דבר יהוה ביד חגי‎ ‏הנביא לאמר‎.

45 On the interrelation and rhetorical function of Hag 1:5, 7 and 2:15a, 18a, cf. esp. Boda, "Haggai," 300–301.

futility curses (cf. Hag 1:6; 2:15b–16) which are well known from the
Hebrew Bible and elsewhere in the ancient Near East.[46] With the implementation of this layer (Hag 1:5–7; 2:15–19*) the text of Haggai now
connects the task of temple building to ancient Near Eastern treaty
traditions and ends with the promise of Yahweh's blessing.

Afterwards, the original date formulae were expanded by the insertion of the addressees of Haggai's prophecies, i.e. Zerubbabel and Joshua as the leaders of the community and the people themselves (Hag
1:1–3, 12a, 14–15a; 1:15b–2:2) in order to identify the 2nd plural of the
oracular material. Also the reaction of the people and their leaders is
reported. Due to this framework the book of Haggai is shaped into a
historical narrative, and this redaction must be more recent than the
addition of the futility curses. Taking up the treaty topic of 1:5–7 and
2:15–19, the obedience of the people is expressed in Hag 1:12a, 14 by
using the deuteronomistic formula שמע בקול יהוה אלהיהם thus explicitly interpreting the task of rebuilding the temple as a covenantal duty.[47]

At the next stage the question regarding the impurity of the people
(Hag 2:10–14) has been inserted between the oracle about the future
glory of the temple and the promise of future blessings. Thus the promise of blessing gets a new precondition. The problem of the people's
impure offerings needs to be solved before Yahweh will provide a
blessing. Kratz and Wöhrle have already identified this piece of text as
a literary expansion, for it does not fit the design and context of the rest
of Haggai.[48] According to Wöhrle the intention of Hag 2:11–14 is obscure, yet I would suggest that it reflects problems similar to those in
Malachi (cf. esp. Mal 1:6–14; 2:1–9; 3:6–12). The people are accused of
unclean offerings which the priests obviously accepted. Thus the

---

46 Cf., e.g., Lev 26:16, 26; Deut 28:30–32, 38–41; Isa 9:19; Hos 4:10; 8:7; 9:12, 16; Amos
    4:8; 5:11; Mic 6:14–15; Zeph 1:13; Hag 1:6, 9; 2:16; Mal 1:4; Job 31:8, further Hos 5:6;
    Amos 8:12; Mic 3:4; the stelae from Sfire (Sfire I A,21–24; II A,2–3); Bukān (lines 5–8)
    and Tell Feḥerīje (lines 18–22 in the Aramaic and lines 30–36 in the Akkadian ver-
    sion).
47 See, e.g., Deut 4:30; 8:20; 9:23; 13:5, 19; 15:5; 26:14, 17; 27:10; 28:1–2, 15, 45, 62; 30:2, 8,
    10, 20; Jer 3:13, 25; 7:23, 28; 9:12; 11:4, 7; 18:10; 22:21; 26:13; 32:23; 35:8; 38:20; 40:3;
    42:6, 13, 21; 43:4, 7; 44:23. On the formula שמע בקול יהוה see Lohfink, Hauptgebot,
    65–66; Fenz, Stimme, esp. 38–39.49.116–117; Veijola, Königtum, 88–89; Levin, Ver-
    heißung, 105–109, on its use in Hag 1:12a cf., e.g., Beuken, Haggai, 33–36; Mason,
    "Purpose," 418; Wolff, Dodekapropheton, 33–34; Kessler, Book, 142–145; Boda, Haggai,
    107.
48 Cf. Kratz, "Serubbabel," 91; Wöhrle, Sammlungen, 302–305.320–321. Without 2:10–14,
    Hag 2:3–9, 15–19 corresponds to Hag 1:4–11 in structure.

priests are criticized as well,[49] and also the term שאל תורה (Hag 2:11)
has its closest parallel in Mal 2:7 (בקש תורה). Therefore Hag 2:10–14
may be dated to a time close to Malachi.[50] The date formula in Hag 2:10
must have been inserted together with v. 11–14.

The last addition is the oracle for Zerubbabel who will be set as
Yahweh's seal (Hag 2:20–23). The dating formula in 2:20 refers back to
the date given 2:10. Given the various literary critical options, the most
probable option would read Hag 2:20–23 as literarily unified, despite
the differences between v. 21b–22 and v. 23.[51] Zerubbabel's designation
(בן שאלתיאל פחת יהודה) appears in the editorial framework (cf. Hag
1:1, 14; 2:2), but is divided between v. 21a (זרבבל פחת יהודה) and v. 23
(זרבבל בן שאלתיאל). These two elements are taken from the framework, but when combined give the complete designation. They are
carefully divided according to their function for the context. In v. 21a
Zerubbabel is called פחת יהודה, because in the following v. 21b–22 the
role of the nations of the earth and their rulers are explained.[52] The last
verse, Hag 2:23, however concentrates on the choice of Davidic Zerubbabel and it consequently names him as בן שאלתיאל.[53] The first part of
the oracle (Hag 2:21b–22) uses material from 2:6–8 and reformulates it.[54]
Thus v. 22 functions as an explanation or illustration of the shaking of
the nations previously described in v. 7.[55] The expression ביום ההוא

---

49 Cf. Petersen, *Haggai*, 84–85; Tiemeyer, "Question," 71–72; idem, *Rites*, 221–
    223.226.237–239. Pace, e.g., Verhoef, *Books*, 116.
50 The book of Malachi may be dated not earlier than the 5th century (cf., e.g., Verhoef,
    Books, 160–162; Steck, *Abschluß*, 33–36; see also Steck and Schmid, "Heilserwartun-
    gen," 28; Redditt, *Haggai*, 149–151; Zenger, *Einleitung*, 583–584; Wöhrle, *Abschluss*,
    259) or even to the late Persian period (cf., e.g., Kaiser, *Einleitung*, 295; Bosshard-
    Nepustil, *Rezeptionen*, 420–422.426–428). Cf. the article of Kessler, p. 223–236, in this
    volume.
51 Among others one could name the military imagery and the nations that are treated
    only in v. 21b–22 whereas v. 23 deals with the choice of Zerubbabel, previously men-
    tioned in v. 21a. Yet, Pss 2 and 110 and other texts attest to the connection of the na-
    tions' abolition with royal terminology; cf. Sauer, "Serubbabel," 202–203; Petersen,
    Haggai, 100.
52 Thus Kessler, *Book*, 223, who thinks the title of governor is used in Hag 2:21a on
    purpose: "The inclusion of Zerubbabel's official title of governor, here as in 2:1 [sic!],
    implies that Yahweh addresses the word to Zerubbabel in the context of the official
    mandate he holds from the Persian throne. This fact proves highly significant in the
    oracle that follows."
53 The title פחת יהודה is used (without the patronymic) in v. 21a but not in v. 23 (here
    we have the patronymic instead) to hint at a change in the role of Zerubbabel, cf.
    Boda, *Haggai*, 164: "Once Haggai has described the overthrow of human power in
    2:22, it is inappropriate to continue to refer to Zerubbabel by his title as a small polit-
    ical player in the bureaucracy of the Persian empire. By calling him 'son of Shealtiel'
    Haggai is alluding to his genealogical connection to the royal line of David."
54 Cf. Petersen, *Haggai*, 98; Kessler, *Book*, 220–221.224; Kratz, "Serubbabel," 88.
55 Cf. Wolff, *Dodekapropheton*, 82.

נאם יהוה צבאות marks the climax of the oracle, and it adds a new, specific thought; namely the promise to establish Zerubbabel as Yahweh's seal.[56] The structure of v. 21b–22 and v. 23 corresponds to the sequence of v. 6–8 and v. 9, each announcement of the shaking of the cosmos and the nations is followed by a salvation oracle.[57] Thus both text passages are related to each other. The changes – apparently caused by Yahweh's theophany – not only affect the construction of the temple (Hag 2:9) but also the builder of the temple (2:23): The חותם imagery in Hag 2:23 clearly relates to Jer 22:24. The rejection of Jehoiachin and the Davidic dynasty is revoked in Hag 2:23.[58] Zerubbabel receives a promise that he will continue the Davidic line.

Kratz and Wöhrle have identified the shaking of the nations in Hag 2:6–8 as a secondary insert. Since Hag 2:21b–22 cites and resumes that shaking of the nations the oracle Hag 2:20–23 cannot be older than that theme. Hence, the oracle for Zerubbabel must be a late addition to the book of Haggai.[59] According to Wöhrle the oracles against the nations in Hag 2:6–8, 21b–22 should be dated to the end of the 5th or to the beginning of the 4th century.[60] However, Steck argues convincingly that universal judgment with cosmic upheavals should be dated to the Hellenistic period and not to the Persian era.[61] While the Persians had to struggle with different riots and wars within the empire and with the Greeks, the end of the *pax persica* and of the old world order is marked with Alexander's conquest and the subsequent wars of the Diadochi.[62] This is the time when the thrones of the kingdoms were overthrown (cf. Hag 2:22). The oracle for Zerubbabel then would be one in the line of

---

56 Petersen, *Haggai*, 102: "In v. 23, *bayyôm hahû'* seems to mark a transition point; it represents the move from a general statement of weal to the more concrete promise addressed to Zerubbabel. Furthermore, the phrase 'on that day' itself reinforces the theme of specific future events contained in this verse." Cf. Rudolph, *Haggai*, 54; Reventlow, *Propheten*, 30; Kessler, *Book*, 226. The three divine-saying formulae in v. 23 also mark the special meaning of this verse.

57 Cf. Beuken, *Haggai*, 226.

58 "The metaphor of the donning of the signet in 2:23 was chosen precisely because it served as a vehicle to contrast the diverse fates of two different Davidides. The implication is that Hag 2:23 views the promises to David as having ongoing validity" (Kessler, *Book*, 236–237). Cf., e.g., Sauer, "Serubbabel," 203–204; Rudolph, *Haggai*, 54; Meyers and Meyers, *Haggai*, 69–70; Redditt, *Haggai*, 32; Boda, *Haggai*, 163–165.

59 Cf. already Böhme, "Maleachi," 215; Sérandour, "Récits," 16–19; Kratz, "Serubbabel," 88.

60 Cf. the article of Leuenberger, p. 157–169, in this volume.

61 See, e.g., Steck, *Abschluß*, 22–23.27–28.63–69.73–87; idem, *Studien*, 163–165; idem, *Prophetenbücher*, 52–54.62–63.70–75.97–98.119; Steck and Schmid, "Heilserwartungen," 9–10.33–34; Schmid, *Buchgestalten*, 181–185.305–310; idem, *Literaturgeschichte*, 192–194.

62 Cf. esp. Steck, *Prophetenbücher*, 119.

other post-exilic texts that have set their hopes on David and the Davidides, and the temple rebuilt by Zerubbabel would be the portent of the restitution of the Davidic line.[63]

2.2 The Formation of First Zechariah

Turning to Zechariah I shall first concentrate on the night visions where various redactional levels can be identified, and one can detect different redactional stages of the literary growth of the night vision-cycle by way of the various angelic beings and their roles within the visions. In the primary layer of the cycle – which consists of the substrata to the visions of the "rider" (i.e., Zech 1:8, 9a, 10, 11b) and the "measuring cord" (i.e., Zech 2:5–6) – two men appear within the vision and talk to the prophet.[64] Their actions (commanding a patrol that roams about the whole earth, measuring Jerusalem) and their knowledge show that they belong to the heavenly realm.[65] Both the rider and the measuring cord scenes have a parallel structure that consists of the description of the vision by the prophet (1:8//2:5), the question to a man (1:9a//2:6a), and the man's reply (1:10, 11b//2:6b) explaining the vision. At this textual level, the description and interpretation of the visions do not depend on "the angel who talked to me" who was not part of the primary layer.[66] The visions were apparently intended to be read in sequence, and the first night vision is the precondition (or better, the signal) for what will be seen in the measuring vision. Silence on earth (1:11b) is the required condition for rebuilding Jerusalem (2:6b). The interpretation of the situation on earth by the man on horseback ("all the earth rests

---

63 Cf., e.g., Jer 33:14–26, which according to Schmid, *Buchgestalten*, 56–66.323–327, can be dated to the first half of the 3rd century B.C.E., or Ezek 17:22–24, which refers back to the kingdom of Jehoiachin and his line. Ezek 17:22–24 is probably the latest restoration expectation within the book of Ezekiel; cf. Klein, *Schriftauslegung*, 234–236. 244–245.250.382. Anyway, texts postdating the rebuilding of the second temple had an interest in Zerubbabel (cf. Japhet, "Sheshbazzar," esp. 218–229), as can be seen in Ezra 1–6; 1 Esd 4–6; Sir 49:11; Josephus, Ant. XI; Matt 1:12–13; Luke 3:27. *Terminus ad quem* for Hag 2:20–23 is in any case Sirach. In Sir 49:11 Zerubbabel – in combination with Jer 22:24 and Hag 2:23 – is praised as a signet ring on the right hand.

64 Cf. the remarks in Kratz, "Serubbabel," 85.

65 For other examples of celestial beings simply called "man" (אִישׁ), see e.g. the three men in Mamre in Gen 18. That the celestial אִישׁ in Zech 1:8 is addressed as אֲדֹנִי in v. 9a (cf. Gen 18:3; 19:2, 18; Josh 5:13–14) may have been the trigger for the later editor to insert the *angelus interpres* in v. 9b, immediately after this address.

66 Cf. Uehlinger, "Policy," 338–343, who reconstructs an original cycle of five night visions (Zech 1:8, 9a, 10*, 11*; 2:1, 2*, 4b, 5–6; 5:1–3a[b?]; 6:1–3* ... [sic!] 5*, 7–8) without "the angel who talked to me." Also according to Kratz, "Serubbabel," 85–86, the *angelus interpres* was inserted secondarily.

quietly," כל הארץ ישבת ושקטת, v. 11b) correlates best to the political situation or at least to the Persian propaganda after Darius I coming to power.[67]

In the next redactional stage the basic visions were expanded by the insertion of "the angel who talked to me" (1:9b, 14; 2:7–8*). At this point most of the other visions that include the interpreting angel were added, most likely not all at once. I would argue that the visions "menorah" (4:1–14*), "flying scroll" (5:1–4), and "chariots" (6:1–8) were composed together and the visions of the "the ephah" (5:5–11) and the "horns and craftsmen" (2:1–4) were added later. Last but not least, the vision of the atonement of Joshua the high priest (Zech 3) was added, a vision that differs considerably from the others and disturbs the concentric symmetry of the cycle of the previous seven visions.[68]

The first expansion of the night visions (1:9b, 14; 2:7–8*; 4:1–14*; 5:1, 3; 6:1–8*) would have formed a cycle of five visions with ch. 4 ("menorah") at the center.[69] The central theme of this redaction could be called "reorganization" and the visions still reflect the situation in early Persian Judah.[70]

---

67 Cf., e.g., Meyers and Meyers, *Haggai*, 115.130; Uehlinger, "Policy," 340, pace, e.g., Wolters, "Earth," 128–143.

68 The most significant variations are the absence of the *angelus interpres* (with the angel of Yahweh appear instead; see also Zech 1:11–12); and the unhidden meaning of this vision (so that the prophet does not have to ask for its meaning). Cf., e.g., Jeremias, *Nachtgesichte*, 201–223; Meyers and Meyers, *Haggai*, lvi–lx.213–227; Reventlow, *Haggai*, 32; Redditt, *Haggai*, 62–63; Floyd, *Prophets*, 373–374; Boda, "Oil," 383–384; Wöhrle, *Sammlungen*, 332–337; Willi-Plein, *Haggai*, 61.84. Pace, e.g., Beuken, *Haggai*, 282–283; Rudolph, *Haggai*, 93–94; Tollington, *Tradition*, 34–35; Hanhart, *Dodekapropheton*, 176–213; Rose, *Zemah*, 37–41; Stead, *Intertextuality*, 45–48, who opt for the originality of Zech 3.
    Since Zech 3 is in all probability a secondary insert, the prophetic sign act of the crowning of Joshua (Zech 6:9–15), which also deals with the role of the high priest and the announcement of the צמח (6:12, cf. 3:8), is secondary as well.

69 Besides Uehlinger (cf. above, note 66), also Schöttler, *Gott*, 165.169–191.223–286, delineates a primary layer of five visions which, however, knows of "the angel who talked to me" and consists of Zech 1:8*, 9abα, 10b, 11b; 2:5–8; 4:1, 2*, 3a, 4–6aα, 14*; 5:5*, 6a, 8aα, 9*, 10, 11*; 6:1a, 2, 3*, 4aβb, 5aβ*, 7aα*b.

70 The issues of the cycle of five visions are: the rebuilding of Jerusalem as an unwalled city (cf. 2:7–8); the leaders of Yehud (cf. 4:14: the two sons of fresh oil in Yahweh's presence); law and order (cf. 5:1, 3: a curse on thieves and perjurers); and the leading role of the Golah (cf. 6:8: Yahweh's spirit is placed in the land of the north). The secondary expansion of this cycle by the vision "the ephah" varies and generalizes the theme of 5:1–4 (5:5–11: the removal of iniquity out of the land, on this vision see esp. Körting, "Unrechtmäßigkeit," 477–492). The vision of the "horns and craftsmen" (2:1–4), which in its initial stage had the form of a Yahweh vision (only Zech 2:3–4*; cf. Schöttler, *Gott*, 60–71), introduces the theme of the hostile nations (cf. 1:15; 2:10–13).

The vision of the menorah (Zech 4) alludes to the temple. Triggered by the temple theme, the epexegetical texts were subsequently added to the night visions dealing with the return of Yahweh to Jerusalem, with the rebuilding of the temple and at a later stage with the return of the diaspora (cf. Zech 1:16–17; 2:10–14).[71] The oracles concerning the temple builder Zerubbabel that were inserted into the vision of the menorah (cf. Zech 4:6–10*)[72] make it plausible that the cycle containing this vision was combined with the growing book of Haggai that had already been expanded by the narrative framework. Here Zerubbabel is introduced and presented as the temple builder. In Zechariah the reference to Zerubbabel is rather abrupt, and therefore it may be concluded that his role is already specified in Haggai. The cycle of five night visions would then have been joined to Haggai via the dating formula in Zech 1:7 which was modeled after Hag 1:1; 1:15b–2:1.

The question about fasting in Zech 7–8 (7:2–3; 8:18–19a), which is the oldest text in the epilogue, was at some time added to the night visions and subsequently expanded by unconditioned words of salvation taking up and resembling the epexegetical texts of the night visions (cf. Zech 8:1–13). The oracles in Zech 8:9–13 are especially noteworthy because they refer back to the prophets who were there when the foundations of the temple were laid. Thus, these oracles also allude to the book of Haggai. Those prophets are of course Haggai and Zechariah, and the call to reflect on their ministry presupposes that some time had elapsed since the day when the foundations were laid.[73] I therefore conclude that the date formula in Zech 7:1 was inserted along with Zech 8:9–13 since this date creates a time span of roughly two years. The date formula in Zech 7:1 also refers to the formulae in Haggai because Zechariah's patronymic is not given and Darius is bearing the title הַמֶּלֶךְ.

With the prologue's call for repentance (Zech 1:1–6) and the epilogue's corresponding admonitions to do social justice (Zech 7:7, 9–14; 8:14–17, 19b) Zechariah's unconditioned words of salvation become

---

71 On these texts cf. Bosshard-Nepustil, *Rezeptionen*, 393–408; Kratz, *Kyros*, 89–90 note 332; idem, "Serubbabel," 83; Wöhrle, *Sammlungen*, 326–332.362–364; Boda, "Hoy," 171–190.

72 That Zech 4:6–10* is a secondary insert to the vision of the menorah was first proposed by Wellhausen, *Propheten*, 182–183.

73 Cf. Ackroyd, "Book," 154; Beuken, *Haggai*, 156–183; Rudolph, *Haggai*, 63.148–149; Petersen, *Haggai*, 305; Reventlow, *Propheten*, 81; Lux, "Zweiprophetenbuch," 23–24; Wöhrle, *Sammlungen*, 382.

preconditioned.[74] I agree with Lux that the date in Zech 1:1 which is different from the date formula in 1:7 belongs to the insertion of the prologue.[75] As has been mentioned before, this date creates an overlap between the ministries of Haggai and Zechariah and the repentance of the people becomes the precondition not only for Zechariah's message but also for the laying of the temple's foundations reported in the book of Haggai.

3. Conclusions: The Formation of the Haggai-Zechariah-Corpus

To conclude, the formation of the Haggai-Zechariah-Corpus is not the work of a single editor. The fact that both books have formal and thematic similarities is due to various, overarching expansions in the formation of each book that aim at interrelating the two prophetic messages. I agree with Wöhrle that the oldest date formulae can be found in Haggai and that Zechariah was linked with Haggai by imitating the dates of Haggai.[76] Moving beyond Wöhrle, I would propose that the dating system in the Haggai-Zechariah-Corpus underwent a rather complex process of reediting. The oldest date formulae can be found with the core material of Haggai (cf. Hag 1:1; 1:15b–2:1), and then Zechariah's night visions were combined with Haggai by the date formula in Zech 1:7, thus adding a wider concept of hope for restoration to Haggai's oracles concerning the rebuilding of the temple. That the date in Zech 7:1 has certain similarities with Haggai's date formulae corresponds to the intention of Zech 8:9–13 which refers back to the time of the laying of the foundations in Hag 2:15–19. The date formula in Hag 2:10, which was inserted along with the question about impurity, is dissimilar to the first and second date in Haggai but similar to Zech 1:7. Thus Hag 2:10 in all probability anticipates the book of Zechariah. The unclean people are a problem for the rebuilding of the temple and for the realization of the restoration proclaimed in the night visions. The date in Hag 2:10 is repeated in 2:20 to introduce the oracle for Zerubbabel and to emphasize the importance of the day when the foundations of the temple were laid. Nogalski has detected several catchwords that

---

74   Cf. Kratz, *Kyros*, 89–90 note 332; idem, "Serubbabel," 83–84; Albertz, *Religionsgeschichte*, 484; Boda, "Zechariah," 55–61; idem, "Fasts," esp. 398–405; Wöhrle, *Sammlungen*, 351–355.362–364.375–380; Lux, "Zweiprophetenbuch," 22–26.
75   Cf. Lux, "Zweiprophetenbuch," 4–8.22–26; idem, "Konditionierung," 225–240.
76   Cf. Wöhrle, "Formation," 9–12; idem, *Sammlungen*, 367–374.

link the last oracle in Haggai with the night visions.[77] The silence on earth (cf. Zech 1:11) is the result of the universal judgment of the nations (cf. Hag 2:22).[78] The date in Zech 1:1 that interrupts the chronological sequence was inserted together with the call for repentance (Zech 1:2–6) so that the repentance of the people becomes the precondition not only for Zechariah's message but also for the rebuilding of the temple and the blessings promised in the book of Haggai.

References

Ackroyd, P.R. "Studies in the Book of Haggai (Part 1)." *JJS* 2 (1950–1951) 163–176.
–   "Studies in the Book of Haggai (Part 2)." *JJS* 3 (1952) 1–13.
–   "The Book of Haggai and Zechariah i-viii." *JJS* 3 (1952) 151–156.
Albertz, R. *Religionsgeschichte Israels in alttestamentlicher Zeit.* 2 vols. GAT 8,1–2. Göttingen: Vandenhoeck & Ruprecht, 1992.
Assis, E. "Composition, Rhetoric and Theology in Haggai 1:1–11." *Journal of Hebrew Scriptures* 7.11 (2007) 1–14.
–   "To Build or Not to Build: A Dispute between Haggai and His People." *ZAW* 119 (2007) 514–527.
Beuken, W.A.M. *Haggai-Sacharja 1–8: Studien zur Überlieferungsgeschichte der frühnachexilischen Prophetie.* SSN 10. Assen: Van Gorcum, 1967.
Bloomhardt, P.F. "The Poems of Haggai." *HUCA* 5 (1928) 153–195.
Boda, M.J. "Haggai: Master Rhetorician." *TynBul* 51 (2000) 295–304.
–   "From Fasts to Feasts: The Literary Function of Zechariah 7–8." *CBQ* 65 (2003) 390–407.
–   *Haggai & Zechariah Research: A Bibliographical Survey.* Tools for Biblical Study 5. Leiden: Deo Publishing, 2003.
–   "Zechariah: Master Mason or Penitential Prophet?" Pp. 49–69 in *Yahwism after the Exile: Perspectives on Israelite Religion in the Persian Era: Papers Read at the First Meeting of the European Association for Biblical Studies, Utrecht, 6–9 August 2000.* Edited by R. Albertz and B. Becking. Studies in Theology and Religion 5. Assen: Van Gorcum, 2003.
–   *Haggai, Zechariah.* The NIV Application Commentary. Grand Rapids: Zondervan, 2004.
–   "Oil, Crowns and Thrones: Prophet, Priest and King in Zechariah 1:7–6:15." Pp. 379–404 in *Perspectives on Biblical Hebrew: Comprising the Contents of Journal of Hebrew Scriptures, Volumes 1–4.* Edited by E. Ben Zvi. Piscataway: Gorgias Press, 2006.
–   "Hoy, Hoy: The Prophetic Origins of the Babylonian Tradition in Zechariah 2:10–17." Pp. 171–190 in *Tradition in Transition: Haggai and Zechariah 1–8 in the Trajectory of Hebrew Theology.* Edited by idem and M.H. Floyd. Library of Hebrew Bible / Old Testament Studies 475. New York: T&T Clark, 2008.

---

77   See Nogalski, *Precursors,* 51–52.255–257.
78   Cf. Lux, "Zweiprophetenbuch," 8–12.

Böhme, W. "Zu Maleachi und Haggai." *ZAW* 7 (1887) 210–217.

Bosshard-Nepustil, E. *Rezeptionen von Jesaja 1–39 im Zwölfprophetenbuch: Untersuchungen zur literarischen Verbindung von Prophetenbüchern in babylonischer und persischer Zeit.* OBO 154. Göttingen: Vandenhoeck & Ruprecht, 1997.

Fenz, A.K. *Auf Jahwes Stimme hören: Eine biblische Begriffsuntersuchung.* Wiener Beiträge zur Theologie 6. Wien: Herder, 1964.

Floyd, M.H. "The Nature of the Narrative and the Evidence of Redaction in Haggai." *VT* 45 (1995) 470–490.

– *Minor Prophets, Part 2.* FOTL 22. Grand Rapids: Eerdmans, 2000.

Hallaschka, M. *Haggai und Sacharja 1–8: Eine redaktionsgeschichtliche Untersuchung.* BZAW 411. Berlin: de Gruyter, 2011.

Hanhart, R. *Dodekapropheton 7.1: Sacharja 1–8.* BKAT 24,7.1. Neukirchen-Vluyn: Neukirchener, 1998.

Horst, F. *Die Zwölf Kleinen Propheten: Nahum bis Maleachi.* HAT 1,14. 2nd ed. Tübingen: Mohr, 1954.

Japhet, S. "Sheshbazzar and Zerubbabel – Against the Background of the Historical and Religious Tendencies of Ezra-Nehemiah." *ZAW* 94 (1982) 66–98; *ZAW* 95 (1983) 218–229.

Jeremias, C. *Die Nachtgesichte des Sacharja: Untersuchungen zu ihrer Stellung im Zusammenhang der Visionsberichte im Alten Testament und zu ihrem Bildmaterial.* FRLANT 117. Göttingen: Vandenhoeck & Ruprecht, 1977.

Kaiser, O. *Einleitung in das Alte Testament: Eine Einführung in ihre Ergebnisse und Probleme.* 5th ed. Gütersloh: Gütersloher, 1984.

Kessler, J. *The Book of Haggai: Prophecy and Society in Early Persian Yehud.* VTSup 91. Leiden: Brill, 2002.

Klein, A. *Schriftauslegung im Ezechielbuch: Redaktionsgeschichtliche Untersuchungen zu Ez 34–39.* BZAW 391. Berlin: de Gruyter, 2008.

Klostermann, A. *Geschichte des Volkes Israel: Bis zur Restauration unter Esra und Nehemia.* München: Beck, 1896.

Koch, K. "Haggais unreines Volk." Pp. 206–219 in *Spuren des hebräischen Denkens: Beiträge zur alttestamentlichen Theologie.* Vol. 1 of *Gesammelte Aufsätze.* Edited by B. Janowski and M. Krause. Neukirchen-Vluyn: Neukirchener, 1991.

Körting, C. "Sach 5,5–11 – Die Unrechtmäßigkeit wird an ihren Ort verwiesen." *Bib* 87 (2006) 477–492.

Kratz, R.G. *Kyros im Deuterojesaja-Buch: Redaktionsgeschichtliche Untersuchungen zu Entstehung und Theologie von Jes 40–55.* FAT 1. Tübingen: Mohr, 1991.

– "Der zweite Tempel zu Jeb und zu Jerusalem." Pp. 60–78 in *Das Judentum im Zeitalter des Zweiten Tempels.* Edited by idem. FAT 42. Tübingen: Mohr, 2004.

– "Serubbabel und Joschua." Pp. 79–92 in *Das Judentum im Zeitalter des Zweiten Tempels.* Edited by idem. FAT 42. Tübingen: Mohr, 2004.

Levin, C. *Die Verheißung des neuen Bundes in ihrem theologiegeschichtlichen Zusammenhang ausgelegt.* FRLANT 137. Göttingen: Vandenhoeck & Ruprecht, 1985.

Lohfink, N. *Das Hauptgebot: Eine Untersuchung literarischer Einleitungsfragen zu Dtn 5–11.* AnBib 20. Rome: Pontificio Istituto Biblico, 1963.

Lux, R. "Das Zweiprophetenbuch: Beobachtungen zu Aufbau und Struktur von Haggai und Sacharja 1–8." Pp. 3–26 in *Prophetie und Zweiter Tempel: Studien zu Haggai und Sacharja*. Edited by idem. FAT 65. Tübingen: Mohr, 2009.

— "Die doppelte Konditionierung des Heils: Theologische Anmerkungen zum chronologischen und literarischen Ort des Sacharjaprologs (Sach 1,1–6)." Pp. 223–240 in *Prophetie und Zweiter Tempel: Studien zu Haggai und Sacharja*. Edited by idem. FAT 65. Tübingen: Mohr, 2009.

Mason, R.A. "The Purpose of the 'Editorial Framework' of the Book of Haggai." *VT* 27 (1977) 413–421.

— *Preaching the Tradition: Homily and Hermeneutics after the Exile*. Cambridge: Cambridge University Press, 1990.

Meyers, C.L. and Meyers, E.M. *Haggai, Zechariah 1–8*. AB 25B. New York.: Doubleday, 1987.

Nogalski, J.D. *Literary Precursors to the Book of the Twelve*. BZAW 217. Berlin: de Gruyter, 1993.

Petersen, D.L. *Haggai and Zechariah: A Commentary*. OTL. Philadelphia: Westminster, 1984.

Redditt, P.L. *Haggai, Zechariah and Malachi*. New Century Bible Commentary. Grand Rapids: Eerdmans and London: Marshall Pickering, 1995.

Reventlow, H. Graf *Die Propheten Haggai, Sacharja und Maleachi*. ATD 25,2. Göttingen: Vandenhoeck & Ruprecht, 1993.

Rose, W.H. *Zemah and Zerubbabel: Messianic Expectations in the Early Postexilic Period*. JSOTSup 304. Sheffield: Sheffield Academic Press, 2000.

Rudolph, W. *Haggai – Sacharja 1–8 – Sacharja 9–14 – Maleachi: Mit einer Zeittafel von Alfred Jepsen*. KAT 13,4. Gütersloh: Gütersloher, 1976.

Sauer, G. "Serubbabel in der Sicht Haggais und Sacharjas." Pp. 199–207 in *Das ferne und nahe Wort*. Edited by F. Maas. FS L. Rost. BZAW 105. Berlin: de Gruyter, 1967.

Schmid, K. *Buchgestalten des Jeremiabuches: Untersuchungen zur Redaktions- und Rezeptionsgeschichte von Jer 30–33 im Kontext des Buches*. WMANT 72. Neukirchen-Vluyn: Neukirchener, 1996.

— *Literaturgeschichte des Alten Testaments: Eine Einführung*. Darmstadt: Wissenschaftliche Buchgesellschaft, 2008.

Schöttler, H.-G. *Gott inmitten seines Volkes: Die Neuordnung des Gottesvolkes nach Sacharja 1–6*. TThSt 43. Trier: Paulinus-Verlag, 1987.

Sérandour, A. "Les récits bibliques de la construction du second temple: leurs enjeux." *Transeu* 11 (1996) 9–32.

Stead, M.R. *The Intertextuality of Zechariah 1–8*. Library of Hebrew Bible / Old Testament Studies 506, New York: T&T Clark, 2009.

Steck, O.H. "Zu Haggai 1,2–11." *ZAW* 83 (1971) 355–379.

— *Der Abschluß der Prophetie im Alten Testament: Ein Versuch zur Frage der Vorgeschichte des Kanons*. Biblisch-Theologische Studien 17. Neukirchen-Vluyn: Neukirchener, 1991.

— *Studien zu Tritojesaja*. BZAW 203. Berlin: de Gruyter, 1991.

— *Die Prophetenbücher und ihr theologisches Zeugnis: Wege der Nachfrage und Fährten zur Antwort*. Tübingen: Mohr, 1996.

– and Schmid, K. "Heilserwartungen in den Prophetenbüchern des Alten Testaments." Pp. 1–36 in *Prophetische Heils- und Herrschererwartungen*. Edited by K. Schmid. SBS 194. Stuttgart: Katholisches Bibelwerk, 2005.
Sweeney, M.A. *Micah, Nahum, Habbakuk, Zephaniah, Haggai, Zechariah, Malachi.* Vol. 2 of *The Twelve Prophets*. Berit Olam. Collegeville: Liturgical, 2000.
Tiemeyer, L.-S. *Priestly Rites and Prophetic Rage: Post-Exilic Prophetic Critique of the Priesthood.* FAT II/19. Tübingen: Mohr, 2006.
– "The Question of Indirect Touch: Lam 4,14; Ezek 44,19 and Hag 2,12–13." *Bib* 87 (2006) 64–74.
Tollington, J.E. *Tradition and Innovation in Haggai and Zechariah 1–8.* JSOTSup 150. Sheffield: JSOT Press, 1993.
– "Readings in Haggai: From the Prophet to the Completed Book, a Changing Message in Changing Times." Pp. 194–208 in *The Crisis of Israelite Religion: Transformation of Religious Tradition in Exilic and Post-Exilic Times.* Edited by B. Becking and M.C.A. Korpel. OTS 42. Leiden: Brill, 1999.
Uehlinger, C. "Figurative Policy, Propaganda und Prophetie." Pp. 297–349 in *Congress Volume Cambridge 1995*. Edited by J.A. Emerton. VTSup 66. Leiden: Brill, 1997.
Veijola, T. *Das Königtum in der Beurteilung der deuteronomistischen Historiographie: Eine redaktionsgeschichtliche Untersuchung.* AASF, Ser. B 198. Helsinki: Suomalainen Tiedeakatemia, 1977.
Verhoef, P.A. *The Books of Haggai and Malachi.* NICOT. Grand Rapids: Eerdmans, 1987.
Wellhausen, J. *Die Kleinen Propheten: Übersetzt und erklärt.* 4th ed. Berlin: de Gruyter, 1963.
Willi-Plein, I. *Haggai, Sacharja, Maleachi.* ZBK 24,4. Zürich: Theologischer Verlag, 2007.
Wöhrle, J. *Die frühen Sammlungen des Zwölfprophetenbuches: Entstehung und Komposition.* BZAW 360. Berlin: de Gruyter, 2006.
– "The Formation and Intention of the Haggai-Zechariah Corpus." *Journal of Hebrew Scriptures* 6.10 (2006) 1–14.
– *Der Abschluss des Zwölfprophetenbuches: Buchübergreifende Redaktionsprozesse in den späten Sammlungen.* BZAW 389. Berlin: de Gruyter, 2008.
Wolff, H.W. *Dodekapropheton 6: Haggai.* BKAT 14,6. 2nd ed. Neukirchen-Vluyn: Neukirchener, 1991.
Wolters, A. "'The Whole Earth Remains at Peace' (Zechariah 1:11): The Problem and an Intertextual Clue." Pp. 128–143 in *Tradition in Transition: Haggai and Zechariah 1–8 in the Trajectory of Hebrew Theology.* Edited by M.J. Boda and M.H. Floyd. Library of Hebrew Bible / Old Testament Studies 475. New York: T&T Clark, 2008.
Zenger, E. et. al. *Einleitung in das Alte Testament.* Kohlhammer Studienbücher Theologie 1,1. 6th ed. Stuttgart: Kohlhammer, 2006.

The *Mas'ot* Triptych and the Date of Zechariah 9–14: Issues in the Latter Formation of the Book of the Twelve

BYRON G. CURTIS

Geneva College

1. Introduction

1. Just as Zech 1–8 bears a system of redactional headings that it shares with the preceding booklet, Haggai, with which it also likely circulated as one composite book, so Zech 9–14 bears a system of redactional headings that it shares with the following booklet, the one we now call Malachi. These *massa'* headings ("oracle"), now found at Zech 9:1, Zech 12:1, and Mal 1:1, mark off three related prophetic units that together may once have been yet another of the literary precursors of the Book of the Twelve.[1] This larger, three-part unit, comprised of Zech 9–11, Zech 12–14, and Mal 1–3 [ET Mal 1–4] perhaps circulated as one composite booklet of prophecy, which I shall call "the *Mas'ot* Triptych."[2] A triptych, a three-paneled painting or altarpiece, makes an alluring metaphor for these three roughly equal and adjacent portions of text.

1.1 My suggestion is that in the redactional assembly of the larger pieces that became the Book of the Twelve, one of the last substantial acts of the redactors was to break apart Haggai–Zech 1–8, making Haggai a separate booklet.[3] Perhaps at the same time the redactors likewise

---

1 Some of the questions pursued in this paper are addressed at greater length in my 2006 book, *Up the Steep and Stony Road*. Two literary precursors to the united Twelve have been well identified by Nogalski, *Precursors*: Hosea–Amos–Micah–Zephaniah, and Haggai–Zechariah 1–8. Schart, *Entstehung*, has successfully argued that early in their history the first four were placed upon a single scroll. Albertz has called this first precursor the "Book of the Four;" see "Exile;" *Israel*, 204–211. Meyers and Meyers, *Haggai*, have likewise successfully argued that Haggai and Zech 1–8 also once circulated on a single scroll. Cf. Wöhrle, "Haggai–Zechariah Corpus," who cites Klostermann as promoting the same view in 1896.
2 In the MT, *mas'ot* is the plural form of *massa'*. Rabbinic Hebrew uses *massa'ot*.
3 I shall use the term "booklet" to denote any of the individually named components of the Book of the Twelve, and reserve the word "book" for the entirety of a scroll. This practice seems more precise than the choice of "writing" for the individual booklets.

broke apart the *Mas'ot* Triptych, assigning the first two panels (Zech 9–11 and Zech 12–14) to follow Zech 8, and assigning the final panel to stand as the final booklet of the set. They gave this final booklet the label *mal'aki*, Malachi, "My Messenger." And so, my unorthodox suggestion is that *two* composite books perhaps once circulated as late precursors to the Twelve:

a) The Temple Book: Haggai + Zech 1–8;
b) The *Mas'ot* Triptych: Zech 9–11 + Zech 12–14 + Mal 1–3.

Those portions that we now label "Zechariah" were united; the non-Zecharian portions were separated out; and so as a three-booklet unit these materials became the end of the formative Twelve: Hag 1–2, Zech 1–14, and Mal 1–3. Haggai + Zech 1–8 may have previously stood for a time at the end of, say, a Book of the Nine, later to be separated in the manner I have described. At any rate, with the union of Zech 1–14, the booklets Haggai, Zechariah, and Malachi now comprised a redactional unit in its own right, a final trilogy placed at the end of the larger order of the formative Twelve.[4]

1.2 In discussing this proposal, I have space enough to address only three main points: the headings of the key texts, the question of a Haggai–Zechariah–Malachi corpus, and the date of Zech 9–14. The question of the date will be divided into two parts: the first in regard to Hellenistic and Persian period history; the second in regard to the question of whether Zech 12–14 is apocalyptic and therefore late. Finally, I shall draw a few tentative conclusions. Now to marshal – in brief space – some of the evidence and argument that may support this thesis.

2. The Headings of Zech 9–11, Zech 12–14, and Mal 1–3

2. As for the union of Haggai + Zech 1–8, I refer the reader to the well-known studies of Nogalski and of Meyers and Meyers.[5] Schart calls the Haggai + Zechariah link "unambiguous."[6]

2.1 As for evidence of the redactional framing of Zech 9–Mal 3, we must first understand the headings. Just as the Deuteronomistic headings of the Book of the Four show some variation in style, alongside stronger commonalities, giving credence to the hypothesis of "the

---

4 Whether late productions such as Joel or Jonah yet appeared in the set is uncertain.
5 Nogalski, *Precursors*; Meyers and Meyers, *Haggai*. For a negative conclusion on this point, see Kessler, *Haggai*, 56–57.
6 Schart, "Visions," 334.

Four," so too the titles and incipits of Zech 9–Mal 3 show some variation but nonetheless stronger commonalities.[7]

2.1.1 First, the commonality:

Zech 9:1 משא דבר יהוה
An oracle, Yahweh's word[8]

12:1 משא דבר יהוה
An oracle, Yahweh's word

Mal 1:1 משא דבר יהוה
An oracle, Yahweh's word

Here we find strong similarity: three identical words in each, followed
by adjacent, roughly equivalent lengths of text, three chapters each in
the Hebrew numbering.

2.1.2 However, the syntax by which each three-word combination
relates to its following text shows differences.

Zech 9:1 משא דבר יהוה בארץ חדרך
An oracle, the word of Yahweh is in the land of Hadrach ...[9]

12:1 משא דבר יהוה על ישראל נאם יהוה נטה
שמים ויסד ארץ ויצר רוח אדם בקרבו
An oracle, the word of Yahweh concerning Israel; the utterance
of Yahweh who stretches out heaven, who founds earth,
and who forms the spirit of a man within him.

Mal 1:1 משא דבר יהוה אל ישראל ביד מלאכי
An oracle, the word of Yahweh to Israel by the hand of Malachi.

Clearly there are differences here. The first is probably best read as a
title (משא) plus an incipit, since the syntax continues; the second reads
as a triple title; and the third as a double title. However, despite differences, the triple appearance of the opening three-word combination
seems to be a unifying redactional framing device difficult to miss.[10]
These three משא דבר יהוה openings are unique in the Hebrew Bible. Of
the seventeen literary units in the prophetic books labeled as משא,
"oracle," none join directly to it the additional דבר יהוה. The phrase

---

7   By "title" I denote a discrete heading, not syntactically linked to what follows; by
     "incipit," I denote the opening syntactical line of a text by which it can be easily
     identified. By "heading" I refer to both types.
8   Or "The oracle of Yahweh's word."
9   Or "The oracle of Yahweh's word is in the land of Hadrach."
10   Childs suggests a contrary view, that these three משא units arose independently of
     each other, and that the משא דבר יהוה phrase is but a superficial similarity of no
     importance for redaction history; see his *Introduction*, 480.492. But this leaves unex-
     plained the strange conjunction of the phrase in these three adjacent, equipoised
     units. His interest is to counter the widespread view that the three משא headings
     frame three anonymous oracles *arbitrarily* assigned to their present places in the can-
     on.

דבר יהוה appears in redactional frames very frequently; משא much less so. Their appearance together as a three-word phrase appears nowhere else, not even in the Twelve.

2.1.3 Within the Twelve we find some similarity in the משא openings of Nahum and Habakkuk, but the differences are far greater.

2.1.4 I therefore suggest that it is likely that the three literary units we now find as Zech 9–11, Zech 12–14, and Mal 1–3 were once a collection, a "*Mas'ot* Triptych," and are therefore yet another literary precursor to the Book of the Twelve alongside the Book of the Four and Haggai–Zech 1–8.[11] So, standing behind our present concluding trilogy of Haggai, Zechariah, and Malachi, we may have two redactional precursors: (a) the Temple Book, Haggai + Zech 1–8; and (b) the *Mas'ot* Triptych, Zech 9–11 + Zech 12–14 + Mal 1–3.

3. Do Haggai, Zechariah, and Malachi Comprise a Corpus?

3. Space does not permit a full review of evidence regarding a Haggai–Zechariah–Malachi corpus, which must await another occasion. Only a few points can be made. In their breaking apart each of these late, composite precursors, Haggai–Zech 1–8 and Zech 9–Mal 3, I suggest the redactors created a larger three-fold set of prophetic booklets, a Haggai–Zechariah–Malachi corpus. Since the work of Mason and Childs, it is now widely recognized that Zech 9–14 shares strong thematic and intertextual links to Zech 1–8, links that in part justify in our minds today the unification of these strange fourteen chapters into one prophetic booklet.[12] This makes for a decisive change from previous opinion, which held that the two sides of Zechariah were not related.[13] Chapters 1–8 belong with chapters 9–14.

3.1 Less widely recognized is the linkage between Haggai and Malachi. I shall cite a few significant links.

3.1.1 Few prophets are ever called מלאך, "messenger" or "angel." Aside from a perplexing text in Judges 2:1–5, we have only Haggai, who remarkably bears the same title, מלאך יהוה, and who speaks "Yahweh's message," מלאכות יהוה (1:13); and we have Malachi him-

---

11 Schart argues well that the *Grundschicht* of Malachi was once attached not to Zech 8 (so Nogalski, *Redactional Processes*) nor to Zech 13, but to Zech 14. See his "Visions," 335–339.
12 Mason, "Inner-Biblical Exegesis;" Childs, *Introduction*, 482–485. I attempt to carry these thematic and lexical connections further in *Up the Steep*, 256–267.
13 Soggin, *Introduction*, 347, could once say that "chs. 9–14 have nothing at all to do with chs. 1–8 of the book."

self, whose name is linked to the coming מלאך הברית, the "messenger of the covenant" in Mal 3:1c. This figure is introduced two lines earlier as "my messenger," מלאכי (3:1a). The name (or title?) "Malachi" involves a word play with this phrase.[14] The prophet Malachi is also the one who reproves the errant priests of Jerusalem so that they too may serve their true function as מלאך יהוה צבאות, "the messenger of Yahweh of the Heavenly Armies" (2:7).[15] Aside from Haggai, Zechariah, and Malachi, the מלאך יהוה appears nowhere else in the Twelve, and is only attested once more in all the Latter Prophets, in the Deuteronomistic story of the plague on the Assyrian army in Isa 37:36.

3.1.2 Another linkage is the great number of questions, often rhetorical questions, asked in both Haggai and Malachi (as well as in Zech 1–8).[16] Haggai and Malachi also share a strong interest in authoritative priestly instruction (תורה in both Hag 2:11 and Mal 2:6).[17] Is Malachi a latter-day disciple of Haggai?

3.2 Both books also uniquely share something in their redactional frames: both are reported as comprised of דבר יהוה given ביד, "by the hand of" the prophet, a phrase that never occurs elsewhere in a heading with דבר יהוה. Thus the heading of Malachi combines two elements: the first it shares with the משא דבר יהוה headings of the *Mas'ot* Triptych; the second it shares with the ביד + PN formula found in Haggai (1:1, 3; 2:1), and almost nowhere else in prophetic headings.[18] Thus we may conclude that the redactor of Malachi looks both to Zech 9–14 and to Hag 1–2 for his introductory formula. This evidence suggests that the tradents who framed the book of Malachi had also received the book of Haggai, or that the same multi-generational tradent community was responsible for both types of headings.

3.3 These three booklets, Haggai–Zechariah–Malachi, share important themes and a mutually congruent theological stance. That stance involves either Jerusalem's temple construction and the prospect of its

---

14 The book is usually taken as anonymous with the claim that "Malachi" is not a personal name; however, good arguments to the contrary are found in Glazier-McDonald, *Divine Messenger*, 27–29, and Childs, *Introduction*, 490.

15 Interestingly, Zech 12:8 has the Davidides fighting in the eschatological battle like the מלאך יהוה. The מלאך יהוה also appears in Zech 1:11–12; 3:1, 5, 6.

16 As noted by Pearce, "Literary Connectors," 283–284. He does observe that Zech 9–14 contains no questions. However, the assignment of the label "corpus" properly belongs to a late redactional stage in which all of Zech 1–14 stands as a united booklet, alongside Haggai and Malachi. For detailed analysis of the interrogatives, see Craig, "Interrogatives."

17 In neither case does the word תורה denote the Mosaic Torah, but rather priestly rulings and instructions. See Meyers, "Use."

18 The only other occasions in prophetic headings are Isa 20:1, and Jer 50:1; cf. the similar Jer 37:2.

ritual and spiritual purity under divinely approved civil and priestly leaders (Haggai, Zech 1–8), or Jerusalem's civil and priestly apostasy and the improper functioning of its temple (Zech 10–11; Mal 1–2), or Jerusalem's present failure in holiness, and the future possibility of the city's radical sanctification (Zech 9; Zech 12–14; Mal 3). Taken together, then, the evidence suggests that in their basic form, these three booklets perform a crucial task for Persian Period Jerusalem, presenting a more profound message than if taken separately, reinforcing the prospect that the three do indeed comprise a corpus at the end of the Twelve.

4. The Date of Zech 9–14:
Issues involving Hellenistic and Persian History

4. Perhaps the biggest obstacle to the acceptance of my *Mas'ot* Triptych thesis is the scholarly tradition of the last one hundred years and more that assigns Zech 9–14 to the Hellenistic or Maccabean age, while assigning Malachi mainly to the Persian Period. The precursors to the Twelve identified so well by Nogalski and others are not so greatly separated in time. Hosea, Amos, and Micah are near contemporaries, though Zephaniah is a century later.[19] Haggai and Zech 1–8 even have interlocking date formulae for the second year of King Darius, 520 B.C.E. A triptych of *Mas'ot* serving as another precursor seems much less likely if the parts are greatly separated in time. However, a Hellenistic date for Zech 9–14, while possible, is unsatisfactory for several reasons. Among recent scholars who likewise reject the Hellenistic dating in favor of the early Persian period are Petersen, Meyers and Meyers, Reventlow, Redditt, Boda, and on linguistic grounds, Hill.[20]

4.1 Critical opinion on the date and origins of Zech 9–14 wavered much in the nineteenth century. However, with Stade's three-part article in the 1881–1882 founding issues of *ZAW*, entitled "Deuterozacharja," a new consensus soon emerged toward a late postexilic date. Stade deemed that Zech 9:13's mention of the sons of "Yavan," the Greeks, was alone (*"allein"*!) persuasive for dating the text to the Alexandrian period or later. He meticulously placed particular text-units in Zech 9–14 at intervals from 306 to 278 B.C.E. Accordingly, Zech 10's mention of Egypt and Assyria referred to the Ptolemaic and Seleucid

---

19 Hagedorn wonders why Wöhrle does not pursue the prospect of a "Book of the Three," namely, Hosea, Amos, and Micah, all responding to the crisis of 701 B.C.E. See his review of Wöhrle's *Die frühen Sammlungen*, 602.

20 Petersen, *Zechariah 9–14*; Meyers and Meyers, *Zechariah 9–14*; Reventlow, *Propheten*, 129; Redditt, *Introduction*, 334; Boda, *Haggai*, 31, and Hill, "Dating."

empires from the time of the beginning of the Five Syrian Wars.[21] Following Stade, many interpreters took the opening passage of Zech 9 with its geographic list as the military itinerary of Alexander the Great in his conquest of Syro-Palestine. Does the evidence support this consensus?

4.2 This roster of cities and regions, Zech 9:1–8 neither reflects Alexander's itinerary, nor that of any other Hellenistic conqueror. Here is the roster in order: Hadrach, Damascus, Hamath, Tyre, Sidon, Ashkelon, Gaza, Ekron, and Ashdod. The name Hadrach, the most northerly on the list, seems an Assyrian-era relic. The region apparently lies adjacent to Issus, where Alexander fought Darius III in 333, yet Hellenistic geography knows no such name.[22] As for the second named site, after the Battle of Issus Alexander headed south along the coast, rather than to Damascus. A smaller force led by Parmenion headed off to subjugate Damascus, while Alexander came to Sidon, which surrendered, and then to Tyre. Zechariah 9:2 shows the opposite order: Tyre, then Sidon. After some dallying negotiations, Tyre resisted and endured a terrible seven-month siege before capitulating. The list then names Ashkelon and Gaza, but Alexander came to Gaza first, which like Tyre resisted. Gaza fell after two months; the other cities put up no resistance. Alexander then subjugated Egypt; only then did he turn to Damascus. This list does not conform to any known Hellenistic military itinerary, and thus Zech 9:1–8 provides no evidence for a Hellenistic date.[23] Almost any date in the first millennium B.C.E. could suit these geographic terms.

4.3 If the geographic list in Zech 9 gives no evidence of a Hellenistic date, what about the item Stade presents as his parade example, the mention of the sons of *Yavan*, the Greeks, in Zech 9:13? Stade believed that this reference was compelling, *"allein ein zwingender Grund,"* to demonstrate that these texts were Hellenistic in origin.[24] The Greek reference certainly permits a Hellenistic date, but such a date is far from demonstrated by it. It may be that Stade did not pay sufficient heed to the geopolitical problem posed by Greece for the Persian leadership in the late sixth and fifth centuries B.C.E. Stade wrote that in Zech 9 the sons of *Yavan* had to constitute the *"Weltmacht"* of the time.[25]

---

21   These details are found in Stade, "Deuterozacharja" (1882), 290–296.305.
22   See the Assyrian imperial texts naming the rarely attested Hadrach/Hattarika in ANET, 282–283.655.
23   Alexander's Syro-Palestinian campaign can be briefly reviewed in Hayes and Mandell, *Jewish People*, 21, or in Briant, *Cyrus*, 857–858, who appropriately cites Arrian, Diodorus, and Quintus Curtius.
24   Stade, "Deuterozacharja" (1882), 290.
25   Stade, "Deuterozacharja" (1882), 275.

The Greek city-states, of course, were not the *dominant* world power of the Persian period, but they did indeed comprise *a* world power; in fact, they proved to be Persia's most insurmountable problem. This strategic role of the Greeks may be sufficient to satisfy the geopolitics latent in Zech 9:13.

4.3.1 Among Yehudeans, Persian political loyalty was a widespread social value, and leaders such as Sheshbazzar, Zerubbabel, Ezra, and Nehemiah were all hand-picked by the imperial administration for their distinctive roles in Yehud.[26] Moreover, there was the coercive power of the empire demanding provision and recruitment from its populations for its immense, expensive, but essential military forces. We should therefore expect that young Yehudean men likely served in its ranks.[27] Armed conflict between Persian forces and the Greeks could well then provide the backdrop to Zech 9:13's oracular declaration, "I will rouse your sons, O Zion, against your sons, O *Yavan*, and make you like a warrior's sword."

4.3.2 Since it is widely thought that no mention of the Greeks in biblical texts is likely until the time of Alexander, a brief review of Persian-Greek conflict in the late sixth, fifth, and early fourth centuries is now in order. Persian conflict with the Greeks began in the aftermath of Cyrus's defeat of the kingdom of Lydia at Sardis in 546 B.C.E. This conquest brought the Persian Empire to the very edge of the Greeks' Aegean domains. Sparta instantly sent emissaries to demand of Cyrus no incursions on Greek cities. Herodotus reports that the astonished Cyrus asked some Greek bystanders who these Spartans were.[28] The answer to that question would haunt his successors. This story begins a long litany of Persian-Greek military confrontation and bloodletting that would not come to a (temporary) close for nearly one hundred years. Here is a survey of some of the clashes between Greek and Persian military in this era.

4.3.3 546–542 B.C.E: after Croesus' kingdom of Lydia falls to Persia, Cyrus systematically subjugates the Greek cities of the eastern Aegean. 525: Greek and Carian mercenary forces give substantial support to Pharaoh Amasis (570–525 B.C.E.) and Psammetichus III (525), but are

---

26   The messianic conspiracy theory involving Zerubbabel in a scheme of anti-Persian revolt cannot be accredited.

27   We know from the fifth century Elephantine archive that many Jews served at the Persian-Jewish-Aramean military colony on Elephantine Island, in the Nile near present day Aswan, the southern extremity of Persian rule in Africa. This archive seems to be our only direct source of knowledge of Jewish service in the Persian military. The archive's Jewish documents date from 471 to about 400 B.C.E. For the archive, see Porten and Greenfield, *Jews*.

28   *Histories*, 1:152–153.

defeated by Cambyses. 522: Polycrates, tyrant of Samos and dominant naval power in the Aegean islands, is entrapped and impaled at a "peace" parley by Oroites, Persian satrap of Sardis. 519: Darius subdues the first Egyptian revolt, but is forced to redeploy his forces to the empire's northwestern hinterlands to hold back Greek incursions. 516: Darius succeeds in subjugating Samos, the Hellespont, and Thrace. 513: after a failed attempt against the Scythians, Darius returns to Sardis, his satrapic capital in the northwest, and ponders the Greek problem. 500–499: the Ionian Revolt begins, abetted much by the Athenians. 498: a joint force of Ionians and Eretrians, with Athenians in the lead, burns Sardis; Cyprus soon joins the revolt. 493: with help from a large and well-paid Phoenician naval force, Darius at last crushes the Ionians. 492: Mardonius, Darius' son-in-law, invades Greece in reprisal. 490: Darius himself invades Greece, but fails at the Battle of Marathon. 486: a second (and hugely popular) Egyptian revolt breaks out at the death of Darius; oppressive taxation levels contribute to the public unrest. 480: after years of preparation, Xerxes invades Greece, succeeds with difficulty against the famously resilient but doomed Spartans at Thermopylae, burns Athens, but meets disaster on the seas at the Battle of Salamis. 464–454: the Libyan king Inaros leads a third Egyptian revolt, with massive Athenian support. As Persia retaliates, Athens loses 250 triremes and countless men in the Nile Delta. An Athenian army is likewise crushed at Kition in Cyprus. 449: the Peace of Callias brings a negotiated end to hostilities, for a time. 411–404: the Persians assist Sparta against the Athenians in the third and final phase of the Peloponnesian War. Athens is defeated, never to recover. 408: the Jewish temple at Elephantine Island is destroyed by Egyptian rebels; Jewish members of the military outpost there write to the governors of Jerusalem and Samaria regarding its reconstruction. 404: the Egyptian revolt achieves independence, which lasts sixty years (404–343). 401: in an attempt to take the Persian throne Cyrus the Younger is killed in battle against his brother, Artaxerxes II; Cyrus' army of perhaps 30.000 holds 14.000 Greeks; the future historian Xenophon serves as an officer in the Greek contingent. 390s: the successful Egyptians now invade Persian Palestine from the Sinai; their Cypriot and Athenian allies occupy the northern coastal plain of Palestine – a Greek invasion of Palestinian territory sixty years before Alexander. 385: Athens withdraws its forces from Palestine, making a separate peace with Persia. 380: the Persians at last succeed in forcefully expelling the Cypriots and the Egyptians from Palestine.

4.3.4 The list could continue in similar style.[29] The point is to show the enormous importance of the Greeks in the geopolitics of the eastern Mediterranean world, including Egypt and Syro-Palestine, and how much effort the Persians expended in countering Greek power. Perhaps the most interesting item on the list is the redeployment of forces to the northwestern/Greek frontier of the empire after Darius pacified the Egyptian revolt of 519 B.C.E. This move intrigues, because Darius had marched the main force of the Persian army through Syro-Palestine twice, into Egypt and out again. Jerusalem and Yehud were almost undoubtedly caught up in these events.

4.3.5 It seems that four times in the 520s and 510s the main force of the Persian army moved through Syro-Palestine, placing extraordinary demands for supply and manpower upon the territories through which it passed. Berquist makes much of the strain imposed upon Yehud in 520 by the duty of preparing for provisioning the Persian army in its upcoming march to Egypt in 519, and interprets the agricultural distress in Haggai and the anxiety over international peace in Zech 1–8 in this light.[30] Men and materiel from along the route were undoubtedly and coercively drawn into the Persian effort. In his redeployment from Egypt in 518 Darius may well have taken new Syro-Palestinian conscripts with him up to the northwestern/Greek frontier. Perhaps this is the *Sitz im Leben* of Zech 9:13's confrontation between the sons of Zion and the sons of Yavan.

4.3.6 Stern, a judicious archaeological excavator and analyst, makes much of Greek presence in Persian period Syro-Palestine. In Phoenicia, Philistia, and often Palestine too, Stern says, Phoenician population and material culture dominate, but a strong second element is Greek and Cypriot population with their distinctive material cultures. Sometimes the Greek evidence is military in nature: bronze Greek helmets are found in the sea off the ports of Dor, Ashdod, and Ashkelon; or bronze Greek arrowheads.[31] At Persian-era Dor, a Greek trading colony boasting its own temple was found; another Greek trading colony is found at Acco; such colonies often date from the sixth century. Stern reports the presence of Cypriot pilgrims or soldiers at Persian-era Sidon, Sarepta,

---

29 Much of the earlier part of this history is discussed in Herodotus, *Histories*. See especially 1:152–153; 3:124–125; 5:96–106. For secondary sources, see Sealey, *Greek City States*, 169–230.369–385; Briant, *Cyrus*, 36–38.52.141–146; Cook, *Persian Empire*, 59–60.64; Stern, *Archaeology*, 353–360; Hoglund, *Administration*, 138–164. In this last source, Hoglund argued that the missions of Ezra and Nehemiah in Jerusalem ought to be understood as part of a general Persian policy to secure Syro-Palestine against the Greek threat in the eastern Mediterranean.

30 Berquist, *Judaism*, 65–72.

31 Stern, *Archaeology*, respectively 410.422.521–522.533.

and Dor. Tel el-Kheleifeh on the Red Sea was a joint Phoenician and Greek trading colony, showing Greek participation in the trade connecting Arabia with the Mediterranean.[32] *Doros* (Dor) also appears on the Athenian tribute lists in the mid fifth century. Hoglund therefore concludes that Dor dared to assist Athens in the Inaros revolt in 454.[33]

4.4 For Persian loyalists in Yehud, the Greek city states must have appeared as an ominous foreign power all too near at hand. A prophet's promise of divine help against them, as in Zech 9, would have been welcomed. This scenario seems at least as plausible as the frequently encountered view that relegates the text of Zech 9–14 to the Maccabean age and fails to connect it to the rest of the book of Zechariah. Zechariah 9:13 does not require the sons of Yavan to be the dominant world power, only a significant world power, one that shall vie against Persia and threaten Zion.

4.5 Thus Stade's best evidences for a Hellenistic date fail to make a strong case.

5. The Date of Zech 9–14: Is the Text Apocalyptic?

5. Another impediment to the acceptance of my Persian-era thesis for the *Mas'ot* Triptych is the frequent claim that Zech 9–14, or major sections of 9–14, are apocalyptic literature, and therefore late in origin.[34] Here I can only briefly suggest a line of argument.

5.1 In 1979 the Society of Biblical Literature's Apocalypse Group, a part of the Genres Project, published a major report on its work, which the group entitled *Apocalypse: The Morphology of a Genre*.[35] In that widely praised report it was judged that Zech 1–8 "anticipates the later apocalypses in manner of revelation and the disclosure of otherworldly realities, but lacks the distinctively apocalyptic eschatology." On the other hand, regarding Zech 9–11 and Zech 12–14, "in form ... these passages are prophetic oracles ... not ... visions with interpretations." Thus, both sides of Zechariah fail to make the grade as apocalypses. Moreover, "in Zechariah 9–14 ... we may recognize some of the major characteristics of apocalyptic eschatology." However, "all these writings must still be categorized formally as prophetic oracles, not as apocalypses, since

32 Stern, *Archaeology*, respectively 458.460.502–503.519.
33 Hoglund, *Administration*, 153–154.
34 These two conclusions do not always go together: Hanson, *Dawn*, 369, labels Zech 14 "full-blown apocalyptic," but nonetheless assigns the text to the Persian period. See also the critique of Hanson in my book, *Up the Steep*, 156–160.278.
35 Collins, *Apocalypse*, v.

they lack the apocalyptic manner of revelation, with an otherworldly mediator."[36]

5.2 Particularly notable is the statement that Zech 9–14 only possesses "some" of the elements of apocalyptic eschatology. A brief review of Zech 14 bears out the lack of a fully apocalyptic, otherworldly or trans-historical eschatology. In Zech 14 after the terrible eschatological battle, there shall indeed be a cosmic transformation. Continuous day seems indicated; Jerusalem's mountain is immensely elevated; the rest of the land is flattened like the Arabah. "Living water" shall flow from Zion east and west, renewing land and sea. The survivors of the nations that fought against Jerusalem will be converted, to join Yehud in worship at the Feast of Tabernacles. There shall be annual pilgrimage; if any nation refuses pilgrimage, drought shall afflict it. Egypt too shall suffer plagues as in the book of Exodus, if it refuses pilgrimage. Holiness shall be so pervasive that the inscription "holy to Yahweh" from the high priest's tiara shall be inscribed even on humble objects like harness bells and cooking pots. Temple purity shall be inviolate. Holiness shall prevail everywhere in Yehud.

5.3 This is not the advanced eschatology of, say, Daniel 12 with its "end of days" and the resurrection of those righteous ones who "sleep in the dust," who shall emerge transformed to shine like the stars. It is the Day of the Lord, but not the end of days. Evil and sin remain in the world; nations might refuse pilgrimage and thus suffer drought or plague. We do not even find the finality of the judgment separating the righteous and the wicked that we see in Mal 3, where the wicked are consumed "root and branch," leaving them as "ashes under the feet" of those who revere God's name (3:19 MT), a text that is usually recognized as Persian era. The eschatology of Zech 14, then, still has one foot within this mortal world. Zechariah 14, while somewhat more trans-historical than Zech 8, is not as trans-historical as the Persian-era Mal 3. If fully apocalyptic texts must be late, Zech 9–14 does not qualify as apocalyptic, and therefore may be early.

5.4 These two impediments that we have reviewed, a Hellenistic date and an apocalyptic genre designation for Zech 9–14, are not borne out by the evidence. The evidence permits a Persian era date for Zech 9–14, and thus makes the *Mas'ot* Triptych proposal more tenable.

---

36   Collins, "Apocalypses," 29.

6. Conclusion

6. Let me very tentatively suggest a concluding historical scenario that may be roughly congruent with the biblical material reviewed above, though simplified.

6.1 The Temple Book, Haggai + Zech 1–8, represents the prophetic materials of the first generation of a prophetic group in Persian-period Jerusalem, 520–518 B.C.E., marked by redactionally framed dated oracles. This material circulates in the larger community of Jerusalem as encouragement to a no-longer moribund temple building project that had so daunted the community. The temple is completed by 516. Whether the Temple Book thereafter remains independent, or is taken up as the conclusion of the formative Book of the Twelve is unclear. The temple begins to function as the cultic center of fledgling Yehud, though Jerusalem itself remains under-populated and under-developed. Various lesser redactional processes lay hold of the prophetic material.

6.2 An unknown length of time elapses, though a Hellenistic date is unwarranted. A second body of prophetic material begins to be produced by members of this prophet-tradent, Persian-era community, perhaps presided over by an aging Zechariah or by his close associates and successors. Much of this new material, produced in various phases, stands in utterly sharp rebuke to the civic and priestly leaders and the people, who represent a new generation lacking the conviction of those who rebuilt the temple. Some of this material seems designed for the members of the inner circle of tradents; other parts are designed for public dispute in the streets of the city. Various redactional processes shape the material.

6.3 This prophetic material is eventually bound together as the *Mas'ot* Triptych, a three-part book whose basic form stems from at least two main hands. The decision is made (when? by whom?) to add this material to the Book of the Twelve. Perhaps at this time the Haggai material is broken off from the Temple Book, conforming Hag 1–2 to the practice of the formative Twelve, since each booklet in the lengthening scroll names one prophet as revelatory agent. The remembered tradition of the tradent group associates the material we now call Zech 9–11 and Zech 12–14 with the prophet Zechariah, though other hands may also have been at work. Hence, all the Zechariah-tradition materials are likewise united into one booklet. The distinctive Malachi material is also added as under one prophetic name. Since Haggai was associated with Zechariah (1–8), Malachi was associated with Zechariah (9–14), and Zech 1–14 is now united, a corpus of three prophetic books now concludes the Twelve. Various lesser redactional processes continue. Whether other late productions such as Joel and Jonah were added at this time remains unclear.

6.4 Perhaps in this way the Temple Book of Haggai + Zech 1–8, and the *Mas'ot* Triptych of Zech 9–11, Zech 12–14, and Mal 1–3, may have been produced and entered the Book of the Twelve, providing an authoritative word to guide, confront, and purify the ancient people of God.

References

Albertz, R. "Exile as Purification: Reconstructing the 'Book of the Four.'" Pp. 232–251 in *Thematic Threads in the Book of the Twelve*. Edited by P.L. Redditt and A. Schart. BZAW 325. Berlin: de Gruyter, 2003.

– *Israel in Exile*. Translated by D. Green. Studies in Biblical Literature 3. Atlanta: Society of Biblical Literature, 2003.

Berquist, J.L. *Judaism in Persia's Shadow: A Social and Historical Approach*. Minneapolis: Fortress, 1995.

Boda, M.J. *Haggai, Zechariah*. NIV Application Commentary. Grand Rapids: Zondervan, 2004.

Briant, P. *From Cyrus to Alexander: A History of the Persian Empire*. Translated by P.T. Daniels. Winona Lake: Eisenbrauns, 2002.

Childs, B.S. *Introduction to the Old Testament as Canonical Scripture*. Philadelphia: Fortress, 1979.

Collins, J.J. "The Jewish Apocalypses." Pp. 21–61 in *Apocalypse: The Morphology of a Genre*. Edited by idem. Semeia 14. Missoula: Scholars Press, 1979.

– (ed.) *Apocalypse: The Morphology of a Genre*. Semeia 14. Missoula: Scholars Press, 1979.

Cook, J.M. *The Persian Empire*. New York: Schocken Books, 1983.

Craig, K.M. "Interrogatives in Haggai–Zechariah: A Literary Thread?" Pp. 222–244 in *Forming Prophetic Literature: Essays on Isaiah and the Twelve in Honor of John D.W. Watts*. Edited by J.W. Watts and P.R. House. JSOTSup 235. Sheffield: Sheffield Academic Press, 1996.

Curtis, B.G. *Up the Steep and Stony Road: The Book of Zechariah in Social Location Trajectory Analysis*. Academia Biblica 25. Atlanta: Society of Biblical Literature, 2006.

Glazier-McDonald, B. *Malachi: The Divine Messenger*. SBLDS 98. Atlanta: Scholars Press, 1987.

Hagedorn, A.C. Review of J. Wöhrle, *Die frühen Sammlungen des Zwölfprophetenbuches: Entstehung und Komposition*. JTS 58 (2007) 601–603.

Hanson, P.D. *The Dawn of Apocalyptic: The Historical and Sociological Roots of Jewish Apocalyptic Eschatology*. Revised ed. Philadelphia: Fortress, 1979.

Hayes, J.H. and Mandell, S.R. *The Jewish People in Classical Antiquity: From Alexander to Bar Kochba*. Louisville: Westminster John Knox, 1998.

Herodotus, *Histories*. Translated by A. de Sélincourt. Baltimore: Penguin Classics, 1954.

Hill, A.E. "Dating Second Zechariah: A Linguistic Examination." *HAR* 6 (1982) 105–134.

Hoglund, K.G. *Achaemenid Imperial Administration in Syria-Palestine and the Missions of Ezra and Nehemiah*. SBLDS 125. Atlanta: Scholars Press, 1992.

Kessler, J. *The Book of Haggai: Prophecy and Society in Early Persian Period Yehud*. VTSup 91. Leiden: Brill, 2002.

Mason, R.A. "Some Examples of Inner-Biblical Exegesis in Zech. 9–14." *Studia Evangelica* 7 (1982) 343–354.

–   "The Use of Earlier Biblical Material in Zechariah 9–14: A Study in Inner Biblical Exegesis." Pp. 2–202 in *Bringing Out the Treasure: Inner Biblical Allusion in Zechariah 9–14*. Edited by M.J. Boda and M.H. Floyd. JSOTSup 370. Sheffield: Sheffield Academic Press, 2003.

Meyers, C.L. and Meyers, E.M. *Haggai, Zechariah 1–8*. AB 25B. Garden City: Doubleday, 1987.

–   *Zechariah 9–14*. AB 25C. New York: Doubleday, 1993.

Meyers, E.M. "The use of *Tora* in Haggai 2:11 and the Role of the Prophet in the Restoration Community." Pp. 69–76 in *The Word of the Lord Shall Go Forth*. Edited by C.L. Meyers and M. O'Connor. FS D.N. Freedman. Winona Lake: Eisenbrauns, 1983.

Nogalski, J.D. *Literary Precursors to the Book of the Twelve*. BZAW 217. Berlin: de Gruyter, 1993.

–   *Redactional Processes in the Book of the Twelve*. BZAW 218. Berlin: de Gruyter, 1993.

Pearce, R.W. "Literary Connectors and a Haggai/Zechariah/Malachi Corpus." *JETS* 27 (1984) 277–289.

–   "A Thematic Development of the Haggai/Zechariah/Malachi Corpus." *JETS* 27 (1984) 401–412.

Petersen, D.L. *Zechariah 9–14 and Malachi: A Commentary*. OTL. Philadelphia: Westminster, 1995.

Porten, B. and Greenfield, J.C. *Jews of Elephantine and Arameans of Syene (Fifth Century B.C.E.): Fifty Aramaic Texts with Hebrew and English Translations*. Jerusalem: Department of the History of the Jewish People, 1974.

Pritchard, J.B. (ed.) *Ancient Near Eastern Texts Relating to the Old Testament*. 3rd ed. Princeton: Princeton University Press, 1969.

Redditt, P.L. *Introduction to the Prophets*. Grand Rapids: Eerdmans, 2008.

Reventlow, H.G. *Die Propheten Haggai, Sacharja und Maleachi*. ATD 25,2. Göttingen: Vandenhoeck & Ruprecht, 1993.

Schart A. *Die Entstehung des Zwölfprophetenbuchs: Neubearbeitungen von Amos im Rahmen schriftenübergreifender Redaktionsprozesse*. BZAW 260. Berlin: de Gruyter, 1998.

–   "Putting the Eschatological Visions of Zechariah in their Place: Malachi as a Hermeneutical Guide for the Last Section of the Book of the Twelve." Pp. 333–343 in *Bringing Out the Treasure: Inner Biblical Allusion in Zechariah 9–14*. Edited by M.J. Boda and M.H. Floyd. JSOTSup 370. Sheffield: Sheffield Academic Press, 2003.

206 Byron G. Curtis

Sealey, R. *A History of the Greek City States ca. 700–338 B.C.* Berkeley: University of California Press, 1976.
Soggin, J.A. *Introduction to the Old Testament*. Translated by J. Bowden. Revised ed. OTL. Philadelphia: Westminster, 1980.
Stade, B. "Deuterozacharja: eine kritische Studie." *ZAW* 1 (1881) 1–96.
– "Deuterozacharja: eine kritische Studie." *ZAW* 2 (1882) 157–172.
– "Deuterozacharja: eine kritische Studie." *ZAW* 2 (1882) 275–309.
Stern, E. *The Assyrian, Babylonian, and Persian Periods (732–332 B.C.E.)*. Vol. 2 of *Archaeology of the Land of the Bible*. ABRL. New York: Doubleday, 2001.
Wöhrle, J. "The Formation and Intention of the Haggai–Zechariah Corpus." *Journal of Hebrew Scriptures* 6.10 (2006) 1–14.

Redactional Connectors in Zechariah 9–14

PAUL L. REDDITT

Georgetown College

Baptist Seminary of Kentucky

Zechariah 9–14 is replete with images of God as shepherd (9:16; 10:1–3) and especially as warrior/king (9:1–8, 11–15; 10:3–5, 9, 11–12; 11:17; 12:1–9; 13:7–9; 14:1–5, 9, 16–17). Two crucial issues in Zechariah 9–14, conversely, are the identities of the human shepherds in charge of God's flock (11:4–17; 13:7–9) and the human king (9:9–10).[1] Understanding these six chapters, therefore, requires understanding the dynamics between the divine and the human shepherds and kings. This paper will focus its attention on redactional passages that seem to guide the overall arrangement of Zechariah 9–14, judging how the final form of the text, and thus the redactor at work within it, views the human "shepherds" and the issue of a human king.

The paper will argue that the final redactor wrote six transition pieces that may be called "redactional bridges" (10:2–3a; 11:1–3; 12:7–8; 13:7–9; 14:18–19; and 14:21b) and three more pieces that may be called "redactional frames" (11:1–3 + 17; 14:12 + 15; 14:9 + 16–17) in building to his conclusion that the "shepherds" had failed to rule well and that YHWH, not a Davidide, would rule in the future. The first section will survey the growth of Zechariah 9–14, paying attention to the redactional word מַשָּׂא (maśśā', oracle) and to the structure of Zechariah 9–14. It also will discuss the phenomena of redactional bridges and redactional frames. The second section will examine the two most fully developed bridges: Zech 11:1–3 and 13:7–9. Zech 11:17, which completes a redactional frame with 11:1–3, will also be discussed at that point. The third section will study four simpler bridges (Zech 10:2–3a; 12:7–8; 14:18–19; and 14:21b), all of which likely derive from the same redactor. The fourth section will study two other redactional passages that one might call redactional frames (Zech 14:12 and 15; 14:9 and 16–17), the second of which also serves as a redactional bridge.

---

1   It is by no means clear that Zech 10:4 even has kings in view or that Zech 12:10–14 anticipates a new Davidic king.

1. The Growth of Zechariah 9–14

1.1 The first redactional element one encounters in the chapters is the redactional word מַשָּׂא, typically translated "Oracle."[2] It is followed immediately by the opening prophetic message, which begins: "The word of YHWH is against/upon the land of Hadrach, and will rest upon Damascus." It is clear that מַשָּׂא is not a part of that sentence. It is, rather, a one-word superscription for at least 9:1–8 and arguably more. That conclusion is reinforced by the fact that Zechariah 12 and Malachi 1 also begin with מַשָּׂא. In both of those cases, however, a second superscription follows. Zech 12:1 reads: "the word of the Lord concerning Israel; oracle of YHWH," the last phrase perhaps forming a separate – third – superscription. In Mal 1:1 the second superscription reads: "the word of the Lord to Israel by the hand of Malachi." The import of the recognition of the nature of Zech 9:1, 12:1, and Mal 1:1 is that a reader is confronted by three collections added to Haggai–Zechariah 1–8, each beginning with מַשָּׂא, and written with an eye on one another.

All three continue with the phrase "The word of the Lord."[3] In Zech 9:1 that phrase is simply the opening of the first line of the oracle, which extends through verse 8 or farther. In 12:1 מַשָּׂא precedes a separate superscription for at least Zech 12:1–9: "The word of God concerning Israel." The word "Israel" had been used previously in 9:1, where it referred to the twelve tribes, and in 11:14, where it designated the northern tribes in distinction from Judah. Zech 12:1 probably uses the word in conscious imitation of 9:1, *but* as a designation for Judah alone. Nothing at all is said of the northern tribes in Zechariah 12–14, so the use of the term appears to be polemical. Although "Israel" in 9:1 was revealed to include Judah and Ephraim in 9:10, 13; 10:7, and "Joseph" was paired with Judah as joint beneficiaries of God's rescue in 10:3b, chapters 12–14 limit the meaning to Judah and Jerusalem. Moreover, the second superscription is followed by the typical opening of a prophecy of destruction: "Thus says YHWH," which in turn is amplified by a hymn-like praise of God: "Who stretched out the heavens, and founded the earth, and formed the human breath within." Mal 1:1 also opens with מַשָּׂא and the phrase "The word of YHWH to Israel," which is followed by the phrase "by Malachi." That addition serves to attribute the three chapters that follow to someone called "My Messenger," a

---

2   On the significance of this word, see Conrad, *Zechariah*, 156; Moseman, "Two Zechariahs," 494, and O'Brien, *Nahum*, 234, among others.
3   For a discussion of the use of this phrase, see Boda, *Haggai*, 41–42.411.480.482, and Nogalski, *Redactional Processes*, 187–188.217.221.227–228.244.

designation probably derived from Mal 3:1: "Behold, I am sending my messenger, and he will make clear the way before me."

1.2 These observations lead to the probable conclusion, long recognized by critical scholars, that the three collections (Zech 9–11, 12–14, and Malachi) were added to Haggai–Zechariah by someone or ones with an eye on all three collections. To be sure those three collections probably grew over time, but ultimately they seem to have come together at the hand of a redactor or redactors who deliberately created similar opening statements for them. Further, the third collection, Malachi, seems to have grown up separately from Zechariah 9–14, since Malachi shares few of the concerns of Zechariah 9–14.

In Zech 9:1 משא *is* the superscription. What follows is the opening sentence of the message. In Mal 1:1 משא precedes the phrase "the word of YHWH to Israel *by Malachi*." The contrived name was added to supply the booklet an author. The name, if not the whole phrase "the word of YHWH by Malachi" was probably added when the booklet took its place after Haggai and Zechariah, i.e., well into the growth of the Twelve as a collection of words from named prophets. משא probably was added then in conscious imitation of Zech 9:1. Zech 12:1, however, is much more complex. It appears to have been constructed in conscious imitation of both Zech 9:1 and Mal 1:1, probably at the same time the three passages Zechariah 9–11, 12–14, and Malachi were joined to Zechariah 1–8. Zech 12:1 contains its own formulaic opening "Thus says the Lord…," plus two separate superscriptions משא and "the word of YHWH concerning Israel." It draws משא from Zech 9:1 (as does Mal 1:1), and claims the designation "Israel" for Judah alone.

1.3 An analysis of Zechariah 9–14 reveals a number of individual passages sewn together redactionally to form a literary mosaic. The first unit is 9:1–17. Verses 1–8 portray YHWH moving from Hadrach, Damascus, and Hamath in the north down the coast from Tyre and Sidon to the Philistine city Gaza before encamping at God's house. In v. 4, God the Warrior strips Tyre of its possessions, in v. 5 the human king of Gaza perishes, and in v. 8 God the Warrior encamps at the house of God to protect it. Verses 9–10 portray God's presentation of a new king, the only place in Zechariah 9–14 where an earthly, Jerusalemite king is explicitly predicted. Verses 11–13 include both Judah and Ephraim in God's new earthly kingdom. Verses 14–15 describe in the third person the Divine Warrior's rescue of his subjects, and v. 16–17 portray the Divine Shepherd caring for his flock.[4]

---

4   Person, *Second Zechariah*, 119.205, excludes a "prophetic" Zechariah 9 from 10–14, which chapters he ascribes to a Deuteronomic scribe/redactor.

1.4 The second redactional unit is Zech 10:1–12, which also envisions a future state including both Judah and Ephraim. The verses do not, however, speak of a future human king. Verse 1 speaks of people's asking for rain from YHWH, the One who sends storms and showers. Verse 2 shifts subjects to mention the teraphim, diviners, and dreamers who are no help, and laments that the people are like sheep without a shepherd. The verse does not mention prophets per se, though the reference to teraphim, diviners, and dreamers exposes the failure of many seers to predict the future. Verse 3a announces God's anger with human shepherds, and 3b envisions God's own shepherd-like care for Judah. Some scholars read the enigmatic v. 4 as a prediction of a king, but the text itself only uses the designation "warrior."[5] In the context of Persian-period Judah, one might expect hopes for liberation from Persia, but those hopes do not surface in Zechariah 10 in anything that actually speaks of a king – Persian or Judean. What is stated is that both Judah (v. 5) and Ephraim (v. 7) will become "like warriors" (כגברים, kĕgibbōrîm) with Israelites who had fled Israel returning home from Assyria and Egypt (v. 10). This prediction in Zech 10:3b–12 is tied to Zech 9:1–17 by 10:1–3a, which will receive further attention below.

1.5 The third unit is Zech 11:1–17, which contains the "Shepherd Allegory" in 11:4–16. The allegory draws upon and revises the vision of Ezek 37:15–23, in which the prophet takes two staffs, writes "For Judah and the Israelites associated with it" on one staff and "For Joseph (the stick of Ephraim) and all the house of Israel associated with it" on the other. Ezekiel was then to fuse the two separate staffs into one, symbolizing the reunion of the old David kingdom.[6] Obviously, that reunion never occurred, and Zech 11:4–16 explained why: poor leadership symbolized by shepherds/merchants. In other words, the priestly leadership of Persian period Judah was incapable of carrying out the Davidic task.[7] The allegory itself appears only in Zech 11:4–16. Zech 11:1–3 and 17 frame the allegory, and derive from a redactor about whom more will be said later.

---

5   The Hebrew reads נוגש (nôgēś), a Qal active participle, masculine singular from the root נגש, variously translated driver, taskmaster, ruler, oppressor, tyrant. The word could, of course, describe a king, but nothing in v. 4 suggests that a king is in view. Rather, the context suggests a warrior.

6   Tai, *Prophetie*, 151, has shown that Zech 11:16–17a also draws upon Ezek 34:2–4.

7   Space does not permit reviewing the long debate about the identity of the shepherds and merchants, but they seem to be two different groups. The shepherds were probably the priests at the temple, and the merchants may well have been their Persian overlords and cooperating Judeans, including the governors. See the forthcoming commentary by Redditt in the International Exegetical Commentary on the Old Testament.

1.6 The fourth unit contains a new account of the future Jerusalem (Zech 12:1–13:9). Its starting point is Zech 12:1–9, a complex account of a future war against Jerusalem defended by Warrior YHWH, but other issues are addressed in 12:10–13:1 and 13:2–6 by way of explanation of the failure of post-exilic hope for a better world. Specifically, Zech 12:10–13:1 anticipates the repentance of the Davidides and the Levites, with 13:1 adding that the Davidides and *all* the people of Jerusalem would cleanse themselves in a fountain. Also, Zech 13:2–6 anticipates the cessation of false prophecy. Zech 13:7–9, in which God fights for God's people, reaches back to Zech 11:1–3, however, and brings together the whole of Zechariah 11 through 13. Zechariah 14 comprises the last unit in Zechariah 9–14, and it – like 12:1–9 – describes a future war, but foresees not only God's intervention to defeat the nations, but also God's reigning in Jerusalem.

1.7 These five collections contain reflections from various time periods, with 9:1–13 or 9:1–17, perhaps arising fairly soon after the career of Zechariah and in light of his hope for a new Davidic king.[8] The other collections probably arose later, perhaps all in the fifth century. The centerpiece of these five collections is Zech 11:4–17, and Zechariah 14 revises the expectation for a human (presumably Davidic) king in 9:9–10 in favor of God as the king in Jerusalem. This structure may be outlined as follows:

9:1–17. God's Future United Kingdom and Earthly King
   10:1–12. The Future of Judah and Ephraim and the Return of Exiles
      11:1–17. The Shepherd Narrative
   12:1–13:9. War Narrative I: Jerusalem and Judah
14:1–21. War Narrative II: Jerusalem and Judah. God as the Future King

1.8 Cook sees in Zech 12:1–14:21 a chiasmus, and argues that it separates the shepherd piece in 13:7–9 from its original home at the end of the shepherd allegory in Zech 11:4–17. This new setting for the image, Cook argues, reverses the negative meaning of the shepherd in 11:15–17, and turns it into a more positive figure in 13:7–9.[9] Nogalski rightly rejects several of Cook's points, but commends him for highlighting the differences between 11:4–16 and 13:7–9. Nogalski argues, moreover, that 13:7–9 is no misplaced part of the Shepherd Allegory, but a separate, redactional passage.[10] One should also note that it is a redactional

8   Redditt, "King," 77–78. That Zech 9:9–10 is derived from a pro-Davidic thinker seems quite clear, but that view appears only in 9:9–10 in the whole of Zechariah 9–14.
9   Cook, "Metamorphosis," 460–463.
10 Nogalski, "Zechariah 13:7–9," 297.

passage that reaches back beyond אשׂמ in 12:1 to Zechariah 11 and the Shepherd Allegory, with which it dialogues.

1.9 What this paper is primarily focused on, however, is the redactional connections in Zechariah 9–14. It will study the major bridges between the main sections (Zech 11:1–3 + 17 and 13:7–9), other bridges that articulate those themes (Zech 10:2–3a and 14:21b), and other redactional verses that appear to derive from the same hand (12:7–8 and 14:18–19). It will also examine two redactional passages (14:12, 15; 14:9, 16–17) that frame earlier material.

2. Two Primary Redactional Bridges: 11:1–3 and 13:7–9

2.1 Zechariah 11:1–3. The first lengthy redactional bridge a reader encounters is Zech 11:1–3. Tai sees the passage as the final piece added to form 9:1–11:3,[11] which seems to connect it too closely to the entirely optimistic Zech 9. Ellul thinks it concludes the redactional unit that began with 10:1.[12] She is correct that it reaches back to chapter 10, but 11:1–3 does not continue the prominent themes of victory and the unity of Judah and Joseph/Ephraim that appear in 10:1–12 and in Zechariah 9 as well. Willi-Plein correctly sees the verses as the first part of a poetic frame (which included 11:17) for the prosaic shepherd narrative in v. 4–16.[13] Curtis, also correctly, calls v. 1–3 a "short linking unit" constituting a taunt song against the house of David, introducing a prophetic report, which he finds in v. 4–16.[14] Actually, however, the Davidides are not mentioned anywhere in 11:4–16/17, and they are mentioned explicitly only in 12:7–8, 10–12 and 13:1. There appears to be room, therefore, for a reinvestigation of 11:1–3.

2.1.1 Zech 11:1–3 does pick up the motif of the "shepherds" (in v. 1) from the redactional insertion 10:2–3a, and it picks up (in v. 3) the reference to Lebanon in 10:10. Zech 11:1–3 also anticipates the negative view of the shepherds in 11:4–16. In other words the verses create a bridge between 10:1–12 and 11:4–16/17. Two remarkable features of this bridge, however, are its literary quality and its awareness and use of other scriptures.

2.1.1.1 First, one could argue that Zech 11:1–3 constitutes a call to lament, especially in view of the opening of v. 2: "Wail, O cypress, for fallen is the cedar [forest]." The command to "wail" is ironic, however,

---

11   Tai, *Prophetie*, 127.
12   Ellul, "Variations," 59–60.
13   Willi-Plein, *Haggai*, 180–182.
14   Curtis, *Steep*, 163.194–195.

if not sarcastic,[15] and the attitude of the speaker is anything but sorrow-
ful. He does not sympathize with the "wailing" of the shepherds in v. 3,
but considers the destruction of their glory just desserts. Petersen objects to calling the passage a lament, and argues that v. 1–2 present the
voice of a prophet calling for destruction, while v. 3 presents the response.[16] Correct though he is about what happens in the verses, the
taunting nature of the passage seems to justify Curtis's identification
also.

2.1.1.2 Second, it is possible to identify several of the sources standing behind Zech 11:1–3, in particular Isa 10:33–34, Isa 2:13, and Jer
25:34–38, all passages of judgment.[17]

Isa 10:33–34	Destruction of trees of Lebanon	Zech 11:1
Isa 2:13–15	Trees of Lebanon and Bashan	Zech 11:1–2
Jer 25:34	Call to lament ("Wail")	Zech 11:2
Jer 25:36	Wailing of the shepherds	Zech 11:3
Jer 25:36–37	Despoliation of pasture/glory	Zech 11:3
Jer 25:38	Lions leave their covert or roar	Zech 11:3

2.1.1.3 It is difficult to avoid the conclusion that 11:1–3 was created
for its position in Zechariah 9–14. These verses, as noted above, pick up
Lebanon from Zech 10:10 in v. 1, and the mention of shepherd(s) in
11:2b–3a anticipates the lengthy discussion of shepherds in v. 4–
16(17).[18] They cohere, moreover, through the repetition of three words.
The verb יָלַל (yll, wail) appears three times: twice in v. 2 as impera-
tives, and once in v. 3 as a participle. The verb שָׁדַד (šdd, destroy, ruin)
also appears three times: once in v. 2 and twice in v. 3. The noun קוֹל
(qwl, sound) appears twice in v. 3.

2.1.2 The interpretation of v. 1–3 is disputed. Some scholars argue
that the cedars, the shepherds, and the lion all symbolize rulers, but
disagree on which ones. More importantly, however, Deut 11:24, Josh
1:4 and 11:17 seem to associate Lebanon with the ideal boundaries of
Israel, and Zech 10:10 includes Lebanon along with Gilead as part of
the future northern kingdom. Curtis, moreover, understands Lebanon
as a reference to the name of Solomon's palace "the House of the Lebanon Forest" (1 Kgs 7:2),[19] and Boda also points out that a lion does not

15 One may note a parallel with the sarcasm about rulers in the fable about the trees
    searching for a tree to rule over them in Judg 9:15, a connection noted by Willi-Plein,
    Prophetie, 73.
16 Petersen, *Zechariah 9–14*, 82.
17 These three passages do not constitute a definitive, but a representative list. Other
    scholars cite similar texts.
18 Cf. Ollenberger, "Zechariah," 817.
19 Curtis, *Steep*, 194.

roar over defeat, but over attack and victory.[20] He notes that Jer 25:34–
38 and Isa 10:33–34, both alluded to in Zech 11:1–3, predict the downfall of Assyria and Babylon, so he thinks those three verses should be
read more positively than is usually suggested. It is not clear, however,
that the verses as a whole are so positive in meaning. It seems better to
see v. 3a as a depiction of shepherds *bewailing* the loss of their flocks,
and v. 3b as a depiction of lions *roaring* over the fall of the shepherds'
majesty. In addition, the verses lead directly into Zech 11:4–16(17).
What "falls" in that passage is Ezekiel's hope for the favor of God
(37:15–23) and the reunion of Judah and Ephraim under a Davidic ruler
(37:24–28). This redactional bridge in Zech 11:1–3 gathers up the hopes
found in Zechariah 9–10 and declares them void. Then, it looks forward
to Zech 11:4–16(17), which explains why. Thus, the overall message of
v. 1–3 is one of destruction: devouring fire, felled forests, ruined majesty of the Jordan; and the piece leads into what will follow in v. 4–16(17).
This taunt against the shepherds in v. 1–3 *anticipates* the allegory about
the shepherds in v. 4–16, and the report in v. 17 *responds* to those verses,
in particular to the "worthless shepherd" God had directed the Narrator to imitate in v. 15–16.[21]

The identity of the shepherds is one of the most contested issues in
the study of Zechariah 9–14. The nominees include three sets of kings
or priests of Israel, various foreign kings of Israel/Judah or enemy nations (Assyria, Babylon, and Persia), other biblical figures (e.g., Moses,
Aaron, and Miriam), later Jewish groups (Pharisees, Sadducees, and
Essenes), and smaller national enemies (Moabites, Edomites, and Ama-
lekites). Hanson's view that the post-exilic hierocratic priests were the
shepherds seems best, however. Focusing on Zech 11:11–13, where the
sheep merchants try to pay the narrator of the so-called Shepherd Allegory only to have the money flung into the temple, Hanson concludes:
"by this act the shepherd identifies the ultimate source of the corruption and the exploitation which are destroying the [Persian period]
community: the temple and its leaders are to blame!"[22] In v. 14 the narrator breaks the second staff, the one named Union. The meaning was
clear: the reunion of Judah and Ephraim (anticipated in Ezekiel and in
Zechariah 9 and 10) was a dead issue. It would not happen. In v. 15–16
God calls the narrator of Zechariah 11 to return to work as a "worth-

---

20 Boda, *Haggai*, 460–461.
21 It is this connection between Zech 11:1–3 and 11:4–17 that Steck, *Abschluß*, 196–197,
    misses. He argues that Zech 10:3–11:3 was added to the growing Zechariah corpus
    between 320 and 315, while 11:4–13:9 (except for part of 12:1–9) was added ca. 311–
    302.
22 Hanson, *Dawn*, 347.

less" shepherd. This time he is called to ignore all the harm suffered by the sheep: death, wandering off, being maimed. Indeed, he – like a wolf – eats the sheep, right down to their hooves.

When Zech 11:4–16 was written, Persia had given the high priest religious but not political power over Judah.[23] That power and how the author of Zech 11:4–16 perceived its use seems to be the background for this passage. This text is an allegory, not an autobiography. The action is partly a reflection on the times of the author, partly sheer imagination, and partly prediction. All constitute an explanation of why the scene reported in Ezekiel was a dead issue. Modern readers should recognize, therefore, that the narrative charges the narrator with disposing of the three shepherds (v. 8), abandoning the sheep (v. 9), and taking on the role of shepherd a second time when the shepherd will simply eat the sheep himself (v. 16). He is the *antitype* of the divine shepherd. He is the shepherd who is cursed in v. 17. Not only is that verse a curse, however, it also completes a poetic frame around the allegory.

2.2 Zechariah 13:7–9. This passage constitutes the second most obvious redactional bridge. It concludes the lengthy discussion of the failures of the Davidides, the Levites, and the false prophets (Zech 12:10–13:6), and it reaches back to the shepherd passage in Zech 11:4–16/17. It too borrows from texts outside Zechariah. A chart will highlight several parallels.

Ezek 34:5	Sheep scattered because of shepherds	Zech 13:7
Ezek 5:3	Two-thirds scattered; one-third refined in fire[24]	Zech 13:8
Mal 3:2–4	Refine people like silver, gold	Zech 13:9
Hos 2:23	Israel is God's people; YHWH is their God	Zech 13:9

2.2.1 First, scholars widely agree that Zech 13:7 reaches back to the Shepherd narrative in Zechariah 11.[25] Specifically, it returns to the motif of the "worthless shepherd" of Zech 11:15–16 and 17. In 13:7, however, God calls that shepherd "my associate." The verse appears to envision an attack on one particular priest, and if so one might be justified in speculating that he was the high priest. The divine warrior commands the sword to strike that priest/shepherd, with the result that the sheep will be scattered. Indeed God the Warrior would turn God's hand against the "little ones," presumably the people of Judah.

---

23 Cataldo, *Yehud*, 90 (Table 2) and 190.
24 Actually, in Ezek 5:2–4 the third group is scattered, and only a part is refined in the fire.
25 Reventlow, *Propheten*, 121, disagrees and understands 13:7 as an older, but independent verse. He argues that the shepherd in v. 7 has no connection with the shepherd/shepherds in chapter 11.

2.2.2 Second, Zech 13:8 says two-thirds of Judah's population would be cut off. A more limited expression of this thought appears in 14:2, where half of the citizens of the city will be sent into exile. O'Brien calls attention to a connection between 13:3 and 13:8 as well. In 13:3 the parents were responsible for stabbing their prophesying children, while in 13:8 YHWH the warrior will strike down the populace.[26]

2.2.3 Third, Zech 13:9a anticipates Mal 3:2b–4.[27] In Mal 3:2b God is compared to a refiner and a fuller, and v. 3 says that God will refine and purify the sons of Levi until they are fit to present offerings at the altar of God. Then, according to v. 4 the offering of Judah and Jerusalem will be pleasing to God again just as it had been in better days. If, as argued in this article, the shepherds are the priests, the connection between Zech 13:9 and Mal 3:2b–4 is much closer than scholars have usually imagined.

Zech 13:9b also looks outside the book of Zechariah. In 13:9b once the people are refined, God will say "They are my people," and the people will say "The Lord is our God," phrases taken from Hos 2:23. Nogalski has called attention to the redactional significance of Zech 13:9 for the Book of the Twelve as a whole.[28] Its purview presupposes at least a partial Twelve, which most likely includes at a minimum the Book of the Four (Hosea, Amos, Micah, and Zephaniah) on the one hand and Haggai, Zechariah, and Malachi on the other. In other words, this redactional connection bridges not just Zechariah 11 and 13, but much if not all of the Twelve.

3. Other Bridges Created by the Redactor of Zechariah 9–14

If Zech 11:1–3 and 13:7–9 are the two most obvious and extensive redactional bridges in Zechariah 9–14, they are not the only ones. This section will examine four more: 10:2–3a; 14:21b; 12:7–8; and 14:18–19, and in that order.

3.1 Zechariah 10:2–3a. The context of these verses is quite positive, opening with a statement that people ("they") request[29] rain from God who makes it. In v. 3b, the thought continues, affirming that God cares for Judah (v. 3b–6aα) and will bring back the house of Joseph/Ephraim (v. 6aβ). Thus, v. 1 + 3b–6aα constitute an entirely self-consistent por-

---

26 O'Brien, *Nahum*, 270.
27 See Nogalski, "Zechariah 13:7–9," 301–304.
28 Nogalski, *Processes*, 234–236.
29 Reading the verb שׁאלו as a third masculine plural indicative ("they ask") instead of as an imperative.

trayal of God's care for Judah, concluded by a transition to a portrayal of God's care for Ephraim. In v. 6b–12, God returns Joseph/Ephraim from Assyrian captivity and makes them warriors.

Verses 2–3a, by contrast, introduce a strident reference to shepherds, anticipating all of the shepherd passages to come. Verse 2b employs the anti-shepherd motif, using it in the comment that the people have no "shepherd," i.e., no reliable guide, whether the guide consulted the teraphim, practiced divination, or interpreted dreams. The verse ends with the sentence: "Therefore they [the people] wander like sheep; they suffer like those lacking a shepherd." The word "shepherd" in this passage seems to designate one who tends sheep, but in light of Zech 11:4–17 the whole of 2–3a takes on a much more sinister connotation. Simply stated, it *foreshadows* the use of the term "shepherds" in 11:4–17 and 13:7–9. Verse 3a also adds a descriptive note in parallelism: "and I will punish the leaders."

3.2 Zechariah 14:21b. This half verse closes Zech 14 as well as the book of Zechariah with a reference to the "merchants" (כְּנַעֲנִי) who figured so prominently in Zech 11:7, 11. Verse 21b appears to deliver one last, sarcastic blow to the people the redactor of Zechariah 9–14 held to be chiefly responsible for Persian period Judah's sad condition: the Persian overlords, perhaps including Judean officials. They were not the religious leaders of the Judean people, but the civil leaders. The half verse is, in fact, quite jarring in its context. Beginning with 14:16, the text had turned suddenly positive with regard to Jerusalem *and* Judah, but 14:21b insists that the merchants would no longer run the temple.

3.3 Zechariah 12:7–8. A third short bridge appears in Zech 12:7–8. That these verses constitute a redactional addition can be deduced from two observations. First, they are the only two verses in Zech 12:1–13:6 that speak of God in the third person; everywhere else God speaks in the first person.[30] Second, the mention of the house of David in this verse anticipates its use three times in 12:10–13:1. These verses are the only places in Zechariah 9–14 that mention the house of David. Not even God's presentation of the future king in 9:9–10 mentions a Davidic king, though it seems quite likely those two verses had one in view.[31] Zech 12:7–8, however, mentions the house of David twice, and the verses say that even the feeblest in Judah would be like him in military prowess. That is faint praise for a warrior king. Verse 8 also says "the

---

30   Elliger, *Propheten*, 168, treats 12:2b and 4a as simple glosses; cf. Reventlow, *Propheten*, 116. Rudolph, *Haggai*, 219, also treats v. 7 as a gloss, but argues that 12:1–14 forms the conclusion to 11:4–17, ignoring the introductory word "Oracle" and the heading "The word of the Lord concerning Israel."

31   See note 8 and, recently, Redditt, "King," 78–80.

house of David will be 'like God,'" but *immediately* redefines the phrase for itself: "like the angels." Wherever the redactor saw the phrase, it would not have been intended literally. It would have emphasized the role of the king in battle, but the redactor toned it down when he used it. Zech 12:10–13:1 emphasizes the need for the house of David to repent and be cleansed from sin and iniquity. Thus, this bridge, 12:7–8, inserted just prior to the last verse about the coming battle over Jerusalem, anticipates the discussion of the house of David in 12:10–13:1 and articulates a negative view of Davidides held by the final redactor of Zechariah 9–14. By including 12:10–13:1 the redactor says that the members of the house of David will be afforded the opportunity to cleanse themselves from sin (13:1), but he nowhere says that they will take advantage of the offer, let alone rule again. Appropriately, Pomykala emphatically argues that these verses offer no evidence of hope for a Davidic king or messiah.[32]

3.4 Zechariah 14:18–19. A fourth bridge to be discussed is Zech 14:18–19, which actually looks outside Zechariah 9–14. Scholars have long recognized that it alludes to Zech 8:22–23 with its presentation of the nations coming to Jerusalem "to entreat the favor of the Lord." Zech 14:18–19 repeats that motif, but excludes Egypt. Earlier Zech 10:9–10 alluded to Egypt along with Assyria as places to which fugitives or captives from northern Israel had fled, and from which they would return. Zech 14:18–19 has quite a different perspective. Those verses seem to single out Egypt for possible future obstinacy. One suspects that the redactor was displeased with something Egypt had done, though some scholars suggest that the verse was directed against Judeans living there. That issue will be left open here.

4. Redactional Frames in Zechariah 9–14

A different type of redactional device appears in Zech 14:12, 15 and in Zech 14: 9, 16–17. This device may be called a "redactional frame" because it introduces and concludes traditions with which it has little to do, thereby providing a new context for verses which it surrounds.

4.1 Zechariah 14:12 + 15. Zechariah 14 as a whole offers a complex program for the future. It opens with the prediction of a future war in v. 1–5, which involves God as the divine warrior. Verses 6–7 discuss changes in the climate, and v. 8, 10–11 to the geography in and around

---

32 Pomykala, *Dynasty*, 124. Petterson, *King*, 221–224, by contrast, still argues that the verses anticipate the messiah.

Jerusalem. Verses 13–14 seem finally to resume the motif of the future war against Jerusalem by discussing a holy war type "panic" that God will send upon the peoples who wage war against Jerusalem. Verses 12 and 15, however, bracket the discussion of the panic with a description of a plague that will befall the nations who experience the panic, including the animals in their camps as well.

What, then, is the function of this frame? It reintroduces (from v. 5) the motif of the holy war that God would fight for God's people, and it says that the means by which God will fight will be a plague (v. 12 and 15). Verse 12 announces the effect of the plague on soldiers: their entire bodies would rot. Verse 15 rounds off the passage by noting that all the animals (horses, mules, camels, donkeys, etc.) in the warring camps will suffer from the same plague. The cues in v. 13–14 for this development were the mention in v. 13 of the panic that God would send upon the enemy forces and in v. 14 of the despoliation of the enemy forces.[33]

4.2 Zechariah 14:9 + 16–17. The second frame appears in Zech 14:9 + 16–17. These three verses proclaim a royal theology that supersedes that of Zech 9. The Davidides had been tried in Zech 12:10–13:1 and found wanting. Repentance and purification lay in the future for them – if they repented. Nothing is said in those verses, however, about their resuming rulership. Zech 14:9 + 16–17 provide the final redactor's alternative. These verses assert the kingship of YHWH, who had presented the king to Jerusalem in Zech 9:9–10 anyway. That king, however, could never have been more than God's earthly representative. Zech 14, probably written later in the Persian period, depicted a future in which YHWH, the real king, ruled.[34] How the author of v. 9 + 16–17 thought such a kingship might actually work, he does not say.

4.2.1 Like Zech 13:7–9 and 14:18–19, however, 14:9 + 16–17 also form a redactional *bridge* with verses outside Zechariah 9–14, namely with Mal 1:14b and its proclamation of the kingship of God. Both passages proclaim God king over all the nations. Although the motif of YHWH as King is relatively widespread in the Old Testament, especially in Psalms, it is fairly rare in the Latter Prophets. It appears three times within four chapters in Deutero-Isaiah, once in the book of Jeremiah, once in Micah, and once in Obadiah, but four times in the two successive chapters Zech 14 and Mal 1. To be sure, God's statement that

---

33 Zech 14:18 mentions another plague, but it is associated with the hypothetical failure of Egypt to observe the Feast of Tabernacles. Thus, it is not the same plague as the one mentioned in 14:12+15.

34 See the similar ascription of kingship to YHWH in Zeph 3:15; YHWH as warrior appears in 3:17–19.

God is a great king in Mal 1:14b makes sense where it stands, but it follows a curse against persons who offer a blemished sacrifice. The last phrase in v. 14 ("my name is great among the nations") fits Malachi 1 like a glove, repeating Mal 1:11. The assertion of the *kingship* of YHWH in v. 11, however, is unique to that verse and stands out both in Malachi 1 and the book as a whole. It appears, then, that it was added in Mal 1:14 to create a bridge between Zechariah 14 and Malachi 1. If so, the writer who created the bridge to Malachi could be the same writer as the redactor of Zechariah 9–14, who used bridges so effectively in pulling together those chapters.

4.2.2 Zech 14:9 + 16–17 brings the six-chapter addition to Zechariah 1–8 to its climax on a high note, with a vision of God defeating the enemies of Jerusalem and becoming king over the earth. Jerusalem would serve as the earth's navel, through which God would nourish its inhabitants, especially the people of Judah. All inhabitants of the (known) world would recognize God's kingship and travel to Jerusalem annually to worship. It completes the promise of Zech 9:8:

> 9:8 Then I shall encamp at my house [as a] guard against all who depart and return,
>   No oppressor will overcome them again, for now I have seen with my eyes."

Verses 18–21, largely redactional, constitute the denouement of Zechariah 9–14.

5. Summary

To summarize, these observations have shown that Zech 9:1–17 details God's presentation of a new king – probably Davidic – to Jerusalem. It was attached to Zechariah 1–8 by means of the word אשׂמ. In view of the expectations for Zerubbabel in Haggai–Zechariah 6, it is possible, maybe even likely that the chapter was added by about the end of the sixth century. Zech 10:1, 3b–12 was added a little later to say the hope for a reunited kingdom was still alive, even if the expectation of a new king over that kingdom was not. After some time, though perhaps before the end of the fifth century B.C.E., hopes for Jerusalem's survival of attacks by the nations (12:1–6, 9), for its triumph under God in a coming battle (14:1–5, 13–14), and for its perfection (14:6–8, 10–11) were added, but with considerable qualification. Specifically, the shepherds, the ruling priests (11:4–16) would have to be punished (11:17), the Davidides and Levites purified (12:10–13:1), and false prophet silenced, even if their parents had to stab them (13:2–6). Zech 11:4–16 was anticipated by 10:2–3a and inserted into Zechariah 9–14 by means of 11:1–3, 17. Zech 14:1–8, 10–14 was attached and supplemented by hopes for God's reign, acknowledged by the nations at the feast of booths (14:9, 16–17, 20–21a).

The redactional bridges in 10:2–3a; 11:1–3, 17; 12:7–8; and 13:7–9 seem to be consistent with each other in abandoning hope for the upper class (Davidides and ruling priests alike as spelled out in 12:10–13:7). Deliberate editing drawing upon Hos 2:23; Zech 8:22–23; and Mal 3:2b–4 suggests that the final editor of Zechariah 9–14 was aware of much, perhaps all of the Twelve. Jonah is often cited as the last collection to be added to the Twelve, but these deliberations keep that issue open.[35]

References

Boda, M.J. *Haggai, Zechariah*. NIV Application Commentary. Grand Rapids: Zondervan, 2004.

Cataldo, J.W. *A Theocratic Yehud? Issues of Government in a Persian Province*. Library of Hebrew Bible / Old Testament Studies 498. New York: T&T Clark, 2009.

Conrad, E.W. *Zechariah*. Sheffield: Sheffield Academic Press, 1999.

Cook, S.L. "The Metamorphosis of a Shepherd: The Tradition History of Zechariah 11:17 + 13:7–9." *CBQ* 55 (1993) 453–456.

Curtis, B.G. *Up the Steep and Stony Road*. Academia Biblica 25. Atlanta: Society of Biblical Literature, 2006.

Elliger, K. *Die Propheten Nahum, Habakuk, Zephanja, Haggai, Sacharja, Maleachi*. Vol. 2 of *Das Buch der zwölf kleinen Propheten*. ATD 25. Göttingen: Vandenhoeck & Ruprecht, 1982.

Ellul, D. "Variations sur le Thème de la Guerre Sainte dans le Deutéro-Zacharie." *ETR* 56 (1981) 55–71.

Hanson, P.D. *The Dawn of Apocalyptic*. Philadelphia: Fortress, 1975.

Mason, R.A. "The Use of Earlier Biblical Material in Zechariah 9–14: A Study in Inner Biblical Exegesis." Pp. 1–208 in *Bringing out the Treasure: Inner Biblical Allusion in Zechariah 9–14*. Edited by M.J. Boda and M.H. Floyd. JSOTSup 370. Sheffield: Sheffield Academic Press, 2003.

Moseman, R.D. "Reading the Two Zechariahs as One." *RevExp* 97 (2000) 487–498.

Nogalski, J.D. *Redactional Processes in the Book of the Twelve*. BZAW 218. Berlin: de Gruyter, 1993.

–   "Zechariah 13:7–9 as a Transitional Text." Pp. 292–304 in *Bringing out the Treasure: Inner Biblical Allusion in Zechariah 9–14*. Edited by M.J. Boda and M.H. Floyd. JSOTSup 370. Sheffield: Sheffield Academic Press, 2003.

O'Brien, J. *Nahum, Habakkuk, Zephaniah, Haggai, Zechariah, Malachi*. Abingdon Old Testament Commentary. Nashville: Abingdon, 2004.

---

35   See Redditt, "Zechariah 9–14," 318–320.

Ollenberger, B.C. "The Book of Zechariah." Pp. 733–840 in vol. 7 of *The New Interpreter's Bible*. Nashville: Abingdon, 1997.

Person, R.F. *Second Zechariah and the Deuteronomic School*. JSOTSup 167. Sheffield: Sheffield Academic Press, 1993.

Petersen, D.L. *Zechariah 9–14 and Malachi*. OTL. Louisville: Westminster John Knox, 1995.

Petterson, A.R. *Behold your King: The Hope for the House of David in the Book of Zechariah*. LHBOTS 513. New York: T&T Clark, 2009.

Pomykala, K.E. *The Davidic Dynasty Tradition in Early Judaism*. SBLEJL 7. Atlanta: Scholars Press, 1995.

Redditt, P.L. "The King in Haggai–Zechariah 1–8 and the Book of the Twelve." Pp. 305–332 in *Tradition and Transition: Haggai and Zechariah 1–8 in the Trajectory of Hebrew Theology*. Edited by M.J. Boda and M.H. Floyd. Library of Hebrew Bible / Old Testament Studies 475. New York: T&T Clark, 2008.

–   "Zechariah 9–14: The Capstone of the Book of the Twelve." Pp. 305–323 in *Bringing out the Treasure: Inner Biblical Allusion in Zechariah 9–14*. Edited by M.J. Boda and M.H. Floyd. JSOTSup 370. Sheffield: Sheffield Academic Press, 2003.

Reventlow, H.G. *Die Propheten Haggai, Sacharja und Maleachi*. ATD 25,2. Göttingen: Vandenhoeck & Ruprecht, 1993.

Rudolph, W. *Haggai – Sacharja 1–8 – Sacharja 9–14 – Maleachi*. KAT 13,4. Gütersloh: Gerd Mohn, 1976.

Steck, O.H. *Der Abschluß der Prophetie im Alten Testament*. Biblisch-Theologische Studien 17. Neukirchen-Vluyn: Neukirchener Verlag, 1991.

Tai, N.H.F. *Prophetie als Schriftauslegung in Sacharja 9–14*. Calwer theologische Monographien 17. Stuttgart: Calwer, 1996.

Willi-Plein, I. Prophetie am Ende: Untersuchungen zu Sacharja 9–14, BBB 42, Köln: Hanstein, 1974.

–   *Haggai, Sacharja, Maleachi*. ZBK 24,4. Zürich: Theologischer Verlag, 2007.

The Unity of Malachi
and Its Relation to the Book of the Twelve

RAINER KESSLER

Philipps-Universität Marburg

1. An Outline of the History of Research

1.1 From Hitzig to the Zurich School

For a long time, biblical scholars read the book of Malachi as an entity unto itself. Ferdinand Hitzig published the 1st edition of his commentary on the Book of the Twelve in 1838. According to him, Malachi did not act publicly. He was the head of a school. His writing was no longer inspired by the powerful spirit of the older prophecy, but consisted of a monotonous and doctrinal teaching.[1] For Julius Wellhausen in the 1890s, the form of the discussion in Malachi "is of course only a literary device."[2] The anti-Jewish paradigm of powerful vivid prophecy vs. doctrinal dry teaching was upheld up to the 20th century, but then Malachi was defended. For Karl Marti (1904), the book of Malachi does not give the impression of "a dry school teaching or merely rabbinical school discussion," but of vivid contact with friends and adversaries.[3] At the end of this line of interpretation, in 1976, we find Wilhelm Rudolph who contends that "without doubt" the oracles of Malachi are the record of real discussions.[4]

In 1993, the next German commentator, Henning Graf Reventlow, already argued against a newly emerging current in the interpretation of Malachi. According to him, the interpretation of the book as a mere product of a writer is not possible ("Die Deutung des Buches als rein schriftstellerisches Erzeugnis ... ist nicht möglich"). In brackets he adds

---

1   Hitzig, *Propheten*, 414.
2   Wellhausen, *Propheten*, 203–204: "natürlich nur schriftstellerische Form."
3   Marti, *Dodekapropheton*, 459: "... macht doch keineswegs den Eindruck eines trockenen Schulvortrags oder blossen rabbinischen Schulstreits."
4   Rudolph, *Maleachi*, 250: "... es kann keinem Zweifel unterliegen, daß hier die Niederschrift von tatsächlichen Gesprächen vorliegt."

three names: Utzschneider and Bosshard/Kratz.[5] Two things had happened in the late 1980s and early 1990s.

First, Helmut Utzschneider had argued strongly for the written
character of the prophecy of Malachi, claiming that this was a form of
true prophecy and not just the degeneration of the older, vivid oral
prophecy.[6] This new interest in the written character of Malachi's
prophecy, however, went further than the early critics of the 19th century. The new phenomenon that came into the focus of the exegetes
was intertextuality. Utzschneider, who restricted his study to Mal 1:6–
2:9, discovered what he called "äußere Kontextualität (Intertextualität)"[7] with all parts of the canon, from Genesis to the Psalms and
Nehemiah. In 1996, Donald Berry presented a table that runs over two
pages in an article that bears the title "Allusions to Canonical Traditions in Malachi."[8] Finally, in 2000 Karl William Weyde dedicated a
book of about 450 pages to "The Use of Traditions in the Book of Malachi."[9]

The second new trend that arose in the late 1980s was an interest in
the formation of the Book of the Twelve as a unity.[10] Erich Bosshard
and Reinhard Gregor Kratz – both rejected by Graf Reventlow together
with Utzschneider – combine the new trends.[11] Their model was fully
accepted later by their teacher Odil Hannes Steck.[12] For these exegetes,
Malachi was written prophecy from the beginning. At the same time, it
was written exclusively as a continuation of the prophecies of Haggai
and Proto-Zechariah. It was mere *Fortschreibung*. Even the original layer, according to them, was never independent from Haggai and Proto-
Zechariah. Its horizon, however, was wider; it included the emerging
book of the Twelve and Deuteronomy. The second layer is a
Fortschreibung of the original layer. It now refers to Zech 9–14 too. The
third layer, finally, makes Malachi an independent book by inserting
the superscription in Mal 1:1. At the same time, the third layer connects
Malachi with the canon of Torah and Prophets by adding the appendix
in 3:22–24.

---

5   Reventlow, *Propheten*, 131.
6   Utzschneider, *Künder*.
7   Utzschneider, *Künder*, 42.
8   Berry, "Dual Design," 270–272.
9   Weyde, *Prophecy*.
10   For the discussion until the end of the century see the review by Schart, "Redak-
     tionsgeschichte."
11   Bosshard and Kratz, "Maleachi."
12   Steck, *Abschluß*.

The Bosshard-Kratz-Steck model has often been criticized. Arndt Meinhold calls it "hypothesenfreudig."[13] Indeed, many of the intertextual relations with Haggai and Zechariah the authors rely on are neither significant nor exclusive.[14] Besides this, Malachi has a very special form, the form of "disputation speech."[15] This form is unique in the whole Hebrew Bible. It is difficult to believe that such a book should be nothing but a literary continuation of Haggai and Proto-Zechariah, which are so different in literary character.

James Nogalski, in his 1991 Zurich dissertation written under the supervision of Odil Hannes Steck and published in two volumes in 1993, goes a step further. First, he formulates a consensus among these scholars: "... the similarities shared by the respective studies [i.e. Bosshard, Kratz, and Steck], together with Utzschneider, independently conclude that Malachi is a literary construction which manifests canonical awareness in its compositional process." He then notes similarities and differences between his own conclusions and those of Bosshard, Kratz, and Steck: "All of these studies, mine included, see Malachi as the redactional continuation of Zech 8:9ff. I differ with their conclusions in that I sense this redactional work already takes place in the Book of the Twelve, and not with the Haggai-Zechariah corpus alone."[16]

In contrast to the somehow apodictic declaration of Bosshard and Kratz that Malachi is a mere *Fortschreibung* of the Haggai-Zechariah-corpus, Nogalski discusses "three possible explanations" for the problem of "the incorporation of Malachi into the Book of the Twelve." "*First,* ... [is] the placing of two completed works next to one another ..." "A *second* possibility argues ... that Malachi was composed for its position as the conclusion to the Book of the Twelve." This option "appears to be" "the most likely solution" for Nogalski. "The *third* option argues that the redactional shaping has been accomplished by adaptation of pre-existing material which skillfully integrated the perspective of a larger corpus with the book of which it was a part."[17] If I understand this last option right, it means that there existed already something like a book of Malachi that was integrated by redactional work into the larger corpus. The task then would be to identify this redactional work.

---

13 Meinhold, "Maleachi/Maleachibuch," 7.
14 See the discussion in Lauber, "Maleachi."
15 Hill, *Malachi*, 34.
16 Nogalski, *Processes*, 211 note 96.
17 Nogalski, *Processes*, 210–211.

1.2 Jakob Wöhrle's Model

In the rest of my paper, I will argue for Nogalski's first explanation, namely that Malachi existed as "a completed work" and was added as such at the end of the Book of the Twelve. Before I do this, however, I will turn to the elaboration of Nogalski's third explanation given by Jakob Wöhrle. Wöhrle rightly states that one has to start with the analysis of the individual books of the collection of the Twelve. He then gives a long analysis of the book of Malachi, where he discovers an original layer ("*Grundschicht*") which was enlarged by a cult-critical redaction and a redaction which inserts the motif of the righteous and the wicked. These redactions nearly cover the whole text of the book of Malachi. The only exceptions are the superscription 1:1, two verses on Edom in 1:4–5, the so-called "grace layer" (*Gnadenschicht*) in 1:9a, and the appendix in 3:22–24. The most important of these few verses are the superscription and 1:4–5. According to Wöhrle, they are part of a redactional layer that covers and unites the whole Book of the Twelve, the "layer of the foreign nations II" (*Fremdvölkerschicht II*).[18]

Wöhrle contends that the book of Malachi was available to the redactors of the layer of the foreign nations II ("lag das Maleachibuch den Redaktoren der Fremdvölkerschicht II bereits vor").[19] Compared with the works of the Zurich school, this is a very strong reduction. For Wöhrle, Malachi is not a *Fortschreibung*, be it of the Haggai-Zechariah-corpus (Bosshard, Kratz, and Steck) or of the emerging Book of the Twelve (Nogalski). Malachi is an independent book inserted by just three and a half verses of redactional origin.

2. The Unity and Intertextuality of Malachi

In my view, no redactional work was necessary to incorporate Malachi into the (emerging) Book of the Twelve. To demonstrate my position I will, in a first step, discuss whether the verses claimed by Wöhrle to be redactional can bear the weight that he lays on them. After denying that they can, I then will develop my own view, namely that Malachi indeed was an independent book and that it was not necessary to do redactional work within the book to add it to the Twelve.

---

18   Wöhrle, *Abschluss*, 255–263.
19   Wöhrle, *Abschluss*, 275.

2.1 Mal 1:2–5 – Unity and Intertextual Relations

Wöhrle presents several arguments for his opinion that Mal 1:4–5 are a secondary addition to 1:2–3. First, he argues that v. 4–5 leave the "basic theme" which, as another commentator claims, "is not the judgment of Edom but God's covenant love for Israel."[20] Besides, the verses do not speak of Edom's present fate, but of its future. Second, Mal 1:4–5 are the only verses in the Book of Malachi that show hostility against foreign nations. Third, v. 4–5 no longer speak of Esau and Jacob but of Edom and Israel. In v. 4a, they even shift from the third person masculine to the third person feminine. Fourth, Wöhrle mentions that 1:4 is the only verse in the book that has the so called messenger formula (כה אמר יהוה).[21]

Concerning the last argument, Wöhrle himself admits that also the formula "says the Lord" (נאם יהוה) in v. 2 is unique in the whole book.[22] So why should the lone messenger formula כה אמר יהוה be secondary while the only example of נאם יהוה is original? Besides, the כה אמר יהוה צבאות in v. 4 is easy to explain. It is part of a longer sentence which begins in v. 4aα with "if Edom says" and continues in v. 4aβ with "then says Yhwh of hosts." The typical introductory formula for divine speech in Malachi is a form of "says Yhwh." Twenty times Malachi uses "says Yhwh of hosts" (אמר יהוה צבאות) (1:6, 8, 9, 10, 11, 13, 14; 2:1, 4, 8, 16; 3:1, 5, 7, 10, 11, 12, 17, 19, 21), three times he uses "says Yhwh" (אמר יהוה) (1:2, 13; 3:13), and once we find "says Yhwh, the God of Israel" (2:16). As the first part of the sentence in 1:4 is a conditional clause ("if ...") its most natural continuation is introduced by "then ..." followed by Malachi's usual "says Yhwh of hosts" (אמר יהוה צבאות).

Wöhrle's other observations are correct and helpful for understanding the text, but they cannot prove that v. 4–5 are a secondary addition to v. 2–3. There is a shift from the present to the future from v. 2–3 to v. 4–5. There also is a shift from the words "Esau" and "Jacob" in v. 2–3 to "Edom" and "Israel" in v. 4–5. The basic theme of Yhwh's love to Jacob is contrasted with a threat against Edom, indeed. But does all this prove that v. 4–5 are secondary? They form a new element after the prophet's refutation in v. 2b, 3. I think Arndt Meinhold is right when he finds four elements in the disputation speeches of the Book of Malachi: the prophetic declaration or opening statement (1:2aα) – the hypothetical audience rebuttal or objection (1:2aβ) – the prophet's refutation or

20 Verhoef, *Books*, 195.
21 Wöhrle, *Abschluss*, 219–222.
22 Wöhrle, *Abschluss*, 221 note 11.

explanation (1:2b, 3).[23] As a fourth part of the disputation speech Meinhold identifies what he calls "consequences."[24] This fourth part can be
found in all six disputation speeches. Why should it be missing in the
first one? It is not missing, indeed, but is to be found in v. 4–5 as an
integral part of the speech.

However, it is not enough to reject Wöhrle's interpretation. One
should be able to give an alternative explanation. Let me start with the
general consensus of most of the authors in the last twenty years that
Malachi is aware of numerous traditions and even written texts. I am
convinced that he knows most parts of the Torah and a great number of
prophetic texts in written form. I would like to demonstrate this on our
text, Mal 1:2–5.

The author of the Book of Malachi – I will call him Malachi for convenience – knows the tradition of the brothers Esau and Jacob. From
the short text of Mal 1:2–5 we cannot say that he must know the text of
Gen 25–36 because the story of the two brothers was certainly well
known in postexilic Israel so that Malachi could just know it from oral
tradition. However, other parts of Malachi demonstrate that the prophet knows pentateuchal texts (see below). So, it is probable that he also
knew the text of Gen 25–36. Be it from the oral tradition, or from the
text of Genesis, Malachi knew that the two brothers were the ancestors
of Israel and Edom. He knew that Jacob was preferred over Esau. But
he also must have known that the story ends in the reconciliation of the
brothers. When their father Isaac died the brothers came to bury him,
and Esau the first-born is even mentioned first: "and his sons Esau and
Jacob buried him" (Gen 35:29). For Malachi, however, God loves Jacob
and hates Esau, as if he knew nothing of their reconciliation. What
happened?

In addition to the basic story of Genesis, Malachi also knew prophetic announcements of the future destruction of Edom, as I will
demonstrate below. How did Malachi proceed from the story of Genesis to these texts of hatred? I think he just continued to read the Pentateuch, where the next time Israel meets Edom is during the wandering
in the wilderness. The story is told in Num 20:14–21. It begins with
these words: "Moses sent messengers from Kadesh to the king of
Edom, 'Thus says your brother Israel ...'" (v. 14). Though the story only
uses the names of the peoples of Edom and Israel, by characterizing
Israel as "your brother" the story gives a hint of the Jacob-Esau tradition. Edom refused Israel to give passage through their territory. Three
times the text of Num 20:14–21 uses the word גבול for "territory." It is

23   Terminology according to Hill, *Malachi*, 26.
24   Meinhold, *Maleachi*, XII ("Folgerungen").

the same word that Malachi uses for the territories of Edom and Israel in 1:4–5.[25]

For the reader of the Pentateuch the reconciliation between the brothers Esau and Jacob is not the end of the story. Edom's hostile attitude towards Israel during the wandering in the wilderness is the bridge to the large number of texts of hatred against Edom to be found in prophetic literature. Of course these texts are not just the result of reading the Pentateuch. They have their roots in the attitude of Edomites after the destruction of Jerusalem in the Neo-Babylonian epoch. Because of these bad experiences, Judahite prophets threatened Edom with destruction. But once you read these texts in the context of the emerging canon, you must find a bridge between the story of the brothers and the actual political tensions.

Malachi seems to know most or all of these prophetical texts. There is a long list of semantic allusions. They include the motif of the brothers (Amos 1:11; Obad 10, 12), the verbal form אשׂים "I have made" together with the words "ruins" and "desolation" in the context of Edom (Ezek 35:4), the root שׁמם for "desolation" (Jer 49:13, 17; Ezek 32:29; 35:3–4, 7, 9, 14–15), the mention of jackals in the devastated territory of Edom (Isa 34:14), the use of a feminine verbal form with the noun Edom (Jer 49:17; Ezek 32:29), the root חרב for "ruins" (Jer 49:13; Ezek 25:13; 35:4), and the word גבול for "territory" (Obad 7). Of course, not all of these allusions are exclusive, nor are they significant when seen in isolation. The cluster they form, however, shows that Malachi must have known at least some of these texts.[26] The closest and densest allusions are with texts from Jeremiah and Ezekiel – and not with any prophet from the Book of the Twelve.

Further, I consider it highly probable that Malachi knew the text of Ezek 36:33–36. In this text Yhwh announces that in the future the ruins of Judah shall be rebuilt. The land that was desolate shall be tilled, and the wasted, ruined, and desolate towns shall be inhabited. We have the same semantic field as in Mal 1:4–5 with the roots שׁמם for "desolation," חרב for "ruins," and הרס for "to tear down." Both texts begin with כה אמר יהוה, both have a reaction of Israel ("you will say," Mal 1:5; "they will say," Ezek 36:35). Malachi's text is a counter-text to Ezek 36. What Yhwh promises to Israel ("the ruins shall be rebuilt") is denied to Edom ("if Edom says ... we will rebuild the ruins etc.").

For the discussion of both positions, those of Nogalski and of Wöhrle, it is crucial to recognize that Malachi's allusions are not exclu-

---

25   Cf. Kessler, "Jakob und Esau."
26   According to Meinhold, *Maleachi*, 49, the author of the Book of Malachi knows Jer 49:7–22, Ezek 35, and Obadiah.

sive to texts of prophets from the Book of the Twelve. To the contrary, the allusions to other prophetic texts from Jeremiah and Ezekiel are much closer. So I think there is no reason to believe that Malachi was formulated with (only) the other books of the Twelve in mind. Nor is there any proof that Mal 1:4–5 which Wöhrle holds to be secondary in Mal 1 form a redactional layer that runs through the Book of the Twelve. The only semantic parallel that Wöhrle mentions is the word גְּבוּל for "territory" in Obad 7. One could add the motif of Esau as "brother." In summary, Wöhrle gives four characteristics of his layer of the foreign nations II.[27] Three of them are not present in Mal 1:4–5: the enslavement of Jews by foreign nations, the expectation of an invasion of the neighboring territories, and the promise of a transformation of nature in favor of better agricultural conditions. Only one of the characteristics in my eyes is discussible: the announcement of judgment against the nations. But even this characteristic is not quite clear because in Mal 1:2–5, judgment is not announced on Edom but has already occurred. Yhwh says: "I have made his hill country a desolation and his heritage a desert for jackals" (v. 3). This is not an announcement but an appraisal. The only threat is directed against plans for future reconstruction.

In my eyes, the example of Malachi's first disputation speech (1:2–5) demonstrates that the author of the book knows and uses traditions and even texts from the Torah and from prophetic books. At the same time, he presupposes that his readers know these traditions and texts. In the next two sections I am going to show how the prophet also in his other speeches makes use of traditions and texts from all parts of the Torah and the Prophets.

2.2 Mal 1:6–2:9 and the Torah

We have already found awareness of the Esau-Edom tradition of Genesis and Numbers in Malachi's first speech. In the next section of this paper we will find the idea of a messenger sent by Yhwh, an image which comes from the book of Exodus. In this section, I turn to the observation that the discussion about offerings in Mal 1:6–14 has close and sometimes literal parallels with Lev 21–22. Both texts end with a paragraph about lay people after having dealt with the priests' duties (Mal 1:14 and Lev 22:17–25). Both texts speak of a "vow" (Mal 1:14 and Lev 22:18, 21, 23), both expressly mention the "male" offering (Mal 1:14

---

27 Wöhrle, *Abschluss*, 273.

and Lev 22:19), both use the rare form מֻשְׁחָת ("blemished") that only
appears in Lev 22:25, Mal 1:14, and Prov 25:26.

However, Malachi also must know the text of Deuteronomy. Deut
15:21 forbids the offering of lame and blind animals, acts which the
priests are doing according to Mal 1:8. Deut 15:21 calls these defects רַע,
something "evil," while the priests of Mal 1:8 who offer these animals
just say "no evil" (אֵין רַע).

From Deuteronomy I turn to Numbers. It is very likely that the text
of Mal 1:6–2:9 is written with the Priestly Blessing of Num 6:23–27 in
mind. The key word "to bless" appears in both texts (Num 6:23, 24, 27
and Mal 2:2). The role of Yhwh's name is central in both (Num 6:27 and
Mal 1:6, 11, 14; 2:2). The Priestly Blessing says: "Yhwh make his face to
shine upon you, and be gracious to you," and Mal 1:9 echoes this text:
"And now appease God's face that he may be gracious to us." Finally,
the wish for שָׁלוֹם should be noted as important for both texts.[28] The
final section of Malachi's first disputation speech confronts the behavior of contemporary priests with that of their ancestor Levi. Yhwh reminds them of "my covenant with Levi" (2:4). The words about this
"covenant" have their closest parallels in Num 25:10–13 and in Deut
33:8–11. Num 25:10–13 mentions a "covenant of perpetual priesthood"
with "Phinehas son of Eleazar, son of Aaron the priest" (v. 10 and 13).
The texts of Malachi and Numbers have some ideas and semantic expressions in common. Phinehas "turned back [Yhwh's] wrath" (Num
25:11), Levi "turned many from iniquity" (Mal 2:6). According to Num
25:12, Yhwh "grants" Phinehas "my covenant of peace," according to
Mal 2:5 Yhwh "granted" Levi a "covenant of life and peace." In both
texts, the covenant "exists" expressed by the Hebrew verb הָיָה ("to be")
(Num 25:13 and Mal 2:5). All these traits point toward an intertextual
relation between the two texts.[29]

One central difference remains: Num 25 does not mention Levi but
refers only to Aaron. Malachi manifests a special interest in emphasizing that the priests of his time, the Zadokites, were not only descendants of Aaron, but of Levi too. In 3:3 he expressly calls them "descendants of Levi." To demonstrate that the Zadokite priests are also "sons of
Levi," Mal 2:4–8 combines the idea of Yhwh's "covenant of perpetual
priesthood" with "Phinehas son of Eleazar, son of Aaron the priest"
and with the blessing of Levi in Deut 33:8–11. In Deut 33:10 as well as
in Mal 2:7, Levi's central task is to teach Israel the Torah. Both texts
mention Yhwh's "covenant" (Deut 33:9). It is true that Deut 33:9 speaks
of Yhwh's covenant with Israel, whereas Mal 2:4–8 addresses God's

28 Cf. Fishbane, "Form," 118–120; idem, *Interpretation*, 332–334.
29 Cf. Utzschneider, *Künder*, 64–70.

covenant with Levi. However, "one would underestimate the midrashic way in which the Book of Malachi deals with the pentateuchal
traditions if one expects only verbal quotations."[30] If Yhwh has a covenant with the priests, and if the priests are teachers of the Torah as Levi
was, then it is only logical that Yhwh should have a covenant with Levi. So we can conclude that Mal 2:4–9 indeed "utilizes two pentateuchal
passages in developing the idea of a covenant with Levi,"[31] namely
Num 25:10–13 and Deut 33:8–11.

I do not have the space to go through the whole Book of Malachi.
The result would be the same: Malachi is aware not only of a great
number of traditions from the Pentateuch, he also knows texts from all
layers of the pentateuchal traditions. The same is true for Malachi's use
of prophetic texts.

2.3 Mal 2:17–3:5 and the Prophets

Malachi knew other writings from the emerging Book of the Twelve. A
look at the fourth discussion in Mal 2:17–3:5 will demonstrate this. The
opposition of "evil" and "good" and the quest for "justice" in 2:17 have
their closest parallel in Amos 5:14–15 and Mic 3:1–2. The question concerning the day of the messenger's coming ("and who can stand when
he appears?" 3:2) echoes Joel 2:11 ("the day of Yhwh is great – who can
stand it?") and Nah 1:6 ("Who can stand before his indignation?"). The
combination of the coming of the Lord (הָאָדוֹן) with his "temple"
(הֵיכָל) and the idea of Yhwh being a witness (עֵד; Mal 3:1, 5) is also
found in Mic 1:2. All this demonstrates that Malachi indeed knew a
collection of prophetic books that later became the Book of the Twelve.

However, the allusions to Joel and Amos, Micah and Nahum are
not exclusive. The root יגע (hif) "to weary Yhwh" in the Hebrew Bible
only appears in Mal 2:17 and Isa 43:24. The same is true for the idea of
clearing the way before Yhwh which is found in Mal 3:1 and Isa 40:3.
So we can be sure that Malachi knew Deutero-Isaiah. The phrase "See, I
am sending my messenger" (Mal 3:1) seems to be inspired by Exod
23:20 and 33:2 ("I will send a messenger before you"). In 3:2–3, Malachi
uses the image of a refiner's fire and a fuller's soap; the refiner will
purify the sons of Levi and refine them like gold and silver. The closest
parallels in concept and vocabulary are found in Isa 1:22, 25, Jer 6:27–
30, and Zech 13:9: the "fire" (Jer 6:29; Zech 13:9), to refine (צרף; Isa 1:25;

---

30   Frevel, "Bund," 90: "Man unterschätzt den midraschartigen Umgang des Maleachi-
      buches mit den Pentateuchtraditionen, wenn man sich auf wörtliche Zitate versteift."
31   Fuller, "Blessing," 37–40.

Jer 6:29; Zech 13:9), the "soap" or "lye" (Isa 1:25), and the "silver" (Isa 1:22; Jer 6:30; Zech 13:9). There is a vivid discussion of the question whether Malachi knew Zech 13:9 – as Bosshard and Kratz claim –[32] or whether Zech 13:9 is dependent on Mal 2:17–3:5 – which is Judith Gärtner's opinion.[33] Whomever we follow, the connection between Mal 2:17–3:5 and Zech 13:9 is not exclusive.

In summary, Malachi must know a form of the Pentateuch that is very close to the one we have in the final form. Additionally, Malachi knew texts from Isaiah, Jeremiah, and Ezekiel, as we have seen in the first (1:2–5) and fourth discussion (2:17–3:5). He also knew texts from the emerging Book of the Twelve. To all the examples I have already given and that one will find in the works of Bosshard and Kratz, of Nogalski, Wöhrle and others, I would like to add Mal 3:7 which is nearly identical with Zech 1:3 ("Return to me, and I will return to you, says Yhwh of hosts"). But the allusions to writings from the Book of the Twelve are not exclusive.

3. Consequences

The first conclusion I draw from the observation of this rich intertextuality of the Book of Malachi concerns the date of the book. I think we should go to the late Persian period, and not to its beginning. The later we go, the more probable it is that an author may know so many texts. Already more than a hundred years ago, Torrey made observations "that ... point distinctly to a late rather than an early date."[34]

Second, Malachi's intertextuality is not restricted to the Haggai-Zechariah-corpus or the Book of the Twelve. It covers the Torah and the prophetic corpus nearly in their final form. Consequently, I cannot see that Malachi was written as a continuation of Haggai and Proto-Zechariah or as a continuation of the emerging Book of the Twelve. Neither can I see that any redactional work was necessary to include Malachi into the Book of the Twelve. The few verses Wöhrle mentions cannot bear the weight they are asked to bear.

In my opinion, Malachi was written as an independent book. Malachi has a message for his time, the message of God's everlasting love towards Israel, of serious problems with priests and lay-people, the necessity of purification, judgment, and conversion, and of the final elimination of the wicked. He brings his message inventively into the

---

32 Bosshard and Kratz, "Maleachi," 41.
33 Gärtner, *Jesaja 66*, 280–283.
34 Torrey, "Prophecy," 13.

form of a continuing discussion. He formulates his message in the light
of the pentateuchal and prophetic texts he has at hand. At the same
time, he reckons with the knowledge of these texts by his readers. In a
review article on the literature of the Persian period, Thomas Willi
notes that Chronicles may be seen as a form of re-shaping and reinterpretation of the older traditions. Chronicles has its own message,
but formulates it in the light of tradition.[35] The same is true with Malachi.

Since in my view Malachi was written as an independent book and
then added to the Twelve, an analysis of Malachi can give no answer to
the question whether Malachi was added to Proto-Zechariah[36] or the
whole Book of Zechariah including ch. 9–14.[37] This question can only be
answered by a thorough analysis of the Book of Zechariah itself which I
cannot deliver here.

A third consequence of my position concerns the superscription of
Mal 1:1. Superscriptions are always secondary because they are not part
of the corpus of the writing itself. In the words of James Nogalski: "Mal
1:1 presents a simple title affixed to the head of the writing."[38] However, this does not necessarily mean that the superscription is redactional.
The author himself could have affixed it to his writing. I think we are
not able to decide the question. As with all superscriptions to prophetic
books, the name therein is meant to be a proper personal name. As in
other prophetic writings, we have allusions to the prophet's name within the text of the book. One should compare the use of the root ישע in
the Book of Isaiah (it appears 52 times in the book against 23 appearances in the rest of the Latter Prophets), the use of the root חזק in the
Book of Ezekiel (22 times in the book), or the מי־אל כמוך as an allusion
to the prophet's name in Mic 7:18. So Malachi uses מלאך three times for
figures who function as mediators between God and Israel: the prophet
himself in 1:1, the priest in 2:7, and God's "messenger of the covenant"
in 3:1. The superscription of Mal 1:1 fits perfectly with the text. Malachi
speaks only to Israel, never to foreign peoples. It is a text where the
word of Yhwh is indeed "in the hand of Malachi," who throughout the
whole book continuously gives Yhwh the floor ("says Yhwh of hosts"
and some other formulae). So it is possible that already the author of
the book added the superscription. It also may have been affixed by
someone else before Malachi was added to the Twelve. We even cannot
exclude that it was affixed only when the book was added to the
Twelve. This however is the least probable interpretation.

---

35   Willi, "Weltkönigtum."
36   Nogalski, *Processes*, 277; Redditt, "Zechariah 9–14."
37   Schart, *Entstehung*, 297–299; Wöhrle, *Abschluss*, 275.
38   Nogalski, *Processes*, 188.

Fourth, Malachi was added to the Twelve and to the whole prophetic corpus by adding 3:23–24 to the book (verses according to the Hebrew text). These verses are an interpretation of open questions in Malachi. Who is the messenger? What is meant by the day that comes? They necessarily are an addition to Malachi and could not have been added to any other writing of the Twelve. At the same time, they connect Malachi with the prophetic tradition from the earlier times by introducing Elijah. From this line of reasoning, it is clear that Malachi was added at the end of the emerging Book of the Twelve. This does not exclude the possibility that other texts were inserted later into the Book of the Twelve, e.g., Zech 9–14. But whatever was inserted later could not have been inserted after Mal 3:24.[39]

In a second step, Mal 3:22 was added before 3:23–24. As has often been seen, this verse, which mentions the Torah of Moses, connects Malachi with the beginning of the Book of Joshua and the end of the Pentateuch. It is the final step of the incorporation of the originally independent Book of Malachi into the emerging canon of Torah and Prophets.

References

Berry, D.K. "Malachi's Dual Design: The Close of the Canon and What Comes Afterward." Pp. 269–302 in *Forming Prophetic Literature: Essays on Isaiah and the Twelve in Honor of John D.W. Watts*. Edited by J.W. Watts and P.R. House. JSOTSup 235. Sheffield: Sheffield Academic Press, 1996.
Bosshard, E. and Kratz, R.G. "Maleachi im Zwölfprophetenbuch." *BN* 52 (1990) 27–46.
Fishbane, M. "Form and Reformulation of the Biblical Priestly Blessing." *JAOS* 103 (1983) 115–121.
– *Biblical Interpretation in Ancient Israel*. Oxford: Clarendon, 1985.
Frevel, C. "'Mein Bund mit ihm war das Leben und der Friede.' Priesterbund und Mischehenfrage." Pp. 85–93 in *Für immer verbündet: Studien zur Bundestheologie der Bibel*. Edited by C. Dohmen and C. Frevel. SBS 211. Stuttgart: Katholisches Bibelwerk, 2007.
Fuller, R.E. "The Blessing of Levi in Dtn 33, Mal 2, and Qumran." Pp. 31–44 in *Konsequente Traditionsgeschichte*. Edited by R. Bartelmus et al. FS K. Baltzer. OBO 126. Freiburg, Schweiz: Universitätsverlag and Göttingen: Vandenhoeck & Ruprecht, 1993.

---

39 One exception is the Qumran manuscript 4QXIIa (DJD 15, 221–232), where Malachi is followed by Jonah. The exceptional order in this manuscript – one of the two oldest manuscripts we have – warns against too far-reaching speculations about the meaning of the order of the writings within the Book of the Twelve.

Gärtner, J. *Jesaja 66 und Sacharja 14 als Summe der Prophetie: Eine traditions- und redaktionsgeschichtliche Untersuchung zum Abschluss des Jesaja- und des Zwölfprophetenbuches*. WMANT 114. Neukirchen-Vluyn: Neukirchener, 2006.

Hill, A.E. *Malachi: A New Translation with Introduction and Commentary*. AB 25D. New York: Doubleday, 1998.

Hitzig, F. *Die zwölf kleinen Propheten*. Kurzgefasstes exegetisches Handbuch 1. 4th ed. Leipzig: Hirzel, 1881.

Kessler, R. "Jakob und Esau als Brüderpaar in Mal 1,2–5." Pp. 209–229 in *Diasynchron: Beiträge zur Exegese, Theologie und Rezeption der Hebräischen Bibel*. Edited by T. Naumann and R. Hunziker-Rodewald. FS W. Dietrich. Stuttgart: Kohlhammer, 2009.

Lauber, S. "Das Buch Maleachi als literarische Fortschreibung von Sacharja?" *Bib* 88 (2007) 214–221.

Marti, K. *Das Dodekapropheton*. KHC 13. Tübingen: Mohr, 1904.

Meinhold, A. "Maleachi/Maleachibuch." *TRE* 22 (1992) 6–11.

– *Maleachi*. BK 14,8. Neukirchen-Vluyn: Neukirchener, 2006.

Nogalski, J.D. *Redactional Processes in the Book of the Twelve*. BZAW 218. Berlin: de Gruyter, 1993.

Redditt, P.L. "Zechariah 9–14, Malachi, and the Redaction of the Book of the Twelve." Pp. 245–268 in *Forming Prophetic Literature: Essays on Isaiah and the Twelve in Honor of John D.W. Watts*. Edited by J.W. Watts and P.R. House. JSOTSup 235. Sheffield: Sheffield Academic Press, 1996.

Reventlow, H. Graf *Die Propheten Haggai, Sacharja und Maleachi*. ATD 25,2. Göttingen: Vandenhoeck & Ruprecht, 1993.

Rudolph, W. *Haggai – Sacharja 1–8 – Sacharja 9–14 – Maleachi*. KAT 13,4. Gütersloh: Gütersloher, 1976.

Schart, A. *Die Entstehung des Zwölfprophetenbuchs: Neubearbeitungen von Amos im Rahmen schriftenübergreifender Redaktionsprozesse*. BZAW 260. Berlin: de Gruyter, 1998.

– "Zur Redaktionsgeschichte des Zwölfprophetenbuchs." *VF* 43 (1998) 13–33.

Steck, O.H. *Der Abschluß der Prophetie im Alten Testament: Ein Versuch zur Frage der Vorgeschichte des Kanons*. Biblisch-Theologische Studien 17. Neukirchen-Vluyn: Neukirchener, 1991.

Torrey, C.C. "The Prophecy of 'Malachi'." *JBL* 17 (1898) 1–15.

Utzschneider, H. *Künder oder Schreiber? Eine These zum Problem der "Schriftprophetie" auf Grund von Maleachi 1,6–2,9*. BEATAJ 19. Frankfurt: Lang, 1989.

Verhoef, P.A. *The Books of Haggai and Malachi*. NICOT. Grand Rapids: Eerdmans, 1987.

Wellhausen, J. *Die kleinen Propheten*. 4th ed. Berlin: de Gruyter, 1963.

Weyde, K.W. *Prophecy and Teaching: Prophetic Authority, Form Problems, and the Use of Traditions in the Book of Malachi*. BZAW 288. Berlin: de Gruyter, 2000.

Willi, T. "Das Weltkönigtum – seine Residenz und seine Regeln: Ein kritischer Blick auf die Diskussion zur biblischen Literatur der persischen Epoche." *ThLZ* 135 (2010) 1055–1070.

Wöhrle, J. *Der Abschluss des Zwölfprophetenbuches. Buchübergreifende Redaktionsprozesse in den späten Sammlungen*. BZAW 389. Berlin: de Gruyter, 2008.

Rattling the Bones of the Twelve: Wilderness Reflections in the Formation of the Book of the Twelve

ROY E. GARTON

Baylor University

> And there was a noise as I prophesied, a rattling, and the bones came together, bone to its bone. Then I looked, and sinew was upon them, and flesh sprung up, and skin covered them over ...
>
> (Ezek 37:7–8)

> And may the bones of the twelve prophets spring to life from where they lie ...
>
> (Sir 49:10)

1. Introduction

The synecdoches of Ezek 37:7–8 and Sir 49:10 are remarkably similar, sharing the same vehicle, dimension, and rhetorical effect.[1] What is lacking from Sir 49:10 – the earliest extant evidence of the twelve minor prophets having coalesced –[2] is any indication as to how these "bones"

---

1   The classical parlance defines synecdoche as a metaphor in which "the part represents the whole" (Eco and Paci, "Scandal," 219–221). As such, the terms "tenor" and "vehicle" – first proposed by Richards, *Philosophy*, 96–97 – for the constituent halves of a metaphor are quite applicable here. The *vehicle*, or metaphorizing idea, in Ezek 37:3–11 and Sir 49:10 is עצמות and ὀστᾶ respectively; while the *tenors*, or metaphorized ideas, are the בית ישראל (Ezek 37:11) and τῶν δώδεκα προφητῶν respectively. The shared *dimension*, or attribute which the vehicle communicates to the tenor, is the vestige of death; the yielded *rhetorical effect* in both synecdoches is the paradox of death springing forth life.

2   Petersen, "Book," 4, rejects this evidence, averring that "Sirach seems to be referring to the prophets as individuals and not the books attributed to them." One must ask, however, whether Sirach's reference to the "twelve prophets" would have been intelligible prior to the editing of the Twelve. In other words, to which twelve prophets would Sirach have been referring? And what vehicle other than a literary collec-

were joined in first place. Ezekiel 37:7–8 artfully portrays this formation process for its synecdoche, and figuratively it is this same process that scholars have sought to uncover regarding the formation of the Book of the Twelve: that is, a description of the editorial processes used to produce the Twelve, or in the words of Ezekiel how the "bones came together, bone to its bone."

Over the last two decades, scholars have marshaled several types of evidences showing cohesion in the Twelve. Stylized superscriptions and incipits, interlocking catchwords at the beginning and ending of the individual writings, the presence of plot progression, intertextual citations and allusions, and other literary framing devices have been variously employed to reconstruct the Twelve's formative stages.[3] Carrying the above anatomical imagery forward, these *literary ligaments* have resulted in a wide-spread recognition of two collections as precursors to the Twelve: namely, Hosea–Amos–Micah–Zephaniah (the so-called Book of the Four) and Haggai–Zechariah 1–8.[4] The question of how to further nuance the formation of the Twelve and its precursors, however, still remains.

This paper explores the reflections on ancient Israel's wilderness traditions within the Twelve as yet another possible literary ligament binding "the bones of the Twelve." A brief discussion that defines *tradition*, sets the parameters of the traditions in question, and delimits what constitutes a reflection of a tradition within those parameters begins our inquiry (§2). Only then can one objectively map the occurrences of these reflections within the Twelve. Afterwards, there is an attempt to categorize these reflections (§3) and a brief assessment of the implications this study may have for redactional models (§4). Though no more than a preliminary investigation, the thesis throughout is that the distribution of these reflections and the diversity they reflect may provide additional corroborative evidence by which future studies may further nuance the formation of the Twelve.

---

tion would have united them as a corporate entity in the first place? With this in mind, it is likely that Sir 49:10 presupposes the Twelve as a literary collection.

3   For a review of scholarship in this vein and its detractors, see Redditt, "Research," 50–80, and Wöhrle, *Sammlungen*, 3–24.

4   Nogalski, "Book," 14–16, brings attention to this emerging consensus, along the relative agreement that the Twelve was formed by deliberate editorial processes and that the Masoretic arrangement holds priority over the Septuagint's.

2. Tradition: Definition and Parameters

As a critical method, tradition-history remains one of the most difficult to pin down due to what Knight calls "the multiplicity of the phenomenon."[5] Tradents can pass down practically any inheritable datum (*traditum*), whether oral or written, through an array of techniques that constitute the traditioning process (*traditio*).[6] Obviously, a full tradition-historical investigation is not within the scope of this study. Rather, the intent is to initiate the task by identifying and categorizing those components within the Twelve that *reflect* traditions pertaining to the Wilderness Tradition complex – that is, those narratives whose locus is ancient Israel's desert sojourn, but which also presume the exodus from Egypt as well as the entrance into the land.[7]

Two caveats, however, are in order. First, it is clear that the tradents active in the formation of the Twelve were not intent on codifying their *traditum* therein. As such, the Twelve contains only *reflections* of the state of traditions coterminous to their entry into the text. A certain lack of conformity, therefore, is not unexpected when comparing reflections in the Twelve with their final, fixed forms in the Pentateuch, or even when comparing one reflection with another within the Twelve. Thus, one simply cannot exclude non-aligned reflections solely on the grounds of their being so.[8] Secondly, in effort to avoid devolving into a

---

5   Knight, "Introduction," 2, goes on to ask, "What cannot be considered a matter of tradition? The term is applied as readily to oral and written literature (of all genres) as it is to customs, habits, beliefs, moral standards, cultural attitudes and values, [and] social and religious institutions." Similarly, Steck, *Exegese*, 127, states that "Der Begriff 'Traditionsgeschichte' ist infolge der Mehrdeutigkeit seines ersten Wortbestandteiles in der exegetischen Literatur alles andere als eindeutig festgelegt."

6   For a discussion of the *tradition-traditum* dynamic, see Fishbane, *Interpretation*, 6–16.

7   Noth, *Überlieferungsgeschichte*, 62, uses the rubric "Führung in der Wüste" to describe "die verschiedenen Erzählungen von göttlicher Hilfe in den Nöten und Entbehrungen der Wüste." While I disagree with Noth assessing this theme as relatively unimportant, his conclusion is understandable as these stories do presuppose and rely on the themes "Herausführung aus Ägypten" and "Hineinführung in das Kulturland."

8   Hosea 2:16–17 is a case in point. Dozeman,"Hosea," 67–68, argues that this text does not reflect "a firmly fixed ancient tradition of wilderness wandering," but is rather "a new interpretation." He bases this assessment on 1) the absence of the preposition on מדבר, which renders the force of Hos 2:16 unclear; 2) the origin of Israel, which elsewhere in Hosea is Egypt, not the wilderness; and 3) the blurring of wilderness with imagery typical of the Promised Land. That this text does not readily align with the fixed tradition, there is no doubt. However, the absence of a preposition (whether ב or כ) on מדבר, though unusual in Hosea, does not overshadow the explicit wilderness tradition components within the text. (Dozeman's rejection of Hos 9:10 is similarly flawed: the simile of כענבים במדבר cannot eclipse the other tradition components within the text.) As well, the "origin of Israel" is not what is represented in Hos 2:16–17, rather an "original desert experience;" Dozeman erroneously con-

study of motifs, this study admits only those texts that contain or are contextualized by 1) an overt expression about a wilderness tradition, or 2) a component integral to it. Lexemes such as מדבר or אבות, or motifs like infertility of the land, are insufficient on their own to constitute a reflection of a wilderness tradition.[9]

3. Reflections in the Twelve

The texts within the Twelve that most clearly reflect one of ancient Israel's wilderness traditions are as follows:

Hos 2:16–17	Amos 2:9–11	Mic 6:4–5	Hag 2:5	Mal 3:22
Hos 9:10	Amos 3:1	Mic 7:14–17		
Hos 11:1–5	Amos 5:25			
Hos 12:10, 14	Amos 9:7			
Hos 13:4–6				

More ambiguous exemplars include Hos 2:5; 8:13; 9:3; Amos 4:6–13; and Mal 2:4–8, which possibly *evoke* wilderness traditions.[10] These passages contain a variety of tradition components which can be categorized and thereby more readily assessed.[11]

·flates the two. Finally, the wilderness tradition is not "blurred" by divine provision of vineyards. Miraculous provision in the wilderness is a common motif in the wilderness tradition: e.g., potable water (Exod 15:22–27; 17:1–7; Num 20:1–13; 21:16–18), food (Exod 16; Num 11:4–9, 31–33), and even durability of clothing (Deut 8:4).

9   Hosea 2:5's relation to the wilderness tradition is an example. For Dozeman, "Hosea," 64–70, the three-fold preposition כ in Hos 2:5 makes it an "extended simile," one infused with desert motifs, not a wilderness tradition. In the end, he concludes that Hosea is not aware of an original wilderness wandering tradition, and so predates it, if not actually inspiring it. In order to arrive at this conclusion, Dozeman restricts his analysis to texts in Hosea with the word מדבר, apparently assuming that the tradition cannot be evoked without it. Not only can the tradition be reflected in other ways, but similes can serve to evoke tradition as well. For example, Wolff, *Hosea*, 34, sees the simile of Hos 2:5 as embedded with a tradition parallel to that seen in Ezek 16:4–8. A closer and more relevant parallel, however, may be seen in the Song of Moses, specifically Deut 32:10.

10 For a brief discussion on Hos 2:5, see note 9 above. Hosea 8:13 and 9:3 is discussed below under §3.1 Regarding Amos 4:6–13, Hadjiev, *Composition*, 147–161, surveys and reacts to scholarship viewing the plagues in Amos 4:6–12 as dependent on either Leviticus 26, 1 Kings 18, or Deuteronomistic theology. What Hadjiev and others miss, however, is that regardless of the provenance of these divine curses, the macrostructure of Amos 4 proceeds along axis of divine censure as portrayed through a grand reversal of cosmic history: from the oncoming censure of Samaria (v. 1–5), to the traditional censures of the land (v. 6–9), Egypt (v. 10), Sodom and Gomorrah (v. 11), and finally creation itself (v. 13). Within this metanarrative, however, the wilderness tradition is at best inferred. Finally, for Mal 2:4–8's reference to the covenant of Levi, see note 29 below.

3.1 The Exodus from Egypt

By far, the most attested wilderness tradition reflected in the Twelve is the exodus from Egypt, occurring at least fourteen times.[12] Ten of these occurrences appear in Hosea, Amos, and Micah; the eleventh occurs in Hag 2:5. Implicitly, Hosea 8:13; 9:3, and 11:5 also reflect this tradition. Thus, every reflection of ancient Israel's exodus from Egypt within the Twelve – save Hag 2:5 –[13] is located within the precursor dubbed the Book of the Four (hereafter, "the Four"). Not surprisingly, despite this focused distribution, these texts reflect a variety of forms by which this tradition finds expression. Two classes, each with two subclasses, emerge for consideration: those texts *explicitly* reflecting this tradition constitute the first classification, while those *implicitly* reflecting it make up the second.

The *explicit* reflections of this tradition predominantly align with the formulas described by Winjgaards.[14] The early form of מצרים +

---

11   It is necessary to clarify the exclusion of Joel 2:13; Jonah 3:9; 4:2; Mic 7:18; Nah 1:2–3, and Mal 1:9a – exemplars of the so-called "Gnadenformel," or grace formula – commonly said to be drawn directly from Exod 34:6–7. Most recently, Wöhrle, "Reflection," 1–17, who describes the grace formula as "from Exod 34:6–7," has argued that these formulas constitute a late redactional layer. Yet despite the extant verbal parallels, more caution is need in assigning this formula's derivation. Franz, *Gott*, 43–93, demonstrates the language of this formula to be extant in Egyptian, Mesopotamian, and Ugaritic literature. Further, the Hebrew inscriptions found at Kuntillet 'Ajrud (COS II.171–172, §2.47b) and Khirbet Beit-Lei (COS II.179–180, §2.53) already contain components of this formula. Given the early dates of these inscriptions (late 9th – early 8th cent. and late 8th cent., respectively) and the elasticity of grace formula's expression in the Twelve, it is likely the above instances are merely variants of a stock *credo* regarding YHWH's character rather than quotations of any singular text. In short, the grace formula does not appear to find its genesis in Exod 34:6–7, but rather in cultic parlance of the broader ancient Near East.

12   Explicitly in Hosea 2:17; 11:1; 12:10, 14; 13:4; Amos 2:10; 3:1; 9:7; Mic 6:4; 7:15; Hag 2:5; but only implicitly in Hos 8:13; 9:3; 11:5. Hoffman, "Myth," 170.177, also recognizes these implicit references. Curiously, Schart, *Entstehung*, 158 note 9, says "Diese Formel findet sich innerhalb des Zwölfprophetenbuchs nur in Am 2,10; 3,1b; 9,7 und Mi 6,4."

13   That Hag 2:5a (אֶת־הַדָּבָר אֲשֶׁר־כָּרַתִּי אִתְּכֶם בְּצֵאתְכֶם מִמִּצְרַיִם) represents a late interpolation scholars widely agree. Though partially extant in the 2nd century MurXII, it is absent from many versions (LXX, OL, Syr Hex) and interrupts the assurances of v. 4b and v. 5b (Wolff, *Haggai*, 71; Gelston, *Biblica*, 132*). More important for our investigation is why a glossator would insert this particular reflection. Nogalski, *Book of the Twelve*, 2:782, suggests the echo of the encouragement to Joshua at the Jordan in Hag 2:4 (presumably the imperative חזק; cf. Josh 1:6, 7, 9, 18), prompted the scribe to insert a gloss about the "exodus experience." Petersen, *Haggai*, 62.66, sees the inspiration stemming from the date formula in Hag 2:1, which falls on the last day prescribed for the feast of booths (cf. Lev 23:33–36).

14   Although dated and reflecting the source critical proclivities of its time, Wijngaards, "Approach," 91–102, remains foundational. Wijngaards discerns two formulas, each

הֶעֱלָה shapes the reflections in Hos 2:17; 12:14; Amos 2:10; 3:1; 9:7, and
Mic 6:4. The late form of מִצְרַיִם + הוֹצִיא, on the other hand, is extant
only in Mic 7:15 and Hag 2:5. This distribution is striking, as the הוֹצִיא
form is the preferred expression of the Deuteronomistic (Dtr) circle,
and yet Amos 2:10; 3:1; 9:7, and Mic 6:4 are widely considered to be
D/Dtr additions.[15] Why would the Dtr editors preserve the הֶעֱלָה form
of this tradition given their preference for הוֹצִיא? Although not in reference to the Four, Wijngaards observes that Dtr typically employs
הֶעֱלָה in context of anti-idolatry rhetoric.[16] Not surprisingly, the same is
true in the Four: all six occurrences of the הֶעֱלָה formula facilitate corrections to Israel's idolatry;[17] the הוֹצִיא formula in Mic 7:15, on the other hand, functions within YHWH's promised restoration.[18]

The *implicit* reflections of this tradition are all within Hosea: 8:13;
9:3, 6; 11:1, 5; 12:9; 13:4. Among these reflections Hos 11:1 is unique, as
no other text in the Hebrew Bible uses קָרָא to evoke the exodus. The
remainder of the occurrences formally fall into two subsets: those employing שׁוּב + מִצְרַיִם (8:13; 9:3; 11:5) and the doublet phrase וְאָנֹכִי יְהוָה
אֱלֹהֶיךָ מֵאֶרֶץ מִצְרַיִם (12:10; 13:4). Regarding the former, the rhetoric of
a return to Egypt not only implies origination and the departure from
it, but in each case the reflection also serves as retribution for ancient
Israel's cultic infidelities (cf. 8:5–13; 9:1–4; 11:2). Concerning the latter,
the מִן-preposition is often rendered duratively: "I have been YHWH
your God *since* the land of Egypt."[19] Formally, however, these phrases

---

containing three fixed components: a verb (a form of הֶעֱלָה or הוֹצִיא), Israel (or one
of its equivalents) as the direct object, and the determinative מִמִּצְרַיִם. The earlier of
the two forms uses הֶעֱלָה (41 times), while the latter and more prominent form uses
הוֹצִיא (83 times). Further, the הֶעֱלָה formula has the possession of the "land" within
its immediate purview and originates from the northern sanctuaries, while the הוֹצִיא
formula expresses freedom from slavery and is the preferred expression of Dtr circles. As expressed by Wijngaards, however, these formulas are too narrowly delim-
ited. For example, in three instances – Hos 2:17; Mic 7:15, and Hag 2:5 – the agency
shifts from YHWH to Israel/Judah.

15 See note 39 below.
16 According to Wijngaard, "Approach," 98.102, the only times the הֶעֱלָה formula
occurs in Deuteronomy and the DtrH are Deut 20:1; Josh 24:17; Judg 2:1; 6:8, 13;
1 Sam 8:8; 10:18; 12:6; 2 Sam 7:6; 1 Kgs 12:28; 2 Kgs 17:7, 36. Of these texts, only two
do not participate in anti-idolatry rhetoric – Deut 20:1 and 2 Sam 7:6 – and Wijngaards considers the latter to be pre-Dtr. This usage leads him to conclude that Dtr
circles preferred the הוֹצִיא formula over the הֶעֱלָה formula, having associated the
latter with idolatry, especially the northern cultic shrines of Dan and Bethel.
17 Even within this commonality there is diversity, however: Amos 3:1 facilitates the
notion of Israel's unique status and so YHWH's right to judge her (cf. Amos 3:2);
Amos 9:7, however, undermines Israel's unique status and so renders her subject to
YHWH's judgment along with the other nations.
18 The הוֹצִיא formula in Hag 2:5 also performs a promissory role.
19 Hoffman, "Myth," 172; NASB.

appear to be no more than an abridged version of the העלה/הוציא formulas. Although Wijngaards does not include Hos 12:10 and 13:4, one
can especially discern the affinities when compared to unabridged formulations such as Exod 20:2; Deut 5:6, and Ps 81:11:[20]

Hos 12:9 // Hos 13:4	מארץ מצרים	ואנכי יהוה אלהיך
Exod 20:2 // Deut 5:6	מארץ מצרים [אשר הוצאתיך]	אנכי יהוה אלהיך
Ps 81:11	מארץ מצרים [המעלך]	אנכי יהוה אלהיך

Clearly, what is omitted in Hos 12:10 and 13:4 is the verbal aspect of the
העלה and הוציא forms.[21] Given this omission, one cannot assume
Wijngaards' rhetorical observations. Although in context, both Hos
12:10 and 13:4 facilitate a polemic against Ephraim's history of infidelity, which evolves from a Canaanite-like treachery (מרמה; cf. Hos 12:1,
8) to explicit Baalism (13:1).

3.2 YHWH's Activity in the Wilderness

Beyond the exodus, one searches in vain for formulaic reflections on
the wilderness traditions in the Twelve. Consequently, though admittedly arbitrary, a heuristic organization is needed to discuss these dis-
parate reflections. In what follows, the portraits of the activities of the
two primary characters within these reflections – that is, YHWH and
Israel – provide this necessary foil.

Aside from Hos 12:14, the reflections on YHWH's activity in the
wilderness are cast on the lips of the deity himself. Most of the texts
preserving this type of reflection occur in the immediate proximity of
an exodus credo.[22] Only a few reflections on YHWH's wilderness activity emerge via the context of another tradition component: Hos 9:10
(by Israel's failure at בעל־פעור); Amos 5:25 (by במדבר ארבעים שנה);
and Mal 3:22 (by תורת משה עבדי אשר צויתי אותו בחרב). When taken

---

20 Hoffman, "Myth," 172, also recognizes this affinity to Exod 20:2 and Deut 5:6, but his
    assessment too narrowly describes Hos 12:10 and 13:4 as variants of the first com-
    mandment. For other close parallels, see Exod 29:46; Lev 11:45; 19:36; 25:38; 26:13,
    and Num 15:41.
21 Note that the LXX fills the verbal gaps in Hos 12:10 and 13:4 with the addition of
    ἀγήγαγόν σε, presuming reading הוצאתיך or העליתיך (Wolff, *Hosea*, 207). More sig-
    nificantly, 4QXII[c] preserves אנכי העליתיכה, which Ulrich et al., *Qumran*, 241, argue
    is evidence for the LXX's reading. Regardless, it is sufficient here to note that these
    tradents also read these doublets as abridged versions of the more common formu-
    las, and perhaps more specifically, according to 4QXII[c], of the העלה form.
22 Specifically, Hos 11:1–4; 13:5; Amos 2:10; Mic 6:5; 7:15, and Hag 2:5. Hosea 2:16–17 is
    excluded on account that YHWH's actions are cast in the future and do not clearly
    reflect a tradition of YHWH having once enacted them in the wilderness.

together, one can discern four thematic types of reflections, the distribution of which is not without consequence.

The theme of YHWH's *pathos toward Israel* in the wilderness is evident primarily in Hosea.[23] Like its expression of the exodus credo, Hos
11:1 also uniquely portrays YHWH's pathos toward Israel: כי נער
ישראל ואהבהו. Contextualized by the credo in Hos 11:1b, YHWH's
love for ancient Israel in Hos 11:1a takes on the metaphor of sonship.[24]
Typically in Hosea, however, it is the metaphor of marriage that nu-
ances YHWH's love toward Israel and conversely Israel's preference for
other "lovers."[25] It is in the face of this cultic infidelity that two further
reflections of YHWH's pathos toward Israel in wilderness surfaces: Hos
9:10 and 13:4–5. The mention of the failure at בעל־פעור (Num 23:1–5)
concretizes retroactively the reflection in 9:10a: YHWH found Israel
כענבים במדבר and he saw her כבכורה בתאנה בראשיתה. While the
focus of the similes embedded in this reflection is "the quality of Israel
in their initial encounter with God,"[26] as Dozeman rightly observes, the
reflection itself shows YHWH's divine delight in possessing such a
rarity. Similarly, it is in the context of Israel's intimately knowing (ידע)
other gods (cf. Hos 13:2, 4) that YHWH recalls having intimately
known (ידע) Israel במדבר בארץ תלאבות (Hos 13:4–5).

Guidance and *provision* make up the second and third themes in the
reflections of YHWH's activity in the wilderness. Set in context of
YHWH calling out his son from Egypt, YHWH recalls how he had tod-
dled Ephraim (*tiphil* of רגל) and led (משך) them as a liberator with hu-
mane cords of love (Hos 11:3–4). In Amos 2:10, YHWH also recalls how
he led (הלך) them in the wilderness forty years to possess the land of
the Amorite (cf. Num 21:21–35). YHWH also remembers how he guid-
ed them through human leadership: he not only sent Moses, Aaron,
and Miriam (Mic 6:4), but he also preserved Israel through the foreign
prophet, Balaam (Mic 6:5; cf. Num 22–24). Finally, in the only reflection
not spoken by YHWH, the prophet recalls how YHWH used a נביא
(presumably Moses) to bring out Israel from Egypt and to keep them in
the wilderness (Hos 12:14).

---

23 One could argue that Amos 9:7 is an example of the deity's lack of pathos toward
    Israel. By comparing Israel's exodus to those YHWH performed for the Ethiopians,
    Philistines, and Arameans, YHWH effectively strips Israel's exodus of its unique-
    ness. The primary rhetorical effect is a negation of ancient Israel's presumption that
    her elect status would protect her from annihilation (cf. Hoffman, "Myth," 181).
24 Although not within the textual parameters of the Wilderness Tradition, the closest
    parallel to this language is in Exod 4:22–23.
25 For YHWH's marital love toward Israel see Hos 2:16–17, 21–22; 3:1; for Israel's pref-
    erence for other "lovers" see Hos 2:7, 9, 12, 14, 15; 9:1, 10.
26 Dozeman, "Hosea," 65.

Along the way, YHWH is not just directly and indirectly guiding Israel through wilderness and foreign territories; YHWH also provides for the journey. In Hosea 11, the deity recalls how he healed (רפא) them (v. 3). Granted, elsewhere in Hosea רפא carries connotations other than caring provision,[27] but the two times that רפא occurs in the Wilderness Tradition are when YHWH heals the waters at Marah (Exod 15:26) and when Moses prays for Miriam's healing (Num 12:13). In the same context, YHWH recalls how he fed them (v. 4) – perhaps a reflection of the manna and quail traditions (Exod 16; Num 11). Next, in Amos 5:24, YHWH remembers that he did not require Israel to present him with sacrifices and grain offerings – a boon, no doubt, for subsisting in the wilderness. Finally, in Mic 7:5, YHWH promises he will show his people wonders like those he performed when they went out from Egypt.

The tradition reflections making up these three themes – YHWH's pathos, guidance and provision in the wilderness – occur only in within the Four, specifically in Hosea, Amos, and Micah. A fourth theme, however, emerges outside the Four: the *law/covenant of God*. The first example appears conceptually in the gloss of Hag 2:5, as את־הדבר אשר כרתי אתכם is clear covenant language.[28] Malachi 3:22 also evinces this theme when the deity recalls having commanded Moses at Horeb (cf. Deut 5:2; 29:1; 1 Kgs 8:9//2 Chr 5:10). A final reflection may be the mysterious covenant that YHWH recalls having given the Levites in Mal 2:4–8; though its derivation and content can only be inferred (cf. Num 25:11–13; Deut 33:9).[29]

3.3 Israel's Activity in the Wilderness

Unlike the reflections on YHWH's activity in the wilderness, those on Israel's activity in the wilderness only occur in the Four. Similar to reflections on YHWH, however, is the fact that – aside from Mic 7:14 in which the prophet is speaking – the reflections on Israel's activity in the wilderness are again cast on the lips of the deity. As well, due to its

---

27 Wolff, *Hosea*, 199, argues that since רפא in both Hos 6:1 and 7:1 refers to political salvation, its occurrence in Hos 11:3 is indicative of YHWH's liberating Israel from Egypt. Actually, Hosea's usage of רפא is more diverse than Wolff admits, as in Hos 14:5 it clearly refers to cultic restoration.

28 Sweeney, *Micah*, 547; Petersen, *Haggai*, 66; Wolff, *Haggai*, 80. Regarding Hag 2:5's status as a gloss, see note 13 above.

29 McKenzie and Wallace, "Covenant," 550–551, survey the texts scholars have proposed as laying behind this covenant, concluding that these references bear little resemblance to Malachi's interpretation of it.

prevalence, the exodus credo contextualizes most of these reflections
(cf. Hos 2:17; 11:2–3; 12:10; 13:4; Amos 2:10; Mic 7:14). Only two other
reflections emerge otherwise: Hos 9:10, with its citation of Israel's failure at בעל־פעור, and Amos 5:25, by its reference to the forty year sojourn. Taken together, one can discern at least two themes whereby to
discuss these reflections.

The first theme is that of ancient Israel's *cultic infidelity* – the reflections of which all occur in Hosea and are rhetorically juxtaposed to
reflections on YHWH's pathos toward Israel. First, in contrast to
YHWH's delight over Israel's initial quality, Hos 9:10 recalls how the
Israelites had joined themselves to the Moabite deity בעל־פעור (cf.
Num 25:1–5) *prior* to their entry into the land. A similar pairing occurs
in Hos 11:2b. Regardless of the precise identity of the subject of קראו in
Hos 11:2a, the rhetoric force of 11:2b sets Israel's devotion to the בעלים
and פסלים in clear contrast to YHWH's adoptive call and wilderness
faithfulness (Hos 11:1, 3–5). Unlike the punctiliar Hos 9:10, however,
the comparative force of קראו להם כן הלכו מפניהם in Hos 11:2a[30] portrays Israel as *continuing* her idolatrous practices indefinitely, from
wilderness sojourn onward. A third and final juxtaposition perhaps
occurs in Hos 13:4–6, which recalls Israel's infidelity arising *after* entry
into the land. Here, an abridged historical recitation progresses from
the exodus (v. 4a), to the giving of the law (v. 4b), to the deity's pathos
and provision in the wilderness (v. 5), and finally to Israel's pasturage,
wherein she becomes satisfied (שבע), prideful (רום), and forgetful
(שכח) (v. 6). This constellation forms what Vielhauer calls a "deutero-
nomische Trias,"[31] seen elsewhere only in Moses' proleptic warning
against cultic infidelity upon entering the land (Deut 8:10–14; cf. Deut
6:10–12).

A second theme to emerge is Israel's *Amorite conquest*. The most
predominant expression of this tradition in the Hebrew Bible takes the
form of nation lists, which record the people groups Israel was to dis-
possess during the conquest.[32] Of these groups, Israel possessed (ירש)

30 The translation of "The more they called to them, the more than walked after them"
    is indicated by the כ + מן-preposition construction (cf. Joüon and Muraoka, *Gram-
    mar*, §174e). That there is no clear antecedent for קראו has prompted some scholars
    to accept the easier reading of LXX's καθὼς μετεκάλεσα (for כקראי); see Wolff, *Hosea*,
    190; Nogalski, *Book of the Twelve*, 1:156.164. The lack of a clear antecedent, however,
    is not unusual within the Twelve and can be an indicator of secondary insertion (cf.
    Hag 2:5a).
31 Vielhauer, *Werden*, 180.
32 Ishida, "Structure," 461–462, cites twenty-seven such lists. The most common type of
    these lists is the six-fold nation list: Canaanite, Hittite, Amorite, Perizzite, Hivite, and
    Jebusite (cf. Exod 3:8, 17; 23:23; 34:11; Deut 20:17; Josh 9:1; 11:3; 12:8; Judg 3:5).

only Amorite land during their wilderness sojourn (Num 21:21–35).[33] In this way, Amos 2:10bβ – לרשת את־ארץ האמרי – likely reflects the prominent tradition of Israel defeating the two Amorite kings: Sihon of Heshbon and Og of Bashan (Num 21:21–35; Deut 2:24–3:14; Judg 9:10).[34] A second example of this theme emerges via toponyms associated with this conquest. Like the victories over the two Amorite kings, tradition frequently couples the regions of Bashan and Gilead,[35] the latter also said to have been once populated by Amorites (Num 32:39). In this way, Mic 7:14b – ירעו בשן וגלעד כימי עולם – constitutes a wilderness reflection quite similar to Amos 2:10 in that prior to crossing the Jordan, Israel occupied Transjordanian Amorite territories.[36]

Two final reflections on Israel's wilderness activity remain, though they resist categorization. The first, in conjunction with YHWH's promise to woo Israel in the wilderness, is the reflection that she once sang (ענה) as a youth, specifically on the day of the exodus (Hos 2:17b).[37] The second is in Hos 12:10, where YHWH declares, עד אושיבך באהלים כימי מועד. While implicit, the deity's threat reflects the tradition that ancient Israelites were once nomadic tent-dwellers (e.g. Exod 16:16; Num 24:5).

4. Distribution and Import for Redactional Models

With the exceptions of Hag 2:5; Mal 2:4–8, and 3:22, the distribution of the wilderness reflections within the Twelve find their locus within the Four, specifically Hosea, Amos, and Micah. Whether this concentration has any editorial significance now demands our attention. Since Nogalski's observation regarding the possibility of a Dtr-corpus[38] (i.e. the Four) as a precursor to the Twelve, several studies have sought to isolate redactional texts crucial to its formation. A significant conflu-

---

33 During their sojourn, Israel also conquered the Canaanite cites under king Arad (Num 21:1–3) – the first to be devoted to destruction (חרם), hence the etiology חרמה (v. 3). As there is no mention of Israel possessing (ירש) this land, like Jericho, these cities may have belonged to YHWH (cf. Jos 6:17, 26; 1 Kgs 16:34).

34 See also Num 21:33; 32:33; Deut 4:46–47; 29:7; 31:4; Josh 2:10; 9:10; 12:2–5; 13:10–12; 1 Kgs 4:19; Neh 9:22; Ps 135:11; 136:19–20.

35 See Deut 3:10, 13; 4:43; Josh 12:5; 13:11, 31; 17:1, 5; 20:8; 1 Kgs 4:13, 19; 2 Kgs 10:33; 1 Chr 5:16; Jer 50:19; Mic 7:14.

36 For a discussion of Bashan and Gilead within the geography of the Transjordanian region, see Ahlström, *History*, 63–65.

37 Though not its primary nuance, the use of ענה in Hos 2:16 to indicate singing is not without precedent. Miriam sings in Exod 15:21; the song at the well of Beer (Num 21:16–18); and the song of Moses (Deut 31:30–32:43).

38 Nogalski, *Precursors*, 84–89, 278–280.

ence emerges when one compares texts exhibiting wilderness reflections in the Four with those to which scholars ascribe redactional significance.

The clearest of these overlaps pertains to the reflections contained within Amos. Schart, Albertz, and Wöhrle all consider Amos 2:9–11; 3:1; 5:25, and 9:7 to be D/Dtr additions.[39] Schart also deems Amos 4:6–11 to be part of a D redactional unit. Admittedly, the wilderness reflections in Hosea and Micah do not coincide with those texts these scholars see as redactionally significant. Still, the proximity of certain of these reflections directly adjoins some of the editorial additions so far proposed. Micah 6:4–5, for example, adjoins a D/Dtr expansion seen by both Schart (Mic 6:2–16*) and Wöhrle (Mic 6:2–4, 9*, 10–15). As well, Wöhrle also sees Hos 13:2–3 as a Dtr addition, to which the reflection of Hos 13:4–5 is also adjoined.

Further corroboration for the editorial significance of these reflections can be seen in the redactional studies of Zapff and Vielhauer. For Zapff, Mic 7:1–20 is not only redactional, but it contains strong thematic links to Mic 6:1–8. These links *coincidentally* pertain to the wilderness traditions reflected in Mic 6:4–5 and 7:14–17.[40] In his study on Hosea, Vielhauer finds Hos 11:1–5* to be foundational to the formation of Hosea.[41] As well, in his analysis, Hos 9:10 constitutes the beginning of a redactional frame (9:10–17; [10:1–8]; 10:9–15) overviewing key portions of ancient Israel's history.[42]

In short, the reflections in Amos clearly align with the texts associated with the Dtr editing of the Four. Further, although not associated with the Dtr editing, the location of most of the reflections in Hosea and Micah lie along what might be called key *redactional seams* in the growth of these writings and the Dtr-corpus. Just in this short review,

---

39   Schart, *Entstehung*, 317, cites the following as D additions: Hos 1:1–2b*; 2:6; 3:1*; 4:1a*; 5:1–2*; 8:1b; 14:2–4; Amos 1:1–2, 9–12; 2:4–5, 10–12; 3:1b–7; 4:6–11*; 5:11, 25–26*; 8:4–7, 11–12; 9:7–10; Mic 1:1, 2b, 5a, 6–7, 13b; 2:3*; 6:2–16*; Zeph 1:1, 6, 13b, 17aβ. Albertz, "Exile," 251, cites Hos 1:5, 7; 3:1bβ; 4:1*, 15; 8:1b, 6, 14; 11:5b; Amos 1:1b, 9–10, 11–12; 2:4–5, 10–12; 3:1b*, 7; 5:25(?); 8:11–12; 9:7–10; Mic 1:1, 5b–7, 13bβ; 5:8(?), 9–13; Zeph 1:1, 3–6, 13b, 17aβ; 2:3a; 2:5–3:8bα*; 11–13 (without 2:7, 9, 10–11; 3:8bβ–10). Wöhrle, "Future," 610, cites Hos 1:1; 3:1–4, 5*; 4:1abα, 10, 15; 8:1b, 4b–6, 14; 13:2–3; 14:1; Amos 1:1*; 2:4–5, 9–12; 3:1b, 7; 4:13*; 5:11, 25–26; 7:10–17; 8:5, 6b, 11–12; 9:7–10; Mic 1:1, 5b–7, 9, 12b; 5:9–13; 6:2–4a, 9aα, 10–15; Zeph 1;1, 4–6, 13b; 2:1–2, 3*, 4–6, 8–9a; 3:1–4, 6–8a, 11–13.
40   Zapff, *Studien*, 233–234, states that "zwischen Mi 6,1–8 und Mi 7,7–20 existieren verschiedene Stichwortbezüge, die aufgrund ihrer Zahl und ihrer formalen Ähnlichkeit ... die Annahme einer reinen Zufälligkeit unwahrscheinlich machen."
41   Vielhauer, *Werden*, 13–43.
42   Vielhauer, *Werden*, 161.

the only reflections in the Four not within, or along the boundaries of, editorially significant texts are Hos 2:16–17 and Hos 12:10, 14.[43]

Finally, the wilderness reflections outside the Four are also not without editorial significance. Haggai 2:5, as noted earlier,[44] is widely considered an editorial gloss, the purpose of which remains relatively unexplored in the context of the Twelve's formation. The reflection in Mal 3:22, on the other hand, likely belongs to the hand of the Twelve's final redactor.[45]

5. Conclusions

The confluence of 1) texts bearing wilderness reflections in the Twelve, and of 2) texts scholars of the Twelve consider editorially significant for the Twelve's formation, beg for further redactional analysis that is sensitive to tradition-historical reflections pertaining to the Wilderness Tradition. The concentration, distribution, and diversity of these reflections within Hosea, Amos, and Micah are particularly salient for the formation of the Four. Given the above, one must now consider whether the D/Dtr redactors of the Four were not also tradents preoccupied with ancient Israel's wilderness wanderings. The frequent and consistent usage of the exodus credo along Dtr lines is evidence of this dynamic. As for the remaining reflections in the Four, the editorial implications wrought by their diversity and development merits further study. The same applies to the placement of both the late interpolation of Hag 2:5a and the concluding reflection of Mal 3:22. No doubt, as scholars continue to rattle the bones of the Twelve, more and more literary ligaments binding them will emerge. Could the reflections on the Wilderness Tradition within this corpus be one of them? Only further rattling will tell.

---

43 One further issue remains: why are these wilderness reflections within the Four extant only in within this precursor's first three writings, especially Hosea and Amos? Zephaniah exhibits some wilderness motifs – e.g, Nineveh becoming צִיָּה כַמִּדְבָּר in 2:13 – but there is no clear wilderness reflection in Zephaniah. Initially, it is tempting to posit the distribution of these tradition reflections as further corroboration for Schart's *Zweiprophetenbuch*, a precursor comprised of Hos 1:2–14:1* + Amos 1–9*. Such an proposition, upon further inspection, immediately encounters difficulties, as Schart attributes all the texts within Amos that contain wilderness reflections to the redactor responsible for the "D-Korpus." Thus, the wilderness reflections in Amos were not extant therein until the formation of the Four, or in other words until *after* the formation of Schart's *Zweiprophetenbuch* (Schart, *Entstehung*, 101–155.316–317).

44 See note 13 above.

45 Nogalski, *Processes*, 212; Schart, *Entstehung*, 317; Wöhrle, *Abschluss*, 251.

References

Ahlström, G.W. *The History of Ancient Palestine*. Edited by D. Edelman. Minneapolis: Fortress, 1993.

Albertz, R. "Exile as Purification: Reconstructing the 'Book of the Four.'" Pp. 232–251 in *Thematic Threads in the Book of the Twelve*. Edited by P.L. Redditt and A. Schart. BZAW 325. Berlin: de Gruyter, 2003.

Dozeman, T. "Hosea and the Wilderness Wandering Tradition." Pp. 55–70 in *Rethinking the Foundations: Historiography in the Ancient World and in the Bible*. Edited by S.L. McKenzie and T. Römer. FS J. Van Seters. BZAW 294. Berlin: de Gruyter, 2000.

Eco, U. and Paci, C. "The Scandal of Metaphor: Metaphorology and Semiotics." *Poetics Today* 4 (1983) 217–257.

Fishbane, M. *Biblical Interpretation in Ancient Israel*. New York: Oxford University Press, 1988.

Franz, M. *Der barmherzige und gnädige Gott: Die Gnadenrede vom Sinai (Exodus 34,6–7) und ihre Parallelen im Alten Testament und seiner Umwelt*. BWANT 160. Stuttgart: Kohlhammer, 2003.

Gelston, A. *Biblia Hebraica Quinta: Fascicle 13: The Twelve Minor Prophets*. Stuttgart: Deutsche Bibelgesellschaft, 2010.

Hadjiev, T. *The Composition and Redaction of the Book of Amos*. BZAW 393. Berlin: de Gruyter, 2009.

Hallo, W.M. and Younger, K.L. (eds.) *The Context of Scripture*. 2 vols. Leiden: Brill, 2003.

Hoffman, Y. "A North Israelite Typological Myth and a Judaean Historical Tradition: The Exodus in Hosea and Amos." *VT* 39 (1989) 169–182.

Ishida, T. "The Structure and Historical Implications of the Lists of Pre-Israelite Nations." *Bib* 60 (1979) 461–490.

Joüon, P. and Muraoka, T. *A Grammar of Biblical Hebrew*. 2 vols. SubBi 14. 3rd reprint 2000. Rome: Pontificio Istituto Biblico, 1991.

Knight, D.A. "Introduction: Tradition and Theology." Pp. 1–8 in *Tradition and Theology in the Old Testament*. Edited by idem. Philadelphia: Fortress Press, 1977.

McKenzie, S.L. and Wallace, H.N. "Covenant Themes in Malachi." *CBQ* 45 (1983) 549–563.

Nogalski, J.D. *Literary Precursors to the Book of the Twelve*. BZAW 217. Berlin: de Gruyter, 1993.

– *Redactional Processes in the Book of the Twelve*. BZAW 218. Berlin: de Gruyter, 1993.

– "One Book and Twelve Books: The Nature of the Redactional Work and the Implications of Cultic Source Material in the Book of the Twelve." Pp. 11–46 in *Two Sides of a Coin: Juxtaposing Views on Interpreting the Book of the Twelve / the Twelve Prophetic Books*. Analecta Gorgiana 201. Piscataway: Gorgias Press, 2009.

– *The Book of the Twelve*. 2 vols. Macon: Smyth & Helwys, 2011.

Noth, M. *Überlieferungsgeschichte des Pentateuch*. Stuttgart: Kohlhammer, 1948.

Petersen, D.L. *Haggai and Zechariah 1–8: A Commentary*. OTL. Philadelphia: Westminster, 1984.

– "A Book of the Twelve." Pp. 3–10 in *Reading and Hearing the Book of the Twelve*. Edited by J.D. Nogalski and M.A. Sweeney. SBLSymS 15. Atlanta: Society of Biblical Literature, 2000.

Redditt, P.L. "Recent Research on the Book of the Twelve as One Book." *CurBS* 9 (2001) 47–80.

Richards, I.A. *Philosophy of Rhetoric*. The Mary Flexner Lectures on the Humanities 3. New York: Oxford University Press, 1936.

Schart, A. *Die Entstehung des Zwölfprophetenbuchs: Neubearbeitungen von Amos im Rahmen schriftenübergreifender Redaktionsprozesse*. BZAW 260. Berlin: de Gruyter, 1998.

Steck, O.H. *Exegese des Alten Testaments: Leitfaden der Methodik: Ein Arbeitbuch für Proseminare, Seminare und Vorlesungen*. 12th ed. Neukirchen-Vluyn: Neukirchener, 1989.

Sweeney, M.A. *Micah, Nahum, Habbakuk, Zephaniah, Haggai, Zechariah, Malachi*. Vol. 2 of *The Twelve Prophets*. Berit Olam. Collegeville: Liturgical, 2000.

Ulrich, E. et al. *Qumran Cave 4: X: The Prophets*. DJD 15. New York: Oxford and Clarendon, 1997.

Vielhauer, R. *Das Werden des Buches Hosea: Eine redaktiongeschichtliche Untersuchung*. BZAW 349. Berlin: de Gruyter, 2007.

Wijngaards, J. "הוציא and העלה: A Twofold Approach to the Exodus." *VT* 15 (1965) 91–102.

Wöhrle, J. *Die frühen Sammlungen des Zwölfprophetenbuches: Entstehung und Komposition*. BZAW 360. Berlin: de Gruyter, 2006.

– *Der Abschluss des Zwölfprophetenbuches: Buchübergreifende Redaktionsprozesse in den späten Sammlungen*. BZAW 389. Berlin: de Gruyter, 2008.

– "'No Future for the Proud Exultant Ones': The Exilic Book of the Four Prophets (Hos., Am., Mic., Zeph.) as a Concept Opposed to the Deuteronomistic History." *VT* 58 (2008) 608–627.

– "A Prophetic Reflection on Divine Forgiveness: The Integration of the Book of Jonah into the Book of the Twelve." *Journal of Hebrew Scriptures* 9.7 (2009) 1–17.

Wolff, H.W. *Hosea: A Commentary on the Book of the Prophet Hosea*. Translated by G. Stansell. Hermeneia. Philadelphia: Fortress, 1974.

– *Haggai: A Commentary*. Translated by M. Kohl. Minneapolis: Augsburg, 1988.

Zapff, B.M. *Redaktionsgeschichtliche Studien zum Michabuch im Kontext des Dodekapropheton*. BZAW 256. Berlin: de Gruyter, 1997.

Dominion Comes to Jerusalem:
An Examination of Developments in the Kingship and Zion Traditions as Reflected in the Book of the Twelve with Particular Attention to Micah 4–5

MARK E. BIDDLE

Baptist Theological Seminary Richmond

In a recently published article, Roberts argues that the beloved vision of universal peace and tranquility often read in the pericope attested in Isa 2:2–4 and Mic 4:1–3 misapprehends the resonances of imperial political power that echo throughout the text. Specifically, Roberts points to intimations, especially in the Isaian context of the material, that it envisions the exercise of God's worldwide sovereignty through the apparatus of the Davidic monarchy. He notes, for example, that the notions of the issuance of the divine word, the divine Torah, and divine judicial rulings implies the functions of prophets, priests, and judges, and concludes that the biblical text reflects an awareness that pure theocracy is impracticable.[1] Without engaging Roberts directly in detail, two of his central observations – namely the imperial status of Jerusalem described in the Isaiah–Micah parallel and the nature of the relationships between King YHWH, imperial Zion, and the Davidic dynasty – invite a fresh examination.

As the context-specific treatments given the pericope in Isaiah and Micah already indicate,[2] ideas associated with Zion's glorious future – a complex of motifs and themes often collectively designated "Zion tradition" – resists monolithic description. Although the complex includes a number of elements or motifs (the *Völkerkampf* motif, the pilgrimage of the nations, etc.), time and space limitations dictate that this paper re-

---

1   Roberts, "End," 121, observes with regard to Isa 2:2–4 that another Isaian "peace" passage (11:10) envisions the Davidic king as "the human agent for rendering God's verdicts to the nations seeking arbitration."

2   Sweeney, "Debate," 113, for example, maintains based on his comparative analysis of Mic 4:1–5 and Isa 2:1–4 and their literary contexts, that Micah and Isaiah testify to a "debate concerning Judah's relationship to the nations in early Persian period Judaism." In his view, Isaiah envisions submission to Persian hegemony as a component of YHWH's plan for Zion, whereas Micah 4–5 advocates the submission of all the nations of the world, including Persia, to reestablished Davidic rule.

stricts itself to the two closely related elements already mentioned: the imperial status of Zion and the character of the exercise of earthly political power. The subsequent examination will deal with the four layers of "kingship" material in Micah 4–5 that correspond roughly to the major structural components of the collection, each of which, conveniently, concentrates on one element of the earthly ruler/divine king/royal city triad.

1. Kings, Kingship and Kingdom and the Structure/Redactional History of Micah 4–5

While the several redactional analyses of Micah 4–5 offered in recent years differ on significant details, they agree substantially that obvious structural features of the collection provide initial criteria for distinguishing layers in its growth.[3] The likely core of Micah 4–5, namely the three "now" sayings (4:9–14), concentrate on Jerusalem's dire situation, which involves the aggression of "many nations" and an absent or ineffective king. In contrast, Mic 4:6–7, tied secondarily to Mic 5:9–13 by the introductory formula, "in that day," and likely constituting part of a redaction of Micah that included Mic 2:12–13, announces the glorious return of the remnant to Jerusalem, gathered and led by their king, YHWH, who will henceforth reign over them on Mt. Zion. Yet another layer of material, characterized by the address to a place (Jerusalem, 4:8; Bethlehem, 5:1), also set in the future day of prosperity, not only stands between the contrasting depictions of the failure of the human monarchy and the wondrous reign of King YHWH, but problematizes the relationship. This paired prediction will be the focus of attention here.

2. The Failure of Human Rule

Accepting arguments for an early form of Micah that ended with the prediction of the destruction of Jerusalem in 3:12,[4] the "now" sayings will probably have been added during or shortly after the Babylonian crisis to announce that the destruction predicted in 3:12 is "now" imminent or in progress. The warning (3:12) that Zion would one day

---

3   Mays, *Micah*, 25–26; Wolff, *Micah*, 85; Zapff, *Studien*, 79–86.296; Lescow, *Worte*, 137; Metzner, *Kompositionsgeschichte*, 78.
4   Nogalski, *Precursors*, 274–275; Schart, *Entstehung*, 316–317; Zapff, *Studien*, 12.

become a "plowed field" (שָׂדֶה) has or is about to come to pass (4:10);
Zion must now dwell "in the open field (שָׂדֶה)." One of the rulers who
rendered judgment (שָׁפַט, 3:11) for bribes, the behavior that resulted in
Jerusalem's distress, now experiences humiliation at hands of those
laying siege (4:14).

The final form of Mic 4:9–14 envisions an inconsistent sequence of
events, however. The secondary expansion in v. 10 refers to exile in and
redemption from Babylon eventuating from Daughter Zion's current
distress. In contrast, v. 11–13* expect, uniquely in the Twelve, that the
"many nations" gathered against Jerusalem have unwittingly played
their assigned role in YHWH's plan for their destruction and spoliation
at Zion's hands.[5] The two views resist harmonization. Either Zion "now"
faces Babylonian conquest and exile, one day to be redeemed, or her
enemies have stepped into a divine trap to be sprung "now." These difficulties only emerge, however, because of the "Arise, thresh!" material in
v. 12–13. After excising this material and the "exile in Babylon" material
in v. 10, the three un-supplemented "now" sayings depict a coherent
situation: Zion faces a threat from enemies gathered against her, indeed,
the earthly ruler has apparently already been taken captive.

The earliest form of the "now"-sayings composition would have
consisted, then, of 4:9–10abβ, 11, and 14,[6] the core perspective on "kingship" in Micah 4–5. The rhetorical question, "Is your king not in you,
has your counselor perished?" – one of only two instances of the root
מֶלֶךְ in the collection – allows for several interpretations. Does it anticipate a positive or a negative response? Is the king in question an earthly ruler or YHWH? On one hand, the statement concerning the slap
administered to "Israel's judge" (v. 14) suggests that v. 9 contemplates

---

5   The closest parallel appears in Jeremianic oracles against Edom (49:20) and Babylon
     (50:45), the only other occurrences of the collocation of the terms מַחֲשָׁבָה and עֵצָה in
     the prophetic literature (cf. Job 5:12–13; Ps 33:10–11; Prov 19:20–21; 20:18).
6   Zapff, Studien, 81, argues that Mic 4:11–13, in its entirety, constitutes an insertion
     because it exemplifies the Völkerkampf (VK) motif and not a historical reminiscence of
     the Babylonian crisis. Unlike typical VK texts, however, Mic 4:11–13 purports to ad-
     dress a situation in the present ("now"). Unlike typical VK texts, Mic 4:11 describes
     the nations as having gathered against Jerusalem on their own volition. The descrip-
     tion of "many nations" assembled against Judah, eager to witness her profanation,
     bears greater similarity to descriptions of Jerusalem taunted by her neighbors (Isa;
     Jer; Ezek; Obad; Lam) than to the depictions of conflict on a universal, even cosmic
     scale (i.e. Joel 4:9–17). Finally, although Wolff's suggestion that Mic 4:11 may have in
     view events such as the attack of Chaldean, Syrian, Moabite and Ammonite forces
     recorded in 2 Kgs 24:1 (Dodekapropheton 4, 110–111) has not found widespread ac-
     ceptance, another report that Nebuchadnezzar led "all the kingdoms of the earth
     under his dominion and all the peoples" (Jer 34:1) against on Jerusalem in Jer 34:1
     lends support to Wolff's view (see also Rudolph, Micha, 92).

a human king, leading some commentators to conclude that the quotation continues Micah's critique of Judah's leadership: 'Isn't your earthly ruler still there, even though he is useless?'[7] Alternatively, if v. 14 alludes to the deposition of a Jerusalemite king, the question in v. 9 may function as a taunt: 'O, you poor thing, you have lost your king, haven't you?' In contrast, some interpreters, relying on the reference to the deity as king in the preceding verses, understand the question as an ironic affirmation of the deity's continued presence in Zion: 'Why are you upset? Your king, YHWH, is still with you, is he not?'[8] Despite a degree of grammatical ambiguity,[9] the second clause in the compound question, which inquires as to the fate of Zion's "counselor" (יוֹעֵץ), supports the human identity of the king in question since, unless Mic 4:9 does so, no text in the Hebrew Bible refers to YHWH as a "counselor."[10]

Final confirmation that Mic 4:9–14 express a negative view of human kingship comes from a consideration of its role in the macro-context. Others have already noted a thematic attitude toward kingship characteristic of the so-called "Deuteronomic/deuteronomistic corpus" (DC: consisting of Hos, Amos, Mic, Zeph).[11] In a synchronic/canonical reading of the Twelve, Leuenberger finds in Hosea a delineation of the programmatic prophetic critique of the institutional monarchy, which YHWH established and can abolish. This dialectic between YHWH's dominion and authority conferred upon temporal rulers, Leuenberger argues, runs throughout the Twelve and culminates in Zechariah 14 (with echoes in Malachi).[12] Similarly stipulating the existence of a DC, Redditt's analysis of kingship in the Twelve finds that Mic 4:9–10abα, with its "anti-monarchial" perspective probably followed originally directly upon Mic 3:12 and comprised the conclusion of the form of Micah incorporated into the Book of the Four.[13]

On balance then, in its likely original context following directly upon Mic 3:9–12, the "now" triplet describes the fulfillment of the earlier

---

7   Mays, *Micah*, 105; Weiser, *Propheten*, 268; Smith, *Micah*, 91; Hillers, *Micah*, 59, who identifies the king as Hezekiah; McKane, *Micah*, 134–140, conveniently summarizes the alternative positions.
8   Wolff, *Micah*, 139, calls attention to Jer 8:19 and Mic 3:11b; idem, *Prophet*, 91: "With deep irony inquiry is made concerning the whereabouts of the king."
9   In Hebrew, the second element in such rhetorical questions can either express an alternative or it can repeat the content of the first element.
10   Although YHWH does "give counsel" (Ps 16:7) and frequently "plans" (Isa 14:24, 26, 27, passim). McKane, *Micah*, 136–137, amends the second reference in Mic 4:9 to a plural (following Syr and Targ) and understands YHWH as the king and the early rulers as "counselors."
11   Cf. Schart, *Entstehung*, 316–317; Zapff, *Studien*, 12.
12   Leuenberger, "Herrschaftserwartungen," 75–111.
13   Redditt, "King," 56–82.

warning. Jerusalem and its ruling class face the consequences of failed leadership. The ambiguity noted above, however, especially with respect to the initial rhetorical question, permitted or even generated a series of reinterpretations through recontextualiztion.

3. YHWH as King

The redactor responsible for including Mic 4:6–7 and 2:12–13, influenced perhaps by the false confidence based on claims that YHWH is "in our midst" asserted by Jerusalem's guilty leadership (3:11), seems to have understood the reference otherwise. This redactor viewed the Babylonian catastrophe, especially the destruction of the Jerusalem temple, as tantamount to YHWH's departure from Jerusalem. Now, he announces the day when YHWH, the king (2:13), will assemble the scattered flock and lead them home thenceforth to reign over them as king (4:7) on Mt. Zion.

3.1 Theocracy?

The language seems straightforward, but the concept of divine rule announced here is far from clear. Does Mic 4:6–7, in concert with the vision of the "latter days" in Mic 4:1–4(5), call for a theocracy or are biblical texts such as this aware that pure theocracy is impracticable, as Roberts and others argue?[14] Does YHWH's kingship necessarily imply Davidic rulership, and, if so, what is the precise character of that rule?[15] Micah 4–5 offers two perspectives on these questions: the vision of world peace in Mic 4:1–4(5) and the prediction of the return of dominion to Jerusalem along with the advent of a Bethlehemite ruler.

3.2 Utopia?

Although Mic 4:1–4(5) looks forward to a period when Mt. Zion will occupy supreme status in the world, its interest lies primarily in defining Zion's relationship to the nations rather than in outlining a form of government. The only active agents explicitly identified in the unit are

---

14   Roberts, "End," 121, observes with regard to Isa 2:2–4 that another Isaian "peace" passage (11:10) envisions the Davidic king as "the human agent for rendering God's verdicts to the nations seeking arbitration."

15   So Redditt, "King," 76.

YHWH, who will "teach [the nations] his ways" (v. 2) and "judge the nations" (v. 3; YHWH is also the agent implied by the twofold *passivum divinum* in v. 1) and the nations, who will "flow to Zion" (v. 1) seeking instruction (v. 2) and who will abandon weapons and warfare (v. 3). The primary image of YHWH here is as lawgiver, not king. Presumably, the scenario envisioned calls for priests to mediate instruction and officials to render judgment, but the text only implies such institutions.

4. Dominion for Zion (Mic 4:8)

The core of Micah 4–5 offers a negative view of Judah's kings, a subsequent redactional layer looks forward to the return of King YHWH to Mt. Zion but goes no further, and the vision of a future era of international peace refrains similarly from describing mechanisms or institutions. Sandwiched between the ironic question concerning the absence of Zion's king (v. 11) and the announcement of the day in which King YHWH will return (v. 7), Mic 4:8, the first component in a structural and redactional layer of material with a counterpart in Mic 5:1, introduces an added dimension. In its immediate context, it responds to the question concerning the absence of Zion's king with a promise that "dominion" and "kingship" will one day return and explicates the preceding announcement of the return of King YHWH. That is, it assumes that King YHWH has indeed departed but will one day return. In the context of its counterpart, however, interpreters commonly read Mic 4:8 as a promise concerning the reestablishment of the Davidic dynasty referenced in Mic 5:1.

Evidence for the full scope – denotations, connotations, allusions, and worldview – of the idea expressed in Mic 4:8 is scant, but tantalizing. Three observations complicate the view that the language employed refers simply to the reestablishment of the Davidic dynasty. First, Mic 4:8 focuses on the return of sovereign authority to Jerusalem. The second of the terms for this authority employed here, מֶמְלָכָה, which exhibits no marked distinction in meaning or usage from other feminine abstract nouns formed on the root מלך (i.e. מְלוּכָה), has a wide range of connotations, roughly equivalent to the semantic field of the English term "kingdom." It can refer to a concrete political entity (e.g. the "kingdom of Israel," 1 Sam 24:20 or the "kingdom of Judah," 2 Chr 11:17) or to the status of a particular ruler or ruling house (e.g., "the kingdom of Og," Deut 3:4, 13). Notably, this usage does not equate the political entity with the status of an individual or dynasty. When Samuel informs Saul that his "kingship" will not endure, he does not

mean that Israel will cease to exist as a nation, but only that God intends to transfer the authority to rule over the nation to another (1 Sam
13:13, 14). Just as God bestows the abstract principle of "kingship" upon individuals and can transfer it (2 Sam 3:10; 1 Kgs 11:11, 13, 31; 12:26;
14:8; cf. 1 Kgs 2:46), as an abstraction, it can pertain to cities as the seat
of such authority (Josh 10:1; 11:10; Isa 17:3). In the Hebrew Bible,
ממשלה, the second term in Mic 4:8, designates either the abstract notion
of "authority," the "power/right/responsibility" to govern (Gen 1:16; Ps
136:8, 9; 145:13; Isa 22:21; Jer 34:1; 51:28; Dan 11:5; cf. Aramaic שלטן in
Dan 3:33; 4:31; 7:6, 12, 14, 26, 27) or, by extension, the realm in which or
over which one exercises this authority (1 Kgs 9:19; 2 Kgs 20:13 ‖ Isa
39:2; 2 Chr 8:6; Ps 103:22; 114:2; cf. Aramaic שלטן in Dan 4:19; 6:26;), in
one case in the sense of "those under [someone's] command" (2 Chr
32:9). Coupled in Mic 4:8 with ממשלה "dominion," ממלכה refers, then,
to sovereignty associated with a place, regardless of the identity of the
human ruler who exercises it. As an abstraction referring to supreme
political authority, it is well-suited for the language of empire. In Jer
34:1, it describes the relationship of the Babylonian "king of kings,"
Nebuchadnezzar, to the "kingdoms" under his authority which partic-
ipated in the attack against Jerusalem, and, similarly, in Jer 51:28, it
denotes "every land under its (Media's) dominion."

Second, according to Mic 4:8, this sovereignty will not come to a
person or a dynasty, but to the personified fortifications of the personified city, "Daughter Jerusalem/Zion." As is true of Micah 4 generally,
she is the focus of attention here, not a human ruler. In context, Mic 4:8
culminates the depiction of her glorious future as the seat of worldwide
– even imperial - authority, located atop the highest of mountains,
attracting the nations of the world to receive YHWH's instruction and
guidance; then she will truly be the "City of Peace," the destination for
the remnant returning to live under YHWH's reign. Like the vision for
Zion's future portrayed in Isaiah 60 and 62, the picture painted here
assumes such grandiose proportions as to render any ordinary human
king inconspicuous in proportion.

Third, lexically, one may understand the expression הראשנה, either
in relation to the immediate context as a reference to YHWH's return,
as a reference to the return of a "previous" human monarchy, or as the
advent in Jerusalem of authority of the first rank (the noun occurs in
the sense of "chief" or "foremost" in Ezr 9:2; 1 Chr 18:17; Dan 10:13;
Esth 1:14; LXX renders the term here with prōtos, which has a similar
range of meanings). More suggestively, finally, LXX qualifies this advent of dominion with the prepositional phrase "from Babylon," not
from Bethlehem. Since nothing in the other versional evidence or in the

condition of the Hebrew text indicates that the LXX addition arose as a misreading of the Hebrew, and no grounds for an omission in the Hebrew exist, it can best be understood as a witness to an early interpretive tradition. LXX understands Mic 4:8 in terms of YHWH's transfer of "mistress of nations" (cf. Isa 47) status from Daughter Babylon to Daughter Zion.

4.1 Mesopotamian and Persian Concepts of Dominion

After the end of the Davidic dynasty, biblical authors conceived of a variety of schemes for the relationship between God's dominion and the exercise of derivative earthly authority. In addition to the hope for a restoration of the Davidic monarchy (e.g., Jer 23:5; 30:9; 33:15; Ezek 34:23–24; 37:23–25), a hope that must have soon faded or evolved in the face of political realities, the Bible also bears witness to the advocacy of proponents of hierocratic governance of a faith community living under foreign political domination.[16] Alternatively, Deutero-Isaiah has no difficulty designating Cyrus as the messiah (45:1), just as the Chronicler can quote, apparently with assent if not approval, Cyrus' alleged declaration that "YHWH, the God of heaven, has given me all the kingdoms of the earth, and has appointed me to build him a house in Jerusalem…" (2 Chr 36:23). Several passages document the transformation of Davidic traditions into a form that applies corporately/democratically/collectively to the people (see, for example Isa 45:14; 49:7, 22–23; 55:3–5; 60:14; Ps 18:44–45).[17] In yet another theological strategy that accommodates monotheistic faith with *Realpolitik*, the book of Daniel operates with a highly-nuanced concept of the "kingdom of God," understanding it, on one level, as synonymous with "empire." God bestows the kingdom on specific empires and emperors (Dan 2–6). On another level, the book also looks forward to the end of world empires when the kingdom of God [the people?] will *replace* secular power.[18]

As early as circa 539 B.C.E., Deutero-Isaiah had laid the conceptual groundwork for Daniel's understanding of the exercise of God's sovereignty in human political affairs. The Deutero-Isaianic scheme of history involves three principal actors: a seat of authority, a "messiah" anointed to exercise authority on the political level, and God who is sovereign over the process. Because of her sin, God had stripped Lady Jerusalem/Zion of her status, transferring supremacy for a time to Lady

---

16   Cf. Ezra 5:14; 6:7; Neh 5:14, etc.; see Kessler, "Haggai," 102–119.
17   Cf. Becker, *Expectation*, 72–73.
18   Kratz, "Reich," 193–194.

Babylon. Now, however, God has in turn removed from the throne Lady Babylon, the "mistress of kingdoms" (Isa 47:5), who had presumptuously thought that her preeminence would endure permanently (Isa 47:7, 10), in order to make room for the restoration of ascendant Lady Zion (49:14–26, etc.).[19] Notably, Deutero-Isaiah's "royal theology" does not link divine kingship with a Davidic agent of human rulership; amid the aspirations for Jerusalem's glorious future, it does not envision the restoration of a Davidic king in Jerusalem. In the prophet's view, for the moment, God had bestowed executive authority on Cyrus. With regard to human agency beyond that moment, Deutero-Isaiah remains silent.

A long tradition of Mesopotamian theopolitical theory probably influenced the axis of thought that runs from Deutero-Isaiah through Mic 4:8 and on to Daniel. With centuries, even millennia, of shifting power dynamics that saw the ascendancy and then demise of first one then another city-state, Mesopotamian thought developed a basic theological rationale to explain how a center of political and religious power, once apparently favored by the gods, could find itself suddenly abandoned. While perspectives differ somewhat according to genre and sometimes with regard to whether the reversal of fortunes in a particular case could be attributed to some specific cause,[20] a basic rationale proved remarkably resilient over time. According to this rationale, the abstraction *kingship* "was let down from heaven," prior to and independent of an actual king, to reside first in Eridu.[21] History, then, is the sequence of holders of this authority.[22] From time to time, by decision of Enlil and the great gods (a decision reached either at the beginning of time or in the given moment), this *kingship* was transferred to another city, a decision tantamount to placing the former seat of *kingship* under curse.[23] Meanwhile, the patron deity of the now cursed city finds

19 Biddle, "Lady," 124–139.
20 See Cooper's discussion of Mesopotamian notions concerning "the divine alienation of political power" (*Curse*, 29–30). He distinguishes four answers offered to explain why the gods occasioned shifts in power, three deal with specific instances, the fourth and more common was that it was simply time for a change.
21 "When kingship was lowered from heaven, kingship was (first) in Eridu" (*Sumerian King List*, l. 1; ANET, 265). Cf. Ningal's description of Ekishnugal as "my seat of kingship" (*The Lament for Ur*, l. 125; Jacobsen, *Harps*, 456).
22 See Clifford, "Roots," 12–15.
23 Jacobsen, *Harps*, 478, observes concerning the decision of the divine assembly that "enemy attack is only the superficial, 'political,' appearance, storm the more profound, 'theological,' reality, Enlil's 'word.'" A sampling of texts illustrates the idea and suggests its prevalence and longevity:
"Utu took away the city's counsel,
Enki took away its wisdom,

it impossible to persuade Enlil and the gods to annul their decision or to avert its enforcement.[24] A passage from the *Lamentation over the Destruction of Sumer and Ur* (ll. 364–369) typifies this Mesopotamian theology of kingship:

> Ur was indeed given kingship (but) it was not given an eternal reign.
> From time immemorial, since the land was founded, until the population multiplied,
> Who has ever seen a reign of kingship that would take precedence (for ever)?
> The reign of its kingship had been long indeed but had to exhaust itself.[25]

Several aspects of the Mesopotamian ideology resonate with the program outlined in Deutero-Isaiah, in Micah 4–5, and in a later form in Daniel. In both, the deity or deities bestow royal status on cities. This status is mobile. The deity or deities can and do transfer it. Like Ur, Lady Babylon mistakenly believed this status to be her permanent possession. Ironically, Lady Zion also had to learn the lesson implicit in the impermanence of this preeminence.

Its (Agade's) radiant aura, that reached heaven"
(*Curse of Agade*, ll. 70–72; cf. l. 225;
see Cooper, *Curse*, 53.61]).
"When the fates of the universe were being decreed ..."
(*Gudea Cylinder* A, Col I, l. 1;
see Wilson, *Cylinders*, 9, and Römer, *Zylinderinschriften*, 9.44).
"That city whose fate has not been decided (favorably)!
That city whose lord does not care for it!
That city against which Enlil rushes!
That city with which Ninlil has started a quarrel! ...
That city which has become ill-fated!"
(*Uru Amirabi*; translation Cohen, *Lamentations*, 2:588).
"(Behold,) they gave instruction for the ravaging of my city ...
and as its destiny decreed that its people be killed."
(*Lament for Ur*, ll. 161–164; Jacobsen, *Harps*, 457).

24   "On that day, after *the lord had been overcome by the storm,*
After, *in spite of the 'lady,'* her city had been destroyed; ...
After they had *commanded* the utter destruction of my city; ...
On that day verily I abandoned not my city. ...
To Anu the water of my eye verily I poured;
To Enlil I in person verily made supplication.
'Let not my city be destroyed,' verily I said unto them; ...
Verily Anu turned not to this word;
Verily Enlil with its "It is good; so be it' soothed not my heart. ...
May Enlil, the king of all the lands, decree thy (favorable) fate.
May *he* return thy city to its place for thee; exercise its queenship!
May *he* return Ur to its place for thee; exercise its queenship!"
(*Lamentation over the Destruction of Ur*, ll. 137–151.382–384;
translation Kramer, *Lamentation*, 31.33.65; see also Römer, *Klage*).

25   Michalowski, *Lamentation*, 59.

5. The Bethlehemite Ruler (Mic 5:1)

It remains only to examine the role of the ruler from Bethlehem in the return of "dominion" to Jerusalem. Disregarding the accretions to Mic 5:1 in v. 2–8,[26] the relationship between the two promises is unmistakable. In the final form of the text of Mic 4–5, these verses constitute yet another framework structure ("and/but you" place name and promise). Both deal with kingship, employing a form of the root מש׳ל. Unless Mic 4:8 has priority of status rather than time in view, both relate a future hope to a foundation in the past ("former dominion," 4:8; "of old," 5:1).[27] The approach of dominion *to* Daughter Zion parallels the exit of the expected ruler *from* Bethlehem.

Despite these structural parallels, however, the promise of the Bethlehemite stands out in comparison for its modesty. Becker argues, for example, that Mic 4:8 and 5:1 do not share a common conception of authority. He argues that, in context, the "kingdom" mentioned in 4:8 must be God's kingdom and that, in any case, the language of Mic 5:8 is not that of "restorative monarchism."[28] Metzner argues for similar reasons but virtually to the contrary that Mic 4:8 was added to the collection as an interpretation of Mic 5:1. In her view, the promise of a Bethlehemite stems from a time when the notion of a king from and in

---

26 Verses 2–5 overbalance the symmetry of Mic 4:8 and 5:1 and the syntax and content of v. 2–5 confirm their secondary character. Divine speech in v. 1 gives way to prophetic speech in v. 2; the conjunction לכן of v. 2 does not introduce an explanation, conclusion, or exposition of v. 1. Apparently, v. 2 picks up the idea of Jerusalem's birth pangs from 4:10, transforming the image into a picture of hope and new life, and applies it to the difficult clause concerning the ruler's "going forth" (Metzner, *Kompositionsgeschichte*, 148–149), now a reference to the ruler's birth. The temporal phrase עד־עת ("until such time as") in v. 2 represents an unusual understanding of the corresponding temporal phrase in v. 1. As v. 2 reinterprets v. 1, YHWH will delay the return of the remnant until the one in labor gives birth to the ruler whose "going forth (from the womb)" will, according to the original prediction, be "before many days." The birth of the Bethlehemite ruler becomes the precondition for the promised return of the remnant. In a similar manner, v. 3b links the ruler's ultimate appearance, or more precisely, his attainment of worldwide grandeur, to the security of the remnant, and v. 6–7 continue the remnant theme. In contrast, the sentiment expressed in v. 4–5 conflicts not only with the tenor of its context. Mic 5:1–3 awaits the arrival of an individual who will rule "in Israel" (v. 1) through YHWH's strength and in YHWH's name (v. 3); instead, Mic 5:4–5 envisions multiple "shepherds" and "princes of men" who will "shepherd" Assyria with the sword. This violent policy of "self-help" contradicts the hope voiced in 5:1–3 (so Rudolph, *Micha*, 99, who argues that this text reflects Maccabeean boasts regarding their victory over the Seleucids; see also McKane, *Micah*, 159).

27 Renaud, *Structure*, 18.

28 Becker, *Expectation*, 75.

Jerusalem was inconceivable. Only the secondary addition of Mic 4:8 declares the "ruler/governor" of Mic 5:1 to be a king.[29]

Assuming that Mic 4:8 and 5:1 constitute a single layer of material, a third option presents itself, namely, that Mic 5:1 depicts the role of a human administrator of the "dominion" that King YHWH returns to cosmopolitan Jerusalem. Several features of Mic 5:1 support the view that by linking the abstract notion of "kingship" primarily with the city, this layer of material seeks, in part, to redefine the status and function of human agency. The overall modest tone of Mic 5:1, similar to that of Amos 9:11 ("booth of David") and Zech 9:9–10,[30] calls attention to the humble origins of the Bethlehemite. Without explicitly mentioning David, the youngest and smallest of Jesse's sons, it notes the insignificance of Bethlehem among the clans of Judah. As Metzner and others have already observed, the use of the root מָשַׁל, which connotes the "exercise of authority on behalf of another" (cf. Gen 45:8, 26; 24:2; Judg 8:22–23)[31] evidences a reticence to employ king language in reference to the Bethlehemite figure. In this regard, Mic 5:1 reflects the hesitancy prevalent throughout the Twelve to employ "kingship" language positively with regard to a human ruler.[32] Its lexicon seems intent upon avoiding kingship language in reference to future human rulers, presumably motivated by embarrassment at the failure of the monarchy, by an interest in avoiding conflict with the imperial power,[33] or, as seems the case here, by a concern for redefining, and in a sense restricting, the role of a human leader under YHWH's authority. The Bethlehemite will exercise authority "for" YHWH (לְ, 5:1), i.e. as YHWH's deputed governor.[34] In a text that reflects awareness of Mic 4:8 and 5:1, Obadiah 21 – "Saviors (ישׁע) go up to Mount Zion to rule (שׁפט) Mount Esau; but the kingdom (המלוכה) shall be YHWH's" – states the relationship between human agents and divine authority envisioned in this layer of Micah material succinctly. Significantly, it, too, avoids "king"

Metzner, *Kompositionsgeschichte*, 147. Cf. Weiser, *Propheten*, 265; Wolff, *Dodekapropheton 4*, 86–87.96.

30 The latter depends redactionally on Mic 5.

31 See Harrelson, "Nonroyal," 156.

32 Only two of scores of uses of the root מלך in the Twelve refer positively to an "earthly" king (Hos 3:5; Zech 9:9). By contrast, the root refers to YHWH as king or as exercising kingship eight times (Mic 2:13; 4:7, 9; Zeph 3:15; Zech 14:9, 16, 17; Mal 1:14). A similar pattern pertains to near synonyms (שׂר "prince;" שׁפט "to rule, to judge," noun "ruler, judge;" ראשׁ "head;" קצין "chief;" רזן "ruler;" רעה "[to] shepherd;" etc.), which appear primarily in contexts critical of human agents.

33 Cf. the title "governor" (פחה) in Hag 1:1, 14; 2:2, 21; Mal 1:8.

34 Metzner, *Kompositionsgeschichte*, 147.

language in reference to human agents, preferring instead terms associated with the activity of Israel's pre-monarchial judges, and defines the abstraction "dominion" as YHWH's sole prerogative.

6. Conclusion

Regarding the issue of the relationship between Zion's imperial status and theocracy, the redactional history of Micah 4–5 reflects a debate concerning the exercise of political power as a theological category. At the extremes, Micah 4–5 acknowledges the historical failures of Jerusalem's monarchy, on the one hand, and expresses hopes for a day when YHWH will again reign from Zion, on the other. Interposed between these extremes, contextually, redactionally, and logically, Mic 4:8 and 5:1 offer the outlines of a theo-political theory based upon the abstract concept of "dominion." Micah 4:8 reflects a theory of history according to which YHWH bestows this authority on one and then another of the world's leading cities, not upon an individual or a dynastic house. Its proper seat, of course, is Jerusalem, to which it will one day return. This concept of authority provides a mechanism for explaining YHWH's continued sovereignty over human affairs even in the absence of Jerusalem's temple and monarchy. Furthermore, it both implies the recognition that "pure theocracy" is impracticable and distances human agents from the ultimate source of political authority. While Micah 5:1 and its context look forward to the appearance of a Bethlehemite in conjunction with the return of dominion to Jerusalem, the description of this deputy falls far short of the lofty imagery associated with the pre-exilic kings. From humble origins, he will "exercise authority" for YHWH, in his might and name and without the tools normally associated with political power – no horses, no chariots, no cities, and no fortresses (5:10–11).

References

Becker, J. *Messianic Expectation in the Old Testament*. Translated by D.E. Green. Philadelphia: Fortress, 1980.

Biddle, M.E. "Lady Zion's Alter Egos: Isaiah 47:1–15 and 57:6–13 as Structural Counterparts." Pp. 124–139 in *New Visions of the Book of Isaiah*. Edited by R. Melugin and M. Sweeney. JSOTSup 214. Sheffield: JSOT Press, 1997.

Clifford, R.J. "The Roots of Apocalypticism in Near Eastern Myth." Pp. 3–38 in *The Origins of Apocalypticism in Judaism and Christianity*. Vol. 1 of *The Ency-*

clopedia of Apocalypticism. Edited by J.J. Collins. New York: Continuum, 1998.

Cohen, M.E. *The Canonical Lamentations of Ancient Mesopotamia,* 2 vols. Potomac: Capital Decisions, 1988.

Cooper, J.S. *The Curse of Agade.* Johns Hopkins Near Eastern Studies 13. Baltimore: Johns Hopkins, 1983.

Harrelson, W. "Nonroyal Motifs in the Royal Eschatology." Pp. 147–165 in *Israel's Prophetic Heritage: Essays in Honor of James Muilenburg.* Edited by B.W. Anderson and W. Harrelson. New York: Harper & Brothers, 1962.

Hillers, D.R. *Micah: A Commentary on the Book of the Prophet Micah.* Hermeneia. Philadelphia: Fortress, 1984.

Jacobsen, T. *The Harps that Once: Sumerian Poetry in Translation.* New Haven: Yale, 1987.

Kessler, J. "Haggai, Zerubbabel, and the Political Status of Yehud: The Signet Ring in Haggai 2:23." Pp. 102–119 in *Prophets, Prophecy, and Prophetic Texts in Second Temple Judaism.* Edited by M.H. Floyd and R.D. Haak. Library of Hebrew Bible / Old Testament Studies 427. New York: T&T Clark, 2006.

Kramer, S.N. *Lamentation over the Destruction of Ur.* AS 12. Chicago: University of Chicago, 1940.

Kratz, R.G. "Reich Gottes und Gesetz im Danielbuch und im werdenden Judentum." Pp. 187–226 in *Das Judentum im Zeitalter des zweiten Tempels.* Edited by idem. FAT 42. Tübingen: Mohr, 2004. (= "Reich Gottes und Gesetz im Danielbuch und im werdenden Judentum." Pp. 435–479 in *The Book of Daniel in the Light of New Findings.* Edited by A.S. van der Woude. BETL 106. Leiden: Brill, 1993).

Lescow, T. *Worte und Wirkungen des Propheten Micha: Ein kompositionsgeschichtlicher Kommentar.* AzTh 84. Stuttgart: Calwer, 1997.

Leuenberger, M. "Herrschaftserwartungen im Zwölfprophetenbuch: Ein Beitrag zu seiner Kohärenz und Anlage." Pp. 75–111 in *Prophetische Heils- und Herrschererwartungen.* Edited by K. Schmid. SBS 194. Stuttgart: Katholisches Bibelwerk, 2005.

Mays, J.L. *Micah: A Commentary.* OTL. Philadelphia: Westminster, 1976.

McKane, W. *The Book of Micah: Introduction and Commentary.* Edinburgh: T&T Clark, 1998.

Metzner, G. *Kompositionsgeschichte des Michabuches.* Europäische Hochschulschriften 23/635. Frankfurt: Peter Lang, 1996.

Michalowski, P. *The Lamentation over the Destruction of Sumer and Ur.* Mesopotamian Civilizations 1. Winona Lake: Eisenbrauns, 1989.

Nogalski, J.D. *Literary Precursors to the Book of the Twelve.* BZAW 217. Berlin: de Gruyter, 1993.

Redditt, P.L. "The King in Haggai – Zecharaiah 1–8 and the Book of the Twelve." Pp. 56–82 in *Tradition in Transition: Haggai and Zechariah 1–8 in the Trajectory of Hebrew Theology.* Edited by M.J. Boda and M.H. Floyd. Library of Hebrew Bible / Old Testament Studies 475. New York: T&T Clark, 2008.

Renaud, B. *Structure et Attaches Littéraires de Michée IV-V.* CahRB 2. Paris: Gabalda, 1964.

Roberts, J.J.M. "The End of War in the Zion Tradition: The Imperialistic Background of an Old Testament Vision of Worldwide Peace." Pp. 119–128 in

Character Ethics and the Old Testament: Moral Dimensions of Scripture. Edited by M.D. Carroll R. and J.E. Lapsley. Louisville: Westminster John Knox, 2007.

Römer, W.H.P. *Die Klage über die Zerstörung von Ur*. AOAT 309. Münster: Ugarit-Verlag, 2004.

– *Die Zylinderinschriften von Gudea*. AOAT 376. Münster: Ugarit-Verlag, 2010.

Rudolph, W. *Micha – Nahum – Habakuk – Zephanja*. KAT 13,3. Gütersloh: Gütersloher, 1975.

Schart, A. *Die Entstehung des Zwölfprophetenbuchs: Neubearbeitungen von Amos im Rahmen schriftenübergreifender Redaktionsprozesse*. BZAW 260. Berlin: de Gruyter, 1998.

Smith, J.M.P. *A Critical and Exegetical Commentary on Micah*. ICC. Edinburgh: T&T Clark, 1912.

Sweeney, M.A. "Micah's Debate with Isaiah." *JSOT* 93 (2001) 111–124.

Weiser, A. *Die Propheten Hosea, Joel, Amos, Obadja, Jona, Micha*. ATD 24. Göttingen: Vandenhoeck & Ruprecht, 1985.

Wilson, J.E. *The Cylinders of Gudea: Transliteration, Translation and Index*. AOAT 244. Neukirchen-Vluyn: Neukirchener, 1996.

Wolff, H.W. *Dodekapropheton 4: Micha*. BKAT 14,4. Neukirchen-Vluyn: Neukirchener, 1982 (= *Micah: A Commentary*. Translated by G. Stansell. Philadelphia: Fortress, 1981).

– *Micah the Prophet*. Translated by R. Gehrke. Minneapolis: Augsburg, 1990.

Zapff, B.M. *Redaktionsgeschichtliche Studien zum Michabuch im Kontext des Dodekapropheton*. BZAW 256. Berlin: de Gruyter, 1997.

Jerusalem – City of God for Israel and for the Nations in Zeph 3:8, 9–10, 11–13

JUDITH GÄRTNER

Ludwig-Maximilians-Universität München

According to the great emphasis Odil Hannes Steck put on 'die Frie-densvorstellungen im Alten Jerusalem' in his eminent study, the bond of YHWH with Zion is the very center of Jerusalem's cultic tradition.[1] For Zion as the Mountain of God and Jerusalem as the City of God represent YHWH's chosen place of his residence. Here YHWH becomes tangible for his own people. From Zion YHWH rules the entire cosmos. On Zion the mundane sphere amalgamates with the heavenly divine and those who pray have a share in the heavenly sphere of YHWH's activity. At the same time,

> "das Wirken des Jahwe vom Zion ... ist die fortwährende Stabilisierung und Erhaltung des Weltganzen als einer planvoll geordneten Totalität, das er in einem einmaligen Akt, der zuweilen noch mit kämpferischen Zügen versehen ist, vorlängst ins Dasein gebracht hat und in Bändigung des Chaos ständig im Dasein hält."[2]

Thus Zion represents the axis mundi, the axis of the known world, the focal point of divine action within the world.

This conceptual imagination of Jerusalem as the City of God, or as God's Mountain is of exceptional significance for the late texts of the Twelve Minor Prophets. It goes back to Jerusalem's cultic tradition, when the prophets conceptualized their vision of the Jerusalem in the end of days. Here it is important to take notice of the fact that Jerusalem's cultic tradition expands over time and changes through this growth. This affects two aspects in particular: First, the imagination of a tribunal, assigned to Jerusalem is developed. And second, the importance of the nations in the Jerusalem of the end of days becomes more and more complex.

These two aspects can be comprehended particularly well in the vision of Jerusalem in the end of times in Zeph 3. Thereby the *Fortschreibungen* [or biblical redactions] correlate to the growth of Jerusalem's

---

1   See Steck, *Friedensvorstellungen*, 13–14.
2   Steck, *Friedensvorstellungen*, 16.

cultic tradition of a tribunal in the City of God and also to the importance of the nations in the eschatological Jerusalem. It is exactly these
processes I want to trace in what follows. The crucial point here is the
quite ambiguous v. 8abα, with which the verdict against Jerusalem in v.
1–8 ends. This verse gave rise to three *Fortschreibungen* in v. 8bβ, v. 9–10
and v. 11–13, which develop the juridical and saving work of YHWH
with respect to Israel and the nations.

1. The Judgment of Jerusalem in Zeph 3:1–8

The oldest part is the judgment in Zeph 3:1–8abα.[3] The word of judgment itself is comprised of two parts: an announcement in v. 1–4, 5 and
an accusation in v. 6–8.[4] The announcement of v. 1–4, 5 develops and
furthers the judgment against the elite of Jerusalem.[5] It addresses the
three important institutions: the state with its officials, the law with its
judges and the cult with prophets and priests. All social dignitaries
have ignored the voice of YHWH and become guilty before YHWH.
Thus the judgment begins with an announcement to Jerusalem that it
has become a violent city (v. 1). This malicious behavior of Jerusalem is
contrasted with YHWH's saving activity for his city in v. 5, which distinguishes itself from the actions of officers, judges, prophets and
priests in that he is just.[6] The announcement of judgment in v. 6–8 starts
with the annihilating tribunal considering the nations. But this punishment is related to the judgment over Jerusalem. Its function was to
be a deterring example for Jerusalem to persuade it to turn back. To
make this point v. 6–8 draw on the verdicts against the nations in Zeph
2:1–15 and arranges the judgment that is described within the greater

---

3   The judgment is usually dated as preexilic, see Irsigler, *Zefanja*, 355, who sees it in
    direct proximity to the destruction of Jerusalem or Rudolph, *Zephanja*, 287.290, who
    assigns the text directly to the prophet.
4   For the structure of Zeph 3 see Neef, "Gottesgericht," 536–537; Nogalski, "Zepha-
    niah," 211–212; Schart, *Entstehung*, 211–213; Rudolph, *Zephanja*, 289–290; Elliger, *Ze-
    phanja*, 77–78; Irsigler, *Zefanja*, 192–193.344–345; Vlaardingerbroek, *Zephaniah*, 164–
    188, and Ben Zvi, *Study*, 318–319. A different opinion is held by Floyd, *Minor Proph-
    ets*, 233–236, who does not see v. 8 as the end of the scolding, but identifies the im-
    perative as an appeal to hope for YHWH. Then, however, the relation to v. 6–7 is un-
    clear. Furthermore, it has been discussed repeatedly whether Zeph 3:6–8 might be an
    extension of the old woe over Jerusalem. See the discussions in Rudolph, *Zephanja*,
    284; Wöhrle, *Sammlungen*, 208–211, and Irsigler, *Zefanja*, 315.356–357.
5   For the literary criticism of Zeph 3:1–5 see Wöhrle, *Sammlungen*, 208–211, and Al-
    bertz, *Exilszeit*, 172–176.
6   According to Irsigler, *Zefanja*, 324, a supplement has to be identified in v. 5. For the
    motif of God providing help in the morning, which is the substratum for this, see Ja-
    nowski, *Rettungsgewissheit*, 182–184.

context of YHWH's judgment against Jerusalem. In this sense the verdicts against the nations in Zeph 2 are summed up and inherit a pedagogical function with regard to Jerusalem.[7] But, despite YHWH's effort
on behalf of Jerusalem, the city acts against God's law and does not
accept godly correction. Thus (לכב) in Zeph 3:8abα only the tribunal
remains with which the judgment concludes. Here it says:

> 3:8 Therefore only wait for me[8] – declaration of YHWH –,
> for the day[9], when I will stand up as a witness.
> For it is my judgment to gather nations and to assemble kingdoms[10]
> to pour out my indignation on them
> all my burning anger
> (...)

Particularly remarkable in this verse is that the antecedent for 'עליהם'
is not clearly determined grammatically. It remains debatable upon
whom (עליהם) YHWH pours out his wrath. This ambiguity leads to
three possible readings of the verse. The first one refers עליהם to Jerusalem and the elite. The context of Zeph 3:1–4, 6–7 implies Jerusalem
and its elite, who already in Zeph 3:3–4, 7 are addressed in the third person plural. They cannot escape the menacing judgment because of their
malicious behavior and their rejection to change for the better. This interpretation of עליהם however takes into account a shift in the mode of
address from imperative plural to the third person plural within just
one clause. What is more, this option of reading the text brings consequences for the representation of the nations. Should עליהם refer to
those who dwell in Jerusalem, the importance of the nations changes
with regard to Zeph 3:6–7. They do not serve YHWH as a daunting
example to bring Jerusalem to reform. He rather assembles them to a
tribunal as a means of punishment, to pour out his wrath. It is in this
sense that Ezek 22:23–31 interprets the verse, which in all likelihood
refers to Zeph 3:1–8. According to Ezek 22:31 YHWH unambiguously
pours out his wrath over the dwellers of Jerusalem (שפך זעם עלם על), thus
interpreting Zeph 3:1–8 as an imminent judgment against God's City.[11]

---

7   For an extensive outline of the references of Zeph 2 to Zeph 3:1–8abα see Gärtner,
     Jesaja 66, 182–185.
8   Irsigler, *Zefanja*, 342, understands ל׳ in contrast to ליום as a free part of the clause, in
     the sense of a dativus commodi. Thus his translation is "You wait for me – declara-
     tion of YHWH – for the day when ..." The differences are minor and both want to
     clarify that for Jerusalem the waiting for YHWH following the accusation in 3:1–4, 6–
     7 can only mean judgment.
9   With the LXX and Peshitta and most recent exegetes like Mic 1:2.
10   For the suffix see Irsigler, *Zefanja*, 343, who understands it as an enclitic suffix to
     especially emphasize YHWH as the subject of the action.
11   For the integration of Ezek 22:23–31 in Zeph 3:8abα see Irsigler, *Zefanja*, 324–326.

A second reading of the text refers עליהם to the nations. Here
YHWH does not pour out his wrath on those who live in Jerusalem, but
on the nations which he had assembled beforehand. In this reading, the
verse describes the assembly of the nations for the purpose of their very
own judgment. Against this interpretation one can argue that, in the
context of Zeph 3:1–7, the judgment against Jerusalem refers back to a
tribunal over the nations that had already taken place but which functions as a pedagogical example for Jerusalem.[12]

The third reading of the text might interpret עליהם within its literary context and take into account the linguistic references of Zeph 3:8
to Zeph 2:1–3. Alongside the keyword of the burning of anger (חרון
אף), the small hope described in Zeph 2:2–3 is included – to avoid the
Day of Wrath with humility and justice. However, this hope has proven
to be an illusion in Zeph 3:6–8. Jerusalem does not accept YHWH's
scolding or his demand to change, and so the city ignores the pedagogical function of the nations' tribunal (Zeph 3:6). Jerusalem has refused
every option for avoiding God's wrath, so judgment is inevitable.
However, this means that Zeph 3:6–7, through the keyword connections of Zeph 3:1–3 and the reference to the declarations over the nations in Zeph 2:4–15, does not include the tribunal over the people that
is described there. A judgment over Jerusalem already preconditions a
judgment over the nations. The wrath of YHWH concerns Jerusalem as
well, although it was directed first at the nations. Consequently עליהם
in the context of the declaration of judgment in v. 1–8 primarily concerns Jerusalem. The nations are implied as a second reference through
the intertextual connections. In this respect the third possible reading
refers עליהם to Jerusalem *and* the nations. But the importance of the
nations in Zeph 3:8abα still remains unclear. One does not know
whether the nations are a means for YHWH's punishment of Jerusalem,

---

12 The assembly of the nations in Zeph 3:8 much more strongly brings to mind Isa 13.
    Here nations and kingdoms are undoubtedly assembled to form an army as a means
    of punishment by YHWH. But in Isa 13:6ff the day of YHWH as the final judgment
    does not include this army of YHWH that had been summoned. Therefore a parallel
    to Zeph 3:8 can be identified in the assembly of the nations, perhaps as a means of
    punishment. But an elaborate concept of the rush of the nations is not developed in
    either text. For this evaluation, see Irsigler, *Zefanja*, 355. Also Irsigler's dating is too
    close to the destruction of Jerusalem by the Babylonians to be plausible since the ear-
    ly exilic text Ezek 22:23–31 (by which he means composed 597–587) already refers
    back to Zeph 3:1–8*. At the same time Zeph 3:1–8 ponders why Jerusalem cannot es-
    cape the wrath of YHWH, and the text, too, could be a reflection formulated after Je-
    rusalem's destruction. Although Rudolph, *Zephanja*, 287.290, ascribes the text to Ze-
    phaniah himself, he understands Ezek 22:23–31 as a text that already refers back to
    Zeph 3:1–8*.

are witnesses for YHWH's judgment on Jerusalem, are being judged themselves; or have all three roles at once.

These three possible readings have given rise to redactions in v. 11–13, in v. 9–10 and in v. 8bβ. These *Fortschreibungen* determine the reference of עליהם and expand v. 8abα extending YHWH's judgment to his eschatological saving work. I want to look at the *Fortschreibungen* diachronically. The first and oldest *Fortschreibung*, in all likelihood, is to be found in v. 11–13. It opens up a perspective of salvation for the guilty in Jerusalem. It refers back, like v. 6–8, not only to Zeph 3:1–5 but also to Zeph 2:1–3. Thus the judgment and salvific work of YHWH on Jerusalem in Zeph 3:11–13 follows the inclinations of what was said previously, so that the section formally and substantively, connects directly to Zeph 3:6–8.[13] If this passage is compared with the second *Fortschreibung* in Zeph 3:9–10, which in the final text precedes 3:11–13, but from a literary critical perspective, is actually a secondary augmentation, then this impression is confirmed. Zeph 3:9–10 features almost no connections to the literary context of the book of Zephaniah and leaves aside the style that can be observed in the incorporation and continuity of the preceding chapter. Content-wise the second *Fortschreibung* opens up an option of salvation for the nations, salvation which transcends the horizon of the book of Zephaniah. Both arguments taken together tilt towards an understanding of Zeph 3:11–13 as the first *Fortschreibung* of Zeph 3:1–8, which later is complemented by the perspective of the nations in Zeph 3:9–10.[14] The third and youngest *Fortschreibung* in v. 8bβ finally interprets YHWH's judging activity as the final judgment over the entire world.

2. The Judgment over Jerusalem – the Separation into Wicked and the Salvific Remnant in Zeph 3:11–13

3:11   On that day you will not be ashamed
      because of your deeds
      with which you have become rebellious before me.
      Yea, then I will remove you from the midst
      those who rejoice in their pride,
      And you will no longer be haughty in the mountain of my holiness.
  12 And I will leave in your midst
      a meek and humble people,
      And they will seek refuge in the Name of YHWH

---

13   See Wöhrle, *Sammlungen*, 211–212.
14   In contrast to Rudolph, *Zephanja*, 295.

13 as the remnant of Israel.[15]
    They shall not do injustice
    and speak no lies.
    And in their mouth there shall not be found
    a deceitful tongue.
    Yea, they will gaze and lie down,
    and no one will make them afraid.

This biblical redaction is characterised by the incorporation of the word
of judgment in Zeph 3:8 and by complementing it with an option for
the salvation of Jerusalem. Here four linguistic references are of importance. First, the inhabitants of Jerusalem from v. 7 are adapted in v. 11.
Standing for the irredeemable Jerusalem in v. 7, which declines to return to God despite YHWH's pedagogical efforts, here in v. 11 they
symbolise the salvific work of YHWH.[16] Second, Jerusalem is addressed, just as in v. 7, in the second person feminine. Third, the keyword 'amidst/in the middle' (קרב) from v. 2–4 is adapted.[17] Fourth, v.
11b connects to the notion that those sacrileges intensified in Zeph 3:7
(שכם), will now come to an end (לא סוף). Thus, all four references to
the word of judgment in Zeph 3:1–8abα indicate a revision of the tribunal described there with the intention of establishing an option for
the saving of Jerusalem. This change occurs when YHWH on the one
hand acknowledges Jerusalem's involvement in iniquity. On the other
hand the change occurs when his wrath does not destroy the entire city,
but only its devious epicenter, so that the poor and humble people stay
as a remnant (3:12). The appellation 'poor and humble people' (עם עני
ודל)[18] is a reminder of Zephaniah's context. It brings to mind the words
of menace in Zeph 2:1–3, urging the 'humble' (עני) to seek 'humility'
(ענוה) and 'justice' (צדק) (Zeph 2:3).[19] The demand in Zeph 2:3 foresaw

---

15 See for the interpretation of שארית ישראל Irsigler, *Zefanja*, 386.
16 For the references see Irsigler, *Zefanja*, 389, who, beyond 3:7, sees a reference to the
    sacrileges described in 3:1–4, 2:1–3 and 1:4–13. As the references to Zeph 1:4–13 can-
    not be based on linguistic evidence, it appears that they are only implicated in Zeph
    3:11.
17 In that process it is significant that Zion, which YHWH refers to as his holy moun-
    tain, joins the city as another landmark. This is important because Zeph 3:9 lacks any
    kind of location and Zion as the destination for the pilgrimage of the nations is im-
    plicitly presupposed.
18 As in Zeph 3:12 not a *humble* but a *poor* people is intended. See Irsigler, *Zefanja*, 393–
    395, who identifies the remnant with those economically poor and those oppressed
    by the elite in 3:1–4. This concept might resonate in the references to 3:3–4. Also the
    characterization in 3:13 does not speak to injustice and life remains open in this re-
    spect.
19 With Irsigler, *Zefanja*, 394–395, it has to be added that Zeph 2:3 already presupposes
    a fixed group of humble people and its constitution already emanates from Zeph
    3:12.

a small hope for escaping the wrath of YHWH. It is precisely this hope that the *Fortschreibung* in v. 11–13 incorporates. But it is modified against the background of the word of judgment in Zeph 3:1–8 so that such an attitude is only possible after judgment in the eschatological Jerusalem.[20] This attitude means an internal differentiation for the people of God. With that internal differentiation an "either/or" of Zeph 2:1–3 and Zeph 3:6–8 in the *Fortschreibung* becomes a "both/and."

3. The Judgment on the Nations – the Transformation of Lips and the Pilgrimage of the Nations in Zeph 3:9–10

The second *Fortschreibung* links to the preceding by a "yea, then" (כִּי אָז) to the nations in Zeph 3:8 and modifies the judgment of the people that was explicated there with an option of salvation for the nations in the eschatological Jerusalem.[21]

> 3:9 Yea, at that time I will change the nations
> the lip(s) to (a) pure one(s).[22]
> That all of them may call the name of YHWH
> that they serve him with one shoulder.
> 10 From beyond the streams of Cush
> they, my worshippers, will bring me the daughter of my
>   dispersed ones[23] as an offering.

---

20 See for this Albertz, *Exilszeit*, 173, whose Book of the Four Prophets (*Vierprophetenbuch*) ends with Zeph 3:11–13. According to Albertz Zeph 3:11–13 is "an exilic basic text, from which stems the piety of the poor in the Persian period" (Albertz, *Exilszeit*, 173). Wöhrle, *Sammlungen*, 211–213, assigns the entire section Zeph 3:1–13 to his conception of a deuteronomistic redaction of the Minor Prophets. With these verses this redaction created a new ending for the book and established YHWH's judgment on his people. At the same time, according to Wöhrle, Zeph 3:1–13 embodies the conclusion of the Book of the Four Prophets, which itself stems from the deuteronomistic redaction of Hosea, Amos, Micah and Zephaniah. For details consult Wöhrle, *Sammlungen*, 255–284.

21 For the *Fortschreibung* in Zeph 3:9–10, see Wöhrle, *Sammlungen*, 212–213.

22 For the translation see Rudolph, *Zefanja*, 292 note 9a, and Irsigler, *Zefanja*, 369.

23 See for the discussion of the difficult expression עֲתָרַי בַּת־פּוּצַי, Irsigler, *Zefanja*, 370–371. The translation above understands עֲתָרַי as nominalisation of עתר. The translation 'my worshippers' is supported by the textual witnesses of LXX and Vg. See Rudolph, *Zephanja*, 292 note 10a. פּוּצַי is most likely participle passive of פוץ and therefore has to be translated as 'my dispersed ones' instead of an abstract plural פוצים (my dispersion). This is suggested, in analogy, by the expressions בת־עמי or בת־ציון, which both denote the collective of the inhabitants of Jerusalem or that part of the people. See further Irsigler, *Zefanja*, 370–371. As the expression 'my worshippers, the daughters of my dispersed ones' is missing in the early LXX tradition as well as in the Peshitta, Irsigler, *Zefanja*, 370, identifies it as a commenting gloss. Against this, I think, it can be argued that the MT represents the *lectio difficilior* and one also has to

In v. 9 the focus is on the entire cosmos of the nations. With that the perspective of the nations from v. 8abα is continued.[24] What is more, v. 9–10 contrast linguistically and conceptually with their literary context. This difference is illustrated in v. 9 which does not utilize the usual 'nations' (גוים see Zeph 2:5; 3:6), but establishes a contrast with the appellation 'peoples' (עמים).[25] Second, YHWH's judging acts on the people no longer imply their destruction and annihilation (as in Zeph 3:6 and 2:5–15), and thus they differ conceptually from the outpouring of his wrath in v. 8abα. The formulation utilized, 'changing of the lips' (הפך שפה), implies overthrow, destruction of the establishment, and abolition of the old status quo. Yet this reversal occurs with the intention of creating a new situation.[26] The lips of the nations will be changed so that they become pure.[27] Thereby these transformed lips are empowered to call upon the name of YHWH and to serve him with one shoulder. The prevalent image of the nations is thus contrasted with a different one. The nations are more important than just serving as a part of YHWH's judgment as in chapters 2 and 3, in that the option of salvation is being opened for the nations. It remains essential, however, in contrast to the salvific word in v. 11–13, that v. 9 does not take the literary context of the book of Zephaniah into account.

The observations made in v. 9 can be repeated for v. 10. First of all v. 10 is linked to the function of Cush in the Oracles against the nations in the book of Zephaniah. With the mention of Cush in Zeph 2:12 and 3:10, a region is invoked that is far away in the worldview of the time and represents the fringes of the known world, which then is also in-

---

consider whether עתרי בת־פוצי has been omitted as a matter of simplification. To approach the question of a possible supplementation, I think, it is necessary to go beyond Irsigler's argument stemming exclusively from textual history and to look why the theme 'assembling the Diaspora' has been inserted in the context of the pilgrimage of the nations. Especially Steck argues against the insertion of a gloss, see Steck, "Zef 3,9–10," 92 note 12.

24 See for this Ben Zvi, *Zephaniah*, 320, and, drawing on him, Wöhrle, *Sammlungen*, 213.

25 The term 'peoples' (עמים) can only be found in the later redactional verse Zeph 3:20, which is presumably redactionally connected to Zeph 3:10, see Gärtner, *Jesaja 66*, 191–192.

26 For הפך see Gen 19:21–29; Amos 5:7; Jer 31:13. הפך can mean 'overthrow' in the sense of destruction (Gen 19:21–29) but also in the sense of transformation into a new condition. The latter presupposes that the old condition will be replaced by the new (Amos 5:7; Jer 31:13).

27 See for this Hamp, "ברר," 843–845. The term used here for the purity of lips is, in contrast to טהר, not primarily cultic. ברר designates especially the purity of hearts (Ps 24:4) and hands (Ps 18:21, 25 par. 2 Sam 22:21, 25; Job 22:30), so that for Zeph 3:9 a morally religious purity of lips can be assumed. At the same time it must be stressed that טהר too, beyond its cultic context, can indicate a holistic purity (Ps 19:8–10; 51:4, 9, 12). See for this the vision of the calling Isa 6, in which the notion of a purity of lips is a precondition to acts considered good in the eyes of YHWH. For Isa 6 see Hartenstein, *Unzugänglichkeit*.

volved in YHWH's judging actions.[28] With the background of Zeph 2:12 and 3:10, Cush stands not only for the outer periphery, but also for the worldwide domain of YHWH's ruling. Linguistically the formulation 'from beyond the streams of Cush' is only attested by Isa 18:1 and explicitly exceeds the literary context of the book of Zephaniah. Thus the option of saving for the nations stands in a larger literary context.

4. The Judgment over Jerusalem as Judgment over the World in Zeph 3:8bβ

The third *Fortschreibung* in Zeph 3:8bβ is a quotation from Zeph 1:18: 'For in the fire of my jealousy the whole world will be consumed.' It connects to the preceding with a substantiating כִּי clause to v. 8bα and refers the previously ambiguous 'עֲלֵיהֶם' to the entire world. Thus, the judgment of YHWH undoubtedly involves Jerusalem and the world of the nations, and it is interpreted as a judgment over the world encompassing both realms. Its intention is to connect the judgment in ch. 3 with the day of YHWH in ch. 1.

It is noteworthy that the third *Fortschreibung*, as with the first one in Zeph 3:11–13, refers back to the literary context of the book of Zephaniah. But now, the previously disregarded first chapter of the book is adapted, and Zeph 1:18 is quoted almost verbatim: 'on the day of the Lord's wrath and in the fire of his jealousy the whole world will be consumed for doom, a sudden end he will make of all who live on earth.' According to the interpretation of Irsigler, Zeph 1:18 is a redactional complement. This conclusion suggests the ascription of both additions to the same hand, because of their great conformity.[29] Both verses want to expand the judgment of YHWH to a universal dimension.[30] Zeph 1:18 is a reading of the day of YHWH, and Zeph 3:8bβ uses it with reference to the judging actions of YHWH over Jerusalem and the nations in Zeph 3:6–8. Thus a connection is established with the first

---

28   See Irsigler, *Zefanja*, 282.376–377, for locating Kush south of Upper Egypt.
29   See for this Irsigler, *Zefanja*, 179–188.
30   If one assumes that both additions come from the same hand, Zeph 1:18 אֶרֶץ must already be understood universally in the sense of 'earth,' and not in the sense of 'land,' because this universal interpretation is presupposed by the context of Zeph 3:8. If it is assumed that Zeph 3:8 is a later extension of Zeph 1:18, then it is possible to understand אֶרֶץ in Zeph 1:18 in the sense of 'land' and to see a universal interpretation only in Zeph 3:8. Against the latter, only Zeph 1:17 with the word אָדָם generalises in a way that does not exclude the notion of the judgment of the world. So I think nothing speaks against assigning the redaction in Zeph 1:18 and Zeph 3:8bβ to the very same hand; see Irsigler, *Zefanja*, 181.

chapters of the book of Zephaniah, disregarded by Zeph 3:6–8, to bring
together the judging acts of YHWH described there with the concept of
the day of YHWH.

Looking at the text from a synchronic point of view, the third *Fortschreibung* specifies the perspective of the first and second. The fire that
consumes the entire world epitomizes the judging of YHWH over nations and Jerusalem. Thus this last Fortschreibung allows one to recognize that the option of salvation for Israel and the nations precedes the
tribunal of YHWH. Only afterwards is the action of YHWH possible as
described in the two subsequent *Fortschreibungen* that move from
judgment to salvation.

5. Conclusions

With the third *Fortschreibung* the interpretations of God's acts of judgment are concluded and the ambiguous 'over them' (עליהם) in v. 8 has
apparently been modified in three different ways. With the first *Fortschreibung* in v. 11–13 the eschatological work of YHWH in Jerusalem
has been extended with a perspective of salvation for God's people by
differentiating among the people of God. The wrath of YHWH only
affects the sinfully infected area in Jerusalem and removes it. Thus a
salvific remnant emerges, which represents the theological existence of
God's people.

The second *Fortschreibung* relates עליהם to the nations and transforms the judgment of YHWH into an option of salvation for the nations. This comes about by the transformation of the lips and the conversion of the nations to followers of YHWH, who move towards him
in an eschatological pilgrimage to present him offerings. In analogy
with the salvific remnant of God's people, this change means that the
theological existence of the nation's eschatological world is depicted in
the pilgrimage of the nations.

The third *Fortschreibung* in 3:8bβ states that before the eschatological
option for salvation there is a final judgment that includes the entire
earth, both Jerusalem and the nations, and is connected to the day of
YHWH in ch. 1.

Thus by comparing all three *Fortschreibungen* it becomes clear that
the first and the third *Fortschreibung* in Zeph 3:11–13 and Zeph 3:8bβ are
woven into the literary context of the book of Zephaniah. The second
Fortschreibung in Zeph 3:9–10 however transforms the judgment on the
people into an eschatological pilgrimage of the nations without referring back to the literary context of the Book of Zephaniah.

6. The Redactional Significance of the Pilgrimage of the Nations in Zeph 3:9–10 for the Formation of the Twelve Minor Prophets

Those references of Zeph 3:9–10 that are of greatest relevance for redactional criticism apparently point toward the book of Isaiah. The first assimilation can be found in the expression 'from beyond the streams of Cush' (מעבר לנהרי־כוש), which has been proven by Odil Hannes Steck's 1990 essay on Zeph 3:9–10 in *Biblische Zeitschrift* to refer back to the woe oracle in Isa 18:1.[31] But this means that in Zeph 3:10 initially a word of judgment is called to mind. The ongoing description of the pilgrimage of the nations deepens the connection to Isa 18 by incorporating the end of the prophecy against Cush in Isa 18:7 with the key-word 'to bring' (יבל). As in the addition of v. 7, the Cushites also present gifts to YHWH in Zeph 3:10. But in contrast to Isa 18:7, the material presented is not merely a gift (שׁי), but is specified as sacrifice or tribute (מנחה).[32]

With the incorporation of Isa 18:1 and Isa 18:7 in Zeph 3:10 exactly this development is traced. The wrath of YHWH in v. 8 leads to the pilgrimage of the nations in v. 10. In contrast to Isa 18:7 the Cushites in Zeph 3:9–10 belong to YHWH's worshippers, who not only bring gifts (Isa 18:7) but tribute, מנחה. In this sense Zeph 3:10 remarkably exceeds the Isaianic pattern it is based on, in which the nations are not included in the cultic events.[33] Second, the difficult-to-understand expression 'my worshippers, the daughter of my scattered ones' (עתרי בת־פוצי) in Zeph 3:10 refers to the Isaianic tradition. If one understands, as Irsigler does, 'עתרי' (my worshippers) as likely to be the converted nations from Zeph 3:9 and 'בת־פוצי' (daughter of my scattered ones) as the Diaspora, the verse can be paraphrased as follows:

---

31 This reference is unambiguous also, because this expression cannot be found elsewhere in the Hebrew Bible. See Steck, "Zef 3,9–10," 90–95.

32 For the complexity of Isa 18–19 see Beuken, *Jesaja*, 164–206.

33 Beyond this the cultic status of the nations is undecided. This is interesting insofar as in Zech 14:16–19 and in Isa 66:18–23 the cultic status of the nations is clearly defined. Whereas the nations in Zech 14:16–19 partake in the Sukkoth, the nations according to Isa 66:23 come to Zion every new moon, every Sabbath. Furthermore YHWH designates a few pious from the nations to be Levitic priests (Isa 66:21). The pure lips of the nations in Zeph 3:9–10 became haphtara to seder 9, the section of the Torah with which Gen 11:1 starts, read in the tradition of the Palestinian synagogue every three years, so that Zeph 3:9 and Gen 11:1 reciprocally interpret each other. The one language of primordial times equals the pure lips of the nations in the eschatological promise; see Irsigler, *Zefanja*, 376.383–384.

> 3:9 From beyond the streams of Cush they
> – the nations as YHWH-worshippers –
> will bring the daughter of my scattered ones
> – the Diaspora – to YHWH as an offering.

This notion, that the nations bring the Diaspora back to Jerusalem is genuine Isaianic tradition and evidenced in Deutero-Isaiah (Isa 49:22) as well as in the great prophecy of the new Jerusalem or Zion in Isa 60.[34] That the nations in Zeph 3:10 bring the Diaspora as מנחה for YHWH can only be found in the eschatological pilgrimage of the nations in Isa 66:20.

Both recourses to the Isaianic tradition in Zeph 3:9–10 serve to render the role of the nations in the eschatological pilgrimage of the nations. With the re-arrangement of the Cush theme, influenced by Isa 18:1–7, the development from a judgment over the nations to the pilgrimage of the nations can be traced. By incorporating the notion of the returning Diaspora as in Isa 66:20,[35] the nations' pilgrimage is complemented with the Diaspora theme.[36] This modification demonstrates the

---

34 For the motif of the Diaspora carried home by the nations see Steck, "Heimkehr," 97–100. For Isa 60 see further Steck, "Grundtext," 49–79; Blenkinsopp, *Isaiah 56–66*, 203–218, and Lau, *Schriftgelehrte Prophetie*, 22–117.

35 For Isa 66 see Steck, "Beobachtungen," 217–228; Blenkinsopp, *Isaiah*, 290–317; Lau, *Schriftgelehrte Prophetie*, 143–151, as well as Gärtner, *Jesaja 66*, 34–54.

36 Furthermore against Steck, "Zef 3,9–10," 90–95, there are no redactionally relevant references to Isa 19 which would bring to mind Ashur or Egypt. According to Steck there is another reference made to Isa 19:22 by עתר which in return can be traced back to Egyptian plague texts, where the verb occurs several times. At the same time the keyword עתר can be found in the word of judgment against Egypt (Jer 46:11), where Egypt is also addressed as daughter as well as in the threat to destroy Egypt in Ezek 30:21. From this Steck, "Zef 3,9–10," 91.94, concludes that 'daugher of my dispersed (*Tochter meiner Zerstreuten*)' goes back to Jer 46 and Ezek 29–30 *via* Isa 19:22 to suspend Egypt's status of judgment. That furthermore with 'daughter of my dispersed' Ashur too is addressed, Steck, "Zef 3,9–10," 92, can be demonstrated with the references to Nah 3:18. Those prophetical 'detours' Steck has to take, however, as the immediate linguistic references to Isa 19 run via עבד (Isa 19:21, 23), עתר (Isa 19:22) and מנחה (Isa 19:21). Those references might actually be present, but they are conceptually not very convincing. Thus Isa 19:21 talks about Egypt serving YHWH with מנחה and victims and vows to him, that is in a cultic act of Egypt, whereas in Zeph 3:10 a pilgrimage of the nations is described, whereby with מנחה deliberately a word is chosen that can mean sacrifice as well as tribute. But Isa 19 is not at all dealing with pilgrimage. The Egyptians will serve YHWH in Egypt. Thus עבד and מנחה in Isa 19 share a conceptually different framework in contrast to Zeph 3:9–10 and cannot provide enough evidence for the incorporation of Isa 19. Furthermore Isa 19 is conceptually closer to Zeph 2:11, because in both texts the nations (Zeph 2:11) or Ashur and Egpyt (Isa 19) worship YHWH in their own lands and do not move to Jerusalem. The notion in Zeph 2:11 and Isa 19 can – in both books – not be found in the Zion chapters, but as additions to the prophecies about the nations. See for Isa 19 Groß, *YHWH*, 17–22.

intention of the second *Fortschreibung* in Zeph 3:9–10, which develops a more open image of the nations with regard to their importance in the eschatological Jerusalem.

This conceptual image of the eschatological pilgrimage of the nations based on the Isaianic tradition contains three aspects. First the judgment on the nations is not an annihilating tribunal, but a judgment of purification. Second, from this judgment the nations come forth as converted worshippers of YHWH. Third, they offer the Diaspora as מנחה. With the composition of these three aspects the image of a differentiated pilgrimage of the nations emerges, in which the different motifs of the nations' pilgrimage as they can be found in other pilgrimage texts in the Twelve Minor Prophets are merged together. The notion of the nations calling upon the name of YHWH and serving him (Zeph 3:9) brings to mind the pilgrimage texts in Isa 2:2, 4 par. Mic 4:1–3, Zech 2:15, Zech 8:20–23 and Zech 14:16–19. In Isa 2:2–4 (par Mic 4:1–3) the nations trek to Jerusalem, to have YHWH pronounce judgment; in Zech 2:15 they join YHWH (לוה), in Zech 8:20–23 the nations come to find shelter with YHWH (בקש) and to plead before him and to worship him (הלך). And in Zech 14:16–19 the remnant from the nations comes to Jerusalem once a year to celebrate Sukkoth. What is more, the bringing of מנחה by the nations in Zeph 3:10 refers to those texts in which the nations present offerings to YHWH (Hag 2:6–7; Isa 18:7; 60:5–9, 11, 13–14). This outline suggests that the different imaginations of the nations' pilgrimage in the Twelve Minor Prophets are compiled in Zeph 3:10 and brought together with the Deutero-Isaianic concept of the pilgrimage of the nations. Thus a complex reflection of the nation theme emerges in which the judgment of YHWH leads to an option of salvation.

Such a multiplex reflection exceeds the framework of a singular prophetic book. It is preferable to assume that this insertion of a theme so important for the Twelve Minor Prophets took place within the process of the development of an overarching book – the Dodekapropheton – particularly since the motifs in the described Isaianic tradition can be found in all the other significant texts dealing with the pilgrimage of the nations in The Twelve. With that said, the pilgrimage in Zeph 3:10 has proven to be a redactional text of reflection in three respects. First, in the literary context of Zephaniah the wrath of YHWH in v. 3:8abα is transformed into a pilgrimage of the nations, so that an option of salvation is established. Second, in the context of the Dodekapropheton it proved necessary to merge the factual connections of the nations' pilgrimage. Third, the importance of the Diaspora from the

Isaianic tradition is inscribed into Zeph 3:9–10, so that besides the Dodekapropheton the book of Isaiah comes into view.

Thus in Zeph 3:9–10 one finds an exceptional example of scribal
prophecy, whose literary horizon not only extends beyond Zephaniah,
but in its final form it interlocks the two great prophetic corpora, Isaiah
and the Dodekapropheton, in a theme that is of crucial importance for
both books. Finally Jerusalem proves to be the City of God for Israel
and the nations beyond the boundaries of the book.

References

Albertz, R. *Die Exilzeit: 6. Jahrhundert v.Chr.* Biblische Enzyklopädie 7. Stuttgart:
Kohlhammer, 2001.
Ben Zvi, E. *A Historical-Critical Study of the Book of Zephaniah.* BZAW 198. Berlin:
de Gruyter, 1991.
Beuken, W.A.M. *Jesaja 13–27.* Herders theologischer Kommentar zum Alten
Testament. Freiburg: Herder, 2007.
Blenkinsopp, J. *Isaiah 56–66: A New Translation with Introduction and Commen-
tary.* AB 19B. New York: Doubleday, 2003.
Elliger, K. *Das Buch der zwölf kleinen Propheten II: Die Propheten Nahum, Habakuk,
Zephanja, Haggai, Sacharja, Maleachi.* ATD 25. 5th ed. Göttingen: Vanden-
hoeck & Ruprecht, 1964.
Floyd, M.H. *Minor Prophets: Part 2.* FOTL 22. Cambridge: Eerdmans, 2000.
Gärtner, J. *Jesaja 66 und Sacharja 14 als Summe der Prophetie: Eine traditions- und
redaktionsgeschichtliche Untersuchung zum Abschluss des Jesaja- und des
Zwölfprophetenbuches.* WMANT 114. Neukirchen-Vluyn: Neukirchener,
2006.
Groß, W. "Wer soll YHWH verehren? Der Streit um die Aufgabe und die Iden-
tität Israels in der Spannung zwischen Abgrenzung und Öffnung." Pp. 11–
33 in *Kirche in der Zeit.* Edited by H.J. Vogt. FS W. Kasper. München: We-
wel, 1989.
Hamp, V. "ברר." *ThWAT* 1 (1973) 841–845.
Hartenstein, F. *Die Unzugänglichkeit Gottes im Heiligtum: Jesaja 6 und der Wohnort
JHWHs in der Jerusalemer Kulttradition.* WMANT 75. Neukirchen-Vluyn:
Neukirchener, 1997.
Irsigler, H. *Zefanja.* Herders theologischer Kommentar zum Alten Testament.
Freiburg: Herder, 2002.
Janowski, B. *Rettungsgewißheit und Epiphanie des Heils: Das Motiv der Hilfe Gottes
"am Morgen" im Alten Orient und im Alten Testament. Band I: Alter Orient.*
WMANT 59. Neukirchen-Vluyn: Neukirchener, 1989.
Lau, W. *Schriftgelehrte Prophetie in Jes 56–66: Eine Untersuchung zu den litera-
rischen Bezügen in den letzten elf Kapiteln des Jesajabuches.* BZAW 225. Berlin:
de Gruyter, 1994.
Neef, H.-D. "Vom Gottesgericht zum universalen Heil: Komposition und Re-
daktion des Zephanjabuches." *ZAW* 111 (1999) 530–546.

Nogalski, J.D. *Literary Precursors to the Book of the Twelve.* BZAW 217. Berlin: de Gruyter, 1993.
– *Redactional Processes in the Book of Twelve.* BZAW 218. Berlin: de Gruyter, 1993.
– "Zephaniah 3: A Redactional Text for a Developing Corpus." Pp. 207–218 in *Schriftauslegung in der Schrift.* Edited by R. Kratz et al. FS O.-H. Steck. BZAW 300. Berlin: de Gruyter, 2000.
Rudolph, W. *Haggai – Sacharja 1–8 – Sacharja 9–14 – Maleachi.* KAT 13,4. Gütersloh: Gütersloher, 1976.
Schart, A. *Die Entstehung des Zwölfprophetenbuchs: Neubearbeitungen von Amos im Rahmen schriftenübergreifender Redaktionsprozesse.* BZAW 260. Berlin: de Gruyter, 1998.
Steck, O.H. *Friedensvorstellungen im alten Jerusalem: Psalmen, Jesaja, Deuterojesaja.* ThSt 111. Zürich: Theologischer Verlag, 1972.
– "Zu Zef 3,9–10,1." BZ 34 (1990), 90–95.
– "Beobachtungen zur Analyse von Jes 65–66." Pp. 217–228 in *Studien zu Tritojesaja.* Edited by idem. BZAW 203. Berlin: de Gruyter, 1991.
– "Der Grundtext in Jesaja 60 und sein Aufbau." Pp. 49–79 in *Studien zu Tritojesaja.* Edited by idem. BZAW 203. Berlin: de Gruyter, 1991.
– "Heimkehr auf der Schulter oder/und auf der Hüfte: Jes 49,22b/60,4b." Pp. 97–100 in *Studien zu Tritojesaja.* Edited by idem. BZAW 203. Berlin: de Gruyter, 1991.
Vlaardingerbroek, J. *Zephaniah.* Historical Commentary on the Old Testament. Leuven: Peeters, 1999.
Wöhrle, J. *Die frühen Sammlungen des Zwölfprophetenbuches: Entstehung und Kompositon.* BZAW 360. Berlin: de Gruyter, 2006.

Historical Issues

Deuteronomistic Redaction of the Book of the Four and the Origins of Israel's Wrongs*

JASON RADINE

Moravian College

1. Introduction

The possible presence of Deuteronomistic redaction or influence in the books of Hosea, Amos, and Micah has long been discussed. Phrases and terms in these books have been identified as Deuteronomistic (hereafter "Dtr"),[1] as well as at least portions of the regnal synchronisms in the books' superscriptions.[2] James Nogalski has proposed that these three books along with Zephaniah formed a Deuteronomistically-redacted "Book of the Four," which was a stage towards the formation of the "Book of the Twelve."[3] Others, most notably Ehud Ben Zvi, have challenged the concept of Dtr redaction of these books. Ben Zvi has argued that many of the Dtr phrases in the four books are not unique to Dtr, and that the books also contain phrases that are distinctive to other collections, such as Ezekiel or Leviticus.[4] The purpose of this article is not to categorically affirm nor deny that there has been Dtr redaction of the books of Hosea, Amos, Micah, and Zephaniah; such redaction is certainly possible but not certain. The purpose here is to raise a problem with the idea of Dtr redaction, and to suggest some solutions to it. The problem is the contrasting ideologies of the reason for the fall of the northern kingdom of Israel, between the Deuteronomistic History (hereafter DtrH) and the books of Hosea, Amos, and Micah.[5]

---

* I would like to thank the Faculty Development and Research Committee of Moravian College for a summer stipend to produce this article.
1 Schmidt, "Redaktion." A primary candidate for Dtr redaction is Amos 3:7, for which also see Wolff, *Joel*, 187, and Blenkinsopp, *History*, 75.
2 Tucker, "Superscriptions," 68–70. On the headings in general: Freedman, "Headings."
3 Nogalski, *Precursors*, 276–82; idem, *Processes*, 274–280. Cf. Schart, *Entstehung*, 304–306, and "Reconstructing," 42–44, with some qualifying comments regarding Dtr redaction.
4 Ben Zvi, "Deuteronomistic Redaction." Cf. also Lohfink, "Deuteronomistic Movement," and Kugler, "Deuteronomists."
5 Only Hosea, Amos, and Micah will be discussed here, because these three, rather than Zephaniah, have significant criticisms of the northern kingdom which can be compared with those of the DtrH.

2. The Deuteronomistic Perspective
on the Fall of the Northern Kingdom

The books of 1 and 2 Kings identify the cause of the fall of the northern
kingdom of Israel with the religious practices instituted by Jeroboam
son of Nebat, and with the Israelites continuing in those practices until
their conquest by Assyria. Regarding Israel in general, 1 Kgs 14:16 features a prophecy by Ahijah, declaring: "He [YHWH] will give up Israel
on account of the sins of Jeroboam which he sinned, and which he
caused Israel to sin." When Israel's fall is finally narrated in 2 Kgs 17,
the indictment concludes (v. 21) with the statement that "when he
[YHWH] had torn Israel from the house of David, they made Jeroboam
son of Nebat king, and Jeroboam drove Israel from following YHWH
and he made them sin a great sin." This is described as setting the standard for Israelite religious behavior, leading straight to exile (2 Kgs
17:23). This passage also makes clear in v. 23 that the Israelites had been
warned repeatedly by "his [YHWH's] servants the prophets." Almost
every time that a northern king is evaluated at the end of his reign
in 1 and 2 Kings, he is compared to this notorious predecessor with
the frequent refrain, "he continued to commit the sins which Jeroboam
son of Nebat caused Israel to commit."[6] Thus, Israel is destroyed because its leadership and population consistently followed the ways
of Jeroboam I, in spite of prophetic admonition.

1 Kgs 12:26–33 portrays Jeroboam as founding an illicit cult including golden calves (or young bulls) installed at Bethel and Dan, a non-
levitical priesthood, and an eighth-month holiday. Paul Ash has pointed out that the gravity of Jeroboam's offenses themselves cannot have
been the actual reason for Israel's fall according to Dtr thought, since
Omri and Ahab are identified as having done more wrong than all
northern kings before them.[7] Ahab is even explicitly described as committing more wrong than Jeroboam himself (1 Kgs 16:31), by marrying
Jezebel and endorsing Baalistic worship. Ash argued that Jeroboam is
specifically identified as the cause of Israel's fall because he is the
founder of the kingdom and was not like David; the fact that his sins
are less than those of later Israelite kings is only incidental.[8] Thus, Israel
is doomed almost from the start, due to the actions of the founder of

---

6   Except for Elah and Shallum (the latter reigning for only one week).
7   Ash, "Jeroboam I," 16. For Omri, 1 Kgs 16:25; for Ahab, 1 Kgs 16:30.
8   Ash, "Jeroboam I," 19: "Jeroboam's construction of the calves is secondary, a specific
    act of being unlike David." Ash observed that Jeroboam functions as an *Unheilsherr-
    scher*, a king who is blamed for the later fall of his kingdom. For this concept, cf.
    Evans, "Naram-Sin."

the new kingdom, regardless of the fact that he was surpassed in wrongdoing by later Israelite kings.

Israel's founding as a separate kingdom from Jerusalem-centered rule is thus key; but it is not the founding itself that Dtr condemns (as this was portrayed as divinely ordained, and the choice of Jeroboam affirmed by the prophet Ahijah), but what Jeroboam does immediately afterward. Even though Israel's secession is not Jeroboam's "fault" (in MT at least),[9] Jeroboam's actions are directly caused by his being the first king of a secessionist kingdom. He endorses the shrine at Bethel specifically to prevent his subjects from going to worship in Jerusalem and thus reverting to Davidic authority (1 Kgs 12:26–28). Thus in the Dtr perspective on Israelite history, Jeroboam is the ultimate source of Israel's sins and demise, and this was apparently part of the prophetic message. If there was a Dtr redaction of the books of Hosea, Amos, and Micah, this theme might be expected to be present in those books. As it turns out, the circumstances of the kingdom of Israel's origin as a cause of its wrongfulness is nowhere clear in these books, and Jeroboam son of Nebat never appears at all. This is the case even if we include the entire final forms of these books. This is a remarkable difference, considering that Hosea, Amos, and Micah all condemn the northern kingdom in various ways; the former two focusing on it.

3. Perspectives on the Origins of the Israel's Wrongdoing in Hosea, Amos, and Micah

3.1 The Book of Hosea

The condemnations of Israel within the book of Hosea are the most similar to the Dtr condemnations, in that they are largely cultic in nature. As stated above, 1 Kgs 12:29–30 states that Jeroboam son of Nebat installed golden calf (or young bull) statues at shrines at Bethel and Dan. While the Bethel shrine is condemned in the books of Hosea, Amos, and Micah, the reader gets no sense that it was explicitly built to provide alternatives to the older Jerusalem site for northerners. The shrine of Dan is mentioned only once in all of the Twelve, at Amos 8:14.

Hos 8:4–6 accuses Israel of setting up their own kings without divine approval, and of worshipping a calf icon in Samaria. Jerome, ibn

---

9   See discussion of LXX below. Note however that in 1 Kgs 17:21 the people of Israel are accused of making Jeroboam king, rather than YHWH doing this (as in 1 Kgs 11:31–39).

Ezra, and Kimḥi identified the reference to unauthorized Israelite kings in Hos 8:4 as referring to Jeroboam I.[10] Macintosh viewed Hosea as seeing idolatry and political apostasy (Israel's secession) as "indissolubly linked," and thus Macintosh followed the above-mentioned early commentators in seeing this passage as referring back to the founding transgression of Jeroboam I.[11] However, Peter Machinist has pointed out that Jeroboam I was given divine authorization to rule (1 Kgs 11:29–31), and that Jeroboam had set up calf images in Bethel and Dan, not Samaria.[12] Machinist is correct that the connection with Jeroboam I is "considerably weakened by the imprecision of the parallel."[13] This weakening is certainly not to say that Bethel's shrine is not condemned in the book of Hosea. A calf statue appears in Bethel (called "Beth-Aven") in Hos 10:5, and the shrine is called the "sin of Israel" in Hos 10:8.[14] However, Hos 9:15 seems to identify Gilgal, not Bethel, as the origin of Israel's wrongdoing. The Hebrew can be translated in several ways; it could be "all of their evils are in Gilgal, for there I hate them" or, more likely, "all their evils are in Gilgal, for there I began to hate them."[15] NRSV translates the verse as "Every evil of theirs began at Gilgal; there I came to hate them." The $k\hat{\imath}$ in the verse may suggest that the past tense reading is to be preferred, and that the $k\hat{\imath}$ clause is here to be read as a past result of a past action. If the past-tense reading is correct, then Hos 9:15 forms an interesting contrast with the Dtr focus on Bethel and Dan. Even if the present-tense reading is preferred, this sharp condemnation of Gilgal by itself is distinct from the Dtr condemnations of northern Israelite worship, except in the sense that DtrH opposes non-Jerusalemite shrines in general. The verse continues with a threat of exile for the wrongs committed in Gilgal, suggesting that exile is at least in part a result of deeds done in Gilgal. Bethel appears

---

10 Macintosh, *Hosea*, 299; there Macintosh states that Kimḥi stated that Ahijah did not authorize Jeroboam's kingship, but only announced that it would happen.
11 Macintosh, *Hosea*, 300, also in reference to Hosea 7:7. See also Mays, *Hosea*, 117, and Emmerson, *Hosea*, 106–108.
12 Machinist, "Ambiguity," 171. Mays, *Hosea*, 117, argued that the calf/bull statue referred to was actually the one in Bethel, and that "Samaria" here refers to the residents of the city, not the city itself.
13 Machinist, "Ambiguity," 171.
14 Bethel is also condemned in general terms in Hos 10:15. Day, "Hosea," 215–216, identified the calf references in Hos 8:5–6; 10:5–6; 13:2 with Jeroboam's golden calves, which he identified as "Yahweh-El" statues. However, from the book of Hosea alone the origin of these statues with Jeroboam cannot be determined.
15 Mays, *Hosea*, 135–136, rendered the verse in the present tense, as "All their evil is in Gilgal. Yea, there I hate them." Wolff, *Hosea*, 161.167, rendered the verse in the past, inchoative: "All their wickedness (became visible) in Gilgal; indeed, then I became their enemy."

with Gilgal in Hos 4:15 (Gilgal first), again demonstrating the importance of Gilgal to the book of Hosea's condemnations of Israel's religious condition. So, while Bethel appears several times in the book of Hosea, there is no reference to it being built by Jeroboam that would be expected from a Dtr redactor associated with 2 Kgs 17.

Additionally, the book of Hosea makes no clear reference to the political side of the Dtr critique; that Jeroboam I was responsible for setting the religious tone of Israel due to his being the founder of it. That is to say, the book of Hosea makes no clear reference to Israel's founding as a factor in its fall, or as an historical event at all. It is not certain that Israel ever was "founded" as a secessionist state in the book of Hosea. This is not to say that the northern kingdom was not founded in this manner, only that it seems unimportant for the book of Hosea.[16] There may be some hints to former Jerusalemite control of the north, however. Hos 2:2 (Eng 1:11) states that the peoples of Israel and Judah will be gathered together and appoint one head for themselves and "go up from the land,"[17] and Hos 3:5 states that the Israelites will return to Yahweh their God and David their king.[18] However, when read independently of the lens of the DtrH, neither of these verses provides clarity on what relationship the northern tribes had with the Davidic monarchy beyond the hint that they had once followed a Davidide, at least in the imagination of the author of this verse if not in reality. There is also no sense in these verses that any such separation led directly to Israel's foundational sin, as is repeatedly the case in the books of Kings. Again, in the brief history of Yahweh's relationship with Ephraim in Hos 11:1–4, no mention is made of Israel's secession leading to its foundational sin. So, the book of Hosea seems to have a significantly different perspective on the nature of Israel's wrongs than does Dtr, and so if there was Dtr redaction of this book, it was minor enough to not include the main Dtr evaluation of the northern kingdom.

16 This argument is also not to say that Jeroboam did not exist. The patronymic for Jeroboam II in Hos 1:1 and Amos 1:1 could suggest that at some point a redactor of these books regarded Jeroboam I as a historical figure, but these two books nonetheless do not seem to regard him as the author of Israel's wrongs.
17 This is often rendered as "take possession of the land" based on Exodus 1:10 (so NRSV; Wolff, *Hosea*, 28).
18 At least as far back as Wellhausen, *Propheten*, 105–108, this has been considered a later addition; cf. also Wolff, *Hosea*, 57.63. Emmerson, *Hosea*, 98–105, however, argued that the David reference here is original to the prophet Hosea.

3.2 The Book of Amos

The lack of reference to the DtrH's foundational indictment of Israel is
even more noticeable in the book of Amos. This book, more than any
other, throws a vast number of attacks on the northern kingdom, charg-
ing it with a variety of social, cultic, and even sexual offences. Yet nowhere does it make the standard Dtr foundational charge. This is striking, since the book of Amos has often been seen as having the most Dtr
insertions of any of the Twelve. As noted above, Dtr redaction in Amos
has been identified at least since Werner H. Schmidt's seminal article
on the topic in 1965; even in Robert Kugler's argument against Dtr redaction of most of the latter prophets, he granted that there was Dtr
redaction in Amos.[19] Like the book of Hosea, the book of Amos also
contains a sacred history of Israel's relationship with Yahweh, in Amos
2:9–12, and again, no reference to secession, no tracing of Israel's sins to
Jeroboam son of Nebat. Bethel remains important in this book, but so
does Gilgal, as in Hosea. Again, like in Hosea, there is no association of
Bethel with Jeroboam I or with the founding of the kingdom.

While there is no appearance of the standard Dtr accusation of Israel's sins being based in the actions of Jeroboam I, several commentators
have argued that at least certain authors of the book of Amos regarded
Israel as a secessionist kingdom that should rejoin Judah. These have
included G. Henton Davies, who interpreted the "motto" at Amos 1:2,
the "seek me" passages at Amos 5:4, 6, and the "fallen booth of David"
in the epilogue at Amos 9:11 as all expressing hope for the northern
kingdom of Israel to rejoin Jerusalemite rule.[20] Max Polley drew from
ancient Near Eastern notions of "correct kingship" to interpret Amos'
criticisms of Israel's political and religious behaviors as urging that
Israel rejoin a reconstituted Davidic kingdom.[21] More recently, Marvin
Sweeney has proposed that the political purpose of the book was to
urge the rejection of the Jehu dynasty as well as the Bethel shrine, and
restore Davidic rule over Israel.[22] He acknowledged that the historicity
of the Davidic-Solomonic rule over the north is open to question (for
which see further below), but wrote that the book drew on Judean traditions of a United Monarchy even if they were not based in reality.[23]
Like Davies above, Sweeney did not regard the "booth of David" in

---

19   Kugler, "Deuteronomists," 136–138.
20   Davies, "Amos," 198. Many scholars have regarded Amos 9:11–15 as a post-exilic
      addition; e.g., Wellhausen, *Propheten*, 96.
21   Polley, *Amos*, 14–16.112–131.
22   Sweeney, *King Josiah*, 285–286.
23   Sweeney, "Dystopianization," 184.

Amos 9:11 as a later addition to the early form of the book. Davies' and Sweeney's views work best if Amos 9:11 is not regarded as a later addition; I have argued elsewhere that the entire text of Amos 9:11–15 should be considered a post-exilic addition, and that the "booth of David" should actually be identified with the Jerusalem temple, not the Davidic kingdom.[24] Even if the passage is retained as dating back to the eighth century, the "booth of David" is not depicted as recovering Israel specifically, but all the nations round about, with only Edom specified. The book of Amos, even in its final form, does not reflect a clear tradition of Israelite secession from Judah nor does it share the Dtr view that Israel's wrongdoings lie in the events involved in its foundation as a separate kingdom.

3.3 The Book of Micah

The book of Micah also presents a somewhat different view or emphasis on the origins and nature of Israel's wrongdoing than does the DtrH.[25] Mic 1:5 reads, "What [or who] is the transgression of Jacob? Is it not Samaria? And what [or who] is the high place of Judah? Is it not Jerusalem?" Samaria is politically the best parallel to Jerusalem, but in the DtrH, Bethel appears to be the anti-Jerusalem. Of course Samaria has nothing to do with Jeroboam son of Nebat, as it was purchased by Omri a century later (2 Kgs 16:24). The Omrides appear specifically as the model of Israelite sin in Mic 6:16, where the people (however defined at this point in the book) are accused of keeping the statutes of Omri and the deeds of the house of Ahab, and of following their counsels. For this reason, the verse continues, Yahweh will make the nation into a desolation and source of shame.

Elsewhere in Micah, the blame is more general, directed to the "heads of the house of Jacob and rulers of the house of Israel"[26] in Mic 3:1 and 3:9. As seen above in the books of Hosea and Amos, when Israel's history with Yahweh is recounted in brief in Mic 6:4–5, Jeroboam is not part of the explanation for Israel's wrongs. Again, the standard Dtr understanding of the origins of Israel's wrongfulness is different than that in the book of Micah. Certainly, it is possible that the Omride references are post-Dtr additions to the text; this is not the place to carry

---

24 Radine, *Amos*, 198–209.
25 For a view in favor of Dtr redaction of the book of Micah, cf. Cook, "Redaction."
26 On the complexities of the addressees of the book of Micah in regard to the identities of "Israel" and "Jacob," cf. Biddle, "Israel."

out a detailed redaction criticism of these books. The point here is that
the standard Dtr explanation for Israel's wrongs is not present in these
three books.

4. The Deuteronomistic Relationship
with the Books of Hosea, Amos, and Micah

It has thus far been observed that while the books of Hosea, Amos, and
Micah all feature sharp condemnations of the northern kingdom, the
standard Dtr condemnation of that kingdom is absent from these
books, in spite of the possible presence of Dtr redaction. This is not just
a matter of the absence of Dtr themes, that is, not an argument from
silence, but a case of contrast. In regard to the observations made
above, one could argue that there is no Dtr redaction in these books,
because if there had been, the chief accusation of the DtrH should be
present. However, Dtr redactors do not need to have always been consistent with the DtrH. Rainer Albertz and Jakob Wöhrle have both suggested ways in which redaction of these books could have happened
under Dtr influence, but without adhering to, and even actively opposing, key Dtr concepts. The DtrH valorizes the reign of Josiah, and by
concluding the history with the house arrest of Jehoiachin, it leaves
open the possibility of the return of the Judahite monarchy. Rainer Albertz wrote that the "Four Prophets Redactor" is aware of the DtrH, but
actively opposed its hopes for a restoration of the pre-exilic monarchy
in Josianic form.[27] Albertz suggested that the Four Prophets Redactor
was influenced also by the original messages of these prophetic books,
and their opposition to trust in military power and the upper class.
Wöhrle saw the redactors of these four books as being aware of and
dependent upon the DtrH, but opposing the Deuteronomists' hopes for
the recovery of the Judahite upper class leadership.[28] In Wöhrle's view,
the redactors of the Four advanced social criticisms that have virtually
no role in the DtrH, and that these redactors may have been among the
Judahites left in Judah during the exile. Thus, the upper class is
doomed, and only the poor remnant will be saved.[29]

As can be seen from these proposals, Dtr influence can occur in redaction of other books without those redactors agreeing with every-
thing that is promoted in the DtrH. So, there could have been Dtr re-

27   Albertz, "Exile," 232–251.
28   Wöhrle, "No Future," 608–627.
29   Wöhrle, "No Future," 625–626.

daction of these three books without those redactors agreeing with the History's view of the origins of Israel's sins in the secessionist leader Jeroboam son of Nebat. This is a matter of degree, because perhaps limits should be set on what we consider to be Dtr when such material differs from or contradicts the DtrH (which itself, of course, is not always internally consistent). Raymond Person has warned against an overly rigid typology of what is and is not Dtr, arguing that "Dtr" should be thought of as a broad literary tradition (or traditions) that went through various permutations and modifications.[30] However, if too broadly defined, the term "Deuteronomist" can dissolve into any authorship or redaction that uses phrases and ideas that happen also to appear in Deuteronomy and the Deuteronomistic History, and thus to become part of what some call "pan-deuteronomism."[31]

If the books of Hosea, Amos, and Micah indeed had Dtr redaction, but of a sort that was not closely following the DtrH's view of Israelite history, one can speculate on why these redactors would not have included the History's standard condemnation of Israel. Perhaps the redactors wanted to hold all of the Israelite leadership directly accountable for their actions, and thus avoided the impression that they had all simply been led astray by one bad man, Jeroboam son of Nebat. It is also possible that the redactors of these books were not aware of Jeroboam I as a particularly blameworthy or important figure as far as Israel's wrongfulness was concerned. This possibility precludes an author or redactor being aware of the DtrH in anything like its current form, of course.

First, there is the possibility of proto-Dtr redaction of the three books that reflects an earlier stage of the DtrH than the final form. There is a notable contrast between how Jeroboam I is initially presented in 1 Kgs 11, and how he is depicted afterwards. Jeroboam is given a prophetic endorsement by the prophet Ahijah in 1 Kgs 11:29–39, and then of course Jeroboam is demonized as the source and standard of Israel's wrongs. Various scholars, such as Antony Campbell, have suggested that the positive promises to Jeroboam I derive from a pre-Dtr, northern prophetic source that endorsed Jeroboam's religious reforms in somewhat the same way as Dtr endorses David's religious innovations.[32] John Van Seters has argued that the "sins" of Jeroboam should

---

30 Person, *Second Zechariah*, 98.
31 Cf. the subtitle of the book in which the articles by Lohfink, Kugler, and Ben Zvi are found, in the reference list to this article.
32 Campbell, *Prophets*, 25–32; also Debus, *Sünde*. 17. Knoppers, *Two Nations*, 1:195–196, counters that the promises to Jeroboam are Dtr, as they have several Dtr idioms and themes, but also argues in *Two Nations*, 2:35–44, that Jeroboam's Bethel shrine was Yahwistic, but has been polemically overlayed by Dtr with implications of worship

be thought of not as historical events, but as a Dtr construction to anticipate the reforms of Josiah.[33] The Jeroboam narrative in the MT clearly has a complicated history, and its complexity continues beyond, into the LXX traditions. There, 3 Kgdms 11:1–14:21 (LXX A) overall follows MT fairly closely, but 3 Kgdms 12:24a-z (LXX B) presents a different narrative, which portrays Jeroboam as more actively leading Israel to secede, and it is this political sedition, more than the religious practices, that earns him condemnation.[34] In view of the diversity of possible traditions about Jeroboam, proto-Dtr elements could have entered the books of Hosea, Amos, and Micah at an earlier stage than the production of the overarching anti-Jeroboam polemics in the final DtrH.[35] The accusations that each king followed in Jeroboam's ways appears as a framing device for the various northern kings' reigns, suggesting a later overlaying on earlier, perhaps annalistic materials. However, such a thesis would require determining the existence of both a distinct Dtr literary identity as well as redaction of the prophetic books prior to the formation of the anti-Jeroboam polemic.

---

of other deities. Pakkala, "Jeroboam," has argued that the calf/bull statues are the latest addition to the text of 1 Kgs 12:26–33. Leuchter, "Jeroboam," has proposed that an original pro-Jeroboam prophecy by Ahijah has been overlayed by a condemnation by the same prophet, after Jeroboam (from Judah [Ephratha] in Leuchter's view) declined to elevate the Shilonite priesthood of which Ahijah was a member.

33   Van Seters, *Search*, 314: "The story about Jeroboam and the golden calves is so thoroughly anachronistic and propagandistic that we must suspect it of being a complete fabrication."

34   Sweeney, "Reassessment," proposed that LXX B was produced in the early 1st century B.C.E. partly in order to clarify the religiously difficult problem that Jeroboam is originally appointed by YHWH through a prophet, and promised a dynasty like David's. Schenker, "Jeroboam's Rise," argues instead that LXX B is in fact older than the surrounding LXX material, and was produced in the 2nd century, from an alternative Hebrew account. Cf. Debus, *Sünde*, 90–92, for another proposal that LXX B derives from a Hebrew *Vorlage* prior to the final form of the MT.

35   Knauf, "Kings," 132–133, argued that the theme of the "sin of Jeroboam" emerged only in the first half of the fifth century B.C.E. with the conflict between returnees from exile and the "people of the land": "the enmity between the returnees and the 'people of the land' is the background to the massive polemic in Kings against the 'sin of Jeroboam.' There is no prior point in history where this polemic would make sense."

5. Archaeological Questions on the History of the Northern Kingdom's Origins

The tendentious nature of the Dtr portrayal of Jeroboam may point toward a second possibility, and that is that the books of Hosea, Amos, and Micah reflect a different and possibly more accurate view of Israel's history than does the DtrH. To assess this historical question, we must turn to archaeology. The Dtr portrayal of the founding wrongs of Jeroboam is predicated on his being the founder of a new kingdom that broke away from Jerusalem-based rule. The archaeological situation however suggests that this may not represent historical reality. 1 Kgs 9:15 portrays Solomon as using forced labor (presumably with Jeroboam's participation in part) for various building activities, including building fortified cities at Hazor, Megiddo, and Gezer. Yigael Yadin excavated nearly identical casemate walls and six-chambered gates at these sites, and proposed that these were Solomonic fortifications.[36] Israel Finkelstein, however, argued that these fortifications in fact date to the ninth century B.C.E., not the eighth (the "Low Chronology"), and pointed out that the fortifications are similar to those at Samaria and Jezreel, which were built by the Omrides in the ninth century.[37] If the comparable fortifications of Hazor, Megiddo, and Gezer are ninth and not tenth-century in origin, then they do not present evidence of Solomonic control of northern Israel, but rather of Omride building projects. In Finkelstein's view, the DtrH took northern achievements and attributed them to David and Solomon, creating a patriotic fiction of a large, Jerusalem-based tenth-century empire.[38]

However, it is not necessary to accept Finkelstein's down-dating of these northern sites for questions to remain about the historicity of the Solomonic building programs. No fortifications like those at Hazor, Megiddo, Gezer, Samaria, and Jezreel have been found for Jerusalem. In fact, Jerusalem used its Middle Bronze Age walls for an entire millennium before getting a fortification upgrade, and that did not happen

---

36   Yadin, "Megiddo," 66–96.
37   Finkelstein, "Omride Architecture;" idem, "State Formation."
38   For an overview, cf. Finkelstein and Silberman, *Bible Unearthed*, and the articles by Finkelstein and Mazar in Schmidt, *Quest*. The notion of Jerusalemite control of the north may have its origins earlier yet, in the time of Hezekiah. Albertz, "Secondary Sources," has challenged those who suggest that the United Monarchy was not historical to answer the question of why various biblical sources refer to it. The appearance of the idea of a United Monarchy in the seventh or even eighth century (including the question of how one dates and interprets Isaiah 7:17), does not mean that it reflects historical reality.

until the defenses built by Hezekiah in the late eighth century.[39] So, even if one dates the fortifications at Hazor, Megiddo, and Gezer to the tenth century, one would still have to explain why Jerusalem was still in such an obsolete condition while these other cities were receiving such elaborate defenses.

This is not to say that there was no active urban life in tenth-century Judah. Eilat Mazar has been excavating a large building in the City of David excavations that she suggests could have been a palace with large walls.[40] However, the dating of these structures is very much in doubt, partly because of the absence of recoverable floors on which to anchor the pottery stratigraphy.[41] Yosef Garfinkel has been excavating the large site of Khirbet el-Qeiyafa in the valley of Elah, and has identified it as tenth-century biblical Sha'araim on the basis of its supposed two gates.[42] While Na'aman has argued that the city was in Philistine, not Judahite, hands in the tenth century B.C.E.,[43] Garfinkel contends that the city was Judahite, and that the city's fortifications demonstrate that Jerusalem wielded considerable power in the area. However, Garfinkel acknowledges that even if the city is evidence of Jerusalem having regional power, the excavation does not provide evidence of Jerusalem ever controlling northern Israel.[44]

In view of the current archaeological situation, there is no conclusive evidence that Jerusalem ever ruled over northern Israel. Thus, the northern kingdom's origins may not be found in any secessionist moment, but rather Israel and Judah may have existed separately side-by-side. Jeroboam I may well have been a real historical figure, but the archaeological picture does not support the notion of his being a labor leader of Jerusalem-controlled building projects in the north, who then led a breakaway kingdom.

---

39   Ussishkin, "Solomon's Jerusalem," 103–115.
40   Mazar, *Preliminary Report*, 52–66.
41   Finkelstein et al., "King David's Palace."
42   Garfinkel and Ganor, "Khirbet Qeiyafa." Na'aman, "Shaaraim," 1–2, has argued that the supposed second city gate is in fact only a palace gate, not a city wall gate.
43   Na'aman, "Shaaraim," 3–4
44   Garfinkel, "Birth," 53. Tubb, "Judah," has pointed out that there is no evidence indicating if the city was governed by any other city, such as Jerusalem. In Tubb's view, it should be understood simply as a city on its own terms.

6. Conclusion

In view of all of the above, it has been observed that the indictments of the wrongs of the northern kingdom of Israel in the books of Hosea, Amos, and Micah are markedly different than those in the DtrH. This is the case even in the final form of the books. Thus, two conclusions are presented here. First, Dtr redaction, if present, did not include the overall Dtr ideological indictment of the northern kingdom. Thus, this redaction would have been either fairly limited or even oppositional to the main indictment in DtrH. Second, the absence of a Jeroboam-focus in the books of Hosea, Amos, and Micah in fact better fits the archaeological picture of ancient Israel than does the DtrH.

References

Albertz, R. "Exile as Purification: Reconstructing the 'Book of the Four.'" Pp. 232–251 in *Thematic Threads in the Book of the Twelve*. Edited by P.L. Redditt and A. Schart. BZAW 325. Berlin: de Gruyter, 2003.

– "Secondary Sources also Deserve to be Critically Evaluated." Pp. 31–45 in *The Historian and the Bible*. Edited by P.L. Davies and D.V. Edelman. FS L.L. Grabbe. Library of Hebrew Bible / Old Testament Studies 530. New York: T&T Clark, 2010.

Ash, P.S. "Jeroboam I and the Deuteronomistic Historian's Ideology of the Founder." *CBQ* 60 (1998) 16–24.

Ben Zvi, E. "A Deuteronomistic Redaction in/among the 'The Twelve'? A Contribution from the Standpoint of the Books of Micah, Zephaniah and Obadiah." Pp. 232–261 in *Those Elusive Deuteronomists: The Phenomenon of Pan-Deuteronomism*. Edited by L.S. Shearing and S.L. McKenzie. JSOTSup 268. Sheffield: Sheffield Academic Press, 1999.

Biddle, M.E. "'Israel' and 'Jacob' in the Book of Micah: Micah in the Context of the Twelve." Pp. 146–165 in *Reading and Hearing the Book of the Twelve*. Edited by J.D. Nogalski and M.A. Sweeney. SBLSymS 15. Atlanta: Society of Biblical Literature, 2000.

Blenkinsopp, J. *A History of Prophecy in Israel*. 2nd ed. Louisville: Westminster John Knox, 1996.

Campbell, A.F. *Of Prophets and Kings: A Late Ninth-Century Document (1 Samuel 1 – 2 Kings 10)*. CBQMS 17. Washington: CBQ Monograph Series, 1986.

Cook, S.L. "Micah's Deuteronomistic Redaction and the Deuteronomists' Identity." Pp. 216–231 in *Those Elusive Deuteronomists: The Phenomenon of Pan-Deuteronomism*. JSOTSup 268. Edited by L.S. Shearing and S.L. McKenzie. JSOTSup 268. Sheffield: Sheffield Academic Press, 1999.

Davies, G.H. "Amos – The Prophet of Re-union." *ExpTim* 92 (1980–1981) 196–200.

300   Jason Radine

Day, J. "Hosea and the Baal Cult." Pp. 202–224 in *Prophecy and Prophets in Ancient Israel: Proceedings of the Oxford Old Testament Seminar*. Edited by J. Day. LHBOTS 531. New York: T&T Clark, 2010.

Debus, J. *Die Sünde Jerobeams*. FRLANT 93. Göttingen: Vandenhoeck & Ruprecht, 1967.

Emmerson, G. *Hosea: An Israelite Prophet in Judean Perspective*. JSOTSup 28. Sheffield: Sheffield Academic Press, 1984.

Evans, C.D. "Naram-Sin and Jeroboam: The Archetypal *Unheilsherrscher* in Mesopotamian and Biblical Historiography." Pp. 97–125 in *Scripture in Context II: More Essays on the Comparative Method*. Edited by W.W. Hallo et al. Winona Lake: Eisenbrauns, 1983.

Finkelstein, I. "State Formation in Israel and Judah: A Contrast in Context, and Contrast in Trajectory." *Near Eastern Archaeology* 62 (1999) 35–52.

– "Omride Architecture." *ZDPV* 116 (2000) 114–138.

Finkelstein I. and Silberman, N.A. *The Bible Unearthed: Archaeology's New Vision of Ancient Israel and the Origin of its Sacred Texts*. New York: Free Press, 2001.

Finkelstein I. et al. "Has King David's Palace in Jerusalem Been Found?" *TA* 34 (2007) 142–164.

Freedman, D.N. "Headings in the Books of the Eighth-Century Prophets." *AUSS* 25 (1987) 9–26.

Garfinkel, Y. and Ganor, S. "Khirbet Qeiyafa: Sha'arayim." *Journal of Hebrew Scriptures* 8.22 (2008) 1–10.

– "The Birth and Death of Biblical Minimalism." *BAR* 37 (2011) 46–53.78.

Knauf, E.A. "Kings Among the Prophets." Pp. 131–149 in *The Production of Prophecy: Constructing Prophecy and Prophets in Yehud*. Edited by D.V. Edelman and E. Ben Zvi. London: Equinox, 2009.

Knoppers, G.N. *Two Nations Under God: The Deuteronomistic History of Solomon and the Dual Monarchies*. 2 vols. Harvard Semitic Museum Monographs 52. Atlanta: Scholars Press, 1993.

Kugler, R.A. "The Deuteronomists and the Latter Prophets." Pp. 127–144 in *Those Elusive Deuteronomists: The Phenomenon of Pan-Deuteronomism*. Edited by L.S. Shearing and S.L. McKenzie. JSOTSup 268. Sheffield: Sheffield Academic Press, 1999.

Leuchter, M. "Jeroboam the Ephratite." *JBL* 125 (2006) 51–72.

Lohfink, N. "Was There a Deuteronomistic Movement?" Pp. 36–66 in *Those Elusive Deuteronomists: The Phenomenon of Pan-Deuteronomism*. Edited by L.S. Shearing and S.L. McKenzie. JSOTSup 268. Sheffield: Sheffield Academic Press, 1999.

Machinist, P. "Hosea and the Ambiguity of Kingship in Ancient Israel." Pp. 153–181 in *Constituting the Community: Studies on the Polity of Ancient Israel in Honor of S. Dean McBride Jr.* Edited by J.T. Strong and S.S. Tuell. Winona Lake: Eisenbrauns, 2005.

Macintosh, A.A. *Hosea*. ICC. Edinburgh: T&T Clark, 1997.

Mays, J.L. *Hosea*. OTL. Philadelphia: Westminster John Knox, 1969.

Mazar, E. *Preliminary Report on the City of David Excavations 2005 at the Visitors' Center Area*. Jerusalem: Shalem Press, 2006.

Na'aman, N. "Shaaraim – The Gateway to the Kingdom of Judah." *Journal of Hebrew Scriptures* 8.24 (2008) 1–5.

Nogalski, J.D. *Literary Precursors to the Book of the Twelve*. BZAW 217. Berlin: de Gruyter, 1993.
– *Redactional Processes in the Book of the Twelve*. BZAW 218. Berlin: de Gruyter, 1993.
Pakkala, J. "Jeroboam without Bulls." *ZAW* 120 (2008) 501–525.
Person, R. *Second Zechariah and the Deuteronomic School*. JSOTSup 167. Sheffield: Sheffield Academic Press, 1993.
Polley, M. *Amos and the Davidic Empire – A Socio-Historical Approach*. New York: Oxford University Press, 1989.
Radine, J. *The Book of Amos in Emergent Judah*. FAT II/45. Tübingen: Mohr, 2010.
Schart, A. *Die Entstehung des Zwölfprophetenbuchs: Neubearbeitungen von Amos im Rahmen schriftenübergreifender Redaktionsprozesse*. BZAW 260. Berlin: de Gruyter, 1998.
– "Reconstructing the Redaction History of the Twelve Prophets: Problems and Models." Pp. 34–48 in *Reading and Hearing the Book of the Twelve*. Edited by J.D. Nogalski and M.A. Sweeney. SBLSymS 15. Atlanta: Society of Biblical Literature, 2000.
Schenker, A. "Jeroboam's Rise and Fall in the Hebrew and Greek Bible." *JSJ* 39 (2008) 367–373.
Schmidt, B. (ed.) *The Quest for the Historical Israel: Debating Archaeology and the History of Early Israel*. SBLABS 17. Atlanta: Society of Biblical Literature, 2007.
Schmidt, W.H. "Die deuteronomistische Redaktion des Amosbuches: Zu den theologischen Unterschieden zwischen dem Prophetenwort und seinem Sammler." *ZAW* 77 (1965) 168–193.
Sweeney, M.A. *King Josiah of Judah: The Lost Messiah of Israel*. New York: Oxford University Press, 2001.
– "The Dystopianization of Utopian Prophetic Literature: The Case of Amos 9:11–15." Pp. 175–185 in *Utopia and Dystopia in Prophetic Literature*. Edited by E. Ben Zvi. Helsinki: Finnish Exegetical Society, 2006.
– "A Reassessment of the Masoretic and Septuagint Versions of the Jeroboam Narratives in Kings/3 Kingdoms 11–14." *JSJ* 38 (2007) 165–195.
Tubb, J.N. "Early Iron Age Judah in the Light of Recent Discoveries at Khirbet Qeiyafa." *PEQ* 142 (2010) 1–2.
Tucker, G.N. "Prophetic Superscriptions and the Growth of a Canon." Pp. 56–70 in *Canon and Authority: Essays in Old Testament Religion and Theology*. Edited by G.W. Coats and B.O. Long. Philadelphia: Fortress, 1997.
Ussishkin, D. "Solomon's Jerusalem: The Texts and the Facts on the Ground." Pp. 103–115 in *Jerusalem in Bible and Archaeology: The First Temple Period*. Edited by A.G. Vaughn and A.E. Killebrew. SBLSymS 18. Atlanta: Society of Biblical Literature, 2003.
Van Seters, J. *In Search of History: Historiography in the Ancient World and the Origins of Biblical History*. Winona Lake: Eisenbrauns, 1997 (orig. 1983).
Wellhausen, J. *Die kleinen Propheten übersetzt und erklärt*. 4th ed. Berlin: de Gruyter, 1963 (orig. 1892).
Wöhrle, J. "'No Future for the Proud Exultant Ones': The Exilic Book of the Four Prophets (Hos., Am., Mic., Zeph.,) as a Concept Opposed to the Deuteronomistic History." *VT* 58 (2008) 608–627.

Wolff, H.W. *Hosea: A Commentary on the Book of the Prophet Hosea*. Translated by
   G. Stansell, Hermeneia. Philadelphia: Fortress, 1974.
–   *Joel and Amos: A Commentary on the Books of the Prophets Joel and Amos*.
   Translated by W. Janzen et al. Hermeneia. Philadelphia: Fortress, 1997.
Yadin, Y. "Megiddo of the Kings of Israel." *BA* 33 (1970) 66–96.

The History of Judah and Samaria in the Late Persian and Hellenistic Periods as a Possible Background of the Later Editions of the Book of the Twelve

Westfälische Wilhelms-Universität Münster

One needs to be reminded that the concept of historical critical research, which became common in biblical exegesis during the last three centuries, is based on a close relationship between literary critical analysis and historical investigations. In recent times several biblical scholars – especially in Germany – are confident that they are able to reconstruct the literary history of a textual corpus in detail, but they doubt whether it is possible to reconstruct the accompanying political and social history with any degree of certainty. The connection between two approaches, however, should not be dissolved. Admittedly, each approach has its material and methodological limits, but our experience with historical critical research during the last centuries, in spite of unavoidable errors, shows that knowledge of the historical background of a biblical passage leads to a more concrete and a better understanding of the text on the one hand. On the other hand, insights into the formation of a biblical corpus help to reconstruct the political, social, and theological history of ancient Israel, and these insights should not be forgotten.

1. Diachronic Literary Approach and Historical Investigations Concerning the Minor Prophets

Concerning the Minor Prophets the results of the historical critical research have been ambivalent. Focusing on the early phases of the prophetical books, several scholars as Rudolph, Wolff, Jeremias, Kessler, Mays, Sweeney, Hanhart and others[1] were able to reconstruct the mes-

---

1   See just the most influential commentaries of these scholars: Rudolph, *Hosea*; idem, *Joel*; idem, *Micha*; idem, *Haggai*; Wolff, *Dodekapropheton 1–2, 4, 6*; Jeremias, *Hosea*;

sage of the prophets Amos, Hosea, Micah, Zephaniah, Haggai, and
Zechariah on their historical background from the 8th to the 6th century,
even though it turned out that it was more shaped by their pupils and
early tradents than some of these scholars were aware. And even for
the early collections of those prophetical books, the Book of the Four
consisting of most of the books of Hosea, Amos, Micah, and Zephaniah
and the Book of the Two containing most of the books of Haggai and
Zech 1–8, suitable historical backgrounds could be found. The former
seems to have come from the late exilic period, when the aims at a new
beginning were at stake (539–520 B.C.E.).[2] For the latter I recently proposed the Babylonian revolts during the early reign of Xerxes (484–
479),[3] which might have nourished new hopes for a complete realization of salvation.

For the later redactional layers of these books and for those books
of admittedly later origin (Joel, Zech 9–14, or Malachi), however, it
remains extremely difficult to find any historical background. On the
one hand, this has to do with the nature of these post-exilic prophetical
texts: representing a kind of scribal prophecy and exegesis, they have
less clear allusions to historical events than the older collections. Even
in those passages that seem to allude to specific events (e.g. Zech 11:8a;
12:10), we do not have the historical knowledge to understand them
and to integrate them into the history of the Persian or Hellenistic Judah and Samaria.[4] On the other hand, from the middle of the 5th century onwards, when the biblical historical accounts end, only a few non-
biblical sources exist for the reconstruction of the history of Judah and
Samaria in the late Persian and early Hellenistic periods (mainly Josephus). These sources have been only slightly amplified by archaeological, epigraphical, and iconographical findings during the last 100 years.
Therefore, combining isolated prophetic passages with specific historical events was often risky and conclusions were dubious. For example,
is it or is it not possible to relate Zech 9:1–8, which mentions YHWH's
judgment on Phoenician and Philistine cities, to Alexander's campaign
through the Levant on the way to Egypt in 332 B.C.E., as Elliger proposed?[5] Or, does the symbolic prophetic act in Zech 11:14, tell us that

---

idem, *Amos*; idem, *Joel*; Kessler, *Micha*; Mays, *Hosea*; idem, *Amos*; idem, *Micah*; Sweeney, *Prophets*; idem, *Zephaniah*; Hanhart, *Dodekapropheton 7,1*.

2 See Nogalski, *Precursors*, 176–177; Albertz, *Exile*, 236–237; Wöhrle, *Sammlungen*, 272–
275.

3 See Albertz, "Streit," 17–19.

4 For the discussion about the identity of the "three shepherds" in Zech 11:8a see
Wöhrle, *Abschluss*, 87–88, esp. note 73, for the speculations about the "pierced one"
in Zech 12:10 see Wöhrle, *Abschluss*, 103–104, esp. note 120–121.

5 See Elliger, "Zeugnis," 89–115.

the brotherhood between Judah and Israel was broken by referring to the schism of the Samarians, as several scholars believe?[6] Apart from the question of whether the material correspondence holds true, the answer depends on one's view regarding the time to which the text should be dated. From an isolated passage, however, this decision is often difficult to make.

Under these poor conditions, a diachronic approach to the Book of the Twelve that covers its entire literary history promises genuine progress. [7] By reconstructing a sequence of redactional layers throughout the books, layers to which specific passages can be attributed, it establishes a relative chronological order, which provides us with a period of time, in which those passages can probably be dated. If this period of time can be fixed, the search for a possible historical background for those passages can proceed with a much higher degree of probability. If a redactional history of the Book of the Twelve can be reconstructed with some degree of probability, we would not only enhance our chances for a better historical understanding of its texts, but also gain a new source for reconstructing the political, social, and theological history of the late Persian and early Hellenistic periods.

2. The Destiny of the Foreign Nations in the Book of the Twelve

It has often been noted that the destiny of the foreign nations belongs to the major topics of the Book of the Twelve.[8] The study of Roth, however, shows, that a topical investigation, which goes without a redaction critical reconstruction, leads to very vague results.[9] Roth merely describes different positions concerning foreign nations, which he attributes to an ongoing discourse of literary prophecy over two centuries, without being able to show any developments or to detect influences from the course of Judean and Samarian history. According to Roth, the oracles on foreign nations intend to construct a counter-world, by

---

6   So e.g. Elliger, *Buch*, 163, and others; for the discussion see Wöhrle, *Abschluss*, 91–92, esp. note 86.
7   See the pioneer works of Nogalski, *Precursors*; idem, *Processes*; Schart, *Entstehung*, and Sweeney, *Prophets*. Most elaborated is the thesis of Wöhrle, *Sammlungen*; idem, *Abschluss*.
8   See the literature mentioned by Wöhrle, *Abschluss*, 139.
9   See Roth, *Israel*, 291–298, even though in this book he starts with an overview of the political, social, and theological history of the late Persian and Hellenistic periods (Roth, *Israel*, 12–55).

which the Jewish identity was defined.[10] But does this rather general information explain the variety and the prominence of the topic?

In his redaction critical study Wöhrle distinguished no less than 4 different literary layers, which are concerned with the destiny of foreign nations:[11] first, a layer announcing a divine judgment on all the nations, including the dominant world power, in connection with the final salvation of Jerusalem and the people (Foreign-Nations-Redaction I), dated at the end of the 5th century; second, a layer announcing specific divine judgments on a number of nations (Phoenicians, Philistines, Edomites, Greeks) for their concrete misdeeds, dated to the beginning of the 3rd century (Foreign-Nations-Redaction II); third, a layer announcing the possibility of salvation for foreign nations beyond divine judgment (Salvation-for-the-Nations-Redaction), dated in the first part of the 3rd century; and finally, a layer reflecting upon the possibilities and the limits of divine grace for foreign nations with reference to Exod 34:6–7, dated in the second part of the 3rd century. Thus, Wöhrle elaborates in detail how reflection about the destiny of foreign nations lasted over a period of two centuries. Indeed, he demonstrates that the destiny of foreign nations was one of the driving forces that enlarged and shaped the Book of the Twelve during the later phases of its formation. Moreover, he shows that the attitude towards the nations changed from a negative one during the late Persian and the beginning of the Hellenistic periods to a more positive one during the later Hellenistic period. According to Wöhrle, this development is not only the result of internal theological reflection by scribal groups, but has also to do with concrete experiences between foreign nations and Judeans during these periods. Do his results, derived from critical literary analysis, fit the historical developments in Judah and Samaria during the Persian and Hellenistic periods?

3. The Late Persian Period as Background for the Foreign-Nations-Redaction I

At first glance, a redaction, which reworked and united eight prophetic books from the perspective of a total divine judgment on all the nations, including the Eastern world power, does not correspond with our typical view of the Persian period. In contrast, the books of Ezra and Nehemiah essentially draw a picture of successful cooperation

---

10   Roth, *Israel*, 292.
11   See Wöhrle, *Abschluss*, 139–171.264–287.335–361.400–419.

between the Persian authorities and Jewish leaders, cooperation which provided the province of Judah, and especially its temple in Jerusalem, with many privileges.[12] Even a more critical view of the imperial policy of the Persians has to admit that their imperial ideology opened the way of integrating the cultural and religious diversity of the subjected nations into the empire in a positive manner,[13] although acts of cultural "tolerance" were granted only to loyal subjects, while disloyal subjects were severely punished.[14] We learn of complaints about the severe economic rule of the Persians (Neh 9:37), especially their strict tax system, which burdened the poor in particular (Neh 5:1–4), but the Judean upper classes and their leaders seem to have enjoyed a considerable degree of freedom under the Persian government.

In order to provide his Foreign-Nations-Redaction I with a suitable historical context, Wöhrle already points to the Bagoses story[15] told by Josephus in Ant. XI.297–301 as a story that shows a totally different picture of Persian provincial policy toward Judah.[16] According to this story the Persian governor Bagoses seriously interfered with Judean self-government. He tried to supplant the ruling high priest Joannes with his brother Jesus. This intervention failed, since Joannes murdered his brother because of a dispute while he was serving in the Jerusalem temple. Afterward, Bagoses forced his way into the temple and deliberately defiled it. Moreover, he punished the entire community by imposing a high tax of 50 drachmae on any sacrifice for a period of seven years. Wöhrle draws a striking parallel between these events and the

---

12 Cf. only Ezra 1:1–11; 6:1–22; 7:1–18; Neh 1:1–2:18; 13:4–6.
13 In difference to the Neo-Assyrian kings, who called themselves 'king of the countries,' 'king of totality,' or 'king of the four world regions,' Persian kings after Darius used titles as 'king of the peoples,' or 'king of the peoples of numerous origins' (see Lecoq, *Inscriptions*, 137.187.219.228 and passim), thus emphasizing not the totality, but the diversity of their empire. In their royal inscriptions, sometimes these peoples, who carry tributes or maintain the royal law, are listed (Lecoq, *Inscriptions*, 228.233). The Behistun inscription lists 23 peoples (188). See also the visual portrayals of this ideology in the palace in Persepolis, where the peoples are depicted carrying tribute or the royal throne (Walser, *Persepolis*, 16–76.80–81; the latter similar to a picture on the mausoleum of Naqš-e Rostam, see Lecoq, *Inscriptions*, pl. 15–16). In Persian royal ideology, ethnic diversity was also accepted on the religious level, because it could also include – apart from the main deity Ahuramazda – "all gods, who exist" in divine support of the king (see §§62–63 of the Behistun inscription; Lecoq, *Inscriptions*, 210). According to Lecoq, *Inscriptions*, 210 note 3, this formula constitutes an archaic grammatical formulation that may have come from the Medes. For the discussion about Persian 'toleration' see Albertz, *Exile*, 114–116.
14 Cf. Darius' statement in the second inscription of his Mausoleum, translated by Lecoq, *Inscriptions*, 222: "L'homme qui aide, lui je le protège selon sa collaboration; celui qui nuit, je le punis ainsi selon sa nuisance."
15 See Wöhrle, *Abschluss*, 162–164.
16 See in the edition of Marcus, *Josephus*, 6:457–461.

literary device that frames the Foreign-Nations-Redaction I with statements in Joel 4:17 and Zech 14:21; namely that after YHWH's judgment
on the nations, the holiness of Jerusalem and its temple will be guaranteed and no stranger will again pass through the city or come into the
temple.[17] Another observation can be added. The statement in Joel 2:20
that YHWH would remove 'the Northern one' from the people[18] can be
interpreted specifically as a hidden indication that Persian rule over
Judah and Samaria would end.

Thus, there are good reasons that the severe and long lasting conflict under Bagoses may constitute a suitable historical background for
the Foreign-Nations-Redaction I. There are, however, some remaining
historical problems: First, the historicity of the story may be doubted.
Second, the identity of that Bagoses mentioned by Josephus is still a
matter of dispute. Third, therefore, the date of the conflict is not established, which should be the prerequisite for any combination with biblical texts. Finally, because of its strangeness, the conflict has, to this
point, not been integrated into the course of the post-exilic Judean history. It appears in virtually none of the textbooks on ancient Israel's
history.[19] Thus, a historical reconstruction of the possible events behind
this episode is still necessary.[20]

---

17 See Wöhrle, *Abschluss*, 163–164. The two passages are not identical since they differ
    in their terminology. Joel 4:17 says that the זרים will no longer pass through Jerusa-
    lem; in the post-exilic period the Hebrew term denotes the stranger (Isa 61:5) and the
    unauthorized one as well (Lev 22:10, 12–13). Zech 14:21 speaks of the Canaanite
    (כנעני), who will not be in the temple of YHWH Sebaoth any longer. Wöhrle, *Ab-
    schluss*, 122–123, convincingly argues that the term should not be rendered by 'trad-
    ers,' but 'Canaanites' in the general sense of 'foreigners.' The meaning 'traders' de-
    rives from the fact that these persons were almost all of foreign (i.e. Phoenician)
    origin.

18 The Masoretic reading הצפוני 'the Northern one' was sometimes altered in
    הצפצפוני 'the chirping one,' because the metaphoric of the verse alludes to a swarm
    of locusts. But the reading is established by the versions, and it is already recognized
    that the rare term alludes to Jeremiah's prophecy of the 'enemy from the North' (Jer
    1:14; 4:6; 6:1, 22), cf. Wolff, *Dodekapropheton 2*, 73–74; Jeremias, *Joel*, 36–37. By this
    concept Jeremiah denoted the Neo-Babylonian Empire. If Joel 2:18–20 did not belong
    to an apocalyptic concept as Wolff supposes, but to a redaction of the late 5th centu-
    ry, then the expression 'the Northern one' probably does not refer to a last aggressor
    at the end of time or to a "Satanlike figure" (so Barton, *Joel*, 88–89), but to the con-
    temporary Eastern world power (meaning the Persians), which used to intrude into
    the Levant from the North. Wöhrle, *Abschluss*, 162–170, is right to emphasize the
    universality of the divine judgment in the concept of the Foreign-Nation-Redaction I,
    but that does not exclude a specific role of the world power, which is also addressed
    by the redaction under the label of Assur in Zeph 2:13–15 and Ninive in Nah 3*.

19 Among common German textbooks Gunneweg, *Geschichte*, 139, is the only excep-
    tion; among the English texts Miller and Hayes, *History*, 474–475, only briefly men-
    tion the episode, but they refrain from any interpretation.

4. A Historical Reconstruction of the Bagoses Story

Since Josephus has only limited knowledge about the late Persian peri-od,[21] the credibility of the Bagoses story, which is reported only by him (Ant. XI.297–301), could be doubted. However, even critical scholars as Grabbe now tend to accept the historical reliability of the story, because "the murder in the temple is not likely to be simply a Jewish inven-tion."[22] Moreover, Williamson has pointed out that Josephus was prob-ably drawing on an independent source (§§298–301), which he framed by his own introduction and conclusion.[23] The event is important enough to be reported and handed down in the temple archive. Thus the formal historicity of the Bagoses event seems to be established.

Before the discovery of the Elephantine papyri, the Bagoses of the story was generally identified with the influential minister of this name[24] under Artaxerxes III (358–337 B.C.E.),[25] but since the papyri TAD A4.7–9 verify a Persian governor of Judah, named Bagohi,[26] who was a contemporary of the high priest Johanan at the end of the 5th cen-tury (at least 410–407), the majority of scholars prefer the latter identifi-cation.[27] Williamson has recently questioned this interpretation, be-cause the Bagoses of the story is called στρατηγός (§§297.300),[28] but since Grabbe has shown that this title was used in Hellenistic Greek not only for military, but also for civil offices, including the office of a pro-vincial governor or satrap,[29] the main counter-argument against this natural identification is removed. Because of his Persian name, Bagohi

20 For a more detailed reconstruction with additional rationale, see Albertz, "Contro-versy," 484–499.
21 For this judgment see Grabbe, *Judaism*, 1:61–62. For example, Josephus did not know that there were three rulers with the name Artaxerxes. Apart from the first one, he mentions only "the other Artaxerxes" (τοῦ ἄλλου Ἀρταχέρξου) in Ant. XI.297. After the Bagoses story Josephus immediately continues with the "last king Darius" (= Da-rius III) and Alexander (§§302–305); Darius II, as the forerunner of Artaxerxes II, seems to have been unknown to him.
22 Grabbe, *Judaism*, 1:62.
23 See Williamson, "Historical Value," 75–79.
24 Cf. Torrey, "Two Persian Officers," 300–301.
25 He is mentioned by Diodorus Siculus, *Bibliotheca Historica*, XVI.47–50, and called a 'general,' a 'commander over the thousands,' who was in charge of the king's body guard and the chief friend of King Artaxerxes III. He seems to have been one of the most influential persons at the Persian court; he poisoned Artaxerxes and later Arses and replaced them with his favorites (first Arses, then Darius III); but no contact to Palestine is attested.
26 See Porten and Yardeni, *Textbook*, 1:68–78.
27 So Galling, "Bagoas," 162–164; Schwartz, "Papyri," 193–194; Grabbe, *Judaism*, 1:62–63; idem, "Bagoses," 54–55; Rooke, *Zadok's Heirs*, 236; Dušek, *Manuscrits*, 593–597.
28 See Williamson, "Historical Value," 81–89; idem, "Judean History," 21–23.
29 See Grabbe, "Bagoses;" idem, *Judaism*, 1:63.

– as well as the Bagoses of the story – should be regarded as a Persian.[30] According to Josephus he was a governor of Judah under Artaxerxes II (§297: τοῦ ἄλλου Ἀρταχέρξου), who was enthroned 404 B.C.E., but according to the papyri he was already in office under Darius II (424– 405). Thus, the events told in the story can be dated, indeed, to the end of the 5th century, in the same period, to which the Foreign-Nations-Redaction I probably belongs according to literary historical criteria.

The severe conflict between Bagohi and Johanan at the end of the 5th century is better to be understood from the new insights granted by two recent archaeological discoveries. First, Lipschits documents a considerable change of Persian policies toward the Levant that seems to have been provoked by the Persian Empire's loss of Egypt.[31] While for most of the 5th century the Persians fostered urban life in the coastal plain, where they built many fortresses in order to safeguard their roads and harbors on the way to their province Egypt, at the end of the 5th and the beginning of the 4th centuries, they put the previously neglected Samarian and Judean hill country under stricter control. During this period, they built several fortresses and administrative centers in Lachish, Ramat Rahel, and in the Negev, because – with the loss of Egypt – Judah had become the southwestern border of the empire. Thus, we probably have to distinguish between two phases of Persian policy concerning Judah and Samaria: a first phase of *laissez faire*, when the Persian government was only interested in the profit they could make from these rural provinces, and a second phase of strict control, when the political stability of that border region came into the Persian's field of view.

Second, the excavations of Magen have shown that the first sanctuary on Mount Gerizim was not constructed in the days of Darius III and Alexander as Josephus reports (336–332 B.C.E; Ant. XI.306–325), but about 100 years earlier in the last third of 5th century.[32] Gerizim temple construction probably followed Nehemiah's decision of expelling a member of the high priest's family from Jerusalem, who had married a

---

30   According to Lemaire, "Administration," 54, Bagohi is the Aramaic spelling of Ba-
     gavahya. This is clearly a Persian name, even if Jews might have adopted it in some
     way, cf. Bigwai in Ezra 2:2, 14; Neh 7:7; 10:17.
31   See Lipschits, "Imperial Policy," 26–38; decisive for this evaluation was the insight
     that the Persian fortress on Tell Lachish was built not in the midst, but at the end of
     the 5th century B.C.E.
32   According Magen, "Samaritan Temple," 176, the sanctuary was constructed in the
     mid-fifth century, but since he himself refers to Neh 13:38 (188–189), the date has to
     be lowered to about 430 B.C.E. at least, since the first term of Nehemiah's office last-
     ed from 445–433, and the expulsion of the high priest's son took place during the se-
     cond term, a date that cannot be determined with precision.

daughter of Sanballat (Neh 13:28).[33] Being excluded from any influence in the Jerusalem temple, the Samarian governor decided to found his own sanctuary, where he could install his Zadokite son-in-law. The foundation of the Gerizim temple could have happened shortly after the accession of Darius II in 424 B.C.E.[34] Thus, Judah got a new cultic rival in a neighboring province, a fact that would have challenged the Jerusalemites to claim their leadership in all cultic and religious affairs. Thus, this rivalry involved the danger of the destabilization of the two border provinces, a situation which the Persians must have tried to avert.

In the light of these two new insights, the conflicts, which are mirrored in the Elephantine papyri, on the one hand, and told in the Bagoses story of Josephus, on the other hand, verify the changing international conditions and their impact on a more rigorous Persian policy toward Judah and Samaria. The course of events can be reconstructed in the following way. The Egyptian fight for independence was a long process. It already started with small riots from 410 B.C.E. onwards, as can be seen from Elephantine papyri.[35] Also, the encroachment on the Jewish temple in Elephantine, initiated by the Khnum priests, can be interpreted in this context; it was not only a religious, but also a political demonstration against foreign elements in the Persian garrison.[36] With the death of Darius II in the year 405 and the length period of battles of Artaxerxes II against his brother Cyrus for executing his claim to the Persian throne (404–401), Armyrtaeus from Saïs seized the opportunity to throw off the Persian yoke with the help of Sparta and became the first Pharaoh of independent Egypt.

Presupposing the typical good relations between the Persian governor and the Judean self-government, Jedaniah, the priest and leader

---

33 Since the son of the high priest Joiada, who was expelled, probably did not marry the daughter of the Samarian governor without the consent of his father, this high priest seems to have felt much more sympathy for the Samarians than did his forerunner Eliashib, who had supported Nehemiah's policy of dissociation, cf. Albertz, "Purity Strategies," 200–205.

34 King Artaxerxes I seems to have supported Nehemiah and his strict anti-Samarian policy, while his follower was probably less obliged to foster Judean interests.

35 Cf. TAD A4.5:1; 6.7:6; 6.10:4; 6.11:2, 4.

36 According to TAD A4.3:7 the hostility with the Khnum priests arose because Hananiah had been in Egypt. Hananiah was probably sent by the central Persian government in order to enhance the public religious status of the Jewish minority in the multiethnic society of Elephantine, for example, by the official acknowledgement of its holidays during the feast of Unleavened Bread (cf. TAD 4.1). This public enhancement of a foreign element obviously bothered the Egyptian priests; they likely regarded it as neglecting Egyptian interests by the Persian government. For the important mission of Hananiah, which can be compared with the mission of Nehemiah in some ways, see Kottsieper, "Religionspolitik," 150–157; Kratz, "Tempel," 65–57.

of the Jewish garrison in Elephantine, addressed his first letter of the
year 410 B.C.E (TAD A4.7:17–19) to the governor Bagohi, the high
priest Johanan, the leader of the congregation of priests, and Ostanes,
the leader of the council of elders,[37] in order to win their support for the
reconstruction of the Elephantine temple that had been destroyed.
Bagohi was probably concerned about recent Egyptian unrest, interested in preventing the success of Egyptian nationalism, and in strength-
ening the morality of the Jewish mercenaries in the Persian garrison.
The high priest Johanan, however, refused to agree and prevented any
quick answer. In competition with the Samarians, Johanan used the
matter of the Elephantine temple as an opportunity to demonstrate the
cultic exclusivity of the Jerusalem temple and the Judean leadership in
all matters pertaining to YHWH religion. As his brother Joshua verifies,
there was also a party among the leading priests and the aristocrats that
pleaded for more sympathy for Persian interests and for a concession to
the Jewish brothers in Egypt. But this party does not seem to have had
the majority in the two councils of the Judean self-government. Thus,
Johanan notoriously used his authority to prevent the council from
making any decision for three years.

This is probably the situation in which the conflict reported by Josephus took place. Frustrated by Johanan's resistance, the Persian governor was no longer willing to accept that the Judean religious ambi-
tions should disturb the Persian strategic interest in safeguarding the
empire at its southwestern wing. Thus, he intervened in the Judean
self-government. By promising Joshua his support in taking over the
office of the high priest (Ant. XI.298b), he tried to replace Johanan, to
change the majority in the Judean councils and to pave the way for a
reasonable decision. However, this attempt failed; the priestly brothers
got into an argument about their opposing political options, and provoked by Joshua's assurance, the high priest Johanan killed his brother
while he was serving in the sanctuary (§299). The murder may have
happened in the year 408 B.C.E.

One can imagine that Bagohi was disappointed and angry about
the failure of his guarded intervention. The shocking sacrilege, however, provided him with the opportunity to teach the ambitious priests of
Jerusalem and the entire Judean community a harsh lesson. Brutally, he
forced his way into the temple and defiled it deliberately (§§300–301).
Moreover, he maligned the high priest in public, who had himself de-

---

37 For this two councils of the Judean self-government below the Persian provincial
    administration see already Galling, "Bagoas," 162–163, and Albertz, *Israelite Religion*,
    2:446–447.

filed the sanctuary by a corpse (§301).[38] Obviously, he wanted to humiliate the Judeans and their ambitious priesthood. Finally, in order to punish the whole Judean community he imposed a high tax of 50 drachmae on each of the daily sacrifices, which had to be paid from the public treasury (§297). This tax was intended to reduce the temple cult to a minimum, to decrease the income of the priests, and to burden to the entire Judean province with severe financial losses. With all these measures Bagohi wanted to demonstrate in a brutal way that in spite of their ambitious claims, the Judeans (including their temple and their priests) were subject to the Persian government. During a long seven year period of punishment they were supposed to learn that their claim to religious leadership was very restricted and should never contradict the Persian strategic interest.

During the years 408 and 407 the Jews of Elephantine heard about the serious disagreement between Bagohi and the Judean community. Thus, they decided to write a new petition in the year 407. This time, however, they wrote two letters and sent one to Bagohi only, and the other to the sons of Sanballat in Samaria, who seem to have carried out the governorship of their old father (TAD 4.7:1, 29). Thus they addressed only the governors of the two provinces and deliberately excluded the high priest Johanan and the Judean councils of self-government. This time, Bagohi no longer felt obliged to show consideration to the Judeans and their claims. As we know from the papyrus TAD 4.9, both governors, Bagohi and Delaiah, immediately made a common decision and supported the reconstruction of the temple with some minor restrictions.[39] Thus, the cult-political decision was made only on the level of the Persian provincial government, without any participation of the Judeans.

During the years of punishment (408–401 B.C.E.), the Judeans probably tried to lodge complaints against Bagohi at the Persian royal court with the help of the Diaspora Jews. But as long as the two rival brothers, Artaxerxes and Cyrus, engaged in their bitter war over succession (404–401), the Judeans did not gain a hearing. The period of harsh in-

---

38 Following Marcus, *Josephus*, 6:459, who rightly preferred the passive variant of the mocking phrase of Bagoses: "Am I, then, not purer than he who was slain in the temple?" instead of "who slew" (Ant. XI.301).

39 The memorandum of Bagohi and Delaiah TAD A4.9:9 speaks of grain-offerings and incense-offerings, but not blood sacrifices, while Jedaniah had also mentioned holocausts in his letter (TAD 4.7:25). This restriction may have to do with the reservations of the Persians against blood sacrifices or it may have been a compromise to lessen any provocation of the Khnum priests. The formulation of the text does not show that the governors took any Judean claim into account, cf. Kottsieper, "Religionspolitik," 169–175.

tervention into Judean affairs lasted so long because of these inner Persian struggles, which also included allies from many nations of the empire.[40] Only after Artaxerxes II emerged successfully, does he seem to have stopped the punitive policy against the Judeans. Assuming it was he who sent Ezra to Judah in 398 B.C.E.,[41] this mission and the implementation of the Pentateuch aimed at pacifying the conflict and stabilizing the southwestern border against Egypt.

5. Interpreting the Foreign-Nations-Redaction I on this Political Background

The political and cultic crisis, which Judah experienced under the reign of the Persian governor Bagohi (alias Bagoses) during the last decade of the 5th century B.C.E. was severe and long lasting enough to provoke theological reflections and literary activities among the scribal elite of Judah. Since the redaction shows many of the basic convictions of Zion theology,[42] its authors probably belonged to the priestly or lay staff of the Jerusalem temple. Thus, they were personally affected by the punitive measures against the temple cult. Confronted with the brutal political intervention of the world power into Jerusalem's cultic affairs combined with high military activity during Egypt's struggles for independence and the succession wars of the royal brothers, they could have gained the impression that Jerusalem and YHWH's people were surrounded by enemies and threatened by all those foreign nations. In light of Zion theology they understood the frightening contemporary events as an onslaught of the peoples against Mount Zion[43] that YHWH would stop.

---

40 See Briant, *History*, 615–634. Cyrus assembled Greek mercenaries and forces from many peoples of Asia Minor. Artaxerxes, who had gathered in 404 B.C.E. an army in Phoenicia against revolting Egypt, mustered troops from Babylonia, Susiana, Media, and Persia against his brother, who attacked him in Babylonia during the year 401. Artaxerxes seems to have intended to use the army of Levantine peoples also for his defense against his brother, but it was probably still on the road, when the decisive battle was fought in Cunaxa near Babylon (see ibid., 629).
41 Whether Ezra's mission should be dated in the 7th year of Artaxerxes I (458 B.C.E.) or the II (398) is still a matter of dispute (cf. Grabbe, *Judaism*, 1:136–138), which cannot be discussed here. Galling ("Bagoas," 161–178), who preferred the later dating, drew a very close connection between the Bagoses crisis and Ezra's letter of appointment (Ezra 7:12–26). Whether all details of this Aramaic text, however, can be regarded historically reliable, is rather improbable.
42 Cf. Joel 4:16–17; Mic 1:2; 4:7, 13; Zeph 3:19; Hag 2:7–9; Zech 12:9; 14:3, 11b–12, 20–21.
43 For this topic cf. Pss 46:7; 48:5–8; 76:4–6.

The existing compositions of the Minor Prophets – the Joel-Corpus and the Haggai-Zechariah-Corpus[44] according to Wöhrle – provided the redactors with a theological basis for both: to understand their present distress as YHWH's just judgment on his own disobedient people[45] and to express the hope that YHWH would judge all the nations including the world power for their unreasonable conduct against YHWH's people and his temple in future. Accordingly, this universal judgment would lead to the salvation of the people, the reestablishment of Jerusalem's holiness, and the enrichment of its cult so it would never be disturbed again by the intrusion of strangers (Joel 4:17; Zech 14:20–21).

This is not the place to unfold all the possible allusions to this historical background that may be detected in the Foreign-Nation-Redaction I. The intention is only to demonstrate that the Foreign-Nation-Redaction I is a reasonable theological response to the historical situation during the last decade of the 5th century, if this period has been reconstructed properly.

References

Albertz, R. *A History of Israelite Religion in the Old Testament Period*. 2 vols. OTL. Louisville: Westminster John Knox, 1994.
– *Israel in Exile: The History and Literature of the Sixth Century B.C.E.* Studies in Biblical Literature 3. Atlanta: Society of Biblical Literature, 2003.
– "Purity Strategies and Political Interests in the Policy of Nehemiah." Pp. 199–206 in *Confronting the Past: Archaeological and Historical Essays on Ancient Israel in Honor of William G. Dever*. Edited by S. Gitin et al. Winona Lake: Eisenbrauns, 2006.
– "The Controversy about Judean versus Israelite Identity and the Persian Government: A New Interpretation of the Bagoses Story (Jewish Antiquities XI.297–301)." Pp. 483–504 in *Judah and the Judeans in the Achaemenid Period: Negotiating Identity in an International Context*. Edited by G. Knoppers et al. Winona Lake: Eisenbrauns, 2011.
– "Der Streit der Deuteronomisten um das richtige Verständnis der Geschichte Israels." Pp. 1–21 in *Geschichte Israels und deuteronomistisches Geschichtsdenken*. Edited by P. Mommer and A. Scherer. FS W. Thiel. AOAT 380. Münster: Ugarit-Verlag, 2011.
Barton, J. *Joel and Obadiah: A Commentary*. OTL. Louisville: Westminster John Knox, 2001.

---

44   See Wöhrle, *Sammlungen*, 285–385.387–460.
45   In the Bagoses story of Josephus the temple's defilement by the Persians and the period of suppression is also understood as a divine punishment, but in this case especially for the crime of the high priest, cf. §300.

Briant, P. *From Cyrus to Alexander: A History of the Persian Empire*. Winona Lake: Eisenbrauns, 2002.

Dušek, J. *Les Manuscrits araméens du Wadi Daliyeh et la Samarie vers 450–332 av. J.-C.* Culture and History of the Ancient Near East 30. Leiden: Brill, 2007.

Elliger, K. "Ein Zeugnis aus der jüdischen Gemeinde im Alexanderjahr 332 v. Chr.: Eine territorialgeschichtliche Studie zu Sach 9,1–8." *ZAW* 62 (1950) 63–115.

– *Das Buch der zwölf Kleinen Propheten II: Die Propheten Nahum, Habakuk, Zephanja, Haggai, Sacharja, Maleachi.* ATD 25. 7ᵗʰ ed. Göttingen: Vandenhoeck & Ruprecht, 1975.

Galling, K. "Bagoas und Esra." Pp. 149–184 in *Studien zur Geschichte Israels im persischen Zeitalter.* Edited by idem. Tübingen: Mohr, 1964.

Grabbe, L.L. "Who Was the Bagoses of Josephus (Ant. 11.7.1, §§297–301)?" *Transeu* 5 (1992) 49–55.

– *Judaism from Cyrus to Hadrian.* 2 vols. Minneapolis: Fortress, 1992.

Gunneweg, A.H.J. *Geschichte Israels bis Bar Kochba.* Theologische Wissenschaft 2. 2ⁿᵈ ed. Stuttgart: Kohlhammer, 1972.

Hanhart, R. *Dodekapropheton 7.1: Sacharja 1–8.* BKAT 14,7. Neukirchen-Vluyn: Neukirchener, 1998.

Jeremias, J. *Der Prophet Hosea.* ATD 24,1. Göttingen: Vandenhoeck & Ruprecht, 1983.

– *Der Prophet Amos.* ATD 24,2. Göttingen: Vandenhoeck & Ruprecht, 1995.

– *Die Propheten Joel, Obadja, Jona, Micha.* ATD 24,3. Göttingen: Vandenhoeck & Ruprecht, 2007.

Kessler, R. *Micha.* Herders theologischer Kommentar zum Alten Testament. Freiburg: Herder, 1999.

Kottsieper, I. "Die Religionspolitik der Achämeniden und die Juden von Elephantine." Pp. 150–178 in *Religion und Religionskontakte im Zeitalter der Achämeniden.* Edited by R. Kratz. Veröffentlichungen der Wissenschaftlichen Gesellschaft für Theologie 22. Gütersloh: Kaiser and Gütersloher, 2002.

Kratz, R.G. "Der zweite Tempel zu Jeb und zu Jerusalem." Pp. 60–78 in *Das Judentum im Zeitalter des Zweiten Tempels.* Edited by idem. FAT 42. Tübingen: Mohr, 2004.

Lecoq, P. *Les inscriptions de la Perse achéménide.* L'aube des peuples. Paris: Gallimard, 1997.

Lemaire, A. "Administration in Fourth-Century B.C.E. Judah in the light of Epigraphy and Numismatics." Pp. 53–74 in *Judah and the Judeans in the Fourth Century B.C.E.* Edited by O. Lipschits et al. Winona Lake: Eisenbrauns, 2007.

Lipschits, O. "Achaemenid Imperial Policy, Settlement Processes in Palestine, and the Status of Jerusalem in the Middle of the Fifth Century B.C.E." Pp. 19–52 in *Judah and the Judeans in the Persian Period.* Edited by idem and W. Oeming. Winona Lake: Eisenbrauns, 2006.

Magen, Y. "The Dating of the First Phase of the Samaritan Temple on Mount Gerizim in Light of Archaeological Evidence." Pp. 157–211 in *Judah and the Judeans in the Fourth Century B.C.E.* Edited by O. Lipschits et al. Winona Lake: Eisenbrauns, 2007.

Marcus, R. *Jewish Antiquities IX-XI*. Vol. 6 of *Josephus*. London: Heinemann & Cambridge: Harvard University Press, reprint 1958.

Mays, J.L. *Amos: A Commentary*. OTL. London: SCM, 1969.

– *Hosea: A Commentary*. OTL. London: SCM, 1969.

– *Micah: A Commentary*. OTL. London: SCM, 1976.

Miller, J.M. and Hayes, J.H. *A History of Ancient Israel and Judah*. OTL. Philadelphia: Westminster, 1986.

Nogalski, J.D. *Literary Precursors to the Book of the Twelve*. BZAW 217. Berlin: de Gruyter, 1993.

– *Redactional Processes in the Book of the Twelve*, BZAW 218. Berlin: de Gruyter, 1993.

Porten, B. and Yardeni, A. *Textbook of Aramaic Documents from Ancient Egypt*. 4 vols. Jerusalem: Bazael Porten & Winona Lake: Eisenbrauns, 1986–1999.

Rooke, D.W. *Zadok's Heirs: The Role and Development of the High Priesthood in Ancient Israel*. Oxford Theological Monographs. Oxford: Oxford University Press, 2000.

Roth, M. *Israel und die Völker im Zwölfprophetenbuch: Eine Untersuchung zu den Büchern Joel, Jona, Micha und Nahum*. FRLANT 210. Göttingen: Vandenhoeck & Ruprecht, 2005.

Rudolph, W. *Hosea*. KAT 13,1. Gütersloh: Gütersloher, 1966.

– *Joel – Amos – Obadja – Jona*. KAT 13,2. Gütersloh: Gütersloher, 1971.

– *Micha – Nahum – Habakuk – Zephanja*. KAT 13,3. Gütersloh: Gütersloher, 1975.

– *Haggai – Sacharja 1–8 – Sacharja 9–14 – Maleachi*. KAT 13,4. Gütersloh: Gütersloher, 1976.

Schart, A. *Die Entstehung des Zwölfprophetenbuches: Neubearbeitungen von Amos im Rahmen schriftenübergreifender Redaktionsprozesse*. BZAW 260. Berlin: de Gruyter, 1998.

Schwartz, D.R. "On Some Papyri and Josephus' Sources and Chronology for the Persian Period." *JSJ* 21 (1990) 175–199.

Sweeney, M.A. *The Twelve Prophets*. 2 vols. Berit Olam. Collegeville: Order of St. Benedict, 2000.

– *Zephaniah: A Commentary*. Hermeneia. Minneapolis: Fortress, 2003.

Torrey, C.C. "The Two Persian Officers Named Bagoas." *AJSL* 56 (1936) 300–301.

Walser, G. *Persepolis: Die Königspfalz des Darius*. Tübingen: Wasmuth, 1980.

Williamson, H.G.M. "Early-Post Exilic Judean History." Pp. 3–45 in *Studies in the Persian Period: History and Historiography*. Edited by idem. FAT 38. Tübingen: Mohr, 2004.

– "The Historical Value of Josephus' Jewish Antiquities XI. 297–301." Pp. 74–89 in *Studies in the Persian Period: History and Historiography*. Edited by idem. FAT 38. Tübingen: Mohr, 2004.

Wöhrle, J. *Die frühen Sammlungen des Zwölfprophetenbuches: Entstehung und Komposition*. BZAW 360. Berlin: de Gruyter, 2006.

– *Der Abschluss des Zwölfprophetenbuches: Buchübergreifende Redaktionsprozesse in den späten Sammlungen*. BZAW 389. Berlin: de Gruyter, 2008.

Wolff, H.W. *Dodekapropheton 1: Hosea*. BKAT 14,1. 2nd ed. Neukirchen-Vluyn: Neukirchener, 1965.

– *Dodekapropheton 2: Joel und Amos*. BKAT 14,2. 2nd ed. Neukirchen-Vluyn:
   Neukirchener, 1975.
– *Dodekapropheton 4: Micha*. BKAT 14,4. Neukirchen-Vluyn: Neukirchener,
   1982.
– *Dodekapropheton 6: Haggai*. BKAT 14,6. Neukirchen-Vluyn: Neukirchener,
   1986.

Diaspora or no Diaspora?
Some Remarks on the Role of Egypt and Babylon in the Book of the Twelve

ANSELM C. HAGEDORN

Humboldt-Universität zu Berlin

Introduction

It is an exegetical truism that words against foreign nations form an integral part of biblical prophecy.[1] This observation allows for the conclusion that ancient Israel defines itself against the background of its neighbours. Normally, such oracles consist of an announcement of future doom on a specific ruler, city, or nation and of a prophetic proclamation that YHWH will enact judgment upon the nations.[2] The audience for such an oracle is almost exclusively Israel and the origin of such oracles might have been war settings.[3]

> "In such cases the punishment announced for the foreign nation might be described not so much in terms of its disastrous consequences for them as conversely in terms of its beneficial consequences for the audience ... The announcement of punishment concerning the enemy nation thus might include elements of an announcement of salvation for the people of Yahweh, to be overheard (as it were) by them ..., so that the prophecy of punishment against a foreign nation functioned for Israel or Judah virtually as a prophecy of salvation."[4]

---

1   Cf. Barton, *Oracles*, 203: "... it seems to have come to be thought normal, even obligatory, for prophetic books to include oracles against a variety of foreign nations." The phenomenon does not seem to be limited to the Hebrew Bible, see Weippert, "Fürchte dich nicht," 1–54, for the ancient Near East and Hagedorn, "Foreigners," 432–448, for Greek parallels.

2   See Raabe, "Oracles," 236–257.

3   Thus Christensen, *Transformations*, whose argument, however, that any word against a foreign nation originated in a concrete oracle of a priest or a prophet immediately before the battle is difficult to maintain and Hagedorn, "Foreigners," 439. The arguments against such a political use of words against foreign people put forward in Geyer, "Look," 80–87, are hardly convincing.

4   Floyd, *Minor Prophets*, 636; for a different view see Albertz, *Exilszeit*, 148: "Die in der Forschung weit verbreitete Meinung, es handele sich bei den Völkerworten um eine

The oracles can be seen as part of a discourse employing stereotypes that shed light on the question how the "other" is constructed in the Hebrew Bible.[5] These oracles are only possible because the hearers/ readers already possess a certain knowledge of the actions/characteristics of the foreigners. Whether such knowledge is historically accurate or based on concrete encounters is not always important,[6] because the imagined community – to use a term applied by Anderson[7] – utilizes the imagined adversary to proclaim salvation for one's own group.

These quasi form-critical remarks should not evoke the impression that the oracle against foreign nations is a fixed category, easily detectable by a certain form or *Gattung*.[8] Rather, we have to stress that these words are only connected by their contents (and probably their intention).[9]

The recent interest in the processes at work in the literary development of the Book of the Twelve beyond simple catchword phenomena and direct literary quotations has also sparked new interest into the role of the nations.[10] After the groundbreaking studies by Odil H. Steck,[11] Burkard M. Zapff has used the perspective of the nations in the Book of Micah as a possible clue to the systematization of the nations' role in Joel, Jonah, and Nahum. Further, Jakob Wöhrle has detected two corpora relating to the foreign nations in the Book of the Twelve as well as an expanded corpus addressing the issue of salvation.[12] These are highly stimulating and truly proposals that pushed the boundaries of scholarship but I have to admit that they sometimes seem to lack a historical anchor.

The following contribution looks at two aspects of the oracles against foreign nations and hopes to offer some historical anchor, or at least an evaluation of the background for their origins. I am well aware that such undertaking is speculative at best but maybe some controlled speculation will provide the desired anchor for the development of theological (and historical) concepts at work in the Book of the Twelve.

---

     indirekte Heilsverkündigung für Israel, weswegen sie häufig den klassischen Gerichtspropheten abgeschrieben wurden, ist in dieser Allgemeinheit falsch."

5   See Hagedorn, "Nahum," 223–239. The rather inflationary use of the term "other" in current anthropological discourse has been critically evaluated by Fabian, "The other," 139–152.

6   For an evaluation of how Israel shapes its identity in the presence of the Assyrian threat see Machinist, "*Rab Šāqēh*," 151–168.

7   Anderson, *Communities*.

8   See the remarks in Huwyler, *Jeremia*, 2–5.

9   See Albertz, *Exilszeit*, 146.

10   See the overview of recent scholarship in Schart, "Zwölfprophetenbuch," 227–246.

11   Steck, *Abschluß*.

12   Zapff, "Perspective," 292–312; Wöhrle, *Sammlungen*, and idem, *Abschluss*.

The above stated prevalence of the oracles against foreign nations in the Book of the Twelve often blinds one in regard to the peculiarities of such collections. So let me again start with some basic observations. Almost all prophetic books within the corpus of a Book of the Twelve contain oracles against foreign nations and some books like Obadiah and Nahum seem to be solely shaped by them. The sole exception here being Hosea.[13] The complicated integration of the Book of Hosea does not need to concern us here and it will suffice to say that – maybe – the book of Hosea has to be seen as a whole as a word against the Northern Kingdom.[14]

The second observation will lead us more directly into the topic under investigation: there is a surprising silence or better to say reluctance to engage directly with the world empires. The absence of any words against Persia has long been noted and can be neglected for our enterprise as we will simply focus on the role of Babylon and Egypt.[15]

1. Babylon in the Book of the Twelve

Babylon (בבל) is mentioned by name only three times in the book of the Twelve: Mic 4:10; Zech 2:11; 6:10. In none of these three occurrences is Babylon addressed directly. Here, Mic 4:10 seems to set the tone:

> 4:10 Writhe[16] and scream,[17]
>   daughter Zion, like a woman in labor
>   for now you shall go forth from the city,
>   and dwell in open country.
>   You shall go to Babylon;
>   there you shall be delivered.
>   There YHWH[18] shall redeem you
>   from the hand of your enemies.

---

13 The complicated literary history of the book of Hosea is a vexing – and maybe un-solvable – issue of biblical scholarship; see the proposals offered in Pfeiffer, *Heilig-tum*; Vielhauer, *Werden*, and the review of scholarship in Rudnig-Zelt, "Genese," 351–386, as well as her own proposal in eadem, *Hoseastudien*.
14 For a proposal of how to integrate Hosea into a larger literary context within the Book of the Twelve, see Wöhrle, *Abschluss*, 429–437; for a more critical view see Viel-hauer's contribution, p. 55–75, in this volume.
15 On the possibility of Hab 1:5–11 being a reference to the Persians see Pfeiffer, *Jahwes Kommen*, 137–141.
16 LXX reads ὤδινε καὶ ἀνδρίζου for Hebrew חול; this can be explained as offering a translation of חיל I. and חיל II.
17 גיח qal is difficult to translate; in Job 38:8; 40:23 it refers to the bursting forth of wa-ter; BHS suggests to emend to נוח or הגה. The translation reflects the context of childbearing; see the discussion in McKane, *Micah*, 138–140.
18 LXX expands and reads κύριος ὁ θεός σου.

Babylon is simply the land of exile. The perspective is clear – only the
impact of conquest and destruction upon Judah is important. The aggressor remains strangely anonymous throughout, even though in the
context of Mic 4:9–10 it can only be Babylon. This anonymity is maintained in the following oracle Mic 4:14–5:1 and is even further stressed
by the impersonal construction מצור שם עלינו which again avoids the
naming of the aggressor. Babylon in Mic 4:10 is simply a geographical
region that designates the future dwelling place of daughter Zion – a
place from which YHWH will redeem (גאל) his people.

This view is echoed in the two other occurrences of Babylon in the
Book of the Twelve. Zech 2:11 is part of various additions to the third
vision in Zech 2:5–9;[19] this addition imitates classic prophetic speech
and thus departs from the language normally prevalent in the nightly
vision in Zech 1–8.[20] Zech 2:10–11 is addressed to a people, living in
Babylon:

> 2:10   Woe, woe! Flee from the land of the North – utterance of YHWH
> for I have dispersed you like the four winds of heaven –
> utterance of YHWH.
> 11   Woe! Escape Zion,[21]
> dwellers by the daughter of Babylon.

The verses belong to the larger context of Zech 2:10–14 and operate
with phrases taken over from other parts of Zech 1–8.[22] Within the context of Zech 2:10–14 the flight is a necessary prerequisite for the judg-

---

19   See the analysis of Hallaschka, *Haggai*, 187–193.
20   For influences of other (earlier?) prophetic material on Zech 2:10–17 see Boda,
     "Hoy," 171–190. Here – as well as in Boda, "Horns," 22–41 – he argues that in Zech
     1:7–6:15 Zechariah employs earlier prophetic material to announce judgment and
     doom to Babylon. Boda sees this adaptation as a being part of a development of a
     "prophetic tradition *contra* Babylon, highlighting that a key signal of restoration
     would have been the judgment of Babylon for their abuse of Israel during exile"
     (Boda, "Hoy," 190). If Boda is correct and the historical context is indeed the Babylo-
     nian revolts under Gaumata it remains surprising why a direct address against Bab-
     ylon is avoided.
21   The question here is whether ציון is a vocative or an accusative of direction. LXX
     seems to think of a direction (εἰς Σιων ἀνασώζεσθε) while the paraphrase of the Tar-
     gum points to a vocative understanding: אכלו לכנשתא דציון ואימרו לה. Since Zion
     is normally used in parallel to Jerusalem in Zech 1–8 (1:17; 2:11, 14; 8:2, 3), Rudolph,
     Haggai, 87, has argued that Zion cannot be used denoting the people of the Diaspora.
     If one follows his proposal (as done by Willi-Plein, *Haggai*, 78), the feminine parti-
     ciple יושבת lacks a clear reference point. Following Hanhart, *Sacharja*, 117, "Zion"
     will be understood as a vocative, denoting the daughter Zion, dwelling amongst the
     daughter Babel.
22   ארץ צפון is probably taken from Zech 6:6, 8 and the same can be said of the addition
     in v. 10b as ארבע רוחות השמים is only found in Zech 2:10 and Zech 6:5. The verse,
     added to v. 10a by כי, expands the perspective as it now also includes the worldwide
     Diaspora (Hallaschka, *Haggai*, 189).

ment against the foreign nations in Zech 2:13a (כִּי הִנְנִי מֵנִיף אֶת יָדִי עֲלֵיהֶם).[23]

The language here is reminiscent of the Book of Jeremiah and other Babel texts in the Hebrew Bible but an important change has happened.[24] While texts like Jer 50:42, 51:33, Isa 47:1, and Ps 137:8 address the daughter of Babylon directly and announce doom to her, such is not the case in Zech 2:11. Here, Babylon is again simply used to designate the dwelling place of the exiled population of Judah. Though Zech 2:12–13 supplements the summons to flee to Zion by an announcement of YHWH's visitation of the nations – Babel is no longer the sole focus here (as is the case in Isaiah and Jeremiah) but it is anonymously subsumed under the general term 'nations.'

In Zech 6:10 Babylon has completely faded into the background:

> 6:10 Take[25] from the gôlah, from Heldai, Tobijah, and Jedaiha,[26] who have come from Babylon,[27] and you come on this day and come to the house of Josiah, son of Zephaniah.

Babylon is only the place from where the Gola returned and the mentioning of the Gola refers back to Zech 6:8,[28] where it is explicitly stated that those who went to the North (אֶל אֶרֶץ צָפוֹן) have placed YHWH's spirit there (הֵנִיחוּ אֶת רוּחִי) – a necessary requirement for the reorganization of the community.[29] Here, in an addition to the original night visions, a peaceful co-existence (Zech 6:9–13) between worldly and spiritual leadership is envisaged as the new order of the post-exilic community and this order is erected and guaranteed by members of the return-group as is the case in Ezra and Nehemiah.[30]

As Babylon and the Babylonians are generally seen as the archetypical enemy in biblical literature, such a scarcity of occurrences of Babylon comes as a surprise. Especially in the Book of Obadiah the absence of Babylon is remarkable as the literary and possibly also the

---

23 Hallaschka, *Haggai*, 189.
24 מֵאֶרֶץ צָפוֹן only in Jer 3:18; 6:22; 10:22; 16:15; 23:8; 31:8; 50:9; Zech 2:10 and without מִן Jer 46:10; Zech 6:6, 8. בַּת בָּבֶל only in Isa 47:1; Jer 50:42; 51:33; Ps 137:8.
25 *Inf. abs.* is used as an imperative here; see GK §113 and LXX (λάβε).
26 LXX reinterprets the names as offices, which is probably triggered by v. 14 (Hanhart, *Sacharja*, 406): παρὰ τῶν ἀρχόντων καὶ παρὰ τῶν χρησίμων αὐτῆς καὶ παρὰ τῶν ἐπεγνωκότων.
27 The position of the relative clause is unusual – because of the 3rd pers. pl. it has to refer to the members of the Gola.
28 Thus also Hallaschka, *Haggai*, 260.
29 See Lux, "JHWHs 'Herrlichkeit'," 220–221, and Uehlinger, "Policy," 347.
30 On the influence of the return-group on the construction of the post-exilic community see Williamson, *Studies*, 25–45; Karrer, *Ringen*, 149–161; Rothenbusch, "Auseinandersetzung," 112–126.

historical setting of the booklet points to the Babylonian conquest and destruction of Jerusalem. An event that left traces in almost all biblical books is carefully pushed into the background here and simply serves as the point of departure for an evaluation of Israel's relationship to Edom. In this process the role of Babylon remains completely un-addressed. This goes so far that Babylon is not even mentioned and simply described as foreign (זר and נכר in Obad 11). We can see that the perspective of this particular nation differs remarkably from the view put forward in the Books of Isaiah and Jeremiah. In those writings – to use an expression applied by Rainer Albertz – vengeance on Baby-lon becomes the *cantus firmus* of the oracles against the foreign na-tions.[31] Such a theology of retribution is alien to the Book of the Twelve but several passages introduced by הנני אליך in the Book of Nahum, however, may point into such a direction. Here we have arrived at a second aspect of the role of Babylon in the Book of the Twelve.

One can trace several literary strata that seem to reflect anonymous-ly the period of Babylonian rule in several books within the Dodeka-propheton.[32] Here – amongst others – Habakkuk and Nahum come to mind. As far as the Book of Habakkuk is concerned, Jakob Wöhrle has shown that a Babylonian layer was introduced into the book that trans-forms its original intention into an oracle against an enemy from the outside.[33] Intriguing as this proposal may be, he has then to concede that the Babylonians – only mentioned in Hab 1:6aα – are used in ex-emplary fashion for any foreign nation that threatens Israel and that they do not represent the historical Babylonians as such.[34] Maybe it is more likely to follow Henrik Pfeiffer here and regard את הכשדים as a gloss to the following הגוי here;[35] this probably explains the apparent lack of the Babylonians in the rest of the book a bit better. Also in the context of (Hos) Nah–Zeph, i.e. the Assyrian period, any reference to the Babylonians would be strangely out of place.

The book of Nahum is a different matter.[36] Here after the fall of As-syria, the fate of Nineveh is transferred to Babylon, which is now seen as the aggressor that threatens Israel and no longer as the welcome

---

31 Albertz, *Exilszeit*, 155–156.
32 See also the literary implications in regard to the redaction history of the Book of the Twelve in Bosshard-Nepustil, *Rezeptionen*, 277–359, who detects an "Assur/Babel-Redaktion" that aligns the Dodekapropheton with the order First Isaiah – Jeremiah.
33 See Wöhrle, *Abschluss*, 319–322.
34 "Die Babylonier dürften daher wohl beispielhaft für eine dem Volk feindlich ge-sinnte Großmacht zu verstehen sein" (Wöhrle, *Abschluss*, 321).
35 Pfeiffer, *Jahwes Kommen*, 138–139.
36 For a detailed literary analysis see Hagedorn, *Die Anderen*, 25–90, and Kratz, "Pe-scher," 123–141.

destroyer of the Assyrian tyrant. Prerequisite for this addition has been the fact that Nineveh indeed fell in 612 B.C.E., thus providing proof for the authenticity of the prophecy. We encounter the first words of this redaction in Nah 1:11, a problematic verse, since the feminine suffix in Nah 1:11a (ממך יצא) is in the need of a feminine reference word and the only feminine word encountered so far has been Nineveh in Nah 1:1a.[37] The linguistic evidence seems to support such a view: The unusual construction מן + suffix followed by יצא is found seven times in the Hebrew Bible (Gen 17:6; Isa 49:17; Ezek 5:4; Nah 1:11; Zech 10:4; Job 28:5; Dan 8:9) and describes in the book of Nahum the going out from a place – thus it is similar to the more common construction יצא מן. In this way, for example, the book of Micah can speak of God, saying כי הנה יהוה יצא ממקמו (Mi 1:3a) and Deuteronomy constructs the idea in a similar way when referring to the Cretans: כפתרים היצאים מכפתור (Deut 2:23). The person who comes forth from Nineveh is called חשב על יהוה רעה; the masculine participle identifies the person as the (Assyrian) king who resides in Nineveh. In contrast to Nah 2:1 the יעץ בליעל is not yet personified.[38] Rather, בליעל is used in an attributive sense here, similar for example to the use in Prov 6:12 (אדם בליעל). Furthermore, YHWH is introduced as the one who will bring destruction to the enemies and salvation to Judah. This is done in the divine speech Nah 1:12–14. The passage is again full of changes in person. At the same time, the passage uses language well known from the deuteronomistic parts of the Bible, when it speaks of פסל ומסכה (cf. Deut 27:15; Jud 17:3, 4; 18:14, 17, 18; Isa 42:17; Hab 2:8) as well as employing elements which show a certain familiarity with the treaty literature of the Ancient Near East.[39] These features of the pericope make it unlikely that the text originated in preexilic times. Furthermore the problematic כי קלות in Nah 1:14b sounds like a conclusion to an oracle of doom for the (Assyrian) king.[40] We encounter the work of this redaction on two further places: Nah 2:14 and Nah 3:5–7*. Both times the addition is introduced with the same formula: הנני אליך נאם יהוה צבאות again stressing that the destruction of Nineveh is now seen as an

---

37 Cf. Cathcart, *Nahum*, 62, different Roberts, *Nahum*, 53, who wants to regard the suffix as referring to Judah; this follows a proposal made by Jeremias, *Kultprophetie*, 53–55, and is recently been taken up by Wöhrle, *Abschluss*, 60–63, who also regards the basic layer (*Grundschicht*) of Nahum addressing Judah rather than Nineveh.

38 Spronk, *Nahum*, 56.

39 VTE 435–436.472.484; cf. VTE 525.538–539.543; Sefire I C 24–25; Sefire II A 4–5; KAI 13:7–8; 14:8–10.11–12; 225:9–11; 226:10; 228:13–14; Bukan line 3.

40 There are many proposals for the emendation of כי קלות. See the detailed discussion in Cathcart, "Curses," 145–146. Since all the versions support the Masoretic Text, we will maintain the reading provided.

act of the hand of God.[41] It is interesting that elements from the compositional layer of the book are taken up and are transformed. For example the image of the powerful family of lions, used in Nah 2:12–13 as an image for the strength of the Assyrian army (cf. the similar use in 2 Sam 1:23; Isa 15:9; Jer 2:15; 4:7; 50:17; Ps 57:4; 58:7; 91:13) now triggers the remark וכפיריך תאכל חרב in Nah 2:14. The same can be said of the image of the harlot. In Nah 3:4 the harlot was used to describe the fascination and power that Nineveh exercises over her enemies (or better, her subjects). In contrast to such a view Nah 3:5–7* takes up the female imagery and transforms it into a public shaming at the hand of YHWH. This second layer from the time of the exile makes it abundantly clear that YHWH will be responsible for the destruction of Nineveh – in accord with exilic theology and thinking, a concrete political entity of the oldest stratum (Babylon) is replaced by the divinity who now acts on behalf of his subjects.

At the same time, Babylon is not mentioned even though the threat of the Babylonians or a reflection about the Babylonian period prompted this addition to the book of Nahum.

2. Egypt in the Book of the Twelve

A similar reluctance can be observed when looking at the role of Egypt in the Book of the Twelve. Out of the 29 occurrences of Egypt (מצרים) in Hosea–Malachi the majority of the passages refer to Egypt simply as a geographical location, i.e. either the place from where YHWH brought Israel or a place where Israel turns in time of (political) need.[42] The name Egypt – it appears – is linked to the Exodus and to go to Egypt for political help is – especially in the Book of Hosea – condemned. Outside such references only Joel 4:19; Amos 3:9; Nah 3:9; Zech 10:11 and Zech 14:18–19 speak of Egypt.

Here Amos 3:9 can be quickly dismissed for our enterprise as the text simply uses Egypt in parallel to Ashdod[43] as addressee for the mes-

---

41 On the formula הנני אליך see Humbert, "Herausführungsformel," 101–108.
42 מצרים in Hos 2:17; 7:11, 16; 8:13; 9:3, 6; 11:1, 5, 11; 12:2, 10, 14; 13:4; Joel 4:19; Amos 2:10; 3:1, 9; 4:10; 8:8; 9:5, 7; Mic 6:4; 7:15; Nah 3:9; Hag 2:5; Zech 10:10, 11; 14:18, 19 and מצור in Mic 7:12.
43 LXX changes to Assur giving the passage a more universalistic outlook. Also Assur and Egypt occur together in texts like Isa 7:18; Hos 11:5 as Israel's archenemies. In Amos 1:8 LXX maintains אשדוד and translates ἐξ Ἀζώτου.

sage against Samaria.[44] Egypt serves a (stereotypical) representative of
a major foreign power here that should witness the social injustices in
Samaria.[45] In the course of the announcement against Samaria that follows in Amos 3:9–4:3 Egypt does not reappear or play any further role.

Nah 3:9 is a complicated verse within the last original oracle against
Nineveh/Assyria (Nah 3:8*–10*, 11–14, 15*).

> 3:8 Are you better than No-Ammon,
>   situated by streams '...'[46]
>   whose strength the sea,
>   water was her wall
>   9 Cush was her strength,[47]
>   and Egypt – there was no end.
>   Put[48] and the Libyans
>   were your[49] allies.

A problematic change of suffixes combined with a certain lack of clarity
regarding who exactly is addressed make interpretation difficult. What
we can deduce however is that Egypt is set in parallel to Cush (i.e.
Ethiopia) and possibly designates the realm of power of Thebes, which
is mentioned in the preceding verses that introduces the last oracle
against Nineveh (התיטבי מנא אמון).[50] The context is then the destruction of a major center of power (Thebes) despite her apparent invinci-
bility.[51] A theological evaluation of such destruction is not given as the
events of the Theban destruction at the hands of the Assyrians in the
year 664/663 B.C.E. are simply reported and used as a foil for the hubris

---

44 Paul, *Amos*, 115, has drawn attention to the fact that the passage seems to comply to
  biblical law (e.g. Deut 17:6; 19:15) where two witnesses are required "to bear eyewit-
  ness testimony to the acts of injustice committed in the north."
45 Jeremias, *Prophet*, 40; Sweeney, *Prophets*, 2:222, comments: "It seems likely that
  Amos' call to Ashdod and Egypt envisions the ultimate collapse of friendly trade relations between Israel and Egypt as a consequence of Israel's 'sin'."
46 Nah 3:8aγ is a gloss (against Fabry, *Nahum*, 202) that wants to explain the unusual
  use of יִם here; as in Isa 19:5 יִם is used to refer to the Nile.
47 Rare suffix of the 3rd pers. f.; see JM §94h.
48 LXX οὐκ ἔστιν πέρας τῆς φυγῆς does not recognize the name and thinks of פלט.
49 On the basis of the Septuagint (βοηθοὶ αὐτῆς) almost all commentators change the
  suffix of the 2nd pers. sg. to בעזרתה (e.g. Roberts, *Nahum*, 68; Spronk, *Nahum*, 130;
  Perlitt, *Propheten*, 31); MT is maintained – as it should – by Cathcart, *Nahum*, 135, and
  Fabry, *Nahum*, 202–203.
50 On the function of Thebes in Nahum see Schneider, "Nahum," 63–73, and Huddlestun, "Nahum," 97–110.
51 "Im Nahumbuch als formativem Text ist der Untergang Thebens bereits von einer
  einmaligen Erfahrung mit assyrischer Eroberungspolitik zum Teil des verteilten
  Wissens des kollektiven Gedächtnisses geworden." (Berlejung, "Erinnerungen,"
  340).

of Nineveh.[52] In other words: The prestige of the conquest of Thebes becomes a paradigm for the doom of Assyria.[53]

The doom of Egypt that was simply reported as historical fact in Nah 3:9, and utilized in a word against Assyria, is paired with the desolation of Edom in Joel 4:19 and moved outside the realm of historical reality:

> 4:19 Egypt shall become a desolation
>   and Edom shall become a desolate wilderness,
>   because of the violence done to the children of Judah,
>   in whose land they have shed innocent blood.[54]

The desolation of Joel 4:19 stands in stark contrast to the arcadian vision of the preceding verse (Joel 4:18) where the fruitfulness of a renewed Judah with its miraculous water supply is described.[55] As such the desolation of the traditional fertile Egypt places a final emphasis on the wondrous deeds of v. 18.[56] Also the verse introduces concrete nations and thus narrows the focus of the otherwise universal outlook of the prophecy of Joel; in all other instances references to non-Israelite entities are simply made to "people" (גוים) the exception to the rule being the late addition in Joel 4:4–8. Both, Joel 4:19 and 4:4–8 can be seen as passages that aim at a concretization of the judgment against the people announced in the book of Joel.[57] That Edom appears in such texts is hardly surprising, if one considers the role of the Edomites in the Book of the Twelve.[58] The mentioning of Egypt, however, is – at least in the context of the Book of the Twelve – surprising. As the verse seems to presuppose an invasion of Judean territory by Edom and Egypt, for which a concrete historical date is difficult to determine.[59] Also the language of the verse seems to fit much better with simply Edom than with Edom and Egypt together. If one takes the subsequent book of Amos into consideration this uneasiness persists, as Egypt is strangely absent from the cycle in Amos 1:3–2:16.

The last references to Egypt are found in second part of the Book of Zechariah (10:10–11; 14:18–19). First, Zechariah 10 pairs Egypt with

---

52   The cuneiform texts relating to the siege and conquest of Thebes are collected in Onasch, *Eroberungen*, 93–127.
53   Berlejung, "Erinnerungen," 340.
54   Translation according to Barton, *Joel*, 109.
55   Barton, *Joel*, 110.
56   Rudolph, *Joel*, 87.
57   See Wöhrle, *Sammlungen*, 433–434, and Hagedorn, *Die Anderen*, 274–276.
58   On Edom see Assis, "Edom," 1–20, and Hagedorn, "Edom," 41–58.
59   Roth, *Israel*, 108 takes up an earlier proposal by Treves, "Date," 149–156, and places the events alluded to in Joel 4:19 during the Ptolemaic period. Similarly Barton, *Joel*, 110.

Assyria as places where dispersed Judeans are living, stating that from both ends of the known earth will the people return:

10:10 I will bring them back from the land of Egypt;
           and from Assyria I will gather them.
       To the land of Gilead and to Lebanon I will bring them,
           till no room is found for them.
   11 He will traverse the sea of stress,
           he will smite the rolling sea,
           and all the depths of the stream will dry up.
       The splendor of Assyria will be brought low,
           and the scepter of Egypt will pass away.
   12 I will make them mighty in Yahweh;
           in his name they will go about – utterance of Yahweh.[60]

Zech 10:10, in a way, offers a concretization to the 'remote places' (מרחקים) mentioned in v. 9,[61] where YHWH has sowed his people and where they live and give birth to sons. Egypt and Assyria in v. 10 are then the places for the Eastern and Western Diaspora whose members are so numerous that they will even populate Lebanon and Gilead.

Zech 10:11–12 seem to belong to a different literary layer as the abrupt shift to the 3rd pers. pl. indicates.[62] The passing away of the scepter of Egypt – possibly a reference to the conquest of Ptolemaic Egypt by the Seleucids – is paired with the decline of the splendor of Assyria.[63] This pairing indicates that both again function as ciphers for both ends of the world, not as concrete nations.[64] If that is the case, Zech 10 does not envisage the destruction of Egypt but simply uses it as pars pro toto for a universal judgment. Also we need to note that the splendor (גאון) of Assur and the scepter (שבט) of Egypt are mentioned – this seems to point to a destruction of the ruling classes rather than to an annihilation of every inhabitant.[65]

---

60 Translation Meyers and Meyers, *Zechariah 9–14*, 179.
61 מרחק as a designation for far away places see Isa 13:5; 46:11; Jer 4:16; 6:20; 31:10.
62 Zech 10:6–10, 12 is shaped as a divine speech that focuses on return and salvation for Israel, while Zech 10:3b, 4–5, 11 are concerned with YHWH's judgment against the nations (see כי פקד יהוה צבאות in Zech 10:3b).
63 Assyria can also be used for Syria as Ezra 6:22 indicates; see also Herodotus, *Hist.* 7.63: οὗτοι δὲ ὑπὸ μὲν Ἑλλήνων καλέονται Σύρια, ὑπὸ δὲ τῶν βαρβάρων Ἀσσύρια ἐκλήθησαν.
64 Willi-Plein, *Haggai*, 175; Steck, *Abschluß*, 78–79, proposes that Assur in Zech 10:11 includes Babylon.
65 Also one has to note that the destruction of Egypt and Assyria is connected with mythological language echoing the Exodus in v. 11a.

Zech 14 is a notoriously difficult text and we cannot even attempt to solve its literary problems here.[66] Egypt is mentioned as part of the description of a general pilgrimage of the nations to Jerusalem in 14:16–19; in the current context of the chapter, this pilgrimage follows the judgment on the people carried out in 14:12–15:

14:16 And it will come to pass: All who survive[67] of all those nations that came up against Jerusalem shall come up year by year to bow low to the King, YHWH of Hosts, and to celebrate the Festival of Booths.
17 Any of the earth's communities (מִשְׁפָּחוֹת)[68] that do not come up to Jerusalem to bow low to the King, YHWH of Hosts,[69] shall receive no rain.[70]
18 However, if the community of Egypt does not come up and does not go, it shall not[71] be visited by the same affliction with which YHWH will strike the other nations that do not come up to observe the Festival of Booths.
19 Such shall be the punishment of Egypt and of all other nations that do not come up to observe the Festival of Booths.

The verse mentioning Egypt is fraught with problems of a text critical and a literary historical nature. It remains unclear whether Egypt will suffer a special punishment or whether it is simply made explicit that Egypt will not escape YHWH's judgment. On a purely agricultural level, withholding the rain from Egypt would not make sense as "Egypt's traditional fecundity ... was a gift of the Nile, not of abundant rainfall. Lack of rainfall would not affect the economy of Egypt the way it would all other areas of the Near East."[72] A second reason for a special treatment of Egypt may be deduced from Zech 10:10 – if Egypt is the home of the Diaspora it is hardly surprising that it is singled out. Furthermore it is clear that Zech 14:16–18 envisages an apolitical

66 See the discussion in Gärtner, *Jesaja 66*, 86–89; Wöhrle, *Abschluss*, 112–124, and Bilić, *Jerusalem*, 172–176.
67 The root יתר also occurs in Zech 13:8 and 14:2 both times referring to Israel. "Thus in employing a term that elsewhere indicates the remnant of God's people, the prophet brings the remnant of 'all the nations' ... into alignment with Israel." (Meyers and Meyers, *Zechariah 9–14*, 463).
68 The term מִשְׁפְּחוֹת הָאָרֶץ is unique in the Hebrew Bible but see הָאָרֶץ מִשְׁפְּחוֹת. On the basis of Ezek 20:32 (נִהְיֶה כַגּוֹיִם כְּמִשְׁפְּחוֹת הָאֲרָצוֹת) it seems clear that the phrase refers to foreign nations (Meyers and Meyers, *Zechariah 9–14*, 471).
69 מֶלֶךְ יהוה צְבָאוֹת only in Zech 14:16–17; but see Ps 24:10.
70 LXX offers a completely different text for v. 17b when it reads καὶ οὗτοι ἐκείνοις προστεθήσονται.
71 LXX drops the negation and reads καὶ ἐπὶ τούτοις ἔσται ἡ πτῶσις, ἣν πατάξει κύριος πάντα τὰ ἔθνη. Tg. thinks of the Nile here and reads: ולא להון יסק נינום ברם; this is taken up by Rudolph, *Haggai*, 233, who emends to ולא יעלה [להם] הים.
72 Meyers and Meyers, *Zechariah 9–14*, 474.

world,[73] i.e. a world where nations are only seen as families, families that can celebrate together with other families the Festival of Booths in Jerusalem.[74] This seems to fulfill the announcement of Zech 2:15 and revises the separation between Judahites and foreigners in worship put forth by Zech 8:20–23.[75]

Conclusion

This overview of the mentioning of Egypt and Babylon in the Book of the Twelve has detected a certain reluctance to address both geographical regions in the same manner as other nations are addressed in Joel–Malachi. As part of this reluctance, the view in the Twelve differs from Isaiah, Jeremiah (and to a certain respect also Ezekiel). Though Israel, in the Book of Hosea is accused of going down to Egypt for help, this does not lead to the development of full-fledged oracles against Egypt in the Book of the Twelve.[76] As far as the other texts are concerned, with the exception of Nah 3:9 and Amos 3:9 all occurrences of either Babylon or Egypt are of late literary origin.

The reluctance to mention or to address Babylon is particularly surprising – at least if one does not want to postulate that Babylon is no longer of interest to the authors or to assume that readers picked up their copy of Jeremiah or Isaiah when wanting to read about Babylon. Also we have to note that Assyria continues to be mentioned and used despite the fact that this Empire has long vanished from the scene. Here, Steck has argued convincingly that Assyria was transformed into a cipher for the Seleucid Empire in the late stages of the formation of the prophetic canon. Naturally one wonders why such a transformation has not happened for Babylon, even though echoes of the Babylonian period can be traced throughout the Book of the Twelve. Yet, within the internal chronology of the prophetic corpus, the Babylonian period is gapped and the books seem to jump from the end of the Assyrian period (Zephaniah) directly to Persian times (Haggai).

---

73   Steck, *Abschluß*, 58.

74   Kunz, *Zions Weg*, 37–38, has argued on the basis of Zech 12:12 (וספדה הארץ משפחות משפחות לבד) that 14:17aα can only refer to members of the Jewish community and he points to the controversy between Jerusalem and Alexandria over Sukkôth reported 2 Macc 1:9, 18; 2:16 – later, however, he has to concede: "Mit den *Sippen der Erde* können nur die Völker gemeint sein." (38).

75   On the relationship between Zech 2:15 and Zech 8:20–23 see Lux, "Überlegungen," 259–263.

76   On the role of Egypt in Hosea see Kratz, "Erkenntnis Gottes," 287–309.

As a solution to the problem I would propose that the authors of the books of the Twelve refrained from addressing Babylon and Egypt directly since both geographical locations were known as places of the Diaspora. If one were to pursue this idea further it might be possible to argue that the biblical authors were aware that it is not always possible to distinguish clearly between indigenous and Diaspora population, a fact that finds support in the new documents from the Al-Yahudu archive as well as in the numerous papyri from Elephantine.[77] Erich S. Gruen has recently argued that "Diaspora lies deeply rooted in Jewish consciousness" and that

> "[i]t existed in one form or another almost from the start, and it persists as an integral part of the Jews' experience of history. The status of absence from the center has demanded time and again that Jews confront and, in some fashion, come to terms with a seemingly inescapable concomitant of their being."[78]

If that is the case it is hardly surprising that such *Diaspora* discourses are already found in the biblical texts themselves – even though we have to admit that the discourse happening in the Book of the Twelve borders on the non-existence.[79] However, in literary surroundings where ancient Israel defines itself in relationship to and distinction from other ethnic nations this might not be surprising at all.

How such an interpretation relates to other prophetic writings such as Jeremiah and Isaiah and how it relates to the ongoing use of the cipher Assyria in the Book of the Twelve is a different matter for another contribution.

---

77 See the evidence on this point amassed in Pearce, "New Evidence," 399–411; Abraham, "Brides," 198–219, and Magdalene and Wunsch, "Slavery," 113–134. This evidence shows how much the Judean exiles were integrated into Babylonian/Persian society. Compare also 2 Macc 8:19–20 where a Jewish military contingent helps to defend Babylon against the Galatians (καὶ τὴν ἐν τῇ Βαβυλωνίᾳ τὴν πρὸς τοὺς Γαλάτας παράταξιν γενομένην); Josephus, *Ant.* 11.338, reports as part of his fictitious Alexander legend that Alexander the Great confirmed the earlier privileges granted to the Jews in Babylon and Media: παρακαλεσάντων δ᾽ αὐτόν, ἵνα καὶ τοὺς ἐν Βαβυλῶνι καὶ Μηδίᾳ Ἰουδαίους τοῖς ἰδίοις ἐπιτρέψῃ νόμοις χρῆσθαι, ἀσμένως ὑπέσχετο ποιήσειν ἅπερ ἀξιοῦσιν. Josephus continues to narrate that Alexander opened his army to the Jews and that many seized the opportunity and joined the military service (πολλοὶ τὴν σὺν αὐτῷ στρατείαν ἠγάπησαν); finally, according to the Letter of Aristeas (§ 25) the Jewish Diaspora in Egypt began during the time of Jeremiah.

78 Gruen, *Diaspora*, 232.

79 On Diaspora discourses see Hagedorn, "Absent Presence," 39–66.

References

Abraham, K. "West Semitic and Judean Brides in Cuneiform Sources from the Sixth Century BCE: New Evidence from a Marriage Contract from Al-Yahudu" *AfO* 51 (2005/2006) 198–219.

Albertz, R. *Die Exilszeit: 6. Jahrhundert v. Chr.* Biblische Enzyklopädie 7. Stuttgart: Kohlhammer, 2001.

Anderson, B. *Imagined Communities: Reflections on the Origins and Spread of Nationalism.* Rev. ed. London: Verso, 1999.

Assis, E. "Why Edom? On the Hostility Towards Jacob's Brother in Prophetic Sources." *VT* 56 (2006) 1–20.

Barton, J. *Oracles of God: Perceptions of Ancient Prophecy in Israel after the Exile.* London: Darton, Longman and Todd, 1986.

– *Joel and Obadiah.* OTL. Louisville: Westminster/John Knox, 2001.

Berlejung, A. "Erinnerungen an Assyrien in Nahum 2,4–3,19." Pp. 323–356 in *Die unwiderstehliche Wahrheit: Studien zur alttestamentlichen Prophetie.* Edited by R. Lux and E.-J. Waschke. FS A. Meinhold. Arbeiten zur Bibel und ihrer Geschichte 23. Leipzig: Evangelische Verlagsanstalt, 2006.

Bilić, N. *Jerusalem an jenem Tag: Text und Botschaft von Sach 12–14.* Forschungen zur Bibel 117. Würzburg: Echter, 2008.

Boda, M.J. "Terrifying the Horns: Persia and Babylon in Zechariah 1:7–6:15." *CBQ* 67 (2005) 22–41.

– "Hoy, Hoy: The Prophetic Origins of the Babylonian tradition in Zechariah 2:10–17." Pp. 171–190 in *Tradition in Transition: Haggai and Zechariah 1–8 in the Trajectory of Hebrew Theology.* Edited by idem and M.H. Floyd. Library of Hebrew Bible/Old Testament Studies 475. New York: T&T Clark, 2008.

Bosshard-Nepustil, E. *Rezeptionen von Jesaia 1–39 im Zwölfprophetenbuch: Untersuchungen zur literarischen Verbindung von Prophetenbüchern in babylonischer und persischer Zeit.* OBO 154. Fribourg: Universitätsverlag and Göttingen: Vandenhoeck & Ruprecht, 1997.

Cathcart, K.J. *Nahum in the Light of Northwest Semitic.* BibOr 26. Rome: Biblical Institute Press, 1973.

– "The Curses in Old Aramaic Inscriptions." Pp. 140–152 in *Targumic and Cognate Studies in Honour of Martin McNamara.* Edited by idem and M. Maher. JSOTSup 230. Sheffield: Sheffield Academic Press, 1996.

Christensen, D.L. *Transformations of the War Oracle in Old Testament Prophecy.* HDR 3. Missoula: Scholars Press, 1975.

Fabian, J. "The other revisited: Critical afterthoughts." *Anthropological Theory* 6 (2006) 139–152.

Fabry, H.-J. *Nahum,* Herders theologischer Kommentar zum Alten Testament, Freiburg: Herder, 2006.

Floyd, M.H. *Minor Prophets: Part 2.* FOTL 22. Grand Rapids: Eerdmans, 2000.

Gärtner, J. *Jesaja 66 und Sacharja 14 als Summe der Prophetie: Eine traditions- und redaktionsgeschichtliche Untersuchung zum Abschluss des Jesaja- und des Zwölfprophetenbuches.* WMANT 114. Neukirchen-Vluyn: Neukirchener, 2006.

Geyer, J.B. "Another Look at the Oracles about the Nations in the Hebrew Bible: A Response to A.C. Hagedorn." *VT* 59 (2009) 80–87.

Gruen, E.S. *Diaspora: Jews amidst Greeks and Romans*. Cambridge: Harvard University Press, 2002.

Hagedorn, A.C. "Nahum – Ethnicity and Stereotypes: Anthropological Insights into Nahum's Literary History." Pp 223–239 in *Ancient Israel: The Old Testament in its Social Context*. Edited by P.F. Esler. Minneapolis: Fortress Press, 2006.

–   "Looking at Foreigners in Biblical and Greek Prophecy." *VT* 57 (2007) 432–448.

–   "The Absent Presence: Cultural Responses to Persian Presence in the Eastern Mediterranean." Pp. 39–66 in *Judah and the Judeans in the Achaemenid Period: Negotiating Identity in an International Context*. Edited by O. Lipschits et al. Winona Lake: Eisenbrauns, 2011.

–   *Die Anderen im Spiegel: Israels Auseinandersetzung mit den Völkern in den Büchern Nahum, Zefanja, Obadja und Joel*. BZAW 414. Berlin: de Gruyter 2011.

–   "Edom in the Book of Amos and beyond." Pp. 41–58 in *Aspects of Amos: Exegesis and Interpretation*. Edited by idem and A. Mein. Library of Hebrew Bible/Old Testament Studies 536. London: T&T Clark, 2011.

Hallaschka, M. *Haggai und Sacharja 1–8: Eine redaktionsgeschichtliche Untersuchung*. BZAW 411. Berlin: de Gruyter, 2011.

Hanhart, R. *Sacharja 1,1–8,23*. BKAT 14,7.1. Neukirchen-Vluyn: Neukichener, 1998.

Huddlestun, J.R. "Nahum, Nineveh, and the Nile: The Description of Thebes in Nahum 3:8–9." *JNES* 62 (2003) 97–110.

Humbert, P. "Die Herausführungsformel 'hinnenî êlékâ'." *ZAW* 51 (1933) 101–108.

Huwyler, B. *Jeremia und die Völker: Untersuchungen zu den Völkersprüchen in Jeremia 46–49*. FAT 20. Tübingen: Mohr, 1997.

Jeremias, J. *Kultprophetie und Gerichtsverkündigung in der späten Königszeit Israels*. WMANT 35. Neukirchen-Vluyn: Neukirchener, 1970.

–   *Der Prophet Amos*. ATD 24,2. Göttingen: Vandenhoeck & Ruprecht, 1995.

Karrer, C. *Ringen um die Verfassung Judas: Eine Studie zu den theologisch-politischen Vorstellungen im Esra-Nehemia-Buch*. BZAW 308. Berlin: de Gruyter, 2001.

Kratz, R.G. "Erkenntnis Gottes im Hoseabuch." Pp. 287–309 in *Prophetenstudien: Kleine Schriften II*. Edited by idem. FAT 74. Tübingen: Mohr, 2011.

–   "Der Pescher Nahum und seine biblische Vorlage." Pp. 99–145 in *Prophetenstudien: Kleine Schriften II*. Edited by idem. FAT 74. Tübingen: Mohr, 2011.

Kunz, A. *Zions Weg zum Frieden: Jüdische Vorstellungen vom endzeitlichen Krieg und Frieden in hellenistischer Zeit am Beispiel von Sacharja 9–14*. Beiträge zur Friedensethik 33. Stuttgart: Kohlhammer, 2001.

Lux, R. "JHWHs 'Herrlichkeit' und 'Geist': Die 'Rückkehr' JHWHs in den Nachtgesichten des Sacharja." Pp. 193–222 in *Prophetie und Zweiter Tempel: Studien zu Haggai und Sacharja*. Edited by idem. FAT 65. Tübingen: Mohr, 2009.

– "'Wir wollen mit euch gehen ...': Überlegungen zur Völkertheologie Haggais und Sacharjas." Pp. 241–265 in *Prophetie und Zweiter Tempel: Studien zu Haggai und Sacharja*. Edited by idem. FAT 65. Tübingen: Mohr, 2009.

Machinist, P. "The *Rab Šāqēh* at the Wall of Jerusalem: Israelite Identity in the Face of the Assyrian 'Other'." *HS* 41 (2000) 151–168.

Magdalene, R.F. and Wunsch, C. "Slavery between Judah and Babylon: The Exilic Experience." Pp. 113–134 in *Slaves and Households in the Near East*. Edited by L. Culbertson. Oriental Institute Seminars 7. Chicago: The Oriental Institute, 2011.

McKane, W. *The Book of Micah: Introduction and Commentary*, Edinburgh: T&T Clark, 1998.

Meyers, C.L. and Meyers, E.M. *Zechariah 9–14: A New Translation with Introduction and Commentary*. AB 25C. New York: Doubleday, 1993.

Onasch, H.-U., *Die assyrischen Eroberungen Ägyptens*. 2 vols. Ägypten und Altes Testament 27,1–2. Wiesbaden: Harrassowitz, 1994.

Paul, S.M. *Amos*. Hermeneia. Minneapolis: Fortress Press, 1991.

Pearce, L.E. "New Evidence for Judeans in Babylonia." Pp. 399–411 in *Judah and the Judeans in the Persian Period*. Edited by O. Lipschits and M. Oeming. Winona Lake: Eisenbrauns, 2006.

Perlitt, L. *Die Propheten Nahum, Habakuk, Zephanja*. ATD 25,1. Göttingen: Vandenhoeck & Ruprecht, 2004.

Pfeiffer, H. *Das Heiligtum von Bethel im Spiegel des Hoseabuches*. FRLANT 183. Göttingen: Vandenhoeck & Ruprecht, 1999.

– *Jahwes Kommen von Süden: Jdc 5; Hab 3; Dtn 33 und Ps 68 in ihrem literatur- und theologiegeschichtlichen Umfeld*. FRLANT 211. Göttingen: Vandenhoeck & Ruprecht, 2005.

Raabe, P.R. "Why Prophetic Oracles against the Nations?" Pp. 236–257 in *Fortunate the Eyes That See: Essays in Honor of David Noel Freedman in Celebration of His Seventieth Birthday*. Edited by A.B. Beck et al. Grand Rapids: Eerdmans, 1995.

Roberts, J.J.M. *Nahum, Habakkuk and Zephaniah*. OTL. Louisville: Westminster/John Knox, 1991.

Roth, M. *Israel und die Völker im Zwölfprophetenbuch: Eine Untersuchung zu den Büchern Joel, Jona, Micha und Nahum*. FRLANT 210. Göttingen: Vandenhoeck & Ruprecht, 2005.

Rothenbusch, R. "Die Auseinandersetzung um die Identität Israels im Esra- und Nehemiabuch." Pp. 111–144 in *Die Identität Israels: Entwicklungen und Kontroversen in alttestamentlicher Zeit*. Edited by H. Irsigler. Herders Biblische Studien 56. Freiburg: Herder, 2009.

Rudnig-Zelt, S. "Die Genese des Hoseabuches: Ein Forschungsbericht." Pp. 351–386 in *Textarbeit: Studien zu Texten und ihrer Rezeption aus dem Alten Testament und der Umwelt Israels*. FS P. Weimar. Edited by K. Kiesow and T. Meurer. AOAT 294. Münster: Ugarit-Verlag, 2003.

– *Hoseastudien: Redaktionskritische Untersuchungen zur Genese des Hoseabuches*. FRLANT 213. Göttingen: Vandenhoeck & Ruprecht, 2006.

Rudolph, W. *Joel – Amos – Obadja – Jona*. KAT 13,2. Gütersloh: Mohr, 1971.

– *Haggai – Sacharja 1–8 – Sacharja 9–14 – Maleachi*. KAT 13,4. Gütersloh: Mohr, 1976.

Schart, A. "Das Zwölfprophetenbuch als redaktionelle Großeinheit." *TLZ* 133 (2008) 227–246.

Schneider, T. "Nahum und Theben: Zum topograpisch-historischen Hintergrund von Nah 3,8f." *BN* 44 (1988) 63–73.

Spronk, K. *Nahum*. Historical Commentary on the Old Testament. Leuven: Peeters, 1997.

Steck, O.H. *Der Abschluß der Prophetie im Alten Testament: Ein Versuch zur Frage der Vorgeschichte des Kanons*. Biblisch-Theologische Studien 17. Neukirchen-Vluyn: Neukirchener, 1991.

Sweeney, M.A. *The Twelve Prophets*. 2 vols. Berit Olam. Collegeville: Liturgical, 2000.

Treves, M. "The Date of Joel." *VT* 7 (1957) 149–156.

Uehlinger, C. "Figurative Policy, Propaganda und Prophetie." Pp. 297–349 in *Congress Volume Cambridge 1995*. Edited by J.A. Emerton. VTSup 66. Leiden: Brill, 1997.

Vielhauer, R. *Das Werden des Buches Hosea: Eine redaktionsgeschichtliche Untersuchung*. BZAW 349. Berlin: de Gruyter, 2007.

Weippert, M. "'König, fürchte dich nicht!' Assyrische Prophetie im 7. Jh. v. Chr." *Or* 71 (2002) 1–54.

Williamson, H.G.M. *Studies in Persian Period History and Historiography*. FAT 38. Tübingen: Mohr, 2004.

Willi-Plein, I. *Haggai, Sacharja, Maleachi*. ZBK 24,4. Zurich: Theologischer Verlag, 2007.

Wöhrle, J. *Die frühen Sammlungen des Zwölfprophetenbuches: Entstehung und Komposition*. BZAW 360. Berlin: de Gruyter, 2006.

– *Der Abschluss des Zwölfprophetenbuches: Buchübergreifende Redaktionsprozesse in den späten Sammlungen*. BZAW 389. Berlin: de Gruyter, 2008.

Zapff, B.M. "The Perspective on the Nations in the Book of Micah as a 'Systematization' of the Nations' Role in Joel, Jonah, Nahum?" Pp. 292–312 in *Thematic Threads in the Book of the Twelve*. Edited by P.L. Redditt and A. Schart. BZAW 325. Berlin: de Gruyter, 2003.

The Book of the Twelve and "The Great Assembly" in History and Tradition[1]

MARK LEUCHTER
Temple University

The Book of the Twelve ("the Twelve") is a tangible reality. Though questions and problems abound regarding how to understand it or the process through which it developed, we nonetheless can read it, mine it for details about how it grew, and see that it existed in some form already in the days of ancient authors who make reference to it.[2] One such reference is found in the famous Talmudic passage, Baba Bathra 14b–15a, which discusses the particulars of biblical authorship:

> [14b] Who wrote the Scriptures? Moses wrote his own book and the portion of Balaam and Job. Joshua wrote the book which bears his name and [the last] eight verses of the Pentateuch. Samuel wrote the book which bears his name and the Book of Judges and Ruth. David wrote the Book of Psalms, including in it the work of the elders, namely, Adam, Melchizedek, Abraham, Moses, Heman, Yeduthun, Asaph [15a] and the three sons of Korah. Jeremiah wrote the book which bears his name, the Book of Kings, and Lamentations. Hezekiah and his colleagues wrote Isaiah, Proverbs, the Song of Songs and Ecclesiastes.[3] *The Men of the Great Assembly* (כנסת הגדולה) *wrote Ezekiel, the Twelve Minor Prophets, Daniel and the Scroll of Esther.* Ezra wrote the book that bears his name and the genealogies of the Book of Chronicles up to his own time. This confirms the opinion of Rab, since Rab Judah has said in the name of Rab: Ezra did not leave Babylon to go up to Eretz Yisrael until he had written his own genealogy. Who then finished it [the Book of Chronicles]? Nehemiah the son of Hachaliah.

The passage is quite clear on who wrote what, but when the text comes to the Twelve, we find the ambiguous assertion that it was written by the men of the "Great Assembly" (כנסת הגדולה; from the Babylonian

---

1 In the present study, the following abbreviations are used: ARN (Avot de-Rabbi Nathan), m. (Mishnah), t. (Tosefta), Targ. (Targum), Gen. Rab. (Midrash Genesis Rabbah), y. (Talmud Yerushalmi/Palestinian Talmud). Talmudic passages without any prefixed abbreviation are drawn from the Talmud Bavli/Babylonian Talmud.
2 E.g., Sir 49:10.
3 This is represented within the Talmudic passage by the acronym ימשהק, that is, the first Hebrew letters of the Hebrew titles of each of these works (שיר, משלי, ישיהו and קהלת השרים).

kiništu).[4] Though the Twelve is an historical entity, the Great Assembly is a phantom. We have next to nothing, save a few brief wisps throughout the Talmud, regarding their origins and function ... and even then, the available evidence is not uniform in what it reveals.[5] So despite a sure and tangible literary corpus called the Twelve, the authors of Baba Bathra 15a credit its authorship to a very elusive group that has defied any concrete definition.

If the Great Assembly did exist, how is it connected, if at all, to institutions attested within the biblical record? Further, how does the ascription of the Twelve to the Great Assembly fit into the other texts this group is reported to have written (Ezekiel, Daniel and Esther)?[6] Finally, what hermeneutical purpose is actually served by having the Great Assembly serve as the authors of the Twelve? Scholars regularly note that Talmudic references to the Twelve in other places do not speak of the entire scroll upon which the prophetic material was collected but of the individual prophetic books contained therein.[7] What do the Rabbis assume about the activity of the Great Assembly in light of prophetic literature and phenomenology?

The Great Assembly in Historical Context

The introduction to Mishnah Avot is the definitive rabbinic model for situating the Great Assembly within some chronological context:[8]

> Moses received the Torah from Sinai and transmitted it to Joshua; Joshua to the elders; the elders to the prophets; and the prophets handed it down to the men of the Great Assembly. They said three things: Be deliberate in judgment, raise up many disciples, and make a fence around the Torah. (m. Avot 1.1)

There was a time when the historical authenticity of m. Avot 1 and other rabbinic references to the Great Assembly were viewed as histori-

---

4   Geller, "Influence," 44; Weinfeld, "Origin," 74.
5   The major rabbinic sources regarding the Great Assembly include ARN i.1; m. Avot 1.1; Gen. Rab. 71; Targ. Cant 7:3; Baba Bathra 15a; Berachot 33a; Megillah 2a; Yoma 69b, and several other references. The present study will focus on only the most relevant of these references in relation to the Twelve.
6   ARN i 1 also ascribes to them the Song of Songs and Ecclesiastes. By the time Baba Bathra 14b–15a was composed, however, a different account of authorship for these works appears to have dominated. See below.
7   Redditt, "Production," 29–30.
8   Mantel, "Nature," 69. This is based in part on the parallel tradition in the collection ARN, which evidences an even earlier version taken over by the Mishnaic editors. See Finkelstein, "Maxim," 457–468.

cally reliable,[9] with a biblical institution attested in Nehemiah 8–10 and founded by Ezra the scribe (as per y. Berakhot 3a; Sanhedrin 21b; Lev. Rab. 2.11; Exod. Rab. 51, Tanchuma Beshallakh 16; etc.) giving way to the Pharisaic pairs and ultimately the birth of rabbinic Judaism. This linear schema is no longer readily accepted. Abraham Kuenen long ago argued that Nehemiah 8–10 was not a testament to an actual "Great Assembly," but that the idea of such an entity was artificially derived from that text.[10] Whether or not a "Great Assembly" formed and endured subsequent to the Persian era (at least as depicted in the rabbinic sources) is also contested among historians of the late Second Temple and early rabbinic period.[11] Moreover, m. Avot 1 is now often viewed as an intellectual foundation myth for the rabbinic movement in general and the Gamalian patriarchate in particular.[12] The chapter is strongly influenced by Hellenistic forms of succession records;[13] it is therefore difficult to view m. Avot 1 as an ancient tradition taken over by Judah the Patriarch and his redactional agents behind the formation of the Mishnah.

This, however, does not demand that the Great Assembly was entirely fictitious. Mnemo-historical considerations demand a more nuanced approach,[14] especially in light of more recent historical investigation and comparative literary evidence.[15] It is much safer to conceive of the term "Great Assembly" as a conceptual trope influenced both by historical memory *and* by the Hellenistic culture in which the Mishnah was produced.[16] The authors of Avot worked during the time of the Second Sophistic, a philosophical trend in the Greco-Roman world that sought to reconnect with the cultural bastions of high antiquity.[17] In his

---

9   Cohen, *Everyman's Talmud*, xxxvi.
10   Kuenen, *Abhandlungen*, 143–158. Pace Finkelstein, "Maxim," 457.
11   Englander, "Men," 149.
12   Tropper, *Wisdom*, 101–106, with the Gamalian genealogy interpolated into earlier sources. See however Strack and Stemberger, *Introduction*, 133–139.
13   Tropper, *Wisdom*, 146–172.
14   I refer here to the method discussed at length by Assmann, *Moses*. See also the application of this approach to the thorny matter of the Exodus by Hendel, "Exodus," 601–622. Mnemonic safeguards were cultivated in early rabbinic tradition through dispassionate and ritualized repetition; see Jaffee, *Torah*, 128–140. For a more general discussion on rabbinic memory regarding the biblical past, see Yerushalmi, *Zakhor*, 15–26.
15   Steiner, "*mbqr*," 636–637.
16   Neusner's term "mythologumenon" is a fitting appellation (*Pharisees*, 1:19). See also Mantel, "Nature," 75–91.
17   By the term "reconnect," I refer to the increased interest especially in traditions relating to Greek politics, oratory and rhetoric of the 5th and 4th centuries B.C.E. in the eastern Mediterranean and Near Eastern world of the 1st through 3rd centuries C.E. Whitmarsh, *Second Sophistic*, 8–9, notes that this intellectual and cultural renais-

recent monograph on the redaction of Avot, Amram Tropper summarizes the implications of this cultural background for m. Avot 1:

> "... given the cultural and political leanings of the editor of Avot, certain common features may probably be viewed as Hellenistic ideas or cultural norms diffused across cultural lines ... in this period, the sophists continued to practise [sic] and teach all the rhetorical forms known in antiquity ... this classicism or self-conscious revival of ancient Greek culture is a distinctive and important feature of the Second Sophistic ... the title 'sophist' itself was probably supposed to bring to mind the sophists of classical Greece and thereby connect new sophists to the Golden Age of Greece."[18]

To be sure, the redactors of Avot possessed some authentic details regarding the Pharisaic masters and some memories of their antecedents rooted in historical experience, and it is quite possible that the Pharisees did organize themselves according to Hellenistic convention. But tying their organizational practices to an institution founded by Ezra – as attested in the rabbinic sources – is a tenuous venture, and the redactors of Avot do so only because it A) served their rhetorical interests and B) conformed to widespread praxes in the culture surrounding them.

Nevertheless, there are some important kernels of historical information that may be gleaned from the incidental presuppositions encoded into the text of m. Avot 1 and related rabbinic works concerned with the Great Assembly. First and foremost, the passages in which it is depicted are not *aggadic* in nature; it is evident that the Rabbis regarded the Great Assembly as a genuine institution and set it alongside concepts of religious leadership culled from the Bibilical record that appeared to conform to the tradition regarding its membership and function. The first named sage in Avot (Moses and Joshua notwithstanding) is Simon the Just (m. Avot 1.2), identified with the high priest Simon I from ca. 270 B.C.E. or Simon II from ca. 170 B.C.E.[19] It is notable that m. Avot 1.2 is explicit that Simon was a *survivor* of the institution that closes the preceding unit in m. Avot 1.1. This statement makes clear that Simon lived at a time that saw the dissolution of the Great Assembly. With the invocation of Simon the Just begins the era of the post-biblical sages that the redactors of Avot saw as culminating in their own time with the Gamalian dynasty – in short, Simon lived in their epoch, not the mythic, biblical past. But the figure initiating this era was neverthe-

---

sance constitutes a response to Roman cultural hegemony (see also his discussion of literary materials ibid., 74–89). See also Tropper, *Wisdom*, 136–146.

18 Tropper, *Wisdom*, 136–145.

19 Neusner, *Pharisees*, 1:19, suggests the rhetorical significance of attaching the institution to the last legitimate member of the Zadokite priestly dynasty, i.e., to Simon II. The ambiguity may be a deliberate hermeneutical tactic; see Steinsaltz, *Essential Talmud*, 18.

less a member of an institution connected to a chain of tradition that began with other figures from the biblical period. By implication, the Great Assembly to which he once belonged was regarded as the gateway between the mythic foundations of Judaism and later rabbinic authority.[20]

There was good reason for the Rabbis responsible for the Mishnah to ascribe the foundation of this gateway institution to Ezra beyond the antiquarian impulses of the Second Sophistic. As careful readers of the biblical text, they must have seen in Ezra a strong parallel to Patriarchs such as Rabbi Judah, learned in *torah*, overseeing scribal and exegetical enterprises and responsible for Jewish life in an imperial world.[21] The picture of the mid 5th century B.C.E., then, seems to fit the background for the origins of the Great Assembly as an entity that straddled mythic past and the social and religious categories of the present as imagined by the redactors of Avot. Simon the Just, the Pharisaic pairs, and ultimately the Gamalian Patriarchs who carried forward the doctrines and values of the (putative) Great Assembly were the intellectual heirs and disciples of Ezra, its founder.

Two considerations must give us pause, however, before accepting the rabbinic tradition that Ezra indeed stands behind the historical entity remembered as the Great Assembly.[22] First, while many rabbinic passages either identify or strongly point to Ezra as the founder of the Great Assembly, Avot does not. The Great Assembly is situated directly after the prophets as the inheritors of *torah*, but Ezra is never mentioned. Scholars have long noted that overt mention of Israel's priesthood appears to be deliberately avoided in the succession list in Avot 1,[23] and one might suppose that the non-mention of Ezra is a matter of his own connection to priestly heritage (Ezra 7:1–5).[24] But the list then goes on in m. Avot 1.2 to engage the words of Simon the Just without hesitation. It is true that Simon's priestly heritage is not mentioned and his qualifying credential is association with the Great Assembly rather

---

20 So also Neusner, *Pharisees*, 1:18–19.

21 Such is the proposal of Williamson, *Ezra*, 104–105. See also Steiner, "*mbqr*." The relationship between Ezra and the Levite scribes of his day (especially in Nehemiah 8–10) factor into this consideration as well. See the summary of views regarding Nehemiah 8–10 by Englander, "Men," 145–146. See further my essays "Ezra's Mission," 173–195, and "Politics," 355–362.

22 Finkelstein, "Maxim," 455–457; Mantel, "Great Synagogue." See also idem, "Dichotomy," 55–87.

23 E.g., Finkelstein, *Introduction*, 9–11.

24 The accuracy of the genealogy in these verses cannot be accepted. For a discussion, see Blenkinsopp, *Ezra-Nehemiah*, 135–136. The genealogy's artifice, however, does not preclude the likelihood that it was devised precisely because Ezra did possess Aaronide-priestly heritage.

than the high priesthood, but one must wonder why the authors could not have done the same with Ezra, especially if Ezra is so often attested as organization's founder. Given the prominence afforded Ezra elsewhere in Rabbinic writings, his excision from the list cannot be accidental.

Second, as most contemporary researchers recognize, there are difficulties with seeing Ezra 7–8 and Nehemiah 8 as transparent indications of Ezra's activity in the mid 5th century B.C.E. Both units of texts show signs of multiple redaction and the introduction of language serving different ideological agendas.[25] Much within the Ezra material has been shaped to anticipate what obtains within the Nehemiah Memoir (Nehemiah 1–6*),[26] the Artaxerxes Rescript in Ezra 7 is inconsistent with Persian diplomatic documents found beyond the Bible,[27] the event depicted in Nehemiah 8 involving Ezra's reading of the Torah seems to be a fairly late addition to the entire Ezra–Nehemiah corpus, and the literary construct following it (the prayer of the Levites in Nehemiah 9 and the pact in Nehemiah 10) likely derive from a similar later redactional enterprise.[28] There is enough detail to flesh out a basic reconstruction that saw Artaxerxes appoint Ezra, a Jewish emissary of the royal court, to oversee the affairs of Jewish life in Transeuphrates.[29] One should expect administrative assistance from literate individuals of appropriate religious pedigree (e.g., Levites, scribes, priests) under such circumstances. But this is a far cry from seeing the establishment of a fixed body of sage-scribes with a set curriculum and exegetical methodology as forebears of the Rabbis.

Still, temporally proximate circumstances may very well stand behind the tradition of the Great Assembly as originating in the Persian period. A scribal/administrative caste did form under the tenure of Nehemiah in which Levites played a major role.[30] The literary Ezra and his Levite and scribal supporters (while rooted in some authentic historical memory, to be sure) become ciphers for the Nehemiah group and those who followed in their footsteps, establishing a legislative/administrative body regulating Jewish life in Yehud that the Nehemiah group used as the basis for their own interests and agendas. It

---

25 See Pakkala, *Ezra*, and Wright, *Rebuilding Identity*. Both scholars see Nehemiah 8–10 as growing over a fairly extensive period of time and in successive editorial waves.
26 Wright, *Rebuilding Identity*, 338–339; Leuchter, "Ezra's Mission," 189–195.
27 Theories regarding the Rescript vary tremendously. See Kratz, *Translatio imperii*, 225–260; Pakkala, *Ezra*, 52–53; Janzen, "Mission," 621–630; Steiner, "*mbqr*," 639–643; Schwiderski, *Handbuch*, 375–382; Hagedorn, "Local Law," 71; Williamson, "Aramaic Documents," 41–62.
28 Wright, *Rebuilding Identity*, 329–330.
29 Williamson, *Ezra*, 104–105.
30 Leuchter, "Politics," 359.

is significant that this group subsumed the Jerusalem temple within their political and religious charter: the sacred space staked out by Nehemiah was one that bound the satellite communities to Jerusalem – rather than to the temple itself – in emulation of the larger imperial structure.[31] And yet, as Nehemiah 13 demonstrates, Nehemiah's supporters eventually incorporated the temple into their sphere of influence, binding its cult to provincial affairs.

This situation comes much closer to the concept of the *kiništu*, i.e., the Babylonian temple assembly with membership extending beyond the priesthood and serving as the mediating interface between temple and the larger community.[32] Joachim Schaper has noted that both priests and Levites hold offices related to matters of state according to sources within the Nehemiah corpus (Neh 10:38–40; 13:13), and that this fits well into the picture of Persian economic policy in the 5th–4th centuries B.C.E.[33] Thus an administrative body staffed at least in part by sacerdotal figures had already begun to form in the era that saw Nehemiah's activity and its immediate impact. Chronicles provides additional detail to this picture: the Chronicler places the Jerusalem temple at the center of the social world but emphasizes the role of Levites as scribes, teachers, librarians, militiamen, jurists and, notably, bearers of *prophetic* traditions and responsibilities (e.g., 1 Chr 25:2–3; 2 Chr 34:30 [cf. 2 Kgs 23:3]).[34]

We must recall here the notice in m. Avot 1.1 that the Great Assembly received the mantle of *torah* directly from the prophets. The language is metaphorical, but beneath the metaphor we may identify a perception informed by texts such as the aforementioned passages in Chronicles. One should not overlook, too, the fact that a good amount of prophetic language – especially from the Jeremiah tradition – is woven throughout Ezra–Nehemiah, and that Nehemiah himself assumes pseudo-prophetic authority in taking up his gubernatorial duties.[35] The redactors of Ezra–Nehemiah color their image of scribal/administrative authority with prophetic tones; the Chronicler seizes upon this in making his bold statements about the multivalent role of Levites as both scribes and prophets.[36] By the Chronicler's time, then, a class of exegeti-

---

31 On Nehemiah's emulation of imperial standards of court conduct, see Wright, "Commensal Politics," 348–351. On the satellite communities Nehemiah connected to a Jerusalem-based administration, see Leuchter, "Politics," 358–359.
32 See Geller, "Influence," 44; Weinfeld," Origin," 74.
33 Schaper, "Temple Treasury Committee," 200–206.
34 On the multiple roles of Levites in this period, see van der Toorn, *Scribal Culture*, 90.
35 Leuchter, "Ezra's Mission;" idem, "Politics," 360–361.
36 Targ. 1 Sam 10:5 and Isa 9:14. It is also important to recall y. Berakhot 3a, where Neh 9:7 – part of the Levitical prayer in Nehemiah 9 – is identified as spoken by the Great

cal authorities connected to the Jerusalem temple (but not limited to it) existed and were charged with the systematizing, interpretation, and application of religious tradition and Scriptural works.[37] If the "Great Assembly" is a trope that reflects back on all of these texts and Levite-scribal groups, then it is no wonder why m. Avot 1.1 does not specify Ezra's activity as their specific point of origin.

In sum: the Rabbinic writers conceived of the Great Assembly in terms that reflect Hellenistic institutions and organizations with which they were more familiar and from which they took cues regarding their own formation as a league with a collective identity. Yet the texts that speak of the Great Assembly preserve some historically significant memories. The fact that the tradition underneath m. Avot 1.1 should be read against the Second Sophistic does point to the Persian period as the basis for the idea of a Great Assembly, but this is a construct that collapses different – though related – scribal institutions into a single entity.[38] Nevertheless, the rabbinic texts that do speak of the Great Assembly present a group that, at least as a symbolic trope, was consistent with the generations of (primarily Levite) scribes of the late Persian and early Hellenistic periods that did serve as the redactors and interpreters of Scripture.

The Great Assembly as the Writers of the Twelve

If the Great Assembly is a *topos* for the different Levite scribes of the 5th–4th centuries B.C.E., we must ask why the authors of Baba Bathra credit this group with the specific texts to which it alludes. Apart from the Twelve, we are informed that the Great Assembly "wrote" Ezekiel, Daniel, and Esther, none of which are particularly "Levitical" in orientation.[39] A classical rabbinic explanation for this is that these three

---

Assembly. Kuenen's suggestion (*Abhandlungen*, 143–158) that any historical connection between Nehemiah 8–10 and a "Great Assembly" is artificial overlooks the role of Levites as both scribal and quasi-prophetic figures in the Persian period.

37   Some dim Rabbinic memory of this may indeed be indicated by the taphonomic association of Nehemiah himself with the completion of Chronicles (Baba Bathra 15a).

38   Such collapsing is not alien to the rabbinic view of the Persian period; Zerubabbel and Ezra live in the same era (Seder Olam Rabbah 29; Targ. Cant 7:3). See also Steinsaltz, *Essential Talmud*, 18, who notes that the references to "Simon the Just" may collapse several priests bearing this name (and even more who do not) into one symbolic literary figure.

39   Ezekiel's view regarding the Levites and the Deuteronomic traditions associated with them is often quite hostile; see Leuchter, *Polemics*, 156–161. The hero of the Esther tale, Mordechai, is a Benjaminite descendant of Saul, who encroached upon Le-

works originated in the Diaspora (or in the case of Ezekiel, during the Babylonian exile) and were thus somehow distanced from the holiness of the homeland.[40] The attribution of these texts to the Great Assembly qualifies them as canonically sound because the latter group was a native institution firmly founded in Jerusalem ... a city carrying mythic overtones in the minds of rabbinic writers who recalled all too well its devastation under the Romans and who sought above all to preserve the essence of its historical and spiritual significance.

Thus, even if Ezekiel (for example) was the originator of the oracles in the book bearing his name, the authors of Baba Bathra characterize it as bearing the holy legacy of Jerusalem by crediting the Great Assembly with "writing" it – that is, transcribing it into an enduring written form.[41] The line between prophet and scribe so often blurred within the biblical tradition is blurred in Baba Bathra as well: writing, in this case, is certainly not "authoring" in the sense of originating the composition.[42] It is perhaps better to characterize the intended meaning of Baba Bathra's terminology as relating to the authoritative *transmission* of text. Reckoned thusly, Baba Bathra 15a informs us that the sage-scribes were responsible for orchestrating, copying, preserving and teaching/contextualizing the contents of the books of Ezekiel, Daniel and Esther, elucidating the ideological essence of these works consonant with the works created on native soil.

There is certainly precedent for this within the biblical tradition, beginning with the late pre-exilic period and persisting well into the Second Temple period that saw textualization itself as a divine, numinous phenomenon. It is not incidental that prophetic works of the time emphasize the literary over the oral and that even the Priestly understanding of *torah* (long restricted to oral contexts) becomes a matter of textual expression.[43] Following Mesopotamian precursors, the scribal craft in early Second Temple Judaism became as potent a vehicle for

---

vitical/priestly social influence (1 Sam 8) and as slaughters Levite priests (1 Sam 22). There is nothing in Daniel to suggest that he is a Levite or priest.

40 Such is already the view of Rashi, though he draws from a much earlier rabbinic dictum that the divine presence was not experienced in exilic or Diasporatic conditions (Mo'ed Qatan 25a). See further Viezel, "Formation," 25; Cheyne and Black, *Encyclopaedia Biblica*, 656.

41 In the case of Ezekiel, this may have to do in part with disputes regarding its inclusion into the canon on the grounds of the danger of its contents or its conflict with the Pentateuch (Hagigah 13a; Shabbat 13b). See, however, Zeitlin, "Study," 122–128.

42 On the fluidity of "authorship," see Carr, *Tablet*, 124–173. The blurring is also evident in rabbinic concepts of textuality and orality; see Shanks-Alexander, "Orality," 38–55.

43 Schaper, "Prophecy," 324–339. On the use of written texts in the promulgation of Priestly instruction, see Leuchter, "Politics," 346–351.

346

Mark Leuchter

revelation as the oral proclamations of earlier prophets.[44] This cultural trait is presupposed in the statement in Baba Bathra that the scribes of the Great Assembly could "write" a text traditional attributed to a different source. For texts that did not originate in the homeland, the exegetical intervention of the Great Assembly subjected them to an authoritative modality possessing a distinctive and numinous genotype.

The ascription of Ezekiel, Esther and Daniel to the Great Assembly constitutes a statement on the necessity of the exegetical process to the vitality of Scripture, but this does not fully account for the Twelve being grouped with these other texts. Unlike Ezekiel, Esther and Daniel, none of the prophetic works within the Twelve were understood to have originated beyond the homeland: all the prophets included therein are presented as carrying out their activity on ancestral soil.[45] Why should native works be categorized alongside exilic/Diasporatic works if the purpose of ascribing the latter to the great Assembly is to legitimize them via a homeland institution? It is certainly true that the placement of the individual prophetic works on one scroll is an essentially scribal act, and the utilitarian benefits of such an act are overtly identified by the authors of Baba Bathra – namely, that smaller works might be forgotten or misplaced unless committed to a single, larger scroll (Baba Bathra 13b; 14b; Pesahim 87b). But mechanical copying seems rather mundane compared to the hermeneutical potency of the Great Assembly in relation to Ezekiel, Esther and Daniel. Whence the categorization of the Twelve with the other works that were made "native" and canonically viable by the Great Assembly?

Three additional considerations may provide an answer to this question, two of which are found within the Talmudic material alongside Baba Bathra 15a. We need not look far to find the first of these, which appears in the same folio as the opening portion of unit ascribing the Twelve to the Great Assembly:

> Our Rabbis taught: The order of the Prophets is, Joshua, Judges, Samuel, Kings, *Jeremiah, Ezekiel, Isaiah*, and the Twelve Minor Prophets ... Let us see ... Isaiah was prior to Jeremiah and Ezekiel. Then why should not Isaiah be placed first? Because the Book of Kings ends with a record of destruction and Jeremiah speaks throughout of destruction and Ezekiel commences with destruction and ends with consolation and Isaiah is full of consolation; therefore we put destruction next to destruction and consolation next to consolation. (Baba Bathra 14b)

---

44   Van der Toorn, *Scribal Culture*, 207–232.
45   A possible exception might be represented by the book of Jonah, but even that book tells the tale of a pre-exilic Israelite prophet whose mission originated in his native land.

The Jeremiah–Ezekiel–Isaiah sequence above has led some scholars to posit a period where the more familiar canonical sequence had not yet been fixed,[46] but it is not necessary to go that far in explaining its contents. The authors are primarily concerned with stressing a particular theoretical standard for textual association, namely, that texts be read or categorized as like-with-like. We may extrapolate from this to the grouping of the Twelve alongside Ezekiel, etc. If the Rabbis advocate the categorization of like-with-like, then in some way, the role of the Great Assembly *vis a vis* the Twelve is akin to their aforementioned exegetical role with exilic and Diaspora traditions, and was not limited to simply copying its contents onto a single scroll.[47] In this light, the redactional seams identified by James Nogalski, Aaron Schart and others that create linguistic connections between the various prophetic corpora in the Twelve evidence an attempt to have the books themselves exhibit this literary character.[48] Certainly, the repetition of keywords and lemmas between these books would facilitate the categorization of these texts akin to the model of like-with-like advocated by the Rabbis. The authors of Baba Bathra may thus be preserving a memory of this redaction of the Twelve, following the like-with-like model of the Jeremiah–Ezekiel–Isaiah sequence in Baba Bathra 13b.

The second consideration is the combined implications of several Talmudic traditions regarding the end of the succession of prophets. The Rabbis recall that the Persian period saw the "last" of the prophets: Haggai, Zechariah and Malachi (t. Sotah 13.2; Sanhedrin 11a). Yet to say that these individuals were the last prophets did not mean that the Rabbis believed that prophecy itself, as an abstract or even mythic concept, ceased.[49] Indeed, one of the passages that identify Haggai, Zecha-

---

46 See among others Rogerson, "Writings," 15–16; Kent and Schmidt, "Bible," 233. Anderson, "Canonical," 140, notes that some French biblical manuscripts follow the order from the aforementioned Talmudic passage. This, however, does not prove the existence of an early alternative canonical sequence but, rather, a later editorial orchestration following the Talmudic passage in question.

47 I would suggest, tentatively, that what we have here is an example of the *middah* of *kal va-chomer* applied to rabbinic discourse itself: a fictive Scriptural typology in Baba Bathra 14b provides the basis for reading Baba Bathra 15a in a particular ideological light.

48 Nogalski, *Processes*; Schart, *Entstehung*.

49 Pace Sommer, "Prophecy," 31–47. Sommer is correct to note a shift from prophecy to exegesis in the Persian period, but this must be qualified since scribal exegesis, at least in the Chronicler's view, is itself a form of prophecy and carries mantic dimensions, and even some of the late classical prophets incorporate scribal emphases into their oracles. See Schaper, "Prophecy," 334.338–339. Though t. Sotah 13.2 and Sanhedrin 11a speak of "the holy spirit" leaving Israel after the death of these prophets, the tradition in Baba Metziah 59b regards written *torah* as the basis for revelatory authority, succeeding prophecy as such a vehicle.

riah and Malachi as the last prophets also identifies them as members of the Great Assembly (ARN i 1);[50] this suggests that their prophetic responsibilities extended beyond the proclamation of oracles.[51] We should thus return to the role of Levite scribes in the late Persian period who the Chronicler clearly understood or advocated as carrying forward prophecy in a new, scribal, form. In short, the prophets (proper) may have ended with Haggai, Zechariah and Malachi in rabbinic thought, but the rabbinic sources preserved a memory of prophecy continuing, at least for a while, in the guise of scribal groups who succeeded the prophets as the trustees of revelation.

It is possible that the redaction of the Twelve was understood in the late Persian period as a sort of prophetic act in and of itself and was carried out by scribes who were connected with the ranks of the Jerusalem temple faculty, Levite or otherwise.[52] Thus like Ezekiel, Esther and Daniel, the contents of the Twelve could be "written" by the Great Assembly because their redactional activity was similarly regarded as prophetic in nature, drawing from the precedent of their Levitical forebears akin to the Chronicler's presentation. For the Rabbis, the contents of the Twelve remained the words of the titular prophets associated with each section, but their weaving into a single scroll and the creation of redactional seams that bound them together revealed a new dimension of meaning between them.[53] A new canonical text was birthed through redaction, and thus a new prophetic word was transmitted through scribal mediation.[54] The Rabbis understood these scribes as members of the Great Assembly, and thereby credited the "writing" of the Twelve to them.

To summarize: Baba Bathra's depiction of the Great Assembly as the writers of the Twelve seems to correspond to the Chronicler's de-

---

50 See further Finkelstein, "Maxim," 456–457 note 6.
51 Indeed, a number of rabbinic passages identify anonymous prophets as among the Great Assembly and charged with scribal duties (Shabbat 104a; Megilla 2a; Yoma 80a).
52 See similarly Englander, "Men," 168. Redaction as subset of prophetic communication is already strongly implied within Jeremiah 36, where the redaction of earlier oracles creates a single scroll with a distinct message (Jer 36:4–8) and where the redactional reconstitution of that scroll carries forward Jeremiah's prophetic words (Jer 36:32).
53 Ergo the notice in Baba Bathra 13b that while four lines should stand between biblical books, only three should separate the contents of the Twelve. The uniqueness of this directive coupled with its similarity to the standard four-line directive indicates that the contents of the Twelve were viewed as both distinct/independent and literarily/canonically intertwined.
54 See once again van der Toorn's discussion of the "holy writ" as a scribal product (Scribal Culture, 207–232).

piction of Levite scribes, and the formation of the scroll as a "new" work of prophecy matches the role of these scribes as quasi-prophets in the late Persian or early Hellenistic period when Chronicles was composed.[55] Considering the Levitical redaction of the Psalter around this time and the characterization of reading and teaching liturgical texts as a form of prophecy in Chronicles, it may be that the redaction of the Twelve was roughly coterminous with the redaction of the Psalter and the composition of Chronicles as well.[56] If this is so, then the scribes who carried on into later period did inherit a form of *torah* from "the prophets" as m. Avot 1.1 claims.

The Hermeneutical Implications of the Great Assembly as the Writers of the Twelve

In the broad strokes, rabbinic tradition paints a picture not completely inconsistent with the fruits of modern critical analysis: the scribes of the Second Temple period took up the mantle of revelatory authority from the prophets via redactional, exegetical and pedagogical activity. However, this does not preclude the possibility that deliberate rhetorical design accounts for the merging of these different historical echoes. In other contexts (such as with the use of *halakha* from before 70 C.E.) the Rabbis abstracted details from the records they possessed or traditions they maintained in order to construct an intellectual paradigm for their own forms of teaching.[57] The new literary context became the definitive way to recall and engage these earlier traditions, but this did not mean that their previous social contexts were to be forgotten or ignored. On the contrary, references to previous contexts supported the validity of the new literary setting. The Rabbinic writings became the conduit to more ancient conditions that dissolved alongside the demolition of the Second Temple and the teachings of earlier sages.[58]

A similar strategy may be at work, at least to a certain degree, with regard to the connection of the Twelve to the Great Assembly. It strains

---

55   Most commentators see a mid to late 4th century to an early 3rd century setting as the most likely background for the Chronicler's activity. See Knoppers, *I Chronicles 1–9*, 101–117.

56   On the redaction of Psalms, see Smith, "Redaction."

57   See especially Sivertsev, *Households*, 199.273.

58   Both the Mishnaic authors and the later Talmudic writers routinely go to great efforts to note the early contexts for practices under discussion, and in all works the authority of a ruling or teaching is founded upon the speaker's reception of it from an earlier Sage. This appears to be in conversation with similar Greco-Roman praxes; see Jaffee, *Torah*, 130.

credulity to imagine that the Rabbis did not discern the literary features of the Twelve that demonstrate both unity and diversity within and between its constituent parts (indeed, the notice regarding line separation in Baba Bathra 13b confirms that they did). If the Great Assembly was a symbolic basis for rabbinic authority, then ascribing to this body an ancient work evidencing both unity and diversity creates an authoritative support to the rabbinic body of tradition that exhibited the same features (Mishnah, Tosefta, various *baraitot*, etc.). The ascription of the Twelve to the Great Assembly not only supports the Rabbis' claim that they had inherited prophetic *torah*, it demonstrates that rabbinic redaction was consistent with redactional processes already at work in the biblical period. The Great Assembly's "writing" of the Twelve legitimized the rabbinic anthologizing of their sources into a comprehensive literary tradition – one that preserved those sources so that they, like the small prophetic scrolls, would not be forgotten. But like the Twelve, those older traditions were set within a literary collection where they countenanced each other and created new ways of conceiving Jewish history, myth, and collective identity.

References

Anderson, G.W. "Canonical and Non-Canonical." Pp. 67–159 in *The Cambridge History of the Bible: From The Beginnings to Jerome*. Edited by P.R. Ackroyd and C.F. Evans. Cambridge: Cambridge University Press, 1970.

Assmann, J. *Moses The Egyptian: The Memory of Egypt in Western Monotheism*. Cambridge: Harvard University Press, 1997.

Blenkinsopp, J. *Ezra-Nehemiah: A Commentary*. OTL. Philadelphia: Westminster, 1988.

Carr, D.M. *Writing on the Tablet of the Heart: Origins of Scripture and Literature*. New York: Oxford University Press, 2005.

Cheyne, T.K. and Black, J.S. (eds.) *Encyclopaedia Biblica*. London: Macmillan, 1899.

Cohen, A. *Everyman's Talmud: The Major Teachings of the Rabbinic Sages*. New York: Dutton, 1949.

Englander, H. "Men of the Great Synagogue." *HUCA Jubilee Volume* (1925) 145–169.

Finkelstein, L. "The Maxim of Anshe Kneset Ha-Gedolah." *JBL* 59 (1940) 455–469.

–   *Introduction to the Treatises Avot and Avot de-Rabbi Nathan*. New York: JTSA, 1950 (Hebrew).

Geller, M.J. "The Influence of Ancient Mesopotamia on Hellenistic Judaism." Pp. 43–54 in vol. 1 of *Civilizations of the Ancient Near East*. Edited by J.M. Sasson. New York: Scribner, 1995.

Hagedorn, A.C. "Local Law in an Imperial Context: The Role of Torah in the (Imagined) Persian Period." Pp. 57–76 in *The Pentateuch as Torah: New Models for Understanding its Promulgation and Acceptance*. Edited by G.N. Knoppers and B.M. Levinson. Winona Lake: Eisenbrauns, 2007.

Hendel, R.S. "The Exodus in Biblical Memory." *JBL* 121 (2000) 601–622.

Jaffee, M.S. *Torah in the Mouth: Writing and Oral Tradition in Palestinian Judaism 200 BCE–400 CE*. New York: Oxford University Press, 2001.

Janzen, D. "The Mission of Ezra and the Persian-Period Temple Community." *JBL* 119 (2000) 619–643.

Kent, C.F. and Schmidt, N. "Bible." *New International Encyclopedia* (²1914) 225–248.

Knoppers, G.N. *I Chronicles 1–9*. AB 12A. New York: Doubleday, 2003.

Kratz, R.G. *Translatio imperii: Untersuchungen zu den aramäischen Danielerzählungen und ihrem theologiegeschichtlichen Umfeld*. WMANT 63. Neukirchen-Vluyn: Neukirchener, 1991.

Kuenen, A. *Gesammelte Abhandlungen zur biblischen Wissenschaft*. Freiburg: Mohr, 1894.

Leuchter, M. *The Polemics of Exile in Jeremiah 26–45*. New York: Cambridge University Press, 2008.

– "Ezra's Mission and the Levites of Casiphia." Pp. 173–195 in *Community and Identity in Judean Historiography*. Edited by G.N. Knoppers and K.A. Ristau. Winona Lake: Eisenbrauns, 2009.

– "The Politics of Ritual Rhetoric: A Proposed Sociohistorical Context for the Redaction of Leviticus 1–16." *VT* 60 (2010) 345–365.

– "From Levite to Maskil in the Persian and Hellenistic Eras." Pp. 215–232 in *Priests and Levites in Biblical History and Tradition*. Edited by idem and J.M. Hutton. Atlanta: Society of Biblical Literature, 2011.

Mantel, H. "The Nature of the Great Synagogue." *HTR* 60 (1967) 69–91.

– "The Dichotomy of Judaism During the Second Temple." *HUCA* 44 (1973) 55–87.

Neusner, J. *The Rabbinic Traditions about the Pharisees Before 70*. 3 vols. Leiden: Brill, 1970.

Nogalski, J.D. *Redactional Processes in the Book of the Twelve*. BZAW 218. Berlin: de Gruyter, 1993.

Pakkala, J. *Ezra the Scribe: The Development of Ezra 7–10 and Nehemiah 8*. BZAW 347. Berlin: de Gruyter, 2004.

Redditt, P.L. "The Production and Reading of the Book of the Twelve." Pp. 11–33 in *Reading and Hearing the Book of the Twelve*. Edited by J.D. Nogalski and M.A. Sweeney. SBLSymS 15. Atlanta: Society of Biblical Literature, 2000.

Rogerson, J.W. "The First Christian Writings." Pp. 15–23 in *The First Christian Theologians*. Edited by G.R. Evans. Malden: Blackwell, 2004.

Schaper, J. "The Temple Treasury Committee in the Times of Nehemiah and Ezra." *VT* 46 (1996) 200–206..

– "Exilic and Post-Exilic Prophecy and the Orality/Literacy Problem." *VT* 55 (2005) 324–342

Schart, A. *Die Entstehung des Zwolfprophetenbuchs: Neubearbeitungen von Amos im Rahmen schriftenübergreifender Redaktionsprozesse*. BZAW 260. Berlin: de Gruyter, 1998.

Schwiderski, D. *Handbuch des nordwestsemitischen Briefformulars: Ein Beitrag zur Echtheitsfrage der aramäischen Briefe des Esrabuches*. BZAW 295. Berlin: de Gruyter, 2000.

Shanks-Alexander, E. "The Orality of Rabbinic Writing." Pp. 38–55 in *The Cambridge Companion to the Talmud and Rabbinic Literature*. Edited by C.E. Fonrobert and M.S. Jaffee. New York: Cambridge University Press, 2007.

Sivertsev, A. *Households, Sects, and the Origins of Rabbinic Judaism*. JSJSup 102. Leiden: Brill, 2005.

Smith, M.S. "The Levitical Redaction of the Psalter." *ZAW* 103 (1991) 258–263.

Sommer, B.D. "Did Prophecy Cease? Evaluating a Reevaluation." *JBL* 115 (1996) 31–47.

Steiner, R.C. "The *mbqr* at Qumran, the *episkopos* in the Athenian Empire, and the meaning of *lbqr'* in Ezra 7:14: On the relation of Ezra's Mission to the Persian Legal Project." *JBL* 120 (2001) 623–636.

Steinsaltz, A. *The Essential Talmud*. New York: Bantam, 1976.

Strack, H.L. and Stemberger, G. *Introduction to the Talmud and Midrash*. Translated by M. Bockmuehl. Minneapolis: Fortress Press, 1996.

Tropper, A. *Wisdom, Politics, and Historiography: Tractate Avot in the Context of the Greco-Roman Near East*. Oxford: Oxford University Press, 2004.

– "Yohana Ben Zakkai, Amicus Caesaris: A Jewish Hero in Rabbinic Eyes." *Jewish Studies, an Internet Journal* 4 (2005) 1–17.

Van der Toorn, K. *Scribal Culture and the Making of the Hebrew Bible*. Cambridge: Harvard University Press, 2007.

Viezel, E. "The Formation of Some Biblical Books According to Rashi." *JTS* 61 (2010) 16–42.

Weinfeld, M. "The Origin of the Apodictic Law: An Overlooked Source." *VT* 23 (1973) 63–75.

Whitmarsh, T. *The Second Sophistic*. New York: Oxford University Press, 2005.

Williamson, H.G.M. *Ezra, Nehemiah*. WBC 16. Waco: Word, 1985.

– "The Aramaic Documents in Ezra Revisited." *JTS* 59 (2008) 41–62.

Wright, J.L. *Rebuilding Identity: The Nehemiah Memoir and its Earliest Readers*. BZAW 348. Berlin: de Gruyter, 2004.

– "Commensal Politics in Ancient Western Asia: The Background to Nehemiah's Feasting." *ZAW* 122 (2010) 212–233.333–352.

Yerushalmi, Y.H. *Zakhor: Jewish History and Jewish Memory*. Seattle: University of Washington Press, 1996.

Zeitlin, S. "An Historical Study of the Canonization of the Hebrew Scriptures." *PAAJR* 3 (1931–1932) 141–156.

Issues Concerning the Canon

Verbal and Thematic Links between the Books of the Twelve in Greek and their Relevance to the Differing Manuscript Sequences

JENNIFER DINES

University of London

1. Introduction

Manuscripts of the Twelve (XII) mostly follow the same order for the last six books but vary in the first six. Masoretic order (Hosea–Joel–Amos–Obadiah–Jonah–Micah) is fully attested in Hebrew from the ninth century C.E. and partially in the first-century B.C.E. Qumran fragments 4QXII[b-g1] and the first to second-century C.E. Murabba`at scroll (Mur88). Masoretic order also occurs in Greek in the mid first-century B.C.E. Naḥal Ḥever scroll (8ḤevXIIgr).[2] The Greek order (Hosea–Amos–Micah–Joel–Obadiah–Jonah) is not attested in any Hebrew manuscript; it occurs first, in Greek, in the third-century C.E. Washington papyrus (W), probably also in a third-century Greek-Coptic Glossary (Rahlfs 829) for Hosea and Amos.[3] Thereafter it dominates the Christian manuscript tradition though, as we shall see, there are significant exceptions. It also occurs in a few Christianized pseudepigrapha of probable Jewish origin. *4 Ezra* 1:39–40 (third century C.E.?) has the standard Greek order.[4] In *Martyrdom of Isaiah* 4:22 and *Lives of the Prophets* (both probably from the first century C.E.), the order is aberrant but based on the Greek sequence.[5] Despite uncertainties about origin and dating, these passages point to at least the possibility that the sequence predates its appearance in Christian manuscripts.[6]

---

1   The earliest fragment, 4QXII[a] (mid-second century B.C.E.), has a unique pairing: Malachi–Jonah.

2   Fuller, "Form," 88–96; Brooke, "Minor Prophets," 20–27.

3   Rahlfs, *Überlieferung*, 221.

4   Metzger, *Fourth Book*, 520.

5   *Martyrdom* switches Hosea and Amos; Knibb, *Martyrdom*, 149–150. *Lives* switches Amos and Micah; Hare, *Lives*, 380.

6   Even Satran, *Prophets*, 50.96, who argues for a Christian origin of *Lives* in the 4th–5th century C.E., allows for some underlying Jewish traditions.

Three linked questions arise from the disparity in evidence for the two sequences. Does the Masoretic order predate the first century B.C.E.? How far back does the Greek order go? Is it of Jewish or Christian origin? For the latter questions, the answer might seem obvious. Since the Greek order occurs in manuscripts of the LXX, the (usually unspoken) presumption is that it dates at least from the time of translation, most likely mid-second century B.C.E., whether as an innovation by the translator or as a reflection of a differently ordered Hebrew *Vorlage*. This is what I wish to test, by borrowing from James Nogalski. Nogalski examined catchwords at the "seams" between component parts of Hebrew XII for signs of editorial activity.[7] I shall similarly look, in first Septuagintal and then Masoretic order, for links in imagery, vocabulary and theme that might indicate connections made by the translator at the "seams" between those books whose order differs in the two sequences, namely Hosea to Nahum. My aim is *not* to establish whether one order was "original," but merely to ascertain the sequence followed by the translator. It is possible that he was himself responsible for a re-ordering; however, given the extent to which he reproduces the word order of a text clearly very close to MT, it seems unlikely that he would make so radical a change. I assume, rather, that he followed the sequence already in his Hebrew *Vorlage*.[8] The question is, which one was it?

2. Hosea–Nahum: Septuagintal "Seams"[9]

2.1 Hosea–Amos

If the translator had the Septuagintal order, he would have passed from Hosea to Amos. There is one possible link. The last words of Hos 14:10 are "transgressors (ἀσεβεῖς פֹּשְׁעִים) stumble." The first words of Amos 1:3 are "for the ... transgressions (ἐπὶ ταῖς ... ἀσεβείαις פֶּשַׁע)." There is, however, nothing in the translation as such to suggest that the translator made a *conscious* connection between the "transgressors" of Hos 14:10 and the "transgressions" listed in Amos 1:3–2:6, since he regularly

---

7   Nogalski, *Precursors*, 13–14.
8   I thus envisage a situation where more than one Hebrew sequence was in existence; cf. Jones, "Book," 69; Sweeney, *Hosea*, xxxv.
9   "Septuagintal" and "Masoretic" are to be understood as "flags of convenience" denoting later manuscript traditions; the terms do not necessarily represent an original division between Greek and Hebrew versions of XII, but "readings" in various Jewish contexts; cf. Sweeney, "Sequence," 56–64.

renders words in the פשע range by words in the ἀσεβεῖν range. The juxtaposition is interesting in both MT and LXX: Amos particularizes Hosea's general warning. The effect is lost when, as in Masoretic ordering, Joel intervenes.

2.2 Amos–Micah

Two words in Amos 9:14–15 recur in Mic 1:2, namely λαός and γῆ. Amos 9:14 has "I will return the captivity of my people (λαοῦ μου עמי);" 9:15 continues with "they shall never again be plucked from their land (ἀπὸ τῆς γῆς αὐτῶν אדמתם)." Mic 1:2 opens with a universal address: "hear, you people (λαοί עמים) ... and let the earth (γῆ ארץ) pay attention." Again, all renderings are standard. But one Greek word (γῆ) renders two different Hebrew ones: אדמה in Amos, ארץ in Micah. This creates a small echo in Greek absent from MT, though whether intentionally is impossible to tell: γῆ is standard for both Hebrew terms. Thematically, Micah's plural universalizes the end of Amos. The shift from Amos to Micah, like that from Hosea to Amos, returns to judgment after a promise of salvation.

2.3 Micah–Joel

Here there is a stronger link. The last words of Mic 7:20 express confidence in the promises made "to our ancestors in the days of old (τοῖς πατράσιν ἡμῶν [לאבתינו] κατὰ τὰς ἡμέρας [מימי] τὰς ἔμπροσθεν)." Joel 1:2 asks if anything like "this" happened "in the days of your ancestors" (ἐν ταῖς ἡμέραις [בימי] τῶν πατέρων ὑμῶν [אבתיכם])." As yet, it is not clear whether "this" is good or bad news: as the end of Micah suggests the former, 1:4 brings another reversal. The contrast remains if Joel follows Hosea, but the link with the ancestors is lost. As in the previous cases, nothing in the actual rendering points to conscious choice on the part of the translator; the result would have been the same wherever he encountered the books.

2.4 Joel–Obadiah

This is a striking transition. In Joel 3:19 Idumea/Edom is singled out for judgment; the whole of Obadiah concerns God's judgment on Idumea/Edom (Obad 1). The transition reads more dramatically than when

Amos intervenes, especially as the reference to Edom in Amos 9:12 MT is further from the end and disappears altogether in LXX. The pairing also highlights XII's concern with Israel/Judah's relationship to foreign nations.

2.5 Obadiah–Jonah

This is the only pairing which is the same in both sequences. There is an interesting thematic balance: Edom's annihilation (Obad 1–9) against Niniveh's reprieve (Jonah 3:10). There are no obvious verbal links, apart from "go up" (ἀναβαίνειν עלה) in Obad 21 and Jonah 1:2, standard renderings that give nothing away.

2.6 Jonah–Nahum

This linkage – another reversal – is clearly significant. Jonah ends with God's question: "shall I not spare Nineue?" Nahum opens with the programmatic "issue (λῆμμα משא) for Nineue," quickly establishing that the city will be destroyed after all. Jonah and Nahum are the only books to end in questions, all the more significant for being adjacent, as they highlight a tension at the very centre of XII: the fate of foreigners. The books are further linked by allusions to Exod 34:6–7 (Jonah 4:2; Nah 1:3), though the *leitmotif* occurs elsewhere in XII. Textually, LXX does not differ in any significant way from MT.

2.7 Summary

The transitions from Hosea to Nahum show that, although the translator *may* have been using a scroll with the component elements arranged in "Greek" order, nothing indicates that he must *necessarily* have done so: shared vocabulary is unremarkable and only demonstrates that the *Vorlage* was very close to MT. The repetition of γῆ in Amos 9:15 and Mic 1:2 may or may not reveal an intention to knit the two books together. Had the translator been constructing a new arrangement, I would have expected more clues. What the exercise does demonstrate is that meaningful connections show up when XII are read in Septuagintal order, in Hebrew as well as Greek.[10]

---

10   See Sweeney, "Sequence," 56–59, for a synchronic reading of LXX.

But supposing the translator was not using a scroll with the books in "Greek" order? What if he already had the Masoretic sequence before him, and the translation was only subsequently rearranged into what is now considered Septuagintal order? Let us, *ad experimentum*, see what happens to the Greek connections if the Masoretic order is followed.

3. Hosea–Nahum: Masoretic "Seams" in Greek

3.1 Hosea–Joel

Nogalski proposed that Hosea and Joel were yoked by catchwords in Joel 1:1–12 anticipated in Hos 14:8–10.[11] Three of these, in Hos 14:8, "corn" (דָּגָן [Joel 1:10]), "vine" (גֶּפֶן [Joel 1:7, 12]), and "wine" (יַיִן [Joel 1:5, 10]), receive standard translations in both passages: σῖτος, ἄμπελος and οἶνος and so prove nothing.

Nogalski's first catchword, however, in MT Hos 14:8; Joel 1:2, is יֹשְׁבֵי, "inhabitants." In LXX, the echo fades: Hosea (presuming יָשְׁבוּ) has καθιοῦνται, "they will sit down."[12] Joel has οἱ κατοικοῦντες, "inhabitants," a stock rendering of a stock phrase. This is one of many places where Nogalski marks down the translator for not recognising or not caring about a catchword.[13] In defence, it could be observed that the contexts here are very different, and that the syntax of Hos 14:8 is awkward.[14] The translator has been attentive to the immediate context (his normal procedure) and has made fair sense of the imagery of a shady tree (v. 6–7). He may also have avoided the repetition for stylistic reasons: elegant variation, even across books, is characteristic of this translator.[15]

If that link is broken, a new one, not in MT, is forged. Hos 14:8 has "they will grow corn," literally "they will make corn live (יְחַיּוּ דָגָן)." Instead of a *piel* LXX understands a *qal* "they will live (יִחְיוּ ζήσονται). דָגָן is treated as instrumental, "by means of corn" (σίτῳ). But between verb and complement, LXX adds "and they will be drunk (καὶ μεθυσθήσονται)."[16] Another characteristic of the translator is to add verbs for clarification.[17] One might have seemed needed here, but get-

---

11   Nogalski, *Precursors*, 21.
12   For the text, see Bons, *Osée*, 166, where MT is already taken to have this sense.
13   Nogalski, *Precursors*, 56–57.
14   Cf. Gelston, *BHQ*, 73*.
15   See Dines, "Invention," 25–31.
16   The verb occurs elsewhere in XII only in Nah 3:11; Hab 2:15.
17   E.g. Hos 7:6; Amos 3:11; Nah 2:6; Hag 2:19; Zech 8:11, 19.

ting drunk on corn is not *prima facie* enlightening.[18] Significantly, however, Joel 1:5 has "you drinkers (οἱ μεθύοντες)," a good rendering of
שְׁכוּרִים, followed by "all who drink wine to intoxication" (εἰς μέθην,
MT עַל־עָסִיס, "over the sweet wine," an equivalence found only here;[19]
the phrase ends the first half of the verse; in MT it opens the second
half). Perhaps the emphasis on drink and drunkenness in Joel gave the
translator the idea of anticipating the theme in Hos 14:8. He is unlikely
to have found the expansion in the Hebrew with its different vocabulary and syntax.[20] Even if there are echoes of Ps 35:8 or Isa 49:26, or
both,[21] the trigger will have been the occurrence of μεθύοντες in Joel
1:5.[22] The link makes sense if the translator met Joel immediately after
Hosea, rather than with Amos and Micah in between.

Nogalski suggests one other link. Hos 14:10 has "those who are
wise understand these things (אֵלֶּה);" Joel 1:2 has "hear this (זֹאת) you
elders," followed by "has such a thing (זֹאת) happened in your days?"
LXX underlines the connection by rendering both אֵלֶּה and the first זֹאת
as ταῦτα.[23] As both Hebrew pronouns are routinely rendered in this
way, this cannot prove that the translator found the passages adjacent.
But if he did, he has created a significant echo, suggesting (as Nogalski
does for MT) that "these things" which the discerning person is to understand in Hosea are also the things which the addressees in Joel are
to hear.[24]

3.2 Joel–Amos

In MT, the opening words of Joel 3(4):16 and Amos 1:2 are identical:
"the Lord roars from Sion and utters his voice from Jerusalem" (וֵ[יהוה]
מִצִּיּוֹן יִשְׁאָג וּמִירוּשָׁלִַם יִתֵּן קוֹלוֹ).[25] LXX differs in two ways. First, Joel

---

18 Hence, doubtless, the addition of, or replacement by, στηριχθήσονται, "they will be
    strengthened," in some manuscripts; Ziegler, *Duodecim Prophetae*, 180. Bons, *Osée*,
    166, refers to Ps 64(65):10, "you visited the earth and intoxicated it (ἐμέθυσας
    αὐτήν)." A closer parallel comes in Ps 35(36):8, "they will be drunk (μεθυσθήσονται
    [רוה]) with fatness." More sinister is Isa 34:7, "the earth will be drunk (μεθυσθήσεται
    [רוה]) with the blood;" also Jer 26(46):10; Isa 49:26 (where καὶ μεθυσθήσονται is a
    plus).
19 But cf. Isa 29:26, "as new wine" (ὡς οἶνος νέος [כעסיס]). Joel 3(4):18, in a different
    context, renders עסיס by γλυκασμός; cf. Amos 9:13.
20 Bons, *Osée*, 166.
21 Cf. note 18. It is as yet unclear whether Psalms and/or Isaiah were already in Greek.
22 μέθυσμα (תירוש), "strong drink" in Hos 4:11 seems too distant to account for the
    choice.
23 The second is rendered τοιαῦτα, perhaps for variation.
24 Nogalski, "Joel," 98 note 15.

has futures, ἀνακεκράξεται and δώσει that match the Hebrew *yiqtols* (ישׂאג, יתן) and fit the context. But Amos has aorists (ἐφθέγξατο, ἔδωκε) that orient the prophecy to past rather than present or future. Secondly, although for נתן the default verb δίδωμι is used each time, שׂאג, is rendered by κράζω in Joel, but φθέγγομαι in Amos. The verbs are effectively synonyms. Does the variation suggest the translator was so far away from the first occurrence when he came to the second that he forgot what he had already put? On the contrary, I think the variation is deliberate, a typical stylistic device that could point to the proximity of the passages in the translator's scroll.

There are other echoes between Joel 3(4):16–21 and Amos 1:1–3 but they are the same in MT and LXX, unremarkable as translations.[26] There is, however, one small link not found in MT. In Joel 3(4):19, the crimes of Egypt and Edom are introduced by אשׁר, "in that," rendered by ἀνθ'ὧν, "because." The same conjunction renders על with infinitive construct in Amos 1:3 to introduce the sins of Damascus. Given the similarity in context, the echo is probably deliberate, especially as the equivalence between על and ἀνθ'ὧν occurs only here in XII.

3.3 Amos–Obadiah

MT creates echoes between Amos 9:12 and Obad 1, and between Amos 9:2 and Obad 4.

Amos 9:12 declares that the survivors of Israel are to inherit the remnant of Edom; it is to Edom that Obad 1 announces the word of the Lord. LXX, however, while addressing the divine word "to Idumea (τῇ Ἰδουμαίᾳ)" in Obad 1, has no previous mention of Edom in Amos 9:12 with which to link it, since אד(ו)ם (perhaps spelt defectively) has been vocalised not as אֱדוֹם ("Edom") but as אָדָם ("humans"), resulting in a very different understanding of the Hebrew.[27]

But the link between Amos 9:2, "from there I will bring them down (משׁם אורידם)," and Obad 4, "from there I will bring you down (משׁם אורידך)," is maintained. LXX translates exactly with ἐκεῖθεν κατάξω αὐτούς / σε. An exact match also occurs in MT between Obad 4 and Jer 49(29):16, though LXX in the latter passage has καθελῶ not κατάξω. The result for Amos and Obadiah is a striking intertextual echo, whether or not the books were contiguous. Obviously, the nearer they were, the more likely the translator was to match his renderings.

---

25   Amos lacks *waw*.
26   E.g. earthquake (Joel 3:16; Amos 1:1); Jerusalem (Joel 3:17, 26; Amos 1:1).
27   See Gelston, *BHQ*, 88*.

Unlike the Joel–Amos repetition discussed in section 3.2, there is no literary variation here, though Jer 29(49):16 shows that other choices were possible had the translator wished; perhaps he found the variation in pronouns sufficient.

3.4 Obadiah–Jonah

What was said about the Greek sequence in section 2.4 holds good here: there is no hint of translational innovation.

3.5 Jonah–Micah

There are no obvious verbal links across this "seam" either. Nogalski points to link-words between Jonah 2:5, 8, 9 and Mic 1:2, 7, especially "temple" (היכל). This is not maintained in Greek, where different words occur, the default ναός in Jonah, the less common οἶκος in Micah.[28]

There is, however, a very striking correlation between the Greek superscriptions in Jonah 1:1 and Mic 1:1. In MT different formulae are used, of which Jonah's is unique in XII as an incipit: "And the word of the Lord came to Jonah (ויהי דבר יהוה אל יונה)."[29] Micah's superscription, however, follows the pattern of Hosea, Joel, and Zephaniah: "The word of the Lord that came to Micah" (דבר יהוה אשר היה אל מיכה). In LXX, the crucial factor is that Jonah 1:1 matches MT: καὶ ἐγένετο λόγος κυρίου πρὸς Ιωναν, but Mic 1:1 does not. Instead it has the same pattern as Jonah 1:1: καὶ ἐγένετο λόγος κυρίου πρὸς Μιχαίαν. Clearly, Mic 1:1 has been conformed to Jonah 1:1, *and not vice versa*, since Jonah's incipit matches the Hebrew and fits the book's narrative genre. It is unlikely that Micah ever started like this in Hebrew, given the regnal setting of the superscription and the prophetic address from 1:2 onwards (Micah has no narrative). This strongly suggests that the translator had already met Jonah before starting on Micah.[30] Had he found Micah in the company of Hosea and Amos, as in the Greek order, and with Joel and Obadiah preceding Jonah, he would have had no reason to adapt the superscription.[31]

---

28 In XII only again in Zech 6:12, 14, 15.
29 It occurs elsewhere as a sub-heading; cf. Hillers, *Micah*, 13, who notes the match with Mic 1:1 as "not altogether without significance"!
30 Perhaps he somehow saw Micah as a continuation of Jonah's open ending; cf. Sweeney, "Sequence," 59–60.

3.6 Micah–Nahum

Nogalski's catchwords for Mic 7:8, 10 and Nah 1:2, 8 include common words like "enemy" and "darkness" which LXX renders unremarkably. There is also a pairing of Bashan and Carmel in Mic 7:18 and Nah 1:4, again identical in LXX and MT. More significantly, both Mic 7:18 and Nah 1:2 LXX have the participle ἐξαίρων, "removing," where MT has different verbs, נשא in Micah, for which ἐξαίρων is an exact match, and נוטר in Nahum, where LXX alters the meaning, since נטר "keep" has the sense of "harbour resentment."[32] An echo not in MT is thus created in LXX.[33] There is also an assonance between ἀδικίας ("injustices," און) in Mic 7:18 and the key verb ἐκδικῶν ("avenging," נקם) in Nah 1:1–3 not found in MT.

3.7 Summary

If LXX XII is read in Masoretic order, we find that some Hebrew links are missing while others appear. In particular, there is a striking link between Hos 14:8, μεθυσθήσονται, and Joel 1:5, μεθύοντες, which seems to be the work of the translator. There is also a surprising move by which Mic 1:1 is brought into line with Jonah 1:1, implying that Micah followed Jonah in the translator's *Vorlage*. There are several other smaller innovations, including ἀνθ'ὧν in both Joel 3(4):19 and Amos 1:3 and ἐξαίρων in both Mic 7:18 and Nah 1:2.

This may not be much to go on, but it is more than emerged from the Greek sequence. I think there is enough to make it plausible that LXX reflects a scroll with XII in Masoretic order. This does not mean that Hebrew scrolls in "Greek" order did not exist at the same time, only that the translator did not use one. There is thus indirect evidence for the existence of the Masoretic order as far back as the mid-second century B.C.E., the same time, that is, as 4QXIIᵃ.[34] 8ḤevXIIgr, which attests Masoretic order, can also be seen in a new light. It is assumed – or at least not questioned – that the order of the books has been rearranged to fit that of an emerging standard Hebrew. But if XII were

---

31 Amos 1:1 is also anomalous, though in a different way; it has not affected Mic 1:1.
32 It occurs only here and Amos 1:11 in XII.
33 Perhaps with a contrast in sense: in Mic 7:18 God "removes" injustices committed by his people, that is he overlooks them; in Nah 1:2 he "removes" his enemies, that is he destroys them.
34 See above, note 1.

translated in Masoretic order, 8ḤevXIIgr would be the earliest witness to the original shape of OG XII.[35] Revision has affected text (Mic 1:1, for instance, matches MT), but not sequence.

4. Afterlife of the Masoretic Order in Greek

LXX XII continued to circulate in Masoretic order well into the Common Era. This calls for some (hesitant) exploration. Evidence for the phenomenon appears mainly in the 4th–5th centuries C.E. patristic writers Theodore of Mopsuestia, Theodoret of Cyrus, and Cyril of Alexandria.[36] All claimed to follow LXX, but internal evidence suggests that the Antiochenes Theodore and Theodoret used the Masoretic order. As with LXX itself, this becomes clear mainly from the "seams" between books.

4.1 Theodore of Mopsuestia (Commentary on XII ca. 375 C.E.)[37]

That Theodore's Lucianic (Antiochian) codex of the XII was in Masoretic order is indicated in several places:[38]

4.1.1 In the Prologue to Joel, Theodore names Joel as Hosea's contemporary. This deduction would have been surprising if, as in Septuagintal order, the two prophets were separated by Amos and Micah, neither of whom is mentioned. It looks as if Theodore passed straight from Hosea to Joel.

4.1.2 When introducing Haggai, Theodore refers back to "Hosea, Joel, Amos, and Micah." This seems to be a mixture of Hebrew and Greek ordering, but Obadiah and Jonah are omitted because, as Theodore explains, they did not prophesy to Israel and Judah. The order is thus Masoretic.

4.1.3 He quotes and expounds the last verses of Malachi in MT order, Moses–Elijah.[39]

It is clear, from these and other indications (especially the Prologues to Micah and Nahum), that Theodore's codex had the Masoretic

---

35 The possibility is noted in passing by Fuller, "Form," 93.
36 Jerome translated XII piecemeal, "not according to the order in which they are read (*iuxta ordinem quo leguntur*);" Prol. Amos (406 C.E.); Adriaen, *S. Hieronymi*, ad loc. But it is unclear if he meant Septuagintal or Masoretic order.
37 Edition: Sprenger, *Theodori*; translation: Hill, *Theodore*.
38 On the text-type, see Dines, *Septuagint*, 103–105; cf. Sprenger, *Theodori*, 66; Hill, *Theodore*, 8.
39 See the article of Fuller, p. 371–379, in this volume.

order. As the earliest Lucianic minuscules of XII date from the ninth century,[40] this indirectly pushes the Lucianic evidence back to the mid-fourth century at least. As this text-type preserves numerous ancient readings,[41] Theodore could have inherited a very old – perhaps even the original – arrangement, though it cannot be ruled out that the ordering was of more recent Christian origin. There is no hint on Theodore's part that he is departing from the normal way of reading XII.

4.2 Theodoret of Cyrus (Commentary on XII ca. 435 C.E.)[42]

Theodoret must also have used a codex with XII in Masoretic order. Similar clues to those in Theodore's Commentary are found at the "seams" of the books, for instance: Joel is contemporary with Hosea, Amos with Hosea and Joel, while Moses precedes Elijah at the end of Malachi.

4.3 Comment

The Antiochene exegetes were not, like Jerome, partisans of *Hebraica veritas*, nor is the order of the books an issue, since no reference is made to it. Their practice seems to result from the nature of their manuscripts. Study of their biblical citations confirms that they used a text type which, even if reworked by Lucian (ca. 250–312 C.E.), can be traced back at least to the first century C.E. (the so-called proto-Lucianic text).[43] Ziegler's *Hauptgruppe* of six Lucianic manuscripts for XII, dating from ninth to twelfth centuries, all follow Masoretic order, as do the vast majority of those in the two *Untergruppen*.[44] The commentaries of Theodore and Theodoret suggest that this was the normal way in which XII were read in fourth and fifth century Antiochene churches. As there is no hint of this being innovative or controversial, it is likely that the sequence derived from even older manuscripts.

Theodoret's biblical commentaries are among those featuring in the later Catena collections.[45] Mathilde Aussedat notes the phenomenon of

---

40   Ziegler; *Duodecim Prophetae*, 8–10.73–75; Rahlfs, *Verzeichnis*, 8.67.84.113.162.173.250. 266.
41   See Fernández Marcos, *Septuagint*, 197; Dines, *Septuagint*, 103.
42   Edition: Migne, *Patrologia Graeca* (PG) 81; translation: Hill, *Theodoret*.
43   See note 41.
44   See note 40.
45   Aussedat, "Regroupement," 172. On the Catenae, see Fernández Marcos, *Septuagint*, 287–301.

Catena manuscripts with Masoretic ordering, attributing it to a "Hebraizing" tendency, perhaps due to Hexaplaric influence on the Catena texts. This may account for some of the evidence affecting the Lucianic elements (the Lucianic Recension shows some Hexaplaric influence) but there may be other factors to consider, since the proto-Lucianic text predates Origen.[46]

4.4 Cyril of Alexandria (Commentary on XII ca. 425 C.E.)[47]

For the Alexandrian Cyril, however, an investigation of the "seams" shows conclusively that, despite reordering in the printed editions (based on Pontanus, 1607),[48] Cyril himself worked with the Septuagintal sequence:

4.4.1 In the Prologue to Joel (which follows Hosea in the editions, but must have followed Micah in Cyril's codex), Cyril says, "blessed Joel apparently prophesies at the same time as those placed (τεταγμένοι) before him – I mean Hosea, and also Amos – can be deemed to have prophesied. For the Jews think he ought to be placed (συντετάχθαι) not after Micah but with them." The two Greek terms show that Cyril is referring to sequence, not chronology. Significantly, he is aware of the difference as a Jewish-Christian divide, perhaps controversial ("ought").[49]

4.4.2 He notes the verbal links between the end of Joel and the start of Obadiah.[50] He is unlikely to have made the connection if Amos intervened.

4.4.3 He links Jonah with those already treated: "Hosea, Amos, Micah, and the rest (Ωσεε τε φῆμι καὶ Αμως καὶ Μιχαίας καὶ οἱ λοιποί)," "the rest" presumably being Joel and Obadiah.[51]

4.4.4 He treats the end of Malachi in the Greek order, Elijah–Moses, with no comment on a different "Jewish" order.[52]

---

46 Aussedat, "Regroupement," 175.
47 Editions: Pusey, *Cyrilli* 1; Migne, *Patrologia Graeca* (PG) 71, 72; translation: Hill, *St Cyril*, 1:2.
48 For problems in identifying Pontanus's manuscripts, see Ziegler, "Bibeltext," 400.
49 Migne, *PG* 71, 328B; Hill, *St Cyril*, 1:6.259, takes this passage as evidence of Masoretic order.
50 Migne, *PG* 71, 581B; Hill, *St Cyril*, 1:152.
51 Migne, *PG* 71, 597A–601C; Hill, *St Cyril*, 2:147.
52 Migne, *PG* 72, 361C.364B.

5. Conclusion

Cyril's sequence links him with W, the Greek-Coptic Glossary, the earliest codices (Vaticanus etc.), *Martyrdom of Isaiah, Lives of the Prophets*, and *4 Ezra*.[53] W and the Glossary belong, like Cyril, in Egypt. The provenance of the great uncials is uncertain, but the pseudepigrapha are usually located in Palestine. Tentatively, one might propose a division between the textual habits of the Egyptian and Palestinian churches in this respect and those of the Antiochene ones. The two sequences would then have co-existed in different parts of the Christian Greek-speaking world.[54]

A crucial missing link is Origen (ca. 185–254 C.E.), who lived in both Alexandria and Caesarea. Practically nothing survives of his work on XII, and it is not known how he organized these books in his Hexapla since Eusebius – surely accidentally – omits XII from his list of books in *Historia Ecclesiae*, 6.25. But, given Origen's provenance, it is likely that he used the "Greek" sequence. Perhaps it was he who brought it from Egypt to Palestine. After that, the powerful influence of his Hexaplaric edition of LXX could have led to the dominance of the Greek sequence over the Hebrew. If, however, Aussedat is right in thinking that Origen started the "Hebraizing" trend, we have to account in another way for the success of the Greek sequence.[55] What is clear from the Antiochenes and their texts is that both sequences existed in different strands of Christian transmission at least from the mid-fourth century C.E. The most likely explanation is that both had already circulated together, in Greek, in Egypt, if my case for an original translation according to Masoretic order holds up. A line of transmission from mid-second century B.C.E. Alexandria to mid-fourth century C.E. Antioch needs to be traced, and the proto-Lucianic text may provide some signposts. The greatest remaining challenge is to explain the rearrangement of the OG translation in "Septuagintal" order. It too appears to have Egyptian roots and if any weight can be put on the pseudepigrapha, is likely to be of Jewish rather than Christian origin. If the earliest translation, in "Masoretic" order, was rearranged to fit a sequence found in other Hebrew scrolls which had the "Greek" order, both sequences must have circulated for a considerable time in Hebrew, to allow some Jewish(?) users of LXX to re-order the translation. This would be the reverse of what is usually taken to have happened, for

---

53 See p. 355.
54 Hill, *Theodore*, 8, refers to Theodore's Antiochian text as "local." Fernández Marcos, *Septuagint*, 245, links Cyril with a localized Alexandrian text.
55 See above, note 46.

instance in the supposed reordering of 8ḤevXIIgr.[56] And if two Greek arrangements co-existed, perhaps it was just a matter of chance as to which fell into the hands of Christian scribes and commentators.

It cannot be ruled out, however, that the "Septuagintal" arrangement was a Christian development, since manuscript evidence still begins only with the third century C.E. This is acknowledged by Marvin Sweeney, whose readings of both sequences point nonetheless to a real possibility that the "Greek" one is of great antiquity, perhaps even reflecting an earlier context than the "Hebrew" one.[57]

Was it purely accidental that XII's translator worked from a scroll apparently in Masoretic order? Or did he select this arrangement because it corresponded to his understanding of XII's meaning and message? The fact that he could occasionally put his own mark on the translation – most notably in Hos 14:8; Mic 1:1 – suggests that the latter is not out of the question. The next step is to ponder why a mid-second century Alexandrian translator would make that choice.

References

Adriaen, M.S. *Hieronymi ... Commentarii in Prophetas Minores (Osee, Ioelem, Amos, Abdiam, Ionam, Michaeam)*. Corpus Christianorum Series Latina 76. Turnhout: Brepols, 1969.

Aussedat, M. "Le Regroupement des Livres Prophétiques dans la Septante d'après le Témoignage des Chaînes Exégétiques." Pp. 169–185 in *XII Congress of the International Organization for Septuagint and Cognate Studies, Leiden 2004*. Edited by M.K.H. Peters. Atlanta: Society of Biblical Literature, 2006.

Bons, E. et al. *Osée*. La Bible d'Alexandrie 23.1. Paris: Cerf, 2002.

Brooke, G.J. "The Twelve Minor Prophets and the Dead Sea Scrolls." Pp. 19–43 in *Congress Volume, Leiden 2004*. Edited by A. Lemaire. VTSup 109. Leiden: Brill, 2006.

Dines, J.M. *The Septuagint*. London: T&T Clark, 2004.

– "Stylistic Invention and Rhetorical Purpose in the Book of the Twelve." Pp. 23–48 in *Et sapienter et eloquenter: Studies in Rhetorical and Stylistic Features of the Septuagint*. Edited by E. Bons and T. Kraus. FRLANT 241. Göttingen: Vandenhoeck & Ruprecht, 2011.

Fernández Marcos, N. *The Septuagint in Context: Introduction to the Greek Versions of the Bible*. Leiden: Brill, 2000.

Fuller, R.E. "The Form and Formation of the Book of the Twelve: The Evidence from the Judean Desert." Pp. 86–101 in *Forming Prophetic Literature: Essays*

56 See above, p. 363–364.
57 Sweeney, "Sequence," 64. The widespread agreement that XII grew out of an original Hosea–Amos–Micah collection could suggest that the Greek order is very early.

on Isaiah and the Twelve. Edited by J.W. Watts and P.R. House. FS J.D.W. Watts. JSOTSup 235. Sheffield: Sheffield Academic Press, 1996.

Gelston, A. *BHQ. The Twelve Minor Prophets*. Biblia Hebraica Quinta 13. Stuttgart: Deutsche Bibelgesellschaft, 2010.

Hare, D.R.A. "The Lives of the Prophets (First Century A.D.)." Pp. 379–399 in vol. 2 of *The Old Testament Pseudepigrapha*. Edited by J.H. Charlesworth. New York: Doubleday, 1985.

Hill, R.C. *Theodore of Mopsuestia: Commentary on the Twelve Prophets*. Washington: Catholic University of America, 2004.

–   *Commentary on the Twelve Prophets*. Vol. 3 of *Theodoret of Cyrus: Commentaries on the Prophets*. Brookline: Holy Cross Orthodox Press, 2006.

–   *St Cyril of Alexandria: Commentary on the Twelve Prophets*. 2 vols. Washington: Catholic University of America, 2007–2008.

Hillers, D.R. *Micah*. Hermeneia. Philadelphia: Fortress Press, 1984.

Jones, B.A. "The Book of the Twelve as a Witness to Ancient Biblical Interpretation." Pp. 65–87 in *Reading and Hearing the Book of the Twelve*. Edited by J.D. Nogalski and M.A. Sweeney. SBLSymS 15. Atlanta: Society of Biblical Literature, 2000.

Knibb, M.A. "Martyrdom and Ascension of Isaiah (Second Century B.C.–Fourth Century A.D.)." Pp. 143–155 in vol. 2 of *The Old Testament Pseudepigrapha*. Edited by J.H. Charlesworth. New York: Doubleday, 1985.

Metzger, B.M. "The Fourth Book of Ezra (Late First Century A.D.)." Pp. 517–559 in vol. 1 of *The Old Testament Pseudepigrapha*. Edited by J.H. Charlesworth. New York: Doubleday, 1983.

Migne, J.-P. *S.P.N. Cyrilli Alexandrini in XII Prophetas*. Patrologia Graeca 71, 72. Paris, 1864.

–   *Theodoreti Cyrensis Episcopi Opera*. Patrologia Graeca 81. Paris, 1864.

Nogalski, J.D. *Literary Precursors to the Book of the Twelve*. BZAW 217. Berlin: de Gruyter, 1993.

–   "Joel as 'Literary Anchor' for the Book of the Twelve." Pp. 91–109 in *Reading and Hearing the Book of the Twelve*. Edited by idem and M.A. Sweeney. SBLSymS 15. Atlanta: Society of Biblical Literature, 2000.

Pusey, P.E. *S.P.N. Cyrilli Archiepiscopi Alexandrini in XII Prophetas*. Vol. 1. Oxford, 1868.

Rahlfs, A. *Verzeichnis der griechischen Handschriften des Alten Testaments*. Berlin: Eidmannsche Buchhandlung, 1914.

–   *Die Überlieferung bis zum VIII. Jahrhundert*. Vol. I.1 of Verzeichnis der griechischen Handschriften des Alten Testaments. Revised by D. Fraenkel. Göttingen: Vandenhoeck & Ruprecht, 2004.

Satran, D. *Biblical Prophets in Byzantine Palestine: Reassessing the "Lives of the Prophets."* Leiden: Brill, 1995.

Sprenger, H.N. *Theodori Mopsuesteni Commentarii in XII Prophetas*. Wiesbaden: Harrassowitz, 1977.

Sweeney, M.A. *Hosea Joel Amos Obadiah Jonah*. Vol. 1 of *The Twelve Prophets*. Berit Olam. Collegeville: Liturgical Press, 2000.

–   "Sequence and Interpretation in the Book of the Twelve." Pp. 49–64 in *Reading and Hearing the Book of the Twelve*. Edited by J.D. Nogalski and idem. SBLSymS 15. Atlanta: Society of Biblical Literature, 2000.

Ziegler, J. "Der Bibeltext des Cyrill von Alexandrien zu den zwölf Propheten in den Druck-Ausgaben." Pp. 400–412 in *Sylloge*. Edited by idem. Göttingen: Vandenhoeck & Ruprecht, 1971.

–   *Duodecim Prophetae. Septuaginta: Vetus Testamentum Graecum XIII.* 3rd edition. Göttingen: Vandenhoeck & Ruprecht, 1984.

The Sequence of Malachi 3:22–24 in the Greek and Hebrew Textual Traditions: Implications for the Redactional History of the Minor Prophets

RUSSELL FULLER

University of San Diego

In this paper I will advance the idea of the necessity of the constant interaction of literary criticism and textual criticism in the study of the biblical text, especially in reconstructing the end stages of the growth of the biblical text and the process of canonization. I will also draw attention to the end of Malachi as an example of the importance of this interaction of disciplines and of the importance of utilizing all the manuscript evidence, especially the Greek, for reconstructing the end stages of the growth of biblical books and the development of the collection of the Twelve Minor Prophets.

In this regard, I have also been influenced in my thinking by the very interesting book of Karel van der Toorn, *Scribal Culture and the Making of the Hebrew Bible*. He proposes an interesting model for the scribal creation of the collection of the Twelve Minor Prophets as part of a greater collection of the Torah and Prophets. Malachi 3:22–24 plays an important role in his reconstruction of the history of Malachi, the Twelve, and the Torah-prophets collection. I will be interacting with his model, which I think is an important first step in recognizing the importance of the ancient scribes in the making of the Hebrew Bible and to contextualizing that scribal activity.

Let me begin by citing a passage from the work of Natalio Fernández Marcos, *The Septuagint in Context*, which clearly lays out the changed relationship between textual criticism and literary criticism:[1]

> „Textual criticism is concerned with the transmission of the text once it has been fixed. Literary criticism, instead, studies the period of the literary formation of a book or set of books until the final edit. The problem arises when parts of a biblical book or early editions of complete books have been put into writing and circulated before the literary editing is complete. This

---

1   Fernández Marcos, *Septuagint*, 79–80.

is the case for the LXX translation: the translation was completed at a particular time in history and later the Hebrew texts of some of the books were
re-edited with expansions, revisions or alterations of a different kind. Editions were put into circulation that were later replaced by new revised editions of the same book, revised editions that became official in the canonization process of the Hebrew text. As a result, the first editions have only
been preserved for posterity either by chance, as in the case of the texts
found in Qumran, or else because they were transmitted by non-Jewish
communities, such as the Christian community in the case of the LXX."

This sentiment regarding the "overlap" of textual criticism and literary
criticism or rather the idea that the two disciplines can not exist in a
rigid sequence, is also strongly argued by Emanuel Tov in his magiste-
rial work, *The Textual Criticism of the Hebrew Bible*, soon to appear in a
3rd edition.[2] It is also stressed by Eugene Ulrich in numerous articles.[3]
We are all familiar with the obvious example of Jeremiah where the
LXX and some Qumran manuscripts are now understood to preserve
an earlier, first edition of the book, which was later revised and expanded in the Hebrew textual tradition – the version which became
canonical in the MT. But, there are also many other cases, none so dramatic, where later changes may be detected between the versions,
which indicate the continued development of the composition. One
such case, I argue, is found at the end of Malachi in the different sequences of the last three verses.

In Malachi 3:22–24 (MT), the passage which is at the heart of the
discussion, the sequence of the last three verses of Malachi in the MT
differs from the sequence of the last three verses in LXX Malachi.

MT Mal 3:22 features a reminder of the Torah/Law of Moses, which
was commanded for all Israel at Horeb. In 3:23–24 we find the promise
of the sending of Elijah before the "great and terrible Day of the Lord."

In LXX Mal, the Moses and Elijah verses appear in the reverse sequence, first the Elijah verses then the Moses verse.

There are other mostly minor differences in the text of LXX compared to MT.

Van der Toorn argues that the temple scribes in Jerusalem published the scroll of the XII in an official edition on a single scroll in ca.
250 B.C.E., in Hebrew, in the proto-Masoretic form.[4] Elsewhere he also
suggests that this final edition of the XII was done by 200 B.C.E.,[5] so he
has the idea that somewhere between 250–200 B.C.E. the Twelve Minor
Prophets were completed in an official edition. At that time, in his

---

2   Tov, *Textual Criticism*, 313–350.
3   See conveniently the articles collected in: Ulrich, *Dead Sea Scrolls*.
4   Van der Toorn, *Scribal Culture*, 252.
5   Van der Toorn, *Scribal Culture*, 255.

model, the scribes created a twelfth prophet by disconnecting one of the *maśśā'* oracle collections (Zech 9–11; 12–14; Mal) from the others and attributing them to a twelfth prophet. The goal was to reach the number twelve so that the collection of all the prophets would correspond to the three patriarchs and the twelve tribes, 3+12 – an idea he borrows apparently from Joseph Blenkinsopp.[6] So his idea of the creation of Malachi as the twelfth prophet follows that described by Rainer Kessler.[7] But he does not agree with the understanding of Rainer Kessler that Malachi existed as a completed work which was then integrated into the XII by the addition of Malachi 3:22–24, with Malachi 3:22 added last. A position I find very attractive.

For van der Toorn, Malachi 3:22–24 comprises an editorial postscript or scribal colophon, he uses both descriptions, not only to the newly completed collection of the XII, but also to the prophets as a whole.[8] The colophon also functions to link the end of the collection of the prophets to the Torah (Deut 34). In this van der Toorn is similar to other proposals. Indeed, he is clearly dependent on the models proposed by or assumed by other scholars of the prophets. He places the time of publication of the prophets in a time of messianic expectations.[9] For van der Toorn, the publication of the XII on a single scroll conveyed the idea that the time of the prophets had come to an end. There would be no more prophets. Regarding the placement of Malachi at the end of the collection of the XII he states:[10]

> "If Malachi is a scribal construct created to obtain the canonical number of twelve, it follows that the Book of Malachi would originally have been placed at the end of the Minor Prophets. In this respect, the Masoretic manuscripts of the Minor Prophets preserve the original order. Further corroboration of the position of Malachi at the end of the Minor Prophets is provided by the occurrence of an editorial colophon, that pertains to the Minor Prophets as a whole."

---

6   Blenkinsopp, *History*, 209: "The reason for this sectioning at the end of the prophetic collection, one would suppose, was the need to arrive at the number twelve and thus permit the entire prophetic corpus to fall into a three plus twelve pattern, thereby symbolizing the three great ancestors and the twelve sons of Jacob/Israel, in other words, the totality of the house of Israel in light of which the reader is invited to read the prophets. This proposal is, as we shall see shortly, congruous with the last verses of Malachi (4:4–6 [MT 3:22–24]), which serve as the finale to the prophetic corpus as a whole,' perhaps even to Torah and Prophets together." See also Bosshard and Kratz, "Maleachi."

7   Kessler, p. 235, in this volume.

8   Van der Toorn, *Scribal Culture*, 253-255.

9   Van der Toorn, *Scribal Culture*, 252–256.

10   Van der Toorn, *Scribal Culture*, 253.

For van der Toorn, Malachi 3:22 reveals the scribal editors' view that the prophets are not meant to take the place of the Law of Moses, but rather to serve as a reminder of its importance.[11] Malachi 3:22 is strongly deuteronomic in flavor. Since there are no new prophets after Malachi, then we have the prediction of the return of an old one, Elijah.

In a footnote, he acknowledges the problem, which the Qumran evidence raises for this model of the priority of the sequence of the XII with Malachi at the end.[12] 4QXII^a becomes problematic to explain for his model, as for most other models. He follows Steck in arguing that the order Malachi-Jonah in 4QXII^a is secondarily derived from the order that becomes canonical in the Masoretic Text.[13]

Van der Toorn's model is a very attractive one, but I have several disagreements with it. I would like to begin with the sequence of the last three verses of Malachi in MT and LXX. A sequence difference, which may be significant. Van der Toorn mostly ignores this variation between the versions.[14] In this he follows the majority of the commentators.

I have argued elsewhere that the LXX sequence represents an older order for these three verses than the order found in MT.[15] I based this in part on the work of Emanuel Tov on sequence differences between LXX and MT where it is also possible to compare biblical manuscripts from the Judean Desert to verify the antiquity of the LXX sequence.[16] Tov argued, and I agree, that we must also start with the assumption that the LXX sequence is the older order where late material has been inserted into the text by scribes. This, I think was the case with verses at the end of Malachi. I also argued that the change in the sequence of verses occurred during the second century B.C.E., perhaps during the Maccabeean revolt and is first attested in 4QXII^a/4Q76 from this time period.

In this understanding, MT preserves a later redaction of the ending of Malachi. This understanding of the difference of the sequence of the verses is in agreement with the idea, advanced by Tov, that when late material was added to a composition, the scribes sometimes put the late material in different places. The LXX version was based on an earlier "official copy" in Hebrew, which became the basis for the translation. The MT preserves a later "official copy" which was redacted later in

11 Van der Toorn, *Scribal Culture*, 254.
12 Van der Toorn, *Scribal Culture*, 362 note 68.
13 Steck, "Abfolge," 251.
14 Van der Toorn, *Scribal Culture*, 363 note 69.
15 Fuller, "Hebrew."
16 Tov, "Sequence Differences."

circumstances, which favored the positioning of the Elijah verses at the very end also highlighting the Day of the Lord.

If I am correct in arguing that the LXX sequence of verses at the end of Malachi is original or older, then the mid second century B.C.E., with the evidence of 4QXII[a], marks the redaction of Malachi 3, perhaps during the early Hasmonean period reflecting a new emphasis on the coming of Elijah.[17]

The scribe moved Malachi 3:22 (MT) from the original position at the end of the chapter to its current position preceding the Elijah verses. This had the effect of emphasizing the Elijah tradition and the Day of Yahweh. Additional evidence of the early importance of the traditions of the return of Elijah before the Day of Yahweh to avert the wrath of God may be found in Ben Sira 48:10, ca. 180 B.C.E. Ben Sira 48:10 alludes to the tradition of the return of Elijah before the Day of Yahweh to avert the wrath of God. Malachi 3:24aα is cited and Malachi 3:24b is replaced with a citation of Isaiah 49:6b, apparently from a variant Hebrew text (also attested in 1QIsa[a]).[18]

Although most commentators either ignore or pay very little attention to this difference in the sequence of verses between the Greek and the Hebrew forms of Malachi, I would like to use this as a starting point and as an example for the discussion of some of the changes in our knowledge of the history of the texts of the Greek and Hebrew Bibles and their interrelationships and for the effect they have on our approaches to the study and reconstruction of the history of the compositions which make up the Twelve Minor Prophets.

In a sense I am working "backwards" in reconstructing the history of the text beginning with the manuscript evidence.

It is crucial to understand that we must look not only at Hebrew biblical manuscripts of the XII, but also especially the various Greek versions of the XII; i.e. the LXX and the Greek Minor Prophets scroll from Naḥal Ḥever (8ḤevXIIgr) which give us important information about the content, order and text of the collection of the XII as it was developing.

---

17 Two compositions from Qumran seem important in this regard, 4Q558 and 4Q521. Both allude to the role of Elijah in Malachi 3:23–24. See the editions of these fragmentary compositions in Puech, *Qumrân Grotte 4 XVIII*, and *Qumrân Grotte 4 XXVII*. This evidence (4Q558) of a focus on the coming of Elijah from the 1st century B.C.E. adds support for the idea of a redaction of Malachi 3:22–24 during this period and indirectly supports van der Toorn's idea of the redaction of the end of Malachi occurring during a time of messianic fervor.

18 1QIsa[a] col. 41.3 להקים את שבטי ישראל ונצירי יעקוב להשיב; MT Isa 49:6 reads: להקים את שבטי יעקוב ונצרי ישראל להשיב.

So to summarize, I would "fine tune" van der Toorn's model slightly to take account of the manuscript evidence regarding the history of
the end of Malachi (LXX) and the evidence for the focus on the Elijah
traditions for which we have new evidence from Qumran manuscripts,
4Q558 and 4Q521.

The original sequence of the verses of the appendix/appendices of
Malachi 3:22–24 is preserved in the LXX where the admonition to "re-
member the Law of Moses my servant" is found in the final position.
This verse in final position forms an intentional scribal *inclusio*, as van
der Toorn and many other scholars have argued, which "brackets" the
entire collection of the Prophets (Josh 1:7, etc.) and also links the collection of the Prophets to the Torah (Deut 34).[19] The final position is the
logical place for an *inclusio* and may suggest that the Moses verse was
added last by redactors. The LXX thus reflects the sequence of verses in
its Hebrew *Vorlage* from the late third or early second century B.C.E.
This time frame assumes the continuation of the translation of the Hebrew Scriptures into Greek between ca. 250–150 B.C.E.

During this time period there is evidence of a completed collection
of the XII from Ben Sira 49:10. Unfortunately, this reference does not
give us any information about the internal organization of the collection that Ben Sira was apparently acquainted with. However, since both
LXX and MT preserve collections in which Malachi was in the final
position in the scroll of the XII, it seems likely that this sequence of the
books was early (since we have it in LXX) and probably the most wide
spread, since we have Malachi in the final position in two out of three
ancient witnesses.

We must acknowledge that there existed some fluidity in the internal organization of this collection from early on. The LXX and the MT
differ in the order of the first six books of the collection, as is well
known. But, given the recognized tendency of the LXX to preserve the
sequence of both large and small textual units which were found in its
Vorlage, and the persuasive arguments that the XII were translated by a
single translator, I am inclined to think that the arrangement of the
Books in the LXX XII reflects the order that the translator found in his
Hebrew *Vorlage* and that this was an arrangement of the collection
which was perhaps older than the organization later found in the MT.[20]
The order of books in the MT collection would then represent a rearrangement, which either occurred after the LXX translation was completed or, alternatively, may represent a variant organization of the XII,

19 Wöhrle, *Abschluss*, 421–427.
20 This assumes that the translator was working from a single scroll. It is also possible
    that the sequence of books in the MT and LXX are equally old.

which was later chosen by the temple scribes as the authoritative form of the scroll. This idea would obviously have implications for theories of the redactional history of the XII.

There is also 4QXII[a], a mid second century B.C.E. manuscript, which almost certainly preserves a third, variant order of at least the end of the collection. This fragmentary manuscript preserves the remains of a scroll of the XII in which Jonah follows Malachi. I find myself unconvinced by the arguments of Steck that 4QXII[a] represents an anomalous collection of the XII which deviates intentionally from the "original order" which he thinks is that of MT. It seems to me more likely that 4QXII[a] preserves a variant order, which was extant before the scribes (perhaps arbitrarily) chose a scroll of the XII for the "official" copy. This scroll was one in the proto-Masoretic tradition. In other words, the period of time before the "official" scroll was created by the temple scribes was a period in which, based on the manuscript evidence, there was variation in the internal organization of the collection. The "official" version of the collection in Hebrew postdates the LXX translation and 4QXII[a]. 4QXII[a], from ca. 150 B.C.E. happens to preserve one of the variant orders that existed before the creation of the "official" copy. The Jerusalem temple scribes created a scroll of the XII in which Malachi was in the final position, perhaps because this was more usual, and Jonah was in the fifth position, a slightly variant order than that preserved from the scroll, which served as the basis for the LXX translation.

There is additional manuscript evidence for the growing dominance of the MT order of the collection, and this presumably dates from after the "official" copy had been made. First, in the Naḥal Ḥever Greek scroll of the XII where the preserved portions in the first six books show that this revision of the LXX collection had adopted the order in the pMT (proto-Masoretic Text). The Greek Naḥal Ḥever scroll of the XII dates to the last half of the first century B.C.E. Second, from the time of the Bar Kochba revolt against Rome (132–135 C.E.) we have the Hebrew scroll of the XII from the Wadi Murabba`at, a proto-Masoretic manuscript which witnesses not only to the canonical order in the Hebrew textual tradition of the XII, but also to the development of a standard text. This is an important stage in the development of the concept of a canon.

For the XII, 8ḤevXIIgr may be an indication of the date of the "official copy" of the XII published in temple circles. 8ḤevXIIgr seems to represent an attempt to revise the older LXX, to bring it into conformity with a Hebrew copy of the XII. This copy was not identical to MT according to both Barthelemy and Tov. This suggests an authoritative

Hebrew text of the XII had been published. In addition, as far as we can determine based on the remains of this manuscript, the sequence of compositions which is later normative/canonical in MT is also followed in this Greek manuscript and this is the earliest evidence for this sequence of compositions and stands in contrast to the *older* Greek sequence. This revision of both the text and the sequence is strongly suggestive of the publication of an official copy of the XII to which 8ḤevXIIgr is conforming. The *Vorlage* of 8ḤevXIIgr may be described as proto-Masoretic or proto-Rabbinic in terms of its text type.

Since 8ḤevXIIgr is dated to the last half of the 1st century B.C.E. (50–1 B.C.E.) this gives us a rough date for the publication of the "official copy" on which it was based; ca. 100–50 B.C.E. or the first half of the 1st century B.C.E.

So, perhaps by the beginning of the 1st century B.C.E., but probably no later than the middle of the 1st century B.C.E., the proto-Masoretic form of the collection had been finalized. This formalized the content, the sequence and the text of the collection. The LXX and Qumran copies of the XII which show variations from the proto-Masoretic form of the collection, such as 4QXIIa and 4QXIIc (close to the LXX), are reflective of earlier forms of the collection and should be taken into account in hypothetical reconstructions of the redactional history of the XII, especially since the proto-Masoretic text form achieved normative status at such a late date.

References

Blenkinsopp, J. *A History of Prophecy in Israel*. Revised and enlarged. Louisville: Westminster John Knox, 1996.

Bosshard, E. and Kratz, R.G. "Maleachi im Zwölfprophetenbuch." *BN* 52 (1990) 27–46.

Fernández Marcos, N. *The Septuagint in Context: Introduction to the Greek Version of the Bible*. Translated by W.G.E. Watson. Atlanta: Society of Biblical Literature, 2000.

Fuller, R.E. "Hebrew & Greek Biblical Manuscripts: Their Interpretations & Their Interpreters." Pp. 101–110 in vol. 1 of *The Dead Sea Scrolls in Context: Integrating the Dead Sea Scrolls in the Study of Ancient Texts, Languages, and Cultures*. Edited by A. Lange et al. Leiden: Brill, 2010–2011.

Puech, E. *Qumrân Grotte 4 XVIII Textes Hébreux (4Q521–4Q528, 4Q576–4Q579)*. DJD 25. Oxford: Clarendon, 1998.

–   *Qumrân Grotte 4 XXVII Textes Araméens Duexième Partie 4Q550–4Q575a, 4Q580–4Q587*. DJD 37. Oxford: Clarendon, 2009.

Steck, O.H. "Zur Abfolge Maleachi – Jona in 4Q76 (4QXIIa)." *ZAW* 108 (1996) 249–253.

Tov, E. "Some Sequence Differences Between the MT and LXX and Their Ramifications for the Literary Criticism of the Bible." *JNSL* 13 (1987) 151–160.
– *Textual Criticism of the Hebrew Bible.* 2nd revised edition. Minneapolis: Fortress, 2001.
Ulrich, E. *The Dead Sea Scrolls and the Origins of the Bible.* Grand Rapids and Cambridge: Eerdmans, 1999.
van der Kooij, A. "The Canonization of Ancient Books Kept in the Temple of Jerusalem." Pp. 17–40 in *Canonization and Decanonization.* Edited by idem and K. van der Toorn. Leiden: Brill, 1998.
van der Toorn, K. *Scribal Culture and the Making of the Hebrew Bible.* Cambridge and London: Harvard University Press, 2009.
Wöhrle, J. *Der Abschluss des Zwölfprophetenbuches. Buchübergreifende Redaktionsprozesse in den späten Sammlungen.* BZAW 389. Berlin: de Gruyter, 2008.

"Aligned" or "Non-Aligned"?
The Textual Status of the Qumran Cave 4 Manuscripts of the Minor Prophets[*]

HANNE VON WEISSENBERG
University of Helsinki

While it is acknowledged by most scholars that the Qumran "biblical"[1] scrolls have revolutionized our understanding of the Hebrew Bible in the Second Temple period, it is, at the same time, becoming increasingly clear that we are only beginning to find adequate ways to understand and describe the evidence we now have at our disposal. For the first time, scholars are able to investigate and analyze "biblical" manuscripts from a period prior to the stabilization of the text form of the individual books of the Hebrew Bible and the closure of the canon. Various attempts have been made to classify the "biblical" manuscripts, and probably the most influential has been the categorization proposed by Emanuel Tov.[2]

In this article, my intention is to revisit the Cave 4 manuscripts of the Minor Prophets, beginning with a brief introduction to the Minor Prophets manuscripts from Qumran. Then, I will continue with an overview of Tov's categories, followed by some criticism these categories have received in recent scholarly discussion. After presenting Tov's categories, I will return to the Cave 4 manuscripts of the Minor Prophets and show how different scholars have ended up with slightly different textual classifications for these manuscripts. The question is whether these differences in scholarly opinions regarding the textual

---

[*]   I wish to thank Mika Pajunen, Hanna Tervanotko, Dr. Charlotte Hempel, Prof. George Brooke, and Prof. Anneli Aejmelaeus for their helpful comments on an earlier draft of this article, and Dr. Robert Whiting for revising my English.

[1]   While acknowledging the problematic usage of the term "biblical" in a late Second Temple context, I am using it in this article simply as a reference to copies of those compositions that in a much later period became a part of the canonical Hebrew Bible. During the late Second Temple period, no closed, canonized Bible yet existed; instead, compositions were still in the process of moving from "authoritative" to "biblical" or "canonical." For the ongoing debate concerning appropriate terminology, see, for example, Ulrich, "The Notion," 21–35; Zahn, "Talking," 93–119.

[2]   See, Tov, *Textual*, 114–117.

affiliation of the Minor Prophets manuscripts result from inconsistent and varying criteria for determining the textual affiliation, or from problematic textual categories. To demonstrate one particular problem, namely the varying significance of the so-called "non-aligned" or "independent" variant readings, I will examine one manuscript, namely 4QXII^c, more closely and present two exemplary text critical cases of "non-aligned" variants in manuscript 4QXII^c to highlight the challenges underlying the classification of the "biblical" manuscripts from Qumran.

Introducing the Minor Prophets at Qumran

When Russell Fuller edited the Cave 4 manuscripts of the Twelve for the *Discoveries in the Judaean Desert* series, he published them as seven manuscripts labeled 4QXII^{a-g} (4Q76–82).[3] In addition to these, one manuscript containing a few verses of Amos (Amos 1:2–5) was recovered from Cave 5 (5QAmos = 5Q4) and published by Józef Milik.[4] In addition to the Qumran scrolls, we have two other important textual witnesses from the Dead Sea region: the Murabbaʿat manuscript of the Minor Prophets (MurXII), and the Greek scroll from Naḥal Ḥever (8ḤevXIIgr).[5] In this article I will focus on the Cave 4 manuscripts and on 4QXII^c in particular.

The Cave 4 manuscripts of the Twelve are dated between the middle of the second century B.C.E. and the last third of the first century B.C.E. Since, according to the new dating of the archaeological data by Jodi Magness, Khirbet Qumran was settled only from c. 100 B.C.E. onwards,[6] at least the oldest manuscripts (4QXII^a and 4QXII^b) must have been copied outside Qumran and brought there from elsewhere.[7] The same could be true, however, even for the younger scrolls since the origin of a manuscript needs to be determined separately in each case.

---

3   Fuller, "Twelve," 221–318.
4   Milik, "Amos," 173–174.
5   Milik, "Rouleau," 181–205. MurXII (Murabbaʿat 88) has 21 preserved columns containing fragmentary passages from the books of Joel, Amos, Obadiah, Jonah, Micah, Nahum, Habakkuk, Zephaniah, Haggai, and Zechariah. The Naḥal Ḥever scroll (8ḤevXIIgr) was published by Tov, *Greek Minor Prophets*. The ms contains fragmentary parts of all the books from Jonah to Zechariah, except for Haggai.
6   Magness, *Archaeology*, 63–69. In a later article Magness, "Methods," 106, proposes that it was only around 80 B.C.E. that the settlement was established by the Qumran sectarians.
7   Thus, these manuscripts cannot be defined as particularly "Qumranic" scrolls.

Some of the Cave 4 manuscripts contain passages from more than one of the Twelve, but none of them preserve all twelve books. However, it is possible that at least two of the Qumran manuscripts (4QXII[b] and 4QXII[g]) contained all twelve books, and the entire collection was also probably copied in the Murabba'at manuscript of the Minor Prophets, and the Greek scroll from Naḥal Ḥever. Additionally, manuscripts 4QXII[a], 4QXII[c], and 4QXII[e] contain fragments from more than one book, but the rest of the manuscripts from only one single book. Altogether, the Minor Prophets are preserved at Qumran in at least eight manuscripts. Depending on how the fragmentary manuscripts are grouped or identified, we might in fact have as many as twelve manuscripts of the Minor Prophets, some of which contain fragments of one of the books of the Twelve while others contain more than one.[8]

Emanuel Tov's Categories for Textual Classification

The categories proposed by Emanuel Tov for textual classification of the "biblical" manuscripts are well known, as well as the criticism offered by his colleagues in the past years. Initially, Tov had a system of five categories; however, he has adjusted his model of late.[9] One of the categories that received most criticism as an inappropriate category for determining textual affiliation was the one called "Texts written in the Qumran Scribal Practice."[10] Recently, Tov himself has modified his position, and refrains from using scribal practices to determine textual affiliation.[11] As a matter of fact, our case example, manuscript 4QXII[c], is at the same time written in "Qumran practice" and textually classified as either close to the LXX or "non-aligned." Of the remaining four categories, the one Tov calls "pre-Samaritan (or harmonistic) texts" is not applicable for the Minor Prophets and therefore will not be discussed further in this article. The three remaining categories that are relevant

---

8   The exact number of manuscripts depends on how the fragments are classified and identified. See von Weissenberg, "Twelve," 359–365.
9   The development of Tov's work is summarized by Lange in his *Handbuch*, 5–7.
10   Several scholars, such as Brooke and Segal, have been critical of the category "texts written in Qumran practice." They have pointed out that rather than being a text type, this group displays certain scribal practices. These practices merely reflect a certain approach to the copying of the manuscripts. Brooke, "Pluribus," 108–109; Segal, "Text," 8. See also Ulrich, *Dead Sea Scrolls*, 86–88.110–113. Certainly, the term "Qumran scribal practice" can be misleading, since these scribal conventions are not necessarily geographically restricted to Qumran, something that Tov never meant to suggest.
11   This he does in a revised version of an earlier article, Tov, "Biblical Texts," 128–154, published in 2008. See also Lange, *Handbuch*, 6.

for the Cave 4 Minor Prophets manuscripts are labelled proto-Masoretic (or proto-Rabbinic) texts, texts close to the presumed Hebrew *Vorlage* of the Septuagint (LXX), and the "non-aligned" texts.

The proto-Masoretic texts have, in Tov's words, "no special textual characteristics beyond their basic agreement with the MT."[12] Eugene Ulrich already some ten years ago stated: "neither the MT, the SP nor the LXX is a text-type or even 'a text' – they are collections of texts, differing from book to book. Thus, they should not constitute 'text-types' to which others either conform or stand 'non-aligned.'"[13] Ulrich's statement has been repeated by others, such as Michael Segal and Sidnie White Crawford. Segal reiterates the important point, made by Ulrich, that the MT is not a textual family but a collection of individual texts – and the same goes for the LXX *Vorlage*.[14] Sidnie White Crawford has also criticized the category "proto-Masoretic." She has two objections: firstly, the term should be abandoned because it gives the final form of the Jewish Bible in its Masoretic text form a privileged position. The main focus of her criticism, however, concerns the lack of textual characteristics of the "proto-Masoretic group," a fact also referred to by Ulrich and Segal: that the Masoretic text group is not a group.[15] It should rather be understood as a collection of individual, separate books all of which have a separate textual history.[16] In a recent article, Tov himself has emphasized the "coincidental textual nature of the ancient scripture collections" and suggested that as a result of their compositional history they are "textually heterogeneous."[17] White Crawford has furthermore highlighted the fact that texts from two scribal traditions have ended up in what became the Masoretic text of the Hebrew Bible. White Crawford calls them "the conservative and the revisionist scribal tradition," and texts from both of these are now parts of the collection we call the Masoretic text of the Hebrew Bible.[18]

---

12   Tov, *Textual Criticism*, 115, states: "They have no special textual characteristics beyond their basic agreement with the MT."
13   Ulrich, "Dead Sea Scrolls," 85. See already Aejmelaeus, "Hebrew Vorlage," 72.
14   Segal, "Text," 8–10.17.
15   See also Tov, *Textual Criticism*, 116, who compares LXX to the other categories: "They [= texts close to the *Vorlage* of LXX] do not form a closely-knit textual family like the MT group or the SP group, nor were they produced by a scribal school."
16   White Crawford, "Understanding," 66–67.
17   Tov, "Textual Nature," 153–169. See also Lange, *Handbuch*, 22–23.
18   Tov, *Textual Criticism*, 189–190, calls the two scribal approaches "exact" and "free." Ulrich, *Dead Sea Scrolls*, 11.23–27.51, uses the terms "exact" and "creative." See also Tov, *Textual Criticism*, 192–195. White Crawford, "Understanding," 67, gives as examples of the "conservative" scribal school 4QJer[b], 4QJer[d] and LXXJeremiah, and of the "revisionist" scribal school 4QJer[a], 4QJer[c], 4QJer[e] and MTJeremiah.

In trying to classify the Minor Prophets manuscripts according to their textual affiliation, there is one particular problem related to the group labelled "texts close to the presumed Hebrew *Vorlage* of the LXX." This is the relationship of the Greek text to the MT. According to George Howard, if the MT is taken as a point of comparison, sometimes the Greek of the Minor Prophets is very close to the MT, and sometimes it differs from it significantly.[19] It is unclear whether the differences – when the LXX is compared to the MT – from book to book depend upon a Hebrew *Vorlage* different from the MT or some other factor. Different solutions have been suggested: sometimes the Hebrew *Vorlage* might have been corrupt and difficult to render, or the *Vorlage* could actually have differed from the Masoretic text. Some scholars have furthermore proposed that the Twelve were translated not by one but by several persons, but this view has been abandoned by most.[20] In order to resolve this issue, much more detailed and comparative text-critical work needs to be done. At this point, it suffices to say that in light of the fact that the proximity of the LXX to the MT differs from book to book inside the collection of the Twelve, the textual classification of a manuscript as something "close to the textual tradition represented by the Septuagint" could mean a variety of things. Accordingly, it is not particularly helpful in clarifying the textual character of the text or manuscript in question.

The last of Tov's categories is labelled "non-aligned or independent texts," i.e., texts with inconsistent patterns of agreements and disagreements with MT, SP, or LXX.[21] Tov defines this category in the following words:

> "Many texts are not exclusively close to any one of the texts mentioned above [MT, SP, *Vorlage* of LXX] and are therefore considered non-aligned. They agree, sometimes significantly, with the MT against other texts, or they agree with SP and/or LXX against the other texts, but the non-aligned texts also disagree with the other texts to the same extent. They furthermore contain readings not known from one of the other texts, so that they are not exclusively close to one of the other texts or groups. – Usually the employment of the term non-aligned merely implies that the texts under consideration follow an inconsistent pattern of agreements and disagree-

---

19 Howard, "Twelve Prophets," 777–781. For instance, while the Book of Hosea, the first three chapters of Micah (1–3) and the book of Habakkuk are quite different from the MT, the book of Jonah seems to be rather close to the MT. According to Howard, Amos is quite close to the MT, although the translator appears to have had some difficulties with the vocabulary; Obadiah, Zephaniah, Haggai, Zachariah, and Malachi are "reasonably close to the MT."

20 For a summary of the different views see Howard, "Twelve Prophets," 780–781.

21 For these categories and their definition, see Tov, *Textual Criticism*, 114–117; idem, "Biblical Texts," 152–157.

ments with MT, SP and LXX –. But the texts which are most manifestly
non-aligned, and actually independent, are texts which contain readings
that diverge significantly from the other texts, such as 4QJosh[a], 4QJudg[a] as
well as excerpted and liturgical texts."[22]

The category has been criticized as inaccurate and anachronistic.[23] The
criticism is understandable: if neither the proto-Masoretic nor the *Vorlage* of the LXX are textual families but rather collections of individual
texts with individual textual histories, we have no textual families left
to align our manuscripts with, and the category "non-aligned" stops
making sense. Moreover, the manuscripts placed in this category can
contain significant individual variant readings and manuscripts that
are valuable for text- and literary-critical purposes.[24]

Cave 4 Manuscripts and their classifications

Several scholars have classified the Cave 4 manuscripts of the Minor
Prophets from Qumran and their textual affiliations by using the categories proposed by Tov, ending up with different proposals.

4QXII[a] (4Q76) contains parts of Zechariah, Malachi, and Jonah. The
scroll is known for the previously unattested Malachi-Jonah sequence.[25]
This manuscript is textually classified as "non-aligned."[26]

4QXII[b] (4Q77) has six fragments from Zephaniah and Haggai; and
the transition from one book to the other is preserved on fragment 3.
Not much text is preserved, but what is left is classified as proto-
Masoretic.[27]

4QXII[c] (4Q78) contains fragments from Hosea, Joel, Amos, and Zephaniah.[28] The scribe of this manuscript prefers *plene* orthography and
the long morphological forms typical of Tov's "Qumran scribal

---

22 Tov, *Textual Criticism*, 116–117.
23 See, for instance, Ulrich, "Dead Sea Scrolls," 97; Segal, "Text," 18.
24 On the other hand, Segal, "Text," 6, cautions against overemphasizing the value of
    individual variant readings.
25 The reconstructed sequence has been supported by some scholars (Steck, "Abfolge,"
    249–253) but questioned by others (Guillaume, "Malachi-Jonah," 2–10; García Martí-
    nez, "Text," 107).
26 Fuller, "Twelve," 221–232; García Martínez, "Text," 106; Brooke, "Twelve Minor
    Prophets," 22; Tov, "Biblical Texts," 156; Lange, *Handbuch*, 336.
27 Fuller, "Minor Prophets," 555; Brooke, "Twelve Minor Prophets," 22; García Martí-
    nez, "Text," 108. Lange, *Handbuch*, 337, refrains from giving a textual classification
    due to the small size of the manuscript.
28 Fragment 35 with text from the Book of Malachi (Malachi 3:6–7) belongs to a sepa-
    rate manuscript; fragment 38 contains text from Ps 38 and belongs to manuscript
    4QPs[a] (4Q83).

school."[29] In the DJD edition, Fuller gives no textual classification for this manuscript. Elsewhere, he states that it "stands relatively close to the textual tradition represented by the Septuagint."[30]

In contrast to Fuller, Tov, Florentino García Martínez, and Armin Lange all classify this manuscript as "non-aligned."[31] George Brooke gives no textual classification for this manuscript; instead, he points out the "striking agreement" with the Septuagint in Hos 13:4 in fragment 8. At this point, the fragmentary text has to be restored according to the longer text of the Septuagint, not according to the shorter MT. In Brooke's words, "[t]his fragment, therefore, raises the important point about how criteria for aligning fragmentary manuscripts are compiled; beyond the way in which the importance can be given to shared distinctive errors, there is still considerable lack of clarity about this."[32]

4QXII^d (4Q79) has two fragments with text from the Book of Hosea (1:6–2:5). There is very little of this manuscript preserved to classify its text type.[33] However, Fuller cautiously suggests that the text stands relatively close to the proto-Masoretic textual tradition;[34] Tov, on the other hand, tentatively classifies it as a "non-aligned" text.[35]

4QXII^e (4Q80) comprises 25 fragments. The identified fragments preserve parts of Haggai and Zechariah. This manuscript is the most peculiar case in that it has been classified in three different ways and will require a more thorough examination in the future. Fuller identifies its textual character as one close to the LXX.[36] Both Brooke and Tov classify this manuscript as "non-aligned." Brooke furthermore points out that "there do not seem to be any significant agreements with the

---

29 Von Weissenberg, "Scripture," 251–252; Tov, *Practices*, 261–273.
30 Fuller, "Minor Prophets," 555.
31 Tov, "Biblical Texts," 156. García Martínez, "Text," 108, states: "In general it is close to the MT, but several readings agree with the Septuagint – Other readings are not attested in any other major witnesses – All of these elements lead me to classify this manuscript as a 'non-aligned' text, although closer to the Septuagint than to MT, another witness of the plurality of the text forms attested in the biblical scrolls from Qumran." Similarly Lange, *Handbuch*, 338: "Texttypologisch repräsentiert 4QXII^c einen eigenständigen Text, der LXX nähersteht als MT."
32 Brooke, "Twelve Minor Prophets," 23. Lange, *Handbuch*, 12, classifies only manuscripts containing more than 100 words and enough evidence of textual variants according to their textual affiliation.
33 Brooke, García Martínez, and Lange give no classification due to the small size of the manuscript; cf. Brooke, "Twelve Minor Prophets," 23; García Martínez, "Text," 109; Lange, *Handbuch*, 339.
34 Fuller, "Minor Prophets," 555.
35 Tov, "Biblical Texts," 156.
36 Fuller, "Minor Prophets," 556.

LXX."[37] García Martínez states that "the text agrees mostly with MT." Lange also tentatively classifies the manuscript as proto-Masoretic.[38]

4QXII^f (4Q81) has four fragments with text from the book of Jonah (Jonah 1:6–8, 10–16).[39] There is so little text left that a textual classification is impossible with certainty, although in the preserved passages the manuscript seems to be close to the proto-Masoretic textual tradition.

4QXII^g (4Q82) is the largest of the manuscripts, with 258 fragments.[40] The identified fragments contain passages from Hosea, Joel, Amos, Obadiah, Jonah, Micah, Nahum, possibly of Habakkuk,[41] and Zechariah. According to Fuller, the manuscript "stands close to the proto-masoretic text form;"[42] García Martínez also states that "[t]he textual character of the manuscript in the best preserved parts is generally close to MT."[43] However, both Brooke and Tov place it in the category of "non-aligned" texts.[44] Lange gives this manuscript the label *"semimasoretisch."*[45]

Where does this leave us with respect to the textual character of the Minor Prophets? In brief, it can clearly be seen that scholars hardly agree on the textual status of the Cave 4 Minor Prophets manuscripts. Whereas the editor classifies only one manuscript as non-aligned, García Martínez and Lange have two and Brooke three "non-aligned" manuscripts, and, finally, Tov classifies four or five of the seven Cave 4 manuscripts of the Minor Prophets as non-aligned. Clearly, there is enough reason to be perplexed: why might the classifications proposed by various scholars differ from one another? Is there a problem with the manuscripts, or with the criteria that have been applied, or with the categories themselves? It is becoming increasingly acknowledged that the classification proposed by Tov does not suffice to describe the ancient evidence. However, to date, there is still not enough information to create an adequate alternative for Tov's classification, as pointed out by Lange:

---

37   Brooke, "Twelve Minor Prophets," 24; Tov, "Biblical Texts," 156.
38   García Martínez, "Text," 109; Lange, *Handbuch*, 339.
39   The Micah fragment (frg. 5) published with 4QXII^f does not belong to this manuscript.
40   In the DJD edition, fragments 106–258 remain unidentified.
41   Of Habakkuk, only one verse can tentatively be identified. See Fuller, "Twelve," 272.
42   Fuller, "Minor Prophets," 556, concludes: "Although 4QXII^g disagrees frequently with both the Masoretic text and the Septuagint, it stands close to the proto-Masoretic textual tradition in most of its readings."
43   García Martínez, "Text," 111.
44   Brooke, "Twelve Minor Prophets," 25; Tov, "Biblical Texts," 156.
45   Lange, *Handbuch*, 341.

"Um die textliche Pluralität des antiken Judentums angemessen erfassen zu können, wäre ein Raster notwendig, das die spätantik-mittelalterlichen Texttypen vermeidet. Momentan ist die Textkritik allerdings noch weit von einem solchen Schema entfernt. Die Forschung zur Identifizierung solcher antiken Textfamilien hat erst begonnen. Ein besonderes Problem besteht darin, dass die Handschriften biblischer Bücher vom Toten Meer nur in relativ begrenzten Textbereichen überlappen. Solche "overlaps" sind aber wichtig, um die Lesarten verschiedener Textzeugen miteinander vergleichen zu können."[46]

It is not possible to sketch a new proposal for textual classification in this short article. At this point we do not know, for instance, whether the manuscripts classified as "non-aligned" share unique textual characteristics and form textual families or not.[47] Here, my intention is to move the discussion forward by pointing out additional problems with the non-aligned texts. In order to do so, I will examine two text-critical cases from manuscript 4QXII[c]. Finally, I will argue that a hasty and superficial labeling of manuscripts can lead to ignoring important information that is hidden in the details of text-critical work.

Variant Readings in Manuscript 4QXII[c]

According to Lange, in ms 4QXII[c] there are 30 variant readings in the 459 identifiable words or parts of words.[48] According to my calculations, there are 32 variant readings; however, many of them are of minor importance; for instance, one of the cases is merely a scribal correction (Zeph 2:15). To summarize the evidence briefly, seventeen, i.e., the majority of these, can tentatively be classified as "independent" or "non-aligned" variants, that is, readings not attested in previously known textual witnesses.[49] In addition, the other variants sometimes agree with the MT against the LXX and at other times vice versa, showing no clear pattern of agreement or disagreement. It should be clear, however, that in trying to determine the textual affiliation or character of a manuscript a simple counting of the variant readings is not

---

46 Lange, *Handbuch*, 15.
47 Segal, "Text," 7. Segal reminds us that manuscripts can only be grouped together according to secondary readings: "Agreement between original readings only demonstrates that two manuscripts can both be traced to a common original author or scribe, but cannot be used to demonstrate a unique, genetic relationship between two texts."
48 Lange, *Handbuch*, 338.
49 The variant readings are conveniently listed in the DJD edition (Fuller, "Twelve," 221–318), as well as in Ulrich, *Biblical Qumran Scrolls*, 590–626.

enough. Not all variants are of equal concern, and the significance of a variant reading needs to be weighed separately in each case. In what follows, I will discuss two independent variant readings in order to demonstrate how greatly they can vary in importance.

Joel 1:17

Here, the Qumran manuscript contains an independent variant reading, although only partially preserved. I will argue that, in this case, manuscript 4QXII^c had a reading closer to the original, which was then modified into the variants attested by the MT and the LXX.

In ms 4QXII^c only the first words of Joel 1:17 are extant: עפ^שו פורות תחת מ[ן "The wine presses / troughs are molding / decaying(?) under ...[."[50]

The MT reads: עבשו פרדות תחת מגרפתיהם נשמו אצרות נהרסו ממגרות כי הביש דגן "The seeds shrivel under the clots, the storehouses are desolate: the granaries are ruined because the grain has failed (NRSV)."

The LXX reads: ἐσκίρτησαν δαμάλεις ἐπὶ ταῖς φάτναις αὐτῶν ἠφανίσθησαν θησαυροί κατεσκάφησαν ληνοί ὅτι ἐξηράνθη σῖτος "Heifers have jumped up at their mangers; storehouses have been annihilated: wine presses have been razed to the ground, because the grain has dried up (NETS)."

The verb in 4QXII^c, according to the supralinear scribal correction,[51] is a qal plural form from the root עבש, which is attested in Mishnaic Hebrew.[52] The subject in 4QXII^c is פורות, a rare word, but most likely a plural form of the word פורה "winepress / winevat / trough." Only the singular is attested in the Hebrew Bible, in Isa 63:3 and in Hag 2:16. Thus, the phrase עפ^שו פורות could be translated "The wine presses / wine vats / troughs are molding / decaying(?)." Although the entire verse Joel 1:17 is slightly ambiguous, this reading suits the context, assuming that the rest of the verse in 4QXII^c had something similar to the MT. The (con)text describes drought and various storehouses and storage vessels that are empty or spoiled.

---

50   Since the text breaks off, it is impossible to know in which of its various meanings the preposition תחת is used here.

51   The linear reading of 4QXII^c, עפו "they flew/were flying," does not make sense in this context, and it must have resulted from a mistake by the scribe as he inadvertently skipped the letter ש. The scribe added it later, probably according to his *Vorlage*. See von Weissenberg, "Scripture," 257–261.267.

52   The root is attested in Mishnaic Hebrew. Jastrow, *Dictionary*, 1100, gives עבש the meaning "to grow mouldy, decay," and the verb is, for instance, used of bread.

In the MT, the entire verse Joel 1:17 is enigmatic and difficult to understand due to several *hapax legomena*. First of all, the verb עבש ("to
dry up, shrivel up") used in the MT is a *hapax legomenon*. The subject of
the clause in the MT (פרדות) is also a *hapax legomenon* in this form and
meaning.[53] The word does not appear elsewhere in the Hebrew Bible in
a meaning suitable for the context of Joel; the word is usually translated
as "grain" or "seed."[54] The phrase עבשו פרדות can thus be translated
"The seeds shrivel / dry up." Assuming the verb attested in 4QXIIᶜ is
closer to the original reading, the *hapax legomenon* עבש in the MT can be
explained as a result of the interchange of *pe* and *bet*.[55] The interchange
from *pe* to *bet* created the form that is in the MT, which is otherwise
unattested in the HB. Further assuming that the subject in 4QXIIᶜ is also
closer to the original reading, the MT variant can be explained as resulting from confusion with the letters *dalet*, *reš*, and *waw*, a common and
frequently attested phenomenon.[56] In short, the rare and difficult reading of the MT can be explained as scribal corruption.[57]

In the LXX, for the verb ἐσκίρτησαν, the Hebrew *Vorlage* probably
had the root פוש "to spring about,"[58] or this is how the LXX translator
interpreted the Hebrew.[59] Orthographically, the word עבש is close to
the possible *Vorlage* of the LXX (פוש), and an *ayin* can sometimes be
dropped during the transmission of the manuscripts. If, however, we
assume, that the *Vorlage* of the Greek also had both the verb and the
subject attested by 4QXIIᶜ, the Greek can be explained as the translator's attempt to deal with difficult Hebrew. The Greek δάμαλις (pl.
δαμάλεις) is often used to render the Hebrew word בקר (i.e., in Numbers) or עגל (i.e., 1 Kgs 12:28; 2 Kgs 10:29; 17:16). For פרדות (sg. פרה),
usually βοῦς is used (i.e., Gen 32:16; 41:2, 3, 18, 19; 1 Sam 6:7, 10). However, in another book of the Minor Prophets, namely in Amos 4:1, the

---

53 פרדות in Ezek 1:11 appears once, but in a completely different context, where four
    humanlike creatures are described: וכנפיהם פרדות "Their wings were spread out ..."
54 Koehler and Baumgartner, *Lexicon*, 963, gives three different explanations: if under-
    stood as a participle from the root פרד, it could be interpreted as something that
    "has been put aside, what has been kept for later, stored provisions." The meaning
    seed-corn is derived from Syriac, and as a third meaning "dried figs" is suggested.
55 See Tov, *Textual Criticism*, 251–252.
56 For the interchange of graphically similar letters see Tov, *Textual Criticism*, 243–244.
    Admittedly, it is difficult to prove in which direction the interchange occurred.
57 Although, in general, the *lectio difficilior* is assumed to be the original reading, there
    are so many exceptions that this rule should not be applied mechanically. See Aej-
    melaeus, "Corruption," *forthcoming*.
58 Ulrich, *Biblical Qumran Scrolls*, 598.
59 This verb, as a reference to jumping cattle, is used in MT Jer 50:11 (LXX Jer 27:11)
    and MT Mal 3:20 (LXX Mal 4:2) and is in both cases rendered with the Greek
    σκιρτάω. See also Ps 114:4/113:4.

MT פרות is translated with δαμάλεις (see also Num 19:2, 6, 9 for the sg.).[60] We cannot know with certainty whether the LXX *Vorlage* had פרות or פורות, although the shorter form is more probable, but it is unlikely that it had a subject with *dalet* (> פרד).[61] If the *Vorlage* had the longer form פורות it is possible that the LXX translator understood the subject as a *plene* form of the word "heifer." Either he first made sense of the subject and then translated the verb accordingly, or he had the reading attested in 4QXIIᶜ in his *Vorlage*, but interpreted פורות as a reference to "heifer" after interpreting the verb עפש as פוש. It is possible that the *Vorlage* of the LXX had the reading ופושו פ(ו)רות(?); however, it is more probable that our earliest Hebrew witness, 4QXIIᶜ, attests the original reading in this case. This reading can also explain the one attested by the LXX, and could have been in its *Vorlage*. This would, in fact, mean that the reading of 4QXIIᶜ can no longer be defined as a "non-aligned" or "independent" variant. Furthermore, although original readings have limited relevance for determining textual affiliation, if the link between 4QXIIᶜ and the LXX that I have proposed is accepted in this case, the reading might in fact be another piece of evidence pointing toward a relationship between these two textual witnesses.

Joel 2:13

The second example of an independent variant reading in ms 4QXIIᶜ is also from the book of Joel. 4QXIIᶜ reads: וקרעו לב⸤כמה ואל גדיכ⸥מה "rend your heart and not your kid(?)." The MT reads: וקרעו לבבכם ואל בגדיכם "rend your heart and not your garments." The LXX has a reading implying a *Vorlage* similar to the MT: ... καὶ μὴ τὰ ἱμάτια ὑμῶν.

---

60 It is generally assumed that the Minor Prophets were translated by one person or group, see Dines, *Septuagint*, 22, and thus, one could expect some consistency in the choice of vocabulary.

61 Judging from the Greek, the *Vorlage* of the LXX had a word containing at least the letters *pe* and *reš* and the plural ending *-ot*, but most likely not the *dalet*: as the verb was rendered with σκιρτάω, a word describing the leaping of calves elsewhere in the Minor Prophets (Mal 3:20/4:2), it is probable that if the Hebrew *Vorlage* had contained a subject with *pe*, *reš* and *dalet* it would have been understood as a reference to "mule" by the LXX translator. The word פרד (pl. פרדים) has the meaning "mule"; even the feminine form exists, but only in the singular in the HB (1 Kgs 1:33, 38, 44). This word (both the masculine and the feminine forms) is usually translated with ἡμίονος in the LXX (see, for example 1 Kgs 1:33, 38, 44; 10:25; 2 Kgs 5:17; 2 Chr 9:24; Ps 32:9). In Mishnaic Hebrew פרד can also mean "mule"; furthermore it can have a collective meaning "split and dried pomegranates;" see Jastrow, *Dictionary*, 1215. The LXX translator appears to have some problems with this passage, judged by the relatively unusual rendering of the preposition תחת as ἐπί.

61 Ulrich, *Biblical Qumran Scrolls*, 598.

In this case, the independent variant reading of the Qumran manuscript, which reads "your kid(?)" instead of "your garments" is a scribal mistake, and has little text-critical relevance.[62] Furthermore, since it has not been transmitted by other textual witnesses, it has little relevance for determining textual affiliation.

Comparing these two "non-aligned" variant readings of manuscript 4QXII[c] suffices to show that mere counting of the variant readings and then classifying them into Tov's categories tells us surprisingly little about the significance of these variants and the textual profile of the manuscript as a whole. Furthermore, it suggests that manuscripts labeled as "non-aligned" can differ considerably from one another in textual profile and quality. For instance, if one compares manuscripts 4QXII[c] and 4QXII[g], it is quite obvious that they are "non-aligned" in very different ways. Both the number and content of the independent variant readings vary from manuscript to manuscript, and also (importantly?) from book to book. Admittedly, the comparison between the manuscripts of the Minor Prophets is hindered by the fact that they have little material overlap, making the comparison difficult or even impossible.[63]

Conclusions

The "biblical" manuscripts from Qumran are a treasure-trove of early textual evidence for the development and transmission of the Hebrew Bible in the pre-canonical era. In the case of the Minor Prophets, we have evidence of a developing collection, as the manuscripts witness both the copying of the individual books and a collection of several, possibly even all twelve books on one scroll. Textually, the Minor Prophets have been classified in various ways. Some of the difficulties in the classification are due to the fragmentary nature of the material, and this fragmentation is probably one of the reasons why scholars currently disagree over the textual affiliation of the manuscripts. A more important issue, however, concerns the definition and usage of Tov's categories: if several of the Minor Prophets manuscripts are classified as "non-aligned," what does this tell us about the textual character of the Twelve in the late Second Temple period? In light of my investigation, it seems that even though (some of) the independent variant readings in the "non-aligned" manuscripts of the Minor Proph-

---

62 See von Weissenberg, "Scripture," 261.
63 As can be seen in the *Biblia Qumranica* volume of the Minor Prophets, where the manuscripts are presented as a synopsis.

ets, and in manuscript 4QXII^c in particular, are interesting and important, none of these manuscripts contain the kind of independent variant
readings that "diverge significantly from the other texts" as in Tov's
examples of "non-aligned" manuscripts, 4QJosh^a and 4QJudg^a. Thus, it
is questionable whether any of the "non-aligned" manuscripts of the
Minor Prophets would qualify as "most manifestly non-aligned or independent" according to Tov's own definition.[64] Regardless, as we saw
with manuscript 4QXII^c, the variants can differ so much from our previously known textual witnesses that the manuscripts do not fall neatly
into any of the other categories.

If Tov's categories are used, it looks like the majority of the Cave 4
manuscripts of the Minor Prophets fall into the category of "non-
aligned" texts. On the other hand, in light of all the problems raised
both in previous research and in this article, this conclusion is not particularly illuminating. Therefore, instead of lumping texts into categories that no longer function, we should consider that the truth is in the
details, and the relevance and value of these details can vary from case
to case. Although preliminary categories are in many ways helpful in
sorting out the vast amount of new material, it is important to acknowledge at this point that they might create more confusion than
clarity, and thus lead us to ignore important textual evidence. Frustrat-
ing though it may seem, in order to fully understand the significance of
the "biblical" manuscripts from Qumran, much more detailed text-
critical work is required.[65] Therefore, we should rather be asking new
questions, such as what happened in the texts, and to the texts, when
the variant readings were developed – to use Anneli Aejmelaeus's
words to search for the story behind the different readings.[66]

References

Aejmelaeus, A. "What can we know about the Hebrew Vorlage of the Septua-
    gint?" Pp. 71–106 in *On the Trail of the Septuagint Translators: Collected Es-
    says*. CBET 50. Leuven: Peeters, 2007.
–   "Corruption or Correction? Textual Development in the MT of 1 Samuel 1."
    Forthcoming.
Brooke, G.J. "E Pluribus Unum: Textual Variety and Definitive Interpretation in
    the Qumran Scrolls." Pp. 108–109 in *The Dead Sea Scrolls in Their Historical
    Context*. Edited by T.H. Lim et al. Edinburgh: T&T Clark, 2000.

---

64   Tov, *Textual Criticism*, 116.
65   I agree with Ulrich, *Dead Sea Scrolls*, 94, who states: "We cannot make our terminolo-
     gy precise until our understanding of the material we are describing is precise."
66   Aejmelaeus, "Corruption," *forthcoming*.

- "The Twelve Minor Prophets and the Dead Sea Scrolls." Pp. 19–43 in *Congress Volume Leiden 2004*. Edited by A. Lemaire. VTSup 109. Leiden: Brill, 2006.
Dines, J. *The Septuagint*. London: T&T Clark, 2004.
Ego, B. et al. (ed.). *Biblia Qumranica 3B: Minor Prophets*. Leiden: Brill, 2005.
Fuller, R.E. "Textual Traditions in the Book of Hosea." Pp. 247–256 in *The Madrid Qumran Congress: Proceedings of the International Congress on the Dead Sea Scrolls, Madrid 18–21 March 1991*. 2 vols. Edited by J. Trebolle Barrera and L. Vegas Montaner. STDJ 11. Leiden: Brill, 1992.
- "The Twelve: 4QXII^a, 4QXII^b, 4QXII^c, 4QXII^d, 4QXII^e, 4QXII^f, 4QXII^g." Pp. 221–318 in *Qumran Cave 4, X: The Prophets*. Edited by E. Ulrich et al. DJD 15. Oxford: Clarendon, 1997.
- "Minor Prophets." Pp. 554–557 in *Encyclopedia of the Dead Sea Scrolls*. 2 vols. Edited by L. Schiffman and J.C. VanderKam. Oxford: Oxford University Press, 2000.
García Martínez, F. "The Text of the XII Prophets." *OTE* 17,1 (2004) 103–119.
Guillaume, P. "The Unlikely Malachi-Jonah Sequence (4QXII^a)." *Journal of Hebrew Scriptures* 7 (2007) 2–10.
Howard, G.E. "The Twelve Prophets." Pp. 777–822 in *A New English Translation of the Septuagint* (NETS). Edited by A. Pietersma and B.G. Wright. Oxford: Oxford University Press, 2007.
Jastrow, M. *A Dictionary of the Targumim, the Talmud Babli and Yerushalmi and the Midrashic Literature*. New York: G.P. Putnam's Sons, 1950.
Koehler, L. and Baumgartner, W. *The Hebrew and Aramaic Lexicon of the Old Testament*. 2 vols. Revised Study Edition. Leiden: Brill, 2001.
Lange, A. *Handbuch der Textfunde vom Toten Meer. Band 1: Die Handschriften biblischer Bücher von Qumran und den anderen Fundorten*. Tübingen: Mohr, 2009.
Magness, J. *The Archaeology of Qumran and the Dead Sea Scrolls*. Studies in the Dead Sea Scrolls and Related Literature. Grand Rapids: Eerdmans, 2002.
- "Methods and Theories in the Archaeology of Qumran." Pp. 89–107 in *Rediscovering the Dead Sea Scrolls: An Assessment of Old and New Approaches and Methods*. Edited by M.L. Grossman. Grand Rapids: Eerdmans, 2010.
Milik, J.T. "Rouleau des Douze Prophètes." Pp. 181–205 in *Les grottes de Murabba`at*. Edited by P. Benoit et al. DJD 2.1. Oxford: Clarendon, 1961.
- "Amos." Pp. 173–174 in *Les 'petites grottes' de Qumran: Exploration de la falaise, Les grottes 2Q, 3Q, 5Q, 6Q, 7Q à 10Q, Le rouleau de cuivre*. Edited by M. Baillet et al. DJD 3. Oxford: Clarendon, 1962.
Segal, M. "The Text of the Hebrew Bible in Light of the Dead Sea Scrolls." *Materia giudaica* 12 (2007) 5–20.
Steck, O.H. "Zur Abfolge Maleachi-Jonah in 4Q76 (4QXII^a)." *ZAW* 108 (1996) 249–253.
Tov, E. *The Greek Minor Prophets Scroll from Naḥal Ḥever (8ḤevXIIgr): The Seiyal collection 1*. DJD 8. Oxford: Clarendon, 1990.
- *Textual Criticism of the Hebrew Bible*. 2nd rev. ed. Minneapolis: Fortress Press, 2001.
- "The Biblical Texts from the Judaean Desert – An Overview and Analysis of the Published Texts." Pp. 152–157 in *The Bible as Book: The Hebrew Bible*

and the Judaean Desert Discoveries. Edited by E.D. Herbert and E. Tov. London: The British Library and Oak Knoll Press, 2002.

– *Scribal Practices and Approaches Reflected in the Texts Found in the Judean Desert*. STDJ 54. Leiden: Brill, 2004.

– "The Biblical Texts from the Judaean Desert." Pp. 128–154 in *Hebrew Bible, Greek Bible and Qumran: Collected Essays*. Tübingen: Mohr, 2008.

– "The Coincidental Textual Nature of the Collections of Ancient Scriptures." Pp. 153–169 in *Congress Volume Ljubljana 2007*. Edited by A. Lemaire. VTSup 133. Leiden: Brill, 2010.

– et al. (ed.) *The Texts from the Judaean Desert: Indices and an Introduction to the Discoveries in the Judaean Desert Series*. DJD 39. Oxford: Clarendon, 2002.

Ulrich, E. "The Dead Sea Scrolls and the Biblical Text." Pp. 79–100 in *The Dead Sea Scrolls after Fifty Years: A Comprehensive Assessment*. Vol. 1. Edited by P.W. Flint and J.C. VanderKam. Leiden: Brill, 1998.

– *The Dead Sea Scrolls and the Origins of the Bible*. Studies in the Dead Sea Scrolls and Related Literature. Leiden: Brill, 1999.

– "The Notion and Definition of Canon." Pp. 21–35 in *The Canon Debate*. Edited by L.M. McDonald and J.A. Sanders. Peabody: Hendrickson, 2002.

– *The Biblical Qumran Scrolls: Transcriptions and Textual Variants*. VTSup 134. Leiden: Brill, 2010.

von Weissenberg, H. "Changing Scripture? Scribal Corrections in MS 4QXII^c." Pp. 247–271 in *Changes in Scripture: Rewriting and Interpreting Authoritative Traditions in the Second Temple Period*. Edited by eadem et al. BZAW 419. Berlin: de Gruyter, 2011.

– "The Twelve Minor Prophets at Qumran and the Canonical Process: Amos as a 'Case Study'." Pp. 357–378 in *The Hebrew Bible in the Light of the Dead Sea Scrolls*. Edited by A. Lange et al. FRLANT 239. Göttingen: Vandenhoeck & Ruprecht, 2012.

White Crawford, S. "Understanding the Textual History of the Hebrew Bible: A New Proposal." Pp. 60–69 in *The Hebrew Bible in the Light of the Dead Sea Scrolls*. Edited by A. Lange et al. FRLANT 239. Göttingen: Vandenhoeck & Ruprecht, 2012.

Zahn, M.M. "Talking about Rewritten Texts: Some Reflections on Terminology." Pp. 93–119 in *Changes in Scripture: Rewriting and Interpreting Authoritative Traditions in the Second Temple Period*. Edited by H. von Weissenberg et al. BZAW 419. Berlin: de Gruyter, 2011.

Scripture Index

Author Index